Organizing and Implementing the Marketing Effort
Text and Cases

Frank V. Cespedes
Harvard Business School

 ADDISON-WESLEY PUBLISHING COMPANY

Reading, Massachusetts ▪ Menlo Park, California ▪ New York

Don Mills, Ontario ▪ Wokingham, England ▪ Amsterdam ▪ Bonn

Sydney ▪ Singapore ▪ Tokyo ▪ Madrid ▪ San Juan

Associate Editor: Christine O'Brien
Production Supervisor: Peggy J. Flanagan
Electronic Production Administrator: Beth Perry
Production Services: The Book Department
Cover Designer: Geralyn Miller
Copy Editor: Carmen Wheatcroft
Manufacturing Supervisor: Roy Logan

Grateful acknowledgement is made to the following publishers for permission to reprint material:

From *The IBM Way* by F. G. "Buck" Rodgers, with Robert L. Shook. Copyright © 1986 by Francis G. Rodgers and Robert L. Shook. Foreword Copyright © 1986 by Harper & Row, Publishers, Inc. Reprinted by permission of the publisher.

From Dennis Kneale, "Working at IBM." Reprinted by permission of *The Wall Street Journal,* April 7, 1986, © 1986 Dow Jones & Co., Inc. All rights reserved worldwide.

Library of Congress Cataloging-in-Publication Data
Cespedes, Frank V., 1950–
   Organizing and Implementing the marketing effort: text and cases
   Frank V. Cespedes.
    p. cm.
   ISBN 0-201-51044-8
   1. Marketing—Management—Case Studies. 2. Sales management—Case studies.
I. Title.
HF5415.13.C47 1991
658.8'02—dc20   90-237
                                            CIP

TO MY PARENTS,
EDWARD and RITA CESPEDES

Preface

As its title suggests, this book addresses organizational and tactical issues in marketing. Unlike most books about marketing, the primary focus here is not on theories and frameworks for strategy development but rather on practical studies of how marketing tasks do (or do not) get accomplished in representative situations. Whereas "big picture" strategic issues are implicated in many of the situations discussed, the focus is on the how-to-do of selected marketing practices rather than the what-to-do of strategy formulation. A growing body of research and informed observation indicates that excellence in organizing and implementing the marketing effort is a characteristic of outstanding firms; and many operating managers at all levels will testify that an understanding of what is required for effective marketing execution has in turn often placed a proposed strategy in a new light and altered their view of the relationship between strategy and implementation.

This book presents its student, faculty, and practioner audiences with an array of implementation problems faced by marketing managers. In contrast to most texts, however, this one does not pretend to offer a comprehensive set of issues, categorized according to the so-called 4Ps (product, price, place, promotion) or a typology of marketing functions and subfunctions. Rather, it focuses on organizational issues in marketing from a certain point of view: that is, deciding how to structure marketing efforts and assign specific responsibilities first requires a detailed understanding of the types of customer encounters and consequent field marketing requirements facing the firm.

Part One, Strategy and Implementation in Marketing, briefly introduces the topic and many of the specific themes explored in more detail in subsequent sections. Part Two, Managing Customer Encounters, then investigates field marketing requirements in various company and competitive settings. Its focus is on the ongoing management of a firm's demand-generation and demand-fulfillment activities and, in particular, on the selection and conduct of field sales, distribution, and account-management activities. The understandings and insights developed with those materials provide a necessary foundation for the topics introduced in Part Three, Managing Marketing Resources: Organization and Control. Here, the marketing organization is examined from three points of view: Key Interfaces (marketing's roles in relation to key external and internal environments); Customer Service (organizational factors that aid or inhibit the provision of an important output of marketing activities in all firms); and Structure, Systems, and Process (some common structures put in place to organize sales and marketing activities and, within each structure, the issues involved in coordinating among the requirements of customers, channels, and internal company systems).

The book's primary means of studying these topics is field-based cases, a form of study that is especially demanding of both teachers and students but one that, for various reasons, is especially appropriate for the study of marketing practice. The topic of marketing organization has received limited systematic study in the past two decades. Major marketing texts devote a few pages to the topic, but their discussions of product- vs. market-oriented forms are increasingly divorced from current context and from the specific combinations of people and data that constitute the core of marketing organizational issues. In addition, for years marketing pedagogy has focused on the content of marketing strategy decisions and the development of selected technical tools to the virtual exclusion of the process of marketing decision making in an organization. But those processes affect how and by whom decisions are made as well as the criteria used to evaluate the outcomes (and the decision makers themselves). As others have noted, moreover, the influence of the study and teaching of marketing processes should increase as the decisions themselves become more organizationally complex.

For all of these reasons, then, studying marketing organization and implementation is particularly suitable to case-study methodology. It requires a solid contextual understanding; in turn, the field studies and concepts discussed in this book can be an important input to marketing decision making and to future research concerning this topic.

If you are using this book in a course or seminar, you will be exposed to a wide range of management situations. You should note at the outset two important characteristics of this collection of case studies.

One is that the book contains a number of "series" cases (i.e., several interrelated cases on a given company or division). These cases reflect the fact that implementation problems tend to recur, resurface, and change over time, especially in marketing. A case that is essentially only a snapshot of events often can distort or obscure the real complexities and options available to marketing managers. Further, in many instances, you may find that the perspective afforded by the later case will change your mind about the analysis and decisions you proposed in an earlier case. Be alert and open to this possibility, and consider what it means for on-the-job conduct where "20-20 hindsight" is usually (and legitimately) disparaged.

Second, some cases in the book have no explicit decision or problem, but they nonetheless pose challenging questions that directly affect marketing actions and implementation. Many students of management (including me) find such cases to be more difficult than material that leads to a clear problem, perhaps in part because such cases demand *more* analysis and preparation time than traditional decision-oriented cases do.

All of the cases are relevant to those working in, or considering careers in, marketing or general management, and all demand rigorous attention. The prevailing thrust of academic research, MBA curriculums, and articles in the business press emphasizes that marketing is concerned with the grand design of strategy. This book can sharpen your understanding and appreciation for the organizational component of marketing: the people, processes, and analytical issues relevant to the implementation of marketing programs and the execution of strategy.

Acknowledgments

Case research spawns many debts. At Harvard Business School, I owe a great deal to Professors Thomas V. Bonoma, E. Raymond Corey, and Benson P. Shapiro. A few years ago, I inherited Tom Bonoma's Marketing Implementation course and a solid foundation for exploring tactical issues in marketing. Tom has also been a valued intellectual sparring partner as well as the generous donator of the Frito-Lay case study in this volume. In working on another book, Ray Corey tutored me in the pleasures, problems, and power of field research and demonstrated professional standards that I hope are reflected in this book. Ben Shapiro ("the greater craftsman of our common art") provided encouragement and much of his own wealth of knowledge about marketing, sales management, case development, and teaching.

Thanks are also due to Professor John Quelch, for permitting the use of his Procter & Gamble case study and for his useful suggestions concerning marketing organization and to Professor V. Kasturi Rangan, for permission to use our joint study of Becton Dickinson & Company as well as for friendship and conversation during the past few years. I am also grateful to Professors M. Bixby Cooper of Michigan State University, Dennis A. Pitta of the University of Baltimore, Donna Santo of Wayne State University, Daniel C. Smith of the University of Wisconsin at Madison, and especially Brown Whittington, Jr. of Emory University for their reviews of the manuscript and suggestions.

During the course of my research and case development, a number of people have used material in this book and provided valuable feedback. These include Kenneth Bernhardt of the University of Georgia, John Cady of the Center for Executive Development, Joel Goldhar of the Illinois Institute of Technology, Thomas Kosnik of Stanford University, Christopher Lovelock of C. Lovelock and Associates, Walter Popper of Index Group, Adrian Ryans of the University of Western Ontario, Carol Smith of UCLA, Frederick Webster of the Tuck School at Dartmouth, and John Whitney, Jr. of Mawarid Holding Company.

Special thanks are also due to four groups: the many companies and executives who cooperated in case development activities; the research assistants who worked with these managers and me in developing the cases: Jon King, Ellen Hattemer, and Susan Vishner; the MBA and executive-program participants who discussed this material and contributed to the thinking underlying the book; and the Division of Research at Harvard Business School for its financial and intellectual support of field research.

Finally, I would like to thank friends and colleagues at the Harvard Business School's Word Processing Center; Mary Fischer, Peggy J. Flanagan, Maribeth Jones, and Christine O'Brien of Addison-Wesley; and Patricia Carda of The Book Department for her professionalism in editing and preparing the manuscript for publication.

Boston, Massachusetts   F.V.C.

Contents

Preface   v

Acknowledgments   ix

Overview: Themes, Emphases, and Plan of the Book   1

PART ONE

Strategy and Implementation in Marketing   15

1   **Strategy and/vs. Implementation**   17

    Case 1   Amerisource   25
    Case 2   Dorio Printing Company   51

PART TWO

**Managing Customer Encounters: Field Marketing
    Requirements**   71

2   **Aspects of Sales Management: An Introduction**   73

3   **Managing Selling and the Salesperson**   86

    Case 3   Cooper Pharmaceuticals, Inc.   94
    Case 4   Cole National Corporation: Turnover   105
    Case 5   Fieldcrest Division of Fieldcrest Mills, Inc.:
             Compensation System for Field Sales
             Representatives   137

4 Deployment, Focus, and Measuring Effectiveness   160

Case 6 Actmedia, Inc. 168
Case 7 Cox Cable (A) 196
Case 8 Cox Cable (B) 219

5 Channel Management   233

Case 9 Westinghouse Electric Corporation (A) 249
Case 10 Westinghouse Electric Corporation (B):
    Control House 273
Case 11 Alloy Rods Corporation 286
Case 12 Becton Dickinson & Company:
    VACUTAINER Systems Division 314

6 Managing Major Accounts   338

Case 13 Springs Industries: Apparel Fabrics Division 358
Case 14 Capital Cities/ABC, Inc.: Spot Sales 381
Case 15 MCI Communications Corporation:
    National Accounts Program 406
Case 16 MCI: Vnet (A) 432

PART THREE

Managing Marketing Resources:
   Organization and Control   453

7 Aspects of Marketing Organization: An Introduction   455

8 Key Interfaces   473

Case 17 Frito-Lay, Inc. (A) 481
Case 18 Imperial Distributors, Inc. (A) 505
Case 19 Peripheral Products Company:
    The Gray Market for Disk Drives 533

9 Customer Service   560

Case 20 Carolina Power & Light Company 569
Case 21 General Electric: Customer Service 598

10 Structure, Systems, and Process   617

**Marketing Organization at Leading Industrial
and Consumer Goods Firms**   631

Case 22 IBM Marketing Organization (A):
    Changes in Structure 632
Case 23 IBM Marketing Organization (B): Process 655
Case 24 Procter & Gamble (A) 666

Case 25 *Pepsi-Cola Fountain Beverage Division:*
  Marketing Organization   *699*

Centralization and Decentralization of Marketing Efforts   **723**

Case 26 *Turner Construction Company*   *724*

Case 27 *Honeywell, Inc.: International Organization*
  for Commercial Avionics (A)   *745*

Getting the Marketing Job Done   **773**

Case 28 *Imperial Distributors, Inc. (B)*   *774*

Case 29 *Pepsi-Cola Fountain Beverage Division:*
  Tea Breeze   *788*

Case Index   **809**

Index   **811**

Overview: Themes, Emphases, and Plan of the Book

A standard thesaurus provides a battalion of synonyms for the verb "implement": "produce, do, carry out, perform, execute, achieve, accomplish, complete, effectuate, realize, bring about by concrete measures." What does this mean in a marketing context? It almost always means time, attention, and resources devoted to two interrelated topics: field sales management and company marketing organization. Sales management, the ongoing management of customer encounters, is important because in most companies the sales force and/or distribution intermediaries are the major vehicles for implementing marketing strategy. Hence getting salespeople or intermediaries "to do what we want them to do" occupies more time and attention for most marketing managers than strategic analysis does. Marketing organization is important because the management of sales and distribution people, relationships, and resources always occurs within an institutional context in which key structures, systems, and processes affect implementation goals, options, and incentives.

This book examines issues involved in implementing marketing strategy by focusing on the allied areas of sales management and marketing organization. Part One considers the relationship between strategy and implementation in marketing and introduces themes that will be explored in more detail later in the book. Figure A summarizes the relationship between Part Two and Part Three.

A company's field marketing requirements will be determined in large part by the market characteristics facing the firm. We can specify some of the more important characteristics as follows: the amount of change in the environment (e.g., new entrants or product substitutes); the relative complexity of field sales and service tasks (e.g., technical complexity of the product or the amount of coordination across product lines or salespeople implied by the customer's

1

Figure A

buying process or the seller's marketing strategy); the relative predictability of those tasks (e.g., standardized across market segments or customized by account); and the influence of competitive forces (e.g., competitors' pricing, promotion, distribution, or product policies). Each of these factors helps to determine the field marketing requirements facing the firm in its encounters with customers and prospective customers. That is, these factors define the nature of the field sales tasks that the firm must be able to perform effectively in its product/market environment. In turn, understanding field marketing requirements is fundamental to any decisions concerning the organization and implementation of the marketing effort. Part Two looks at different product/market environments and their implications for specific aspects of field marketing: managing selling and the salesperson; deploying and measuring the effectiveness of the sales force; working with and through channel intermediaries; and the ongoing management of major accounts.

A primary purpose of any marketing organization is to implement strategy by aligning the firm's resources and capabilities with field marketing requirements. This means making decisions and monitoring at least three aspects of organization: (1) structure (e.g., the reporting relationships within the marketing and sales functions as well as between marketing and sales and other functions, the activities of which affect the company's conduct of customer encounters in the field); (2) systems (e.g., the recruitment, training, and measurement and evaluation systems for various people in the marketing organization); and (3) process (e.g., the kinds of formal and informal interactions that characterize management at different levels of the organization and the implications of these interactions for the company's base of marketing information, its priorities, and the focus of managerial skills and attention). Part Three compares strategies in different product/market environments and the implications of these strategies for these important dimensions of marketing organization.

Let's look in more detail at some of the issues embedded within each section of the book.

SECTION ONE
Strategy and Implementation in Marketing

In broad terms, strategy refers to the what-to-do of marketing activities (see Figure B). At a minimum, a coherent strategy: defines objectives (what a firm seeks in the marketplace and the nature of its potential competitive advantage); establishes strategic plans (road maps for achieving those objectives); and allocates resources across the product categories, markets, and channels in which the company competes. In contrast, implementation refers to the how-to-do-it aspects of marketing. Implementation deals with organizational issues, with the development of specific marketing programs, and with the execution of programs in the field. Field execution includes sales efforts, service capabilities, and systems for generating feedback about both the company's strategy and its implementation.

The two cases in the introductory section illustrate a range of issues inherent in these aspects of marketing implementation. Each case includes a management team that has defined certain objectives, allocated important resources, and (in one case) developed a general strategic plan. The management teams face several issues: the appropriate marketing organization for the company's strategy; the development of specific marketing programs in keeping with that strategy; and the details of execution in the field. In both cases,

Figure B

Strategy	=	**What To Do**
		• Definition of Objectives
		• Strategic Plans
		• Resource Allocations
		(products, markets, channels)

Implementation	=	**How To Do It**
		• Marketing Organization
		• Marketing Programs
		• Field Execution
		(sales, service, feedback)

moreover, management is considering changes in the structure of its sales and marketing organization, in the systems used to manage and monitor sales and marketing personnel, and in the selection and motivation of these personnel. Several important questions are introduced by these cases:

- Which of these areas—structure, systems, people—will have the greatest impact on the firm's ability to implement its strategy?
- Which changes will have immediate effects?
- Which changes will be more or less difficult to implement?

Among other things, what these field studies show is that there is no neat, positive correlation among these factors. Those changes likely to have the greatest impact on a firm's ability to implement a new strategy are also likely to make their impact felt later rather than sooner and are relatively more difficult to implement (i.e., expensive, time-consuming, more disruptive of established ways of doing business). The challenge facing management in these firms (as in most organizations) is that they must recognize the constraints that impede optimal implementation and, at the same time, craft an appropriate course of action that *can* be implemented. These interactions among the structures, systems, and people put in place to implement strategy recur throughout the situations examined in this book, as do the long-term vs. short-term tensions facing marketing management in these cases and in the real world.

SECTION TWO
Managing Customer Encounters: Field Marketing Requirements

In implementing marketing strategies one focal point must be the management of customer encounters in the field. In most companies, field encounters are the responsibility of the sales force, and therefore, decisions dealing with organizing and implementing the marketing effort should begin with a solid understanding of the firm's field marketing requirements.

Sales management can be thought of as consisting of three processes: (1) formulation of a sales program; (2) development of systems, policies, and procedures to implement the sales program; and (3) implementation at the field sales management level. The cases in Part Two illustrate representative tasks, responsibilities, and practices within each set of processes. As Figure C indicates, the organization of topics implies a movement outward from a focus on the individual salesperson to various systems intended to deploy, focus, and measure the sales force's efforts to sales management issues raised by multi-channel selling systems to the customer interface and, in particular, the daily management of major accounts.

These topics are closely related both in concept and practice: If the management of customer encounters is to be effective, these four com-

Figure C

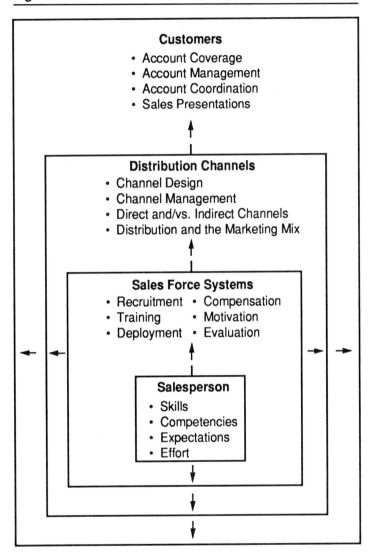

ponents—people, systems, channel policies, and account interactions—must be coordinated.

Managing Selling and the Salesperson

The cases in this chapter introduce basic selling tasks and tensions. Each case focuses on one or more salespeople, but the cases also provide pertinent information about the larger sales management system within which those people are recruited, trained, compensated, and evaluated. There are several important questions in each of these cases:

- What is the role of a salesperson in this company, and how well or how poorly has each individual performed this role?
- What are the key requirements for effective sales management in this company, and how well or how poorly does each firm perform these tasks?
- Who ultimately "owns" the customer in each of these situations—the salesperson or the company? What are the implications for action in the decisions posed by these cases?

These cases require detailed, quantitative attention to matters such as call patterns, the mechanics of incentive systems, and selling costs and budgets. But, more than many other aspects of business, sales management is also "people intensive": Decisions directly impact individuals' livelihoods, relations with colleagues, and sense of self. Hence these cases raise core management issues such as: the role of "nature" (the individual's effort or abilities) vs. "nurture" (training and environment) in evaluating and rewarding performance; the possible extent and limits of a firm's responsibilities for the actions of its employees and the often unintended consequences of these actions; the difference between consistency and inertia; and the requirements of change vs. the impact of change on the personal relationships developed within a different set of norms and expectations.

Part of the fun and challenge of studying sales management is that it requires the articulation of a point of view, or management style, with respect to these issues. You should recognize this from the outset and should track whether your own understanding of the values involved changes during your exploration of these issues in various case studies.

Deployment, Focus, and Measuring Effectiveness

Deployment is the assignment of the sales effort to territories, customers, products, and functions (e.g., opening new accounts vs. servicing existing accounts). Decisions about deployment ultimately affect the primary focus of the sales force: its goals in the revenue stream represented by potential customers and the best use of the individual salesperson's limited time with customers. A coherent deployment program includes policies, procedures to implement those policies, and clarity about the appropriate measures to use in evaluating sales efforts. Several important questions throughout this chapter are:

- How is money made in each business considered? What is the most profitable use of the sales force's efforts? What are the implications of this focus for (a) the longer-term nature of the company's customer base and (b) budgeting criteria for the sales force?

- Within the relevant market segments, what are the implications of typical selling cycles and buying processes for (a) deployment of sales resources, (b) skills and tools required by salespeople, and (c) compensation and performance-evaluation criteria?
- In each case, how should we measure sales effectiveness? What role should any of the following factors play in developing appropriate measures of effectiveness: (a) What information is required to make these measures accurately? (b) What kinds of behavior are encouraged by these measures? (c) Does (or should) the measurement cycle parallel the sales cycle? (d) How should "defensive" vs. "market development" considerations be treated in establishing measures?

We will revisit deployment issues in a larger context in Part Three. The issues involved in measuring sales effectiveness will recur throughout the remainder of the chapters in Part Two.

Channel Management

Reasons for the growing prominence of distribution in marketing strategy have been well documented. They include: increased direct selling costs in many industries; the impact of just-in-time inventory practices on the role of intermediaries; concentration within many traditionally fragmented distribution channels; the growing power of the retail trade vs. national brand manufacturers in consumer goods marketing; more computerized links among manufacturers, distributors, and user-customers; and the appearance of new channels that perform a variety of value-added services in addition to distributors' traditional functions of breaking bulk and providing fast, local deliveries. All of this has escalated the scale and complexity of channel relationships for many marketers, heightened changes in the balance of power between suppliers and resellers, and increased the salience of multichannel management as a component of how to succeed in marketing and sales in many companies.

Cases in the Channel Management chapter illustrate these trends and raise issues concerning the following:

- What factors are relevant in shaping distribution strategy and channel policies for manufacturers? What roles do distributors perform in a given channel strategy? What are the key options available to manufacturers in motivating resellers to perform these roles effectively?
- What factors promote cooperation or conflict in indirect and multichannel selling systems? What criteria are relevant to analyzing the inevitable trade-offs facing supplier and distributor in these systems?
- What factors increase supplier or distributor power in a channel?

In addition, an important theme throughout the cases in this chapter concerns the mutual relationships between distribution decisions and other elements of the marketing mix, such as product policy; pricing; promotional emphases; and sales management practices, including training, compensation, and evaluation criteria. Because distribution decisions implicate so many other aspects of a company's marketing programs, channel issues also will arise in a larger context in Part Three.

Managing Major Accounts

Ultimately, sales management activities should focus on the development and maintenance of profitable accounts. For most companies, "all customers are *not* equal" in the sense that some account for large shares of a company's sales volume and margins, whereas others make up small shares. Some sales managers refer to this as the 80/20 rule, meaning that approximately 20% of the accounts in a customer base may generate in many instances as much as 80% of the company's sales. The final chapter in Part Two focuses on issues encountered at the customer interface and, in particular, on the selling and management of major accounts. Pertinent issues include:

- Account selection. What is a "good" account? What criteria are relevant in deciding whether or not to commit resources to one or another potential major account?
- Account strategy. What factors must be considered in developing an account strategy? What are the implications of each factor for other areas such as manufacturing capacity, product mix, channel relationships, and longer-term marketing strategy?
- Account management. As well as economic and strategic factors, what are some of the organizational and interpersonal issues that typically arise in selling and managing major accounts?

Within this chapter, there are also cases that focus on a core requirement in field marketing: the development and delivery of sales presentations. Although this book is not about selling, it would be remiss to discuss customer encounters and account management without a look at the dynamics of such presentations. Also, while you may not be considering a career in selling or sales management, you will discover that the issues involved in discussing these presentations are pertinent to most managerial positions in a wide variety of occupations, including marketing and nonmarketing, line and staff, and manufacturing and service.

SECTION THREE
Managing Marketing Resources: Organization and Control

Few subjects concern top managers (especially senior marketing managers) as much as organizational structure and processes. By its nature, marketing occurs at the boundaries between the firm, its customers (and prospective customers), and its means of reaching those customers (direct and/or indirect distribution channels). Furthermore, marketing's primary responsibility is to manage the often-conflicting demands among customers, channels, and company policies and so keep the firm's products, services, resources, and focus aligned with the changing needs of various market segments. These factors make organizational issues both crucial and contentious in marketing. Effective marketing managers continually reinvestigate these issues because of their strategic importance for the firm. The way a company organizes its marketing activities helps determine the focus of managers' attention, the kinds of capabilities developed by field and headquarters personnel, and the kinds of marketing strategies that can be implemented by the firm.

The chapters in Part Three illustrate (1) the varied purposes, and demands, placed on marketing organization; (2) the strengths and limitations of different marketing structures and control systems; and (3) how organization affects what skills will (and will not) be developed by marketing managers and companies. Figure D provides an overview of the chapters in this section.

The Key Interfaces chapter focuses on the organizational and control issues designated by **A** and **B** in Figure D. It provides a look at marketing activities in relation to key internal and external environments facing marketing managers. The Customer Service chapter focuses on a link among the activities designated by **B.** It highlights organizational factors that aid or inhibit the provision of customer service, which is a crucial output of marketing activities in all firms.

Figure D

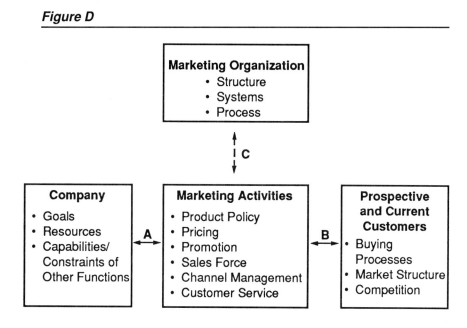

The Structure, Systems, and Process chapter focuses on the interactions designated by **C.** It offers a look at common structures put into place to organize and control marketing activities. Throughout the cases in this section, the insights generated in Part Two concerning the management of field marketing requirements will be critical in analyzing the larger issues of organizational structure and systems at these companies.

Key Interfaces

This chapter raises general issues about the role of marketing in relation to the external market environment and a firm's internal organizational environment. The chapter considers the impact of different market conditions, a company's resource base, and various internal measurement systems on the organization and control of marketing activities.

The chapter introduces these topics by focusing on two consumer goods companies that sell to the same group of customers through similar means but in different competitive environments. What are the elements of good implementation and marketing organization in each situation? How does, or should, the external market environment facing each firm affect the priorities each establishes in its marketing operations? How can we relate what occurs in these two firms' marketing organizations to the insights developed in Part Two concerning the analysis and implementation of field marketing requirements in different environments?

The chapter concludes by looking at an industrial high-tech company and the issues the marketing managers face in coordinating manufacturing, product management, and field sales activities. As well as considering a rapidly changing and technologically dynamic external environment, these managers must look at key internal measurement and performance-evaluation criteria in making decisions. How do each firm's internal systems affect marketing's relations with other functional areas? What are the implications for managing marketing effectively in each firm? What should each manager do about the decisions he or she faces?

The cases in the Key Interfaces chapter also introduce two themes that will recur throughout this section. First, different external and internal environments require different types of conceptual and interpersonal skills. If you are a student considering a career in marketing, consider the different skill requirements placed on marketing management in each case and provide coherent action plans for each case decision. Second, given the practical constraints facing each manager in these cases, there is often a substantial gap between what a manager *should* and *can* do. This raises an issue pertinent to most managers: Textbooks tell us that an organization should create a "fit," or compatibility, between a firm's internal and external environments, but given the often-conflicting demands facing an individual manager, what is a "good decision" in each case? What managerial skills are essential for marketing effectiveness (and perhaps the individual manager's survival) in the face of these conflicting demands?

Customer Service

Nearly all definitions of marketing cite "customer service" as central to the activity. Pressed for a description of their fundamental raison d'être in the organization, most marketing practitioners cite "customer service/serving customer needs." Indeed, in recent years, books such as *In Search of Excellence* have emphasized that "the magic of the excellent companies . . . is simply service, overpowering service, especially after-sales service."

Yet customer service, which is understood to be essential to good marketing, seems to get short shrift in the ongoing activities and resource-allocation patterns of many (if not most) companies. Why? Is it, as many seem to stress, basically a question of "culture," "theme," or the lack of a "service obsession"? Or, are other factors more relevant? What *is* "customer service" in a given situation, and how should we define "good service" (and hence the accompanying assumptions and measurement criteria) for a given company? What are the important organizational factors that aid or inhibit the provision of customer service? Finally, how do service needs influence a firm's product strategy and field marketing requirements, and what can a marketing manager do to improve a firm's customer service?

These questions are considered in the brief Customer Service chapter. The interactions explored in these cases are pertinent to most marketing decisions. They are, moreover, important background for considering the issues and decisions encountered in the final section of the book.

Structure, Systems, and Process

This chapter considers representative structures put in place to organize sales and marketing activities and the issues within each structure involved in coordinating customers' service requirements, channel management demands, and internal company measurement systems. The companies studied in this chapter include industrial firms in both growing and mature markets, consumer goods firms in different market environments, and both industrial and consumer service firms. Hence this concluding chapter allows us to consider as a whole issues that were considered separately in the previous chapters. Within this chapter, the cases have a deliberate mix of situations (consumer vs. industrial, service vs. manufacturing firm, large vs. small firm, field vs. corporate headquarters) because compare-and-contrast is essential in thinking about marketing organization.

The chapter begins by looking at marketing organization and control systems at two leading U. S. companies. IBM and Procter & Gamble have long been cited as especially effective marketers in industrial and consumer markets, respectively. These cases give details about the traditional conduct of marketing activities at each of these firms and illustrate the changes that have pressured each firm's traditional marketing organization and control system during the past decade.

Centralization vs. decentralization of various activities is a perennial issue in marketing organizations in part because effective marketing requires both the attention to local differences appropriate for good field execution and companywide consistency and alignment of resources appropriate for coherent development and implementation of strategy. Global markets and international competition have made this perennial tension particularly salient in the 1990s. Cases in this section of the chapter focus on the issues involved in developing and implementing companywide marketing programs in traditionally decentralized organizations and also contrast the different structures, systems, and processes inherent in a global vs. multinational approach to international markets.

The concluding cases (Getting the Marketing Job Done) provide domestic, consumer-goods contexts that require broad decisions about organization and control systems at companies in which field marketing requirements are changing. These cases examine two companies and provide the kind of knowledge of organizational history required for changes in marketing organizations. The case situations encourage the integration of learning about topics treated throughout the book by raising questions concerning the criteria that are particularly relevant to judgments about what is, or isn't, a well-organized marketing operation.

Before We Begin . . .

Marketing is about managing customer encounters, and so organizing and implementing the marketing effort raises issues crucial to every profit-seeking business. By the end of this book, you will have studied organizational and implementation issues in a wide variety of businesses that face very different field marketing requirements and levels of available resources. Among othe things, you should be sensitive to the dual external and internal requirements that face a boundary function such as marketing. You should be able to move beyond an appreciation for the importance of activities such as field sales management or customer service to the diagnosis of organizational factors that help or hinder good field execution and the provision of appropriate customer service. You will have been exposed to many representative marketing structures and the intricate interactions among structure, systems, and processes in marketing decision making.

This overview has sketched the important themes and issues to consider throughout the book. The chapters provide additional frameworks and specific questions to consider for the materials covered in each chapter. Your primary means of learning, however, will be immersion in, and engagement with, the case studies. In addition to providing realistic decision-making exercises, many of the cases provide valuable background information about a topic. All of the cases illustrate general management concerns about the conduct of marketing activities.

Thus in addition to providing frameworks and concepts relevant to organizational and implementation issues in marketing, I hope the materials in this book will also help to develop skills and attitudes that are especially well nurtured by case pedagogy and especially relevant to effective management practice. These include: the ability to discern complex patterns of organizational cause and effect while respecting particularity and avoiding false analogies; the capacity to realize that not all problems have solutions and that most organizational solutions involve the creation of enabling constraints as well as new capabilities; the analytical and interpersonal capabilities to recognize when the rearrangement of an organization addresses important problems and when it is simply an exercise or excuse for avoiding more fundamental issues; and the willingness to appreciate that indifference to the structures and processes of decision making can make our decisions unwitting prisoners of those organizational factors.

## PART ONE

Strategy and Implementation in Marketing

1. Strategy and/vs. Implementation
- Amerisource
- Dorio Printing Company

## Chapter 1

Strategy and/vs. Implementation

In this book, strategy refers to the what-to-do questions in marketing. What goals should be set in a given time frame? What market segments should be selected for attention? What resources should be allocated among the product categories, target segments, and distribution channels in which the firm competes? Implementation refers to the how-to-do-it aspects of marketing. How should available marketing resources be organized to achieve stated goals? How should marketing requirements in the relevant segments be analyzed? How should marketing programs be executed effectively at the customer interface?

The aphorism "strategy drives implementation" expresses common assumptions about the proper relationship between strategy and implementation in marketing as in other business activities. The belief is that good management and good marketing begin with strategic analysis because "if you don't know where you're going, any road will take you there." To that end, the management literature of the past two decades has been rife with heuristics for strategy development in the form of eight rules for excellence, seven S's, five competitive forces, four product life-cycle stages, three generic strategies, and countless two-by-two matrices.[1]

This way of approaching the relationship between strategy and implementation leads to the sort of picture depicted in Figure A, which implies a series of one-way, cause and effect relationships and, for most companies, a hierarchy of attention. Nearly all strategy theories, and most corporate planning systems, assume a hierarchy in which corporate goals guide business unit strategies and business unit strategies in turn guide functional tactics. In this hierarchy, senior management creates the strategy, and lower levels execute it through the development of specific programs, tactics, and, sometimes, report-

Figure A
Traditional Conceptualization of Strategy-Implementation
Relationship

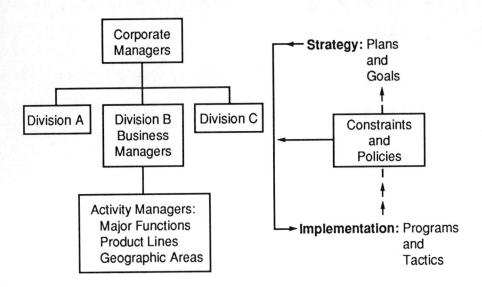

ing systems to alert senior management about how "the strategy" is being implemented in the field.

This dichotomy between formulation and implementation is widely practiced. For a number of reasons, though, there is growing dissatisfaction with this view of the relationship between strategy and implementation, especially in the conduct of marketing activities.

First, there is much evidence that the true relationship between strategy and implementation is inherently reflexive and iterative. As well as feedback loops from the field about how well or how poorly strategies are being implemented, the arrows in Figure A also point to a stronger and more interesting relationship between ends and means. While one purpose of corporate and marketing strategies is to establish goals and, through resource-allocation decisions, the conditions in which field implementation can occur, the quality of the implementation itself quickly and inevitably affects the goals and conditions. To phrase this differently, *how* a company implements its marketing strategy quickly determines *what* strategic goals and plans are feasible. Further, "marketing's strategic flexibility often is constrained by execution behavior in a particularly insidious manner, since management does not always recognize the linkage between how it does the marketing job and what marketing jobs subsequently can be planned."[2] This implies that strategic analysis without recognition of the specific implementation requirements is incomplete at best and actually subversive of strategic goals and options in the long run. The cases in this section look at the implementation requirements of companies developing and altering their marketing strategies.

Second, the traditional dichotomy between strategy formulation and implementation, in practice, has often produced damaging side effects and unforeseen competitive requirements. The formulation/implementation hierarchy often "undermines competitiveness by fostering an elitist view of management that tends to disenfranchise most of the organization. Employees fail to identify with corporate goals or involve themselves deeply in the work of becoming more competitive." [3] The now-standard tools of strategy formulation are shared widely, easily imitated, and often tend to "reduce the number of strategic options management is willing to consider. They create a preference for selling businesses rather than defending them. They yield predictable strategies that rivals easily decode. . . . Competitiveness ultimately depends on the pace at which a company embeds new advantages deep within its organization, not on its stock of advantages at any given time." [4]

This implies that an organization's capacity to simultaneously improve existing skills and learn new ones is its most important and sustainable source of competitive advantage. It also implies that field implementation is a key factor in achieving and building competitive advantage. This is especially true in an increasingly data-rich world where few strategic insights are proprietary or long-lasting and thus where growth and profits often go to that company capable of out-executing its competitors in the implementation of a common strategy. Part Two looks at field marketing requirements: that is, how they relate to different firms' marketing goals and the issues involved in building and improving skills among a company's sales personnel, those people who are responsible for the implementation of marketing strategies through the management of customer encounters.

Third, the formulation/implementation dichotomy assumes and encourages a view of strategizing that is often unrealistic and counterproductive. Effective strategies rely on facts, figures, and forecasts. But strategies also evolve through experimentation as well as deductive analysis. They most often emerge as organizations that are capable of good field execution innovate and respond to their markets. Finally, strategies almost always involve a highly political process as managers weigh the benefits and costs of sponsoring a project in light of the company's reward and measurement systems. A key aspect of effective strategizing is the ability to redefine and indeed manipulate the organizational context in which strategic proposals are put forth, thereby influencing the type of proposals that will be considered and supported. [5]

This suggests the importance of organizational factors in any actionable discussion of strategy or implementation. Organizational structures, measurement and reward systems, and informal processes are central to understanding how goals are established and how marketing tasks actually do (or do not) get accomplished in companies. Part Three surveys marketing organizations at a variety of industrial and consumer-goods companies and considers the implications for managers charged with developing and implementing marketing strategies in each organization.

What do these comments imply for the management of marketing activities and, in particular, for the implementation of marketing strategies?

The Boundary-Spanning Nature of Marketing

Marketing is about getting and keeping customers. Hence it focuses on managing the interface between the firm and its market environment. People who operate at the periphery or boundary of an organization with elements outside that organization are, in the language of the social sciences, "boundary spanners." [6] Boundary spanners serve two important purposes: information transfer and representation. They collect and analyze information from the environment and disseminate it into their organization, and they communicate with the environment on behalf of their organizations. As Figure B indicates, marketing occupies a boundary-spanning role in two senses of that phrase.

Marketing is responsible for managing customer encounters; this means keeping the company's marketing strategy in alignment with customers' buying behavior, the nature and needs of distribution channels used to reach important customer segments, and threats and opportunities posed by competitors' product offerings and competitors' strategies. In turn, dealing with the external environment requires marketing managers to work toward the coordination of important inputs to marketing strategy: for example, manufacturing, product engineering, and various aspects of company operations such as logistics, credit policies, or service terms. In performing this part of their tasks, marketing managers must often cross internal boundaries between other departments at their firms.

Figure B
Marketing as a Boundary-Spanning Role

Thus the essence of the marketing job is to help manage a series of external and internal boundaries. Marketing helps to interpret for the organization the often ambiguous mosaic of information that usually *is* the external environment, or market, of a firm. At the same time, it seeks to keep other functions focused on market realities by acting as the voice of the customer within the organization. Performing this boundary-spanning role is not easy; it usually requires a certain blend of managerial as well as analytical skills. In most firms, marketing managers are responsible for customer and channel relationships, but they do not have formal line authority over parts of their companies that directly affect those relationships. Furthermore, in dealing with other parts of the company, marketing managers often encounter different measurement systems, established administrative procedures, and operating constraints. This suggests some of the conflicts and stresses inherent in many marketing tasks. In turn, the case studies in the book suggest a great deal about the kinds of interpersonal, influence-building, and political skills required to perform effectively in a boundary-spanning role such as marketing.

Figure B can also help to make another point. In marketing, we tend to speak about "target markets," and this metaphor breeds a view of the marketing job as one in which, like William Tell, the task is to hit an external stationary target: "Find a need and fill it," as the old saying goes. But a target market is usually a moving target due to continuing changes in customer demographics, buying behavior, channel structures and capabilities, the firm's own product or service technologies, and competitors' strategies. Hence managing marketing is more of a balancing act than target practice because its boundary-spanning character necessarily entails an ongoing attempt to keep the changing capabilities of the firm aligned with the changing characteristics of a dynamic environment. This view of the marketing job underlines the importance of a point made earlier: An organization's capacity to simultaneously improve existing skills while learning new ones is its most sustainable source of competitive advantage, and field implementation is thus a key factor in achieving and building competitive advantage. In turn, the boundary-spanning requirements of marketing suggest an important criterion useful in evaluating marketing structures and processes encountered in the case studies: the extent to which each helps the organization to manage current field marketing requirements effectively while also providing a necessary balance, or flexibility, in the links established between the firm and its changing environment.

Introductory Case Studies

In dealing with these internal and external boundaries, marketing managers become involved in a variety of areas that span both strategic and tactical concerns. But, effective implementation always requires attention to two important dimensions of marketing: (1) the management of field marketing tasks by the sales force or other personnel responsible for customer encounters and (2) the structures and systems used to organize major marketing activities, direct attention, and monitor performance. The first two cases in this book introduce these marketing implementation concerns.

Amerisource, a subsidiary of a diversified telecommunications company, is a retailer of computers, telephones, and other equipment. The company has been growing rapidly but unprofitably. In response to market and competitive changes, the president of Amerisource and the vice president of marketing and sales recently have initiated a "marketing reorientation," including a change in the company's target markets and marketing strategy. The case focuses on how best to implement the new strategy in the context of slowing market demand, ambitious revenue goals, and increased cost-reduction pressures from the parent company.

As you analyze the situation presented in this case, consider the following questions:

1. What is your evaluation of Amerisource's performance to date? Specifically, what are the areas of potential strength and weakness in the firm?
2. Is the change in marketing strategy warranted? Do you believe this new strategy can succeed?
3. Consider management's market-segmentation analysis and its view of its three target markets. What factors distinguish each segment? What is the role of each segment in the new strategy? What is required in the field to market effectively in each segment?
4. What should Amerisource's management do with regard to the possible changes being considered in sales force deployment, sales management systems, product-line breadth, and market focus?
5. Finally, consider the broader question posed by Amerisource's president in the final paragraph of the case: "What is the role of elements like recruiting criteria, training, compensation, deployment, and other factors when you're involved in the kind of marketing reorientation initiated at Amerisource?" In your view, which of these factors will have the greatest impact on the firm's ability to implement its new marketing strategy?

This first case highlights a situation that most marketing managers encounter repeatedly: Market changes have motivated a change in the firm's strategy, so what must change in marketing and sales policies, programs, and personnel in order to execute that strategy? Since managers must often implement significant changes while continuing to grow short-term revenues and earnings, how can a manager think about the inevitable trade-offs involved in making changes in structure, systems, and people—three areas that tend to have different types of impact on the firm's ability to implement strategy, different time horizons before the impact is felt, and different degrees of difficulty in making changes in each area.

Dorio Printing Company is a small, privately held firm with recently increased production capabilities but static sales volume. Management seeks to increase the firm's sales and profits and is considering hiring new salespeople, but hiring criteria, sales management policies, and the role of personal selling in the firm's strategy are undefined.

As you analyze the situation facing Dorio's management team, consider these questions:

1. What is the sales task at Dorio Printing Company? Specifically, what must the salesperson do in order to succeed, and how (if at all) do these tasks differ by: type of customer; type of product sold; and salesperson?

2. What is the nature of the product being bought by Dorio's customers? How does Dorio provide that product, and what are the implications for market selection; focus of selling efforts; and range of personal-selling styles illustrated in the case?

3. How should Dorio's management define its marketing strategy, and what are the key components of implementing that strategy? In particular, what sales management policies are important to enable Dorio to build sales profitably?

4. Beyond marketing and sales, are there other issues that the management of this company must address? How do these issues affect the marketing strategy and implementation concerns outlined above?

Whereas Amerisource is a subsidiary of a large, multibillion dollar corporation, Dorio is a small, traditionally family-run firm. Amerisource sells high-tech computers and related software whereas Dorio sells printing products and services. Amerisource's management participates in a formal corporate planning process and has outlined a marketing strategy whereas Dorio's management has traditionally operated without any formal plans or strategies and indeed seems to take pride in its "laissez-faire philosophy of managing sales and marketing." As you analyze these cases, consider these differences between the two companies' resource and corporate situations, the nature of their products and selling tasks, and their general management processes. How do these differences affect the key capabilities and constraints involved in organizing and implementing the marketing effort at each firm? Like fingerprints, companies are unique—singular combinations of people, structures, and resources—but we can observe useful patterns of marketing requirements. Compare-and-contrast techniques will be important means for distinguishing such patterns throughout this book.

References

1. For reviews of strategic management frameworks see, for example, Peter Lorange and Richard F. Vancil, *Strategic Planning Systems* (Englewood Cliffs, N.J.: Prentice-Hall, 1977); Charles W. Hofer and Dan E. Schendel, *Strategy Formulation: Analytical Concepts* (St. Paul, Minn.: West Publishing, 1978); Robert Lamb, ed., *Competitive Strategic Management* (Englewood Cliffs, N.J.: Prentice-Hall, 1984); Kenneth J. Hat-

ten and Mary Louise Hatten, *Strategic Management: Analysis and Action* (Englewood Cliffs, N.J.: Prentice-Hall, 1987); or David W. Cravens, *Strategic Marketing* (Homewood, Ill.: Irwin, 1987).

2. Thomas V. Bonoma, *The Marketing Edge: Making Strategies Work* (New York: The Free Press, 1985), pp. 8–9.

3. Gary Hamel and C. K. Prahalad, "Strategic Intent," *Harvard Business Review* (May-June 1989): 75.

4. *Ibid.*, pp. 69, 72.

5. See Joseph L. Bower, *Managing the Resource Allocation Process: A Study of Corporate Planning and Investment* (Boston: Harvard Business School Press, 1970, 1986); and Henry Mintzberg, "Crafting Strategy," *Harvard Business Review* (July-August 1987): 66–75. For applications of this research to the formulation of marketing strategies in particular, see Nigel F. Piercy, "The Marketing Budgeting Process: Marketing Management Implications," *Journal of Marketing* 51 (October 1987): 45–59; and Michael D. Hutt, Peter H. Reingen, and John R. Ronchetto, Jr., "Tracing Emergent Processes in Marketing Strategy Formation," *Journal of Marketing* 52 (January 1988): 4–19.

6. A seminal discussion of boundary roles in organization is J. D. Thompson, *Organizations in Action* (New York: McGraw-Hill, 1967). Other important discussions of boundary-spanning behavior and the academic literature about such roles are J. Stacy Adams, "The Structure and Dynamics of Behavior in Organizational Boundary Roles," in *Handbook of Organizational and Industrial Psychology,* ed. by M. Dunnette (Chicago, Ill.: Rand McNally, 1976), and Howard Aldrich and Diane Herker, "Boundary Spanning Roles and Organizational Structure," *Academy of Management Review* 2 (April 1977): 217–230.

Case 1
Amerisource

On January 15, 1986, Mr. Brian Pemberton, president of Amerisource, Inc., a retailer of computers, telephones, and other equipment, was meeting with Mr. William Lenahan, Amerisource's vice president for sales and marketing. Mr. Pemberton said:

> Bill, in 1985 we made 102% of our revenue goals, which was great considering the computer retail market this past year. But you know that at planning meetings with our corporate parent we set $125 million as our sales goal for 1986, and so far industry conditions show little sign of improving. We must make sure our marketing programs do everything possible to achieve that goal.

Mr. Lenahan replied:

> I agree, and I'm concerned about a few areas, especially the execution of the new value-added marketing strategy we adopted last year. We recognized before most computer dealers that there was little money to be made by continuing to "push boxes." And we decided last year to shift our strategy from retail business to various value-added marketing programs. But now most computer retailers plan to adopt strategies similar to ours. The difference will be in how much better we execute the strategy, especially through the field sales force at individual locations.

"We must do it well," noted Mr. Pemberton. "Bill, I'd like to review the marketing programs already in place and think about where we might improve things. Let's take a zero-based perspective on our marketing programs and discuss *any* changes that seem appropriate."

This case was prepared by Associate Professor Frank V. Cespedes and Research Associate Susan Gruber Vishner as the basis for class discussion rather than to illustrate either effective or ineffective handling of an administrative situation.

Company Background

Amerisource was a wholly owned subsidiary of United Telecom Inc. (UTI). In 1985, Amerisource operated 37 stores, which the company called Business Centers, in 22 cities. Each Business Center sold software, computer supplies, telephones, typewriters, printers, and microcomputers. Amerisource had revenues of $74.7 million in 1985, up from $4 million in 1983 and $26.7 million in 1984 (see Exhibit 1).

UTI was a diversified telecommunications company. Its core business, United Telephone Systems, provided telephone service in 19 states and had a regulated rate of return of approximately 14%. UTI also had several subsidiaries providing long-distance service, mobile telephone services, and data communications networking. Amerisource was part of UTI's diversified operations group, which included companies producing computer graphics systems, applications software, computer services, and telephone equipment. In 1985, diversified operations accounted for one-sixth of UTI's revenues of $3.2 billion (see Exhibit 2). Also in 1985, UTI's management announced that it would spend approximately $2 billion on expanding the firm's long-distance network and adding capabilities for transmission of high-speed data as well as voice communications. These capital investments had increased UTI's debt considerably.

Amerisource was founded by UTI in 1982 to sell personal computers and telephones. UTI's corporate management believed that computers and telephones would be a better way than phone stores alone to reach retail customers. The first store opened in Prairie Village, a suburb of Kansas City, Missouri, in November 1982. Initially, the store sold computers, cash registers, telephones, game computers, business software, home software, and more. In 1983, $3 million of Amerisource's $4 million in revenues came from the Prairie Village store.

Amerisource was incorporated in August 1983 (it had been a department of UTI). In September 1983, Mr. Pemberton was hired from Mitel (after 16 years with IBM) to head Amerisource. Mr. Pemberton reported to Mr. Charles Battey, vice chairman of UTI, who reviewed Amerisource's performance monthly. Amerisource offices were located at UTI headquarters in Kansas City, one floor below UTI's executive offices. Amerisource received funding from UTI in the form of 70% equity and 30% debt (UTI loaned money to its subsidiary at sub-prime rates). UTI conducted a formal planning and budgeting process, in which Amerisource participated. Through 1985, UTI had invested about $36 million in Amerisource.

History of Store Operations

Mr. William Lenahan joined Amerisource in January 1984, after 12 years with IBM where he had managed the expansion of IBM's Product Centers from 3 in 1981 to 72 by 1983. "When I first came to Amerisource," Mr. Lenahan said, "our sales reps were overwhelmed by the number of products we had. I felt we had to have a clearer focus if Amerisource was to grow." Amerisource had originally defined its customer as a small business owner or home computer user. Stores were placed in suburban shopping areas and the product line featured Apple, Commodore, and other microcomputers as well as residential telephones. Advertising stressed Amerisource's prices. Sales reps provided customer support such as setting up equipment. Each store had its own repair technician.

Amerisource did not have stores in the largest 30 cities. The company felt smaller, "second-tier" markets were less competitive and therefore it would be easier to achieve substantial local market share.

Stores had about 3,500 square feet of space, comparable in size to Computerland stores. Initially, one wall of the store displayed telephone systems and supplies. Another wall had personal computers displayed at desk areas, often with printers and other peripheral equipment. The center of the store had modular cubes showing other computer systems. In the rear was a Learning Center for training classes. Against the rear wall computers for use with information services were displayed. Sales reps focused on people who walked into the store. According to one manager:

> Each sale required a lot of time because customers were inexperienced and technically unsophisticated. There was often no follow-up purchase from a sale, and sales reps were constantly providing support for small systems. Products were oriented toward both home and business use, and the same amount of effort was put into each sale. Discounting off retail price was common. The reps had many products to cover and could not keep up with all the new developments.

In 1984, Mr. Pemberton and Mr. Lenahan decided to focus on business customers rather than the retail consumer. New stores were located in business areas where the target customer worked. Amerisource opened 21 additional stores in 1984, usually clustering more than one store in each of a number of areas in 16 states.

With the change in customer focus came a change in product focus. The product line was cut to three microcomputers (IBM, Compaq, and AT&T) and peripheral equipment for those microcomputers. Also retained were some of the advanced telephone products. Software packages were primarily business packages such as spreadsheets and work processing. Games and children's educational software were no longer carried.

The stores' physical layout was also changed. In the front, 2,200 square feet were used to display computer systems and for sales reps to demonstrate systems for three or four people. Each store retained a Learning Center (600 square feet) for teaching classes on specific systems or software. Inventory was assigned 200 square feet, and the manager's office 100 square feet. Additional space was used for the store's service technician and desks for four or five sales reps.

In 1985, opening a Business Center required approximately $350,000 (including a corporate overhead assessment of $100,000 per year per store) while rent averaged $14.41 per square foot annually. Break-even sales volume for each center was about $2 million. Exhibit 3 indicates top-store rankings according to various criteria.

Defining Amerisource's Target Markets

In late 1984, Amerisource adopted a new marketing strategy, based on what management termed a "value-added selling" approach to business accounts. There were three target markets: 1) corporate accounts, 2) walk-in retail accounts, and 3) value-added accounts, small- and medium-sized businesses without significant microcomputer experience.

According to Mr. Pemberton, this strategy was selected primarily because, "in dollar terms, the business market accounts for more than 75% of the value of personal computer shipments annually and promises greater year-to-year growth than any other user group." Mr. Lenahan added:

> In 1982–83, people rushed out and bought microcomputers and used the games, but they didn't know what to do with the computers afterwards. Small- and medium-sized businesses are really just beginning to think about personal computer purchases, and Amerisource can build a significant customer base in this market segment.

Each type of account had different characteristics. *Corporate accounts* (50% of 1985 revenues) typically purchased large quantities of hardware, some software, and very little service or training since corporate accounts generally had in-house support capabilities. The average microcomputer sale to corporate accounts totaled $4,000 per system, of which 4% was software and support services and 96% was equipment. The average sale took 12 hours of sales representative time and a few hours of a Business Center manager's time.

Corporate accounts were *Fortune* 1000 companies or any company that bought in volume. Amerisource required minimum purchases of 50 machines annually to qualify for its corporate discount of 25–30% off retail list price. To start the sales cycle, an Amerisource rep would contact a large local company's purchasing or MIS department. The rep would try to get an appointment to show what products Amerisource carried and what services Amerisource could provide.

During the early 1980s, many microcomputers were bought by corporate managers on an ad hoc, individual basis. But by 1985 large companies often purchased microcomputers through their MIS departments to ensure compatibility and to qualify for volume discounts. Many corporate accounts used at least two local sources for microcomputers and peripherals, although Amerisource sales reps often did not know how many other vendors they might be selling against.

Once a company had become an established account, the sales rep would check on hardware/software needs, assemble equipment, track orders, and stay visible and accessible to the purchasing agents. Corporate accounts usually planned their purchases months ahead. An Amerisource rep often had sales throughout the year, on a regular basis, from corporate accounts. Mr. Pemberton noted:

> Pricing and product availability are the keys to corporate account sales, but there is little vendor loyalty and intense competition in this high-volume, low-margin segment. In the Midwest, we have the multiple locations required to provide service to corporate accounts but not locations in other major metropolitan areas where many corporate offices are located.
>
> We want corporate business because it allows us to maintain purchases from our suppliers at the maximum discount levels. In addition, corporate accounts provide the sales force with exposure to sophisticated user environments, and that's useful in selling to smaller accounts. But corporate accounts should not be our major thrust.

Retail accounts (30% of 1985 revenues) were usually individuals or operators of small businesses who purchased simple equipment, in terms of operating capability, and some service, training, and support. The average microcomputer system sale to a retail account totaled $3,500 of which 6% was standard word processing and spreadsheet software and support. The average discount from list price was 21%. The average sale took 8 hours of sales rep time. Mr. Pemberton explained:

> The concept of "retail sales" tends to be understood in the industry as traditional retailing, with an emphasis on site selection, store layout, etc. But we view this segment as inbound marketing which utilizes mass marketing techniques such as seminars and direct mail.

"Value-added" accounts (20% of 1985 revenues) referred to small- and medium-sized businesses[1] seeking to use computers but also uncertain about appropriate hardware and software applications. Mr. Lenahan noted that,

> The value-added segments are seeking solutions to business problems. These segments have some of the highest growth rates, and present the greatest opportunity for Amerisource to sell its services and support capabilities.

Within the value-added market, management distinguished between (1) Local Area Network applications (LANs), and (2) vertical markets.

LANs enabled users to exchange data and usually required continued support and training from the vendor. Forecasts in 1985 indicated that by 1990 50% of all business microcomputers would be networked. Amerisource targeted LAN applications that involved 4–15 work stations. According to Mr. Lenahan:

> LAN sales are a prime opportunity to improve margins and a vehicle to move our sales force to higher-value system sales. In addition, there is higher vendor loyalty in this segment, and that can produce significant add-on business.

---

[1] By "small business," Amerisource's management meant companies with 50 or fewer employees and $1–$10 million in sales. Medium-sized companies fell between this designation and *Fortune* 1000 companies. According to one research firm, in 1985 fewer than 10% of the 3.2 million U.S. companies with 50 or fewer employees owned any sort of computer.

> The keys to developing a strong niche in the LAN market are a sales force with technical and systems selling capabilities and good service and support capabilities. We have the latter, but our sales force is still learning as far as system sale capabilities are concerned.

After extensive training of the sales force during the third quarter of 1985, LAN sales accounted for 150 installations and $1.7 million in revenues for Amerisource in the fourth quarter.

Vertical markets referred to computer systems tailored to particular industries and occupations. According to Mr. Lenahan, an emphasis on vertical markets could yield the following benefits:

> First, the focus can optimize the sales time for our marketing representatives. For example, most contractors have similar needs in computing systems, and learning those needs can make for more efficient sales calls among our sales force. Second, discounts can be minimized, and complete system sales maximized, with a focus on selected vertical markets.
>
> Third, we can build a strong reference base with this sales strategy, and that in turn can build our market presence and revenues. Fourth, add-on business is likely to be greater with systems that are designed as solutions for specific industries or applications. Fifth, the potential for big ticket sales is greater with solutions. For example, in 1985 a package we put together with a software vendor for the construction industry had an average sale of $16,500, and the software and service content of the sale was about 50%.

Mr. Lenahan had selected six vertical markets (CPAs, manufacturing, distribution, medical, legal, and construction) after looking at national surveys of the penetration rate of computers in various markets. The dollar value of the markets was evaluated and then regional surveys were done to see if the same trends held true for Amerisource's markets. In addition, Amerisource looked for segments which would use intensive computing and which hadn't been penetrated in Amerisource's areas.

Surveys indicated that 34% of all business software purchases was accounting software. Most vertical market software sold by Amerisource was based on accounting functions and then customized for each industry. For example, a legal software package included general bookkeeping functions and a module for tracking lawyers' billable time.

Sales reps were expected to learn specific vertical market packages and "to sell up the product line." Each software package could be upgraded to a networked system and ranged in price from $500 to $4,000 per package. Amerisource planned to use direct mail, telemarketing, and industry seminars to draw qualified prospects into Business Centers. Each center manager was required by Amerisource corporate headquarters to assign at least one salesperson to one or more of the six vertical markets, but, as Mr. Pemberton noted, "We did not provide the field with a formula dictating which kind of people should be assigned to which kinds of vertical markets." Mr. Pemberton believed the criteria used by center managers in assigning salespeople to vertical markets differed from one center to the next. Mr. Lenahan commented:

> In the vertical markets we do best in manufacturing, followed by distribution and legal areas. These markets have the widest selection of products. The medical section hasn't done that well. We don't have enough product offerings to address that market, nor are there many good packages yet available for us to choose from.
>
> In manufacturing and distribution, we target companies with less than 100 employees and around $50 million in revenue. These companies are still using manual systems and want to get control of their growing businesses. Our reps can deal directly with the owner, who makes the decision to buy.

Exhibit 4 indicates potential accounts in various cities and vertical segments targeted by Amerisource.

With its new strategy, Amerisource's ideal customer was a smaller business which required, in addition to the basic hardware, software for problems specific to its business, service contracts, training, and advice on system operations for some period after the purchase. Amerisource had service technicians in each Business Center trained to repair equipment at the center or at the customer site. If repairs took longer than 24 hours, Amerisource provided free replacement equipment until the customer's system was repaired. Amerisource also offered free customer support through an 800 telephone number for 90 days following a purchase.

Customers were also encouraged to enroll for training classes taught in the Business Centers (for a fee) and to use the 800 number for additional questions. Training was provided in the Business Centers by local, independent computer training firms in Amerisource's markets. Amerisource provided the customers, allowed the training firm to use the center's demonstration equipment and software on nights and weekends, and split training revenues equally with the independent training firm; in return, the training firm provided all training personnel and incurred the variable costs of the training seminars. Other services included a 30-day trade-in period for software if the customer was not satisfied and installation of equipment. In general, these support services generated much higher margins for Amerisource than equipment sales. During 1985, Amerisource changed its advertising strategy to emphasize its support capabilities (see Exhibit 5).

Computer Retailing: Industry Background

The first computer retail store was opened in 1975 in California and sold computer kits for hobbyists and engineers wishing to build their own systems. Software was limited and often needed to be written by the user. In 1977, Apple, Commodore, and Tandy–Radio Shack introduced microcomputers which were easier to use and, as more software was developed, sales of microcomputers soared.

In 1981, the IBM PC was introduced, and Apple, which had been the best-selling microcomputer, was overtaken by IBM. Many companies developed IBM-compatible microcomputers which allowed their customers to use software developed for the IBM PC. The most successful was Compaq Computer: its original personal computer, introduced in 1982, sold at retail for $2,995, $800 below the price of a comparable IBM PC. Other companies entered the market, and it was estimated that in 1985, 150 companies sold in the United States, while over 250 sold microcomputers throughout the world.

Distribution Channels

The first microcomputers were sold by mail. Early computer retailers were generally independent merchants with single store locations that served primarily the home buyer. In 1977, Computerland opened its first franchised store, and Tandy opened the first manufacturer's store with the Radio Shack Computer Center. By 1980, other manufacturers including Digital, Xerox, Control Data and IBM had established computer retail outlets. But by 1985, only Tandy–Radio Shack maintained a substantial presence in the retail market. Other computer outlets included large retailers such as Sears. In 1985, there were 4,300 computer specialty stores represented as follows:

Type	Number of Locations	% of Stores
Independents	1,900	44.2%
Franchised Stores	1,200	27.9
Manufacturer-Owned	650	15.1
Company-Owned	550	12.8
	4,300	100.0%

Independents were privately owned and typically had one to three locations in the same area; 47% had only one location. *Franchised stores* were owned by individuals or corporations who purchased the franchise for a particular site from the parent company. The franchisor usually provided dealer training, merchandise distribution and advertising copy and charged a percentage of the gross sales for their services in addition to initial fees. Fifty-nine percent of franchisees owned more than one store. *Manufacturer-owned* stores generally sold and serviced only that company's products. *Company-owned* stores were outlets such as Amerisource, Sears Business Centers, or Businessland stores. Telecommunications companies such as former Bell operating companies had also entered the computer retail market by 1985. Their stores were expected to combine voice and data communications products as well as personal computers.

In 1985, about 30,000 outlets sold computers, but computer specialty stores accounted for 50% of all microcomputer sales. Other outlets included consumer electronics stores, appliance outlets, catalog showrooms, office equipment dealers, department stores, and some toy store chains. Often with previous experience selling calculators or video games, these outlets had gradually extended their product lines to incorporate personal computers primarily for home use.

In addition, a channel known as the "value-added reseller" (VAR) had become increasingly important in recent years. VARs sold computers to businesses after adding additional hardware or software for specific markets. Unlike retailers, VARs did not have storefronts. A value-added reseller which did have a storefront was known as a "value-added dealer" (VAD). Some observers considered retailers such as Computerland and Entre to be value-added dealers because some of their franchises had begun providing technical support and service.

In 1984, VARs accounted for an estimated 18% of all personal computer sales and about 7% of spreadsheet and database management software sales. Of the estimated 4,000 personal computer VARs operating in 1984, nearly 50% had sales of less than $1 million annually, 33% had sales of $1–$5 million, 7% had sales of more than $50 million.

Computer manufacturers (including those carried by Amerisource) had increased their participation in VAR channels, offering equality with retail accounts in terms of discounts, hardware support, access to manufacturers' service centers, training support, and marketing assistance. In turn, VARs bought in quantity and provided manufacturers with access to specialized markets ranging from pet shops and racquetball clubs to hospitals and automobile dealers. A survey indicated that in 1985 VARs sold computer systems to small and large businesses as well as federal, state, and local governments. But the majority of VAR sales were to businesses with less than 500 employees and especially in service industries. Mr. Lenahan noted:

> There are three types of VARs in our local markets. The first and most prevalent type is a small, often one- or two-person firm begun by a former systems engineer of a computer company. These VARs customize specific applications for specific firms in their local areas by writing code for their limited number of customers and helping with installation and training. These VARs do not have the capital to expand outside their limited market area, and competition is by specific Business Center.
>
> Unlike these VARs, Amerisource does not write code and does not have the same customization capability: we're selling standardized packages to our various vertical markets. But we have a nationwide presence, are better capitalized than these VARs and so have more staying power, and aim to provide customers with consistency of support over a long period of time. These points are important because many small VARs go bankrupt or decide to leave the business, and their customers often can't find anyone else to service the specialized software that's been installed by the VAR.
>
> A second type of VAR is the former dentist, lawyer or veterinarian who understands in detail the jargon and administrative procedures of a profession, and

has written a specific software program. Their programs are tailored precisely to the flow of work at a given profession, and you will find literally hundreds of these VARs at various industry trade shows. But they tend not to be able to provide customer support and often lack financial staying power.

A third type of VAR is a big company that's been authorized by a computer OEM to sell its equipment along with a specific software package. For example, some of the "Big-8" accounting firms have developed accounting packages that they sell, along with the hardware, to DP/MIS management at large corporations.

Exhibit 6 provides data concerning the use of personal computers by industry. In most segments, manufacturers' direct sales forces, as well as their authorized dealers, sold products to larger accounts.

Mr. Pemberton characterized industry conditions in early 1986 as follows:

> A few years ago, when IBM PCs were in short supply, computer stores could sit back, take orders, and enjoy full margins. But those easy sales are gone. Today's customers are trying to determine how to use the computers they have. Some are delaying purchases in anticipation of new technologies. As a result, price cutting has been rampant, and a shakeout that began among manufacturers has now spread to computer retailers.

> Competitors have adopted different responses. Several chains feel private label products offer profit opportunities. Others with the financial and marketing resources are moving toward a full-service, full-price strategy. Amerisource was among the first to adopt this strategy. Here, computer retailers seek to do for small businesses what a data processing department does in a large company—things like selecting and installing equipment, training employees, choosing the right software, and modifying it for a specific business. Such support can boost profits: dealers can charge $75 an hour for services that cost them as little as $25 an hour.

> A basic problem in the industry, however, is the slowed growth. For the foreseeable future, there may simply be too many computer stores chasing too few customers.

Manufacturers' Retail Distribution Strategies

IBM had increased the number of its dealers from 1,500 to an estimated 2,500 in 1985. In late 1985, IBM announced it would not sign additional dealers. In 1984, IBM's retail dealers accounted for 65% of the company's U.S. sales of personal computers and systems. Additionally, IBM PCs were sold by VADs and VARs. In 1985, most of IBM's PC sales went through third parties, although IBM did maintain a direct sales force for larger volume PC sales. Amerisource was an IBM dealer.

Compaq computers were sold through many of the same dealers as IBM's PC, since in 1982, when Compaq was founded, IBM PCs were in short supply and dealers were seeking similar products. Unlike IBM and AT&T, Compaq sold its computers solely to dealers and had no direct sales force. Compaq's management felt that using multiple channels would result in competition for the same end user, which would result in price cutting and price erosion. Compaq had approximately 1,700 dealers in the United States and approximately 2,600 worldwide. Compaq's computers were priced so that dealers grossed higher dollar and percentage margins when selling at list price than IBM. Compaq's dealers were also given a liberal return policy and substantial co-op advertising support.

AT&T 's microcomputers were introduced in June 1984, and by mid-1985, AT&T had over 1,000 computer dealers. AT&T's PC 3600 was manufactured by Olivetti SpA, of which AT&T had purchased a 25% share. AT&T's direct sales force was trying to develop *Fortune* 2000 business.

Amerisource's top selling computer in 1985 was the IBM PC followed by the IBM XT, Compaq, IBM AT, AT&T 6300 and the Compaq Plus. In 1985, IBM equipment accounted for 70% of Amerisource's CPU sales and about 50% of revenues, Compaq for 17% of CPU sales and AT&T for 13%.

Mr. Pemberton was a member of the IBM Dealer Advisory Council and Mr. Lenahan was a member of the AT&T Dealer Advisory Council. Amerisource received the maximum discounts possible from its suppliers. IBM gave a 40% discount with the purchase of 400 units/month. Compaq's discount was 41% with an additional 3% for co-op advertising with purchases of 300 units/month. AT&T gave a 46% discount and 3% for co-op advertising. AT&T's official terms were 300 units/month but AT&T was often flexible in order to get its products into retail stores.

Amerisource's best-selling software was Lotus 1-2-3, DOS 2.1, Smart, Symphony, Multimate, BPI Accounting, and Open Systems Accounting. Amerisource's retail competitors sold the same or similar software.

Amerisource sold telephones made by AT&T and TIE, a Japanese company. Amerisource sold a more advanced telephone than the basic desk phone and some sales reps had done well selling telephones. Installation was arranged by the purchaser. According to Mr. Lenahan, telephone customers did not upgrade their equipment frequently and tended to be small businesses that were moving or growing rapidly. In Amerisource's market areas, telephones were sold by AT&T and Faxon stores (which specialized in phone systems), department stores, discounters, electronics stores and other computer retailers.

Amerisource: Marketing Organization and Programs

Amerisource was organized as depicted in Exhibit 7. Marketing and sales represented over 80% of Amerisource's 470 employees in 1985. Field marketing personnel were regional managers (responsible for the operations and profitability of Business Centers in their areas), Business Center managers (responsible for managing the center's staff and operations), and sales representatives. Supporting each center was an administrative coordinator and an assistant manager. The center also provided customer service through a full-time technician. Each center was staffed with four to eight sales representatives.

Business Center Managers

In 1985, the average age of center managers was 32, and most had an undergraduate or graduate degree in business. Prior to joining Amerisource, they had an average of eight years in the office products or office automation industry. Many had worked in sales and marketing with previous employers including IBM, Wang, Xerox, and others. Once employed by Amerisource, center managers attended a two-week sales and product training seminar and a program covering retail merchandising and accounting techniques.

Center managers were responsible for meeting revenue and gross margin quotas for their stores. One manager offered the following scenario for a typical day:

Business Center Manager Time Allocations

Task	Percent of Day
1. Ensuring Product Availability from Corporate Supply for Customer	40%
2. Direct Customer Sales Activities	15
3. Sales Force Supervision	10
4. Customer Assistance by Telephone	10
5. Managing Vendor Relations	10
6. Managing Accounts Receivable	10
7. Merchandising/Store Display	5
8. Paperwork[a]	_____
	100+%

[a]Paperwork was often done at night. Many center managers reported that work weeks of 60 or more hours were not uncommon.

Managers divided their territories into "regions," provided sales assistance, and set revenue and gross margin quotas for each salesperson. They also assigned "vertical" markets to salespeople.

Center managers received a base salary of about $25,000 and incentive compensation: at 100% of quota, center managers received about $57,000 in 1985. During the past 16 months, Amerisource had added 30 center managers, 25 of whom were hired from outside the company. Mr. Mike Connors, vice president of Human Resources, commented:

> With our new emphasis on the business market, we developed a profile of the type of person we wanted to hire as a center manager: ideally, a branch manager at IBM, Xerox or 3M, or someone with 10–12 years of similar sales experience but who had not been given a chance to be a manager.
>
> We hired 90% of the people we made offers to in 1984, and not because of the base salary: most were already making $40–50,000 at their old firms. They were attracted by the opportunity to run their own little businesses in each Business Center, to the entrepreneurial autonomy, no detailed corporate manuals, and the potential for $2–$3 million in center revenues in the near term.

Each manager was hired from the area where the center was located: we wanted managers who knew the customers, the city and the business community. No other staff was hired until the manager was in place.

The Sales Force

In 1983 and early 1984, almost all sales came from inbound (walk-in) customers, and most sales reps and managers came from retail backgrounds. Few of the sales reps did prospecting for sales leads and Amerisource provided little training in prospecting or selling skills. To carry out Amerisource's new strategy, Mr. Lenahan felt almost all the original sales reps and store managers needed to be replaced. Accordingly, in 1984 Amerisource hired 130 sales reps and in 1985 an additional 100 sales reps. According to Mr. Connors,

> We looked for people with college degrees in marketing, business, or finance. We also talked to people with computer science degrees but were not primarily interested in technical expertise; we were looking for sales reps who could relate to business problems of the president of a small- to medium-sized company.

Mr. Pemberton added that "center managers did the hiring, but we encouraged them to take into account (a) an experienced salesperson's established customer base: we needed increased revenues in the short term, and so especially liked people who had already sold products to our targeted markets in an area; and (b) some form of industry-specific knowledge, since we knew it would take time to train adequately the many new salespeople we were hiring in the paperwork, procedures, and jargon of different vertical markets."

Once hired, salespeople received two weeks of training at headquarters where they were introduced to the company, its senior management, and the products and services offered by Amerisource. Within 6–12 months, the reps returned for training in "verticals"—systems specifically designed for particular industries—and in advanced systems such as local area networks. Each representative also spent nine hours each month in "applications training" at the Business Center. This program was designed to ensure that reps became familiar with new software and communications technologies. Center managers administered monthly tests to determine the comprehension of these in-store training programs.

Once in the field, salespeople were assigned a geographic region within a Business Center territory, and some were also assigned to a specific vertical market that cut across the geographic sales regions. Salespeople had quota objectives for revenue, sales to vertical user groups, sales of advanced hardware, and gross margin achieved on all sales. If a sales rep not assigned to a given vertical market provided a lead to the rep who was assigned to that market, then the former received a percentage (10%–30% depending upon the Business Center) of the latter's commission on the sale.

The 1985 compensation plan for Business Center managers and sales representatives is summarized in Exhibit 8. Sales reps received a base salary and commissions tied both to individual performance and the quota-attainment performance of the center. In 1985, the base salary for sales reps was $14,000, with no cap on earnings. Average total compensation for a salesperson was $35,000, with a high of $78,000 and a low of $18,000. Sales reps were reviewed quarterly by the center manager concerning their performance in areas such as training, administrative responsibilities, and sales of specific products or services.

Amerisource also had various motivational programs for the sales force. In 1984, the Century Club was established for salespeople who exceeded quota. The primary incentive was a trip to a resort for three days. In addition to sales contests sponsored by Amerisource, some suppliers provided "spiffs," or incentives, to the sales force for selling their products. For example, in 1985 AT&T gave a cash bonus for every PC 6300 microcomputer sold. But Mr. Lenahan commented: "We don't like vendor spiffs because in effect they tell our reps what to sell. We may want to move higher margin items, but the rep wants the spiff from the vendor."

The casewriter spent a day with a sales representative, Ms. J. R. Irwin, who worked out of Amerisource's City Center Store in Kansas City. Located in a shopping plaza in the business district, City Center did much of its business from customers who walked into the store during lunch hours or after work. Sales reps at City Center, as in most Business Centers, spent some days in the store working with walk-in customers and some days on outbound sales calls. Directly across the courtyard from the City Center store was a Computerland outlet.

After graduating from the University of Missouri, Ms. Irwin spent nine years on active duty in the Navy. She was a line officer when she left the Navy in 1976 and joined IBM as a marketing representative. By 1982, Ms. Irwin noted she was "ready to leave IBM: it was great training and a fine organization, but I didn't like the bureaucracy and I didn't see many promotional opportunities ahead." She then joined a graphics design firm, bringing in over $250,000 worth of business before that company decided to eliminate its sales force in 1985. On the advice of a friend who was also a sales rep for Amerisource, Ms. Irwin joined Amerisource in March 1985.

Ms. Irwin noted that on a typical day in the center,

> I arrive between 7:30 and 8:00 A.M. and usually stay until 6:00 P.M. In the center, the sales job is mainly handling telephone calls and working with walk-ins. I try to do other work, such as calling prospects or working on the specifications of a potential sale, but this is not always possible in the walk-in environment. On "out" days, I follow up on leads directly from my home and make sales calls.

Ms. Irwin estimated that "an average sale in outbound accounts is $5–$6,000. A great sale would be in the $45–$50,000 range, but even a good rep only hits those home runs once or twice a year." Ms. Irwin noted she had recently sold a $43,000 system and credited an Amerisource training course with helping to make the sale. She explained that a friend had casually mentioned that the maintenance contract on his firm's computer system had recently expired. From the training course, Ms. Irwin knew this meant certain tax advantages had therefore expired. In addition, the system's age suggested it was probably obsolete, and so the user would soon be in the market again for a new system. Making these assumptions, she contacted the president of the firm and soon made the sale.

Based on her observations, Ms. Irwin believed that "value-added" marketing was not yet a major emphasis among the Amerisource sales force.

> It's easier for new reps to focus on a vertical market because they don't yet have established accounts or customers. Some other reps tend to gravitate toward certain products, based on their liking for either the hardware or software. With that interest, they may then find themselves selling more to certain types of customers or certain types of applications. But I don't believe that selling solutions is yet a major thrust for most of the salespeople.

Conclusion

In their discussions, Messrs. Pemberton and Lenahan focused on two related issues: how best to meet Amerisource's 1986 sales target in the context of continued slow growth throughout the computer retail industry and, in particular, how to improve implementation of the firm's "value-added" marketing strategy.

Mr. Lenahan introduced the possibility of reorganizing the sales force into two categories: Corporate Account reps and Value-Added Account reps. Such a move would mean that some salespeople would have to trade accounts, and it would require changes in the compensation plans for each group. Mr. Lenahan also suggested the possibility of adding a sales manager in each Business Center to work with reps in value-added sales:

> The center manager must now work with 25–30 employees, and that probably doesn't leave much time to provide daily guidance to salespeople trying to crack value-added accounts. A sales manager in each center would mean more overhead, but it could focus our value-added selling efforts more effectively. On the other hand, we could try to work within the existing structure and deployment of the sales force, and focus on how current efforts could be improved through changes in recruiting, compensation, training, and motivation.

Mr. Pemberton wondered whether Amerisource was trying to target too many, or too few, vertical market segments and whether the firm should add to its computer product line. He noted:

> Slower growth in PC sales means we will encounter more competition from other retailers, and that means we want to explore all segments with the widest array of products and services possible. However, expense control must be a priority for us in 1986 given our budget, and that means we must focus our training efforts and improve sales force productivity.

Summarizing the discussion thus far, Mr. Pemberton commented:

Bill, UTI has supported our expansion thus far, but as we discussed at the last planning meeting, the corporation will measure us by our ROE performance just as it does its other business units. Our strategy is aimed at improving profitability, but it means a radical reorientation in marketing programs. And 1986 will be tougher than 1985. If anything, the current environment seems to me to reaffirm our basic strategy, but it also requires us to take another look at specific elements of execution. What's the role of elements like recruiting criteria, training, compensation, deployment, and other factors when you're involved in the kind of marketing reorientation we've initiated at Amerisource? For example, can we spell out the criteria for a successful vertical-market sales rep and, if so, should we standardize across our Business Centers or continue to let individual Center managers evolve their own criteria? More generally, given our goals and resource constraints, what more can and should we do to execute the strategy?

Exhibit 1 Amerisource

Amerisource Revenue Performance (1985), by Category

Computers	$62,284,020
Software	5,261,585
Telephones	2,230,355
Supplies	1,244,626
Service	2,353,749
Typewriters	1,383,859
	$74,758,194

Cost of Goods Sold	70% of sales
Operating Expenses	31%
Profit (Loss)	($1,226,000)

Store Locations

Kansas City, Missouri (3)	Minneapolis, Minnesota
Tulsa, Oklahoma (3)	(2: Edina, St. Paul)
Oklahoma City, Oklahoma (2)	Memphis, Tennessee (2)
Norman, Oklahoma (1)	Milwaukee, Wisconsin (2)
Austin, Texas (2)	Shreveport, Louisiana (1)
San Antonio, Texas (2)	Richmond, Virginia (2)
St. Louis, Missouri (3)	Columbia, Missouri (1)
Lincoln, Nebraska (1)	Jacksonville, Florida (2)
Wichita, Kansas (2)	Little Rock, Arkansas (1)
Lexington, Kentucky (1)	Altamonte Springs, Florida (1)
Omaha, Nebraska (1)	Orlando, Florida (1)
Des Moines, Iowa (1)	

Source: Company records.

Exhibit 2 Amerisource

Consolidated Statement of Income: United Telecom, Inc.
(Years Ended December 31, 1985, 1984 and 1983)
(thousands of dollars)

United Telephone System	*1985*	*1984*	*1983*
Operating revenues			
Local service	$ 743,953	$ 702,963	$ 716,352
Toll service	1,326,056	1,304,935	1,176,845
Miscellaneous	231,796	137,269	73,125
	$2,301,805	$2,145,167	$1,966,322
Operating expenses			
Maintenance	432,914	393,577	375,209
Depreciation	527,623	450,033	395,305
Other operating expenses	591,466	495,326	445,986
Taxes	341,277	367,278	341,094
	$1,893,280	$1,706,214	$1,557,594

(continued)

Exhibit 2   (continued)

United Telephone System	1985	1984	1983
Other income, net	17,262	4,097	1,686
Interest charges	132,357	139,675	137,883
Preferred stock dividends	3,024	3,061	3,222
Income Applicable to United Telephone System	$ 295,406	$ 300,314	$ 269,309
U.S. Telecom			
Nonaffiliated operating revenues	341,196	221,029	148,828
Affiliated operating revenues	1,414	1,055	11,817
	$ 342,610	$ 221,084	$ 160,645
Operating expenses	537,167	332,695	220,870
Writedowns for partnership valuation and transition costs	303,000	—	—
Interest charges, net of capitalization	(1,772)	12,358	10,521
Federal income tax (benefit)	(240,416)	(54,054)	(22,259)
	$ 597,978	$ 290,999	$ 209,132
Loss before minority interest	$ (255,978)	$ (68,087)	$ (48,487)
Minority interest	2,674	828	1,444
Loss Applicable to U.S. Telecom	$ (252,694)	$ (68,087)	$ (47,043)
Diversified Operations			
Nonaffiliated sales	$ 398,078	$ 337,074	$ 301,994
Affiliated sales	171,846	153,515	146,670
	$ 569,924	$ 490,589	$ 451,664
Cost of sales	457,514	383,465	339,832
Operating expenses	119,849	107,220	100,814
Interest charges, net of capitalization	7,613	4,042	4,524
Federal income tax benefit	(9,363)	(2,748)	2,085
	$ 575,613	$ 491,979	$ 447,225
Income (Loss) Applicable to Diversified Operations	$ (5,689)	$ (1,390)	$ 4,409
Net Income	$ 20,773	$ 235,238	$ 198,971
Preferred Stock Dividends	3,973	4,233	4,550
Earnings Applicable to Common Stock	$ 16,800	$ 231,005	$ 194,421
Earnings per Share from Continuing Operations			
Assuming no dilution	.18	$2.36	$2.36
Assuming full dilution	.18	$2.32	$2.31

Note: A nonrecurring charge reduced income by $1.75 million in 1985.

Exhibit 3   Amerisource

Amerisource Top-Store Rankings (1985) by Various Criteria

Store Rankings by Sales Volume	SMSA Ranking	Sales Volume
1. Edina (Minneapolis, Minnesota)	14	$4,369,730
2. St. Louis (Manchester), Missouri	13	4,294,739
3. Jacksonville (Downtown), Florida	57	3,695,452
4. Des Moines, Iowa	92	3,079,391
5. Richmond, Virginia	59	3,053,488

Store Rankings by Gross Margin	SMSA Ranking	Gross Margin
1. Memphis, Tennessee	43	27.8%
2. Shreveport, Louisiana	94	25.1
3. Austin, Texas	68	24.2
4. Altamonte Springs, Florida	58	24.2
5. Kansas City (City Center), Missouri	27	22.7

Store Rankings by Supply Sales	SMSA Ranking	Sales Volume
1. K.C./Prairie Village, Missouri	27	$75,462
2. Edina (Minneapolis, Minnesota)	14	63,727
3. K.C./City Center, Missouri	27	60,951
4. Little Rock, Arkansas	82	52,643
5. St. Louis (Manchester), Missouri	13	51,369

Store Rankings by Computer Sales	SMSA Ranking	Sales Volume
1. Edina (Minneapolis, Minnesota)	14	$4,047,308
2. St. Louis (Manchester), Missouri	13	3,744,263
3. Jacksonville (Downtown), Florida	57	3,454,398
4. Richmond, Virginia	59	2,655,982
5. Little Rock, Arkansas	82	2,492,582

Store Rankings by Software Sales	SMSA Ranking	Sales Volume
1. Oklahoma City, Oklahoma	39	$365,356
2. Edina (Minneapolis, Minnesota)	14	323,114
3. Richmond, Virginia	59	277,321
4. St. Louis (Manchester), Missouri	13	205,682
5. Memphis, Tennessee	43	200,259

Store Rankings by Telephone Sales	SMSA Ranking	Sales Volume
1. Des Moines, Iowa	92	$557,454
2. Wichita (Downtown), Kansas	78	109,025
3. Kansas City (City Center), Missouri	27	107,057
4. St. Louis (Woodcrest), Missouri	13	86,193
5. Wichita (Rock Road), Kansas	78	85,673

Store Rankings by Typewriter Sales	SMSA Ranking	Sales Volume
1. Omaha, Nebraska	65	$313,936
2. St. Louis (Woodcrest), Missouri	13	177,138
3. Wichita (Rock Road), Kansas	78	157,956
4. St. Louis (Downtown), Missouri	13	113,714
5. Lincoln, Nebraska	175	95,317

Note: SMSA = Standard Metropolitan Statistical Area.

Exhibit 4   Amerisource

Vertical Market Counts: Estimated Number of Each Type of Firm or Professional Group in Amerisource Market Areas

Market	Construction	Lawyers	Doctors	Dentists	CPAs	Target Total
Austin	720	410	440	170	150	1,890
Columbia	700	350	400	240	200	1,890
Des Moines	680	250	270	180	150	1,530
Jacksonville	1,000	610	620	420	350	3,000
Kansas City	1,600	730	770	440	390	3,930
Lexington	660	300	310	190	150	1,610
Lincoln	400	250	275	110	80	1,115
Little Rock	800	410	460	150	110	1,930
Memphis	810	400	400	250	240	2,100
Milwaukee	1,400	710	720	370	330	3,530
Minneapolis/ St. Paul	2,150	1,220	1,300	770	640	6,080
New Orleans	1,380	700	800	400	310	3,590
Oklahoma City	1,330	660	700	340	300	3,330
Omaha	830	480	530	230	190	2,260
Orlando	800	400	400	210	160	1,970
Richmond	800	380	450	180	140	1,950
San Antonio	1,200	520	540	310	270	1,280
Shreveport	550	250	300	100	80	2,840
St. Louis	2,600	1,200	1,350	700	600	6,450
Tulsa	1,100	600	610	320	270	2,900
Wichita	790	400	420	250	200	2,060
Totals	22,300	11,230	12,065	6,330	5,310	57,235

Source: Dun & Bradstreet estimate.

Exhibit 5   Amerisource

How to Put a Computer to Work

Exhibit 6   Amerisource

PC Office Use in U.S., by Industry
(in percent)

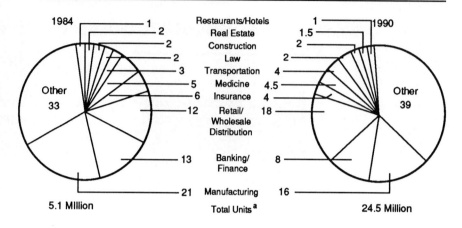

	Total Units[a]	
	Restaurants/Hotels	
1984	Real Estate	1990
	Construction	
	Law	
	Transportation	
	Medicine	
	Insurance	
	Retail/Wholesale Distribution	
	Banking/Finance	
	Manufacturing	

	1984		1990
Restaurants/Hotels	1		1
Real Estate	2		1.5
Construction	2		2
Law	2		2
Transportation	3		4
Medicine	5		4.5
Insurance	6		4
Retail/Wholesale Distribution	12		18
Banking/Finance	13		8
Manufacturing	21		16
Other	33		39
Total	5.1 Million		24.5 Million

aExcludes government workers

PC Industry Use, by Units

Electrical machinery manufacturing	350,000
Industrial conglomerates	335,000
Petrochemical firms	285,000
Life insurance	252,000
Grocery, drug, liquor	230,000
Industrial machinery manufacturing	225,000
Commercial banks	223,000
General merchandise	210,000
Food manufacturing and processing	205,000
Other business services	180,000
Transportation equipment	166,000
Computer related	142,000
Fabricated metals manufacturing	136,400
Lumber/wood/pulp/paper	133,500
Printing/publishing	130,500
Automobile dealerships	126,000
Management consultants and PR firms	124,800

(continued)

Exhibit 6 (continued)

Durable good wholesalers	120,000
Nonelectrical machinery manufacturing	116,000
Law firms	108,000
Miscellaneous Manufacturing	105,500
Casualty insurance	92,000
Accounting and bookkeeping	91,000
Engineering and architecture	85,000
Building equipment retailers	75,000
Eating places	73,000
Metal and machinery wholesalers	70,500
Lodging industry	63,200
Health services	62,000
Nondurable wholesalers	60,000
Grocery wholesalers	52,000
Savings banks	48,000
Equipment leasing companies	44,300
Construction firms	41,000
Research and development labs	36.800
Advertising companies	26,000
Chemical and drug wholesalers	16,000

Source: Wall Street Journal, September 16, 1985.

Exhibit 7 Amerisource

Organization

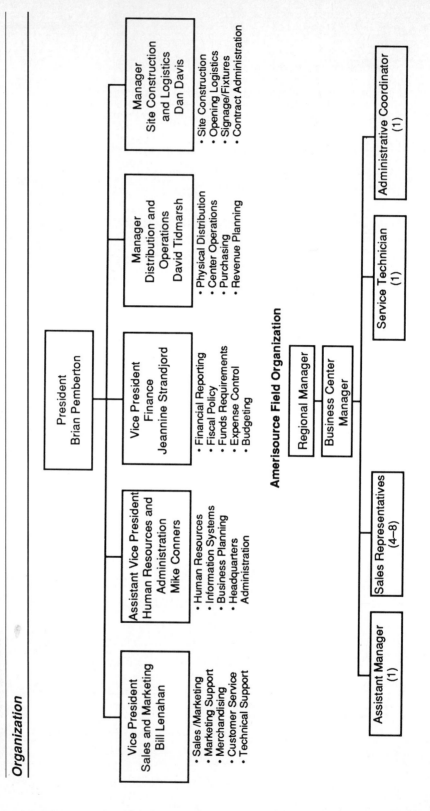

President
Brian Pemberton

Vice President
Sales and Marketing
Bill Lenahan
- Sales/Marketing
- Marketing Support
- Merchandising
- Customer Service
- Technical Support

Assistant Vice President
Human Resources and
Administration
Mike Conners
- Human Resources
- Information Systems
- Business Planning
- Headquarters
  Administration

Vice President
Finance
Jeannine Strandjord
- Financial Reporting
- Fiscal Policy
- Funds Requirements
- Expense Control
- Budgeting

Manager
Distribution and
Operations
David Tidmarsh
- Physical Distribution
- Center Operations
- Purchasing
- Revenue Planning

Manager
Site Construction
and Logistics
Dan Davis
- Site Construction
- Opening Logistics
- Signage/Fixtures
- Contract Administration

Amerisource Field Organization

Regional Manager

Business Center
Manager

Assistant Manager
(1)

Sales Representatives
(4–8)

Service Technician
(1)

Administrative Coordinator
(1)

Exhibit 8 Amerisource

1985 Compensation Plan: Business Center Manager

Element	Description
Salary	Paid semi-monthly
Center revenue attainment	Paid monthly, based on 1% of all Center C.D.V. revenue[a]
Center quota attainment	Value is $9,000 annually paid at 100% of quota; value will increase or decrease with actual quota attainment; paid monthly on a year-to-date basis; sales quota set by headquarters
Service income incentive	Value is $4,000 annually at 100% of service quota; service quota is 4% of sales quota; paid monthly on a year-to-date basis
Expense control incentive	Value is $1,000 annually; minimum qualification is to meet 100% or less of expense budget
Customer education incentive	Value is $1,000 at 100% of education sales quota; paid quarterly; education quota set by headquarters
Profit incentive	Value is $5,000 at 100% of objectives; paid on actual percentage of objective attained, not to exceed $1,500 per quarter; minimum qualification is to meet 85% of objectives to qualify
"Fast Start" bonus	Value is $500, paid for attainment of first quarter sales quota; minimum 100% of sales quota to qualify

1985 Compensation Plan: Sales Representatives

Element	Description
Salary	Paid semi-monthly
Individual commission	Paid monthly on C.D.V. revenue[a] *C.D.V. commission schedule:* 0 – $10,000 in sales volume 1% 10,001 – 20,000 3% 20,001 – 30,000 5% 30,001+ 6%
Center quota attainment	Value is $3,600 annually paid at 100% of center quota; value will increase or decrease with actual quota attainment; paid monthly on a year-to-date basis; center quota set by headquarters, individual rep's quota objective set by Business Center manager

(continued)

Exhibit 8 (continued)

Element	Description
Emphasis incentive	Tied to sales of specific products or services, general criteria set by headquarters; paid quarterly
Service/Support/Education	Paid monthly at 10% of sales volume in these categories
"Fast Start" bonus	Value is $500, paid for attainment of first quarter sales quota; minimum 100% of quota to qualify

[a]C.D.V. referred to "Commissionable Dollar Value": the commission portion of sales compensation was tied to the margins achieved on each sale. For example, sales booked at 93–100% of Amerisource's list price received 100% of available commission while those made at 76–80% of list price received only 20% of available commission.

Dorio Printing Company

In August 1987, Mr. Bob Peterson, executive vice president of the Dorio Printing Company, was seeking an approach to increasing sales $1.5 million in the next two years. In the past few years, he had participated in major acquisitions of new printing equipment. This equipment had meant a significant capital investment for the company and allowed Dorio to produce more printing products faster and at consistently high levels of quality. For the past five years, however, sales volume had remained essentially stable (see Exhibits 1 and 2). Mr. Peterson wondered if he could increase the sales output of his present four-person sales force and how he should go about recruiting new salespeople.

Industry Background

Printing applications included general commercial printing such as annual reports and brochures, direct mail advertising, catalogs, calendars, labels, letterheads, business forms, greeting cards, posters, packaging, folding boxes, coupons, trading stamps, and art reproduction, as well as business forms, newspapers, reprinted newspaper inserts, catalogs, books, encyclopedias, and magazines. Dorio had traditionally concentrated on general commercial printing applications.

Printing and publishing was the seventh largest industry in the Baltimore metropolitan area according to "value added" (i.e., selling price minus the cost of purchased materials) and the largest according to number of plants employing more than 10 persons, roughly 800 compared to a total of 5,000 plants listed. Approximately 70% of all commercial printing firms in Maryland employed

This case was prepared by Associate Professor Frank V. Cespedes as the basis for class discussion rather than to illustrate either effective or ineffective handling of an administrative situation. It is based on an earlier case prepared by Warren D. Nelson and Professor Benson P. Shapiro.

nine or fewer persons; only 15 employed 100 or more persons, and only three of these employed 250 or more. Printing was the industry with the largest number of individual firms in the United States.

A trade association study found that the printing industry had roughly paralleled the growth of all manufacturing and was more profitable than three-quarters of American industries, with an average return on investment of 10%. However, the study found a highly uneven distribution of profits among printing firms: of every five printing firms one lost money, three averaged about 6% return on assets, and one earned three times more ROA than the other firms.

Company Background

Production

In 1983, Dorio moved from an old three-story plant to a new single-level facility in a suburb convenient to downtown Baltimore. Dorio personnel designed the plant and oversaw every detail of the construction and moving efforts. They continued to operate the old plant while moving equipment— some old and some new—into the new plant. According to trade sources the move went smoothly and customer service continued satisfactorily throughout the move.

In 1987, total company employment was 150. Production equipment was geared to the product mix in 1987—85% offset and 15% letterpress. Two modern 4-color sheet-fed offset presses, two 2-color offset presses and two single-color offset presses were operated on two shifts during most of the year. Older letterpress equipment, including 17 presses of various sizes, handled the declining portion of letterpress jobs.

The first step in preparing a printing job for an offset press was work-up of a "board," or layout of the art work in full color. A full-time artist was retained on Dorio's staff to prepare layouts or consult with customers and salespeople on art problems.

After a job was printed, it was usually further processed. "Stitching" machines bound sheets into pamphlets or books. Cutting, folding and packaging were also often performed after printing. Dorio maintained its own delivery fleet. To ensure that jobs could be processed promptly, an extensive inventory of paper was maintained in a warehouse adjacent to the press rooms. A typical job could be shipped within two weeks after a final specification was received, and faster if desired. Roughly 2,500 jobs per year were processed during the 1985–1986 period.

The specifications for each order were transmitted by the individual salesperson to the production supervisor. An estimator assisted during the initial work-up of specifications and estimation of price and delivery time for the salesperson to submit to the customer, especially on those jobs requiring competitive bidding. Dorio's estimator was able to handle the estimating function by devoting only half of his time to it. Thus he was also able to handle a large portion of the company's purchasing activity. Four "customer service reps" worked in the production department in liaison capacities between the sales force, customers, and the production department. These reps received customer phone calls and handled the customer's request or problem when that customer's salesperson was not in the office. The customer service reps also expedited orders, making sure that jobs were processed according to specifications, and in general followed through to satisfy the customer after the salesperson obtained the order. According to Mr. Peterson, this back-up capability was a unique strength of Dorio, since many competitive printing companies required their salespeople to perform the duties handled by Dorio's service reps. The service reps ranged in age from 40 to 50 and earned between $36,000 and $48,000 per year. All had substantial printing production experience. Each tended to work with a particular salesperson and a particular group of customers.

The process for preparing bids, on those jobs requiring competitive bidding, consisted of the following steps, with average times estimated for each step:

Step	Time Required (Minutes)
1. Sales rep records initial customer specification	15–30
2. Sales rep completes specification form	5
3. Sales rep transmits form to estimator	5
4. Estimator prepares bid from standard rates	30–45
5. Sales rep reviews bid	5
6. Sales rep decides on price quotation	15
7. Sales rep submits and explains bid to potential customer	10
8. Sales rep prepares written confirmation of bid	5
9. Written confirmation typed and mailed by secretary	5

Organization and Management

Steve Dorio, president, was a grandson of the founder, Carmine D. Dorio, who started out as his own salesman and pressman in 1905 in Baltimore. Steve had been president since 1980 when his father, Vincent Dorio, retired from the presidency at the age of 80. Bob Peterson, executive vice president, had started out as a printing salesman with no background in the industry after a stint in the military. He had been so successful as a salesman that in 1973 he was offered status as a principal stockholder, which he accepted. In 1987 Messrs. Dorio and Peterson controlled all of the stock.

Mr. Dorio and Mr. Peterson were joint decision makers on all management questions. Mr. Dorio concentrated on operations, while Mr. Peterson concentrated on sales, but both principals conferred frequently and preferred to

reach agreement before making management decisions. Alex Petroski, sales
manager, assisted in managing the sales effort.

Steve Dorio gave his views concerning the company:

> We are a tightly run company. I personally review internal operating and finan-
> cial data every day. Our production crew is young and well trained. Our
> craftsmen and supervisors are very company-minded, and they really care about
> doing good work. There is no union.[1] We pay very good wages and we have
> liberal fringe benefits—group hospital and medical plans, dental insurance, a
> profit-sharing retirement plan, free flu shots, free eye exams, and even a tax ex-
> pert who comes in to help employees with their income tax returns. We are a
> quality-minded company, and the main element in quality is our top production
> crew—they give us a real competitive advantage. Our approach has paid off in
> the past: we have been in the top 20% of printing companies as far as
> profitability is concerned, except for one or two of the past five years. Right now,
> unfortunately, sales volume is static.
>
> As for the future, I am enough of a realist to admit that we cannot succeed by
> remaining static. If we could be assured of maintaining a static, profitable level it
> would be ideal. But we cannot—we have to grow just to stay even. Right now we
> are not as profitable as we should be. Our existing plant could produce an
> added $6–9 million of work, and we have allowed room for expansion to handle
> more. Expanding our production capacity is no problem.
>
> We do not use so-called sophisticated management techniques. We do not set
> our sights on future targets and push to make them. As to how we grow, we try to
> follow the market and respond to it rather than trying to anticipate where the
> market is headed and get there first. I would not say we have the inventive kind
> of management that could develop new techniques; we stay with the stable, estab-
> lished technology, because we have a sound company and good strategy. Natural-
> ly we avoid risks we do not have to take. We have a lot to lose if we make
> mistakes.
>
> Our main problem for the future is to increase sales. But we want to increase
> sales volume profitably. The trouble with a lot of the high-volume work is that it
> is low margin. We are profit oriented, not sales volume oriented. We need to
> hire some proven, experienced salespeople who have some accounts to bring
> along, and who would appreciate our company for the excellent production sup-
> port we can give them. If we could hire a trained sales force from outside, and
> have them bring their business along, it would be Utopia.

Marketing Print in the Baltimore Area

The major characteristics of print marketing—huge primary demand, intense
competition, wide diversity of demand, and long-established customer-vendor
relationships—were both the keys to success and the barriers to expansion of
Dorio's marketing efforts, in Mr. Peterson's opinion.

The market for print in Baltimore generally followed the trends and
practices in the major customer groups served—retailers, manufacturers, ad-

---

[1]Casewriter's note: Few competitors were unionized either.

vertising agencies, publishers, financial companies, educational institutions, etc. For example, in the early 1980s the trend was away from "showpiece" annual reports, coveted business for reasons of both prestige and profit, because companies had become more frugal in response to the recession. Another recent trend among many print buyers was toward requests for competitive bidding for printing jobs. In the past many buyers had done business primarily on the basis of past service and quality rendered by the printer, or on the basis of the printer's reputation. One Dorio salesperson estimated that 60% of his jobs were sold on a bid basis four years ago, but that 90% of his jobs were sold on a bid basis in 1987.

The casewriter accompanied a Dorio salesperson during a call on a typical customer, a publisher. During the call, the buyer commented that an average of six print sales reps called on him daily. Following the call the Dorio salesman estimated that ten print sales reps per day called on major buyers of print, such as the publisher. The salesman commented that, while the list of companies competing for business from such a buyer was too long to list, he believed that his serious competition came from seven of the larger and more highly regarded printing firms in the area (see Exhibit 3).

Marketing Strategy

Mr. Peterson described Dorio's marketing strategy as follows:

> Our product is the best in the area for the kind of work our customers want. We provide the highest quality work, absolutely on-time delivery, strict adherence to customer's special instructions or changes, and expert professional consulting and personal service from our salespeople. We do have a reputation for being higher priced than most of our competitors. Our prices are up to 10% higher than the low bid on many jobs. As a result, we have to hire the best salespeople we can get, because it is entirely up to them to carry out our strategy and make sure that our customers are satisfied that they get the service they are paying for.
>
> Our profits for the past five years have been somewhat erratic and we have not increased our sales volume, but we are confident our strategy is sound. Our problem has been implementation.

Sales Force

All customer accounts were classified either as "house" accounts or as "field" accounts. House accounts were handled directly by Mr. Dorio or Mr. Peterson, and often involved long-standing "understandings" or relationships that required minimal effort to maintain. Many of these understandings had existed for as long as 25 years. Almost all printers, according to Mr. Peterson, had a few such accounts. It was standard practice in the industry for owners of the companies to handle their own house accounts. Field accounts were handled by a four-person sales force including Alex Petroski, who was the sales manager.

A breakdown of major accounts for the past five years, by salesperson, is given in Exhibit 4. Further information on the sales force is given in Exhibit 5.

Mr. Peterson described the Dorio philosophy of managing sales as "laissez-faire." He commented that sales reps had to be "creative," and adapt themselves to each unique situation. This required, according to Mr. Peterson, that each rep be allowed to work independently, develop his or her own style, and learn the kinds of customers he or she could succeed with.

Sales reps were paid a commission of 7 ½% of sales.[2] If a salesperson cut price to obtain a sale, however, commission was reduced for that sale. The amount of reduction was negotiated with Bob Peterson and varied according to company need for business and other factors. In no case, however, was the commission reduced below 5%. During sales slumps, a sales rep's draw could be continued even if not covered by commission, but the rep was then expected to make it up during following months so that annual salary worked out to 7 ½% of his or her sales. In addition to commission, each sales rep was furnished a company car and expense account.

Exhibit 5 includes two salespeople who were no longer employed with Dorio. Frank Barr was considered a high-potential salesman when he was hired, and he had been highly successful selling locks in quantity to motels, hotels, and office buildings. The locks were purchased in large quantities by a few buyers. However, he was unable to sell print and he was fired. Bob Peterson commented on Barr's failure:

> He was the stereotype of a good salesman—if he walked in here tomorrow, unknown, I would hire him immediately. He was well-groomed, well-spoken, smooth and likeable. But selling print is unlike selling anything else, and it is almost impossible to tell beforehand who will be able to sell print. Frank's problem may have been a failure to learn the technical aspects of printing, or possibly that he was simply calling on the wrong customers. We do not really know why he failed. There was no attempt to diagnose the reasons he could not close sales.

Robert Darman, on the other hand, had been highly successful. He had some art talent and could sell well to ad agencies. He was selling $1.2 million of print per year when ad agency business was booming; then, when their business turned down, his sales fell off, and he got behind in his ability to "make up" the salary he was drawing. Also, he encountered some problems in his personal life. He quit "owing" back salary. As of August 1987, he was working as a printing salesman for another company.

Selling Approaches

The casewriter interviewed Bob Peterson and each of the Dorio people. All of the following comments are paraphrased.

---

[2]New salespeople were paid salaries between $30,000 and $45,000 (plus automobile) until they had developed enough sales so that their commissions equaled their salaries.

Bob Peterson. *Bob continued to sell in addition to his management responsibilities:*

Selling print is like selling "blue sky." There is nothing tangible to sell—the product is press time, along with some attendant services. Of course, we offer premium service and strict attention to quality, but these are intangibles and it is often difficult to find customers who appreciate these factors, let alone convince them that we are better than the competition. Of course, after getting an initial order we have to live up to our claims in order to get repeat business.

Selling blue sky requires salesmanship at its creative best. A good print sales rep has to have all the usual qualities—good appearance, charm, empathy with the buyer—and has to use all the other expected influences: tickets to athletic events or the theater, holiday presents, and wining and dining. But a top sales-person has to do these things plus something else—the extra variable that clinches the sale.

When I first began selling, I had no printing background at all. Nor did I have much knowledge of practices or terminology in the industries I was selling to. But I was extremely successful because I relied on my intuition and tried to do something extra besides the things all the competitors were doing. Probably the most effective thing I did was to make sure that I invited the buyer and his or her spouse to an occasion or event as my guest. I made the buyer feel comfort-able and welcome as a friend, not just a business prospect. Many of the people my wife and I have met through this process have remained good friends, above business considerations. Because I had a good deal of charm and taste in this type of "social selling," many buyers were willing to overlook some of my shortcomings in the technical areas. One factor about selling print in the Dorio company that allows this "social selling" to succeed is that a sales rep needs only 10 good accounts to earn a good income. The rep then has ample time to con-centrate on each of his or her top customers.

In cultivating customer relationships, of course, it is vital to know who really influences the purchase decision. Most buyers in purchasing departments base decisions on price and delivery—only a few really care about quality and special service. It is usually the creative people—the ones in the advertising depart-ment—who are willing to pay a higher price to get exactly the quality they want. So we concentrate on the people in the advertising departments of companies. In some companies, though, purchasing will not take suggestions from advertis-ing, or there is a purchasing director with set ideas, a lot of power, and little sym-pathy with the "creative types" who care more about quality than price. We have trouble with such companies. Fortunately, most companies do have creative people in influential positions, and many of these people like their work and stay in their positions for a long time. This has been the case with some of my best customers I have served for up to 25 years.

Many young salespeople tend to withhold information about their customers from their company. Our people do not do this; they cannot and still be success-ful. The opposite is true. They can help themselves by bringing their customers in to see our plant and meet our people in production and customer service. Then if a customer calls when a sales rep is not in the office, one of our produc-tion or service people can handle this call. If the call had to be turned away, the first thing the customer would do would be to call another printer. Another reason our sales reps must be open with our service reps is that they can help immensely by handling many of the details of customer orders. To earn, say $150,000, a sales rep would have to do $2 million of business a year. Servicing even one-half that much business would be impossible without relying on our service reps to handle a good deal of customer work. This adds another dimension to the talents required of our salespeople: they must be able to coordinate their work with our inside service reps, keep them informed, and maintain excellent working relations with them.

Our four inside service reps are very important in providing high-quality service to our customers. Few of our competitors use such inside people to beef up their service capabilities.

In a small company like ours, we don't have time to do market analysis. We just get out and call on as many customers as possible. I don't really even have time to be talking to you—I have six phone calls I should be making right now.

We do not have the time or money to "train" salespeople. They have to be top people who can make it on their own. Most prefer it that way, in fact.

Alex Petroski.   *The casewriter traveled with Alex Petroski, the salesman–sales manager, for one day:*

9:00 A.M. The first half hour of the day was spent in the office on paperwork. Along with other work, Alex dictated a letter inviting a high potential company buyer and his wife to spend a weekend in September at the Petroski summer home in a nearby resort area. Alex indicated that the buyer had expressed interest in the resort area during his last sales call. Alex spent a few minutes with the estimator.

Alex then explained his first sales call. He had obtained an order for 10,000 copies of a 4-color direct mail flyer. He indicated that he had shaved the price to $3,600 from $3,780 to get the order, but that the standard price for a volume of 15,000 copies was only $4,800 due to scale economies. He said he would convince the buyer to take 15,000 copies, and this would allow Alex to earn his full commission.

9:30 A.M. Left the office for first call, a publishing company. While driving to the call in a suburban location, Alex commented that he would make $360 for the morning's work.

10:00 A.M. Arrived in the customer's lobby. The receptionist admitted Alex to see the buyer.

10:10 A.M. Alex introduced the casewriter to the buyer, then began small talk. When the talk turned to details of the printing job, Alex said to the casewriter that he would now see a "professional" buyer dealing with a professional salesman, and he requested the buyer to act out his usual professionalism as well as he could. After several details were taken care of, Alex suggested that the buyer should order 15,000 copies instead of 10,000 because of the great price break, which Alex then explained. The buyer became noticeably tense and commented that he would like to order the higher volume but was already in trouble with his budget. Alex did not comment further and left the conversational initiative with the buyer for the next portion of the visit. The conversation turned to small talk and the buyer asked if Alex had heard of another printing firm that was about to go out of business. Alex expressed interest and ignorance on the matter. Later in the discussion Alex agreed to take the "boards" to the buyer's artist in downtown Baltimore later in the day. Toward the end of the call the buyer appeared more relaxed and said he would purchase 15,000 units instead of 10,000.

10:40 A.M.   First call completed, Alex headed back to the office to set up two sales calls in downtown Baltimore. During the return trip, Alex answered questions about Dorio's sales programs, and selling print in general.

> No, our salespeople have no way of knowing the actual profit to the company of various kinds of orders. This is a problem to management but we have not had time to solve it.
>
> I am recognized as one of the three or four best nonowner print sales reps in the Baltimore area, and I have been in the business 14 years. The only generalization I can make about how to sell print is that each sale is different.
>
> I have toyed with a possible sales idea: a new marketing outlet for the Dorio company. Students on many university campuses would be our sales representatives to their schools. They ought to be in a better position to find out who buys the print, and on what basis, than our regular sales reps. And the 7 ½% commission should look quite attractive to them.
>
> A print sales rep can probably make at most five meaningful sales calls in a single day. I did at one time request our reps to fill out call records so we could begin to establish some data on numbers of calls, where the calls were, etc. But the sales reps lost interest after the first few weeks, and started "fudging" the data. So we dropped the program.

11:10 A.M.   Back at the office, Alex promptly set up two calls in Baltimore.
11:25 A.M.   Left office for second call.
11:35 A.M.   Arrived at customer's store, an old-line specialty retail outlet catering to the carriage trade. The objective was a repeat order for a color catalog. Throughout the call, Alex acted as if it were a foregone conclusion that Dorio would get the repeat order. He said that in situations like this the objective was to make it as easy as possible for the potential customer to give the order. During the call Alex obtained a "dummy" of the catalog from the advertising manager. After the call Alex mentioned that last year was the first time he had obtained the order for the catalog. He had called on the advertising manager for three years before getting the order, and his problem had been in thinking that the advertising manager had responsibility for the catalog. Alex finally learned that the president of the company actually made the decision about the design and printing of the catalog. With this knowledge, Alex said it was easy to get the order because he talked directly to the president, who had been somewhat displeased with the service rendered by the printer who had done the last catalog.

12:00 noon.   The next stop was to drop off the material at the studio of the artist who did the work for the publisher called on earlier in the day. The studio was two doors away from the previous call. Alex made small talk and expressed a great deal of interest in an old nickelodeon that the artist, a young bearded man dressed in an open pull-over shirt, old jeans and sandals, was playing full blast. Alex told a story of how he barely missed purchasing an old nickelodeon from a boardwalk arcade that had gone out of business a few years ago.

12:20 P.M. After the call, Alex asked the casewriter if he had noticed the layout that the artist had been doing. Alex said it was obviously a big printing job and that he would keep in touch with the publisher to find out when selection of a printer was to begin. He said that keeping in touch with a customer's artist was a good way to learn of potential printing jobs.

12:40 P.M. Arrived at the office of the next call, a recently founded, four-person investment banking firm. Dorio would be printing an advertising brochure, and a principal of the firm was making the selection of paper from samples Alex had brought. The customer was quite hesitant about choice of paper, and Alex expressed confidence in her choice. Alex then turned the discussion to some oceanfront real estate the firm was developing, and Alex got the principal to talk about the project. Alex then mentioned that he had a chance to buy land in a particular resort area and the customer said no one had ever lost money buying land in that area. Alex said his problem was coming up with the cash, and the principal said that was what banks were for. Following the call Alex stopped in at his bank, located a few doors away, and confirmed that financing was indeed available for this type of investment. The bank visit took approximately five minutes.

1:15 P.M. During lunch Alex asked if the casewriter thought that a job selling print would have an appeal for an MBA graduate from a top-rated business school. Alex asked about aspirations of MBA graduates, and how they might view working for a family-owned and -managed company. He commented that if he had held an MBA degree when he first started working, he would have expected his business efforts to earn some equity, since that was the only way to make "real" money. The discussion then turned to the problems and opportunities of owning one's own business.

2:00 P.M. On the return trip to his office, Alex talked further about his role as sales manager:

> It is frequently difficult to get salespeople to give up accounts they have cultivated without success. For example, one of our reps had called on an account for years without success but refused to give it to another rep because the buyer had become such a good personal friend and golfing partner.

Donna Shea. *Donna had the strongest technical background on the Dorio sales force. She had worked for Dorio in production and estimating for 10 years, and subsequently moved to the sales position five years ago. Donna talked about various aspects of printing sales:*

> In estimating and production I became interested in sales because I could see the potential earnings that were available. Before that I had never wanted to be in sales and at times I still question my interest in a sales career. I was convinced by others that I could succeed in sales, so I tried it with the knowledge that I

could always fall back on my production knowledge if I could not succeed in selling.

I am not a strong "stand-up" sales rep like Alex Petroski, and I have no design talent or artistic taste. That is a serious flaw in print sales. But I have been successful because of my strong technical background. I sell best to two types of buyers—the ones who are true professionals and demand a true technical salesperson, and the ones who know little or nothing about print and need the education I can give them. My part-time job at a college, teaching graphic arts cost estimating, helps my image as a competent technical salesperson.

A sales rep could probably make six "hello" calls in a day, but four calls per day to active accounts is the maximum. After two calls in the morning, it is invariably necessary to return to the office to do paperwork in support of the sales calls.

During a sales call I spend a good deal of time working with the technical aspects of the job. Frequently I am in two- or three-on-one situations, trying to solve problems, looking at details of preliminary proofs. Frequently I will refer back to the preliminary proof book or the original outline to solve the problem. Also, during a sales call to an active account, there is a check list of technical information that has to be obtained and this takes time.

The customers I prefer the most are the ones with a good deal of technical expertise; for example, paper companies or consumer goods manufacturers who are large enough to have a competent professional purchasing department. I have thought about ranking print buyers on the basis of expertise, and I would give the following rankings on a 1 to 10 basis: paper companies, 10; publishers, 9; mutual funds, 7–8; miscellaneous medium-to-large industrials, 3 to 7; and advertising agencies, 1. All small buyers I would rank 1. The reason funds are sophisticated is that they buy so much print and can afford to have good buyers. But I cannot sell to funds because I do not "talk the language" of investments, stock market, etc. I should probably make more of a study of the mutual fund industry, and learn their terminology.

One of my best customers is a large consumer-goods manufacturer. Their purchasing department does all of the purchasing for other departments in the company. It took me three years to get a sizeable order from them. The way they operate is to investigate vendors and classify them on their ability to handle certain types of work. Then when a job comes along, they will ask the qualifying print vendors to bid—usually I am competing against five or six other vendors—and they generally give the business to the low bidder. However, they cultivate their vendors by spreading the work around; if they didn't, a printer would probably stop bidding. For this reason the potential of this business is limited on the upside, but there is also some minimum amount of business a vendor can count on with good service and quality at reasonable prices.

When I started selling I quoted strictly list price, even with padding in some cases. But lately I have been negotiating more, and I will cut my commission if I feel it is desirable for a particular job. Another technique I have been using more lately is quoting alternates to the specifications that a purchaser has submitted for bids. By altering the paper, the largest single cost component of most printing jobs, I can sometimes meet the intent of the specifications at a lower cost. Of course, a danger in this technique is that the buyer may adopt my standard the next time he requests bids and my advantage disappears.

One of the things I dislike about selling is making cold calls. I do have somewhat of a lack of confidence, and the thing you must do on a first call is sell *yourself*. It takes a strong "standup" sales rep to do that. I am more of a service than a standup rep like some of our other people are.

I once trained four weeks to sell pharmaceuticals. Their method was to memorize a canned sales pitch to deliver to the pharmacist on the first call, but I found that I hated this approach. The first Monday morning after the training program, I sat in the car with the district manager outside my first drug store and argued about the canned approach. I resigned on the spot.

Dick Peterson. *(Bob Peterson's son). Dick had joined the firm in 1986 after receiving an MBA from Columbia:*

The key to selling print is having a personality that will win the buyer over. It helps to have something in common with the buyer—age, for example. I can usually sell better to younger buyers than older ones.

Eight calls in one day is probably the limit. I average four or five every day. We try to spend as much time as possible making calls. I may spend more time in the office—one and a half hours per day—than the other salespeople because I spend a lot of time on the phone.

The only way to find prospects is to keep your eyes open. I use the classified section of the newspaper to get leads since companies hiring personnel frequently will also have more activity in others areas of their business, and I make a lot of calls. It may take months of making calls before a buyer will even trust you enough to ask you to quote on a job. Then, the buyer will be suspicious if your first bid is low, but may still give you a chance. This is largely a function of how well the other printers are serving that customer.

I bid on six different jobs at an insurance company, which I initially considered a good prospect. I finally concluded that they always took the lowest bid, and that quality of work did not enter into the purchase decision. As soon as I discovered that fact, I dropped them as a prospect.

Our company's image is that we have no late deliveries, and consistently high quality. We have to live up to it because we also have a reputation for being more expensive than our competitors.

The recent trend toward competitive bidding may be hurting us. We did a study a couple of years ago showing that we obtained roughly one job for every three bids submitted. Now the ratio is probably one sale for every four jobs we bid on. The problem is that many buyers believe they should be able to get the high-quality service we offer for the lower prices they paid during the recent recession or for the lower prices our competitors quote. I would guess that prices for printing sales in this area have risen 10% in the last 15 months.

Many purchase decisions by print buyers are based on politics or social connections. For example, a buyer may throw business to a printer if the buyer represents a company with a service that the printer uses—accounting, legal, etc. A sales rep always has to be careful not to waste time on buyers with established ties that cannot be broken on the basis of a better printing service.

Most of our salespeople have not intentionally tried to match their customers to their special talents. But through the process of making many sales calls, that fit is usually established naturally.

Harry Cohen. *Harry held undergraduate and graduate degrees in graphic arts design-*
ing. Harry was hired as art director at Dorio, a position he held for two
years before entering sales:

When I first started selling, I had no background in sales at all. I would have
liked more training and guidance than I received, but it is company policy that a
salesman learns mostly on his own.

Of course with my background I go after the accounts that can use my talent.
I often give away a design service to obtain the printing order. The trouble with
this approach is that it limits the volume of business I can handle, since it takes
time to produce good designs.

When I began selling I got leads on prospective customers any way I could; I
even wrote down names from trucks I passed on the road. One of my best customers today I read about in the Sunday paper when the company first moved to
Baltimore. I got in touch with the advertising manager and gave her a lot of
good advice about art services in Baltimore. I set her up with an agency and
helped on initial designs. I was able to make sure that the design specifications
fit our printing capability best, so I naturally got the printing business.

I accumulated more than 600 entries in a notebook on potential customers. I
don't use it any more, however. I really spend less time prospecting for new customers than I should. It is much easier to concentrate on my present customers.

I become deeply involved in all phases of processing an order for my customers. I follow it all the way through the production sequence; this ensures that
the job is done exactly the way the customer wants it.

In a sales situation, I sell myself—all aspects. For example, I have a farm and I
bring it into conversations. At Christmas I do not give my customers the usual
gift certificate or liquor; my wife cans jams and pickles and I give these. They
mean a lot more; they're something personal.

I stay away from purchasing agents because all they know is the unit cost at
the bottom of the line. They do not see the total package. Also, I cannot relate
to most purchasing agent types. I also stay away from most ad agency production
managers for the same reason. The last thing ad agencies need is my design
talent. Some of my best customers are mutual funds who can really use my
design talent. If I design a piece, it saves them a fee; I am really selling on the
basis of economics when I give away free design work.

Every printer tells potential buyers that the printer has high quality. That may
get you the first order, but you have to provide acceptable quality to get repeat
business. A print jobber[3] once won a competitive bid from me, and the job he
delivered looked like an out-of-tune color television picture. I had no trouble
with competition from the jobber after that.

The Situation in August 1987

Bob Peterson had several courses of action in mind for increasing Dorio's sales.
He was actively trying to recruit salespeople from other printers, but it was always

---

[3]A print jobber was an independent salesperson who obtained orders from customers, then
selected a printer to do the work. The jobber's profit was the difference between the price charged
customers and the price paid the printer to do the work.

difficult to lure away a good sales rep. Another possibility was to promote an employee with good technical knowledge of printing production, but no sales background, to a sales position. Such a salesperson could certainly service existing accounts, freeing up more experienced salespeople to call on potential new accounts.

The success of his son, Dick, had led Mr. Peterson to consider recruiting from an MBA program. He was confident such a person would have the talent, general knowledge of business, and personal drive required of the high-caliber sales rep he was seeking. However, he was still unsure of how to select a person who had the particular qualities that would make a good print sales rep. Mr. Peterson knew there was a considerable element of chance involved in hiring an unproven salesperson. Also, he wondered what it would take to attract and motivate a high-caliber MBA to a career in printing sales. He thought that the monetary incentive was a strong lure, and that the broad range of customers should interest and challenge an MBA graduate.

Mr. Peterson had compiled some data on potential customers (see Exhibit 6). He wanted a new sales rep to call on these customers. He knew that some printing companies had succeeded by hiring persons with knowledge of certain customer groups, and then training these persons to sell to these customers. But any training effort would have to take time away from present sales efforts, and could cause a net loss to the company, especially in the short run.

Mr. Peterson believed that the sales plateau of the Dorio Printing Company would result in decreases in profit as costs in general rose faster than revenues. He wanted a plan to increase the sales in the short run and to build a foundation for longer-term growth at a good profit level.

Exhibit 1 Dorio Printing Company

Recent Sales History

Year	Company Sales Volume
1986	$10,920,000
1985	10,992,000
1984	11,730,000
1983	10,374,000
1982	11,067,000
1981	9,575,000
1980	7,950,000
1979	5,580,000
1978	7,010,000
1977	5,450,000
1976	5,025,000

Exhibit 2 Dorio Printing Company

Income Statement 1986
(in 000s)

Net Sales	$10,920
Cost of Sales	
Materials	$ 4,059
Direct labor	3,396
Variable factory expense	480
Fixed factory expense	660
Total	8,595
Gross profit	2,325
Selling and administrative expenses	1,875
Net profit (before taxes)	$ 450

Exhibit 3   Dorio Printing Company

Primary Competitors

Name of Competitor	Estimated Sales 1986 ($ millions)	Comments[a]
Foremost Printing Company	10.5	Quality closest to Dorio in 4-color work.
Wood Printing Company	12.0	Recently purchased large web offset press.
Quality Press	6.0	—
A.T. Berg Company	10.5	Lower prices, lower quality.
Morris Printing Company	4.5	Lower prices. No 4-color capability.
AAA Lithographers	6.0	—
Robinson Printing Company	3.0	Has one top-notch salesperson.

[a]Comments based on opinions expressed by Dorio managers and salespeople.

Exhibit 4   Dorio Printing Company

Sales Data
($000s)

	1982	*1983*	*1984*	*1985*	*1986*
Accounts over $300					
House accounts					
Old Ironside Distiller & Bottler	486	603	657	564	426
XYZ Paper Company	612	507	459	597	297
Industrial Valve Company	225	162	237	255	378
Consumer Package Goods Co.	5,370	4,746	4,584	3,249	4,821
Sterling Silver Company	699	585	618	684	375
Subtotal	7,392	6,603	6,555	5,349	6,297
Alex Petroski					
ABC Mutual Fund	264	234	369	321	300
Donna Shea					
TVW Paper Company	21	132	132	348	219
Educational Associates	501	90	27	90	111
Over $300 Total	8,178	7,059	7,083	6,108	6,927
% of Total Company Sales	74%	68%	60%	56%	64%
Accounts $90 to $300					
House accounts					
Clothing Mfg., Inc.	111	63	81	78	54
White Paper Company	129	165	18	30	0
Black Paper Company	78	87	105	102	42
Subtotal	318	315	204	210	96
Alex Petroski					
Misc. Indust. Inc.	0	0	12	186	3
AA Publishing Company	288	21	219	102	36
BB Publishing Company	165	195	150	147	261
AA Mutual Fund	234	186	201	108	60
CC Publishing Company	102	51	9	6	18
Top Food Company	0	138	105	87	102
Church Press	51	114	15	48	0[a]
Industrial Goods, Inc.	0	6	156	156	15
BB Mutual Fund	63	126	147	273	153
Subtotal	903	837	1,014	1,113	648
Donna Shea					
Ace Consumer Mfg.	0	15	36	237	18
Ideal Ad Agency	117	126	147	111	150
Industrial Mfg. Company	0	12	294	30	30
Plastics Mfg. Company	0	0	0	111	0
Home Products, Inc.	0	9	24	57	270
DD Publishing Company	0	0	0	6	93
Creative Ad Agency	108	162	180	183	24
Subtotal	225	324	681	735	585
Harry Cohen					
Admirable Ad Agency	33	93	60	0	60
CC Mutual Fund	0	12	75	171	159
Industrial Electronics Co.	0	3	123	84	78
DD Mutual Fund	0	60	162	111	0
Subtotal	33	168	420	366	297

(continued)

Exhibit 4 (continued)

	1982	1983	1984	1985	1986
Dick Peterson					
Eastern University	162	240	180	114	182
Andrew Ad Agency	0	33	96	123	120
Consumer Electronics Mfg.	114	108	243	54	15
EE Mutual Fund	0	0	0	0	105
Subtotal	276	381	519	291	422
Frank Barr[b]					
Arnold Ad Agency	0	0	0	132	3 [a]
Albert Ad Agency	93	60	78	45	15 [a]
Subtotal	93	60	78	177	18
Robert Darman[b]	—	—	—	—	—
$90 to $300 Total	1,848	2,085	2,916	2,892	2,046
% of Total Company Sales	17%	20%	25%	26%	19%

Accounts under $90 (There were 150 accounts in this category in 1986.)

% of Total Company Sales	9%	12%	15%	18%	16%
Total Company Sales	11,067	10,374	11,730	10,992	10,920
"House" Sales $	7,710	6,918	6,759	5,559	6,393
"House" Sales %[c]	70%	67%	58%	51%	58%

[a]Gone out of business.

[b]Some of Frank Barr's and Robert Darman's sales are included in sales of persons to whom their accounts were reassigned.

[c]For first six months of 1987 "house" sales were 57% of total.

Exhibit 5 Dorio Printing Company

Sales Personnel

Name	Age	Years of Service	Background	Sales Volume ($000's)			
				1987 1st 6 mos.	1986 1st 6 mos.	1986 Total	1985 Total
Steve Dorio President	42	20	Administrative			6,972	6,162
Bob Peterson Exec. V.P.	53	25	Sales		(House Sales)		
Alex Petroski Sales Manager-Sales Representative	39	13	Sales Qualified as stockbroker	660	576	1,521	1,494
Donna Shea Sales Representative	34	15	Sales—5 years Estimating & Production—10 years	702	636	1,350	972
Harry Cohen Sales Representative	32	7	Sales—5 years Art Director—2 years art education	585	345	600	1,089
Dick Peterson Sales Representative	25	4	MBA '86—Columbia Extensive part-time printing experience prior to 1986	294	—	—	—
Frank Barr[a]	28	2	Sales—Industrial	72	—	33	—
Robert Darman[b]	30	4	Sales Art education	—	144	315 (through Sept.)	1,275

[a]Dismissed, June 1987.
[b]Quit, September 1986.

Exhibit 6   Dorio Printing Company

Market Information—Print Buyers with Potential of $75,000 and Up Per Year

Customer Group	No. of Accounts Potential	No. of Accounts Sold	Purchase Decision Maker
1. Mutual funds	20	10	Advertising Manager[a] Purchasing Agent
2. Advertising agencies	15	6	Production Manager
3. Paper companies	12	6	Advertising Manager
4. Universities, colleges	75	6	Special Print Buyers, P.R. Directors, others
5. Consumer and industrial manufacturers	100+	20	Product Managers, Advertising Managers Purchasing Agents, Art Directors
6. Insurance companies	4	0	Purchasing Agents
7. Banks	6	1	Advertising Manager, Purchasing Agent
8. Publishers	3	3	Advertising Manager, others
9. Financial report buyers[b]			Vice Presidents of Finance, Advertising Managers, Treasurers, or attorney who works on documents
A. Annual reports	200	20	
B. Proxies, prospectuses	100–200[c]	5	

[a]The title "Advertising Manager" was used for any marketing executive with influence over printer selection.

[b]While many other customer groups included financial report buyers, this segment was important enough to form a special group.

[c]If the firm were to enter this market in a major way, it would need $225–$300 thousand worth of new equipment, most of it for typesetting. The company presently had no typesetting equipment and relied on outside contractors for that function. This market segment demanded fast delivery: prospectuses would often be delivered to a printer early in the evening with delivery required at the start of the following working day.

Managing Customer Encounters: Field Marketing Requirements

2. Aspects of Sales Management: An Introduction

3. Managing Selling and the Salesperson
- Cooper Pharmaceuticals, Inc.
- Cole National Corporation: Turnover
- Fieldcrest Division of Fieldcrest Mills, Inc.:
  Compensation System for Field Sales Representatives

4. Deployment, Focus, and Measuring Effectiveness
- Actmedia, Inc.
- Cox Cable (A)
- Cox Cable (B)

5. Channel Management
- Westinghouse Electric Corporation (A)
- Westinghouse Electric Corporation (B)
- Alloy Rods Corporation
- Becton Dickinson & Company: Vacutainer
  Systems Division

6. Managing Major Accounts
- Springs Industries: Apparel Fabrics Division
- Capital Cities/ABC, Inc.: Spot Sales
- MCI Communications Corporation: National
  Accounts Program
- MCI: VNet (A)

## Chapter 2

Aspects of Sales Management: An Introduction

For some decades now, marketing textbooks and professors have assiduously distinguished between sales and marketing. The best statement of the difference emphasizes that "selling is preoccupied with the seller's need to convert his product into cash; marketing with the idea of satisfying the needs of the customer by means of the product and the whole cluster of things associated with creating, delivering, and finally consuming it."[1] Nonetheless, whatever else marketing encompasses, it certainly includes selling—the getting and keeping of customers and the revenues they represent. As the old saying goes, "In most companies, sales is the only revenue-generating function; everything else is a cost center." The importance of sales as a source of revenue looms large in defining the form and substance of companies' marketing programs, for both good (e.g., close attention to buying processes at specific accounts) and ill (e.g., confusion between sales and marketing).

In implementing marketing strategies, managing customer encounters through the field sales effort is crucial. In most companies, the sales force *is* the major vehicle for implementing strategy. As a result, sales-management policies and procedures are core dimensions of organizing and implementing the marketing effort. Part Two looks at field marketing requirements in different company and competitive settings and the implications for specific topics in sales management: selecting, training, and compensating salespeople; deploying and measuring the effectiveness of the sales force; working with and through channel intermediaries; and the ongoing management of major accounts.

This chapter discusses only certain aspects of sales management. It is not intended as a primer on selling skills or as an overview of the issues involved in developing a selling strategy; these topics are discussed in many excellent books and articles. Instead, this introduction considers certain general characteristics

73

that affect field marketing and sales management requirements in most companies: (1) the nature of the salesperson's boundary role in the organization; (2) a general classification of sales tasks relevant to considering the kinds of behaviors and skills required in a firm's field marketing efforts; and (3) an overall sales-management framework useful in analyzing sales situations encountered in our case studies and on the job.

The Salesperson

What is a salesperson? What does it take to be good in sales? These questions have been posed by generations of researchers and sales managers. Research concerning sales effectiveness generally has focused on uncovering the behaviors, personality traits, and capabilities related to performance. The results of this research are, at best, ambiguous.[2] One stream of research has examined different types of messages delivered by salespeople. Whereas some research has found that a "good presentation" is generally more effective than a "poor presentation," these studies have uncovered few significant differences in the effectiveness of a product-oriented vs. a personal-oriented message (academic terminology for the sales manager's distinction between "selling a product" and "selling yourself"). These same studies have also found few differences between "hard sell" emotional appeals and "soft sell" rational appeals (in response to the manager's question, "How should we talk to customers?") or between different personality traits such as "forcefulness" or "sociability" (arising from managerial curiosity concerning "what kind of person should we hire for a sales position?").

A second stream of research has examined the link between the salesperson's performance (e.g., meeting or exceeding sales goals) and specific traits presumably related to a person's ability to persuade another to buy something. These studies indicate that sales effectiveness *is* related to the salesperson's ability to develop accurate impressions of the customer's beliefs about product functions and the ability to articulate these beliefs—qualities that some researchers call "empathy." But, depending upon the product and/or market situation, the links between sales performance, salesperson traits such as age, education, sales experience, product knowledge, training, intelligence, and empathy are inconsistent and often contradictory. Even those variables that can be assessed with high accuracy and reliability (e.g., age, education, and sales experience) are related to performance in some studies and unrelated (or negatively related) in others.

What can a manager take away from such studies? First, the fact that academic studies in these areas are statistically inconsistent and inconclusive does *not* mean that the links are nonexistent or unimportant. Clearly, depending upon the sales situation, many of these traits will be vital. It will be very difficult for a manager to train and motivate poorly selected people to effective sales performance. Many experienced sales managers, reflecting on what it takes to sell effectively in a given situation, can legitimately claim, "I know it when I see it."

Second, the inconsistency of the results generated by these studies is itself significant. It strongly suggests that a search for universal selling rules or guidelines is probably misguided. So much depends on the specific sales situation facing a company that a contingency approach (i.e., one that incorporates situation-specific circumstances) is necessary. Stated another way, it suggests that common stereotypes of a good salesperson (e.g., a loud voice, forceful personality, deep inventory of stories, and a pleasing personality) are precisely that—stereotypes. Selling jobs vary greatly in several ways: in the kind of product or service sold; in the number of customers a salesperson is responsible for; and in the ancillary requirements of the job such as travel, technical knowledge, number and types of people contacted during sales calls, and the pertinence of sales-related dinners and entertainment. As one observer notes, "Selling is a demanding job but a great personality is not one of the demands." [3]

Third, the different results generated when one looks at the same factor in different product or market contexts can remind both researchers and managers that the customer's characteristics as well as the salesperson's must be considered. *The starting point for analyzing sales effectiveness, sales performance, and salesperson requirements should be the nature of the sales task.* In turn, the nature of the sales task will vary according to the customer's buying process and the selling organization's marketing strategy.

Boundary Role Person

Thus the answers to the questions, "What is a salesperson? What does it take to be good in sales?" vary, depending upon the specific industry, marketing, and buying situation. In Part Two, we will have opportunities to observe and analyze different manifestations of the salesperson in different buying and selling situations.

In the marketing programs of most companies, the salesperson is at the heart of the company's encounters with customers and therefore at the heart of marketing's boundary-spanning role in the organization as described in Part One. By definition, the salesperson is at the boundaries of two different organizations and therefore required to manage and respond to the often conflicting rules, procedures, and task requirements of each organization (see Figure A).

The sales representative—the salesperson—must represent the buying organization in the selling organization as well as his or her own organization to the customer. As a result, salespeople (more than most personnel in the company) must interact internally with sales managers, marketing personnel, product managers, production and engineering managers, credit personnel in finance, and so on, and they must deal externally with purchasing managers and, depending upon the product and buying process, a host of other people at their client companies.

Figure A
Boundary Role Person

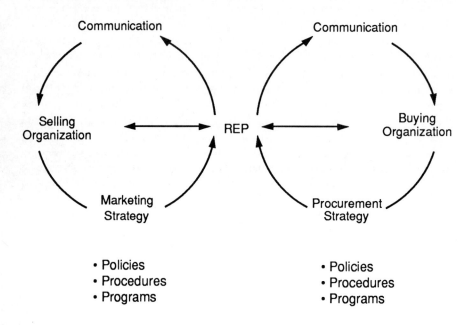

In performing this boundary role, field sales representatives are often placed in circumstances that help define the sales manager's goals, problems, and opportunities. For example, most sales jobs require travel; cold calls (i.e., calling on prospects who do not know the salesperson); nonselling activities; and reporting back to the selling organization different customers' concerns, complaints, and requirements. The sales representative, therefore, is often the focus of conflict and controversy within the selling organization and, due to the boundary role, likely to feel a certain psychological as well as physical distance from the organization. Indeed, some have argued that boundary role personnel are often distrusted by members of their own organizations and that many sales force policies and procedures can be viewed as attempts to "keep the sales rep under control." [4]

More generally, however, this view of the sales representative as a boundary role person emphasizes that *the prime objectives of sales management should be to aid, focus, and evaluate the effective performance of a boundary role.* This view of the salesperson focuses attention on how sales policies, procedures, and programs do (or do not) encourage the behavior required to perform the boundary role effectively. To evaluate the factors, we must pay attention to the important differences among the sales jobs in the case studies and consider the implications for the kinds of people, training, motivation, and evaluation policies relevant to the activities that a sales representative must perform.

A Classification of Sales Jobs

Can sales tasks be classified in a meaningful, orderly scheme? Again, research in this area has generated diverse, sometimes conflicting, results, and common sense suggests that the range of sales tasks is not likely to remain constant in a competitive economy.[5] Nonetheless, Robert McMurray provided the basis for one influential categorization of sales jobs some years ago when he classified salespeople into the five categories that are briefly described below.[6]

Missionary

A missionary salesperson attempts to build goodwill and/or educate the potential user about the company's product line. This salesperson may never book an order personally. Instead, he or she focuses on building sales volume by persuading end users to order from the firm's wholesalers or other channels of distribution. An example would be a sales representative for a pharmaceuticals firm, soft-drink company, or distillery who calls on a doctor, restaurant, or bar, respectively, even though the customers in each instance buy from a pharmacy, bottler, or distributor, not directly from the salesperson.

Delivery

A delivery salesperson's primary responsibility is to increase business from current customers by providing good service, especially order-delivery service and perhaps promotional assistance. This salesperson often calls on the trade (retail or wholesale intermediaries) rather than end users. The goal of the delivery salesperson is to perform tasks aimed at "selling through" the channel rather than "selling to" user customers. This sales emphasis is especially common in consumer goods such as furniture, apparel, textiles, and food, and it is the focus for salespeople in that substantial part of most economies known as wholesaling.

Order Taker

The order taker in McMurray's scheme is a salesperson who may also call on the trade but does little in the way of service support, merchandising assistance, or creative selling. The sales process focuses on rebuys of familiar, frequently purchased goods. Salespeople for some consumer goods companies often deal with store personnel on this basis; similarly, salespeople at many industrial distributors often interact with customer purchasing personnel on the basis of price and in-stock availability of the goods listed on a purchase order.

Technical Sales

The technical salesperson attempts to increase business (usually from current customers) by providing them with technical assistance in the form of engineering support, applications development, user training, documentation, or perhaps advice and help in setting specifications. The technical salesperson, unlike the missionary or delivery salesperson, usually sells directly to end users. Many salespeople in industries concerned with chemicals, computers, office products, and heavy machinery do this kind of selling.

Create Demand

This final category refers to the salesperson whose primary responsibility is to obtain new accounts for the company through extensive cold calling (or, in the language of some industries, "canvassing" or "bird-dogging"). In this sense, the sales task "creates demand" for a product by persuading people unfamiliar with the company's product to switch from the customer's existing vendor or make a new, previously unconsidered purchase. Like technical selling, this sales task focuses on the users of a product (the end user or a key intermediary such as a building contractor for many electrical, houseware, and other goods), and it often requires the salesperson to provide a good deal of information about the product to the customer. But in this type of selling, unlike technical selling, "customer education" is perhaps secondary to qualities such as sheer persistence, aggressiveness, frequent call patterns, and the ability to withstand rejection.

These five categories are not mutually exclusive. The same salesperson calling on the same account may perform a number of these roles during the sales process and account-management cycle. Furthermore, depending upon the selling company's marketing strategy and sales-management systems, the sales job may differ significantly even among companies employing similar kinds of sales personnel in the same industry or product category. Thus this and other such schemes require more than a few grains of salt in their application. But the virtue of such a scheme is that it focuses our attention in a given situation on a key dimension of the salesperson's boundary role: the nature of the sales task to be accomplished and the kinds of behaviors and skills to be encouraged, discouraged, or developed. This is an essential starting point in establishing or changing a sales management system.

Managing Sales Tasks

Whatever the sales position, the nature of the sales task should depend upon an analysis of market conditions and customer behavior in important segments or accounts. Beginning with this analysis, marketing managers attempt to fit their available resources to the opportunities and constraints presented by the environment. This fit is essential to developing a coherent marketing strategy: a definition of marketing objectives, a plan for achieving those objectives, and decisions concerning the resources to be allocated among the product categories, markets, and channels in which the company competes. In turn, if a company has a marketing strategy (as opposed to an abstract set of objectives), then the strategy should have specific implications for what behavior is desired among the company's sales personnel.

Thus a core issue facing sales managers is how to encourage that desired behavior among sales personnel. As Figure B indicates, a number of factors influence the behavior of sales personnel: recruitment and selection policies; training; and the components of effort among salespeople.

At one level, then, managing customer encounters means achieving sales performance consistent with marketing strategy by guiding field marketing efforts toward desired behavior. This view has two important implications. First, despite the importance and salience of individual abilities, the sales representative ultimately is not an individual contributor within the organization; rather, he or she should be viewed as the agent of the firm's marketing strategy and the components of that boundary role should be influenced accordingly. Second, recruitment, training, and the factors affecting sales effort should be linked coherently in the policies established to manage sales tasks. Otherwise, the performance of these tasks is likely to vary from the behavior required by the firm's marketing strategy.

Figure B
Framework for Considering Factors Influencing
Salesperson's Behavior

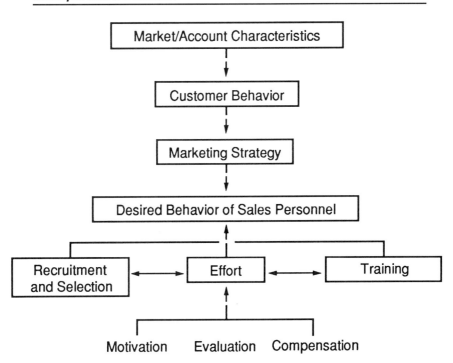

Figure C suggests one way to consider the important links among motivation, effort, evaluation, and compensation.

Motivation is a core function of management. The question, "How do I get other people to do as much as possible of the right kind of work?" may lack the elegance of business school terminology, but it is a question at the heart of most managerial responsibilities. In sales, motivation involves many factors.

One is the individual salesperson's personal characteristics, including knowledge, skills, and attitudes. Some people work harder than others, and some are smarter than others. Recruitment criteria and training policies are factors in accounting for and mitigating these differences. In most sales organizations, however, there is a range of personal abilities that must be developed and managed. Another factor is the salesperson's territory or account characteristics, which define the opportunity available to the salesperson and often provide a direction for the salesperson's efforts. Some of our cases, for example, demonstrate that some territories and accounts seem to have an inherently higher "yield rate" for sales efforts, independent of the salesperson assigned to that territory or account. Another factor affecting motivation is the salesperson's perceptions of the connections among effort, results, and rewards. In some instances, working harder or smarter may not translate into better sales results due to factors such as the firm's product policy, pricing, or competitive situation. In other instances, better efforts by the salesperson may lead to better sales results, but these results are not necessarily acknowledged by the firm's compensation and recognition systems.

Figure C
Links among Motivation, Effort, Evaluation,
and Compensation

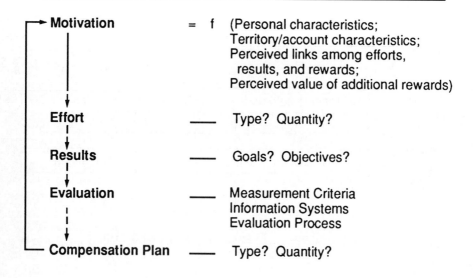

Finally, motivation is also influenced by the perceived value of additional rewards. Effort, results, and rewards may be linked, but the amount of required effort may be perceived as disproportionately high relative to the rewards received. Many sales incentive systems, for example, pay salespeople for incremental volume increases over previous year's results. Often, the intention is to motivate field salespeople to develop new business. In many selling situations, however, the effort required to develop this business is not perceived as worthwhile by the sales rep who has a base of mature, steady accounts in his or her territory.

An important outcome of motivation is effort. In a sales organization, effort has two important dimensions: type and quantity. Type of effort refers to such factors as the focus of the sales force's account development vs. account-maintenance activities, the relative emphasis on new vs. established products, or (in some situations) an emphasis on selling products that generate revenue and manufacturing volume vs. products that may have higher margins but lower unit sales. Quantity of effort refers to the amount of effort expended by salespeople as measured by factors such as call frequency, number of accounts, orders booked, or other measures of output. Compensation plans play a role in influencing both types of effort.

Effort presumably leads to results. The issue in sales management is what goals or objectives should be established in an attempt to guide efforts toward desired results. Some important choices in goal setting and rewarding results will be discussed in the chapter entitled Deployment, Focus, and Measuring Effectiveness.

Once goals are established, results must be measured, raising issues about the appropriate (or feasible) measurement criteria, the information systems in place to provide the data for such measurements, and the processes by which evaluations of effort and results are conducted. Sales performance can be evaluated by several criteria. Often, however, the company's information systems do not gather the relevant data, or sales force call reports (an important source of sales data in most companies) may be unreliable. Equally important, but often overlooked, is the process by which the evaluation is administered. As illustrated in some of the cases, salespeople may receive tangible, significant monetary rewards. But, the process of providing this compensation may be at odds with the company's formal performance evaluation of that person. The result is demotivation or, perhaps worse, motivation to perform the wrong type of sales effort. Many managers assert that they "pay for product, not process"; but if process is ignored in a sales environment, these managers often don't get what they have paid for.

Finally, the mechanics of the compensation plan must be considered. The important decisions here are again type and quantity. Type refers to issues such as the relative emphasis on base salary vs. incentive pay; quantity refers both to the total amount of compensation provided relative to industry norms and, within a sales organization, the amount of compensation provided for performing a given sales task. Both topics are examined in the chapter, Managing Selling and the Salesperson.

The important point, however, is the inevitable links (intended or unintended) among sales compensation, evaluation, and motivation. Faced with these links, the framework sketched in Figure C provides the following advice: start with the engine (the motivational objectives relevant to the sales situation) and then build the transmission (the specific evaluation and compensation policies aimed at encouraging certain kinds of efforts and behaviors by the sales force).

A Sales Management System

More than most aspects of business, effective sales management requires the ability to recognize the interaction among a set of complex factors while also being able to translate the understanding into specific action plans that can be implemented by the company's field personnel. By their nature, sales management decisions directly affect a company's revenue stream and interactions with customers. As a result, marketing managers must understand the consequences of field selling decisions on many other aspects of the organization. The emphasis in sales management policies and practices will affect the quantity and kinds of orders received by manufacturing; the cash-flow profile of the business managed by finance; the recruitment and training needs facing marketing and personnel; and the daily organizational interactions between sales and all of these other functional areas.

Figure D serves two purposes. First, it suggests a framework that will help to place in context some of the topics discussed here, such as the nature of the salesperson's boundary role, the central importance of an analysis of sales tasks, and the roles of different elements of sales management in influencing appropriate selling behaviors by the sales force. Second, it can serve as a reminder of other aspects of sales management that have *not* been discussed but that are important in analyzing sales situations.

In Figure D, Sales Force Control Systems refers to aspects of sales management that are relatively quantitative and measurable in nature, susceptible to management by objectives or policy direction on the part of sales management. These aspects include attention to the impact on sales personnel of the performance measurement, evaluation, compensation, and training systems in place at a company. By contrast, Sales Force Environment refers to more qualitative issues concerning the impact of human resource patterns (e.g., amount of turnover in the sales force); communication patterns (amount and types of communications among sales personnel); interaction patterns (e.g., how conflicts are managed); and management patterns (e.g., how goals are set and results rewarded). The policy—quantitative aspects of control systems— and the process—qualitative aspects of the sales force environment—affect each other. That is, what a company measures and rewards will affect process in its sales force; conversely, how salespeople interact should affect what a

Figure D
A Sales Management Framework

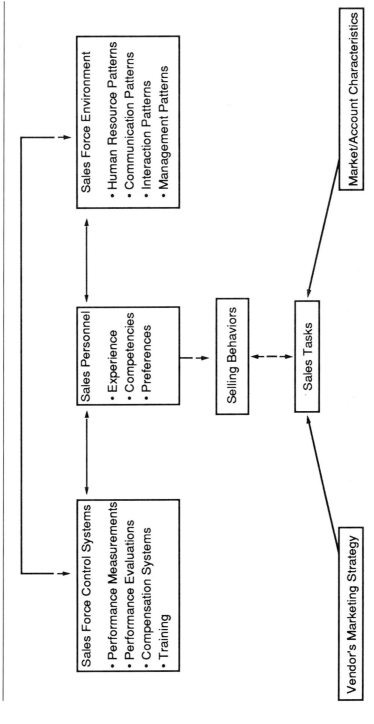

company decides to measure, train, and reward. In turn, both the control systems and the environment will affect the focus of the company's sales personnel, their selling behaviors, and their performance.

Using the framework shown in Figure D, you might want to consider the following as you analyze each of the cases in this section:

1. What is the vendor's marketing strategy for its product(s) or service(s), and what does this strategy imply for the role of personal selling activities at the company?

2. What do specific market-segment conditions, or account characteristics, imply for the kinds of tasks that must be performed effectively by the company's field sales personnel?

3. Who are the salespeople at the company (both the formal sales force and other personnel responsible for customer encounters)? What is the nature of their experience, skills, competencies, and selling preferences?

4. What control systems are used by management to influence sales force behavior? To what extent are sale force productivity measurements, performance evaluations of individual salespeople, emphasis in the compensation systems, or the nature of current sales training programs in line with your analysis of the requirements of the sales task?

5. How well or poorly are these control systems being implemented? What is the effect of human resource, communication, or interaction patterns between sales representatives and sales managers on sales force behavior? How would you describe the overall style or culture of the company's sales force environment?

6. Finally, what gaps exist between the requirements of sales tasks and current selling behaviors, and what should the company do to address these gaps?

The basic idea behind this perspective is that a sales management system must integrate three factors internal to the sales organization: the people involved; the systems established to try to influence those people's behavior (Sales Force Control Systems); and how those systems are applied or misapplied in the sales organization (Sales Force Environment) with two sets of factors external to the sales organization. The external factors include the vendor's marketing strategy (e.g., push vs. pull emphasis and the consequent impact on the role of sales personnel) and key market/account characteristics (e.g., buying processes and market structure). These two external factors largely determine the nature of required sales tasks; the three internal factors influence selling behaviors so that these sales tasks are performed optimally.

When there is coherent integration among these factors, the company is focusing on customer encounters and selling has traveled a long way toward effective marketing.

References

1. Theodore Levitt, "Marketing Myopia," *Harvard Business Review* 38 (July-August 1960): 26.

2. For good reviews of academic research concerning salespeople, see Barton A. Weitz, "Effectiveness in Sales Interactions: A Contingency Framework," *Journal of Marketing* 45 (Winter 1985): 85–103; David M. Szymanski, "Determinants of Selling Effectiveness: The Importance of Declarative Knowledge," *Journal of Marketing* 52 (January 1988): 64–77; and Thomas W. Leigh and Patrick F. McGraw, "Mapping the Procedural Knowledge of Industrial Sales Personnel," *Journal of Marketing* 53 (January 1989): 16–34. Similarly, chapters in Gilbert A. Churchill, Jr., Neil M. Ford, and Orville C. Walker, Jr., *Sales Force Management,* 2nd ed. (Homewood, Ill.: Irwin, 1985) provide the results of research concerning different topics in sales management.

3. Benson P. Shapiro, *Sales Program Management* (New York: McGraw-Hill, 1977), p. 9.

4. See J. S. Adams, "The Structure and Dynamics of Behavior in Organizational Boundary Roles," in *Handbook of Industrial and Organizational Psychology,* ed. by M. Dunnette (Chicago: Rand McNally, 1976); and Robert E. Spekman, "Organizational Boundary Behavior: A Conceptual Framework for Investigating the Industrial Salesperson," in *Sales Management: New Developments from Behavioral and Decision Model Research,* ed. by R. P. Bagozzi (Cambridge, Mass.: Marketing Science Institute, 1978).

5. For a review of various classifications of sales tasks and a suggested taxonomy, see William C. Moncrief, "Five Types of Industrial Sales Jobs," *Industrial Marketing Management* 17 (1988): 161–167.

6. Robert N. McMurray, "The Mystique of Super-Salesmanship," *Harvard Business Review* 39 (March-April 1961): 113–122. Another influential classification is that by Derek A. Newton, "Get the Most out of Your Sales Force," *Harvard Business Review* 47 (September-October 1969): 16–29, where four kinds of selling are emphasized: new-business selling (similar to McMurray's create demand category); trade selling (similar to McMurray's delivery salesperson but with more emphasis on promotional/merchandising assistance); and, identical with McMurray's scheme, missionary selling and technical selling.

⊓⊓⊓⊓⊓ | Chapter 3

Managing Selling and the Salesperson

Recruiting and selecting salespeople along with training, compensating, and evaluating them are core tasks in organizing and implementing the marketing effort. These tasks are often the fundamentals of a marketing program. Each company represented in this chapter approaches these tasks differently. But in all companies, certain generic questions are relevant to the effective management of the activities.

Recruitment and selection processes have a direct impact on a company's field marketing capabilities. Recruitment refers to the generation of applications and the labor pool from which the company seeks to hire salespeople; selection refers to the choice of hirees from among the applicants. Theoretically, the company's marketing strategy should define the role of personal selling within the marketing mix; that role, in turn, should determine recruitment and selection criteria throughout the sales force. In practice, the exigencies of time, the constraints of the relevant labor markets, or the inattention to implementation requirements in the strategy itself make recruitment and selection a more improvised process in many companies.

In each of the following cases, consider:

1. Who in the company has the primary responsibility for recruiting and selecting salespeople? What is the role of first-level sales managers in this process? What are their formal and informal qualifications for making these judgments?
2. What are the stated recruitment and selection criteria at each company studied? Do the criteria seem to differ from the official criteria in any of these situations? If so, why?
3. Finally, "experience" is probably the most frequently cited recruitment criterion by marketing managers. But as has been pointed out,[1]

in a sales context, experience is a multidimensional attribute. It may refer to experience with any of the following:

- A customer group (e.g., a banker, broker, or other financial-services executive hired by a computer firm to call on financial-services prospects).
- A product technology (e.g., an applications engineer or field-service technician hired to sell that category of equipment).
- A company or division of an organization (e.g., an expediter or customer service representative moved to a sales position).
- A geography or territory (e.g., an inexperienced salesperson hired to sell in his or her hometown or college campus).
- Selling activities (e.g., an insurance agent or copier salesperson hired to sell computers or software).

The relevance and importance of each type of experience vary with the nature of the sales tasks in a given situation and with the amount of training the company can offer. In each case in this chapter, consider what experience is relevant to important sales tasks, and what systems or processes (if any) the company has established to find or to build this experience.

Training decisions, which are related to a company's recruitment and selection decisions, generate a lot of attention both within and outside the sales organization. Individual product managers, for instance, are likely to take great interest in how much training the company's salespeople receive in the specifications and technologies of their products whereas individual market managers are likely to take a similar interest in how much training salespeople receive in the demographics, buying processes, or other relevant characteristics of their markets.

Nonetheless, training is also an aspect of sales management that, at many companies, is honored more in theory than in practice. For example, a recent survey of sales and marketing managers found that of nearly 1300 respondents drawn from industrial firms in the United States and Canada, 43% said their companies did not train salespeople in selling at all; 34% solely or predominantly used internally developed sales training; and 23% used professional training services. The same survey also found that the five most preferred training topics for salespeople were identified as effective listening, closing and gaining commitment from customers, maintaining self-motivation, time management, and guidelines and techniques concerning how to do cold calls.[2]

In evaluating training needs in sales, at least three issues are always relevant:

- Who should be trained? In most organizations, new sales recruits receive a combination of training and orientation to company policies and procedures. But this raises the issues of training for different types of salespeople and, depending upon how market or competitive changes may have altered the nature of sales tasks, training for different stages of the same salesperson's career.

- What should be the primary emphasis in the training program? Sales training can encompass the following: product knowledge; company knowledge; customer knowledge; and/or generic selling skills (e.g., time management or presentation skills). All of these may be important, but the relative importance of each type of training differs depending upon the selling situation, the feasible scope and costs of sales training, and the nature of the company's marketing strategy.
- How should the training process be structured in terms of the following: on-the-job training and experience vs. a formal and more consistent centralized program; field initiatives and participation vs. headquarters programs; and in-house training vs. outside expertise?

Finally, selling is an art, not a science or checklist of attributes. Correspondingly, sales training is a complex subject with no easy, measurable answers. What seems clear is that effective sales training, like most types of worthwhile education, cannot be accomplished in a single event. Participants need reinforcement, periodic upgrading and adaptation of pertinent skills and attributes, and the motivation and healthy self-confidence that tend to be by-products of a good developmental process. In most organizations, these important aspects of training are in effect the responsibilities of first-line sales managers. Thus other questions to consider in each case are the role of sales supervisors in developing their salespeople and the success with which each supervisor defines and executes that role.

Compensation is probably the most visible and tangible aspect of sales management; undoubtedly, it affects the salesperson's performance of his or her boundary role. Therefore, it is probably the most discussed aspect of managing selling and the salesperson, but it is not necessarily the most important. Many other factors besides money affect the accomplishment of required sales tasks; an exclusive concern with compensation issues often can obscure the larger sales context in which those issues are only one part. Nonetheless, addressing the question of how to pay the people responsible for customer encounters is a fundamental part of organizing marketing efforts. It requires attention to the following questions.

What must the salesperson do to succeed? Selling, directly or indirectly, is almost always a key function. Developing a compensation plan, however, requires breaking this category into its constituent parts. How much of selling in a given situation is attention to delivery? Price negotiations? Distributor network relations? Customer education? Technical expertise? Personal relationships? Service of different kinds? Cold calling? Sheer persistence? Like other aspects of sales management, the compensation plan should be based on a coherent picture of important sales tasks and reinforce the salesperson's role in the company's marketing strategy.

What is the relevant labor pool? This question, important for determining general compensation levels, has two dimensions. The first is the amount and kind of compensation offered by competitors. This information is always

around the sales office, and comparisons are inevitable. A firm with uncompeti-
tive pay levels will inevitably lose its best sales personnel. The second dimension,
which follows from analyses of the sales task, concerns the salesperson's potential influence on the buying decision and the abilities required to exert this
influence. In many industries, technical skills are essential to the sales task; this
means recruiting highly trained people who often may have a variety of options
in different industries and in different functions besides sales. This also affects
pay levels. More generally, however, what some economists call "transaction-
specific assets" are relevant to sales compensation plans.[3] These assets are the
specialized knowledge and working relationships built up over time by the
people selling a product and specialized to the task of selling that product.
These aspects may include technical skills or simply detailed knowledge of the
decision makers and decision-making process at an important account. When
salespeople have developed transaction-specific assets, the company's costs of
losing these personnel may be prohibitive, which will be reflected in the
compensation plan.

What should be the salary/incentive mix? The questions here concern the
relative emphasis on fixed salary vs. incentive compensation (commission,
bonuses, etc.). Although some sales forces are straight salary and some are
straight commission, surveys indicate that about two-thirds of companies with
sales forces use some combination of salary and incentive compensation. The
following factors tend toward a higher salary component: (a) the difficulty in
measuring the impact of a salesperson's performance in a reasonable period
of time; (b) the need for salespeople to coordinate efforts (e.g., team selling or
national account programs); (c) the complexity and length of the selling task;
(d) the importance of nonselling activities such as after-sale services; (e) the
amount of missionary selling required; and (f) the volatility of demand in a
product market.

These factors tend to make salary a more important factor than incentives
in the total sales compensation mix. As some of our cases illustrate, however, a
company can have a highly leveraged (i.e., high commission component)
compensation plan and still sell highly technical, complex products in a market
environment in which nonselling activities and long-term relationships are
important *if* other aspects of the sales management system support the required
sales tasks. Because salary plans are easier to administer, they are often the
default option for companies lacking the information systems or managerial
skills required to administer more complex compensation plans.

What should be the form of the incentive component? Although their
variations are legion, the major forms of sales compensation are few: straight
salary; salary plus bonus; salary plus compensation; and compensation with or
without a "draw" (i.e., permitting the salesperson to draw commission in
anticipation of actual sales).

Bonuses and commissions are forms of incentive compensation. Bonuses
are lump sums paid for the attainment of specific objectives. Sometimes
bonuses are based on a quantitative formula and sometimes on qualitative

objectives (e.g., reaching certain decision makers at a key account) or administered at a particular manager's discretion. Commissions are typically a percentage of sales volume or margins. Most companies apply a standard commission rate to all sales, but others vary the commission rate by product or category of customer in order to reflect profitability or important competitive objectives. Sometimes commissions are paid only when sales are above quota, or different commission rates are used for sales above and below quota.

Close attention to the details just described is important. Salespeople study the plan closely, and many look for what managers often call loopholes and what a salesperson might well call "the best use of my time in order to maximize income." Apparently incidental matters, such as paying commissions when orders are booked vs. when payment is received, can make major differences in the company's cash flow, order patterns, production schedules, and focus of selling efforts. Hence close attention to the specific company context is crucial.

Performance evaluations are an integral dimension of the sales environment, whether or not the company has a formal, scheduled sales performance evaluation program. Without defined performance evaluation criteria, the company is likely to incur significant opportunity costs in the form of poor sales personnel decisions. There are also likely to be many inconsistencies in the evaluation criteria that are applied, which in turn lead to mixed signals that ultimately damage sales force morale and effectiveness.

At the same time, salesperson evaluations are particularly complex forms of performance evaluations, in part because sales evaluations are inextricably linked to issues considered later in the chapter on Deployment, Focus, and Measuring Effectiveness. At this point, three questions can help to guide our judgments about performance evaluation practices in sales:

- Does the evaluation focus on actionable behavior that the salesperson can control? Many sales evaluation systems focus solely on sales results. This approach emphasizes the importance of results, not just effort or good intentions, in a sales environment. But many of the factors that affect sales results are out of the salesperson's control (e.g., macro-economic developments, a customer's unforeseen demise, competitive moves). Although performance evaluations can encourage attention to these factors, they should focus on factors the salesperson can control. Otherwise, the links among motivation, effort, and evaluation (see Aspects of Sales Management: An Introduction) are broken.

- Are evaluation criteria consistent with the company's measurement systems and compensation plan? Even when performance evaluations focus on actionable items, that focus may be at odds with the company's measurement system for sales performance or with the criteria that drive sales compensation. A common instance concerns team-selling situations: In major-account situations, the coordination of different salespeople calling on different locations or levels of the same account usually is critical. As a result, account managers often spend much time and energy on specific coordination issues in their evaluations of individual salespeople. But the company's measurement systems may not gather data relevant to these team-selling activities, and the compensation plan often focuses on individual sales results.

■ What is the nature of the performance-evaluation process and the roles of the field sales manager and the individual salesperson being evaluated? Effective evaluation processes are a combination of coaching as well as appraisal, a two-way transfer of information between sales representative and sales manager as well as a set of directions and expectations from management concerning selling behaviors. This process relies on managers and their subordinates to communicate effectively about performance. Unfortunately, few companies actually train sales managers in the process of giving and receiving feedback.[4] The challenge is considerable. An effective evaluation process takes time—the scarce resource in most sales organizations. Furthermore, sales environments attract a fair share of highly motivated, achievement-oriented, strong-willed individuals, and as others have pointed out, "no amount of human relations techniques can change the fact that evaluations represent the exercise of power and authority by superiors over subordinates."[5]

Nonetheless, without a good process, the result of performance evaluations can often be demotivation or, perhaps worse, motivation to perform the wrong type of sales effort.

Case Studies

The cases in this chapter provide an introduction to basic selling tasks and sales management issues. In each case, there are one or more salespeople and a great deal of pertinent information about the control systems and sales environment within which those people are recruited, trained, compensated, and evaluated.

The Cooper Pharmaceuticals, Inc. (CPI) case follows the twelve-year career of an ethical drug salesman, Bob Marsh. After a series of events, Marsh is terminated, and certain customers complain. As a result, the vice president of sales at CPI has been instructed by the company's president to examine the Marsh case to determine whether Marsh's firing was a "management failure" and, if so, to decide what should be done to correct the situation.

As well as information about Marsh's performance and sales tactics throughout his career with CPI, the case also provides information about the company's sales policies, recruitment criteria, training procedures, compensation structure, and performance evaluation processes. Thus the case is an excellent introduction to the basics of sales management and to the intricate combination of market conditions, company policies, and individual personalities that usually comprise important issues in the management of customer encounters. As you analyze this case, consider the following questions:

1. What is a good salesperson in this situation? How good a salesperson was Bob Marsh?
2. What is a good district sales manager in this situation? How good was each district manager encountered by Marsh during his career with CPI?
3. What do you think of the recruitment and selection criteria, training, compensation, performance evaluation, and termination policies at CPI?
4. What should be done about the situation in the short term? In the long term?

In the Cole National Corporation case, management is concerned with the issue of turnover in the sales force. As Cole's management sees it, the need is "to reduce turnover or alter substantially the role of the field sales force in the division's marketing program." Thus where the CPI case focuses on an individual salesperson and the human resource management implications of recruitment, training, compensation, and evaluation policies, the Cole case provides a systemwide perspective on a sales force and its role within a marketing strategy. Among other things, the Cole case illustrates that sales management entails managing people but also a certain call capacity, an aspect of field marketing examined in more detail in the chapter on Deployment, Focus, and Measuring Effectiveness.

In the Cole case, the products sold and serviced by the sales force are seemingly simple: keys, knives, letters, numbers, and signs carried by retail stores. The issue of turnover in this sales force, however, raises a number of complex questions concerning strategy, implementation, and sales management:

1. What is the marketing strategy of Cole's Consumer Products Division? What is the role of personal selling within this strategy?
2. How many sales calls should the division's sales force make annually in order to execute this strategy effectively? What does this imply for the optimum number of salespeople in the division?
3. Is Bill Bonnie (a Cole salesperson) a good salesperson? What are the key tasks of a salesperson in this situation?
4. Has Cole management correctly identified the problem in this situation? What should be done about turnover in Cole's sales force?

The Fieldcrest case looks in depth at one aspect of sales management: developing the annual compensation plan. The case describes Fieldcrest's compensation policies in the early 1970s and requires you to understand and analyze the behavioral implications of a fairly complex compensation plan with definite objectives. This case is also an excellent opportunity to discuss the roles, purposes, and limitations of compensation in a sales context. The discussion inevitably touches on fundamental issues concerning how to motivate and manage people so it is relevant to all managers, not just those in marketing. As you analyze the Fieldcrest case, consider the following:

1. How does this compensation plan work? What are the specific steps involved in tabulating a salesperson's total compensation (including bonus) under this plan? What are the strengths and potential vulnerabilities of this plan?
2. What types of selling behaviors are encouraged and discouraged by this compensation plan? How well does it support Fieldcrest's marketing strategy and competitive position?
3. Evaluate the various perspectives and concerns about the compensation plan mentioned in the case. How valid is each concern?
4. What should Fieldcrest's management do about the changes in the compensation plan they are considering?

Together, these three cases provide a solid overview of key issues involved in managing selling and the salesperson. All three examine recruiting, training, compensation, and evaluation policies at the companies studied. Each exhibits, in a different manner, the important linkages required among these policies if the management of customer encounters in the field is to be effective.

References

1. Benson P. Shapiro, *Sales Program Management* (New York: McGraw-Hill, Inc., 1977), p. 455.
2. See "Study Reveals Sales-Training Needs of Business Marketers," *Marketing News* (July 28, 1989): 8. The study involved a series of mail surveys conducted in 1987 and 1988 by Princeton Research and Consulting Center.
3. The notion of "transaction-specific assets" is developed most fully by the economist Oliver E. Williamson, "The Economics of Organization: The Transaction Cost Approach," *American Journal of Sociology* 87 (November 1981): 548–577 and in *The Economic Institutions of Capitalism* (New York: The Free Press, 1987). Applications of Williamson's theory to sales compensation in particular include George John, Allen M. Weiss, and Barton Weitz, "An Organizational Coordination Model of Salesforce Compensation Plans: Theoretical Analysis and Empirical Test," *Journal of Law, Economics, and Organization* 3 (Fall 1987): 231–251; and an interesting application of transaction-costs theory to more general issues in sales management is Erin Anderson and Richard L. Oliver, "Perspectives on Behavior-Based Versus Outcome-Based Salesforce Control Systems," *Journal of Marketing* 51 (October 1987): 76–88.
4. For more detailed discussions of this important topic, see John Anderson, "Giving and Receiving Feedback," in *Organizational Change and Development*, ed. by G. W. Dalton et al. (Homewood, Ill.: Irwin, 1970), pp. 339–346; Michael Beer, "Performance Appraisal: Dilemmas and Possibilities," *Organizational Dynamics* 9 (1981): 24–36; and Linda Micheli, Frank V. Cespedes, Donald Byker, and Thomas J. C. Raymond, *Managerial Communication* (Glenview, Ill.: Scott, Foresman and Company, 1984), pp. 105–126.
5. D. W. Brinkerhoff and Rosabeth Moss Kanter, "Appraising the Performance of Performance Appraisal," *Sloan Management Review* 21 (1980): 8.

Case 3
Cooper Pharmaceuticals, Inc.

In 1990, executives of Cooper Pharmaceuticals, Inc. (CPI) received a number of letters from irate customers who complained about the firm's terminating the services of one of its detailers, Bob Marsh. Because customer reactions of this nature were rare, and because CPI's reputation for "excellent" management practices appeared to be in question, the sales vice president (at the urging of CPI's president) decided to look into the Marsh case in detail to determine whether Marsh's discharge was a management failure and, if so, what could be done to correct the situation. Accordingly, the sales vice president collected all the data in company files relevant to the Marsh case, including managers' comments that allegedly gave insight into Marsh's feelings toward company management personnel.

Background Information

CPI was a major manufacturer of prescription drugs for the medical and dental professions. All its products were carried by drug wholesalers and drugstores for resale to the general public by prescription or to hospitals and physicians. CPI competed with such firms as Abbott, Lilly, Merck, Upjohn, and Schering. CPI's 1989 sales exceeded $1 billion.

CPI fielded a sales force of over 500 *detailers* who called regularly on hospital personnel, doctors, and dentists to describe the product line and to persuade these medical personnel to use and prescribe CPI drugs. A typical CPI detailer was responsible for about 200 physician and hospital accounts within

This case was prepared as the basis for class discussion rather than to illustrate either effective or ineffective handling of an administrative situation. It is a revision of an earlier version by Professor Derek A. Newton, Olsson Professor of Business Administration, University of Virginia.

Copyright © 1990 by the President and Fellows of Harvard College. Harvard Business School case N9-590-111.

an assigned geographic territory, and he or she was expected to make between six and nine doctor or hospital calls per day.

Most CPI detailers were pharmacy school graduates who had joined CPI after a few years' experience as registered pharmacists in retail drugstores. Each new CPI detailer received a month's training in product characteristics and selling (detailing) skills at the company's headquarters. In addition, both new and experienced detailers received regular on-the-job training from the 35 district managers. A CPI detailer could expect between 10 to 15 days of these field visits in a year, depending on his or her experience and performance. All CPI representatives returned to headquarters regularly for continued training throughout their careers.

CPI executives considered these detailers second to none in the business. About 60% of the detailers had 10 or more years with the company; 25% had fewer than 5 years. About half were age 40 or older, and one-fourth were under 30. Senior executives also were gratified that turnover in the sales force was much lower than the industry average. Only about 8% were lost each year from resignation, discharges, retirements, and deaths.

CPI detailers were salaried and received an annual bonus based on corporate performance. In 1989 CPI detailers' total earnings ranged from $40,000 to $80,000. The corporate bonus typically amounted to about 15% of these totals. In addition, each detailer was provided with a company automobile, generous fringe benefits, and reimbursement for all normal business expenses.

Every CPI detailer was evaluated in terms of both sales volume and improvement in his or her relationships with customers. Quotas were established yearly for each of the dozen or so major product categories to stimulate proper concentration of detailing efforts. Every CPI detailer received a formal performance evaluation from his or her district manager once a year and informal evaluations whenever necessary.

Almost all of the 35 CPI district managers had been chosen from among the sales force for leadership and good performance in administrative and selling activities. Evaluated chiefly on ability to develop personnel, each was expected to spend three to four days per week on field visits with detailers. The individual district managers reported to one of the 6 zone managers who reported in turn to the sales vice president.

Bob Marsh

In June 1978 Bob Marsh, the 32-year-old manager of a prescription department in a major drugstore in Toledo, Ohio, submitted his application to CPI for employment as a sales representative. Marsh presented a good academic record and a history of successful drugstore experience since his graduation from a top-flight pharmacy school in 1972. He was also an experienced U.S. naval pilot with a fine officer-service record. Marsh had grown up in a Toledo suburb and married a woman from the same town 12 years before. The couple now owned their own home in this suburb, where they were active in community and church affairs. They had two children.

Marsh considered joining CPI for over a year. He knew several career ethical drug detailers and had talked with them about the job. Since the earliest days of his training in pharmacy, Marsh had considered CPI one of the finest firms in the industry. After a few rewarding but unexciting years in retail pharmacy, he had decided to become a sales representative. His first territorial preference was his home state, although neither he nor his wife felt that moving to another part of the country would deter his joining CPI. Marsh also expressed interest in being considered for an international assignment in the future, as he and his wife had lived in or visited almost every major European country during his years in the Navy.

A CPI detailer who knew Marsh quite well arranged for him to meet John Meredith, the district manager in Toledo. Meredith was impressed with Marsh and rated him highly in sincerity, aggressiveness, attitude, enthusiasm, learning ability, judgment, character, affability, and appearance. His personal refer-´ences were outstanding. In a note to his zone manager, Meredith said, "I am quite hopeful that we will be able to obtain the services of Bob Marsh. I have every reason to believe that he will develop into an excellent salesman."

Working with John Meredith

About a month after the interview with Meredith, Marsh joined the CPI sales force and was assigned to a territory in Toledo, which greatly pleased the Marsh family. Although his new salary level of $35,000 a year was below his salary at the drugstore, he believed that his earnings potential with CPI would be considerably greater in the long run. Marsh had an advantage in that he knew personally many of the physicians and hospital personnel whom he would be calling on.

Marsh's initial field training went smoothly, and Meredith was certain that he had made an excellent decision in hiring Marsh. Marsh quickly grasped all facets of the job, including product characteristics and basic selling skills. He was exceptionally well received by physicians, office receptionists, and hospital personnel. His district associates also welcomed him cordially. The only characteristics that caused Meredith even momentary concern were Marsh's seeming lack of attention to organization, planning, and follow-up, and his tendency to question the logic of some of the company's major promotion programs. But since these attitudes were not unusual with beginning salespeople, Meredith wrote them off to inexperience.

After four months on the job, Marsh joined a group of other recently employed representatives at CPI headquarters for a month-long sales training program. The new detailers studied customer preferences, product characteristics, and sales promotion practices, as well as the pharmaceutical industry and CPI's competition. Top CPI executives lectured on corporate history,

policy, goals, and philosophy. In addition, the salespeople had ample opportunity to share their problems and experiences with other novice detailers
during social get-togethers. The training department's report on Marsh was
excellent.

Shortly after Marsh's return to the territory, Meredith spent a couple of
days in the field with him. Although it was apparent to Meredith that Marsh
had benefited greatly from the home office training program, Meredith was
disappointed with Marsh's seeming indifference to organization. Meredith felt
that Marsh gave little advance thought to the physicians he hoped to see—and
worse yet, he had no definite plan or approach once in the physician's office.
On each call, his attitude was "catch-as-catch-can," as Meredith phrased it.
Marsh's visits to hospitals were similarly unplanned. He also displayed more
interest in developing his own promotional programs than in following the
plans outlined at district meetings; he tended to second-guess scheduled
promotions by deciding himself which products to promote.

Meredith also thought that by this time Marsh should have better records
of physicians and should know more about their backgrounds, practices,
hospital affiliations, and product preferences. Meredith was especially concerned about Marsh's tendency to prejudge his customers' interests. His sample
bag was cluttered and poorly organized, and often he did not have appropriate
promotion literature to accompany the product being discussed. Materials
stored in his automobile or at home were in no better shape.

Meredith reminded Marsh that serendipity was not the pattern of a successful salesperson, and he pointed out that Marsh ought to change those bad work
habits early in his career. Meredith also suggested that Marsh should do less
visiting during his hospital calls and use this valuable time for more sales
presentations. Nevertheless, a good number of Marsh's physicians had increased their CPI prescriptions in recent months, indicating Marsh's ability to
influence physicians favorably. There was also an increase in the number of
physicians buying CPI products for office use. Marsh's hospital sales also were
showing gains.

In January 1979 Marsh's salary was increased to $37,500, the same amount
he had been earning on his previous job. Marsh seemed to be increasingly more
comfortable with his physician and hospital accounts, and sales throughout his
territory were growing steadily. Meredith continued to stress the need for better
planning, follow-through, and responsiveness to company policies. He reiterated that Marsh could do much better with his good customer rapport if he
were better organized and if he pressed harder for commitments to adopt CPI
products.

Near the end of his first year, following another two days with Meredith,
Marsh received his first formal performance review. As on all previous occasions, Meredith instructed Marsh about ways to improve his performance.
Meredith did most of the talking and there was little discussion. From the
interview Meredith gained a clear impression that Marsh had found his suggestions helpful and would try to do better.

Meredith also drew up a written appraisal to be reviewed by the zone manager and sales vice president. On the favorable side of the report, Meredith had this to say:

- A hard worker—loyal and dedicated
- Well received by physicians and hospital personnel
- Anxious to do well
- Appreciates and follows instructions and suggestions
- Cooperative and helpful with fellow associates

The following notations were made on the adverse side:

- Should overcome the tendency to prejudge customers and promotion programs
- Should be more responsive to management directives
- Should give more attention to planning and organization

Marsh's overall work performance was recorded as Below Standard.

In June 1980, Marsh's salary was increased to $40,000. In July 1980, his second year-end performance review resembled the first: work performance, Below Standard; attitude, Standard. At this time the zone manager and sales vice president took note of these performance reports and asked Meredith for his assessment of Marsh's potential. Meredith replied that Marsh was making substantial progress and that he expected him to overcome his deficiencies in the near future.

In January 1981 Marsh's salary was raised to $42,500 and in July, as Meredith had predicted, Marsh's progress review indicated substantial improvement. His overall performance was now Standard. The only areas still needing improvement were planning and organization.

The July 1982 performance appraisal report was even better. Marsh's effort to improve his call planning and overall organization had impressed Meredith to the point that he now rated this aspect of the job as Completely Satisfactory. Meredith also indicated that Marsh's attitude could not be better and that he had made great strides in overcoming his tendency to prejudge management, customers, and promotion programs. Marsh's judgment and responsiveness to supervision were now Excellent, and his overall rating was Above Average. In January 1983 Marsh's salary was raised from $45,000 to $50,000.

Working with Bill Couch

In March 1983, Meredith was transferred to another district. He was replaced by a new district manager, Bill Couch, an experienced and highly regarded supervisor. Couch's initial field visits with Marsh went well. Couch was impressed with Marsh's customer rapport throughout his territory. Couch frequently heard doctors refer to Marsh as one of the best detailers in the area. A prescription audit of several of the larger drugstores in Marsh's territory confirmed an impressive share of prescriptions for all major CPI products. CPI products were being used in every hospital pharmacy. In July, Marsh's first performance review under Couch recorded Satisfactory ratings across the board, with the exception of planning and record keeping.

Later in July, on the occasion of Marsh's fifth anniversary with CPI, the firm's president sent Marsh a personal letter congratulating him on this important anniversary and expressing "sincere gratitude for your fine contributions during your first five years with Cooper."

Over the next three years with Bill Couch, Marsh's performance ratings remained Satisfactory and he was given steady salary increases. In 1985, he was given the added responsibility of overseeing a distributor. Couch suspected, however, that while Marsh considered this activity interesting, he found the attendant work with drugstores a bit time consuming.

Marsh's salary progress in five years was impressive: his salary reached $60,000 in 1986. His final progress review with Couch in July 1986, a few months before Couch was transferred to another district, was the best yet. Couch recorded:

- Outstanding reception in physician offices and drugstores is a great asset
- Most gratifying improvement in drugstore sales
- Good acceptance by fellow associates
- Contributions at district meetings greatly appreciated
- Excellent attitude and company loyalty

Marsh's overall work performance was recorded as Well Above Average. His attitude was graded as Well Above Average.

Working with Jim Rathbun

In September Marsh began reporting to Jim Rathbun, who was gaining a reputation in the company as a bright, young, energetic manager with many new ideas about how to increase sales. Marsh appeared to find Rathbun's emphasis on team work stimulating.

At first Rathbun was complimentary about Marsh. Like previous district managers, Rathbun was quick to observe Marsh's excellent rapport with virtually everyone in his territory. According to Rathbun, however, Marsh was not using this selling asset to the fullest advantage. Rathbun pointed out more opportunities for increased sales than previous supervisors had ever mentioned. First, Rathbun expressed dissatisfaction with Marsh's record in establishing new products with physicians. Second, he criticized Marsh's poor penetration with dentists—a facet of Marsh's job that previous supervisors had not noted. Rathbun asserted that an improved attitude as well as better organization, planning, and follow-up would remedy Marsh's performance. Rathbun also outlined some preliminary sales goals for Marsh to attain within the next four months.

During the next four months Rathbun made several specific suggestions to Marsh. Rathbun advocated pinpoint detailing, that is, presenting one or two items of particular interest to each physician, depending on his or her type of practice, rather than rambling on, as Rathbun put it, about five or six products. Rathbun also talked about getting the doctor involved during the detail call. Rathbun also announced that the disorder in Marsh's detail bag and automobile was deplorable. Rathbun could not understand how any detailer could operate effectively with working tools in complete disarray. Marsh's lack of an organized record and filing system was also beyond Rathbun's comprehension.

During the four-month period, Rathbun spent five different days with Marsh in various parts of his territory. During one of these field visits Rathbun expressed interest in seeing a specific physician. Marsh informed him that the doctor was never in on that day. On his return to the zone office, Rathbun discovered that Marsh's doctor call record showed that he had seen the physician in question regularly during the past two years on various days of the week—including the day in question. During his next visit, Rathbun called Marsh's attention to this discrepancy. Rathbun referred to the gravity of falsifying reports and reminded Marsh that company policy provided for dismissal in such situations.

Marsh explained that although this physician did not have office hours on that particular day, she did occasionally see salespeople in the morning while catching up on her paperwork. Marsh had sometimes taken advantage of this opportunity and had then saved the call report slip for days when he had not been able to meet his doctor call quota. Marsh stated that he would never do so again and that his future record keeping would be flawless. Rathbun confirmed that nothing less would be acceptable. "Rules are rules, and that's the way it's going to be," he said.

In January 1987, Rathbun and Marsh had a lengthy discussion. After notifying Marsh that he would get no salary increase for 1987, Rathbun cited several specific incidents in which Marsh's poor attitude, careless organization, and inattention to planning and follow-up had been responsible for missed sales opportunities. Many of the sales goals that Rathbun had set four months ago had not been met. Marsh's new product placement was seriously deficient, and his sales from special promotions to retailers and hospitals ranked in the lower half of the district. Rathbun closed the discussion by challenging Marsh's attitude toward management directives and company sales objectives.

Most of this lengthy discussion was carefully committed to paper. An apparently stunned Bob Marsh signed a statement confirming that he was now on probation and that failure to improve within 90 days would lead to dismissal.

At the end of the probationary period, after spending several days with Marsh in the field, Rathbun informed Marsh that his intense efforts to measure up to Rathbun's expectations during the past months had paid off. The most dramatic changes were his newly organized detail bag and automobile, and his spruced-up records. His reporting accuracy was unquestioned. Rathbun also complimented Marsh's change in his detailing approach from rambling discussions to pinpoint presentations. Marsh also now was sticking to the promotion schedule outlined by the home office and reviewed at district meetings. His increased effectiveness in drugstore selling was confirmed by recent special orders. Several new product goals had been reached in selected hospitals. His attitude toward the detailer's responsibilities met Rathbun's criteria. Accordingly, Marsh was removed from probation. His performance was now recorded as Satisfactory on all counts.

In January 1988, Marsh was given a salary increase to $62,500 and in July his performance, according to Rathbun, was still Satisfactory on all counts. In August, shortly after Marsh was sent another letter by CPI's president congratulating him on his 10 years of "fine, loyal service" there was another change in district managers.

Working with Vince Reed

The new district manager was a much newer and younger person that Rathbun. Toledo was Vince Reed's first supervisory assignment. He had been with the company only half as long as Marsh but had established himself as a competent detailer and promising management candidate.

According to Reed, his first few visits with Marsh were pleasant and uneventful. Reed had access to Marsh's complete file and felt thoroughly familiar with Marsh's background and past obstacles to his development. The two men talked frequently about Marsh's ups and downs with previous district managers, and it seemed to Reed that Marsh appreciated these opportunities to discuss problems of the previous years.

Reed found Marsh's performance generally satisfactory, especially in view of his earlier problems. Reed was impressed with Marsh's customer rapport, as previous supervisors had been. Reed talked with Marsh about the progress he had made in planning, organization, following directions, and effective use of time on physician calls. Reed also commended Marsh's attainment of sales goals. Reed still questioned the slow acceptance of new products among Marsh's customers, however, and he indicated that physician sales in general were not what they should be. He felt that Marsh could follow district and home directives more promptly. And he felt that Marsh's organization will still deficient—his records of hospital and wholesaler personnel were inadequate, and the samples and promotional literature in his bag and car were disordered.

Reed recommended a salary increase of $2,500 for Marsh in January 1989. But later that spring Reed made some substantial additions to Marsh's file. In a carefully detailed letter to his zone manager, Reed outlined several of the points that he and Marsh had talked about on many previous occasions. Specific instances of Marsh's failure to comply with Reed's suggestions were itemized.

By July Marsh's overall performance had slipped, and he was notified during his annual review that his rating had gone from Satisfactory to Completely Unsatisfactory. Reed closed with an admonition that Marsh's performance would now have to reach an acceptable level within 90 days. Once again,

Marsh was on probation. Marsh was instructed to submit to Reed's office a written plan outlining his intended approach to extricating himself from his current status. Reed provided the basic outline for this master plan, and Marsh had only to fill in the details. Marsh found this easy to do, since he merely needed to agree with Reed's ideas on how the job should be done.

Working with Antonia Wilkens

Vince Reed was being transferred to another district in September 1989 and, therefore, did not follow up on Marsh's performance. The new district manager, Antonia Wilkens, whose background was comparable to Reed's, was only able to spend two days in the field with Marsh before she too was reassigned to another district in March 1990. In view of her brief exposure to Marsh, Wilkens made no change in the record, although she confirmed some of the observations made by Marsh's four previous supervisors. Although she did not discuss Marsh's probationary status in detail, Wilkens implied that the time limit set by Reed was no longer valid. Marsh received no salary increase in January 1990, but his probationary status had "evaporated."

Working with Ted Franklin

In the spring of 1990 (Marsh's twelfth year with CPI) his sixth field supervisor, Ted Franklin, arrived on the scene. Franklin also was younger than Marsh, but he had been a supervisor a year or two longer than had the previous two district managers. Although Marsh had not had a salary increase during the past two years, his 1990 base salary, plus annual bonus and other allowances and benefits, placed him in an income bracket enjoyed by few of his pharmacy school contemporaries.

Before his first meeting with Marsh, Franklin went over Marsh's sizable personal history folder in detail. Franklin also assured the zone manager that with proper guidance Marsh could be remodeled into an above-average performer. In view of the complex history of the Marsh case, Franklin took considerable time writing a detailed narrative report to use as a guide in his interview with Marsh.

Franklin began by summarizing all of Marsh's deficiencies as seen by earlier supervisors. He pointed out that the record was not good and that the time was fast approaching when substandard performance could no longer be tolerated. Franklin then turned to a long list of survival procedures that would save Marsh's career and his job. Marsh would have to improve his sincerity, company loyalty, job interest, enthusiasm, cooperation, deference to supervision, and his work habits. Nothing but complete success could prevent dismissal.

Franklin set no time limit for the necessary turnabout. Instead, he instructed Marsh to call him at an appointed time each week to discuss his adherence to the outline and to review his progress. Franklin's program also included a weekly reading assignment of technical and promotion literature, designed to help Marsh establish new products. Marsh was to submit written summaries of the reading assignments each week. Marsh also was required to complete questionnaires on each of his major hospitals. These forms were designed to give Marsh the market intelligence he needed for improving his hospital sales. Marsh agreed to every point in the step-by-step program. Franklin required that he sign each page of the master plan to indicate his complete understanding of what had to be done as well as the consequences of failure.

By now the zone manager had also been transferred. The new manager, Pete Mallick, was a seasoned field executive with an excellent reputation in the company. He and Franklin carefully reviewed the blueprint for Marsh's rehabilitation. Mallick approved of the program and asked that Franklin submit periodic reports on Marsh's progress to the zone office.

Subsequent weeks did not go well for Marsh. He got off to a bad start with late phone calls and written reports. He began to fall behind schedule in reading assignments and in collecting the required market data for his files. Sales volume within his territory was unchanged. In Franklin's judgment, Marsh appeared moody, unfriendly, indifferent, and lethargic. He had less and less to say, and he offered fewer and fewer explanations about his failures on each subsequent weekly report.

Franklin's field visits also did not elicit the kind of response that he hoped for. Even reminders that time was running out for the dismissal decision no longer appeared to have any stimulating effect on Marsh. The only attitude that seemed constant was his professed fondness for the company and his job and his desire to do better.

By July 1990, after several interim conferences, Mallick and Franklin agreed that time had run out—Marsh should be separated from the company. Franklin arranged a hotel meeting with Marsh. The discussion was short and centered on the well-documented facts that Marsh had been given ample opportunity to succeed, and that in view of his long history of failure he had no alternative but to resign.

According to Franklin, Marsh accepted the ultimatum with surprisingly little resistance or comment. He told Franklin that he understood why the job was no longer for him. Franklin felt that Marsh was relieved that it was all over. He expressed gratitude for all the help he had received through the years, and he said that he would always have a warm spot in his heart for Cooper Pharmaceuticals and his colleagues. At age 44, he planned now to return to the same pharmacy from which his sales career had been launched 12 years before.

Franklin reported to Mallick that the dismissal session had gone exceptionally well. Marsh had understood the decision completely, and agreed with it. Marsh was leaving the company with no ill will. The only touchy spot in the entire session was Marsh's request to talk over the decision with his family. Franklin pointed out that the conditions of his employment were no longer negotiable and that no point would be served in his discussing the situation with anyone. Marsh also understood that his entire case had been reviewed many times with the zone manager and corporate headquarters. The decision was irreversible.

The Aftermath

A week later Marsh called the CPI zone office for an appointment with Mallick. He said that he had been treated unfairly and that he would like to talk over several other circumstances regarding Franklin's handling of his case, as well as Franklin's overall management of the district. Mallick replied that he was thoroughly familiar with every detail of Marsh's history and that he was in complete agreement with Franklin's action. He saw no reason to meet with Marsh.

During the following week, the president of Cooper received a lengthy and thoughtful letter from a prominent physician in Marsh's territory. The doctor expressed disappointment and chagrin over Marsh's dismissal. He was stunned that a representative of Marsh's reputation and stature with so many of his medical colleagues could be dismissed so abruptly and for such arbitrary and flimsy reasons. He also cited irregularities in some of the company's management and promotion practices in the area. He wondered what was happening to the long-standing ethical policies that had given CPI such a fine reputation among physicians, pharmacists, and hospitals.

The president promptly replied that he was requesting an immediate investigation and that the zone manager, Mallick, would contact the physician. A meeting between the doctor and Mallick was quickly arranged. Mallick attempted to explain to the doctor the long history of Marsh's unsatisfactory performance, poor attitude, and reluctance to improve. He also related the abundant patience and help that Marsh had received from each of his district managers. He reiterated the long and thoughtful managerial consideration that preceded Marsh's dismissal. He also reminded the doctor that Marsh had completely agreed with the decision.

The doctor was not satisfied since this explanation failed to agree with his and other physicians' impressions of Marsh as an outstanding detailer. The doctor asserted that many other physicians and pharmacists in the area were talking about Marsh's dismissal, expressing similar surprise and concern. Since Mallick's explanation was not satisfactory, the doctor wrote to the president to tell him so.

In the meantime, the district and zone offices received several similar letters and calls from other physicians and pharmacists. The sales vice president also heard from several doctors and druggists throughout Marsh's territory. The main theme was the same—surprise, disbelief, and perplexity over the abrupt and unexplained dismissal of one of the finest and most helpful career detailers in the area. The central question seemed to be, How could this possibly happen to someone like Bob Marsh in a company like Cooper?

Cole National
Corporation: Turnover

In spring 1975, Mr. Boake Sells, executive vice president of Cole National Corporation's Consumer Products Division, was troubled by what he termed excessively high turnover among field salespeople. Despite several reorganizations of the field sales force Mr. Sells believed he would have to reduce turnover, or alter substantially the role of the field sales force in the division's marketing program.

Cole National and the Consumer Products Division

Cole National sales had grown from $65 million in 1970 to almost $111 million in 1974. During the same period net income had grown from $1.2 million to $4.4 million. Exhibit 1 contains corporate financial data.

The corporation had three major operations: specialty retailing, visual merchandising, and Consumer Products Division. Consumer Products sold keys, knives, and letters, numbers and signs (LNS) to 56,000 retail stores through 90 sales representatives. This field force also provided the retailer with in-store services designed to improve the salability of Cole products. Services included training store personnel in key duplicating equipment installed by the company, maintenance of displays, and introduction of new products suitable to a particular store.

In addition, the division created occasional national advertising programs. In 1972, cooperative advertising for 1¢ key sales[1] was arranged with large variety

---

This case was prepared by Associate Professor Frank V. Cespedes as the basis for class discussion rather than to illustrate either effective or ineffective handling of an administrative situation. It is a revised version of an earlier case prepared by Professor Benson P. Shapiro. Confidential data have been disguised but are deemed useful for discussion.

Copyright © 1989 by the President and Fellows of Harvard College. Harvard Business School case 9-590-031.

[1] In these sales, a consumer was offered two keys for the price of one plus one cent. Cole adjusted its prices to make such sales profitable for both the store and itself.

chains such as Woolworth's. Full-page color ads extolling the qualities of the "Kabar" line of hunting knives (Cole's best quality line) appeared in *Field and Stream* and other magazines. For 1975, there was a national consumer sweepstakes planned to promote colored keys. This sweepstakes would include advertising in magazines and point-of-purchase materials placed in the stores by the field sales forces.

Segments of the product line could be found in different departments in a large store—hardware, sporting goods, housewares, notions and jewelry. The one feature common to all products, according to management, was their need for fairly frequent servicing and reordering. This implied a high degree of personal contact between the field sales force and store management. Sales by product line were:

	1973	1974
Keys and key accessories	$10,538,000	$11,154,000
Pocket and hunting knives	4,820,000	6,000,000
Letters, numbers and signs	5,679,000	6,787,000
Total	$21,037,000	$23,941,000

Average gross margins for the product lines were: keys 70%, knives 40%, letters, numbers and signs 50%. Exhibit 2 contains a division income statement for 1974.

Mr. Sells was responsible for three headquarters departments and the chain and field sales forces (see Exhibit 3). One other headquarters department, marketing research, had been authorized but not yet staffed.

For each product line the division's basic merchandising and service program consisted of an initial assortment of merchandise arranged on a display fixture, in-store promotional materials, training retail clerks in how to sell the products and reorder them by mail, and periodically checking individual store displays to provide additional assurance of balanced inventories. The objective of the merchandising and service program was, as one executive put it, to establish a retailer in a particular line of business and then do almost everything to run that business except taking cash from the ultimate consumer. Because of its emphasis on in-store service, the division shipped its merchandise direct to individual stores, bypassing wholesalers and chain store warehouses.

The Key Product Line

The division's key program involved more in-store service than the knife or LNS programs. The division provided, at no charge to the retailer, a key-duplicating machine similar to those sold by other manufacturers for prices between $100–$200. In addition, the division's field salespeople trained retail clerks to select the correct key blanks from the assortment it provided and to cut keys on the machine. Division salespeople also periodically adjusted and maintained the key machines.

The division's program enabled a retail clerk with very little training to produce an exact copy of almost any key brought in by a customer. Once an operator had learned how to select key blanks quickly and to operate the machine, duplicate keys typically could be produced in less than a minute.[2]

In most stores, only the one or two clerks who serviced the hardware counters typically were trained to operate the key-duplicating machine. If these clerks resigned or were transferred to other departments, new clerks had to be trained.

To eliminate retailer loss from miscut keys, the division exchanged miscut keys for new key blanks. This policy, management believed, was instrumental in the success of the key-product line. In 1974, the division issued credit or exchanged over $740,000 (at division selling price) of miscut keys.

The suggested retail selling price (which most stores followed) was 69 cents for a brass key and 69 cents for a colored aluminum key. Since retailers paid 26 cents each for brass key blanks and 26 cents for aluminum key blanks, the division stressed that retailers' gross margin was 62% on key sales, whereas it was seldom more than 30% to 40% on most hardware items which were priced below $1. In addition, on other items, part of the gross margin defrayed the expense of damaged merchandise, display maintenance, and warehouse distribution—all of which the division's key program covered at no charge.

The division offered programs for both brass and aluminum keys in four bright colors. A popular initial assortment (Exhibit 4) consisted of 40 dozen brass and 36 dozen color fast-selling key blanks. The retailer's cost was $237 ($ .26 × 76 × 12). Brass key sales had been increasing faster than color keys, the reverse of the mid-1960s, situation when color keys had been introduced. The division prepaid freight charges on keys as well as on all other product lines.

Sales of initial assortments of keys accounted for 2% to 4% of total key sales. This figure had been stable for many years and was expected to remain so. All other key sales were reorders. About one-third of the reorders, according to management estimates, were mailed in directly by individual stores rather than submitted by field sales personnel.

In discussing the reorder business, one division executive described a situation in a territory consisting of a large metropolitan area. The territory was over quota because of a high volume of mail reorders even though no one was in the field for several weeks. "Nevertheless," this executive commented, "even though a high percentage of our sales come from mail orders, the salespeople generate those orders. We can't do without them."

Management believed Cole emphasized a different philosophy of selling than competitors. Division executives estimated Cole's service program was more aggressive and comprehensive, and Cole's total sales were considerably

---

[2]The machine could not produce original keys. If a customer had no key for a particular lock, he or she had to go to a locksmith.

higher than competitors' sales. Only one major competitor offered a similar service program. This company sold key blanks direct to chain and independent retailers for 24 cents each.

Most other manufacturers of key blanks provided no service program with their products. They sold key blanks to retailers either directly or through hardware jobbers. Blanks customarily cost the jobber 4 cents to 8 cents apiece. Retailers paid 6 cents to 11 cents and sold duplicate keys for 25 cents to 50 cents. Most retailers who purchased key blanks from jobbers and owned their own key-duplicating machines were locksmiths, repair shops, and small hardware stores.

The Knife Product Line

The division's knife program was similar to the key program. The division offered eight different assortments of knives, each available in a display case. The case contained reserve stock of the displayed items behind the front display. Display cases, as well as monthly mailings of promotional, display, and training material, were free to the retailer.

The division's field sales force was supposed to check the knife inventory in each store regularly and to make up reorders for the approval of the store manager. Between salespersons' visits, however, store managers were encouraged to mail reorders directly to the division. Mail orders accounted for approximately one-third of the total sales of knives. However, mail orders seldom were orders for initial assortments, which accounted for an estimated 15% to 20% of all knife sales. The most popular assortment contained 15 types of imported pocket and hunting knives, ranging in price from $1.99 to $10.95. The total retail value of this assortment was $283. On individual items, the division offered discounts of 40% off retail list price to independent stores and 50% off to chains.

Although hundreds of jobbers and importers offered popular-priced knives, the division was the only supplier which provided a complete service program. Competitors, however, sometimes offered discounts of 50% and 10% to jobbers and large chain accounts. Jobbers usually priced knives to retailers at 40% off list price. According to management estimates the division accounted for a much smaller share of the popular-priced knife market than the key market.

Letters, Numbers and Signs

After acquiring the Gene Upton Company in 1966 the division offered a line of letters, numbers and signs (LNS). Like the key and knife programs, the LNS program provided initial assortment, display fixtures, promotional materials, a mail order program for reorders, and service by the sales force.

The most popular assortment of plastic, adhesive-backed letters, numbers and small signs contained more than 100 individual items housed in a revolving floor rack. The retail value of the assortment was $165. Small letters and numbers were priced at 35 cents each at retail; large numbers at 69 cents apiece; and signs at $1.29 each. The division offered discounts of 40% off retail list price to independent stores and 50% to chains. Competitors regularly offered discounts of 50% off list price to independents and to chains.

During 1974 between 35% and 40% of LNS sales were initial assortments. Management regarded this percentage as high. It attributed it to the placement, since the acquisition of the Gene Upton Company, of many initial assortments in accounts which already carried one or more of the division's other product lines. An analysis of LNS showed that sales were concentrated among relatively few standard items in the line. One executive estimated that volume was also concentrated among relatively few items in the division's key and knife lines.

Management estimated that approximately 40% of all sales of LNS came through mail orders. These mail orders seldom included initial assortments. The remaining 60% of sales came through orders obtained from field salespeople.

Division executives estimated that Cole's LNS sales accounted for more than 50% of the total market for plastic and metal LNS, and more than twice those of the nearest competitor. Although this firm also offered a service program, management did not believe that it was competitive with that offered by Cole since its products were sold through manufacturers' representatives who carried several lines in addition to the competitor's LNS line. The third largest firm in the industry, which accounted for an estimated 10% of the market, sold through wholesalers and offered no service program. The remainder of the market was served by a large number of small regional companies. Exhibit 5 shows a Cole LNS display.

Channels of Distribution

The Consumer Products Division sold its products through 56,000 stores composed primarily of hardware, automobile supply, variety, drug, and discount stores. The division's customers included both independent stores and chain organizations such as Western Auto, F. W. Woolworth and Sears. Chain organizations differed from independent stores: part or all of the buying and general management functions in a chain were performed by a headquarters staff, whereas the owner or manager of an independent store typically made all the buying and management decisions at the store level.

Chain organizations could generally be classified into corporate chains (chains which owned or leased their retail stores and employed their own store managers and personnel), or franchise chains (locally owned stores which paid an annual fee or percentage of profit to use a name and to receive management, buying, and promotional services from a headquarters organization). Chain headquarters typically approved particular purchases for member stores and typically approved only one supplier's line of keys, knives, or LNS. Although franchised stores had almost complete freedom to refuse "approved" items, whereas managers of corporate chain stores were less independent, most followed the "approved" list fairly carefully, as did managers of corporate chain stores.

The retail outlets of 1,100 chains (both corporate and franchise) accounted for 60% of the stores serviced and 80% of sales during fiscal 1974; 15 large chain accounts accounted for one-half of the chain store sales. Sales to independent stores accounted for 20% of sales, 80% of which was obtained from 50% of the independent accounts.

Of the retail outlets the division served, 31,000 carried only one of the division's four product lines: brass keys, keys in color, knives, and LNS (for this purpose, brass and colored aluminum keys were considered separate product lines). About 14,700 carried two lines, 8,200 carried three, and fewer than 2,100 carried all four product lines. Generally, chain store outlets were more likely to carry several of the division's product lines than were independent stores.

Of the stores which carried only one line, 13,400 carried standard brass keys, 9,800 carried LNS, and 7,800 carried knives. Among stores carrying two lines, common combinations were both standard and colored keys and standard keys plus knives. The most common three-line combination was standard keys, colored keys, and knives.

Prior to acquiring Gene Upton, the division had few customers among stores carrying the Upton line. Similarly, the Upton line had been poorly represented in most stores to which the division sold keys or knives. Since the acquisition in 1966, however, the division's field salespeople had begun to place the Upton line in existing accounts and had introduced the key and knife lines to stores which had been Upton customers. Executives expected to continue this cross-selling process.

Variety stores were losing market share to large discount stores, home centers and various types of specialty stores. Sales by channel were:

Discount and variety stores	33%
Automotive and hardware stores	26
General merchandise and department stores	13
Drug stores	7
Wholesalers and distributors	4
Other	17
	100%

Advertising and Sales Promotion

The division's advertising and sales promotion budget of $646,000 focused on materials directed to the trade. Expenditures for 1974 were:

Direct mail to stores (including postage)	$226,000
In-store display materials	53,000
Catalog sheets	31,000
Trade advertising	61,000
Consumer advertising	161,000
Agency fees, administration and miscellaneous	114,000
Total	$646,000

The division mailed at least one promotional piece on each product line every month. It typically provided display and selling suggestions. In addition, the division sent dealers point-of-purchase display materials. Management believed the promotional program was the strongest in the industry, and that dealers welcomed the support. The division had not generally advertised its products directly to consumers, except for an occasional advertisement whose purpose was to build trade acceptance of the division's products rather than consumer demand.

Chain Sales

The chain sales group, a director of chain store sales and three assistants, was headquartered in Cleveland and called on the headquarters' buying offices of chain stores throughout the country. They maintained regular personal contact with the buying offices in 75% of the division's chain accounts. Contact with buying offices in the remaining 25% was handled by the national sales manager and field sales managers and, in some cases, by field salespeople. In addition, Mr. Sells and the president of Cole would occasionally call on chains when particular problems arose.

Only chain accounts which agreed to increase the number of the division's lines they carried, or which were dealing with the division for the first time, would purchase initial assortments outright for some or all of their stores. When a chain headquarters placed a definite order, field salespeople received notification of items purchased, date shipped, and the address of every store affiliated with that chain within each territory. Each field salesperson received credit for all such sales within his or her territory, and was expected to call on each store to set up displays and train store personnel. On the other hand, when a chain headquarters "listed" a division product as "approved for purchase," the task of selling individual stores then fell to the field sales force.

The chain sales specialist at Cole often suggested a test to convince a chain's buyer that the division's program was superior to their present purchase arrangements. He typically proposed a test in two to six stores within the chain. The sales to be attained within a specified time period were designated in advance. If unsuccessful, the division agreed to take back unsold merchandise. Management estimated the vast majority of such tests were successful and resulted in a chain ordering or approving for purchase one or more of the division's programs.

The chain store sales group continued to call on chain headquarters after the initial sale. The purpose was to ensure that all retail outlets had ordered the division's product if the initial "sale" to chain headquarters had been an "approval" and to ensure that each store was producing as high a volume of sales as possible. To support these service calls, the chain sales group received a computer-generated quarterly report, which summarized sales by product line to each store in every chain, so that chain store sales specialists could identify stores whose sales of the division's products were low.

Field Sales Organization

The field sales force was responsible for calling on the individual stores in chains which had listed[3] the division's products and for contacting independent stores. Field sales expenses were $3,807,000 (Exhibit 6). The field sales effort was directed by Mr. George McGonagle, who had been national sales manager (NSM) since early 1972. The NSM headquarters staff in Cleveland consisted of:

1. An administrative assistant responsible for developing and monitoring reports, resolving problems with salespersons' bonuses and quotas, and conducting research for Mr. McGonagle.
2. A Customer Service Department responsible for resolving all customer complaints, from credit problems to defective key machines. If possible, Customer Service attempted to handle problems without contacting the salesperson. Each salesperson was required to call Customer Service at least weekly to report activities and all problems not related to compensation. Customer Service was regarded highly by the salespersons because it made their jobs easier.
3. A national sales trainer position which was vacant.

Reporting directly to the NSM were three zone managers, a relatively new position created when the increasing number of districts had become impossible for one person to manage. Each zone manager was responsible for supervising three district managers who in turn supervised between nine and eleven salespeople, referred to as territory managers.

The district manager's supervision included motivating and training salespeople to perform their selling, servicing, and order-processing activities. Hirings and terminations were also handled by the district manager with the approval of the zone manager. District managers were expected to spend as

---

[3] "Listed" meant chain headquarters personnel had approved the product for sale in the stores if the store manager concurred. For some chains, listing almost required that the store manager carry the line. In others, listing was little more than a "hunting license" for the salesperson.

much time as possible in the field calling on accounts with their salespeople and to talk by phone with every salesperson in the district every week to discuss progress and/or any problems encountered. The district manager also conducted quarterly district sales meetings to review the district's performance against plan and to discuss operating procedures for the next quarter. Bonus checks were distributed by the district managers at these meetings.

The number of salespeople had gradually risen from 50 in 1964 to approximately 118 in 1970. Growth of the sales force as the primary means of growth fell out of favor in 1970 and was replaced by the strategy of stabilized territories which would become increasingly more profitable through increased salespeople efficiency and wider product lines offered. With this in mind, territories were reduced to 90 in 1970 and maintained at that level.

Compensation of district managers included salary and a bonus. Salaries ranged from $10,000 to $18,000. Bonuses, based on district contribution (the gross margin on shipments made into the region minus district expenses), ranged from 15% to as high as 25% of a district manager's salary.

In performing their supervisory duties, district managers relied upon personal observations of field salespeople's activities and the weekly District Representative's Performance Evaluation (DRPE) which indicated, according to one division executive, what a salesperson had done. A sample DRPE is included in Exhibit 9. Copies of the DRPE for each person were available to home office personnel, field managers, and the salesperson.

The Salesperson

Salespeople were accountable for producing profitable sales within a geographic territory equal to, or in excess of, the quotas assigned to him or her for each of the three main product lines. The salesperson had approximately 600 accounts, 450–500 of which were active at any given time. The salesperson called upon major accounts (volume in excess of $1,000 per year) once every six weeks, made six to eight calls per day, and was required to establish a call schedule designed to insure maximum exposure to major accounts while minimizing sales expense.

On each call, salespeople took inventory of all merchandise on hand, insured proper display, serviced the key machine, trained new personnel operating the key machines, and wrote an order for the needed merchandise in quantities that would provide the store with a balanced inventory and prevent overstocking. The salesperson also attempted to meet with store management personnel accountable for the product lines to discuss and resolve any problems and, where possible, to sell additional merchandise. Management believed it was imperative that the salesperson concentrate on selling all product lines to ensure territory profitability.

The chain headquarters sales force was responsible for obtaining listings with the chain buying group. Chain accounts carried only products approved in their listings. The procedures for individual chains were presented in a manual, and the field salesperson was required to adhere to it strictly. Although salespeople were limited in what they could sell to a chain account, they attempted to convince each store manager to carry all merchandise approved in the listing. The salesperson also sold special deals or promotions that had been approved by chain store management, such as 1¢ key sales. The salesperson attempted to obtain business from independent accounts not previously serviced and to expand the lines carried by existing independents. He or she developed mailing lists from the Yellow Pages and knowledge of the territory and sent brochures to prospective accounts in hopes of creating interest in the lines.

The field salesperson was also responsible for responding to and promptly resolving customer complaints to their satisfaction and within the best interest of the division. Most frequently, the customer would contact the salesperson at his or her home. However, some complaints were relayed through the home office or field management. The salesperson evaluated each request and determined if it required immediate response or if it could be fit into the existing call schedule. The type of problem and the volume of the account determined the course of action. To minimize service requests and customer complaints, the salesperson attempted to ensure that each account was properly serviced on a normal call and all orders were placed in accordance with established procedures.

The manager of Customer Service was the salesperson's principal contact with the home office and the channel for resolving customer complaints regarding credit or billing problems, incomplete or delayed orders, or order processing. The salesperson also ordered supplies through the Customer Service manager, mailed daily call reports to this manager, and received reports from this manager.

The salesperson was accountable for completing and submitting a Daily Call Report, Automotive Report, Expense Report, and Monthly Summary Report, copies of which were mailed to the district manager and the home office. The salesperson had weekly telephone contact with the district manager regarding service requests, questions relative to information reflected in the various reports, and negative trends or complaints which might have occurred.

Sales Calls

On average, field salespeople were expected to make about 8 calls per day. This average varied from 5 calls per day in some territories to 16 in others. To service existing accounts properly, management thought each salesperson should call on the average store four to six times per year. It was recognized that some stores—usually but not always the larger ones—needed monthly service calls.

In addition to servicing existing accounts management believed that "prospecting" for new accounts was an essential part of each salesperson's job; two out of every ten calls, it was asserted, should be "prospecting" calls. A salesperson could search for new customers both among the chain stores where approvals but not purchases had been obtained, and among independent stores or small, locally headquartered chains. New business was expected to represent 10% of a person's sales, but in fact sales to new accounts averaged 3% of sales.

Having sold an initial order to an independent account or to the headquarters of a chain which operated solely within his or her territory, the salesperson could call back personally for "fill-in" orders or have the customer mail the orders. The latter course was often taken with smaller stores. Management did not disapprove of this practice if additional personal visits would not adequately stimulate a store's sales of the division's products, and if key machines and displays were kept in serviceable order. But management expected each salesperson to write personally about twice as many orders as came in by mail.

Sales Force Composition

The division's employment records showed almost all field salespeople had at least one full-time job before joining Cole, but fewer than 20% had worked longer than two years for any nongovernment employer.

With few exceptions, all the field salespeople had had previous selling experience, although the products they had sold varied from window shades to life insurance. A few had either technical, clerical, or supervisory experience. All the field salespeople had at least a high-school education. In addition, about 10% had attended trade schools, and more than 40% had some college experience. Nearly half were 30 years old or younger, and more than three-fourths were 40 or under.

Recruiting and Selection

The recruiting and selection process had changed only marginally since the mid-1960s. Recruiting decisions were made by the district manager with the approval of the zone manager. The recruiting process began as soon as a salesperson gave notice or was given notice by a district manager. Salespeople who intended to leave the division typically gave notice one week (i.e., one pay period) before the intended departure.

As soon as a district manager became aware of an impending vacancy, the manager advertised in one or more Sunday newspapers within the open territory and contacted a local employment agency, usually one with which the company had previously dealt. The Sunday newspaper ad included a telephone number at which either the district manager or a secretary could be telephoned on Sunday. When prospective candidates telephoned, they were asked several specific questions relating to family status, income, etc. Answers deemed inappropriate would disqualify a person for further interviewing, unless the person administering the "knockout" questions thought the candidate nevertheless possessed unusual qualities.

The telephone interview and the employment agency screening usually reduced the number of applicants from 15 to 25, to 10 or 12. These people would be scheduled for interviews by the district manager on Monday and Tuesday. In the first personal interview, district managers asked about educational background and work experience and attempted to evaluate appearance, poise, and manner. The division wanted people experienced in dealing with customers and programs similar to its own. People with experience in the hardware, tobacco, and food business often met this standard. After the first personal interview, the district manager hoped to have three or four candidates left for another similar interview within a day or two.

Whenever possible, if the prospective salesperson were married, this second interview was supplemented by having dinner with the prospect and his or her spouse. When practical, the interviewer also visited the prospect's home. One division executive said he had found that meeting a spouse and visiting the home provided one of the best single indicators of potential success with the division sales force. "It's important that the salesperson has a stable home life," this executive stated, "and be willing to travel. In six out of seven of our territories a salesperson must be 'on the road' at least one day, and often up to five days a week. If that person can't travel or tries to cover too much ground in too little time, our customers don't receive proper service—and service is what we sell."

Within five to six days after the appearance of the Sunday newspaper ad, the district manager had usually selected a person, checked references, and arranged for him or her to begin training immediately.

Training

Regardless of previous experience, all new salespeople, after spending a week or ten days in the field with an experienced salesperson, were sent to Cleveland for a week of training. New people generally went through the training program in groups of two to eight.

The training program included instruction in the operation and maintenance of a key machine, as well as lectures on the division's and customers' policies and procedures. Management considered it essential that each salesperson be familiar with the merchandise-ordering procedures of chain accounts. Each salesperson was given a manual which described each chain's procedures in detail. Salespeople were expected to follow these procedures to the letter.

Upon completion of the week of training, the new salesperson began to work a territory. For the first week, the district manager worked with the salesperson, typically in a major metropolitan area so as to minimize travel time. District managers often suggested that the new salesperson concentrate upon large, high-volume accounts with which the division had good working relationships. Selection of these accounts hopefully built confidence by enabling the new salesperson to generate a large volume of sales in the first week. The district manager was expected to spend another week with the new salesperson after he or she had worked alone for two to four weeks. In practice, however, district managers often could not return to work with their new salespeople for several weeks.

Compensation

Salespeople received bi-weekly salaries, quarterly bonus payments, and, occasionally, prize money won in a divisional or district sales contest. In addition, the division provided field salespeople with cars which they were free to use for their own activities on evenings and weekends. Field salespeople were given an expense allowance of $23 for every night their work required them to spend away from home.

In 1975, new salespeople typically started at $200 per week. The median salary for the sales force was $210. In general, weekly salaries of $210 or more were paid to field salespeople who had been with the division more than a year. As a rule, the higher salaries tended to go to the older people. Half of the people with three or more years' service who earned more than the median salary of $210 per week were 40 years old. Two-thirds of those earning the median salary were in their 30s. Finally, over 70% of the people who earned less than $210 per week were 30 or younger.

Each salesperson's bonus depended partly upon the amount by which sales in his or her territory exceeded the quota established by the NSM's office. Until 1966, annual sales quotas for each territory had been established "largely by 'feel,' " according to one division executive.

A new plan was introduced in 1967. Since the final thee months of the fiscal year customarily accounted for 30% of the total sales in each territory, the sales for those months were to be multiplied by 3 $\frac{1}{3}$ to determine the sales quota for the coming fiscal year. For example, if total sales in a particular territory from August 1 to October 31, 1974, were $36,000, the sales quota for the period November 1, 1974, to October 31, 1975, would be 3 $\frac{1}{3}$ × $36,000 or $120,000. Quarterly sales quotas were computed by seasonally adjusting the annual sales quota. Quotas were not set for any territory until the salesperson had at least three months' experience in the territory.

According to one division executive, this new system of setting quotas generally increased quotas. She added that reports from field salespeople indicated that more than 90% regarded the quotas as fair.

The bonus plan related each salesperson's personal bonus to (1) the amount, in dollars, by which the salesperson's sales in each product line exceeded quota, (2) the particular product lines which exceeded or fell short of quota, and (3) the number of product lines on which he or she exceeded quota. For every dollar of sales over each line's quota, a salesperson received points. For each dollar of sales over quota in standard and colored keys and LNS, a salesperson received three points. Every dollar of sales over quota in knives received two points. This differential in points had been included because the gross margin on keys and LNS was substantially greater than gross margin earned on knife sales. Management believed, however, that salespeople who did a particularly good business in knives relative to other products would not be adversely affected by the differential because the average reorder for knives was about twice as large as that for the other products.

Each point was worth one, two, or four cents, depending upon the number of product lines in which the salesperson had exceeded quota. If a salesperson exceeded quota in all three product lines (standard and colored keys, knives, LNS), each point was worth 4 cents. If a salesperson exceeded total quota through sales in excess of quota on two out of the three lines, each point was worth 2 cents. If a salesperson was over total quota because of sales in excess of quota in only one product line, each point was worth 1 cent. No bonuses were paid, however, unless a salesperson exceeded total quota. The purpose of valuing points differently depending on the number of lines over quota was to encourage a balance of sales among all three product lines. A sample calculation of a salesperson's personal bonus follows:

Product Line	Quota	Actual Sales	Sales Over Quota	Bonus pts/$ Over Quota	Total Points Earned	Bonus Point Value	Total Personal Bonus
						Sales over quota:	
Keys: standard & colored	$ 70,000	$ 90,000	$20,000	× 3 =	60,000	1 line—1 cent	
Knives	90,000	94,000	4,000	× 2 =	8,000	2 lines—2 cents	
LNS	60,000	86,000	26,000	× 3 =	78,000	3 lines—4 cents	
Total	$220,000	$270,000	$50,000		146,000	@ $ .04	= $5,840

Bonuses averaged slightly over $4,000 in 1974, with salespeople having at least 5 years' experience receiving almost $5,400 on average and people with less than 1 year's experience about $1,800 on average. Although management could retain any portion of a salesperson's bonus until the end of the division's fiscal year, payments were typically made quarterly. Furthermore, if a salesperson earned and was paid a personal bonus in one quarter and fell below quota in succeeding quarters, the salesperson was not expected to return money to the company.

Previously, salespeople had also been eligible for a district bonus if sales exceeded quota in the district of which the salesperson's territory was a part. The district bonus amounted to 25% of the salesperson's personal bonus if the district exceeded quota in all three product lines. If the district exceeded quota in only two product lines, the salesperson's district bonus was 20% of personal bonus, and, if district sales exceeded quota in only one line, the district bonus was dropped to 10% of the personal bonus. District bonuses had been paid only at the end of the division's fiscal year. They were discontinued in 1971.

In addition to salary and bonus, a salesperson could earn prize money from divisional sales contests. In 1974, the division spent approximately $10,000 on contests. To qualify for prizes in one contest which ran for eight weeks in the fall of 1973, salespersons had to exceed their individual quotas for orders written per call and calls made per day. Average goals were 0.75 order per call and 11 calls per day. According to management, these goals ranged from 100% to 115% of a particular salesperson's recent performance. A salesperson exceeding both of the individual contest quotas could win up to $100 in each of eight weeks. Management estimated that more than 30% of the salespeople had won at least one prize in the contest.

To compare the new compensation plan with plans used in other companies, division executives had obtained a published research report which contained information on compensation in companies in a wide variety of consumer industries. The report indicated that for inexperienced sales trainees, the median starting salary was $9,000.

Turnover

Exhibits 7 and 8 indicate the rate of turnover in the sales force. This turnover was, however, substantially lower than in the 1960s.

Division executives cited two major reasons for turnover among the field sales force: management limitations and a generally tight labor market. One executive believed the lack of management attention had resulted in a failure to detect problems and an inability to take corrective action once a problem had been discovered. This executive believed the division was beginning to "manage" rather than "fight fires."

Management was disturbed by the lost sales which resulted from high salesperson turnover. Executives estimated that a new salesperson had to be with the division for more than six months before becoming a "productive salesperson." Although indirect consequences of the turnover problem included selection and training expense, management estimated that out-of-pocket expenses were approximately $1,000 for each new salesperson hired. More disturbing to management, however, was the time which the selection and training process required.

To obtain firsthand information on the activities and attitudes of field salespeople, the casewriter spent a day with a field salesperson. This information is presented in the appendix.

The Future

The president of Cole National and Mr. Sells had similar views on the division's major problems and objectives. Mr. Sells commented:

> Our future lies in *servicing* independent stores, franchised stores and chain operations with a growing variety of products. We offer not a product, but a com-

plete merchandising and field service program. This program is our strongest competitive advantage.

Our program has helped to establish good relations with the chains at two levels. At headquarters, they like us because of the profit we produce and the store services we perform for them. In the stores, managers welcome our complete ready-to-display assortments and our training of store personnel to operate a key, knife, or sign department.

As I see it, the chains we're in—variety, automotive, drug, hardware, discount—as well as most of our independent outlets, will continue to grow and prosper. So far, no competitor has been able to hurt us seriously either by taking accounts away from us or by preventing us from taking some accounts away from them. Our customer relations are very good, and we should be able to find additional products to keep us growing.

The division's immediate problem is to solidify the organization and to improve our effectiveness as executives. Being executives is something new to many of the top people in the division. Most of our sales managers, for example, have excellent field sales records, but little experience as executives. Even now, they often have to act as salespeople in "problem" territories. But as our field salespeople become more experienced, these managers will become executives.

Ninety percent of our problems revolve around the field sales personnel. We must be able to attract, train, and keep the kind of people we need if we're to continue to offer the unique field service program on which our continued success depends.

Exhibit 1   Cole National Corporation: Turnover

Corporate Financial Data

Statement of Income	Year Ended October 26, 1974	Year Ended October 27, 1973
Net Sales	$110,729,000	$96,161,000
Costs and Expenses:		
Cost of goods sold	42,033,000	36,997,000
Operating expenses	56,395,000	48,001,000
Depreciation and amortization	2,679,000	2,309,000
Interest expense, net	1,146,000	829,000
Other income, net	(156,000)	(166,000)
Total Costs and Expenses	$102,097,000	$87,970,000
Income Before Income Taxes	$ 8,632,000	$ 8,191,000
Provision for Income Taxes	4,241,000	4,112,000
Net Income	$ 4,391,000	$ 4,079,000
Earnings per share	$ 2.12	$ 1.95

Five Year Review*	($000 Omitted)				
	1974	1973	1972	1971	1970
Net sales	$110,729	$96,161	$83,562	$70,100	$65,145
Income before Income Taxes	8,632	8,191	6,662	4,622	2,403
Income Taxes	4,241	4,112	3,237	2,249	1,215
Income Before Extraordinary Items	4,391	4,079	3,425	2,373	1,188
Extraordinary Items	—	—	109	(1,555)	—
Net Income	4,391	4,079	3,534	818	1,188
Earnings per Share**					
Income before extraordinary items	2.12	1.95	1.65	1.14	.56
Extraordinary items	—	—	.05	(.79)	—
Net income	2.12	1.95	1.70	.35	.56
Dividends per Common Share	.52	.47	.445	.44	.44
Working Capital	20,375	18,690	14,212	12,715	10,099
Current Ratio	2.51	2.51	2.23	2.01	1.73
Shareholders' Equity	26,653	23,281	20,226	17,527	17,753
Total Assets	55,090	49,832	40,785	39,454	42,213

*The above financial information includes, for all periods presented, businesses acquired in pooling of interests transactions.

**The earnings per share are based upon the weighted average of common shares outstanding and common share equivalents.

Exhibit 2   Cole National Corporation: Turnover

Consumer Products Division, 1974 Income Statement ($000)

Sales	$23,941
Cost of Goods Sold [a]	10,217
Gross Margin	13,724
Expenses	
Field sales expenses[b]	3,807
H.Q. sales administration	709
Advertising & sales promotion[c]	646
Chain store sales	192
Division general overhead	2,921
Total Expenses	$ 8,275
Division Contribution to Corporate Overhead and Profit	5,449

Source: Company records.
[a]Includes total manufacturing costs and outbound freight charges.
[b]Detail in Exhibit 6.
[c]Detail on page 111.

Exhibit 3   Cole National Corporation: Turnover

Condensed Division Organization Chart

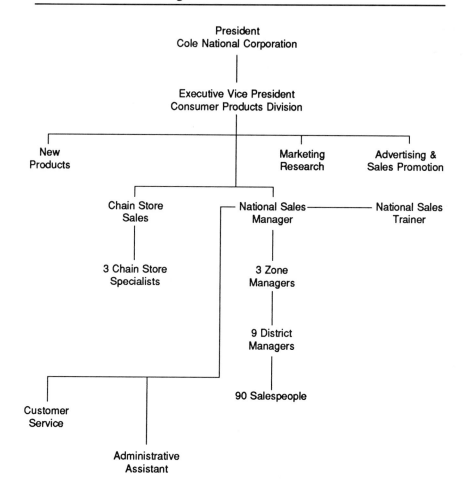

Exhibit 4　Cole National Corporation: Turnover

Key and Accessory Display

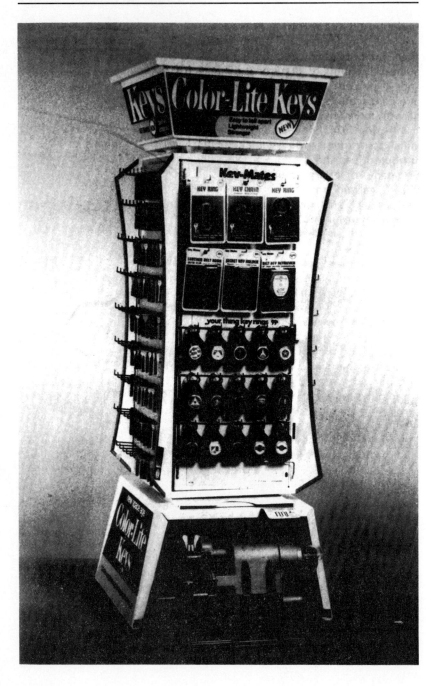

Exhibit 5   Cole National Corporation: Turnover

Letters, Numbers, and Signs Display

Exhibit 6   Cole National Corporation: Turnover

Field Sales Expenses—1974

	($000)	%
Compensation — territory salespeople	1,333	35.0
Compensation — field management	362	9.5
Fringe benefits	190	5.0
Auto expense	453	11.9
Travel expense	403	10.6
Other	1,066	28.0
	$3,807	100.0

Exhibit 7   Cole National Corporation: Turnover

Sales Force Composition

Year Hired	Before 1968	1968	1969	1970	1971	1972	1973
Western zone	7[a]	4	5	2	2	7	2
Central zone	8	2	0	2	7	8	3
Eastern zone	7	2	2	2	3	9	5
Total [b]	22	8	7	6	12	24	10

[a]To be read "7 salespeople of those now in the Western zone were hired before 1968."
[b]The total number of salespeople for each zone was:

Western	29
Central	30
Eastern	30
Grand Total	89

Exhibit 8   Cole National Corporation: Turnover

Consumer Products Division—Training Program
New Hires, Terminations, and Resignations 1969–1973

Month	Number of Territories	New Hires	Termination	Resignation
Nov. '69	116	NA	14[a]	
Dec.	116	10	7[a]	
Jan. '70	117	7	5[a]	
Feb.	NA	NA	6[a]	
March	NA	NA	10[a]	
April	116	7	14[a]	
May	115	9	8[a]	
June	114	9	7[a]	
July	112	8	5	11
Aug.	112	9	5	7
Sept.	111	8	1	10
Oct.	94	1	17	5
Nov.	89	3	1	4
Dec.	82	2	—	1
Jan. '71	82	5	—	7
Feb.	90	6	1	5
March	89	5	4	5
April	89	5	2	3
May	89	5	5	1
June	89	5	1	5
July	89	5	2	2
Aug.	89	1	—	—
Sept.	89	1	6	—
Oct.	89	6	—	1
Nov.	90	7	1	3
Dec.	90	—	1	2
Jan. '72	90	5	1	3
Feb.	90	5	1	2
March	90	3	2	4
April	90	4	1	1
May	90	1	1	2
June	90	5	3	2
July	90	4	2	1
Aug.	90	2	—	—
Sept.	90	4	1	5
Oct.	90	6	2	1
Nov.	90	2	2	4
Dec.	90	3	—	1
Jan. '73	90	6	1	3
Feb.	90	2	1	4

[a]Breakdown of terminations and resignations not collected before July 1970 or after Feb. 1973.

Exhibit 9   Cole National Corporation: Turnover

Consumer Products Division
DRPE—William Bonnie

COLE NATIONAL CORPORATION DISTRICT REPRESENTATIVES PERFORMANCE EVALUATION

DIST. NO. 101	REP. NAME William Bonnie			CUMULATIVE MONTH TO DATE SALES THROUGH		MO. 10	DAY 31	YR. 74

PRODUCT LINES	MAIL ORDERS		WRITTEN REORDERS		WRITTEN NEW ORDERS		TOTAL ORDERS	
	NO.	AMOUNT	NO.	AMOUNT	NO.	AMOUNT	NO.	AMOUNT
NATIONAL KEY	210	13,887	31	5,600	9	1,725	250	21,212
LETTERS NUMBERS SIGNS	32	1,655	16	1,927	6	1,665	54	5,247
AMERICAN KNIFE	14	2,740	23	3,867	4	1,430	46	8,037
TOTALS	261	18,282	70	11,394	19	4,820	350	34,496

TO DATE					YEAR TO DATE			
NK	LNS	AK	TOTAL		NK	LNS	AK	TOTAL
19,296	3,232	5,566	28,094	QUOTA	60,054	12,499	15,993	88,546
21,212	5,247	8,037	34,496	ACTUAL	66,413	21,331	21,784	109,528
1,916	2,015	2,471	6,402	DIFFERENCE (− UNDER)	6,359	8,832	5,791	20,982
109.93	162.34	144.60	122.79	PERCENT REALIZATION ACTUAL/QUOTA	110.59	170.66	136.20	123.70

COMMENTS:

STORE CALL ANALYSIS

NUMBER OF CALLS			DAYS WORKED	SATURDAYS WORKED	CALLS PER DAY	WRITTEN $ PER CALL	WRITTEN ORDERS PER CALL	DAYS OFF	CALLS LOST	DOLLARS LOST	TOTAL ORDERS PER CALL	TOTAL SALES PER CALL
CHAINS	INDEPT	TOTAL										
136	71	207	23	4	9.00		.34				1.69	166.64

AVERAGE ORDER	NK		LNS		AK		PERCENT MAIL TO TOTAL BUSINESS				PERCENT NEW BUSINESS TO TOTAL BUSINESS			
	MAIL	REORDER WRITTEN	MAIL	REORDER WRITTEN	MAIL	REORDER WRITTEN	NK	LNS	AK	TOTAL	NK	LNS	AK	TOTAL
	66.12	180.63	51.72	120.38	144.24	168.12	65.5	31.5	34.1	53.0	8.1	31.8	17.8	14.0

REPRESENTATIVE COPY

TA 26-83

Casewriter's notes:
1. Representative copy means that this was William Bonnie's copy.
2. NK is the key line (National Key), and AK is the knife line (American Knife).

Cole National Corporation: Turnover

On November 14, 1974, a casewriter visited with Mr. William Bonnie, a district sales representative, and accompanied him on his calls. This appendix describes Mr. Bonnie's background and his reactions to his job. The appendix also includes a description of Mr. Bonnie's activities on November 14, together with excerpts from two sales calls.

During the eight years before he joined Cole National Corporation, Mr. Bonnie had attended college on a part-time basis. He estimated that he needed one more year on a full-time basis in order to graduate.

While in college, Mr. Bonnie had held a variety of jobs including one as a hospital orderly from June 1972 to June 1974. His wife, a registered nurse, had also worked since their marriage but was planning to stop work after the birth of their third child in early 1975. Mr. Bonnie joined Cole National Corporation in July 1974. After completing the division's week-long training course, Mr. Bonnie began to work his territory on July 8, 1974. Although the district manager had been unable to accompany him during his first week in the field, the national sales trainer traveled with Mr. Bonnie during his first week on the job.

According to Mr. Bonnie, the district manager telephoned him weekly for the first ten weeks after he began to work his territory. At the end of September, the district manager spent a week making calls with Mr. Bonnie. "Frankly, I like the freedom this job allows," Mr. Bonnie stated. "I don't impose any rigid structure on my daily activities, nor do I do things 'by the book.' Management looks at the figures, not the methods you use. I like to treat my customers as individuals, not just account numbers. This takes time and may mean that I'll have to call back two or three times to get an order that a higher-pressure salesperson might close the first time. But I think my method builds better customer relations."

Mr. Bonnie's territory included Maine, Vermont, New Hampshire, and portions of northern Massachusetts (not including Boston). He serviced this territory from his home in Portsmouth, New Hampshire. Mr. Bonnie estimated that, on the average, he did not have to remain away from home for more than one night a week. Mr. Bonnie stated: "I have between 700 and 800 stores, spread throughout four states. My largest concentration of stores is in Portland, Maine, where I have 18 stores. On most days, however, I drive more than 200 miles from the time I leave home in the morning until I return at night."

Mr. Bonnie estimated that he made, on the average, eight or nine calls in a day. His district manager continually encouraged him to raise his average to 15 calls per day. "I'd rather get more sales from each store by selling in additional product lines," Mr. Bonnie stated, "but my boss thinks it's more important to 'get our foot in the door' in a larger number of stores." Mr. Bonnie estimated that fewer than 10% of his calls were made on stores which did not carry the division's products.

Mr. Bonnie continued: "I try to cover the really high-volume stores once every five weeks. That way they never have to mail in an order. Although I haven't yet been around my territory to all the medium-volume stores, I hope to call on them once every three to four months. As for the small outlets, I'll be lucky to get around to them once or twice a year. Right now, I call on them only when they need service or want a salesperson to call."

Although Mr. Bonnie had been among the top 25% of the people in his district in terms of bonus payments received for exceeding sales quotas, he had not been able to meet his quotas for the sales contest in the fall of 1974. Mr. Bonnie's quotas for this sales contest, as distinct from the annual sales quota, were 10.5 calls per day in September and 9.1 calls per day in October. His quotas for orders per call were 0.45 in September and 0.41 in October.

Mr. Bonnie believed that a number of people had met their quotas for calls per day and orders per call simply by paying courtesy calls on particular stores and writing up small, token orders. In contrast, Mr. Bonnie preferred to spend more time with each store manager and to write fewer, large orders. Mr. Bonnie recalled one instance in which he had met a chain buyer at the opening of a new store in that chain, and had sold $1,600 worth of assortments of colored keys, one assortment for each store in that chain. In another instance, Mr. Bonnie had sold a large order to each of several stores in a chain whose headquarters buyer had approved the division's programs for purchase. In Mr. Bonnie's words, "Sandy Feder [a chain store specialist] opened the door, and I walked in." He recalled another case in which he called on a store manager whom no field salesperson from the division had visited for over a year. Mr. Bonnie recalled that he had persuaded the store manager to reinstate the division lines and obtained an order in excess of $1,200.

Between 10:00 A.M. and 4:30 P.M. on November 14, Mr. Bonnie made six calls. On a typical day, when not accompanied by a visitor, Mr. Bonnie made his first call before 10:00 A.M. and continued to work until 5:00 P.M. or later. A schedule of Mr. Bonnie's activities between 10:00 A.M. and 4:30 P.M. on November 14 appears in Exhibit 1A; Exhibit 2A contains a summary of the data in Exhibit 1A; Exhibit 3A contains an analysis of sales by product line for each store called on. A copy of Mr. Bonnie's DRPE is included in the text as Exhibit 9.

Mr. Bonnie's first call was a service station affiliated with a major oil company.[a] The station, which had three gasoline pumps and two bays for mechanical work, was located on the main road about five minutes from the center of a northern suburb of Boston. On the door of the service station was a "Keys Made" sign furnished by the division. The key machine and attached displays of standard and colored keys were clearly visible through the service station window.

The service station owner had mailed a request to Cleveland for a service call on his key machine, which had not been cutting properly. When Mr. Bonnie arrived, the owner asked him for credit for miscut keys. Mr. Bonnie explained that he could not do so. He told the owner to accumulate miscuts until he had about 100, and then ship them to Cleveland where credit would be issued.

Mr. Bonnie then adjusted the key machine and showed the service station owner how to make minor adjustments if they were needed. At the owner's request, Mr. Bonnie cut a key for the station's rest room to demonstrate that the machine was functioning properly. He also left the owner some spare parts for the machine. The entire procedure took about 25 minutes. The station owner and Mr. Bonnie then engaged in the following conversation:

OWNER:

I received this machine in February and figured out how to use it. The salesperson [Mr. Bonnie's predecessor] didn't come back 'til April. You know, every dealer in town who has your machines is always running out of key blanks. We have to get them locally. If it's profitable, you ought to put on more salespeople. Of course, I don't have to see you too often—every two months ought to do it.

MR. BONNIE:

I'll try to make it every three months. Here's my home phone if you have any problems. Have you thought about adding our house keys in color to your car keys in color? It's the same deal, an initial assortment of 12 dozen keys. . . . How about putting it on?

OWNER:

No, not now. Better wait and see how things go now that the machine's in order.

MR. BONNIE:

OK, maybe after you see that service has improved, you'll be interested. By the way, your key blank inventory is low.

_____

[a]Oil companies allowed their lessees complete freedom in purchasing items such as keys.

OWNER:

Go ahead and figure out your order. Be sure to add some L4s [a specific key blank]. They're big sellers around here. Don't make the order too big—just include the popular ones. Don't give me any slow sellers.

MR. BONNIE:

OK, low inventory, more frequent reorder. That's fine with us.

Mr. Bonnie spent the next 5 to 10 minutes taking inventory of the key blanks and making up an order. The owner signed the order, and Mr. Bonnie said goodbye and left.

Mr. Bonnie's fourth call was the hardware, housewares and toy department of a discount department store. The store covered about 18,000 square feet and was located in a small shopping center off a major highway. A "Keys Made" sign was on the door. The department itself was operated by a firm which leased space in which to operate such departments from several stores throughout Mr. Bonnie's territory. The hardware and housewares sections occupied about 1,500 square feet. Merchandise was piled on some counters to a height of more than ten feet. The aisles were narrow and crowded with cartons and merchandise. Displays of brass and colored keys, knives, and LNS shared a booth with the department's cash register.

After greeting the department manager and the clerk, Mr. Bonnie discovered that almost 90 keys had been miscut since his last visit.

MR. BONNIE:

You've got too many miscuts for two months.

CLERK:

So we've got too many miscuts. I can't help it. [Clerk looks on while Mr. Bonnie adjusts key machine.] Sometimes it's hard to find the right key blank for a customer.

MR. BONNIE:

If it gets to take too long to look for it, tell them you don't have it. It's a high-profit, but low-dollar sale.

CLERK:

It's not just the odd ones I have trouble with.

MR. BONNIE:

If it takes too long, don't bother.

CLERK:

We've got about 80 miscuts.

MR. BONNIE:

Who trained you? I didn't.

CLERK:

The manager did.

MR. BONNIE:

Who has more miscuts?

CLERK:

He does.

MR. BONNIE:

Show me how you cut a key.

The clerk cut a key while Mr. Bonnie watched and made suggestions. Mr. Bonnie discovered that the key machine needed additional adjustment, performed the required adjustment, and showed the clerk how to adjust the machine. The clerk then cut a key while Mr. Bonnie explained why the machine might need adjustment from time to time. The entire key-machine servicing procedure had consumed about 35 minutes. Mr. Bonnie spent an additional ten minutes inventorying the key blank stock and made out an order for $117 while exchanging banter with the department manager.

MANAGER:

How come it takes you so long to make out an order?

MR. BONNIE:

If I made it out fast, without a careful inventory, you'd be overstocked, and that's no good for you or me.

MANAGER:

How about my letters? They're stealing them at a good clip.

MR. BONNIE:

How're your knives? Would you open the case? [Knife cabinets were kept locked to avoid pilferage.]

MANAGER:

I don't know about knife sales. I don't have time to check.

MR. BONNIE:

Not even on a high-profit item? [While he checked the knife inventory and put in an order, Mr. Bonnie and the department manager exchanged jokes.] Do you sell many linoleum knives? Guess I'd better get you some more. You've sold half your assortment.

While he made up a knife order which totaled $70, Mr. Bonnie chatted with the department manager about personal matters. Servicing the knife cabinet and making up the order required about 15 minutes. Mr. Bonnie then checked the LNS display and told the manager that he would make up an order for three dozen each of the letters which had sold best.

MR. BONNIE:

I won't get you many of these larger letters. You don't need many. OK?

MANAGER:

If you say so.

MR. BONNIE:

Do you have to keep these plastic signs down so low? Can't you put them where people can see them?

MANAGER:

Not a chance 'til after Christmas. Need everything I have right now for toys. When are you coming down to get the kids' presents?

MR. BONNIE:

We'll probably be down next week or the week after.

Mr. Bonnie then made up an order for $158 worth of LNS. The department manager signed the order and then insisted that Mr. Bonnie inspect the department's new stockroom. After a five-minute tour, Mr. Bonnie excused himself and left.

Exhibit 1A   Cole National Corporation: Turnover

Mr. Bonnie's Schedule, 10:00 A.M. – 4:30 P.M., November 14, 1974

10:00 – 10:20	Drove to first call, gasoline station which had requested service on a key machine.
10:20 – 11:00	First call.
11:00 – 11:05	Wrote report[a] on first call.
11:05 – 11:10	Drove to second call, a nearby gas station.
11:10 – 11:25	Second call.
11:25 – 11:30	Wrote report on second call and walked to third call, a national chain variety store.
11:30 – 11:45	Third call.
11:45 – 11:50	Wrote report on third call
11:50 – 12:05	Planned route for remainder of day.[b]
12:05 – 12:35	Drove to fourth call, a large leased hardware department located in a discount department store.
12:35 – 1:55	Fourth call.
1:55 – 2:00	Wrote report on fourth call.
2:00 – 2:15	Drove to restaurant (located on direct route between fourth and fifth calls).
2:15 – 2:55	Lunch.[c]
2:55 – 3:10	Drove to fifth call, a large variety store, operated by a regional chain.
3:10 – 3:25	Fifth call.
3:25 – 3:30	Wrote report on fifth call.
3:30 – 3:45	Drove to sixth call, a large self-service department store.
3:45 – 4:25	Sixth call.
4:25 – 4:30	Wrote report on sixth call.

[a]Making out the complete daily report typically took Mr. Bonnie an additional hour after he returned home in the evening.

[b]On days when he was not accompanied by a visitor, Mr. Bonnie planned his route before leaving for his first call.

[c]Mr. Bonnie estimated that lunch typically took no more than 15 to 20 minutes. The presence of the casewriter, however, prolonged lunch on this particular day. The presence of the casewriter did not, however, noticeably affect the remainder of the schedule.

Exhibit 2A   Cole National Corporation: Turnover

Summary of Salesperson's Activities on November 14, 1974

Time spent in stores	3 hours & 25 minutes
Time spent writing call reports	30 minutes
Time spent planning calls and driving between stores	1 hour & 55 minutes
Lunch	40 minutes
Total Time: 10:00 A.M. – 4:30 P.M.	6 hours & 30 minutes

Exhibit 3A   Cole National Corporation: Turnover

Sales by Store and Product

	Brass Keys	Colored Keys	Knives	LNS	Total
First call	$ 44	$ 23	not carried	not carried	$ 67
Second call	51	161	not carried	not carried	212
Third call	119	—	not carried	not carried	119
Fourth call	91	26	70	158	345
Fifth call	—[a]	—[a]	not carried	not carried	—
Sixth call	161	65	—	—[b]	226
Total	$466	$275	$70	$158	$969

[a]Store had recently sent an order in by mail.
[b]Sign assortment had been on display less than a week.

Fieldcrest Division of Fieldcrest Mills, Inc.: Compensation System for Field Sales Representatives

In December 1973, Fieldcrest management was reviewing the compensation system for field sales reps. Complaints about the system had been minor. Most felt this was because the plan was fair and sales reps were well compensated; others argued that the system was too complex for anyone to know what to complain about. "Ideally, we would have a separate system tailored to each salesperson," said Mr. O. G. Grubbs, Vice President and Director of Sales. "However, the more simple and uniform the system, the easier it is to understand and administer."

In addition to deciding about the overall plan, management had to decide how to structure the system for 1974 to direct the sales reps' efforts among products and/or accounts in the best manner.

Company History

When Fieldcrest Mills was spun out of a parent company in 1953, its lines included domestic products such as sheets, towels, blankets, automatic blankets, and bedspreads, and rugs and carpets. Separate marketing divisions handled bed and bath fashions on one hand, and rugs and carpets on the other.

This case was prepared by Associate Professor Frank V. Cespedes as the basis for class discussion rather than to illustrate either effective or ineffective handling of an administrative situation. It is a revised version of an earlier case prepared by Research Associate Nancy J. Davis and Professor Benson P. Shapiro.

(Hereafter, "Fieldcrest" refers to the Fieldcrest Marketing Division, not to the total corporation.)

Fieldcrest, like its competitors, originally sold plain white sheets, towels, blankets, automatic electric blankets, and bedspreads on a utilitarian basis. They were usually the least profitable items in a department store and sold in poorly located linen and domestic departments. In 1953, Fieldcrest initiated design, merchandising and marketing innovations which transformed the industry into a fashion business. After studying color and design trends in apparel and home decorating, Fieldcrest stylists created new designs and colors for their products. Fieldcrest worked with store management to secure dominant locations and better lighting and display for domestics. They often succeeded in establishing "Fieldcrest Shops" in which the total Fieldcrest line was displayed.

In 1957 Fieldcrest acquired St. Mary's, a well-established manufacturer of quality woolen blankets, and used the St. Mary's name for a product line targeted at the rapidly expanding mass merchandiser market.[1] Management believed this would not jeopardize Fieldcrest's luxury/quality image since the Fieldcrest name would be reserved for items sold to fashionable department stores and specialty shops.

During the late 1960s and early 1970s, Fieldcrest introduced new production processes and fiber blends. Moreover, focusing on contemporary consumer interests, it pioneered haute couture by introducing collections designed by Yves St. Laurent, Pierre Cardin, and Marimekko.

In 1972, Fieldcrest's sales were $167,110,000 with operating income before interest of $10,026,000. Volume divided as follows:

Fieldcrest	40%
St. Mary's	15%
Private label	25%
Seconds and discounts	4%
Institutional and military	16%

Over the next five years, management anticipated a 68% increase in sales and a 250% increase in operating income. In 1973, corporate management decided to invest $20 million in expanding production facilities for bed and bath products.

The Bed and Bath Fashion Industry

In 1972, total industry wholesale volume was over $1.5 billion (see Exhibit 1). Of fifty manufacturers, many specialized in only one or two product lines. Since

---

[1]The mass merchandiser market primarily consisted of discount houses such as K Mart and Zayre and variety stores such as Kress and Woolworth.

manufacturers increasingly targeted specific market segments, overall market share was not necessarily the best indication of success. For example, Fieldcrest ranked seventh among all sheet manufacturers but first in the high-quality sheet market.

Since the mid-1950s, products were offered in more colors, sizes, and textures. Bedsheets, for example, progressed from cotton to no-iron, flat to fitted, white to color to fancy, full size to queen size to king size. Stylistic proliferation meant shorter product life cycles and so a constant flow of new styles was essential. By 1973, major manufacturers were hiring well-known designers, and styling had become an important competitive area. Each brand introduced two major products annually, and the multiplicity of items made accurate forecasting both essential and difficult while increasing the inventory investment.

By 1973, moreover, raw material shortages had increased costs. For example, between October 1972 and October 1973, wholesale cotton costs ranged from 27¢ to 90¢ per pound. Comparable increases occurred for plastic film to wrap the products, cartons to ship them, and fuel to run the mills. Thus, while consumer demand produced a sellers' market for manufacturers (a rare situation for the textile industry), maintaining desired profitability was difficult because government price controls (in effect since 1972) did not allow manufacturers to pass through many of their increased costs.

Bed and bath fashions were sold primarily through department stores, specialty shops, and mass merchandiser outlets including discount houses, chains, and variety stores. Since the mid-1950s, department store operations had become increasingly complex and competition had increased with the rise of mass merchandisers. By 1973, most large retailers used computerized inventory systems to calculate turnover rates for individual items: they dropped slow moving items at the earliest sign of weakness and placed smaller, more frequent orders than in the past.

Fieldcrest Operations, December 1973

Fieldcrest had different product lines and channels for each target market. Fieldcrest brand was targeted at well-educated, fashion-conscious, affluent consumers. (Twenty-two percent of all consumers were in the $15,000-plus income group vs. 48% of Fieldcrest brand consumers.) They tended to be young suburban homemakers with young children and to shop in department stores which offered fashion, wide selection, quality and service. Fieldcrest sold through 1,780 department stores and bed and bath specialty shops.[2] In 28 of the top 40 marketing areas, Fieldcrest had exclusive distribution[3] through what

---

[2]These numbers refer to corporate entities, not individual outlets. For example, a department store with ten branches counted as one store.

[3]Exclusive distribution was the policy of selling through only one retail store (and its branches, if any) in a given trading area.

management considered the top quality store in the area. Company policy was to increase Fieldcrest brand volume by better account management rather than by opening new accounts. Working with an account in advertising and merchandising, Fieldcrest tried to increase the account's total volume and Fieldcrest's share of that volume. New accounts had to be reviewed and recommended by a Fieldcrest regional manager and approved through company headquarters.

St. Mary's brand was positioned for younger, price-conscious consumers who shopped primarily in mass merchandisers. St. Mary's sold to 420 stores including discount houses, chains, and variety stores. A small number of stores accounted for a large share of sales.

Fieldcrest also sold both brands to a few wholesalers and over 300 other customers including premium accounts, stamp plans, the military, institutional customers, and several private label customers. In October 1973, sales of Fieldcrest brand products were running about 16% and St. Mary's about 36% ahead of 1972. Total division sales had increased 12% over 1972. Mr. David Tracy, Fieldcrest President, commented:

> This is essentially a fashion business. Our concepts and designs will be accepted only if we stay on top of consumers' ideas, interests, and activities and then design to meet those interests. Our company's strength, our ability to cope with this fashion business, is due in large part to our "people orientation." We feel strongly that this same "people orientation" permeates the atmosphere of our company, our recruiting programs, and our compensation plans.

(See Exhibit 2 for organization chart, and Exhibit 3 for sales data.)

The Merchandising Organization

Fieldcrest's merchandising organization consisted of a design department and five product departments—blankets, bedspreads, sheets, automatic blankets, and bath fashions (i.e., towels, rugs, and shower curtains). Each department was headed by a division vice president located in New York who had a counterpart located at the mill which manufactured the products. Together, they were responsible for departmental profitability, including mill operations. Working with top sales executives, the department heads in New York selected and priced the product line, determined quantities produced, and assigned customer priorities. They ranged in age from 37 to 47, and most had come up through the sales organization. They received an annual salary of $27,000 to $49,000, plus a bonus of up to 35% of their salary. (Twenty-five percent was related to the profitability of their departments and 10% to the profitability of the Fieldcrest Marketing Division.) In addition, under a new incentive program they could aspire to certain stock incentives.

Under the blanket, bedspread, automatic blanket, and sheet department heads were one or two product managers. In the bath fashions department, three managers (two for towels and one for rugs and shower curtains) were between the department head and product managers. A product manager had similar responsibilities as a department head, but was usually limited to either the Fieldcrest or St. Mary's line. Most product managers had previously worked in the sales organization. They ranged in age from 26 to 35, had base salaries from $15,000 to $32,000, and a bonus of up to 20% of their base salary (15% was based on the department's profitability and 5% on the division's profitability).

One department head commented on the merchandising organization:

> It's almost as if we have six or seven different companies sharing the same sales force. Each has different products, different competitors, different opportunities and challenges, and often different buyers to sell to.

In 1973, the major concern of department heads and product managers was not volume so much as profit. In five of the seven product areas, sales had shown significant increases over 1972. However, raw material shortages and skyrocketing costs had cut deeply into profits. The need to eliminate marginally profitable items and emphasize the more profitable items in each line had become increasingly apparent.

The weakest sales areas were sheets and bedspreads. Since 1971, retailers and consumers had moved away from percale blends toward less costly muslin blends.[4] Muslin blends were especially important in mass merchandisers, and even department stores were increasingly interested in muslin as raw materials costs threatened to drive percales out of the market. Through 1972, Fieldcrest's muslin production capabilities inhibited an aggressive sales posture. By 1973, however, half of its looms had been shifted from percale to muslin. Most Fieldcrest brand sheets still were percale, and they were selling well. If the department store market did shift to muslin, Fieldcrest would either have to change over more looms (a complex process) or increase its total capacity. It had one muslin capacity expansion program, but that was designated for the St. Mary's brand. Fieldcrest brand sheet sales were up 8% over the first three quarters of 1972, but this was 3% below target. St. Mary's brand sales were down 1% and private label sales down 16% from 1972.

Sheet department personnel felt sales of other products were strongly affected by sheet sales because sheets represented the cornerstone of a coordinated program in retail domestics departments. Sheets, they argued, accounted for a high percentage of domestics departments' sales, were style coordinated, and were packaged to expose the Fieldcrest and St. Mary's names and build brand awareness. Special sales incentives on sheets might be in order, they thought, because other manufacturers were increasingly competitive in styling and aggressively seeking the business of better department stores and stronger mass merchandisers.

---

[4]Percale blends used thinner yarns woven more tightly than muslin blends. The fibers were costlier and the products softer than muslin blends.

In the bedspread department, St. Mary's brand sales were up 14% over the previous year and 98% of budget had been attained. However, Fieldcrest brand sales were 18% short of target, and though overall sales increased 1% over 1972, sales to traditional department stores decreased 5%. Private brand volume was down 1% but still accounted for 70% of total bedspread sales and was concentrated in a few large accounts. Bedspread department management felt strongly that they should decrease their dependence on so few customers. Further, they felt they had to increase total volume considerably to run their mill at capacity, a condition almost essential to profitable operation.

The Sales Organization

The sales organization, headed by Mr. Grubbs, consisted of five divisions: national accounts, customer relations, Fieldcrest sales, St. Mary's sales, and regional sales. The first four divisions were headed by vice presidents (ages 37–49), who received salaries ranging from $33,000 to $47,000 plus a bonus of up to 35% of salary based on the profitability of the Fieldcrest Marketing Division. They also received the same stock options as vice presidents in merchandising.

National Accounts Division

The National Accounts Division had three sales managers who ranged in age from 35 to 49. They received a base salary of from $20,000 to $29,000 plus a discretionary bonus determined by the Fieldcrest Marketing Division president. It usually amounted to about 10% of their base salary.

The manager of Commercial and Military Sales worked with product departments to determine the products and prices offered to hospitals, hotels, and other institutional customers. He had sole responsibility for selling to a few accounts but made most customer contacts with the Fieldcrest sales representative who normally handled the account. The manager of Premium and Stamp Plan Sales had the same tasks as the manager of Commercial and Military Sales, but his customers used the products as promotional devices. For example, a bank might offer a free Fieldcrest blanket to customers who opened a savings account, a company might use specially printed towel sets as sales force incentives or Fieldcrest products might be part of a stamp redemption company's program. The National Accounts manager handled Fieldcrest's private label business with large chains such as J. C. Penny and Sears, and supervised the private label business which field sales reps did with small accounts.

Customer Relations Division

The vice president for Customer Relations was responsible for recruiting and initial training of sales personnel and for supervising the Fieldcrest and St. Mary's showrooms. In addition, Fieldcrest's market week activities were channeled through her office. (Market week, held in New York three times a year, was sponsored by a trade association and allowed buyers to view manufacturers' new lines. It was an important industry sales effort.) In December 1973, her major activity was the creation of a development program for both trainees and established employees.

Fieldcrest Sales Division and St. Mary's Sales Division

The Fieldcrest and St. Mary's sales managers (both division vice presidents) worked with merchandising executives to determine product lines and volume, supervised regional managers and sales reps, collected market information, and maintained close contact with major customers.

Because headquarters of many major St. Mary's customers were located in the Northeast, three sales reps who sold only St. Mary's products operated out of the New York office and reported directly to the St. Mary's assistant sales manager. Also located in New York was a St. Mary's specialty sales manager who handled large accounts in all areas except where there were special St. Mary's sales reps. For compensation purposes, these three sales reps and the specialty sales manager were considered regular regional sales reps.

Regional Sales

Five division vice presidents served as regional managers. They were not really on the same level with other division vice presidents but had been given the title to increase their prestige in dealing with customers. They were ages 35–52, with experience in Fieldcrest sales and/or merchandising. Each was responsible for field training, directing, and evaluating 6 to 10 sales reps (42 in all) and 1 to 4 sales/service reps (9 in all). One regional manager estimated he spent 40% of his time on the road with his salespeople. Regional managers maintained strong relationships with the management of key accounts in their regions. While a region might contain 500 customers, the regional manager would probably visit 80 or 90. Regional managers received salaries ranging from $23,000 to $37,000 plus bonuses of up to 45% of salary. One-half of the bonus was based on the region's total volume, one-fourth on target account volume within the region, and one-fourth on top management's evaluation of the regional manager's performance.

Fieldcrest's 42 sales reps were each responsible for 16 to 120 accounts. Most had 50 to 60. While some sold only St. Mary's brand products and others only Fieldcrest brand products, most were responsible for both lines and for calling on a wide variety of customers—department stores, specialty stores, mass merchandisers, institutional and premium customers, and wholesalers. Ninety percent of the sales representatives were college graduates. They received base salaries ranging from $10,000 to $28,000 plus bonuses of up to 35% of their base.

Sales territories ranged in volume from $1,400,000 to $3 million. Geographically, the smallest territory covered New York City, while the largest covered Wyoming, Utah, Colorado, and half of New Mexico. Call frequency varied according to the sales location, territory, and account size. A sales rep in New York City might visit a major Manhattan customer four times a week, while another might visit a minor account in a remote area once every six weeks. Normal contacts were with buyers and merchandise managers. Salespeople usually made one to three calls a day depending on the size and complexity of customers visited. Occasionally, one person could make purchase decisions for all products. More frequently, however, contact with at least two buyers and/or merchandise managers, and sometimes as many as six, within a single account was necessary.

Fieldcrest's account dominance program initiated in 1970 brought multi-level executives of Fieldcrest and the client company into the selling situation. This was a comprehensive program of advertising, sales promotion, and product mix designed to help the retailer improve penetration over a three-year period and enable Fieldcrest to attain a larger share of the retailer's business. Fieldcrest management felt this program had been generally successful, especially in strengthening relationships with customers from the top down. However, a few sales reps reported that the program generated negative feelings among some buyers. "If we sell in at a high level, we take away much of the buyer's prerogative," said one executive. "If angry enough, that buyer can do a lot to make our products flop. It's up to our salespeople to maintain a good relationship with that buyer, and that isn't always easy."

Fieldcrest's nine sales/service reps went into retail outlets, counted stock, and took orders on items included in the basic inventory the account maintained. They were paid a salary of $8,000 to $13,000.

In addition to salaries and incentives, Fieldcrest paid salespeople's travel and selling expenses and supplied cars to all regional managers, sales reps, and sales/service reps. In 1972, the average sales representative's travel and selling expense, car included, was $6,891. Other benefits included comprehensive medical and retirement plans.

The Compensation Plan for Field Sales Representatives

The compensation system for Fieldcrest field sales reps was developed in the 1960s to replace discretionary bonuses determined by the Fieldcrest president. The aims were to motivate salespeople to accomplish company objectives for each item in a multiproduct line and yet retain as much of the "human element" of the former system as possible. In 1970, the president, general sales manager, and manager of operations revised the system to encourage concentration on target accounts which they felt offered Fieldcrest the best opportunities for increased sales.

Sales reps received a salary plus a bonus based partly on sales above quota and partly on overall account management. The salary of a new trainee with no previous selling experience was $10,000. The salaries of experienced salespeople ranged from $15,000 to $28,000 with the midpoint being $21,300. Theoretically, salespeople earned bonuses up to 35% of salary. In reality, reaching that level required a perfect score on a very complex rating system. In 1972, the average bonus was 18.6% of base salary. In December 1973, company sources estimated it would be "20% or better" in 1973. (See Exhibit 4 for salaries and bonus levels.)

Several steps were involved in computing a bonus. At the beginning of the year, each sales representative's target accounts were identified. After discussing with sales reps various accounts, company executives selected target accounts for the Fieldcrest and St. Mary's lines. Occasionally, a sales rep would have only one or two accounts of sufficient size to be considered target accounts. The sales rep and regional manager together assigned percentage values to each target account and to "all other" of the rep's accounts. For example, the following evaluations might be made:

Target Account A is worth	30%
Target Account B is worth	25%
Target Account C is worth	20%
Target Account D is worth	15%
All other accounts are worth	10%
	100% = total potential bonus or 35% of base salary

Assuming the sales rep's gross income was $20,000, the bonus earned on each account would be:

On Target Account A, s/he could earn	30% of total potential bonus or	$2,100
On Target Account B, s/he could earn	25% of total potential bonus or	1,750
On Target Account C, s/he could earn	20% of total potential bonus or	1,400
On Target Account D, s/he could earn	15% of total potential bonus or	1,050
On All other accounts, s/he could earn	10% of total potential bonus or	700
	100%	$7,000

The target accounts and their values were then typed onto a Sales Compensation Plan Summary Sheet. (See page 150.)

The next step was to establish volume quotas for each target account. From headquarters, a regional manager received regional sales quotas for each category of Fieldcrest and St. Mary's brand, total private label, and total promotional products. Each sales rep then submitted quotas which the sales rep had set both by product category and by target account. Regional managers repeatedly found that sales reps tended to set unrealistically high quotas, so the quotas they eventually sent to the Fieldcrest and St. Mary's sales managers for final approval were usually arrived at only after much discussion with the sales reps. The Fieldcrest and St. Mary's sales managers said they tried to agree to quotas which were "challenging and obtainable but not requiring windfall or a lot of luck."

Different procedures and evaluation forms were used for Fieldcrest and St. Mary's accounts. Performance on a Fieldcrest target account was evaluated in five areas—volume, product mix, establishing a constructive and complete merchandising plan, effectiveness and utilization of plan, and coop advertising control. Performance on a St. Mary's target account was evaluated in two areas—volume and achievement of special tasks.

Computation of Bonus on Fieldcrest Target Accounts

At the beginning of the year, actual sales for the preceding year and targeted sales for the current year were typed onto Part I of a form entitled Sales Compensation Plan, Fieldcrest Account. At year end, actual sales and percent of quota achieved were filled in. Part I of a sample form is given below:

Sales Compensation Plan: Fieldcrest Account

SALES REPRESENTATIVE   A. L. Powell

ACCOUNT   Martin's Department Store

LOCATION   Louisiana   VALUE   30%   OF PLAN

I   VOLUME (75 Pts)

	Actual Prior Year	This Year Quota	This Year Actual	Quota % Achieved
Fieldcrest Brand				
Blankets	30.2	35.0	11.3	32%
Bedspreads	28.1	33.5	23.9	71%
Sheets	78.3	88.5	109.7	124%
Towels	52.7	62.9	56.6	90%
Bath products	15.3	19.9	13.1	66%
Automatics	4.5	6.2	5.2	84%
Total Brand	209.2	246.0	219.8	89%
Private & St. Mary's	.1	.1	2.1	2100%
Promotional	20.4	20.4	16.4	80%
Total Volume	229.7	266.5	238.3	89% = 19 Pts

The percent of quota achieved was converted into points using the Sales Compensation Rating Chart (see Exhibit 5). This chart had been constructed by management consultants in the 1960s.

Part II centered on the mix of Fieldcrest brand products sold to the particular account. The form looked like this:

II PRODUCT MIX (5 Pts on Brand)

	Points Earned
No line less than 5 points below the average	5
1 line less than 5 points below the average	4
2 lines less than 5 points below the average	3
3 lines less than 5 points below the average	2
4 lines less than 5 points below the average	1
5 lines less than 5 points below the average	0

Rating __2__ Pts

This meant that if none of the first six lines in the Quota, % Achieved column of Part I was less than five points below the percent of quota achieved by the total brand, the sales rep earned five points. If one line was less, only four points were earned, and so on. For example, in the sample Part I above, three lines are less than five points below the average, 89%. Therefore, the sales rep earned two points on Part II.

Parts III, IV, and V consisted of the regional manager's evaluation of certain elements of the sales rep's performance. Part III focused on the quality and completeness of the merchandising plan which the sales rep constructed for each of his or her target accounts:

III ESTABLISHMENT OF A CONSTRUCTIVE AND COMPLETE PLAN (5 Pts)

	Points Earned
Outstanding	5
Excellent	4
Above average	3
Average	2
Fair	1
Inadequate	0

Rating __3__ Pts

Part IV dealt with how well the merchandising plan was executed:

IV EFFECTIVENESS AND UTILIZATION OF PLANS (5 Pts)
Rating of the use of planned programs and accomplishment of goals during the year.

	Points Earned
Outstanding	5
Highly effective	4
Very effective	3
Effective	2
Somewhat effective	1
Inadequate	0

Rating __4__ Pts

Finally, Part V was a yes or no response to whether the sales rep had effectively controlled the account's cooperative advertising program:

V   COOPERATIVE ADVERTISING CONTROL (10 Pts)

	Points Earned
Effective	10
Ineffective	0

Rating ____10____ Pts

Total Pts:__38__

After the sales rep's performance was scored in each area, the points were tallied. The total became the percentage of the total bonus on that particular account which the sales rep received. In the above example, the sales rep received a total of 38 points on the Martin's Department Store account. This meant the bonus from this particular account was 38% of $2,100, or $798.

Computation of Bonus on St. Mary's Target Accounts

Part I of the bonus plan for St. Mary's target accounts was similar to that of Fieldcrest target accounts:

Sales Compensation Plan
St. Mary's Target Account

SALES REPRESENTATIVE   A. L. Powell

ACCOUNT   Redford's 5 & 10

LOCATION   Mississippi   VALUE   25%   OF PLAN

I   VOLUME (80 Pts)

	Actual Prior Year	*This Year Quota*	*This Year Actual*	*Quota % Achieved*
St. Mary's Brand				
Blankets	18.3	25.0	8.4	34%
Bedspreads	—	5.0	3.2	64%
Sheets	—	10.0	14.7	147%
Towels	126.6	149.3	81.9	55%
Bath products	—	—	—	—
Automatics	58.3	61.3	61.9	101%
Total Brand	203.2	250.6	170.1	68%
Private & Fieldcrest	10.4	15.0	(1)	0%
Promotional	387.5	387.8	422.5	109%
Total Volume	601.1	653.4	592.5	91%
				= 22 Pts

Part II, which in the past had also been used for Fieldcrest target accounts, was structured to enable sales management to focus on whatever specific problems arose. The regional manager assigned the tasks and rated sales reps on how well they accomplished them. (In the past, sales reps had rated themselves, but it was found that the better the salesperson, the greater the tendency to give himself or herself a low rating.)

II   SPECIAL TASKS (20 Pts) Redford's 5 & 10

1.   Task: In 1972 place at least one coordinated One Look in better stores consisting of at least 3 classifications.

     Weight   ___50%___   Rating*   ___5___   Pts

2.   Task: Place a promotional package for towels consisting of a jacquard, print or solid in a chainwide promotion. This must be an ensemble promotion (bath, hand, wash).

     Weight   ___50%___   Rating*   ___5___   Pts

3.   Task: _____

     Weight   _____   Rating*   _____   Pts

4.   Task: _____

     Weight   _____   Rating*   _____   Pts

Total
Weight   ___100%___

*Rating Schedule
Accomplishment of Task:

	Points Earned
Outstanding	5
Excellent	4
Above average	3
Average	2
Fair	1
Inadequate	0

$50 \times 5 = 250$
$50 \times 5 = 250$

Total Rating Part II   ___500___ ÷ 25 =   ___20___ Pts[a]

Total target account: ___42___ Pts

When the bonus for each target account had been calculated, the Sales Compensation Plan Summary Sheet was completed as follows:

---

[a]To determine total points earned on Part II, multiply the weights times rating points earned, add total rating points earned, and divide by 25.

Sales Compensation Sheet
Summary Sheet

SALES REP___A. L. Powell___   REGION ___S. E.___   YEAR___1972___

Maximum Potential Bonus per Account[**]	Target Accounts[a]	% of Plan	% of Maximum Potential Bonus Earned[**]	Value of Bonus Earned
$2,100	Martin's Dept. Store	30%	38%	$ 798
1,750	Redford's 5 & 10	25%	42%	735
1,400	Cobb's Dry Goods	20%	21%	294
1,050	Morton Dept. Store	15%	61%	640
700	All Other[b]	10%	79%	553
$7,000	Total	100%		$3,020 = total bonus

VOLUME (100 Pts)		VALUE: 10% of Plan
Quota	$643.5	
Actual	$791.5	
% of quota	123%	
Points earned	79	

[**]These columns were placed here by the casewriter to help clarify the calculations.

[a]In 1973, a special incentive was placed on bathroom rug sales, worth 30% of a sales rep's bonus. On the "Summary Sheet," the special rug program was listed as a target account.

[b]All other account responsibility (excluding target accounts).

The gross income of the sales representative in the above example was:

Salary ($20,000) + Bonus ($3,020) = $23,020.

Management and Sales Force Reaction to the Compensation System

Mr. Grubbs stated there had been "some criticism but no major complaints" about the compensation system. He felt sales reps definitely preferred it to some competitive systems which offered a straight 1 ½ % commission. Other competitors had salary and bonus systems comparable to Fieldcrest's, but Mr. Grubbs was sure Fieldcrest's compensation level and fringe benefits were better than its competitors. Mr. Grubbs admitted that Fieldcrest's system had some weaknesses. One regional manager commented:

The beauty and the horror of our compensation system is that it gives me the opportunity to treat each of my salespeople as individuals. It's difficult to evaluate
your people fairly because personalities get involved. You naturally like some
people better than others, so remaining impartial is like fighting yourself.

Another regional manager stated that setting tasks for sales reps to accomplish with their St. Mary's accounts, a job which normally took about three
full working days, had caused some problems:

I try to set tasks that are meaningful, reasonable, attainable, and challenging,
but it's difficult to repeatedly meet those criteria. It's especially hard to set tasks
for the few salespeople who sell primarily to small stores. You have to focus on
sales of a particular product line to a group of small accounts in the "all other"
classification rather than on the mix sold to any single account, and often a total
dollar volume goal just won't accomplish what you want it to. For example, one
of my people had been having trouble selling a particular bedspread, so I assigned him the task of increasing total sales of that bedspread by a certain percent. Early in the year, he stumbled across an account and got all the dollar
volume increase he needed right there.

One executive stated he felt regional managers spent much less time
identifying problems and setting tasks than they did in the early days of the
system.

Another problem was that situations beyond a sales rep's control sometimes
prevented accomplishing tasks. For example, one regional manager had instructed a sales rep to sell a certain amount of St. Mary's sheets. Two months
later, because of labor problems, the mill could not deliver the sheets. The sales
rep was unable to accomplish the assigned task. The regional manager then
had to devise a new task even though the selling season was well underway.
Similarly, a leading target account encountered unexpected financial difficulty
and was unable to purchase the amount of merchandise projected. The
Fieldcrest sales rep would have been unable to make quota in any area of this
account, so the regional manager selected a new target account and assigned
new tasks.

A frequent criticism of the compensation system was that it might place too
much emphasis on target accounts. "That stifles sales because it encourages us
to concentrate on four to six big customers and limit our efforts among our
smaller customers," said one sales rep. "The weight given to the 'all other'
category is so small that it's meaningless for us to go after those accounts."

Additional criticism concerned the method of selecting target accounts.
Though sales reps had considerable input in the decision, a few top executives
had the final say about which customers would be target accounts. One sales
representative said there had been "a few times" when top management had
inadequately appraised target accounts and selected accounts with very limited
growth potential.

Pros and cons were voiced about using the compensation system to encourage sales of one particular product line. "In 1973, 30% of a rep's bonus was

determined by his or her sales of bathroom rugs, and we ran a special sales contest on bathroom rugs," said one executive. "During this time, sales increased 75% in total and 635% in the St. Mary's line. That suggests to me that the strategy works pretty well." "I maintain that the increase was due more to the expanded and strengthened product line than to the special incentives," one sales rep replied.

Some executives felt special incentives for one line meant salespeople often neglected their other products. Others felt a nationwide special incentive program for one line was of limited value because of many regional variations in demand. "Demand for higher priced towels is generally greater on the West Coast," said one regional manager. "Therefore, if we offer special incentives on the sale of towels, sales reps in the west will have an advantage over those in other areas. Similarly, heirloom bedspreads are strong in the northeast and south central states but hardly sold at all in western states."

Even when regional variations were taken into account by regional managers directing their sales reps to emphasize certain products, there were still problems. For example, one regional manager mentioned the tendency of salespeople to overload customers in the particular line being emphasized. "One year I instructed one of my people to increase his sales of automatic blankets to a group of small accounts by some percent. That year he sold automatic blankets hand over fist. For the next two years, however, automatic blanket sales to those accounts were severely depressed." Other regional managers stated that this was "really an oddball situation" which almost never occurred.

Another criticism of the compensation system was that the sales force could outguess it. "We know our accounts better than anyone else," said one sales rep. "So when we work out product quotas with our regional managers, we make sure we agree to figures we can attain. Furthermore, when we assign different values to our accounts, we give the most weight to those accounts we think we have the best chance with. There's no way Ed Molitor and Gene McCarthy [Fieldcrest and St. Mary's sales managers who gave final approval to quotas] can know details like the buyer's idiosyncrasies or the potential for muslin sheets or Temptation towels in every one of our target accounts." Mr. McCarthy stated that runaway inflation and price increases in 1973 made setting quotas more difficult than ever.

Other sales reps disagreed that they negotiated figures they could attain. "I almost never achieve the mix the quotas call for," one person stated. "If I do all right with a target account, it's usually because I've sold a lot more of one or two products than I expected to. Those extra sales compensate for my failure to make quota in other areas."

Another sales rep said focusing only on existing accounts meant there was no incentive to force new distribution. "That's what the company is after with the Fieldcrest line," she said. "With the St. Mary's line, however, we want mass distribution, but we really don't get paid for opening new accounts. Of course, our position with some present St. Mary's customers needs to be strengthened, and that's what our compensation system is structured to do. But I think we should be encouraged more to find new customers." Top executives believed using the compensation system to help develop major accounts had worked, as those accounts had grown "phenomenally." They wondered, however, if continuing this focus might now be counterproductive.

A different complaint was voiced by a former sales rep recently promoted to product manager in the merchandising department. "I was happy about my promotion until I realized what would happen to my bonus," he said. "As a salesman, I could earn up to 35% of my salary in bonus, and how much I earned was largely dependent on how hard I worked. Now, my bonus is limited to 20% of my salary—15% is based on the profitability of my mill and 5% on the profitability of the whole Fieldcrest Marketing Division. We have control over too few of the factors that determine profitability for this to be fair. I was better off as a salesman. I had more control over my income, and I got a company car."

Additional Considerations for Structuring the 1974 Compensation System

As Fieldcrest executives considered the compensation system's structure for 1974, they were keenly aware of certain situations which might call for special sales force incentives. During 1973, the Fieldcrest brand had not grown in half of its top twenty accounts. Total volume of these accounts was increasing very slowly, competitors had become extremely aggressive, and some of the accounts had not cooperated with Fieldcrest's advertising and promotional programs as completely as in the past. To reverse this situation, management felt it should help solve problems related to merchandising, inadequate influence with buyers, and inadequate inventories. They wondered if special incentives should be offered to encourage salespeople to assist in tackling these more complex problems.

Fieldcrest executives were also considering special incentives on problem products. The bathroom rug incentive plan in 1973 was seen as evidence for such a program. The two areas which needed sales increases most were sheets and bedspreads. A possible capacity shortage in sheets made executives reluctant to initiate an aggressive sales program there. In bedspreads, however, though Fieldcrest ranked first in the market, its position was due to private label volume. Sales to traditional department stores had decreased by 5%, and over half of the company's bedspread sales were to chain stores. At the November sales meetings, the sales force was told that company management was considering revising the compensation program so that bonuses would be tied more closely to bedspread sales. Reaction was immediate and negative. One sales rep commented:

What you are saying is that we haven't been doing our job, haven't been pushing bedspreads as hard as we should. That just isn't the case. I've shown that line so many times my buyers have gotten bored with it. Let's face it. We need new merchandise and a whole new program like we had with the rugs. Simply tacking a bonus on to the old merchandise isn't going to help at all.

Exhibit 1 Fieldcrest Division of Fieldcrest Mills, Inc.

Industry Data and Fieldcrest's Position Within the Industry (1972)

Product	Total Industry Sales (000)	Fieldcrest Sales (000)	Fieldcrest Market Share	Number of Manufacturers in the Industry	Fieldcrest's Rank
Blankets	$ 125,600	$ 25,800[a]	20.5%	10	2
Automatic blankets	41,500	15,700	37.8	3	2
Bedspreads	226,000	24,100	10.7	13	1
Sheets	597,000	34,700	5.8	10	7
Shower curtains	28,000	500	1.8	7	6
Towels	361,500	61,700	17.1	11	2
Bath rugs	141,000	4,000	2.8	18	16
Total	$1,520,600	$166,500	10.9%		

Source: Company records.
[a]Includes channels for automatic blankets sold to other manufacturers.

Exhibit 2   Fieldcrest Division of Fieldcrest Mills, Inc.

Abbreviated Organization Chart [a]

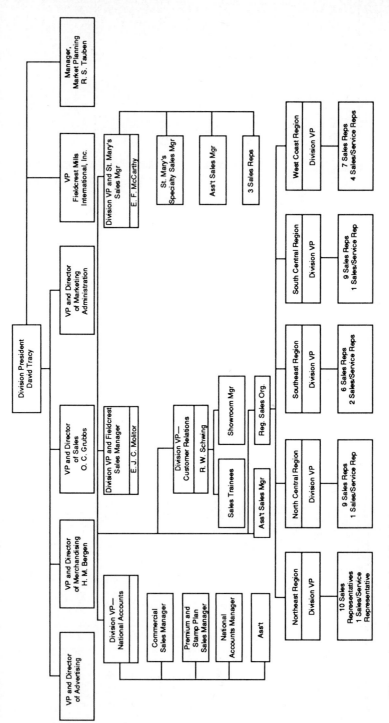

aThe complete sales organization is included.

Exhibit 3   Fieldcrest Division of Fieldcrest Mills, Inc.

Budgeted and Actual Sales (000 omitted)

	January – September			Total Year	
	1972 Actual	1973 Budget	1973 Actual	1972 Actual	1973 Bduget
Fieldcrest					
Blankets	$ 4,158	$ 4,515	$ 5,054	$ 6,264	$ 7,592
Bedspreads	3,070	4,159	3,411	4,530	5,426
Sheets	13,790	15,329	14,882	19,971	23,065
Towels	18,955	20,158	22,643	26,877	31,572
Bathroom rugs	1,727	2,130	2,718	2,701	4,599
Shower curtains	283	339	317	426	560
Automatic blankets	2,758	2,909	2,758	5,158	5,423
Total Fieldcrest	$ 44,741	$ 49,539	$ 51,783	$ 65,927	$ 78,237
St. Mary's					
Blankets	$ 2,270	$ 2,774	$ 3,730	$ 3,568	$ 5,167
Bedspreads	1,466	1,713	1,677	1,865	1,956
Sheets	4,418	4,869	4,363	6,721	7,255
Towels	6,502	7,193	10,461	9,352	13,485
Bathroom rugs	53	312	390	628	628
Shower curtains	—	—	—	—	—
Automatic blankets	2,185	2,127	2,393	3,727	4,397
Total St. Mary's	$ 16,894	$ 18,988	$ 23,014	$ 25,861	$ 32,888
Private Label					
Blankets	$ 2,895	$ 2,836	$ 3,170	$ 5,090	$ 5,158
Bedspreads	10,357	10,924	10,251	14,416	15,275
Sheets	1,264	1,708	1,065	1,718	1,701
Towels	11,011	13,369	11,667	14,831	17,148
Bathroom rugs	583	754	774	778	1,012
Shower curtains	—	—	—	—	—
Automatic blankets	2,982	3,658	3,503	5,512	6,198
Total private label	$ 29,092	$ 33,249	$ 30,430	$ 42,345	$ 46,492
Military					
Institutiona[a]	$ 18,321	$ 16,752	$ 15,900	$ 26,175	$ 21,201
Seconds & Drops	6,921	8,376	8,283	7,329	11,045
Total	$115,988	$126,884	$129,410	$167,110	$189,863

Source: Company records.

[a]While these products normally carried the Fieldcrest or St. Mary's label, company accounting practice was to consider them separate from regular branded sales.

Exhibit 4 Fieldcrest Division of Fieldcrest Mills, Inc.

Salary and Bonus Data for Fieldcrest Sales Representatives, 1972

Salary Ranges		
At Least	But Less Than	Number of Sales Representatives
$10,000	$15,000	12
15,000	20,000	21
20,000	25,000	8
25,000	30,000	1
		42

Bonus Ranges
Lowest bonus paid	$1,352
Highest bonus paid	4,888
Average bonus paid	2,887
Lowest % to base paid	11.3%
Highest % to base paid	26.6%
Average % to base paid	18.6%

Exhibit 5 **Fieldcrest Division of Fieldcrest Mills, Inc.**

Sales Compensation Rating Chart

% of Quota Attained		Points Earned		
At Least	But Less Than	Fieldcrest Target Accounts	St. Mary's Target Accounts	All Other Account Responsibility
0 –	80	—	—	—
80 –	82	5	5	6
82 –	84	9	10	12
84 –	86	12	13	16
86 –	88	16	17	21
88 –	90	19	20	25
90 –	92	21	22	28
92 –	94	23	25	31
94 –	96	25	27	33
96 –	98	26	28	35
98 –	100	27	29	36
100 –	102	28	30	38
102 –	104	30	32	40
104 –	106	32	34	43
106 –	108	35	37	46
108 –	110	37	40	50
110 –	112	40	43	54
112 –	114	44	47	58
114 –	116	47	51	63
116 –	118	51	54	68
118 –	120	54	58	72
120 –	122	57	61	76
122 –	124	59	63	79
124 –	126	62	66	82
126 –	128	64	68	85
128 –	130	65	70	87
130 –	132	67	71	89
132 –	134	68	73	91
134 –	136	70	74	93
136 –	138	71	76	94
138 –	140	72	77	96
140 –	142	73	78	97
142 –	144	74	78	98
144 –	146	74	79	99
146 –	148	75	80	100
148 –	150	75	80	100

Deployment, Focus, and Measuring Effectiveness

Deployment refers to the assignment of the sales effort to territories, customers, products, or functions (e.g., opening new accounts vs. servicing or building existing accounts). Decisions about deployment are ultimately decisions about the primary focus of the sales force: the center of salespeople's attention and the best use of the salesperson's limited time with customers. A coherent deployment program requires clarity about the appropriate measures to use in evaluating the effectiveness of sales efforts.

Deployment and Focus: A Conceptual Framework

Figure A presents a framework for considering relevant factors that affect sales force deployment. Any sales organization needs, at a minimum, ongoing and accurate information about customers and the product (or services) the organization sells to those customers. The extent to which required product information should affect deployment is related to several factors: the type of product sold (e.g., high or low unit prices; salience to the customer's purchasing personnel); the product's complexity (and hence the relative effort required for salespeople to maintain good product technical information); its after-sale service requirements; and the number of products in the vendor's product line, since any individual salesperson has some limit on the amount of product-related information he or she can understand and transmit to customers.

The amount and type of customer information required to conduct field marketing effectively is also a key dimension. Depending upon the buying process, relevant customer information may include data about: the buying company (its competitive and financial situation; management organization; formal and informal procedures for making purchasing decisions); an in-

Figure A
Factors Affecting Sales Force Deployment

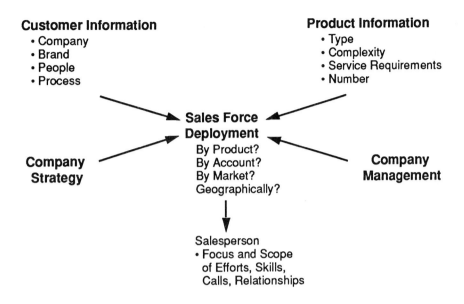

dividual brand or product group at the buyer's company (their marketing strategy and history of purchase preferences in the seller's product category); the people involved in the purchase decision (both their economic and political decision-making criteria in the relevant category of purchases); and, especially, the mechanics of customers' budgeting and purchasing processes, since the other information is of limited use unless the salesperson can utilize it at the appropriate juncture within the customer's purchasing process.

Another relevant factor is the vendor's company strategy. For example, plans for future product introductions can affect deployment decisions independent of the number of products currently sold by the sales force. Similarly, the marketing strategies of many firms are based on selling relevant "bundles" of products (e.g., equipment and related supply items; hardware and customized computer software; systems sales of various sorts). This strategy affects deployment decisions because the sales force often must know about the various items in the bundle while interacting with different purchasing personnel in the customer's organization. In some businesses there are significant speed-to-market or first-mover advantages: The first company to market in a product category may reap the advantages of any switching costs incurred by customers, develop a large installed base that generates scale economies in production and distribution, and use these advantages to fund future product development and sales. In such situations, speed to market and administratively simple structures often are key considerations in deploying the sales force.

Finally, company management is also relevant. Top management faces a series of financial and human-resource constraints and opportunities in other areas besides marketing, which may affect deployment decisions for the sales force. Similarly, within the marketing and sales area, managers typically have developed their skills and preferences within a certain deployment arrangement. Redeployment decisions must take this into account, since there is little sense in establishing a new arrangement that lacks the commitment of key managers in the company or that requires skills not possessed by the relevant managers.

All of the factors just described may be relevant to the selling process, but any one deployment option (e.g., deploying the sales force by product, market, geography, or major-account criteria) usually gathers only certain kinds of information effectively. In essence, analyzing the customer's buying process and buying criteria means judging what types of information and interactions are relatively more important to the selling process and then making deployment decisions according to how well each option generates the relevant kinds of information and interactions. In turn, the deployment decision helps to determine the focus and scope of the individual salesperson's efforts, call patterns, selling skills, and account relationships that are (and are not) developed over time.

This relationship between deployment and focus is a crucial one that should be borne in mind in analyzing attempts at organizing and implementing the marketing effort. Indeed, in many situations, the allocation of sales force effort across product and markets—the deployment decision—is more critical than the size of the sales force itself.

Measuring Effectiveness

Effectiveness refers to some summary measure(s) of outcomes for which the sales and marketing organization is responsible, such as sales volume, market share, or profitability. Deployment and measurement decisions are usually intertwined. On the one hand, deployment decisions have a major effect on sales results and therefore on what can be measured. On the other hand, relevant measurement criteria influence managers' evaluations of deployment options and therefore what will be measured.

At the same time, objective assessment of marketing performance, often called marketing productivity analysis, remains a particularly complex subject with manifold possibilities.[1] The reasons for this include the nature of the marketing effort. Marketing activities involve not only many other functions internal to the corporation, such as production, but also external entities, such as independent distributors and other re-seller channels. Any accurate measure of marketing performance must consider these complexities, which involve a series of more and less controllable factors.

Nonetheless, goals must be established and performance evaluated. For our purposes, certain basic criteria are relevant to considering issues in measuring sales effectiveness and the conduct of field marketing efforts (see Figure B).

First, behavior and performance in the management of selling efforts must be distinguished.[2] Behavior refers to what sales representatives do—that is, the tasks they expend effort on while working. These tasks might include sales calls, preparing orders, formulating and delivering sales presentations, developing formal proposals, and so on. Performance is behavior evaluated in terms of its contributions to the organization's goals. Both behavior and performance are influenced by deployment decisions. Deployment criteria, however, are developed with desired behaviors in mind, whereas performance criteria are intended to measure the outputs of those selling and marketing behaviors in the marketplace.

Second, efficiency and effectiveness in measuring field marketing activity must be clarified. As Peter Drucker once noted, efficiency refers to "doing things right" whereas effectiveness refers to "doing the right things."[3] Depending upon the selling situation, some field marketing activities require efficiency-oriented (usually, cost-efficiency) measures, whereas others require effectiveness-oriented measures. This distinction is stressed here because, in practice, probably the most commonly used benchmark for evaluating field marketing efforts is the selling expense-to-revenue ratio (E/R ratio). E/R ratios can shed light on the relative cost efficiency of certain marketing activities, but they, by themselves, do not illuminate their cost effectiveness, which is a more complex relationship among the selling costs, sales revenues, sales margins, and market share achieved through one or another means of organizing and implementing marketing efforts.[4]

Third, in measuring the effectiveness of sales performance, summary measures of both individual salesperson performance and aggregate field

Figure B
Measuring Effectiveness: Basic Criteria

Behavior (What reps do)	vs.	**Performance** (Contribution to goals)
Efficiency (Doing things right)	vs.	**Effectiveness** (Doing the right things)
Individual Measures (e.g., Sales volume)	and	**Aggregate Measures** (e.g., Call capacity)
Short-term Measures	and	**Long-term Measures**

(Long-term goals and performance measures must usually be complemented and reinforced with short-term incentives, rewards, and goals.)

Importance of Consistent Sales Performance Measures

Internally consistent

Consistent with managerial measures

selling performance, such as the overall call capacity of the sales force, must be developed. Managing a sales force involves managing both individual salespeople, who typically demonstrate a range of efforts and skills as well as a certain aggregate capacity to make sales calls independent of the individuals involved. Call capacity can be expressed in any of a number of ways, depending upon what the sales task requires:

- The number of sales calls
- The quality and length of the calls
- The amount of service, rather than selling, provided by each call
- The amount of selling, rather than service, provided by each call

Further, the relevant index of call capacity is likely to change over the course of the product's life cycle or as an industry evolves. Early in a product's life cycle, for example, market-development concerns typically make the sheer number of calls an important consideration. Later in the course of the product life cycle, the nature of the call (e.g., applications development or merchandising assistance) and the service component of field marketing activities typically assume greater importance.

Fourth, for most sales organizations both short- and long-term measures of effectiveness are relevant and required. Short-term measures typically take the form of quotas or other measures tied to quarterly or annual sales results. Long-term measures typically look at market share, profitability, or customer satisfaction. Recently, there has been legitimate criticism of the excessively short-term orientation of many management decisions at U.S. companies. These types of decisions often bolster quarterly or annual numbers at the expense of longer-term competitive advantage. Nonetheless, in most sales organizations, long-term performance measures usually must be reinforced and complemented with short-term goals, incentives, and rewards. Selling in most situations entails more rejections by customers than sales successes; this often means that short-term motivators and measures are necessary to a sustained field-marketing effort.

Fifth, appropriate sales performance measures require consistency along a number of dimensions. Such measures should not only be internally consistent with each other but also consistent with the measures considered important by top management. If these measures are inconsistent with top management measures, the result is, at best, contention and conflict between the sales organization and other parts of the firm, and, at worst, internal miscoordination problems that result in the mismanagement of customer encounters.

Case Studies

The three cases in this module examine the allied issues of deployment, focus, and measuring effectiveness.

The Actmedia, Inc. case concerns a company founded in 1971 to provide in-store advertising and promotional services for consumer packaged goods sold in supermarkets. Its major product is ads placed on shopping carts. After losing money for 10 years, the company began to grow dramatically in the 1980s and, at the time of the case, is planning to double the size of its sales force. The company's president is grappling with two sets of decisions: How to deploy the sales effort, and whom to recruit for expanded sales efforts.

Precisely because deployment is such a complex decision in this situation, the Actmedia case is an excellent introduction to the topic. Further, it illustrates the ties between deployment decisions and other aspects of sales management considered in the previous chapter. Therefore, when you analyze the Actmedia case, remember some of the lessons learned from those previous case discussions: (1) the factors that should influence recruiting and selection criteria; (2) the importance of fitting selection, motivation, and supervision policies to the sales task and the business system inherent in the company's strategy; and (3) the relevance and limits of compensation policies in guiding selling behaviors. Consider also the following questions about the particular situation at Actmedia:

1. How does this company make money? What are the fundamental economics inherent in the services provided by Actmedia, and what are the firm's current competitive strengths and vulnerabilities?
2. Who buys Actmedia's services? What is the role of each party in influencing the purchase decision?
3. What are the advantages and disadvantages of each deployment option being considered? What are the implications of each option for the recruiting and selection decisions faced by management?
4. Among other things, the case presents the history of this company from start-up, through near-bankruptcy, to growing a successful firm. Is this history relevant to the decisions being considered by management in this case?

As well as being a decision-oriented case, moreover, Actmedia offers information concerning recent developments in packaged-goods marketing: for example, the impact of retail information systems and the fragmentation of advertising media on marketing budgeting allocations at packaged-goods manufacturers; the increase in the numbers of working women and the impact on in-store shopping behavior; and changes in the role of brand managers at packaged-goods manufacturers. These developments have revised the nature of field marketing requirements at consumer packaged-goods firms over the past decade. (You might want to reference this information as you analyze later cases dealing with these firms.)

The Cox Cable cases concern a different business situation in which deployment, focus, and measuring effectiveness are key concerns for management. The case series focuses on one of the company's franchises (Jefferson

Parish, Louisiana, a suburb of New Orleans), but the issues represent those faced by many other companies, especially in service businesses.

Asked to address the problem of "churn" in the franchise's customer base ("churn" refers to the number of customers who disconnect or downgrade their installed service for various reasons), a new marketing manager is considering changes in deployment, training, compensation, and the selling orientation of the sales force. The Cox Cable (A) case provides background information about the industry, company, franchise, the selling process, customer base, and options being considered. The Cox Cable (B) case, which you should read after analyzing and discussing (A), explains what the company did and raises two additional issues: How should we evaluate the results of these actions? What should the marketing manager do next, given your evaluation as well as top management's criteria for measuring effectiveness?

When you analyze the Cox Cable (A) case, consider these questions:

1. What are the important characteristics of the cable business? How has the business changed during the past few years considered in the case?
2. What is your evaluation of the financial and marketing performance of the Jefferson Parish (JP) franchise since its beginning in 1978?
3. What is the economic value of a customer in JP? Does this value differ by type of service? Type of customer? Over time? If you were a salesperson for Cox Cable in JP, where would you spend your time in order to maximize your compensation?
4. What is your evaluation of the options being considered by marketing management for dealing with the problem of churn? What are the important measures of performance for marketing? For general management? Given these measures, what should management at JP do about churn?

When you analyze the Cox Cable (B) case, consider these questions:

1. What is your evaluation of Cox management's response to the problem of churn in the JP franchise? Consider both the substance (i.e., the specific actions taken) and the process (i.e., how these actions were developed and implemented) of their response.
2. If you were a salesperson under the pilot program, how would you allocate your time in order to maximize compensation? What are the characteristics of a "good" territory under the revised deployment and sales management program?
3. What is the purpose of a sales quota? Do quotas serve a purpose in the sales tasks appropriate to Cox JP? Do you agree with the decision to abolish the kind of sales quota previously in place at JP?
4. Evaluate the interim results of the pilot program. What, specifically, is the good news and the bad news from Mr. Arrington's perspective? Mr. Kidd's perspective? Mr. Bowers's perspective?

5. What should Mr. Kidd do next with regard to the deployment, compensation, and other issues discussed in this case?

As well as providing an opportunity for quantitative and qualitative analyses of important issues in sales management, this case series also illustrates a common situation facing marketing managers: Actions taken to correct one problem require management to address a different set of human and economic issues in the sales force. Many aspects of organizing and implementing the marketing effort exhibit this iterative nature, since problems in marketing implementation must be addressed in a dynamic marketplace with human factors as the agents of strategy. The challenge facing marketing managers in this case series, as in many business situations, is not only to recognize the constraints but also to craft an implementable course of action.

References

1. For a review of the literature dealing with marketing productivity analysis, and a suggested model for conceptualizing and measuring marketing productivity, see Thomas V. Bonoma and Bruce H. Clark, *Marketing Performance Assessment* (Boston, Mass.: Harvard Business School Press, 1988).
2. See John P. Campbell et al., *Managerial Behavior, Performance and Effectiveness* (New York: McGraw-Hill, 1970), and Gilbert A. Churchill, Jr., Neil M. Ford, and Orville C. Walker, Jr., "Behavior and Other Performance Analyses," in *Sales Force Management* (Homewood, Ill.: Irwin, 1985), pp. 623–647.
3. Peter F. Drucker, *Management: Tasks, Responsibilities, Practices* (New York: Harper & Row, 1974), p. 45.
4. For a more detailed discussion of E/R ratios and their application as measures of sales and distribution productivity, see E. Raymond Corey, Frank V. Cespedes, and V. Kasturi Rangan, *Going to Market: Distribution Systems for Industrial Products* (Boston, Mass.: Harvard Business School Press, 1989), pp. 60–83.

Case 6
Actmedia, Inc.

In December 1986, Mr. Bruce Failing, Jr., president and CEO of Actmedia, Inc., was reviewing issues raised by the company's rapid growth. Since Actmedia's initial public stock offering in 1983, revenues had risen from $15 million to $65 million. Mr. Failing intended to maintain a 50% annual growth rate throughout the 1980s through expansion and maximum utilization of resources. Between 1984 and 1986 the company's sales force had doubled, and in the first quarter of 1987 it was scheduled to double again. In the meantime, new products and channels had been added.

During its first decade Actmedia had one product and one sales force, but in 1983 the company began introducing new products and in 1985 had divided the sales force into two groups: one for sales of the company's ad products and another for its promotions products. With more product introductions scheduled, organization of the sales force, motivational systems, and recruitment criteria were decisions that had to be made by the start of the new year.

In-Store Marketing

Actmedia was founded in 1971 to provide in-store advertising for consumer packaged goods sold in supermarkets. The company's initial product was multicolored displays, typically 8 ½ " × 11", placed on shopping carts in supermarkets and designed to recall the graphics and slogans of the manufacturer's TV or other media advertising. By 1986, Actmedia had expanded into point-of-sale consumer promotions and was the only national independent company with its own field service staff providing a range of marketing services in supermarkets. Actmedia was in 19 of the 20 largest grocery chains (which

This case was prepared by Research Associate Jon E. King, under the supervision of Associate Professor Frank V. Cespedes, as the basis for class discussion rather than to illustrate either effective or ineffective handling of an administrative situation.

accounted for about 50% of total U.S. grocery store sales in 1986), and its services were purchased by 250 different brands from over 65 different companies, including the 20 largest packaged-goods advertisers. Five companies accounted for a third of Actmedia's revenues in 1986, a proportion in keeping with the percentage of total packaged-goods advertising attributable to these companies.

Most packaged-goods firms conducted three major types of marketing activities: advertising, consumer promotions, and trade promotions. Consumer promotions included discount coupons, premiums, sweepstakes, and samples. Trade promotions were discounts or other incentives aimed at encouraging retailers or distributors to promote a given manufacturer's product. Although philosophies differed among firms, advertising was generally used to increase customer awareness of the product, build "brand loyalty," and develop the product's image over the long term. Trade and consumer promotions were more likely to be aimed at immediately increasing sales volume or gaining new users.

During the 1970s and 1980s new-product introductions accelerated. By 1985, food companies as a group were introducing about 30 new products weekly, twice as many as in 1980; estimates indicated that 70% of all grocery store products available in 1985 had come on the market since 1975. Meanwhile, supermarkets were growing larger and had opened their aisles to other items from plants to greeting cards, office supplies and auto equipment. In 1985 the average food store was 30,000 square feet, compared to 13,000 in 1975. Some warehouse stores were 100,000 square feet and carried 15,000 different products.

Demographics and demand were also changing. Consumers were less typically housewives on errands than shoppers purchasing on their way home from work. The average length of a shopping trip dropped from 28 minutes in 1975 to 21 minutes in 1985, according to trade reports. Bureau of Labor Statistics indicated that the percentage of women working outside the home had increased from 39% in 1970 to 71% in 1985, and male involvement in purchasing decisions rose concurrently. Furthermore, studies indicated that men shopping alone were less likely to preplan the trip, make a list, check newspaper advertisements, or bring coupons to the store than women were. Men also tended to make more impulse purchases than women, were more brand-loyal and less price-conscious, although relatively few shoppers of either gender included brand names on their shopping lists. A 1977 survey indicated that 65% of every dollar spent in the supermarket resulted from in-store decisions; a similar survey in 1987 indicated 81%.

With computerized point-of-sale systems, moreover, supermarket managers had access to detailed sales information on individual items, broken down by brand, size, flavor and color. Computers allowed retailers to tie these data to handling costs, warehousing expenses, and shelf space in order to calculate direct product profit (DPP). This figure represented income per square foot of shelf space and dollar invested, and potentially could be determined for every product in the store. With such knowledge, store managers depended less on the recommendations of the packaged-goods sales force, and instead often dictated stocking terms and shelf space allocation. Noted one industry observer, "It used to be that the manufacturers knew what was going on and would tell the retailers. Now it's the other way around." High DPP contributors were given more space and visibility in order to maximize sales potentials, and low contributors would often be discontinued. In this environment, product life cycles were often shorter, and could be swiftly discontinued in a given chain if performance wasn't high from the start.

In response, manufacturers relied more heavily on consumer and trade promotions to establish new products or boost sales of older products. By 1986, packaged-goods companies were spending about twice as much on promotions as on advertising; 15 years earlier, that ratio had been reversed.

Network Advertising

The three national television networks, the traditional conduits for most packaged-goods advertising, were shrinking as a percentage of television viewing, while the viewing shares for cable channels and videocassette machines were growing swiftly in the 1980s. Estimates indicated that the networks' combined share of prime-time audience fell from 91% in 1978 to 73% in 1985. Additionally, traditional 60-second advertisements were being replaced by 30-, 15-, and 10-second spots, leading to a state often referred to as "clutter" which interfered with a given ad's effectiveness. Surveys indicated a decline in the level of attention paid to TV advertisements: in 1965, 18% of TV viewers in phone interviews could correctly identify what brand was advertised four minutes after seeing a commercial; in 1974 that figure was 12%, and in 1981 7%. "Zapping" from one channel to another during commercials was reportedly more frequent as 35% of all TV households owned remote-control devices by 1985, and in a 1984 Video Story Board survey 20% of viewers claimed they paid no attention to commercials.

Moreover, daytime audiences (a traditional target for packaged-goods advertisers) had changed as more women entered the work force, and although packaged-goods advertisers attempted to target young, affluent viewers, Nielsen showed that the growing segments of the daytime audience were older and lower-income groups. Some media buyers therefore concluded that national TV advertising was less efficient and harder to focus, since the audience was not as large or monolithic as it had appeared in the 1960s. Said one media director at a large packaged-goods firm in 1985, "We expect the networks' audience to continue to diminish, so we're looking for other outlets. We're not going to sit and do nothing."

Company Background

In 1971 Bruce Failing, Sr., a former vice president of a food brokerage firm, founded Actmedia to provide advertising on grocery carts in upstate New York. One problem was that many others had tried unsuccessfully to develop such in-store marketing systems, leaving grocery store management with a clutter of unusable fixtures, no payoff, and residual skepticism. Yet Mr. Failing saw a large market if the chains could be convinced. He also knew that, executed properly, in-store advertising could represent income without capital investment for supermarkets, which was significant in a business that typically operated on 1% net margins.

With $70,000 raised from friends, Mr. Failing spent two years designing the ad frames to be attached to shopping carts. His food brokerage experience had given him broad contacts in the food business and familiarity with chain headquarters operations. By 1973, the ad frames were designed and tested, and advertisers and chains were signed on for free tests of eight-week runs. Audits & Surveys Inc., an independent research group, then collected data to determine the impact on sales.[1] Results indicated an average sales increase of 10–12% for the products advertised.

Early History

Mr. Bruce Failing, Jr. joined Actmedia after graduating from Harvard Business School in 1973. In 1974, a venture capital firm and a group of private investors headed by Mr. Richard Watson (brother to Thomas Watson of IBM) agreed to provide Actmedia with $175,000. However, Mr. Failing, Jr. recalled, "The VC firm ran out of funds and folded. But Dick Watson said, 'Gentlemen don't walk out on deals' and provided the difference out of his own pocket. That was one of many life-saving incidents in our company's history."

During this period, Mr. Failing, Jr. and two friends who had joined Actmedia, John Stevenson and Jeffrey Sturgess, approached brand managers at packaged-goods firms in order to sell the company's shopping-cart ads service. They found that budgeting processes at these firms were lengthy (with 6–12-month lead times the norm for marketing allocations), an obstacle for a business with high fixed costs and limited working capital. Further, brand managers were often skeptical about the concept despite test results. Mr. Failing, Jr. commented:

> Actmedia started with stores in Syracuse, New York, but it became clear that potential clients weren't interested in a service that covered only one city. We therefore started to expand and that, in turn, increased the pressure on us to generate more sales revenue more quickly. Sometimes we were so aggressive we got thrown out.
>
> For years, we didn't fully appreciate the length of the decision-making process at the manufacturer, and all the different internal and external parties

---

[1]Since 1974, Actmedia's shopping cart ads had been tested over 380 times with independent research firms. The basic testing format was a controlled store test consisting of a number of pairs of supermarkets matched by chain, dollar volume, location and demographics. The matching was designed to minimize variables other than Actmedia programs, such as other advertising, promotions or pricing. Actmedia ads were then placed in half the stores, and sales results for the advertised product in controlled and noncontrolled stores were compared.

involved. As a result, we consistently overprojected sales and underprojected our losses. In addition, the oil crisis of 1974–75 hurt us badly: every dollar in additional sales was soon swallowed up in gasoline costs for our field service personnel.

Mr. Sturgess added:

> By 1977 we'd had about a hundred independent tests done to corroborate the sales impact of our product, and we thought clients would beat a path to our door. That misconception almost killed us: no one believed the test results. Some even took us on for test periods just to prove us wrong, and therefore didn't keep us when we were right. We eventually halved our presentation figures to 5% sales increases. This understatement became critical to our success later, since when actual results came back at twice the estimated levels, the brand manager became a hero to his superiors.

During this period, the company survived primarily on revenues from regional advertisers and, in Mr. Failing, Sr.'s words, "through the willingness of the grocery chains to accept consistently late payments on the spaces we leased on shopping carts: we didn't dirty their stores, and they understood they would get nothing if the company went bankrupt." In the mid-1970s, Actmedia needed more funds for expansion to additional cities and management again approached Mr. Watson. He committed to another $300,000 but died before any documents could be signed. However, his wife decided to honor the obligation.

By 1976, Actmedia covered stores in New York City and Atlanta as well as upstate New York, and was approaching profitability. However, management had decided that only national coverage would provide the reach necessary for significant sales to major packaged-goods firms. Actmedia raised $1.25 million from a consortium of venture capital firms, but found that most potential clients had already made their 1977 budgeting decisions. As a result, sales slowed and losses doubled (see Exhibit 1 for financial information). Mr. Failing, Jr. recalled the subsequent events:

> The venture capitalists were angry and pulled the plug. They fired my father and demoted me from president to a sales representative. An HBS alumnus who worked for the VC firm was brought in to fix things: he did so well that sales decreased the next year and losses tripled. By April 1978 the company was out of money.
>
> However, we caught the venture capitalists on the fact that they had not reconstituted the board. So one Saturday, we called a board meeting, fired the president and his people, and put ourselves back in charge. On Monday morning, the venture capitalists showed up in my office to put us into Chapter 11. But we hired an aggressive lawyer who ranted and raved and threatened to sue them for putting the company under. We also pointed out that we had no assets, so liquidation of the company wouldn't generate cash. They took the last $200,000 in the company's bank account and left us alone for a few years.

By 1978, we were a million dollars in debt, but we kept at it for two reasons: a) we really thought it would work, and b) we were all guaranteed utter bank-ruptcy if it didn't. We missed three consecutive payrolls, and HBS notified me that I was the first one in my class to have my school loan go into collection. Stur-gess, Stevenson, and I drove hundreds of miles on sales calls to packaged-goods firms, because it was cheaper than flying and on weekends we delivered ads to the field. My father was in almost constant negotiations with the chains and creditors, and my mother worked on convincing the field service people to stay.

In 1979 Actmedia nearly broke even on sales of $2 million. But in 1980 the company tallied a loss again as Los Angeles and Chicago were added. However, with New York City, those additions proved to be, in Mr. Failing, Jr.'s words, "the magic triangle that provided us with the national presence demanded by packaged-goods firms. Beginning in 1980, it became somewhat easier to be-come part of their budget planning processes." Sales doubled in 1981 and Actmedia showed its first profit.

In 1982, management presented its forecasts to the venture capitalists who dismissed it since past forecasts had been consistently overoptimistic. Mr. Failing, Jr. noted that "we were trying to bring good news, but they had written off the investment. They said, 'If you believe those projections, why don't you buy out our share?' They had originally put in $1.25 million and asked for $3 million." The Failings borrowed money and bought the venture capitalists' 36% interest. In 1983, when Actmedia went public, its market value was $60 million. For much of 1986, after another public offering, the company was trading at a price/earnings multiple approaching 50 and its market value was more than $250 million. Reflecting on the company's history, Mr. Failing, Jr. remarked:

> We sold stock on the leverage built into this business, which the market recog-nized even if our VC friends didn't: once we had the national position, we had more selling potential with manufacturers and a base for highly profitable in-cremental sales revenues, since putting additional ads in the same store has low variable costs. Also, timing was important. In a sense, we were ahead of our time in the 1970s, but more people now recognize the demographic and media trends that make in-store marketing more important.
>
> "Entrepreneurship" is now a buzzword and the focus of elegant theories. However, Actmedia was not the first or last company to develop an in-store marketing program; I estimate that over 18 such firms failed before we even started. But apparently no one was willing to fail for 10 years!

Growth and New Product Development

From its founding to 1983, Actmedia had one product: ads on supermarket shopping carts. The next three years, however, saw a rapid expansion into additional products and retail outlets. In 1986, Actmedia's products (see Exhibit 2) included advertising services (shopping cart displays, Aislevision and

Shelftalk), coupon distribution (Actnow), and an in-store sampling and demonstration service (Impact). In 1986, shopping cart displays accounted for about 40% of company revenues, Aislevision 24%, Shelftalk 3.6%, Actnow 30%, and Impact for 4%.

1. Actmedia's initial product, shopping cart ads, consisted of a two-sided plastic frame attached to the front of each cart in participating stores. The company's field force placed up to 12 noncompeting ads in each store, and each advertiser's ad was on a minimum of one-sixth of the shopping carts in every store. In 1986, Actmedia ad displays appeared on over 1.1 million shopping carts in 67 Areas of Dominant Influence (an industry designation which defined each geographic market exclusive of all others) through more than 7,200 supermarkets operated by 220 chains. The ads, which were designed by Actmedia's customers and their ad agencies, were changed every four weeks by Actmedia's field service staff, consisting of 300 full-time and about 10,000 part-time personnel in 1986. Actmedia offered a set calendar of four-week ad cycles, or "flights," thereby enabling advertisers to limit their participation to a minimum of four weeks. During each flight, Actmedia's field reps visited each store at least weekly to maintain and service the displays.

   During 1986, Actmedia ad displays were purchased for 155 different brands manufactured by 65 different companies reaching 50% of U.S. households. The company's largest clients for ad displays included Procter & Gamble, General Foods, Kimberly-Clark, PepsiCo and General Mills. Each ad was billed to clients at a rate of $.80 per thousand store transactions per month. Transactions at the check-out counter were a measure of total store traffic and therefore an index of consumers exposed to the ad. The retail chains received from Actmedia a 25% commission on these revenues, based on the number of monthly transactions in a given store. In general, the client's ad agency also received from Actmedia its customary 15% commission for advertising developed for that manufacturer.

2. Aislevision was the company's second advertising product, introduced in 1985. This product consisted of an overhead aisle directory, a two-sided plastic-molded sign installed in a supermarket aisle and with 20" × 30" ads on each side (typically for brands in that aisle) as well as the names of product categories shelved in that aisle. Participating supermarkets typically had 12 Aislevision directories, containing 24 ads which were designed by the client and its ad agency and changed every four weeks by Actmedia field personnel. The Aislevision directories were manufactured by another company from a mold owned by Actmedia, and Actmedia's cost of producing and installing each directory was approximately $100.

Actmedia did not accept ads for directly competing products for a given Aislevision flight but did not exclude competing ads in different products (e.g., in a given flight, one brand of shampoo could be advertised on carts and a competing brand through Aislevision displays in the same stores). Aislevision ads were priced at $.50 per thousand store transactions monthly, with retailers receiving 25% and ad agencies 15%. By 1986, Aislevision was in over 7,000 stores, and 1,100 new stores were scheduled to add the product in 1987.

3. Shelftalk, introduced in 1986, was a 5" × 6 ½" two-sided display attached to the supermarket shelf in front of the product being advertised. Actmedia placed up to 60 noncompeting ads in each participating store. Like the traditional "shelftalkers" used by packaged-goods firms, the ads were designed by the client and its ad agency, and changed every four weeks by Actmedia's field personnel at the same time they changed ads for the shopping cart and Aislevision programs.

   Shelftalk ads were priced at $12 per store per flight, regardless of store traffic levels, although retailers received a 25% commission based on monthly store transactions. In 1986, the Shelftalk program was used for 90 different brands in 152 ADIs through more than 5,000 supermarkets.

4. "Actnow," the name of Actmedia's promotions division established in 1984, developed two sets of in-store promotions: coupon programs and a sampling-and-demonstrations service called Impact.

   Through the Actnow coupon program, booklets containing up to 20 coupons were handed directly to shoppers as they entered a supermarket. The program was supported by a prominent entrance display of all participating products and by shelf displays throughout the store. The program was typically executed in 7,000 stores over two consecutive weekends, and utilized by clients for test marketing of new products as well as promotion of existing products. In 1986, Actmedia conducted 5 national programs, which distributed over 11 million coupon booklets. Manufacturers provided the samples and were charged $18 per thousand coupons and $50 per thousand samples distributed by Actmedia, while the retailer received a 25% commission.

Impact, started in 1985, typically involved one product although two or more could participate. In this program, Impact demonstrators prepared the product for in-store trial (e.g., a cup of coffee or bowl of cereal) and distributed samples and coupons. The programs were conducted over a 2–3 day period in each participating store by Actmedia field personnel situated inside the store. In 1986, Actmedia conducted 57 Impact sampling and/or demonstration programs, distributing over 71 million coupon booklets as well as 144 million samples and solo coupons.

Over the past 12 years, Actmedia and its clients had repeatedly tested Actmedia programs through independent research firms. According to company literature, these studies indicated, on average, the following impact of various Actmedia products on the sales of client products:

- Shopping Cart ads: 8.2% sales increase (based on 390 independent studies)
- Aislevision: 7.5% sales increase (based on 70 independent studies)
- Shelftalk: 4.0% sales increase
- Shopping Carts and Aislevision: 12% sales increase

In addition, Actmedia claimed that its Actnow coupon program generated a redemption rate twice that of standard free-standing-insert programs in magazines (9% redemption rate for Actnow versus an average of 4.2% for FSI programs in magazines or newspapers), with a corresponding effect on sales of the client's products. Further, the company believed that, on a cost-per-thousand basis (CPM, a traditional measure of advertising efficiency), its products were more efficient than many standard ad media.[2]

Actmedia's management noted that it took significant time and effort to build client interest in each new product but that the company had accelerated its expansion into more outlets and more products for a variety of reasons, including competition and developing scale economies. Although Actmedia believed it was currently the only company with its own national field service staff providing in-store marketing services, it also believed that new product introductions were required to preempt such direct national competition. Further, there were relatively few entry barriers at the local level for many different types of in-store marketing suppliers. In addition, ad agencies and packaged-goods manufacturers themselves were potential competition. Management also saw Actmedia in indirect competition with other media, including TV, radio, magazines and newspapers. Expansion helped to make Actmedia's services increasingly cost competitive with these media.

Another reason to introduce new products was, in Mr. Failing, Jr.'s words, "to leverage existing store relationships: since our reputation with the chains is good, we tend to encounter less resistance to placing additional products in the stores. More products also leverage the time of our field force, since a single store visit can now accomplish more revenue-generating tasks and since the new products generally require fewer visits and less time to change than shopping cart displays. Therefore, we have been able to move into remote locations economically."

In 1983, with its Cart program in 3,300 stores, Actmedia could advertise 12 different brands of 40,000 ad spaces during each four-week cycle. By 1986, with five programs in 13,000 stores, Actmedia had the capacity to advertise or

---

[2]According to Actmedia, CPM rates in 1986 were, on average, as follows: TV, $10.20; Print, $5.60; Radio, $3.60; Outdoor ads, $2.25; Actmedia Carts, $.80; Aislevision, $.50; Shelftalk, $.25.

promote 112 different products on 647,000 spaces per cycle. At capacity, Actmedia's combined programs had a revenue potential of over $500 million, according to company estimates. Further, the company was planning to expand beyond supermarkets into major chain drug stores and mass merchandisers in 1987. Commenting on the company's recent expansion, Mr. Failing, Jr., said, "We introduced new products faster than would have been ideal, but we felt it was competitively necessary. The organization would probably like to take a breather for a while, but growth is essential to our position and plans."

Organization

Exhibit 3 indicates Actmedia's organization in 1986. The three major operating functions were: retail store relations (signing on chains and leasing space in stores); field service (executing the in-store marketing programs); and marketing and sales (selling the company's services to packaged-goods manufacturers).

Store Relations

In 1986, Actmedia leased the advertising rights to over 1 million shopping carts, 100,000 aisle directories and 74,500 Shelftalk displays in stores operated by 238 retail food chains such as Safeway, Kroger, Lucky Stores, A&P, Stop & Shop and Grand Union. On average, each chain's headquarters was visited monthly by one of the company's 12 store relations staff. Mr. Leighton York, vice president for store relations, noted that "no chain has ever withdrawn from a relationship with Actmedia."

Actmedia operated in 209 ADIs, comprising 47 different sales markets in the United States. In return for a percentage of Actmedia's advertising revenue, the retailer gave Actmedia exclusive, contractual use of its shopping carts, aisle directories and Shelftalk displays for a period of one to five years. Other than providing Actmedia with traffic and sales information about its stores, the supermarket chains invested no money, labor or management time for the income they received from Actmedia.

Field Service

Mrs. Betty Failing (wife of Mr. Failing, Sr.) was in charge of the field service force, which placed and maintained the ads. Field operations were divided into 3 zones, 11 regions and 35 districts, each run by a district manager responsible for executing ad and/or Actnow events. Advertising districts were frequently organized in a different geographical manner than promotions districts, since not all participating stores carried all services offered by Actmedia. The company also employed 8 assistant district managers for the larger districts as well as 36 project managers and 13 assistant project managers for Actnow programs.

In 1986 the field service force for ads included 209 full-time area service representatives (ASRs), each responsible for servicing cart ads in 25–40 stores. During the ad-change period (the first four days of each cycle), ASRs supervised approximately 6,000 part-time personnel, called "contract labor" because ASRs were responsible for recruiting and hiring these assistants. Similarly, Actnow project managers hired and supervised nearly 4,000 part-time personnel for promotional events.

Mrs. Failing commented on her challenges in building the field:

> I would have preferred a bigger management staff, but from the start most of Actmedia's resources had to go into sales in order to generate revenue. I had to hire people interested in other things besides maximizing salary.
>
> We decided to build a predominantly female field force for several reasons. First, women felt natural in the supermarket environment and, second, we saw housewives as a huge, relatively untapped labor pool interested in part-time work. We offered enthusiasm, some flexibility, and a personal touch. To this day, I know every one of our full-time employees across the country, and I recognize them on birthdays or special occasions. By contrast, we really couldn't offer competitive salaries until 1984.

Most ASRs and project managers (98%) were women in their 20s and 30s. Salary ranged from $10,000 to $18,000 plus a car and benefits which Mrs. Failing valued at about $7,000. "The car and flexibility are real incentives for a family seeking to augment its income," noted Mrs. Failing. "If a mother needs to pick up the kids from school, she can easily plan that into her schedule. Working hours are predictable, since each ASR has a specified route and the flights are at set times established here at headquarters. Also, the field managers find that the hiring of part-time personnel, and car-pooling together as they execute programs during each flight, generates a certain kind of hectic camaraderie."

Beyond supervising part-time personnel at the start of each cycle, ASRs also maintained the ads throughout the cycle. This entailed replacing ads that had been removed or damaged, as well as adding ads to carts that had been missed at the start of the cycle due to customer use or repairs at the time. ASRs also maintained detailed records on each Actmedia project in each store. During 1987, the company planned to issue hand-held computers to aid in these record-keeping activities.

Actnow field managers supervised part-time personnel who distributed coupons or samples in stores on designated weekends. Field reps for Actnow had a standardized greeting for each event which introduced the particular product or coupon book to customers. About 50% of Actnow reps were more than 50 years old. One rep pointed out that "the work week is relatively short (three 7-hour days), the pay is $6 per hour, and for retirees Social Security benefits are not affected if the rep earns less than $5,000 annually." Many Actnow reps also worked part time for other sampling companies that competed locally with Actmedia. Unlike ASRs for the advertising services, Actnow field managers could offer incentives to employees, such as bonuses for exceeding distribution quotas or for working several consecutive events.

All field personnel had required uniforms of blue skirts or slacks and white blouses or shirts, with aprons and red bow ties for Actnow sample distributors. In addition, noted Mrs. Failing, "Our people are instructed to be meticulous in maintaining the store's appearance, because that's what store managers care about. We emphasize that, if there is a disagreement with a store manager, the customer is *always* right."

Sales and Marketing

Actmedia's 24-person sales force was divided in 1985 into Advertising Sales, under the direction of Mr. Stevenson, and a sales force for Actnow and Impact programs, under the direction of Mickey Goodman, although both groups sold the Shelftalk product. Salespeople were compensated on commissions which were a percentage of net sales revenues (i.e., sales minus any ad-agency fees). In 1986, the commission rate was 1% for shopping cart ads, and 2% for other Actmedia products. Sales reps' expenses were paid by Actmedia. In 1986, compensation for sales personnel ranged from $70,000 to $210,000, with a median salary of about $100,000. During his or her first year with Actmedia, a new salesperson received a guaranteed draw on commission of $100,000. Including compensation, expenses, benefits and other relevant costs, the fully burdened costs of fielding a salesperson were, on average, approximately $250,000 annually.

Each Actmedia product had annual sales goals, but sales reps' goals were not broken down by product. Mr. Sturgess, senior vice president for sales and marketing, noted: "The fact is, we aren't very good at setting sales targets; but we're good at meeting them. It's hard to figure which product will get the best sales when they're all new. Our sales forecasting is rule of thumb, but morale and motivation are high." Each year, Mr. Failing, Jr. established a target for company growth, which had varied between 50% and 70% annually in the past five years. Mr. Sturgess then established growth targets for each product. Then Messrs. Stevenson, Goodman and their salespeople reviewed each brand at each account, and established overall goals for each salesperson. At 100% of target quota, the salesperson received a 15% bonus, and every sale made beyond quota yielded thrice the normal commission on that product.

In hiring salespeople, Actmedia looked for previous sales experience. Experience with a packaged-goods firm was considered a plus and experience with an ad agency a "slight minus," according to one manager, "since ad people tend to have preconceived notions about our product." Mr. Sturgess commented that "we can teach someone about our product and our customers, but we can't teach them to sell. We're selling a concept and one that still encounters lots of misunderstanding and rejections. We look for aggressive, bright, persistent people. Only one of our reps didn't make quota last year, and our best rep previously sold toys." Most salespeople were in their late 20s and early 30s, "about the same age as most brand managers," noted Mr. Stevenson.

Each salesperson was given an intensive three- to six-month training program that focused on the details of budgeting processes at packaged-goods firms, common concerns and misunderstandings about Actmedia's products, and the nature of the competitive environment facing each client's brands. Training culminated in a "final exam" role play: the trainee was instructed to prepare a 15-minute presentation about Actmedia for Messrs. Failing, Jr., Stevenson and Sturgess (who acted as brand managers and agency representatives), but when the trainee arrived, he or she was told that only five minutes could be allocated.

As well as meeting sales goals, salespeople were evaluated on "quarterly account plans, accuracy of call reports and feedback about accounts, their attitude of commitment and enthusiasm" and a factor described by Mr. Stevenson as "creative lateral thinking: the ability to brainstorm new sales tactics in the heat of the moment at an account." Mr. Sturgess pointed out that although call reports were filed, they were used by management primarily to track products sold. "Our sales-management philosophy is flexible by necessity. Our product requires our clients to change the way they do things and they still don't have a predisposition to consider or buy it. We therefore give our salespeople the freedom and responsibility to develop accounts how they think best. John, Mickey, and I try to make calls and maximize 'face time' with the salespeople to review account planning and management, rather than relying on paperwork or systematic procedures for that communication. Of course, that ongoing, direct contact becomes harder to sustain as we grow."

Sales Tasks: Advertising Products
(Shopping Carts, Aislevision, Shelftalk)

Actmedia's sales force divided its time between manufacturers' product management groups and ad agencies. Salespeople utilized presentation packages customized for a specific product or category, and stressed that in a cluttered media environment Actmedia guaranteed product category exclusivity (i.e., for each category Actmedia provided ads in each region for only one product, a feature generally unavailable in TV, radio or print advertising). Salespeople also stressed the cost efficiency of Actmedia programs compared to alternative media. A number of Actmedia's clients (e.g., in 1986 PepsiCo, Procter & Gamble, and Kimberly-Clark) had purchased all of the firm's shopping cart spaces nationally for a product category for periods of time—ranging from six months to one year. In 1986, about 30% of Actmedia's sales were from such extended-term purchases.

There were three important groups typically involved in a potential Actmedia ad sale (see Exhibit 4). The brand management group (see Exhibit 5) included the brand manager, a marketing assistant, the group product manager, and (depending on the company) perhaps the vice president of marketing. The advertising agency's account group included an account manager and an assistant as well as senior management in certain ad firms. The third group was the advertising agency's media group, which developed copy and purchased media space and usually included a media planner and media supervisors. Mr. Sturgess noted, "Informally, we subscribe to the 'two-out-of-three' theory: you need the strong support of the brand manager and then either the group product manager or an agency executive to close a sale for our ad products."

Brand managers who bought Actmedia, particularly in the early years, were described by Mr. Stevenson as "young Turks: aggressive and iconoclastic. Remember that most brand managers stay with a given brand for only one to three years, and their goal is to get promoted as soon as possible. By definition, their supervisors made their marks through media other than ours, and a perceived 'failure' usually lingers longer in the corridors of a large corporation than an in-store success."

Mr. Sturgess emphasized the importance of the client's ad agency in influencing the brand's advertising strategy and channels:

> In the early years we tended to ignore ad agencies because they wouldn't support us, and that was a mistake. We now give the agency a 15% commission on Actmedia sales even though it is atypical for an agency to be a strong supporter of Actmedia. They often have veto power over a brand's ad expenditures and, once the overall annual ad budget is established for a brand, it's very difficult to alter it. Therefore, it's important that our salespeople maintain good relations with the agencies.
>
> Despite its reputation, Madison Avenue is very conservative. For years, agencies have touted TV as the best mass medium for consumer advertising, and for a while that might have been true. But note that a multimillion dollar TV campaign requires relatively little time from agency account personnel in proportion to the 15% commissions generated, whereas it does take time for an agency media planner to figure out how to best spend, say, $100,000 on Actmedia. And few ad personnel know much about point-of-sale marketing.

Mr. Stevenson explained that "we typically get one big chance to make an ad presentation for a brand's annual budget, so we must match our proposed program to the brand's needs very closely. Therefore, the salesperson's first mandate is to learn everything possible about the client's ad plans, budgeting cycle and authorization process, meaning the people involved both formally and informally in that process." Management preferred that its salespeople find a specific problem at a brand and then present one or two Actmedia solutions, rather than presenting the range of Actmedia services, because clients were unlikely to give salespeople sufficient time or attention for the latter approach. In addition, Actmedia rarely sought more than 10% of a brand's ad budget. One reason, noted Mr. Stevenson, "is that we're still perceived as relatively new and therefore risky. But the ad agencies are another reason. Most agencies will concede, say, 5% less TV advertising in favor of Actmedia, since annual budget growth often covers that. But they'll try hard to block a sale if we usurp a large proportion of TV advertising."

Mr. Ira Lewis, an Actmedia salesman, believed an obstacle was that client budget allocations were often simply repeated from year to year. As a result, adding Actmedia meant cutting some other item. "Therefore," noted Mr. Lewis, "a salesperson has to know which portion of the ad budget performed poorly in the previous year, but this is often difficult due to the confidentiality of budgets. Also, brand managers are usually too busy during budgeting time to accept sales calls. In fact, many brand managers use their ad agencies as a 'front office' to screen callers during this crucial period." Mr. Lewis also noted that sales calls to those unacquainted with Actmedia often required the salesperson to educate the person about vehicles other than TV or coupons:

> Comfort with the concepts behind our products is the most important factor, and that takes time to develop. First, we point out how we resemble TV advertising, in order for them to put us into perspective. Then we show how we're different and better, or at least complementary. If we don't go through these steps, the client is not likely to recognize the special value of our point-of-sale presence, and will instead write us off as some gimmick since they were never taught about us in their training programs.

Marketing provided Actmedia salespeople with presentation cards outlining Actmedia's concepts, services, and advantages. These cards included numerical and graphic representations of each product's cost and scope. Each rep also had ad samples. Another tool was a fill-in-the-blanks card informally called "the game" (see Exhibit 6). The page listed several current national ad slogans with the brand names missing; the prospective buyer would be asked to identify the brands. Scores were consistently low, with entire product categories often missed. Mr. Lewis commented that "at this point brand managers would start listening harder because it reinforces fears of product interchangeability and demonstrates the low residual effect of TV ads. My favorite analogy is that, after months of advertising on TV, a political candidate would like to be at the polling booth on election day, but that's illegal. A brand manager, however, can be in the store through Actmedia."

Sales Tasks: Promotions Products (Actnow, Impact)

Actmedia's ad and promotions sales forces called on many of the same clients, but coordination at the same account was only informal. Some salespeople felt close coordination was helpful, since intelligence could be shared and certain crucial decision makers "double-teamed." But others felt this was "a waste of time," and that a joint presentation by different reps from the same company could alienate or confuse a busy brand manager.

When Actnow promotions were introduced in 1984, they did not get much sales attention. Salespeople said that promotions were new and that no explicit goals were stated. They also felt that selling the company's ad products was made more difficult by the addition of the promotions products. Mr. Goodman recalled, "Within a year, we established a dedicated sales force for Actnow, despite the fact that one reason for adding promotional services was to capitalize on existing relationships."

Mr. Goodman also noted several differences between selling Actmedia's ad and promotional services. First, promotions typically comprised twice as much of the typical brand's budget as advertising. "On the advertising side, we're a small piece of the pie; but we represent a much larger chunk of the promotions budget and a larger dollar commitment." Second, promotions were usually organized as discrete events rather than continuous policies. Consequently, clients' promotional budgets were frequently revised throughout the year, in contrast with fixed annual ad budgets. Third, "there are a limited number of companies with big promotional budgets," Mr. Goodman noted. "Consequently, word-of-mouth spreads fast." Fourth, within these companies, more functions were involved with promotions than advertising. Mr. Goodman explained:

> Often, a coupon promotion is a means for getting more or better trade placement so coordination with a manufacturer's sales force is very important. Their sales force may also need to coordinate our programs with their own trade promotions and, in some packaged-goods firms, the sales vice president often oversees all in-store merchandising programs. Unfortunately, at many of these same firms, brand management and sales management rarely talk to each other. Headquarters doesn't like brand managers explicitly competing with each other for limited sales resources, and some sales vice presidents run their organizations like "black boxes" from the brand manager's point of view. But we need to coordinate Actnow with both groups.
>
> Similarly, many manufacturers have corporate staff groups for promotional activities. These groups can sometimes be a source of "not-invented-here" resistance to our programs. But even when they support our programs, they're not always the best conduit with brand managers at that company. Each brand manager wants promotions for his or her product to be unique, but the corporate promotions group is thinking in terms of scale economies and spreading costs across regions or products. Thus, brand and promotional groups often argue or simply go their own way. In fact, we're probably one of the very few promotions vendors that even speak with brand management; most sell entirely through the promotions group.
>
> Smooth coordination and follow-up with all these internal groups is often the key to additional Actnow business at a client. By contrast, Actnow salespeople almost never speak with the ad agency.

Although costs varied depending upon the campaign, a client typically incurred the following costs for a four-week national flight of each Actmedia advertising product: Shopping Cart Ads, $320,000; Aislevision, $160,000; Shelftalk, $60,000. Promotion products were sold as two-weekend events; the average prices for national coverage were: Actnow Couponing, $300,000; Actnow Sampling, $1,000,000; Impact Demonstrations, $1.3 million.

Account Management Issues

In recent years Mr. Failing, Jr. and others had become aware of several issues that affected the company's sales efforts. One issue concerned the ambiguous positioning, in many clients' eyes, of Actmedia as an advertising or promotions firm. Actmedia initially sold its shopping cart ads primarily on the basis of increased sales results. "Hundreds of tests corroborated our effect on product movement," noted Mr. Failing, Jr., "and we stressed this fact." In the past few years, however, management had come to feel that this meant the company's ad products were perceived as promotions and that this, in turn, limited potential sales of these products due to evaluation criteria for advertising versus promotions at many packaged-goods firms. Promotions were typically evaluated in terms of incremental sales provided for a given level of spending. Advertising, on the other hand, was typically evaluated by the number of consumers exposed to it, a more abstract measure intended to provide an estimate of "consumer awareness" or "brand image" stimulated by the ad. One Actmedia manager noted:

> No one really tests advertising. Nielsen counts the people who watch a TV program and records gross demographics, but the cost of a TV ad is based on the show's ratings, not the number of purchases resulting from an ad. For most media advertising, scope is measured and effectiveness is assumed. In our clients' budgets, moreover, media costs are essentially treated as fixed while promotions are incremental costs measured on a per-item, return-on-sales basis.
>
> As a result, when our shopping cart, Aislevision or Shelftalk products are perceived as promotions (because anything in-store *must* be a promotion, according to the conventional wisdom), we must do business with our accounts on a zero-based basis each year, starting from scratch and repeatedly explaining the concept behind our service. In addition, our ad products are not intended to be—nor are they priced as—promotions. They look even better, and can sell more, when they're rightly understood as in-store advertising.

During the early 1980s, Actmedia had sought to reposition itself in clients' budgeting and measurement criteria. The company began pricing its products on a cost-per-thousand basis, as most ad media were priced, so clients could directly compare Actmedia costs with alternative ad media.

Another issue concerned the different selling dynamics that tended to accompany sales of each product. One manager commented:

> Cart ads reach nearly 100% of the consumers in a store, whereas Aislevision may reach less than 50%. But a big 20" × 30" Aislevision ad strikes some clients as more "powerful" than a smaller shopping cart ad.
>
> Nonetheless, Aislevision and cart ads are variations on the same theme compared to Shelftalk. We view Shelftalk as an ad product, but shelftalkers have a long tradition in supermarkets of being used in promotional events. So we sell Shelftalk as a crossover product through both sales forces.
>
> Finally, our products mean very different up-front costs to clients, and that also affects both the sales and account management tasks.

Some managers believed that Shelftalk, while a successful new product for Actmedia, had cannibalized a portion of Aislevision sales during 1986. "A number of brand managers see them as potentially redundant, rather than complementary, in-store vehicles," noted one manager. "They still don't make the same distinctions we do."

A third issue concerned deployment of the sales forces. Mr. Stevenson explained:

> Instead of assigning salespeople based on types of manufacturers' products, ad agencies used, or geography, we try to organize based on the individuals who do the buying at packaged-goods firms. So when we assign a salesperson to a firm, we recommend initially focusing on one or two brands. As our supporters at those brands spread to other parts of the firm, we'll try to follow them. Remember that brand managers can be rotated through several brands in less than two years. We try to keep continuity with the people who have bought us, even when they move on to other brands or other companies.
>
> Frequency of contact is also important for us. We'll be part of a client's budget for advertising only if we get there at the right time, since brands tend to work on long cycles that are fairly rigid because of production scheduling, trade promotions, and the involvement of other functions with a given brand. If we miss a client's budgeting period, we can lose the entire year's ad business at that client. So it's important to have a supporter inside brand management to alert us to critical budgeting periods and issues.
>
> We still sell to brands, not companies. So when we find supporters, we don't want to lose track of them. But these contacts and this deployment of the sales forces become harder to manage as we grow, add more salespeople, products and channels, and as our champions move within and across manufacturers.

A salesperson for Actmedia added:

> The rapid movement of brand management can help to spread allies, but it also tends to limit the time horizons for buying our products. Within a given brand, I must develop new relations and credibility almost annually. It's not uncommon, for example, to find that new brand management is unaware that previous managers for that brand have already tested Actmedia's products two or three times.

During the mid-1980s, moreover, a number of large packaged-goods firms appeared to be moving toward increasingly regionalized marketing programs and organizations. This trend appeared to be in response to scanner-generated data that revealed important regional differences formerly hidden when these data were not collected. One result of "regional marketing" was often an additional layer of marketing management at these firms in order to coordinate different regional programs, and restrictions on a brand manager's ability to develop national programs. Conversely, regional sales managers at these firms often had increased influence on the development, as well as execution, of local ad and promotional efforts. Managers at Actmedia were unsure if regional marketing was indeed a meaningful long-term trend at packaged-goods firms and, if so, what the implications might be for Actmedia's sales and account management practices.

Conclusion

Commenting in December 1986 on Actmedia, Mr. Failing, Jr., said:

> Our biggest constraints are personnel related. In sales, for competitive reasons, we need more people selling more spaces into more stores. Right now, however, our growing product line and new retail channels for those products are outstripping our sales and marketing capacity. We're also planning a number of new products for 1987, some of which are similar to existing programs and some of which are new departures for us. That's why we will double the sales force during the first quarter of 1987, and perhaps add more people throughout the year.
>
> More generally, at the rate we've grown during the past five years, management systems can easily wear thin. We still manage more by intuition than is perhaps desirable at this stage of our company's growth.

Given these changes, Mr. Failing, Jr., was considering several options for reorganizing Actmedia's sales efforts: by product, by account size or account type, and a hybrid organization combining account and product specialists.

Although Actmedia had divided its sales force into Ads and Promotions products in 1985, some managers felt the company's growth required a further subdivision of the sales force in order to ensure better product knowledge and concentration of effort by salespeople, especially for new products and new channels. Some managers believed new products would not get the attention they needed to become successful if they were sold by a full-line ad sales force, and that rapid roll-out of new products into new channels was strategically important. "Time, Inc. has a different sales force for each magazine," noted one manager, "because each provides a different audience and medium to potential advertisers, and because effective selling requires a dedicated 'champion' for each magazine. A full-line sales force would gravitate to the established magazines and neglect the others. We're evolving toward a similar situation. Our salespeople can lose touch with the dynamics of each product, and neglect new products in favor of established vehicles at established accounts."

Other managers were worried that separate sales forces would "confuse" customers or perhaps cause Actmedia salespeople to "compete" with each other for a given customer's time and money. Further, these managers believed that attention to new products and channels did not require redeployment of the sales force. "We can accomplish this objective either by changing the commission rates by product or by giving our salespeople individual quotas for each product," suggested one manager.

Another option was to organize the sales force by account size. One proponent of this idea explained:

Our products don't differ as much as our customers do. You can learn about
Aislevision quickly, but understanding the subtleties of selling to P&G via
Benton & Bowles is a long, complex and ever-changing process. Also, because of
cost considerations, some of our products seem better suited for larger companies and some for smaller companies. Focusing our salespeople by account
size could allow the rep to develop insights common to the group concerning
budgetary constraints, timing, brand development, product introductions and
other matters.

Other managers located the important differences in account type rather
than account size. "We should organize the sales force by the nature of the
product category being sold by our customers," said one manager. "The
dynamics of selling in-store programs for salty-snack companies is different than
those for coffee companies, and these differences between product categories
are more important to our sales efforts than the differences between a big
account and a little account."

A fourth option was what one manager described as a "hybrid" approach:

We sell to the brand, not the corporation; so distinctions between companies are
not as important as distinctions between brands. Brands from national and
regional firms, big and little firms, new and established brands, can still compete
for the same shopper and the same market. At the same time, our selling
process requires continuity with individual companies, because our supporters
in brand management move frequently.

Therefore, we should have a team organization in our sales efforts: an account manager assigned by company and Actmedia product specialists (shopping cart specialists, Aislevision specialists, etc.) assigned by the account
manager to specific brands within that company. This way, we can keep continuity of contact, familiarity with a given company's budgeting processes, and
still focus attention on our different products.

Other managers believed the "hybrid" approach was "an interesting idea," but
"probably a pain to manage. We must keep things simple administratively; at
the pace we're going, we can't afford to work in fancy structures that require a
lot of coordination."

Finally, some in Actmedia believed the company should not be concerned
with issues of sales organization. "We're growing like crazy and still building
primary demand for our in-store programs," said one manager. "So questions of
reorganization are irrelevant, sap precious management time and energy, and
can demotivate the sales force by making them wonder if taking time to develop
business at a given account will pay off for them. Besides, all the options I've heard
run the risk of turning this place into a bureaucracy. Keep things as they are now."

Another issue facing the company was recruitment criteria for the
salespeople. "We're doubling our sales force soon," noted Mr. Failing, Jr., "but
we haven't really clarified what kind of people we want. In recent years, we've
hired about two salespeople for every one we keep, and that takes a toll in terms
of expenses, opportunity costs at accounts, and management time and atten-

tion. What should we be looking for when we expand our sales efforts? Is there any common denominator or background experience that can help us make our recruitment efforts more focused and efficient? Have the selling requirements changed since John, Jeff and I *were* the sales force for Actmedia?"

Exhibit 1 Actmedia, Inc.

Financial Performance
(all figures in thousands of dollars)

Year	Sales	Profit (Loss)
1974	$ 180	($ 476)
1975	649	(534)
1976	1,336	(196)
1977	1,913	(388)
1978	1,615	(965)
1979	2,084	(13)
1980	2,311	(253)
1981	4,740	401
1982	8,452	460
1983	14,690	1,304
1984	23,587	2,243
1985	44,014	3,694
1986	64,500	5,100

Statement of Operations

(dollars in thousands, except per share amounts)

	Year Ended December 31,		
	1984	1985	1986
Revenue			
Net advertising and promotion revenue	$20,518	$38,707	$56,361
Production revenue	2,383	4,878	8,522
Testing and other revenue	685	429	529
Revenue	$23,586	$44,014	$65,412
Cost of Sales			
Store commissions	$ 4,749	$ 6,933	$12,119
Production costs	2,052	5,495	8,551
Testing and other costs	870	495	770
	$ 7,671	$12,923	$21,440
Field Expenses			
Field salaries and related costs	$ 4,113	$12,983	$15,861
Field force expenses	2,033	2,934	3,510
Other field expenses	952	3,302	4,734
	$ 7,098	$19,219	$24,105
Gross Profit	$ 8,817	$11,872	$19,867
Selling Expenses	$ 2,900	$ 3,213	$ 6,436
General and Administrative Expenses	2,436	4,751	6,006
Interest, Dividend and Sundry Income	(832)	(1,586)	(1,225)
Income before income taxes	$ 4,313	$ 5,494	$ 8,650
Provisions for Income Taxes	2,070	1,800	3,700
Net income	$ 2,243	$ 3,694	$ 4,950
Earnings per share	$.24	$.34	$.42

(continued)

Exhibit 1   (continued)

Balance Sheet
(dollars in thousands)

	December 31, 1985	December 31, 1986
Assets		
Current assets:		
Cash (includes $1,234 and $2,631 of interest bearing deposits)	$ 1,374	$ 2,696
Marketable securities at cost (which approximates market value)	15,874	18,087
Accounts receivable—trade	10,010	11,527
Display devices	1,617	2,177
Prepaid store commissions		1,207
Refundable income taxes	397	
Prepaid expenses	867	1,025
Other current assets	1,025	999
Total Current Assets	$31,164	$37,718
Marketable securities at cost (which approximates market value)	4,165	3,616
Aisle directories, leasehold improvements and equipment at cost, less accumulated depreciation	6,602	9,118
Contract rights	1,779	3,269
Other assets	953	778
	$44,663	$54,499
Liabilities and Common Stockholder's Equity		
Current liabilities:		
Accounts payable—trade	$ 2,228	$ 2,824
Store commissions payable	1,606	4,060
Accrued payroll and related cost	958	1,674
Accrued expenses	1,266	308
Income taxes payable		590
Deferred income taxes	103	208
Deferred income	1,416	2,502
Total Current Liabilities	$ 7,577	$12,166
Commitments and contingencies		
Common stockholders' equity:		
Common stock—40,000,000 shares authorized	$ 116	$ 117
Additional paid-in capital	32,324	32,620
Retained earnings	4,646	9,596
Total Common Stockholders' Equity	$37,086	$42,333
	$44,663	$54,499

Exhibit 2   Actmedia, Inc.

Actmedia Product Line: 1986

Shopping Card Ads

Ads inside every Actmedia
Cart keep the product's message in front of the shopper
pushing the cart; ads on the
outside of every cart present
a "rolling billboard" to every
other shopper.

Aislevision

With the dominant presence
of an AisleVision directory,
the advertised brand virtually
"owns the aisle" in which it is
located.

Shelftalk

In 1987, a second version of
the ShelfTalk program will be
introduced, allowing manufacturers to place "take one"
coupons on the shelf adjacent
to the product being
promoted.

Impact

The Impact program allows
consumers to see, in person,
how a product works or what it
tastes like. Free samples and
coupons maintain their interest and encourage purchase.

Actnow

Actnow Co-op events are supported throughout the store
with product displays, the
"personal selling" efforts of
our in-store representatives
and reminders on the shelf

Exhibit 3 Actmedia, Inc.

Actmedia, Inc. Organization

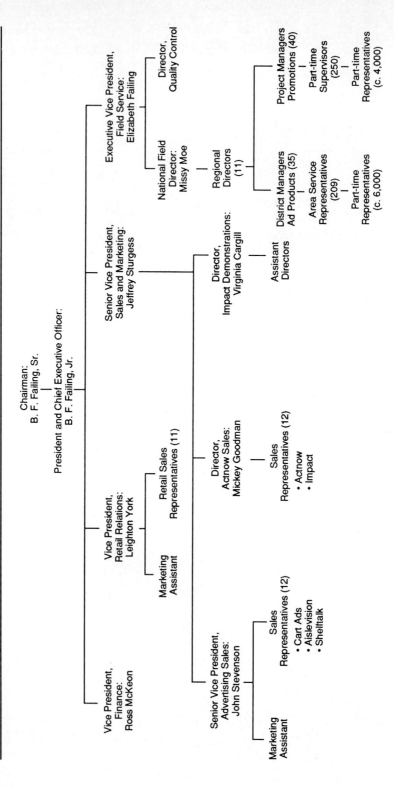

Exhibit 4 Actmedia, Inc.

Personnel Typically Contacted During Sales Process

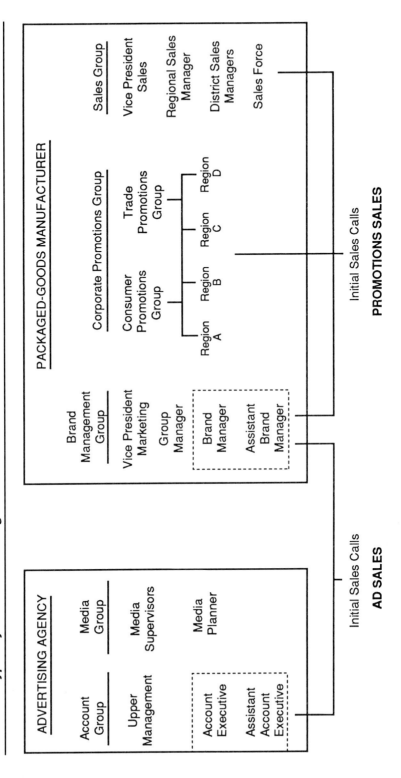

Exhibit 5 Actmedia, Inc.

**Brand Management Organization at a Large Consumer Packaged-Goods Company:
Desserts Division Organization Chart**

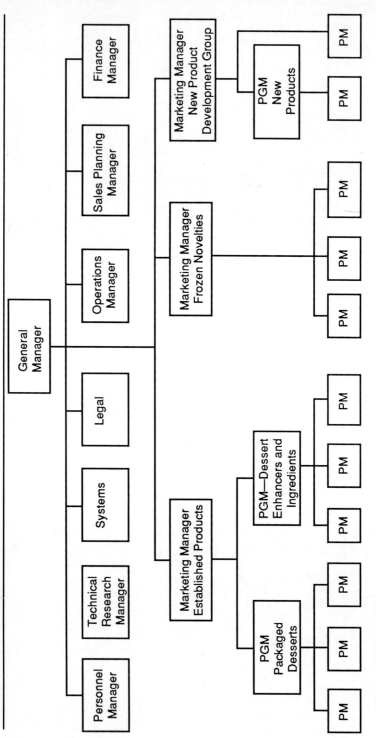

PM = Product Manager
PGM = Product Group Manager

Exhibit 6 Actmedia, Inc.

The Game

Actmedia fills in the blanks

1_____ : "Helps hands look younger."

2 Extra-Strength_____ :
  "Nothing you can buy is stronger."

3_____ : "America's leading
  high nutrition cereal."

4_____ : "Stops wetness better than any
  leading anti-perspirant spray."

5_____ : "For your best coffee times"

6_____ : "A clean so clean, you can
  feel it."

Some of the country's leading advertisers have spent millions of dollars establishing these campaigns. Are they getting their money's worth? If you can't fill in the blanks in 30 seconds, they're not!

Cox Cable Jefferson Parish
250 Plauche Street
Harahan, Louisiana 70123

To: Kevin Kidd, Customer Operations Manager
From: Franklin Bowers, General Manager
Date: Monday, April 30, 1984
Re: Greetings!

Glad to have you on board at last! Sorry I could not be in the office to welcome you personally, but meetings with city and county officials will keep me busy this week. As promised, though, I have enclosed information about our situation here in Jefferson Parish.

Some vital statistics: so far this year, we are behind budgeted forecasts for the number of subscribers on the system, and despite heavy promotions, new subscribers are getting harder to find in JP. We also lose about three percent of our subscriber base each month to "churn"—i.e., people disconnecting the service for some reason. A particular concern is the number of subscribers we must disconnect because they do not pay their bills. These non-pay disconnects cost us a lot of time and money.

You will find that different people have different opinions about churn and how to deal with it. But we must address this problem soon. On Friday, I would like to meet with you to hear your preliminary plans concerning our marketing efforts here in JP.

On his first day as customer operations manager for Cox Cable's Jefferson Parish franchise (JP), Mr. Kevin Kidd sat sweating in his new office. Jefferson Parish, a suburb of New Orleans, was in the midst of an early heat wave, and the air conditioner in Mr. Kidd's office was awaiting repair.

This case was prepared by Associate Professor Frank V. Cespedes and Research Assistant Ellen R. Hattemer as the basis for class discussion rather than to illustrate either effective or ineffective handling of an administrative situation.

Since 1982, Mr. Kidd had been a director of marketing at Cox Cable's headquarters in Atlanta; before joining Cox, he was director of marketing for a large Atlanta bank. When the previous JP customer operations manager left the company, Mr. Kidd had accepted the opportunity to hold a key line position in the field. Now, as the clanking of tools signalled the arrival of air conditioning repair personnel, Mr. Kidd stared at the stack of sales and marketing data on his desk. He reflected that, by comparison, the climate in Atlanta had been balmy.

Industry Background

Cable television was developed in the late 1940s to serve areas unreachable by over-the-air television broadcasts. Cable companies constructed tall antennas to process signals from remote broadcast transmissions. Then the signals were fed past households by coaxial cable, either attached to utility poles above the ground or installed underground. A "cable drop" connected a subscriber to the cable system. In 1974, the advent of satellite broadcasting transformed the cable industry: formerly a distribution mechanism for network television, the cable industry widened its marketing horizons to include nearly every U. S. household with a television set by offering viewers a greater assortment of programming than that available on network television.

Between 1978 and 1984, the cable industry's installed plant more than doubled to approximately 616,000 miles of cable, passing more than 61 million homes. During this same time period, the number of "basic" cable subscribers grew to about 34 million and the number of "premium" or "pay"[1] cable subscriptions increased to 29 million. Estimates indicated that 85% of all U.S. households with television could be reached by cable; of these, about 86% were passed by cable plant by the end of 1984.

Cable companies incurred high fixed costs since a company had to pass all homes in a given area with cable plant to sign up typically half of those homes as subscribers. As a result, according to one observer, "Pricing and other elements of marketing were driven by return-on-assets goals and operating cash flow requirements. Cable was originally an engineer's business, dominated by technicians and pole-climbers; then a sales business where the focus was (and is) on selling a package door-to-door. It is just starting to become a marketing-oriented business."

By the early 1980s, most cable systems offered more than 30 channels of programming. A subscription for basic cable cost the viewer $6.00 to $12.00 per month and typically included the following choices:

1. network broadcasts via local affiliates;

---

[1]To subscribe, a customer had to purchase basic cable service, and could then choose to pay additional monthly fees for premium or pay channels.

2. community access programming which covered local government, health care, education topics, and sometimes a variety of ethnically oriented programs;
3. broadcasts from unaffiliated local TV stations;
4. satellite-transmitted broadcasts from "superstations" such as Turner Broadcasting's WTBS, the Christian Broadcasting Network, and ESPN (22 hours of sports and 2 hours of business news daily); and
5. news, weather, and other information in text format.

Subscribers could also choose to pay an extra $5.00 to $15.00 for a premium or pay channel, such as:

6. Home Box Office (movies, plays, and special shows);
7. Showtime (movies and shows);
8. Cinemax (principally movies);
9. Disney ("children's entertainment"); or
10. Playboy ("adult entertainment").

Most cable systems offered subscribers at least two pay channels, and some offered discounts on subscriptions to multiple premium services. Although many homes opted only for the basic service, 1983 data indicated that users in dual pay systems subscribed on average to 1.4 pay services and those in triple pay systems to 1.6 pay services.

Programs were purchased by a cable system for a fee, with the exception of network broadcasts (which were free of charge) and community access programming (which was developed jointly by the cable company and local organizations). Cable companies negotiated with program suppliers a monthly rate for services in categories 3, 4, and 5 based on the number of system subscribers, and they turned over to the suppliers of premium services (items 6 through 10) a percentage, ranging from 30–50%, of the monthly fee paid by each subscriber.

The Franchise

The right to build and operate a cable franchise was granted by local governments on a competitive bid basis. Firms interested in a given franchise submitted proposals detailing program offerings, subscription rates, franchise fees, and any additional services the company was willing to provide. Once granted a franchise, the cable operator had the right and responsibility to build and manage the system as agreed upon in the franchise contract (see Exhibit 1 for excerpts from the JP contract). However, each time the cable company wanted to amend the terms of the agreement (e.g., raise rates or change the number of channels) more interaction with the local government was required.

Cable operators ranged from small companies having only one franchise to multiple system operators such as Cox Cable and American Tele-Communications Inc., each operating more than fifty franchises. Since 1974, multiple system operators had grown rapidly by acquiring existing systems or developing new systems.

In the late 1970s, cable entrepreneurs moved aggressively to secure franchise rights and to construct major metropolitan systems. One observer noted, "Those were the halcyon days, with visions of 128-channel systems, two-way interactive services, pay-per-view, three-to-one pay to basic penetration levels, and $50 per subscriber monthly revenues. In this context, some unreal agreements were signed to secure franchises from local authorities. In the franchise-frenzy phase, moreover, many cable firms focused on the activities necessary to acquire franchise rights, while often ignoring the daily operations of existing franchises." By 1984, several prominent cable operators were losing money and had petitioned their local governments for changes in the original franchise agreements. Additionally, revenue growth through new franchise development had become limited. As a result, many cable operators had begun to emphasize selling additional advertising during programming hours as a source of revenue growth.

Passage of the Cable Communications Policy Act of 1984 had potentially significant implications for the industry. Among the act's provisions were:

1. entitlement for all systems to increase basic rates by 5% per year in 1985 and 1986, unless rates were explicitly fixed under the franchise agreement;
2. by 1987, rate deregulation for systems in markets categorized as having "effective competition"—i.e., a certain level of broadcast TV coverage as defined by the Federal Communications Commission (JP was expected to qualify);
3. procedures for a franchise renewal process that would protect cable operators from arbitrary challenges; and
4. capping of franchise fees and other monetary contributions to the local governments at 5% of a system's gross revenues.

Some observers believed these deregulatory developments would increase industry profitability greatly. Others were skeptical of the actual impact of federal policy on local governments' behavior. In the words of one cable manager:

Cable is a beautifully visible issue for local politicians, and they won't give it up easily. Besides, while the Cable Act may deregulate subscription rates in some areas by 1987, local governments will still control enough other aspects of cabling, such as the use of utility poles, to influence strongly the prices we charge. In addition, you can bet local governments will be monitoring their cable operators especially closely during the interim.

Competition

Except in the initial bidding for a franchise, cable companies rarely competed with each other for local markets. Instead, competition for a cable operator included other services or products that vied for consumers' discretionary entertainment dollars. Sporting events, the theater, concerts and restaurants were perceived as some of the alternatives to cable subscriptions.

In addition, there were competing technologies for the provision of in-home entertainment and information services. By 1984, over 11% of U.S. households (over 20% in California) had video cassette recorders (VCRs), which allowed users to play video tapes on their TVs and in most cases to tape TV programming. Penetration by VCRs was expected to increase dramatically in coming years as equipment prices fell and local outlets for tape rentals became more numerous.

Industry observers were divided about the future impact of VCRs on cable subscriptions. Some believed VCRs would adversely affect cable sales, particularly sales of multipay packages. Others believed that cable and VCRs were complementary products: since customers could use their VCRs to record programming, cable's many program offerings might be more attractive to households with VCRs.

Another competing technology was the satellite dish, which was originally marketed in 1980 to the 15% of U.S. homes unreachable by cable. Costing $3,000 on average, a satellite dish allowed the purchaser to receive free satellite transmissions, including up to 115 channels of broadcast, cable, and foreign programming. By early 1984, about 350,000 dishes had been sold, many to customers with access to cable.

However, the major premium services such as HBO and Showtime, unhappy with the lost subscriber revenues, had announced plans to scramble their transmission signals. Dish owners would then need to buy an unscrambling device, estimated at $400, and also pay a monthly fee to the premium services. Some observers believed the combination of high equipment price and the impending inability to get movie channels for free lessened the threat to cable.

Company Background

Cox Communications, Inc. (CCI) was formed in 1934 by James Cox, Democratic Presidential candidate in 1920 and former governor of Ohio. Originally involved in radio broadcasting, the company branched into television in 1948 with the start of WSB-TV in Atlanta. In 1984, CCI operated in three business segments: broadcasting (radio and television stations as well as TeleRep, a firm which developed and sold programming to 45 independent television stations, including six Cox-owned operations); wholesale automobile auctions; and Cox Cable. (Exhibit 2 provides financial information about the corporation.) Although CCI went public in 1964, the Cox family owned 40% of the company's common stock. CCI had an unbroken history of increased earnings per share since 1964.

Cox Cable

In 1984, Cox Cable was the fourth largest cable company in the United States with 54 franchises and over 1.4 million subscribers (see Exhibit 3). During the past five years, the corporate parent had invested more than $600 million in its cable subsidiary. Mr. David Van Valkenburg became president of Cox Cable in 1982. Mr. Van Valkenburg was a graduate of Harvard Business School and had worked as an investment analyst and then as chief operating officer for another cable firm before joining Cox.

Senior vice presidents for finance, engineering and technology, human resources, marketing and programming, and operations reported to Mr. Van Valkenburg (see Exhibit 4). Corporate marketing functions included market and industry research, assisting the field in developing telemarketing, promotional, and direct selling techniques, interfranchise communication, and program acquisition. Corporate Cox Cable negotiated with the suppliers of programming to determine monthly rates. Then the local franchises chose which of the numerous program offerings to air. Sometimes corporate Cox guaranteed a supplier a certain number of subscribers in order to get the programming; in these cases, local franchises had to air that programming.

Four senior vice presidents were responsible for the operations of Cox's 54 franchises. These senior vice presidents worked with the franchise general managers to develop annual operating budgets based on targets for the number of subscribers in a franchise. General managers were held accountable for their franchises' performances against these budgets: compensation included bonuses of up to 40% of salary, and 60% of a general manager's bonus was determined by performance against budget. The remainder of the bonus depended upon the attainment of other objectives agreed to at the beginning of the year, such as total employee headcount or turnover.

The Jefferson Parish Franchise

Cox Cable began operations in Jefferson Parish, Louisiana, in 1978, and by 1983, over 91,000 subscribers made JP Cox's third largest cable system. From 1980 to 1983, revenues grew at a compound annual rate of 52% as the number of basic subscribers increased annually by 23% and the number of pay subscriptions by 37% (see Exhibit 5).

The Market

By early 1984, Cox had provided cable access to most homes in JP, and new construction had all but ceased. Basic cable penetration had leveled off at close to 60% of homes passed by cable plant, and the pay-to-basic penetration level was approximately 1.5.

Like Louisiana, JP was poorer than the rest of the country with a 1980 median income of $21,921, 5% lower than the national average. Within the parish, the poorest neighborhood had a median income of $13,235 while the wealthiest neighborhood averaged $26,202. One in ten residents was unemployed.

During the 1970s, JP grew by one-third to over 430,000 people. Since 1980, growth was concentrated in the Black and Hispanic populations. Three-fourths of the households in JP were single family, of which 60% were owner-occupied; the remaining one-fourth were apartments.

A telephone survey in JP showed that basic cable penetration varied by race, income, age and time in residence (see Exhibit 6). Of Cox's subscribers, over half were white-collar workers, one-sixth blue-collar workers, and the rest were retired or unemployed.

Residents of JP had a wide range of entertainment options. In addition to seven regular television stations, the county had 32 movie theaters with tickets priced at about $5.00. The greater New Orleans area offered cultural events including opera, symphony, theater and concerts, as well as sports events such as professional football, wrestling, thoroughbred racing, and golf tournaments. Louisiana, billed as "A Sportsman's Paradise," provided numerous hunting and fishing opportunities, although outdoor activity was limited during the late spring and summer by the humidity and frequent showers.

JP residents could purchase a satellite dish from two local vendors for about $3,150, while 33% of Cox subscribers owned VCRs.

Marketing at JP

Basic cable service in JP consisted of 30 channels including the seven publicly available (see Exhibit 7). For a monthly fee of $10.95, increased from $7.50 in April 1984, viewers received basic programming which included the Nashville Network, MTV, and Cable News Network. Cox grossed 84% on basic cable service after programming expenses. Pay services were Showtime, Cinemax, Home Box Office, and the Playboy Channel; customers paid an additional $11.00 monthly for the first pay channel, $9.00 for the second pay channel, and $8.00 for each additional one. Gross margins on pay services averaged 39%.

In March 1984, the distribution of new sales was as follows: 13% were basic service only; 23% were basic plus one pay channel; 27% were basic plus two pay channels; 32% were basic plus three pay channels; and 5% were basic plus four pay channels. Installation cost a new subscriber $25.00 but this was discounted to $10.00 for customers ordering two or more pay channels.

Marketing promotions had three sources: corporate Cox Cable, the pay services, and the local marketing budget. Corporate Cox Cable provided bill inserts, direct mailings, industry market research, preview tapes of the next month's program offerings, and other promotions which would be prohibitively expensive on the scale of one franchise. Pay service suppliers individually negotiated with local franchises to offer cooperative advertising (typically a 50–50 expense split) and promotions such as incentive contests for sales representatives and subscription prizes for new customers. At any given time, there was usually a promotion running from at least one of the pay channels.

Roughly half of the local marketing budget paid the sales reps' commissions. The remainder was used to pay the marketing and sales staff, to match the pay services' expenditures on cooperative advertising, and to advertise on radio and television. However, franchises frequently offered discounted or free installation, or a free month of basic cable, and charged these promotions against revenues instead of listing them as marketing expenses.

The Sales Force

As customer operations manager, Mr. Kidd was responsible for marketing, sales, and customer service; 85% of Cox's JP sales were made by the 25 sales representatives, with 15% initiated by the customer through a phone call to one of JP's 20 customer service representatives. The sales force was supervised by two general sales managers.

In March 1984, all JP sales reps were between the ages of 23 and 35. All had high school educations and some had college degrees. Half had been with Cox for less than 18 months and, for most, Cox Cable JP was their first or second experience as a salesperson.

Cox hired sales reps frequently because 50% of new hires left within two weeks. The sales managers ascribed this turnover to the "arduous nature of door-to-door selling." Most applications to Cox Cable were referred by Cox employees or attracted by recruiting ads which appeared in the local papers. Training consisted of a five-day program concentrating on product knowledge and selling techniques.

Sales reps were paid bi-weekly and the average annual compensation was $23,000. Payment was entirely on commission which varied with the service level purchased by the customer (see Exhibit 8). So far in 1984, commissions were averaging about $19 per sale. Sales reps earned their commissions upon installation of cable service in the customer's home. Average earnings for six experienced JP reps over the past two years are presented in Exhibit 9. Management believed that, by industry standards, the JP sales force was both more stable and better paid than the typical cable sales force.

Most reps worked three to four hours in the evening, usually starting at 5 P.M. selling cable door-to-door to meet their bi-weekly quotas.[2] Reps were free to sell anywhere within the parish and they often travelled together to neigh-

---

[2]Reps were expected to sell 140 "units" of cable every two weeks. Each basic cable subscription and each pay channel counted as a unit. Thus, an order for basic plus three pay channels counted as four units.

borhoods and apartment complexes, competing informally to make sales. Some sales leads came from telephone inquiries to the sales office[3] and were shared each morning among the reps. Reps not meeting quota were excluded from these leads.

Selling Cable Television

Sales reps relied on certain themes to gain residents' attention. To add urgency to the purchase decision, reps told potential customers when Cox Cable installation trucks would be in their area for a neighbor's installation and emphasized any current promotions or installation discounts. Reps also stressed that customers had to pay $10 to $25 to upgrade their service (e.g., add a pay channel), but that downgrades were free. Similarly, sales reps pointed out that customers could cancel the service at any time with no penalty. One rep commented:

> The thing I hear most from people is, "I don't need cable." My reaction is that they're absolutely right—cable TV is not a necessity, but I can list a lot of reasons why they should want cable.
>
> Persistence is the key to success: a door-to-door salesperson can't take no for an answer. I've closed many a sale after the customer has "rejected" me four or five times. The first thing I try to do is to get in the door. If I can capture the resident's interest just long enough to get inside, my chances of making a sale improve dramatically.
>
> Here in JP, there is good camaraderie among the reps; we always sell together, which makes the constant rejections easier to take. Of course, I like the relatively short hours and freedom of the job, too.

When a customer purchased cable, the sales rep completed the application form (Exhibit 10), scheduled the installation, and collected the deposit. The rep submitted the paperwork and payment the following morning, and posted the previous evening's sales on chalkboards in the sales office before attending a one-hour daily sales meeting at 10 A.M. (After the meeting, reps were free to schedule appointments by phone, make other selling arrangements or go home.) On the agreed installation date, Plant Operations sent a truck to install the cable service: the cable passing the customer's house was brought inside, and the customer was given a converter box wired for the specified program offerings. The customer was then billed one month in advance for the specified cable service.

In general, reps preferred to sell to apartments versus single-family residences, both because the distances were shorter and because apartment residents seemed to move more frequently, opening up new customers for cable.

---

[3]The advertised phone number for Cox Cable connected potential customers with the customer service reps who sold cable over the phone. Calls to the sales office were usually generated by flyers which the sales reps distributed door-to-door.

Customer Behavior and Costs

Like many cable franchises, JP lost about 3% of its customers each month. Mr. Bowers had recently commissioned a survey to determine why subscribers disconnected (see Exhibit 11).

Mr. Bowers had also commissioned a study of historical customer behavior in JP. One result of the study was an analysis of the status of subscribers sold in recent months (Exhibit 12). Another result was an indication of the costs of various transactions. Data from 1983 concluded that the average installation cost Cox Cable $54.00, including the sales commission, paper processing, and installation costs. Nonpay disconnects cost $127.50 on average: $33.50 for the labor, vehicle, customer service, and collection costs to disconnect the customer; $29.00 for the unrecovered converter box; and $65.00 for bad debt expense. Other disconnects, downgrades, and upgrades cost $18.50 for the labor and vehicle costs to pick up or swap the converter box. A summary of transactions by residence type (apartment or single-family home) in one month, October 1983, is included as Exhibit 14.

The study also examined customer behavior over time by pay level (Exhibit 13) and by type of residence (Exhibit 14). The study also found that, after five months as subscribers, 65% of pay customers had received at least one delinquent notice as compared to 52% of basic-only subscribers; similarly, after five months 66% of apartment subscribers had received at least one delinquent notice as compared to 44% of single-family home subscribers.

Management also estimated that a basic customer had to be a subscriber for six months before the JP franchise recouped its costs of installing and servicing that customer, franchise fees, and other variable costs. Including the amortized costs of plant construction, a basic customer had to be a subscriber for 11 months before JP recouped its total costs of servicing that customer.

Conclusion

During the week, Mr. Kidd spoke with sales reps, the sales managers, and others in Jefferson Parish. Many suggestions were offered about how to increase sales and reduce churn. One suggestion was to assign territories to the reps, segregating apartments from single-family residences. Another suggestion was to change the basis of the sales commission from new sales to "net gain" in revenues. For example, commissions might be tied to a rep's new installs less the number of disconnects over a period of time. Others questioned the make-up of the sales force: should Cox employ full-time or part-time people, and were career people preferable to people who worked only a few months as a JP salesperson?

On Thursday evening, Mr. Kidd remained at his desk long after sundown, shivering under the blasts of his rejuvenated air conditioner. He reviewed what he had learned about the JP market and about Cox's sales and marketing programs. As he began to formulate an initial marketing plan, he recalled several comments he had heard during the past week:

Cable sales reps are migrant workers—there is little you can do to motivate them besides commission.

Churn is a fact of life in cable. The only way to combat it is to add bodies faster than you lose them. Besides, retention is harder to measure than acquisition.

The issue is not whether the churn level is high or low, good or bad, but can you do a few effective things which will provide a good return on your marketing investment?

The meeting with Mr. Bowers was scheduled for 10 A.M. the following day.

Exhibit 1   Cox Cable (A)

Cox Cable Jefferson Parish
Excerpts from the Franchise Agreement

01.   FRANCHISE GRANT.   In consideration of the faithful performance and observation of the conditions and reservations herein specified and in consideration of the payments of the amounts provided herein, the right is granted to Cox Cable to erect, operate, and maintain a system of electronic transmission and distribution facilities . . . for the period provided for in this contract.

03.   POLES.   Cox Cable shall make attachments to poles already in existence within the Parish of Jefferson, Louisiana, and shall make such installations so as to preserve the best possible esthetic standards of the community. To the extent that existing poles are insufficient for its purposes, Cox Cable may erect and maintain its own poles with the approval of the appropriate authority of the Parish of Jefferson.

06.   ACCESS CHANNELS.   Cox Cable shall provide at least one educational access channel and one public access channel free of charge.

08.   SUBSCRIBER CONTRACT.   No contract as to length of service for a regular monthly subscriber shall be required by Cox Cable. Additionally Cox Cable shall not charge a fee for disconnecting or downgrading the service level.

09.   RATES.   The original maximum charge which may be levied for installations is $25.00 for the first connection or reconnection or transfer of service and $20.00 for each additional connection in the same dwelling. Cox Cable shall not increase its rates without prior approval by the Parish Council.

12.   COMPENSATION.   In further consideration of the granting of this franchise Cox Cable will pay to the Parish of Jefferson for the first through fifth years 2% of gross subscriber revenues and during the sixth through the fifteenth years 3% of gross subscriber revenues.

Exhibit 2 Cox Cable (A)

Cox Communications, Inc.: Financial Data by Business Segment

For the Year Ended December 31 (thousands of dollars)	1983	1982	1981	1980	1979
Net Revenues					
Broadcasting	$231,457	$216,085	$181,664	$155,140	$133,678
Cable television	337,421	261,525	188,492	125,888	90,869
Automobile auctions	44,103	33,986	30,886	25,769	22,113
Other operations	1,642	3,150	2,455	2,435	2,152
Consolidated	$614,623	$514,746	$403,497	$309,232	$248,812
Operating Income					
Broadcasting	$ 87,125	$ 76,029	$ 66,562	$ 57,501	$ 51,184
Cable television	45,446	37,684	30,520	21,840	21,791
Automobile auctions	17,005	13,361	12,735	9,705	7,645
Other operations	211	56	(69)	333	(310)
Corporate expense	(8,705)	(8,955)	(4,840)	(4,006)	(3,267)
Consolidated	$141,082	$118,175	$104,908	$ 85,373	$ 77,044
Income from Continuing Operations Before Income Taxes					
Operating income	$141,082	$118,175	$104,908	$ 85,373	$ 77,044
Interest expense	(17,422)	(12,783)	(12,145)	(6,957)	(5,093)
Other income (Expense) net	2,920	(4,785)	1,085	4,617	1,682
consolidated	$126,580	$100,607	$ 93,848	$ 83,033	$ 73,633
Identifiable Assets					
Broadcasting	$236,563	$213,861	$179,529	$164,407	$143,112
Cable television	633,644	541,157	391,125	252,490	186,151
Automobile auctions	42,050	34,552	25,590	23,871	21,281
Other operations	1,888	2,217	3,254	5,138	5,703
Corporate	26,118	8,359	4,874	15,439	6,665
Discontinued operations					16,179
Consolidated	$940,263	$800,146	$604,372	$461,345	$379,091
Depreciation and Amortization					
Broadcasting	$ 8,870	$ 9,063	$ 6,228	$ 5,008	$ 4,188
Cable television	65,975	46,111	32,443	22,446	16,896
Automobile auctions	1,522	1,145	1,054	1,159	1,099
Additions to Plant and Equipment					
Broadcasting	$ 13,457	$ 21,367	$ 11,503	$ 15,861	$ 7,847
Cable television	158,358	215,095	141,476	77,373	54,124
Automobile auctions	8,167	6,421	1,289	3,023	1,596
Net income	$ 77,950	$ 65,421	$ 55,490	$ 56,399	$ 43,767

Exhibit 3   Cox Cable (A)

Cox Cable Systems

System Locations	Basic Subscribers	Premium Service Subscriptions	Number of Premium Services
San Diego, California	235,320	183,056	6
Norfolk, Portsmouth & Virginia Beach, Virginia	99,780	131,718	5
Jefferson Parish, Louisiana	91,126	136,113	4
Omaha, Nebraska	64,724	101,846	8
New Orleans, Louisiana	62,891	146,264	7
Santa Barbara, California	58,744	30,987	7
Oklahoma City, Oklahoma	49,360	84,270	4
Davenport, Iowa; Moline, Illinois	48,269	39,054	4
Spokane, Washington	45,589	40,249	5
Cleveland, Ohio	44,052	60,041	5
Pensacola, Florida	39,360	41,642	4
Hartford, Connecticut	36,795	30,072	7
Roanoke, Virginia	34,516	29,501	4
Gainesville, Florida	33,639	20,191	3
Macon, Georgia	32,585	23,144	5
Fort Wayne, Indiana	29,424	26,943	3
Cedar Rapids, Iowa	29,208	26,131	4
Lubbock, Texas	28,664	23,005	3
Saginaw, Michigan	23,585	18,159	5
Vancouver, Washington	23,530	43,975	8
Tucson, Arizona	23,152	55,167	10
Bakersfield, California	20,937	11,189	4
Cranston/Johnson, Rhode Island	18,121	20,271	5
Ocala, Florida	17,207	9,161	4
Eureka, California	16,762	5,740	2
Burlington, Vermont	16,351	8,863	2
Warner Robins, Georgia	15,210	13,441	5
North Adams, Massachusetts	12,968	4,484	3
Assortia/Seaside, Oregon; Long Beach, Washington	12,809	3,504	3
Aberdeen, Washington	11,658	4,916	4
Pan Oklahoma (Oklahoma City), Oklahoma	11,532	18,838	4
Yakima, Washington	11,364	9,507	4
Peru/Wabash, Indiana	11,184	5,956	3
Myrtle Beach, South Carolina	10,323	5,119	2
Rutland, Vermont	9,544	3,436	2
Denton, Texas	9,027	10,855	4
Sebring/Avon Park, Florida	8,297	2,012	2
Lake County, Illinois	8,188	14,007	6
Columbus, Indiana	8,148	6,259	3
Great Neck, New York	7,922	16,350	9
Lewiston, Pennsylvania	7,462	1,934	2
Porterville, California	7,379	3,094	2
Michigan City, Indiana	7,292	10,508	4
Jacksonville Beaches, Florida	7,028	10,562	6
Saranac Lake/Lake Placid/Tupper Lake, New York	5,944	2,531	2
The Dalles, Oregon	5,597	2,097	3
Lock Haven, Pennsylvania	5,236	1,297	2
Park Forest, Illinois	5,007	8,614	6

(continued)

Exhibit 3   (continued)

System Locations	Basic Subscribers	Premium Service Subscriptions	Number of Premium Services
Montpelier, Vermont	4,664	1,364	1
Orland Park, Illinois	4,417	8,167	6
Owosso, Michigan	3,922	1,910	3
Robinson, Illinois	3,606	2,761	3
Tyrone, Pennsylvania	3,118	700	2
Maywood, Illinois	2,812	6,389	6
Total	1,445,347	1,527,364	
Total Homes Passed, as of 12/31/83		2,578,000	
Total Homes in Market, as of 12/31/83		2,984,000	

Exhibit 4   Cox Cable (A)

Organization

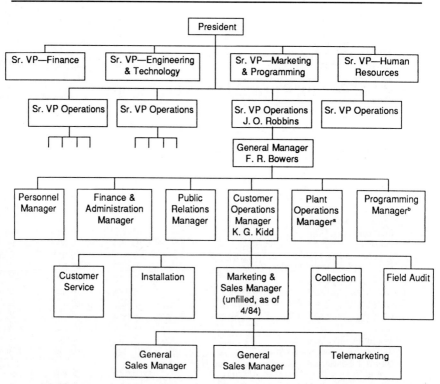

[a]The Plant Operations Manager handled the technical aspects of cable television such as construction.

[b]The Programming Manager coordinated programming for the local access channels only.

Exhibit 5   Cox Cable (A)

Cox Cable Jefferson Parish Historical Data
($000s)

	1979	1980	1981	1982	1983
Revenues					
Basic	$ 708	$3,714	$ 6,018	$ 7,771	$ 9,140
Pay	617	3,475	7,411	12,206	15,030
Other	1	18	20	143	948
Total Revenues	1,326	7,207	13,449	20,120	25,118
Expenses					
Plant [a]	130	972	1,525	2,374	3,339
Programming	404	2,011	4,256	5,928	6,863
Marketing	144	466	694	1,048	1,100
General and Administrative	290	1,388	2,454	4,264 [b]	5,834 [b]
Total Expenses	968	4,837	8,929	13,614	17,136
Gross Profit	358	2,370	4,520	6,506	7,982
Depreciation and Amortization	326	1,376	2,369	3,090	4,443
Operating Income	$ 32	$ 994	$ 2,151	$ 3,416	$ 3,539
Basic Subscribers	21,565	49,071	70,173	80,136	91,126
Pay Subscriptions	19,779	53,451	99,532	122,496	136,113
Number of Employees	50	99	144	186	219

[a]Includes construction, installation and plant maintenance.

[b]1982 & 1983 G & A includes corporate overhead allocations.

Exhibit 6 *Cox Cable (A)*

Basic Cable Penetration Rates in Jefferson Parish

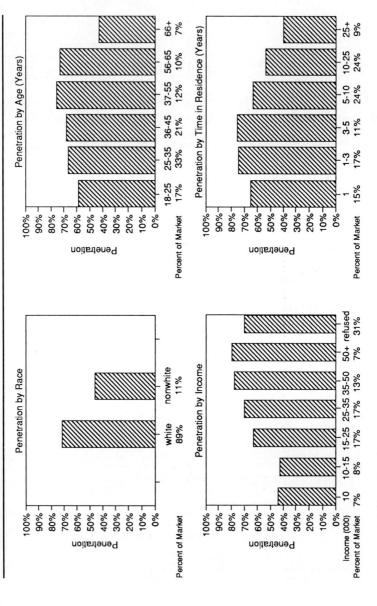

Source: Telephone Surveys, Jan.–March, 1984.

Exhibit 7 Cox Cable (A)

Program Offerings in Jefferson Parish

*Subscribe today and
see all the fabulous T.V.
you've been missing!*

CABLE CHANNEL	SERVICE
2	WCOX—Community Programming
3	WWL TV-4—CBS
4	GOVERNMENT ACCESS
5	HBO (HOME BOX OFFICE)—Great Movies, Sports, Specials, Original Programs-24 Hours
6	INFO-TO-GO
7	WDSU TV-6—NBC
8	PROGRAM GUIDE
9	WVUE TV-8—ABC
10	JEFFERSON PARISH SCHOOL SYSTEM
11	WGNO TV-26—Independent
12	WYES TV-12—PBS
13	CNHN—Cable News Headline News 24-Hours News in Brief
14	ESPN—24-Hour Sports
15	AMERICA'S SHOPPING CHANNEL
16	SHOWTIME—Movies, Comedy, Broadway, Specials-24 Hours
17	WTBS TV-17—Atlanta Independent Movie Classics, Hit Series, Sports
18	NICKELODEON—Award Winning Programs for Children and Teens ARTS & ENTERTAINMENT
19	THE NASHVILLE NETWORK— Country Music, Specials, Comedy

CABLE CHANNEL	SERVICE
20	CINEMAX—Movies, Comedy, Classic Hits-24 Hours
21	CNN (CABLE NEWS NETWORK) In-depth News, Sports, Weather-24 Hours
22	FNN (FINANCIAL NEWS NETWORK) DOW JONES
23	THE PLAYBOY CHANNEL—Adult Entertainment
24	CHRISTIAN FAMILY TELEVISION
25	WGN TV-9—Chicago Independent Movie Classics, Hit Series, Sports
26	USA NETWORK—Sports, Movies, Specialty Programs
27	MTV: MUSIC TELEVISION 24-Hour Video Rock Music
28	WLPB—PBS (Baton Rouge)/Special Events
29	THE WEATHER CHANNEL
30	
31	SIN—Spanish International Network Movies, Sports, Weather in Spanish
32	LIFETIME—Programs on Health, Fitness Fashion, Lifestyles and Nature-24 Hours
33	WLAE TV-32—Educational
34	WNOL TV-38—Independent
35	CBN CABLE NETWORK Family, Religious, Classic Series and Movies 24 Hours
36	C-SPAN—Coverage of the U.S. House of Representatives-24 Hours

...at a price you can afford.

Basic	$10.95	4th Premium service	3.00
1st Premium service	11.00		
2nd Premium service	9.00	On Cable Guide	1.25
3rd Premium service	8.00	Remote Control	4.00*

*With three premium services, Remote Control is only $1.00, and with 4 or 5 it is only a penny!

Call: _____ *At* 733-8817

Exhibit 8   Cox Cable (A)

Jefferson Parish Pricing and Compensation Structure

		Service Level			
	Basic	1-Pay	2-Pay	3-Pay	4-Pay
Pricing					
Monthly service	$ 11	$ 22	$ 31	$ 39	$ 47
Installation fee	25	25	10	10	10
Remote control	4	4	4	1	0
Total Deposit Required for Installation	$ 40	$ 51	$ 45	$ 50	$ 57
Compensation					
Sales commission	$ 9	$ 14	$ 21	$ 25	$ 27

Salespeople also received additional commissions for selling other services: Remote Control: $2; Extra Outlet: $3; On-Cable Magazine: $.50; FM Stereo Service: $3.

Exhibit 9   Cox Cable (A)

Earnings Trends – Six Experienced Sales Representatives in JP

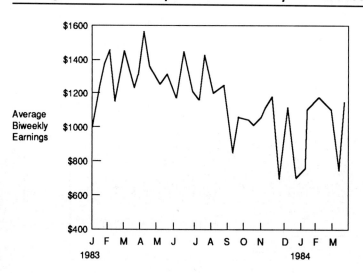

Exhibit 10   Cox Cable (A)

Application Form for Cable Service

Cox Cable
Jefferson Parish
250 Plauche St.
Harahan, LA 70123

Sales Department (8:15-5:00)	733-8817
Installation/Rescheduling (8:15-5:00)	734-1015
Customer Service/Billing (8:15-5:00)	733-4161
Service Repair (8:15-9:00) (7 days a week)	733-5688

APPLICATION FOR CABLE TELEVISION SERVICE

NAME: _____

ADDRESS: _____

APT #:_____CITY:_____ZIP:_____

OWN ☐   RENT ☐

PHONE: HOME _____WORK _____

SOC. SEC. #: _____EMPLOYER: _____

LICENSE #: _____

PREVIOUS ACCT: YES ☐   NO ☐   WHEN _____

SPOUSE NAME: _____ WORK PHONE:_____

RELATIVE/FRIEND: _____PHONE:_____

ADDRESS: _____

SPECIAL INSTRUCTIONS _____

_____

_____

_____

_____

INSTALLATION TIME

8:00 A.M. - 12:00 P.M.   ☐

12:00 P.M. - 5:00 P.M.   ☐

DATE: _____DAY: _____

MONTHLY RATES

Basic Service	$10.95
Premium Services	$11.00 ea.
Remote Control	$ 4.00
Extra Outlet	$ 5.00
FM Stereo Service	$ 3.00
On Cable Magazine	$ 1.25

	CATV	HBO	CIN	SHOW	PLAYBOY	DISNEY	GUIDE	REMOTE	FM	DROP STATUS	ACCT. #
INSTALL											
A/O											

AMOUNT COLLECTED/BILLED

CASH_____

CHECK _____

BILL _____

MONTHLY
CHARGE _____

CONNECTION
CHARGE _____

NOTICE TO BUYER

• You, the buyer, may cancel this transaction at any time prior to the end of the third business day after the date of this transaction.
• Money collected will be applied against your old balance if any is outstanding.
• THIS IS NOT A CONTRACT — ONLY AN APPLICATION.

_____   _____   _____
APPLICANT   REPRESENTATIVE   DATE

Exhibit 11 Cox Cable (A)

Reasons for Disconnection in Jefferson Parish

Move out of franchise	33.0%
Nonpay disconnect (NPD)	32.8
Move within the franchise	13.9
Service	7.5
Programming	6.5
Financial	3.4
Other	3.0
	100.0%

Exhibit 12 Cox Cable (A)

Customer Account Status as of 1/31/84
By Month of Original Sale [a]

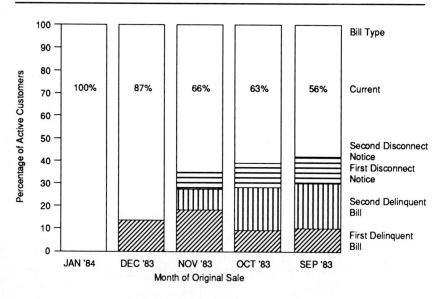

[a]To read this chart: for example, 56% of the sales made in September 1983 that were still active at the end of January 1984 were in good standing, while 44% were at least one month behind in payment.

Exhibit 13 *Cox Cable (A)*

Customer Distribution by Pay Level over Time

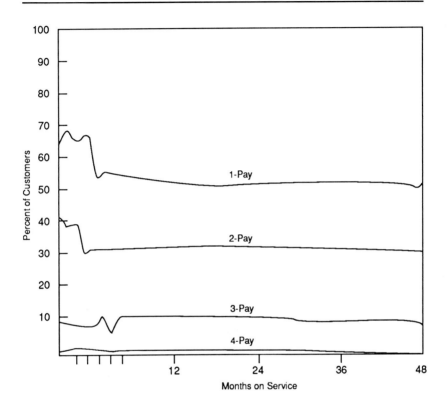

Exhibit 14   Cox Cable (A)

Apartments Compared to Single-Family Homes in Jefferson Parish October 1983 Transactions

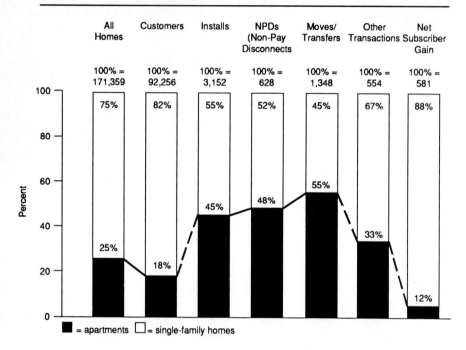

= apartments ☐ = single-family homes

Apartments Compared to Single-Family Homes Time on Service

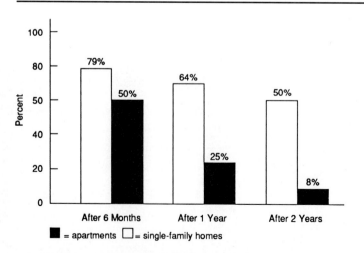

■ = apartments ☐ = single-family homes

To read this chart: for example, after 6 months 79% of single-family home customers and 50% of apartment customers were still subscribers to the cable service.

Cox Cable (B)

On September 14, 1984, Mr. Vic Arrington, director of operations support at Cox Cable Communications, was evaluating the interim results of a sales management program he had helped to develop and implement for Cox Cable's Jefferson Parish franchise (JP). Three months earlier, Mr. Arrington and Mr. Kevin Kidd, customer operations manager at JP, had agreed that changes in sales force deployment, sales compensation, and the sales information system might help to address the problem of churn in JP's customer base. Since that time, Mr. Arrington had assumed responsibility for implementing those changes among a portion of JP's sales force.

By mid-September initial results from the pilot program had been tabulated. In those areas where the changes had been implemented, certain elements of churn appeared to have improved but there had also been a net loss in the total number of customers. In addition, issues of sales force morale had also arisen.

After receiving the initial results, Mr. Kidd had requested a meeting with Mr. Arrington for that afternoon to discuss the results and what changes, if any, might be warranted in the sales force program. "Vic," Mr. Kidd had said, "you know that my boss, Frank Bowers, and your boss, the people at corporate headquarters, will be evaluating our program in December. And I don't want to present them with a program that results in a net loss in subscribers and problems with sales force morale. Let's talk about what we've learned so far from this program and what we can do over the next 3 months to shore up any deficiencies."

This case was prepared by Associate Professor Frank V. Cespedes and Research Assistant Ellen R. Hattemer as the basis for class discussion rather than to illustrate either effective or ineffective handling of an administrative situation.

Company Background

Cox Cable Communications was in 1984 the fourth-largest cable company in the United States and JP, with over 90,000 customers, was Cox Cable's third-largest franchise. (See Cox Cable (A) for background information about the company and the JP franchise.)

In late April of 1984, Mr. Kevin Kidd became customer operations manager at JP with responsibility for directing the marketing, sales, customer service, installation, and collection operations in the franchise. After a review of JP's marketing and sales operations, Mr. Kidd had reported his findings and initial recommendations to Mr. Franklin Bowers, general manager of JP, in early May:

> I believe that, as you suggested, the problem of churn[1] in our customer base demands immediate attention. Not only do disconnects keep us constantly struggling to meet our budgeted subscriber levels, but the number of nonpay disconnects and the volume of downgrade activity cost us a lot of money—more than had previously been estimated.
>
> But I also believe much of this churn is controllable if we change our marketing and, in particular, our sales programs. First, we should differentiate our sales efforts in the residential and apartment segments, since these segments differ in terms of profitability and customer characteristics. Second, we should also consider changes in our sales compensation structure in order to encourage more after-sale service and more effort at identifying customers likely to stay on the system for some time.
>
> I like the idea of assigning territories to our salespeople. I also feel we should change sales compensation so that individual sales reps' objectives are more in line with the company's objectives. To reduce churn and build our customer base profitably, we have to investigate ways of shifting our focus from just acquiring new customers to serving both new and existing customers.

Mr. Bowers agreed with Mr. Kidd's recommendations and urged him to investigate specific actions that might implement these objectives.

The Jefferson Parish Sales Pilot Project

Shortly after his meeting with Mr. Bowers, Mr. Kidd met with Mr. Arrington at Cox Cable's headquarters in Atlanta, Georgia. As corporate director of operations support, Mr. Arrington performed an internal consulting role for field operations while reporting directly to the president of Cox Cable. Mr. Arrington had been with Cox Cable for 15 months; previously, he had worked with MacDowell & Company, a prominent management consulting firm, for a number of years.

During the past months, Mr. Arrington had studied the problems of churn throughout Cox Cable's systems and had developed recommendations that he

---

[1]"Churn" referred to the number of cable subscribers who disconnected the service, or who "downgraded" their service levels from, for example, 3-pay to 2-pay or from pay to basic.

believed would address this issue. In May of 1984, Mr. Arrington was actively seeking a Cox Cable franchise that would agree to implement these recommendations as a way of testing their applicability to a number of other franchises facing similar problems.

During their conversations, Arrington and Kidd found that they had reached similar conclusions about the causes of churn and the changes necessary to deal with it. Within a week of their meeting, Mr. Kidd had received Mr. Bowers' approval to volunteer JP as the pilot site for a revised sales management program and, ten days later, Mr. Arrington arrived in JP to begin the implementation of a pilot sales program.

Mr. Arrington noted that JP was one of Cox Cable's larger franchises. He expected any pilot program to receive considerable attention at corporate headquarters since it would be dealing with issues common to many of Cox Cable's franchises. He also knew that any franchise chosen as the pilot site would still be expected to meet budgeted sales and financial performance objectives.

After an initial meeting, Arrington, Bowers, and Kidd agreed to limit the pilot project to the portion of JP west of the Mississippi River (the "West Bank") and to limit the duration of the project to 6 months. About one-third of JP cable subscribers resided on the West Bank, and this area traditionally had lower basic cable penetration as well as higher churn than the East Bank (see Exhibit 1). It was also agreed that at the end of 6 months the results would be evaluated both by Mr. Bowers, general manager of JP, and by Mr. Jim Robbins, senior vice president of operations and the person to whom Mr. Bowers reported.

In addition, Mr. Arrington received approval to assemble, for the duration of the project, a "sales pilot team" responsible for developing and implementing specific recommendations and whose expenses would be paid by corporate headquarters. As members of the pilot team, Mr. Arrington assembled Mr. Robert Losaw (Cox MIS) and Mr. Michael Morton (from Operations Support). Mr. Arrington also received approval to hire the services of MacDowell, which had previously worked with Cox Cable on a variety of projects. In particular, Mr. Douglass List, a consultant in MacDowell's Atlanta office, and Ms. Jeanne Lasala, a research analyst with MacDowell, were assigned to the project.

By late May, the pilot team had established its "command post" in a small house trailer parked next to Cox Cable's JP headquarters. During the next months, List and Morton established nearly permanent residence in JP, while Mr. Arrington divided his time between JP and his other responsibilities as corporate director of operations support in Atlanta.

The Area Manager Concept

Area management was the central idea in the pilot team's proposal. Sales reps would be designated "area managers" and assigned specific territories. The area manager's principal concern in selling a customer would be establishing a long-term relationship rather than maximizing the initial billing rate. New responsibilities included preventing nonpay disconnects (NPDs) and other disconnects as well as servicing current customers (see Exhibit 2). Mr. Arrington noted:

> Area management pushes accountability for sales and for net gain down to the level of the sales rep. Having one area manager in a well-defined territory also facilitates the tracking of sales and service results and gives the customer a "name and face" to associate with Cox Cable. Additionally, a change to area management should lend greater stability to the sales force and attract higher caliber people.
>
> The key question was, how do we draw up the territories? We saw a significant difference in apartment versus single-family home cable subscribers, and therefore wanted to separate those sales efforts. But geographic segmentation was also attractive because of its simplicity. Once we decided on the basic structure, we still needed to decide how to define specific territories. Based on homes passed? Churn? Customer base? Demographics? And how should we determine how many territories were necessary?

Sales Force Compensation

Mr. Arrington commented on the existing sales compensation system:

> It stressed volume of sales, while ignoring the profit impact of those sales. It treated apartment sales the same as residential sales even though apartments were easier to sell, more costly to serve because of the high number of transactions, and produced less revenue since customers stayed on the system for less time. The compensation plan also discouraged nonselling activities by only rewarding sales.

A new compensation scheme was structured to support the new definition of responsibility for the area manager and to focus the sales rep on certain activities. Mr. Arrington discussed the pilot team's plan:

> We wanted the new compensation structure to motivate the area managers to avoid unnecessary service calls such as billing inquiries, to ensure that customer service problems were quickly resolved (e.g., missed installation appointments), to avoid sales to customers who did not really want the service or who had no intention of paying, and to educate customers more fully at the time of the sale.
>
> Therefore, we abolished sales quotas and designed a compensation system composed of a "service commission" to pay area managers for servicing existing customers, a "growth commission" to compensate for a net gain (and penalize for a net loss) in subscribers in a territory, and a chargeback for nonpay disconnects which would essentially reclaim any commissions for "bad" sales. Previously, a sale that lasted two weeks paid the same as a sale that lasted two years. But under the new plan, with no compensation for sales per se, when a customer disconnected, the sales rep would have to make an additional sale to stay even on net gain and avoid a "negative commission." So one two-year sale would theoretically be worth 12 two-month sales.

Implementation of Pilot Team Recommendations

Despite JP management's support for the program, the pilot team encountered obstacles to the implementation of their plan. First, although JP's operations were computerized, management had little of the information needed to manage the changes in sales practices. For example, Cox managers could not measure the six-month sales retention rate by sales representative, which would be key in measuring both sales force performance and the impact of the new system on churn. The pilot team also discovered inconsistencies in the way internal data were recorded, especially critical disconnect information. The team, therefore, contracted for external software development to meet these and other data needs. Total cost of the additional data processing capability was approximately $100,000.

Additionally, local resources proved to be a constraint as management vacancies and tight limits on the number of total JP franchise employees limited available support. Corporate Cox Cable had recently initiated cost-reduction measures throughout the company. As one part of those cost-cutting measures, limits—in some cases, reductions—in total employee "headcount" within each franchise became one of the key performance measurement criteria for Cox Cable general managers. The JP pilot team operated within these constraints and made adaptations. For example, Mr. List acted as de facto West Bank sales manager at JP for the duration of MacDowell's association with the project.

By early June, enough information was available to allow the pilot team to finalize territory and compensation plans. (See Exhibit 3 for a comparison of new and old sales information capabilities.)

Territories and Compensation on the West Bank

Nine sales reps sold cable service on the West Bank before the pilot. The pilot team decided to separate the area geographically into six residential and four apartment territories, with one residential and one apartment territory "closed" to direct sales activity. The closed territories would allow the team to measure the incremental effect of direct sales activity, since the only activity within these territories would be churn or sales initiated by the customer to JP's customer service office. Mr. List explained that "the intent was to provide something like a 'control' group and also to allow a judgment about the incremental impact of the sales force on sales. Since a cable company is the only such service in town, Cox would get a certain amount of sales without *any* sales force, and we wanted some judgment about that level for planning purposes."

The team decided to establish territories based on the number of existing customers within a geographic area. In addition, reps with historically stronger performance were given larger territories in order to allow the reps to earn their historic average compensation. (See Exhibit 4 for residential territories established by the pilot team.)

Under the new sales compensation plan (Exhibit 5), the service commission was $.30 to $.60 per month per existing account, depending on the pay level of the customer (the higher the number of pay stations bought by the customer, the higher the commission). Sales commission could be positive or negative: a specific growth budget was negotiated for each territory, and then each customer above or below the budget was worth $3.00 to $6.00 per month, again based on the pay level sold. In addition, a nonpay disconnect (NPD) chargeback was set at $8.00 to $15.00 per NPD (by pay level). However, the area managers were given an allowance for the first three months of the pilot (based on the three-month average of nonpay disconnects in JP prior to the launch) since they had not made the initial sales to this group of NPD customers. For the first three months of the pilot, therefore, area managers were levied NPD chargebacks only if the monthly number of NPDs in their areas exceeded the monthly median number of NPDs in JP for the three months prior to the pilot launch.

Pilot Launch

Mr. Arrington described the actual start-up:

The last decision we had to make before implementing the changes was whether or not to keep the current sales reps. We recognized that the sales role would change from a "hunter" trying to meet the sales quota to a "farmer" cultivating current and potential accounts. We decided to go with the current reps even though they might not meet the ideal profile of an area manager. After all, if the pilot were successful, but with a whole new staff, we had to think about the message this would send to Cox Cable's sales forces around the country.

We announced the changes at the reps' regular sales meeting on Friday, June 8. The salespeople were very receptive but quickly brought the area manager concept down to specifics. Basically, they said, "O.K., I understand that I'm responsible for all of these functions, but how should I spend my day?" They needed a new inventory of skills. We gave them suggestions such as: 1) Sell, but sell responsibly: work harder than you've worked before at identifying and maintaining good accounts; 2) call after the installation to see how the customer likes the service and 3) stop doing things that eventually hurt the franchise—for example, don't sell customers more pay levels than they really want, and don't sell to people who are going to move very soon.

We didn't have a formal training program, but we couldn't wait months and probably lacked the resources to develop a comprehensive training program. We also respected our current reps' abilities and believed we could accomplish a great deal of the area management objective without training.

Initial Results of the Pilot Program

Throughout the summer, the pilot team continued to upgrade the information capabilities and to monitor the results of the pilot. During the six weeks following the launch, sales of basic cable service dropped to an average of 97 per week from an average of 116 per week for the six weeks prior to the launch. The pay-to-basic ratio on new sales fell from 200% to 150%. The percentage of sales from apartments also dropped significantly.

Other aspects of the pilot program were more encouraging. In one week in July, for example, the area managers saved 60% of the customers scheduled to be disconnected for nonpayment. In addition, one Saturday each month came to be designated "Nonpay Saturday" when all area managers would visit delinquent accounts in their territories either to collect payment or retrieve the converter box. In addition, the area managers seemed to like their new responsibilities. Many spent hours in the office phoning customers in the early evening to check on the quality of the service.

By September 10, results were as follows. The West Bank pilot territories showed a net gain of 144 residential subscribers and a net loss of 160 apartment subscribers (75 from the "closed" apartment territory) since the launch of the pilot on June 10. During this period, the East Bank showed a slight net loss of 2 residential subscribers and a net gain of 243 apartment subscribers. On the West Bank, revenues from pay subscriptions had dropped sharply due to a lower pay-to-basic ratio in new subscriptions (see Exhibit 6). On the other hand, downgrade performance showed improvement (Exhibit 7), and churn among customers of the "basic" service had decreased (Exhibit 8).

Morale among salespeople on the West Bank was falling as the "growth commission," reflecting the cumulative net decrease in total customers in the pilot territories (see Exhibit 8), became a deduction against their compensation. Mr. List described the sales force's attitude:

> The sales force had perceived more stability in their compensation than there really was: they viewed the service commission as a salary, and I think they hadn't really grasped the idea of being charged a "negative" commission for net losses in their customer base. Also, the sales meetings had become more clinical than inspirational—there was no hoopla over daily sales production. I was also disturbed by complaints about the unfairness of the territory assignments, especially since our best reps were grumbling the most.

The pilot team was losing members. Mr. Losaw returned to corporate headquarters to work on other MIS projects. Mr. Morton had resigned from Cox to enroll at Harvard Business School. And on September 1, Mr. Arrington learned that because of corporate budget considerations, he would have to cut short MacDowell's involvement with the project. On Thursday morning, September 13, Mr. Arrington drove Mr. List to the New Orleans airport. Waiting for his flight back to Atlanta, Mr. List commented:

> Vic, I believe we're on the right track with these changes. But you don't have much time left to demonstrate this. The focus of concern has been on the number of customers on the system and total monthly revenues. But it's important not to let people forget the substantial hidden costs of churn for Cox. That was

the main objective of the pilot program, and it's been a success in that area. The problem, however, is that it's hard to devise a way of measuring costs *not* incurred by adopting this form of sales management.

The following day, September 14, Mr. Arrington prepared for his meeting with Mr. Kidd. He knew Mr. Kidd would review the sales force deployment and compensation schemes under the pilot program, and would have concerns about the interim results. Mr. Arrington considered changes in each area. He wondered whether sales rep complaints about the "unfairness" of territory assignments had any substance and was disturbed by the inability of even the most experienced reps to show a positive net gain in the number of subscribers. He also wondered if the compensation plan could be adjusted to improve pilot results. During the past month, for example, some sales reps had complained about the "complexity" of the compensation plan and the fact of "negative commissions." Reviewing the interim results, Mr. Arrington noted that selling expenses were a larger proportion of revenues under the area-management form of sales force deployment but total marketing expenses were a lower proportion of revenues under area management.

The role of the sales force as area managers was another issue that would probably be part of his discussions with Mr. Kidd. Some JP managers had recently argued that, now that the sales force had shifted its focus from only selling to customer relations as well as sales, the area managers should also take on duties such as installation and minor repairs.

Mr. Arrington also knew that both local and corporate managers were scrutinizing the pilot project closely and would soon demand quantifiable results. Corporate was watching the project for its potential transferability to other franchises and, in total, corporate had thus far spent $300,000 on the pilot project: $100,000 for data processing services purchased through an outside firm, and $200,000 for other expenses such as travel, lodging, and the time devoted to the project over the past months by Mr. List of MacDowell and members of the pilot team from Cox headquarters, including Mr. Arrington himself. Locally, Mr. Bowers and Mr. Kidd were concerned about the lower pay-to-basic ratio generated under the pilot program, and were anxious to have their sales force reunited under one sales management plan.

Exhibit 1 Cox Cable (B)

West Bank and East Bank Characteristics, Jefferson Parish

	West (Pilot)	East
Internal Data		
Total customers	27,709	63,840
Basic penetration	48.62%	58.84%
Basic churn (%/Month)	4.73%	2.87%
1980 Census Data		
Average income	$19,207	$22,937
% of population with income more than $20,000	43.06%	51.01%
% of population with income less than $9,999	27.83%	20.71%
% of households with children under 18	48.25%	37.57%
% of population over 55 years	14.28%	19.96%
% of population with college degree	7.30%	17.80%
% of population renting	31.31%	32.11%

Source: Company records; U.S. Census Bureau.

Exhibit 2 Cox Cable (B)

Role Comparison—Sales Representative vs. Area Manager

	Traditional JP Sales Representative	New Area Manager
Market focus	Unrestricted; can sell apartments or residences	Specialized in either apartments or residences
Selling area	Unrestricted, but given leads in specific areas	Restricted to specific geographic area
Source of leads	Telephone inquiries distributed by sales manager	Receives all leads in own area; emphasis on using apartment managers, other lead sources
Sales responsibility	Closes sale, collects first payment. Emphasizes trial of product.	Sees sale through to complete installation via telephone follow-up; emphasizes long-term benefit
NPD[a] responsibility	None	Responsible for all NPDs in assignment area; telephones new delinquent accounts
Disconnect responsibility	None	All disconnects count against sales in calculating net gain; tries to prevent controllable disconnects
Service responsibility	None	Responds to problems in order to lower chance of disconnect; serves as a "safety net" when regular channels do not work
Performance measure	Sales	Net gain

[a] "NPD" = Non-Pay Disconnect.

Exhibit 3   Cox Cable (B)

Comparison of Pre- and Post-Pilot Sales Information

Management Level	Existing Information	New Information	New Management Capabilities
General Manager/ Marketing Manager	Net gain by service Customers by service combination (more than 100 different) Disconnects by reason	Basic and pay net gain by: Pay level Dwelling segment Transaction type (e.g., upgrade vs. new sales) Geographic area Customers by segment and pay level Disconnects by reason and segment	Assess specific problems and opportunities Initiate action to address specific segments Evaluate potential value of alternative strategies Develop and track impact of segment and transaction-specific programs
Sales Manager/ Sales Representative	Telephone leads (sales office only) Daily sales results	Basic and pay net gain by sales territory Components of net gain by territory Penetration, churn by area and street Daily record of pending opportunities[a] to influence net gain and actions taken	Direct sales efforts toward areas of highest opportunity Take action against nonsales situations influencing net gain Ensure follow-through on leads, sales, service problems, etc. Evaluate quality of sales being made

Source: MacDowell & Company.

[a] "Opportunities" here refers to information indicating potential changes in the customer base such as new residents in an area, a record of information requests by residents, and reasons given by previous customers for discontinuance of the service.

Exhibit 4   Cox Cable (B)

Residential Territories: West Bank (Pilot)

Area Manager	Territory Characteristics: [a]		
	Homes Passed	Number of Customers	Penetration
1. Larry	11,987	5,663	47.2%
2. Al	12,164	6,039	49.6
3. Terry	5,636	2,478	44.0
4. Lou	8,170	5,127	62.8
5. Hollis	8,159	4,499	55.1
6. (Closed)	2,436	999	41.0

Source: Company records.

[a]These numbers refer to the characteristics of each territory at the time the pilot program began in June 1984.

Exhibit 5   Cox Cable (B)

Comparison of Jefferson Parish Compensation Programs

	Original Program	Initial Pilot Program (June–September)
Territory Assignment	None assigned	Varying sizes, with larger territories assigned to more successful salespeople
Base Compensation	None	Service commission based on number of accounts in territory 30–60 cents per month per customer Varies by "points" that reflect incremental contribution of pay levels
Sales Commission	$9–27 per sales depending upon number of pay units sold and other services sold (e.g., extra outlet = $3; remote control = $2); no difference between apartment and residential sales	None

(continued)

Exhibit 5   (continued)

	Original Program	Initial Pilot Program (June–September)
Net Gain Growth Commission	None	Commission or chargeback based on actual accounts vs. growth budget Specific growth budget negotiated for each territory $3–6 per month per customer above or below growth budget (varies by pay level points)
NPD Incentive chargeback	None	$8–15 per NPD (varies by pay level points)
Allowance/ retention	None	Allowance equal to 3-month average prior to launch
Quota	140 units every 2 weeks. Each basic and each pay subscription count as a unit	None

Exhibit 6   Cox Cable (B)

Pay-to-Basic Ratio for New Installs

Month Beginning	Residences		Apartments	
	East Bank	West Bank Pilot [a]	East Bank	West Bank Pilot [a]
3/10/84	1.87	2.03	2.07	2.38
4/10/84	1.83	1.92	2.06	2.10
5/10/84	1.80	1.95	1.96	2.02
6/10/84 pilot launch	1.65	1.50	2.02	1.80
7/10/84	1.75	1.61	2.10	1.50
8/10/84	1.83	1.57	1.90	1.40

[a]Excluding closed territories.

Exhibit 7 *Cox Cable (B)*

Downgrade Performance Before and After Sales Pilot Launch

Residence

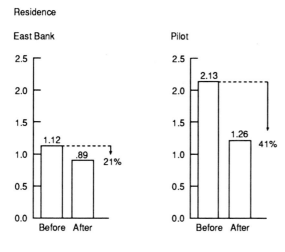

Apartment

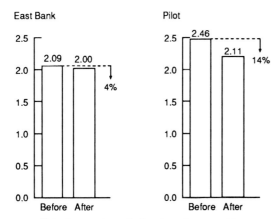

Note: downgrades as % of customer base monthly average; period is 12 weeks before pilot launch and 12 weeks after pilot launch date 6/10/84.

Exhibit 8   *Cox Cable (B)*

Percent Net Change in Number of Customers
(June 10, 1984 through September 10, 1984)

Area Manager	Residential Territories	Area Manager	Apartment Territories
Larry	−0.2%	Ken	−0.8%
Al	+1.4	Barry	−2.0
Terry	−0.3	Lenny	− .9
Lou	+2.1	Closed	−3.7
Hollis	−0.6		
Closed	0		

Basic Churn in Residential Territories
(June 10, 1984 through September 10, 1984)

Area Manager	Residential Territories
Larry	2.6%/month
Al	2.5
Terry	2.3
Lou	1.9
Hollis	2.3
(Closed)	2.8

Channel Management

The term *channels* refers to the ways in which a product reaches its end users. Some products are sold directly to their ultimate buyers whereas others pass through one or more intermediary (or indirect) channels on their way to end users. A common channel arrangement is:

Manufacturer → Wholesaler → Distributor → Retailer → Consumer

In managing customer encounters, an increasingly important task facing many companies is channel management. Although textbooks often use the term *sales management* to refer solely to the management of a direct sales force, most products are sold through a combination of direct and indirect distribution channels. Managing these multichannel arrangements affects all aspects of sales management and is often a key dimension of organizing and implementing a firm's overall marketing effort.

This chapter illustrates: (1) reasons for the growing prominence of multichannel arrangements in marketing efforts; (2) key components and choices of channel management; (3) major factors that affect producer–reseller relations; and (4) trade-offs between control and resources inherent in most distribution systems.

Growth in Multichannel Systems

During the past two decades, the share of sales volume attributable to distribution intermediaries has grown significantly in many industries.[1] According to U.S. Commerce data, wholesalers increased their share of total sales volume from about 50% in 1972 to 58% in 1982, while sales through manufacturers' direct sales forces declined from 37% to 31% during that decade. During the

1980s, wholesale trade real growth increased faster than real growth in GNP in the United States and, according to many observers,[2] will continue to do so at least through the 1990s. One result is that a recent survey indicates less than one-quarter of industrial manufacturers sell solely through direct channels whereas more than three-quarters use some intermediary channel in addition to a direct sales force.[3]

A combination of two external trends and two changes in intermediaries themselves accounts for the increased prominence of multichannel systems in marketing efforts.

Selling Costs

The cost of personal selling rose by 160% between 1975 and 1987. Businesses selling direct to user-customers incurred the highest cost per sales call, averaging $291 in 1987; those selling to intermediaries averaged $204.[4] Resellers are able to cluster the product lines of many manufacturers and so gain selling economies, enabling them to reach accounts that could not be cost-effectively sold by any single manufacturer's sales force. Moreover, winning a new customer often requires multiple sales calls. When the cost of these calls is added to the overhead and support costs inherent in most direct sales efforts, the differentials between direct and indirect selling costs can be compelling for many firms.

In addition, mergers, acquisitions, and an increase in international sourcing strategies mean that, in many product categories, user customers frequently require deliveries at multiple receiving locations. This trend means a further increase in physical distribution costs and often favors the multilocation (especially large chain) distributor who can network needed inventories in regional locations, thereby keeping lower stock levels in each of many local warehouses, deliver multiple product categories on the same order, and so spread these distribution costs over more items than any single manufacturer typically can.

Just-in-Time Inventory Management (JIT)

Spurred in part by a general interest in Japanese management practices in the 1980s and a more specific interest in lowering inventory-carrying costs during a period of high interest rates, JIT is now common practice in many industries. This approach to inventory management affects the channels systems in two ways.

First, it compresses the order cycle, placing a premium on the presence of inventory when and where it is needed. Wider product lines and other economies of scope mean intermediaries are often better able than manufacturers to react quickly to this field marketing requirement.

Second, it increases customers' order fill-rate expectations, since the essence of JIT is to deliver materials at the time they are needed. Conversely, failure to fill a given order when scheduled can mean a costly stoppage in more aspects of production for the industrial customer. Intermediaries managing the flow of multiple items from producers to user-customers often become a more prominent part of the distribution channel under JIT management patterns.

Two related changes in the distribution infrastructure itself have also affected channel-management requirements in many industries.

Concentration

In recent years, many industries' larger multilocation intermediaries have grown and taken increased shares of market from smaller, local distributors. This trend has important implications for producer–reseller relations.

First, these larger intermediary organizations typically have greater purchasing power than traditional distributors do and, often, greater management sophistication and cost controls that enable them to bargain especially aggressively with their suppliers.

Second, any one supplier typically accounts for a smaller proportion of total sales volume at the large intermediary than at the traditional distribution organization. This often means a proportional loss in supplier influence and more emphasis on sales tactics and strategies designed to increase the supplier's "share of mind" at its intermediaries. Often, this means directing more of the supplier's product line through its resale channels, which in turn increases the potential for conflict between its direct and indirect channels.

Third, the scale and scope of the large distribution chain can enable it to offer user-customers a variety of marketing programs not feasible for smaller intermediaries. Such programs include so-called bundled purchasing agreements that often lower user-customers' order-acquisition costs; prime vendor programs in which larger customers agree to purchase a certain percentage of their needs in a product category from the intermediary in exchange for quantity discounts and various materials-handling services; or systems sales contracts in which user-customer and intermediary establish a long-term agreement for the ordering and warehousing of many frequently ordered products. Over time, such intermediary programs can affect the producer's brand preference at user-customers and the directions of the producer's own marketing programs.

Computerization

For resellers, sourcing from many manufacturers and selling to hundreds or thousands of user-customers, automation of order receipt, shipping, invoicing, inventory management, stock replenishment, and accounts receivable often mean major cost reductions. As a result, during the past two decades many distributors and wholesalers have been aggressive in automating these aspects of their operations. They have also taken the lead in many industries in establishing computerized communications with customers and suppliers, thereby reducing costs further through reductions in clerical and telemarketing personnel while also frequently increasing switching costs for other channel members.

While establishing these automated links with user-customers is an option available to manufacturers, the required investments are often more feasible and have a faster payback for large intermediaries, for three reasons. First, the more items sold, the greater the advantage inherent in automating order entry and order processing activities, and intermediaries typically sell many more items than any one manufacturer; second, the subsequent reductions in transaction costs usually have a much greater impact on the cost structure of a distribution, rather than manufacturing, business; and third, by pulling together many suppliers' different ordering formats into a single system, the intermediary often provides user-customers with a level of purchasing convenience difficult for any single supplier to emulate cost effectively.

For all of these reasons, then, intermediaries have assumed a growing prominence in many firms' marketing strategies. In turn, organizing and implementing the marketing effort increasingly requires a clear understanding of key components and choices in channel management, the major factors that affect supplier–reseller relations, and tactics and systems aimed at coordinating direct and indirect field marketing efforts.

Components and Choices

A channel typically performs certain functions: (1) demand generation, or selling; (2) carrying of inventory; (3) physical distribution; (4) after-sale service; (5) extending credit to customers; and, depending upon the product category and nature of demand, (6) product modification and maintenance in the form of customization, applications engineering, or specialized support services. In getting its product to end-user markets, a producer must either assume all of these functions or shift some or all of them to intermediaries. As the old saying goes, "You can eliminate the middle man, but not the middle man's functions."

In performing these functions, a channel may include any of the following components, each typically having distinct capabilities and constraints within the marketing strategy of the producer.[5]

A *direct sales* force usually calls on decision makers and decision influencers within user accounts in an attempt to get the producer's product specified in purchase decisions. Many buying decisions—especially those involving business-to-business transactions—involve multiple personnel at user accounts, including purchasing, production, engineering, and/or financial personnel. Salespeople often contact, negotiate with, and seek to persuade this array of personnel.

In a multichannel system, the direct sales force often also has responsibility for contact with distributor personnel as well as user-customers. The sales force may train distributor personnel in the supplier's product technology and accompany sales reps from the distributor on sales calls at user accounts. The direct salesperson also often is responsible for checking the intermediary's inventory in the supplier's product line; this is important since user-customers often purchase from distributors on the basis of product availability and fast delivery. Further, the direct salesperson may also be responsible for implementing special promotions, co-op advertising programs, or new product introductions with assigned intermediaries. Finally, the direct sales force also typically seeks to develop and maintain good personal relationships with intermediaries in an effort to increase that supplier's support and awareness at the reseller level of the channel.

Distributors purchase goods from suppliers, take title to those goods (and so assume the risks associated with ownership), and then sell those goods to user-customers or to other resellers. (A distributor who sells primarily to other resellers is often called a wholesaler.) Traditionally, the primary function of a distributor is to play a cost-transfer role in the channel: That is, because of their economies of scope, distributors can often perform certain functions for suppliers and user-customers more economically than they can perform these functions themselves. Figure A depicts the distributor's cost-transfer role.

The scope and focus of a distributor's business are usually defined in product-market terms. That is, the distributor may operate as a steel warehouse, chemical distributor, or construction equipment dealer; or the distributor may be identified with a particular customer segment such as a hospital supply distributor, office supply dealer, or mill supply house. In formulating marketing programs, the segment emphasis of a given intermediary is a key consideration for many producers.

Figure A
Distributor's Traditional Economic Role

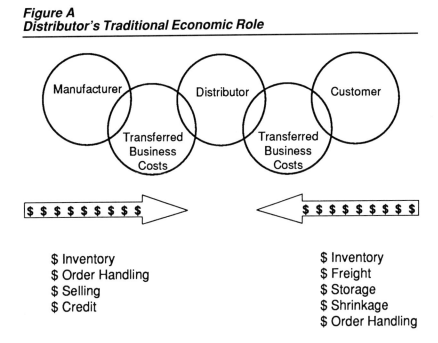

In industrial markets, industrial distributors typically carry hundreds, thousands, and sometimes more than 100,000 items in their inventories. Similarly, in consumer goods, supermarkets and other retailers have grown larger in the past decade and opened their aisles to products ranging from plants to greeting cards and automotive supplies as well as traditional food products. Hence any one product sold by a supplier often cannot attract special attention at distributors, and an important task in channel management is the ongoing development and maintenance of reseller attention and sales support.

Captive distributors function like independent distributors, but they are owned by particular suppliers and typically operate as business units within a larger corporation. Thus captive distributors often have a dual mission: to maximize their own sales volume and product margins while also maximizing the sales volume and margins of products produced by other business units in the corporation.

Agents, like distributors, sell the products of various suppliers to user-customers. Unlike distributors, however, agents typically work on commission and do not take title to the goods they sell. For example, the manufacturers' rep (MR) sells on commission, usually carries a limited number of product lines, and represents fewer suppliers than the typical distributor. As a result, MRs can often provide more attention and support to the lines they carry, and their commission compensation makes them a variable cost channel from the supplier's perspective. At the same time, their compensation structure often implies that MRs are not effective channels for products with long-selling cycles; and since MRs do not take title, the supplier must assume certain risks and costs with MR as opposed to distributor channels.

Brokers, like MRs, also operate on commission and do not take title to the goods they sell. But unlike MRs, brokers tend to represent a number of different producers at any one time and often only for short periods. Brokers are important in areas such as used equipment or in agricultural commodities, where supply and demand characteristics mean ongoing opportunities to sell large lots of products to buyers seeking low price and no service in times of excess supply or to buyers seeking emergency deliveries or products in shortage in allocation periods. Often, brokers never warehouse or deliver the products they sell. Instead, they function as deal makers (or "market makers") between producers and individual accounts.

The key issues in distribution strategy and channel management concern the alignment of available components with the distribution functions that must be performed in getting a product to market. For the supplier, this means (1) seeking to place a given function where it can be performed most cost effectively, and (2) managing the evolving relationships among different channel components. In turn, these tasks pose a series of choices inherent in distribution decisions.

- Channel structure: the relative balance between direct sales and sales through intermediaries

- Reseller type: independent distributor, captive distributor, agent, or broker
- Market coverage: within the reseller network, exclusive, selective or intensive franchising policies
- Terms and conditions: the specific discount structure, support policies, and other terms and conditions that help to define supplier and reseller responsibilities

Part of what makes channel management an especially interesting, and difficult, aspect of marketing implementation is that these choices pose dynamic constraints and opportunities. Most companies usually must manage channel relationships across a number of product-market boundaries, and the relative importance of different components and functions changes over the course of the product life cycle or as competition develops. Thus there is often a tension at the heart of many channel-management policies. When a market is entered or a product introduced, elements of channel management cohere around the particular market circumstances and business objectives held at the time. But as markets evolve, new channel policies are required. However, each dimension of the existing arrangement tends to cement established patterns, making it difficult for the supplier to alter its channel policies. Further, while change may be necessary, attempts to alter established channel policies often threaten established channel relations and the current revenues and margins generated by those relations.

Channel Relations

An important aspect of channel management is the development and maintenance of good relations between suppliers and resellers. No contract, however detailed, can foresee all the circumstances that are likely to arise during the course of a franchise agreement. When the reseller is an independent wholesaler or distributor, these requirements must be addressed by multiple firms (supplier and one or more resellers), each a separate business entity with different objectives, capabilities, and constraints. At least two factors typically affect such relations: (1) the varied goals, or tug-of-war, that typically characterize supplier–reseller relations; and (2) the multiple agreements, or entangling alliances, that usually comprise competition at each stage of a channel.

Tug-of-War

Certain facts condition supplier–reseller relationships. On the one hand, the fact that exchange occurs between supplier and distributor means that each has something deemed valuable by the other, and thus both have mutual interests in maximizing the sales or margins of the producer's product or service in question. On the other hand, channel relations also typically involve each party in an implicit struggle to retain a larger share of profits and control concerning the product or service in question. Also, the goals and operating constraints of producer and resellers are often very different, leading to conflicts in the implementation of marketing strategies designed to maximize a product line's sales or margins with user-customers.

Because supplier and reseller simultaneously have mutual interests and inherent conflicts, the rhythm of these relationships is analogous to an ongoing tug-of-war. Figure B emphasizes this aspect of channels relations through the "seesaws" used to depict the comparative interests and goals of a producer and its channel intermediary.

Suppliers selling through intermediaries must develop capabilities at two levels: as sources of product and revenues for those intermediaries and as the locus of brand preference with end users. In the former role, suppliers try to act as marketing partners with their distributors, building levels of trust and influence that motivate resellers to stock and actively support that supplier's product line(s) rather than the many other product lines carried by the reseller. In the latter role, suppliers seek to have their products specified by end users,

Figure B
Supplier–Reseller Relations: Mutual Interests and
Different Priorities

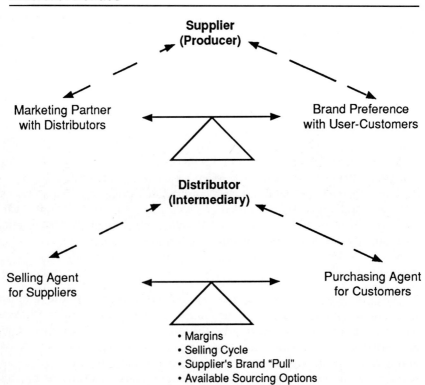

which often requires terms and conditions that can conflict with resellers' preferences.

Conversely, resellers act simultaneously as selling agents for suppliers and as sources of supply for certain groups of customers. In the former role, resellers seek to develop with individual suppliers marketing programs that can build demand for particular brands at user accounts. In the latter role, resellers typically seek to assemble a package of products that will serve particular customers' desires for purchasing convenience or lower transactions costs. This latter goal often motivates distributors to give preference, first, to the generic package of products appropriate to a customer segment and, second, to the selection and promotion of particular brands capable of completing the package.

How these seesaws tip in a given supplier–reseller relationship will depend upon various factors, including the profit margins available to each party through one or another mode of distribution, the supplier's ability to develop and maintain brand pull with user-customers, and the distributor's other sourcing options in a product category. Decisions and actions concerning these factors are usually crucial in the implementation of marketing strategies in multichannel systems.

Entangling Alliances

In practice, most producers and resellers are usually members of multiple (often competing) channel systems. Producers often sell through a number of intermediaries, whereas resellers often carry the products of competing manufacturers as well as the lines of many other suppliers in different product categories. Hence the tug-of-war described above also occurs within the context of a set of entangling alliances implicating suppliers, resellers, and user-customers.

For example, a supplier's pricing decisions must often be considered not only in terms of the impact on user-customer demand patterns but also in terms of the impact on reseller margins and the continued support of the supplier's distribution network in relation to other suppliers that may sell competing lines through those resellers. For resellers, a decision concerning whether to carry and support a given supplier's product line must often be considered not only in terms of customer demand and the particular line's margins and working capital requirements but also in terms of the potential addition's impact on that reseller's relations with other suppliers.

These entangling alliances can play an important role in making or breaking a particular marketing program. Supplier–reseller relationships in many industries can endure for years. Therefore, decisions concerning the implementation of a particular marketing program must often address the capabilities and constraints inherent in this network of alliances as well as the marketing requirements inherent in the purchasing behavior of user-customers.

Control vs. Resources

Channel management tactics and supplier–reseller relations are also affected by the interplay between control and resources inherent in distribution.[6] In most marketing situations, the producer faces a trade-off between its ability to control important channel functions and the financial and/or human resources required to exercise that control.

The more intermediaries involved in getting a supplier's product to market, the less control that supplier generally can exercise over the flow of its product through the channel and the way it is presented to customers. As the number of intermediaries in a distribution channel increases, so generally do the opportunities for transshipment, differing levels of service and delivery by various intermediaries, different stocking levels, and perhaps overlapping sales efforts. In addition, as the number of intermediaries increases, the supplier's ability to influence prices to user-customers generally decreases. On the other hand, reducing the length and breadth of the channel generally requires that the supplier perform more channel functions itself. In turn, this generally requires the supplier to allocate more financial or field marketing resources to activities such as warehousing, shipping, credit, field selling, or field service. Hence as Figure C suggests, there is typically an inverse relationship between control and resources (especially available financial resources) in many distribution situations.

With this inverse relationship in mind, we can make two further observations. First, some business units have the financial resources needed to perform most or all channel functions for their product lines *if* management so desires whereas other business units, operating with constrained financial resources (and/or in markets where a dispersed user-customer base simply increases the resources required for adequate market coverage), lack the ability to perform

Figure C
Control vs. Financial Resources in Channel Design

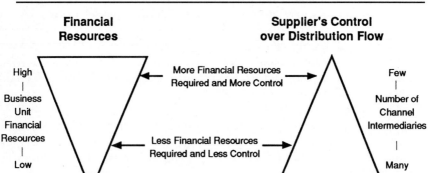

many channel functions, regardless of management's desire for direct control over these functions. Second, depending upon the nature of the product or market, management's need for control over a given channel function may be relatively high or low. That is, because of the nature of the product technology (more or less complex), the required ongoing information exchange between supplier and user-customer (e.g., the amount of technical training or applications development required), or the importance of the product in users' production processes (e.g., a "line stopper" vs. a component or packaging product added at the finished inventory stage), the producer will find it more or less important to exercise direct control over a given channel function such as selling, field service, or fast delivery.

Thus, business units differ in terms of available financial resources and in their *capacity* for performing directly various channel functions, as well as in their relative *need* for direct control over various distribution functions. Arranging these factors on a matrix (Figure D) yields the following distinctions.

In the upper-right cell of Figure D, where the business unit's financial resources are high (i.e., adequate to perform directly important channel functions because of the business unit's gross profit base, financial subsidies from other business units in the corporation, or other factors), and where the need for control over these functions is also high (because of the technology involved or the nature of the buyer–seller relationship required to market the product), a direct sales channel is likely to be the preferred and typical mode of distribution. Such is the case for many highly engineered products sold by large, financially stable companies to a relatively concentrated customer base.

Conversely, in the lower-left cell, where the business unit's financial resources are constrained and where the need to control channel functions is relatively low, multitier distribution is likely. In this situation, supplier management can delegate many functions to intermediaries and conserve financial resources for other purposes, because the incremental value of a direct buyer–seller relationship is not great in the product category. One way to envision this

Figure D
Control vs. Resources: Typical Patterns

| | | Business Unit Financial Resources | |
		Low	High
Business Unit's Need for Control Over Channel Functions	High	Financial resources as *limiting* factor in channel design	Control as determining factor in channel design: direct
	Low	Control as subordinate factor in channel design: multitier distribution	Financial efficiency as *determining* factor in channel design

trade-off is to consider some of the circumstances that, in a sense, preempt resources for purposes other than distribution-related investments. In many situations, the company's strategic priorities (e.g., low-cost manufacturing position) make distribution investments a lower priority in the company's capital-budgeting process. In other situations, manufacturers' reps, wholesalers, distributors, or other intermediaries can be attractive channels for a business with limited resources and under pressure to get its products out into the market quickly. This can be especially important for start-up firms, which must generate revenues quickly and find that rep organizations or distributors offer established customer contacts at a variety of firms in many industries.

In the upper-left cell, where the business unit's financial resources are low but management's need to control channel functions is high, financial considerations tend to act as *limiting* factors in channel design. That is, the supplier tends to perform directly as many important channel functions as possible within the limits of its financial resources. This is the case where a producer has a relatively high need to ensure that applications development and customer education functions are performed effectively by its distribution channel, but at the same time management operates under constrained financial conditions. In such situations, wholesalers or manufacturers' reps are often used to achieve wide market coverage with minimal additions to the fixed distribution costs incurred by the producer. In this situation, distribution costs act as a constraint, not a determinant, of the producer's channel management policies. The producer can be expected to assume more functions if its financial condition improves, and this goal will be reflected in the terms and conditions it seeks to negotiate with its resellers.

Conversely, in the lower-right cell, where the business unit's financial resources are high but the need to control important channel functions is relatively low, low-cost distribution tends to become a *determining* factor in the channel-design decisions. That is, where in the channel a given function is performed is determined primarily by cost-efficiency criteria rather than by the manufacturer's desire to maintain direct control over the function. This is often the case in mature product categories where product applications and specifications are well established and where competition has major suppliers focused on reducing costs, including distribution-related costs.

Besides resource and control considerations, many other factors affect channel-management decisions and tactics. This perspective, however, can highlight the interplay between two particularly important concerns of marketing managers and suggest issues to consider when examining channel-management situations:

1. What is the basic role of intermediaries within the marketing programs of a supplier? Is it in fact cost-efficiency that drives the use of intermediaries for a given producer, or are intermediaries being used primarily to supplement certain scarce resources in an area such as warehousing, field selling, or after-sale service? This is a conceptual

difference that makes a practical difference in areas ranging from the extent of distributor discounts to the roles performed by company salespeople with intermediaries.

2. What level of quality control is required for a particular channel function? Too often, marketing managers speak of distribution as an undifferentiated, homogeneous category in their marketing plans. But as noted earlier, distribution refers to a set of discrete activities including demand generation, carrying of inventory, physical distribution and delivery, after-sale service, credit, and perhaps product modification and maintenance. Depending upon the producer's product and marketing strategy, different channel functions require different levels of quality control. Similarly, the distribution networks of most companies contain different types of intermediaries who perform different functions with different levels of quality control. Effective channel management policies analyze and recognize, through terms and conditions, these differences.

3. In line with this, periodically the options available for shifting a given function to a different point in the channel should be evaluated. As products mature and the technology becomes more standardized, for example, many suppliers find that postsale maintenance and repair services, which initially required an extensive parts inventory and specially trained personnel, often can be performed more efficiently and just as effectively by third-party service firms rather than at manufacturer or distributor locations. Similarly, as user-customers gain more familiarity with a product category, they often develop in-house personnel capable of performing functions previously handled by manufacturer or distributor.[7]

For most companies, sales management means the management of both direct and indirect channels of distribution. In turn, this requires clarity concerning key components and choices in channel management, an understanding of factors that inevitably condition supplier–reseller relationships, and management of the trade-offs between control and resources inherent in distribution. The effective management of customer encounters in the field increasingly revolves around these issues.

Case Studies

The cases in this chapter focus on complex, multichannel systems and the roles of different channel institutions, ranging from independent distributors to captive distribution to direct sales efforts. Each case illustrates a different set of issues involved in aligning channels systems to meet the requirements of different market segments and changing field marketing requirements.

The first two case studies concern businesses within the Industries Group at Westinghouse Electric Corporation, a major supplier of electrical and electronic equipment. In the Westinghouse (A) case, Mr. Chuck Hawks, the manager of distribution for the Industries Group, is reviewing channel policies and, in particular, the role and performance of Westinghouse's captive distributor, Westinghouse Electric Supply Corporation (WESCO). He has been asked to offer a general evaluation of WESCO, including any recommendations ranging from maintaining current channel policies to possible divestment of the captive distribution organization.

When you analyze the Westinghouse (A) case, consider these questions:

1. What factors affect relations between WESCO and the various businesses in Westinghouse's Industries Group?
2. What criticisms are being levelled at the captive distributor, and how should we evaluate these criticisms?
3. What generally are the advantages and disadvantages of captive distribution? What are the implications for Westinghouse product divisions?
4. What is your evaluation of the three options being considered concerning WESCO?

In the Westinghouse (B) case, Mr. Hawks must decide on a new distribution program for programmable controllers (PCs) and certain other industrial control products manufactured by Westinghouse. A task force has recommended establishing a new distribution channel for these products. This new channel would represent a significant departure from current channel management policies and affect relations between the product divisions and WESCO. Mr. Hawks must review the task force's recommendations, suggest any modifications necessary for effective implementation, and present any recommendations to top management.

As you analyze the Westinghouse (B) case, consider these questions:

1. What are the important marketing requirements for PCs and related control products and the implications for the appropriate channels system for these products?
2. Does the proposed channels program address these requirements? Is it, given both the external and internal factors in this situation, a good idea?
3. What is at stake in this decision: For WESCO? For the affected product divisions? For potential independent distributors of these products?
4. What changes (if any) should Mr. Hawks seek in the task force's recommendations?

The Westinghouse cases provide a comprehensive look at the key choices involved in channel management: the balance between direct and indirect channels; reseller type to be used; extent of market coverage; and specific terms and conditions for the supplier–reseller agreement.

The next case, Alloy Rods Corporation, presents a very different competitive situation. Whereas Westinghouse is a large corporation, Alloy Rods (a manufacturer of welding electrodes) is a relatively small firm facing new competition from a much larger company. Lincoln Electric Company, Alloy's principal competitor and a company with nearly six times the annual sales volume of Alloy, has launched a new lower-priced product targeted at Alloy's most profitable and fastest-growing product line. In addition to a nearly 25% price difference, Lincoln has a large direct sales force, a full line of welding equipment, and an aggressive stance in the marketplace. In this seemingly David-and-Goliath situation, Alloy's vice president of marketing must decide how to respond to Lincoln's new product and, more generally, how to implement Alloy's marketing programs in the face of the increased competition.

The following questions might be helpful in considering Alloy's situation:

1. How do market trends, customer demographics, and buying processes for welding electrodes affect competition and field marketing requirements in this business?
2. What are the respective roles of the direct sales force, wholesalers, and distributors in Alloy Rods' channels network? What are the roles of these entities in Lincoln Electric's channels network?
3. Which distribution strategy is more congruent with user and channel behavior in this business? What factors have motivated each firm to market its products in the manner it does?
4. What does Lincoln's new product mean for Alloy Rods? How big a threat does it pose? What are the major constraints and opportunities that should guide any response by Alloy?

Finally, the Becton Dickinson case concerns a drama of shifting channel power and entangling alliances among a major supplier, buyer, and distributor in a marketplace undergoing significant changes due to new governmental regulations. Becton Dickinson's VACUTAINER Systems Division (BDVS) produces products for sale to hospitals, commercial labs, and other health-care centers. The case focuses on contract negotiations between BDVS and Affiliated Purchasing Group (APG), a large hospital buying group. The immediate issue is how to respond to APG's demands concerning pricing, labeling, and distribution terms. But the outcome of APG negotiations will almost certainly affect BDVS's negotiations with other buying groups, relations with its current distributors, and the focus of the division's sales and marketing programs.

In analyzing this situation, consider the following:

1. What are the important changes occurring in the health-care marketplace, and what are the implications for Becton Dickinson and its BDVS division?
2. How important is the APG contract for BDVS? APG's member hospitals? APG's top management? BDVS's distributors? BDVS's competitors?

3. How important is each aspect of the negotiations (pricing, brand name, and distribution terms) to each party?

4. Given your analysis, what should BDVS managers say at the next scheduled round of negotiations with APG?

The BDVS case raises all the channel management issues discussed in this chapter and illustrates how these issues affect other elements of the marketing mix. But, as the suggested questions indicate, this case also concerns a crucial and common task in field marketing: the conduct of important, high-level, face-to-face contract negotiations with big and important accounts. Thus as well as illustrating issues in channel management, this case also serves as a bridge to the topics considered in the next chapter, Managing Major Accounts.

References

1. For a fuller discussion of these trends and their implications, see Frank V. Cespedes and E. Raymond Corey, "Managing Multiple Channels," *Business Horizons* (July-August 1990), on which much of this section dealing with the growth of multichannel systems is based.

2. See the results of interviews with over 600 managers at manufacturers, wholesalers, and customers as reported in Arthur Andersen & Company, *Facing the Forces of Change* (Washington, D.C.: Distribution Research and Education Foundation, 1987).

3. "Industry Markets Goods Through Dual Channels," *Industrial Distribution* (April 1985): p 15.

4. William A. O'Connell, "A 10-Year Report on Sales Force Productivity," *Sales and Marketing Management* (December 1988): 33–38.

5. A more extensive discussion of channels components and the factors that affect the design of channels networks is available in E. Raymond Corey, Frank V. Cespedes, and V. Kasturi Rangan, *Going to Market: Distribution Systems for Industrial Products* (Boston, Mass.: Harvard Business School Press, 1989), Ch. 1–5.

6. Frank V. Cespedes, "Control vs. Resources in Channel Design," *Industrial Marketing Management* 17 (August 1988): 215–227, further analyzes the implications and managerial concerns inherent in this trade-off.

7. For an analysis of changing buyer behavior over the course of the product life cycle, see F. Stewart DeBruicker and Gregory L. Summe, "Make Sure Your Customers Keep Coming Back," *Harvard Business Review* (January-February 1985): 92–99. For a discussion of how these changes often affect the relative importance of different channel functions, see Frank V. Cespedes, E. Raymond Corey, and V. Kasturi Rangan, "Gray Markets: Causes and Cures," *Harvard Business Review* (July–August 1988): 75–82.

Case 9

Westinghouse Electric Corporation (A)

In early 1986, Mr. Chuck Hawks, manager of distribution for the Industries Group at Westinghouse Electric Corporation, was reviewing distribution policies. His major concern was whether the traditional strengths of Westinghouse Electric Supply Corporation (WESCO), the captive distribution arm of Westinghouse and the major distributor for many product divisions within the Industries Group, fit the short- and long-term requirements of Industries' business units. He had also been asked to offer a general evaluation of the role and value of WESCO as a Westinghouse business unit. Mr. Hawks therefore decided to review the history and recent performance of WESCO.

Westinghouse

A major supplier of electrical and electronic equipment, Westinghouse was organized into four major operating groups (see Exhibit 1).

- The Energy and Advanced Technology Group designed, developed, manufactured, and distributed nuclear energy systems, power-generating apparatus, transportation systems, robotics, and high-technology defense equipment.
- The Commercial Group included businesses such as beverage bottling, real estate development, transport refrigeration, elevators and escalators, insulating and plastic materials, and watches.

This case was prepared by Associate Professor Frank V. Cespedes as a basis for class discussion, rather than to illustrate either effective or ineffective handling of an administrative situation. Certain company data, while useful for discussion purposes, have been disguised.

- The Broadcasting and Cable Group owned and operated six television stations, 11 radio stations, a production company, and cable television systems.
- The Industries and International Group (Industries) designed, manufactured and marketed transformers, switchgear, electrical distribution products, circuit devices, motors, electronic components, and industrial controls. (See Exhibit 2.) In addition, WESCO was a business unit in the Industries Group.

Industries Marketing: Organization and Markets

Within Industries, a variety of businesses focused on products designed for industrial applications of electrical and electronic equipment. Each was a profit center.

Three Industries Marketing field sales organizations sold Westinghouse products direct, and through both WESCO and independent distributors, to three major customer segments:

1. *Electric utilities* accounted in 1985 for more than half of Industries Marketing sales volume, of which about 90% went direct and the remainder through WESCO and independent distributors. In this segment, there were three types of customers: a) investor-owned utilities, b) municipal utilities, and c) rural electrical cooperatives, which received low-interest loans from the federal government. To investor-owned utilities, Westinghouse sold products such as distribution transformers and meters through its direct sales force. Distributors sold these products as well as wire, poles, and pole-line hardware to the rural co-ops and municipals.

2. *Industrial* customers accounted in 1985 for about one-third of Industries Marketing sales volume, of which more than half went direct and the remainder through WESCO and independent distributors. In this segment, an Industries sales force sold electrical supply products such as motors and motor controls direct to electrical OEMs, machine tool manufacturers, mechanical OEMs, and large end users of electrical products in the paper, petrochemical and steel industries.

   In the industrial segment, price was important, but quick service and "one-stop" shopping were often more important to customers who used many electrical products for maintenance in their factories and/or in the manufacture of their products. As a result, industrial buyers often developed strong relationships with local distributors over a number of years. Industrywide, it was estimated that about 50% of electrical product sales to industrial customers went through distributors, and the proportion sold through distributors had increased steadily in recent years.

3. *Construction Sales* accounted for the remainder of Industries Marketing sales volume. In this segment, the sales force sold products such as switchgear, switchboards and panelboards to electrical contractors. By policy, all sales to electrical contractors were through distributors, either WESCO or independent distributors. Typically, three or four contractors would request price quotes from local distributors and then submit bids on a construction project. Brand preference was usually not a factor in this segment unless the specifying engineer insisted on a specific brand. Since contractors were usually spending their own money and provided only a one-year guarantee on their work, moreover, construction sales were the most price-sensitive customer segment. In addition, many contractors operated with little working capital, often living from project to project; thus, the credit risks in this market were also significant.

In construction sales, the distributor's sale of Westinghouse products was often as small as one load center selling for $150 to a small residential contractor. A medium-sized construction project (e.g., a small office building) would typically include a switchboard, transformer, and several panelboards worth $10,000 in total. The electrical portion of a 20-story office building (including labor and materials) could be over $1 million; of this, 10–15% was typically equipment of the kind manufactured by Westinghouse. Distributors typically stocked the kinds of products purchased for residential and smaller commercial and industrial projects. By contrast, the special equipment often ordered for larger projects was not stocked but shipped direct from the manufacturer to the job site. Distributors tended to specialize either in the ship-from-stock residential construction segments or in the more complex large-project segments where products were shipped direct from manufacturers.

Distribution Channels

Within Industries Marketing, Westinghouse products were classified into three categories. "Class 1" products such as safety switches went completely through distributors (either WESCO and/or independent distributors), while "Class 3" products such as power transformers were sold entirely direct; "Class 2" products such as switchgear went to market through both distributors and direct sales. Mr. Gary Clark, vice president of Industries Marketing, noted that in recent years the sales mix for Westinghouse "has shifted toward distributors and away from direct sales for two reasons":

One reason is that we can achieve, under the right circumstances, lower selling expenses through distributors. Another reason is the increasing maturity of many of our product lines. As a product matures, it generally requires more service and less applications-development expertise. Distributors can provide field service more cost effectively than our direct sales force can. Overall, the majority of Industries group volume is sold direct. Of the portion sold through distributors, more than half is sold through WESCO.

Most salespeople in the three Industries Marketing sales forces were electrical engineers. They had traditionally sold Westinghouse products to companies developing large construction or utility projects and for large-volume OEM applications. Their average compensation was about $40,000, most of which was fixed salary. Including salary, benefits, expenses and support services, it cost Westinghouse more than $100,000 annually for each salesperson. Mr. Clark noted:

> . . . large project sales have long selling cycles, and it can be two to three years before a salesperson's efforts result in booking an order. At the same time, however, our sales force must evolve from its traditional big-ticket orientation to a more distributor-oriented selling effort, because there are fewer new "greenfield" projects in the United States and more retrofits, which are done in smaller pieces. In addition, the just-in-time inventory policies adopted by many manufacturers mean one-stop shopping and quick, local delivery are increasingly important to our customers. That also raises the relative importance of distributors in our marketing programs.

Commenting on the role of distributors in Westinghouse's marketing programs, Mr. Hawks noted that "the distributor provides important value added in at least three areas":

> First, a local presence in the marketplace, providing frequent and familiar contact with the customer. This is crucial in many of our product segments.
>
> Second, the ability to act as a total source of supply for a particular customer installation. For example, a motor cannot stand alone; it needs conduit, fittings, motor starters, circuit protection, power distribution systems, and so on. Westinghouse cannot provide all of the items a customer needs for a job. But that customer desires one-stop shopping, and that's what the distributor provides.
>
> Third, a properly trained and motivated distributor is an extension of our salesperson's ability to cover a marketplace. But this can only be achieved if the salesperson recognizes the importance of the distributor and acts as a manager of the distributor. However, because Westinghouse has so many product lines going through our sales forces, and because our salespeople have been traditionally oriented to the big-ticket project sales, it's often difficult to get the salespeople to focus on and manage the distributors.

To support Westinghouse's distribution sales efforts, Mr. Hawks established in 1982 a program in which a Westinghouse salesperson in each district was designated a "Lead Salesman" with responsibility for training and coordinating sales efforts through distributors, including WESCO (see Exhibit 3). The Lead Salesman received a base salary and incentive compensation tied to the total sales of Westinghouse products to assigned distributor accounts. Mr. Hawks explained:

> Because of the number of products we sell, the Westinghouse-distributor interface can easily become fragmented. Under the Lead Salesman program, one person has the responsibility for resolving any problems with a given distributor,

and for acting as the visible point of contact with Westinghouse for that distributor.

The channel policy statement for Industries Marketing noted:

> To best service the needs of its customers, Westinghouse believes that distributors provide the best sales channel for many of its products.
>
> Westinghouse policy will be one of selective distribution. The numbers and character of the full-line, specialty independent and WESCO houses appointed will be on this basis to encourage the loyalty of the distributor and protect the investment they make in behalf of Westinghouse. Westinghouse market share will be of prime consideration in determining the adequacy of its distribution.

Management also believed that no one distribution outlet within a given trading area could adequately represent Westinghouse in all the product/market segments in which it competed. It was common to have two or more distributors in a market/trading area, one of whom was often a WESCO branch.

WESCO

Along with Graybar (1985 sales of approximately $1.6 billion), General Electric Supply Company (GESCO; estimated 1985 sales of $940 million), and Consolidated Electrical Distributors (CED; estimated 1985 sales of $690 million), WESCO was one of the four full-line, national electrical distributors in the United States. Most industry observers ranked WESCO as the second-largest electrical distributor in terms of sales volume.

WESCO competed with about 3,000 other U.S. distributors of electrical products, including 38 regional chains,[1] 155 other multibranch firms, and many single-location independents in addition to the four national distribution organizations. In 1985, sales through electrical distributors accounted for an estimated 56% of total sales of electrical products in the United States. The largest 20 electrical distributors accounted for about 30% of electrical sales through distributors and the "big four" for about 14% in 1985. Exhibit 4 provides data concerning market size and typical product and customer mix for electrical distributors.

History and Organization

WESCO began operations in 1922 when George Westinghouse acquired seven bankrupt independent distributors in order to maintain Westinghouse distribution in certain areas of the country. Through World War II, WESCO continued to expand primarily by acquiring bankrupt or faltering independent distributors. After World War II, WESCO expanded both by developing its own

---

[1] A national chain was defined as a distributor with a total of at least 125 branches in 40 or more states, while a regional chain was a distributor with at least 10 branches in at least 3 states.

branches in many locations and by acquiring smaller, local distributors. By 1985, WESCO had 243 U.S. branches, 37 in Canada (where WESCO was among the largest electrical distributors), 4 in Saudi Arabia, and 1 in Singapore.

In the 1950s, when WESCO had about 100 branches, it was organized into 16 districts that reported to the president of WESCO. In 1962 came a change to a regional concept: the then-150 branches were divided into 25 districts in 7 regions that reported to the president. According to Mr. William Taylor, president of WESCO since February of 1985 and a WESCO manager since 1958, the regional reorganization was an initial attempt to put greater control in the hands of field people but "that did not really happen until 1978 with the switch to the divisional structure in place today: four divisions with headquarters in Pittsburgh, Philadelphia, Chicago and San Francisco reporting to me at WESCO corporate headquarters in Pittsburgh." (See Exhibit 5.)

Mr. Taylor explained that the divisional structure had two objectives. One was to move decision-making from headquarters to the divisional offices where "we can be more responsive to the needs of the field and to customer requirements." Another was the need to put financial planning responsibility closer to the field in order to control key assets (inventory, receivables) more effectively. According to Mr. Taylor,

> After the divisional reorganization, the divisions became very strong very quickly. Headquarters staff in Pittsburgh is small, with primary responsibility for goal setting, guidance, and review of plans and performance. We have a pretty informal structure at headquarters. It's pretty easy to go from top to bottom without getting caught up in politics.
>
> Further, it's significant that, with the structural changes over the years, we never changed the district or the branch in terms of their functions. We changed things at the levels above that.

In 1984, about 42% of sales were to electrical contractors in construction markets; 36% to industrial customers; 14% to utilities; and 8% to various commercial, institutional, and governmental customers. During the past decade, the proportion of WESCO's sales to construction markets had decreased while the proportion sold to industrial customers had increased. Mr. Taylor noted that "WESCO grew up in construction, especially large construction jobs, and we are the sole representative for Westinghouse in many construction markets. But we have been stressing further penetration in industrial markets in recent years."

WESCO distributed products for over 600 electrical manufacturers but did not carry product lines competitive with Westinghouse products. Sales of Westinghouse products in 1985 accounted for about one-third of WESCO sales. (Prior to the divestiture of lighting products in the late 1970s and the Westinghouse Lamp Division in 1983, Westinghouse products accounted for nearly 50% of WESCO's sales volume.) Mr. Taylor noted that "Westinghouse has far fewer independent distributors than, for instance, GE does. So WESCO plays a more leading role in the distribution of Westinghouse products. Our growth rate has been higher than the industry by 20% over the last 5 years, and our intent is to be the largest, most progressive and most aggressive electrical distributor in this country."

Branch Operations

Each WESCO branch operated as a profit center. Mr. Taylor explained:

This concept is fundamental to the company and has not changed during the years. The branch manager is the person in charge. He or she develops both financial and marketing plans for the branch each year, provides overall guidance, manages the sales force, hires the staff, and selects customers (although a district credit office does the actual collections work). The branch manager also determines both the levels of inventory (with monthly financial crosschecks from higher up each month) and the mix of products to carry (although the supplier must be on the approved list that comes out of WESCO headquarters).

One branch manager commented, "The best part of my job is the freedom, control, and accountability of this position." Compensation for branch managers was directly related to performance in the areas of income-before-taxes and return-on-investments. In addition, WESCO branch managers were often moved among branches and within WESCO's corporate structure.

- *Sales Volume.* Branch sales ranged from $3 to $30 million annually. Profitability also varied among branches. Personnel, about 70% of branch operating expenses, included outside and inside sales forces and, in larger branches, one or more sales managers. Branches with more than $10 million in annual sales often had (in addition to the branch manager) a sales manager for industrial or contractor sales.

- *Sales Force.* WESCO's field (or "outside") sales force called on current and potential accounts, and set pricing guidelines for inside salespeople. Depending on the territory and mix of accounts, an outside salesperson might concentrate on one major customer or service a number. Some branches focused on one customer segment (e.g., electrical contractors).

Most outside salespeople had previous sales experience from a variety of backgrounds. They were paid entirely through a guaranteed-draw commission based on their billing margin dollars plus additional compensation for exceeding objectives set for certain products. The amount of the monthly guaranteed-draw was deducted from their total commission payments.

Inside salespeople at the branch took customer orders by phone and made pricing and quotation decisions within established guidelines. It was not uncommon for one or more inside salespeople to serve only one major customer who ordered frequently.

At WESCO branches, the outside salesperson was considered the "problem-solver," while the inside salesperson was "easier to reach" and important for "getting the right answer, right product and right price."

■ *Inventory.* Product lines carried at WESCO branches were similar, with some variation based on major local industries. Branch managers determined the products to carry as well as the stocking level for particular items. One branch manager noted that "electrical distributors generally focus on 'earn and turn': they try to maximize their margins and their inventory turns, while minimizing their inventory carrying costs. But a WESCO branch doesn't carry products that compete with Westinghouse products, so 'earn and turn' is not precisely appropriate to our situation, since there are limits on the branch manager's freedom to choose the branch's specific product mix."

WESCO management distinguished among three types of products carried by the distributor:

1. *Commodities* were standardized items sold mainly on price and delivery. These included items such as wire and cable, lamps, circuit breakers, fittings, conduit, load centers, and others. Commodities provided more than half of WESCO's total gross margin dollars in 1984.

2. *Engineered products* were standard, catalogue products which faced heavy competition but were somewhat technical and could be sold to some customers on the product benefits rather than strictly on price. These products were generally sold to large-project customers and included items such as distribution apparatus and switchgear, switchboards, motors, pumping panels and transformers. Relative to the typical electrical distributor, WESCO sales reps were considered to have a "large-project orientation" in their selling efforts.

3. *Specialties* were sophisticated, technical products bought and sold primarily on a price/performance basis. These included items such as power transformers, metering equipment and instruments, programmable controllers, and a number of other products made by Westinghouse and other manufacturers. These higher-technology products were the growth area in electrical distribution.

Of the Westinghouse products carried by WESCO, about two-thirds were considered to be "engineered products."

Computer Systems

WESCO was an acknowledged leader in the use of computers within the electrical distribution industry. Management believed WESCO's computer systems provided an operating cost advantage over most competitors by eliminating errors and lowering labor costs in areas such as order entry and inventory management.

With its Direct Order Entry System (DOES), WESCO put computer terminals in various customer locations. The customer could dial directly into WESCO branch computers to check inventory and place orders. This computerized process improved information flow, cut transaction costs, and increased productivity for both buyer and seller. It also helped WESCO to secure systems contracts in which major customers described their service requirements, products to be ordered, and the vendor's stocking responsibilities. Once a contract had been negotiated, DOES was frequently the major communications method, speeding transactions and—due to the presence of the DOES terminal on customer premises—frequently solidifying the relationship between the customer and WESCO.

WESCO's WESCOM computer system covered all branches and connected WESCO with many of its suppliers. Each WESCO branch had a minicomputer linked to a mainframe at WESCO headquarters; each night the mainframe updated back orders to be released and the pricing guidelines, and every Monday morning branches received a district inventory analysis. According to management, WESCOM improved control of both assets and costs, helping to reduce WESCO's inventory investments while improving service.

WESCO also had computerized links with a number of Westinghouse product divisions. Orders were automatically processed through WESCO's computer system and directed to the appropriate Westinghouse stocking location. Both WESCO and a number of Westinghouse product divisions hoped to expand this system in coming years.

In 1973, WESCO had pioneered in the development and use of computerized systems within the industry. In 1985, WESCO's management planned to make another major capital investment to expand WESCO's computer capabilities and make the systems more compatible with Westinghouse computer systems and to allow more customers the ability to enter orders with WESCO branches via computerized links.

Competition

In electrical distribution, WESCO competed with the other national chains, regional chains, and local, independent distributors.

In 1985, most industry observers ranked WESCO in the number 2 position behind Graybar (which had an estimated 5% share in electrical distribution) and ahead of GESCO and CED, the other *national distributors*. Graybar, due to historical ties with Western Electric, was especially strong in the growing telecommunications area. GESCO had undergone a number of management changes during the early 1980s and had recently cut a number of its locations. GESCO, like WESCO, had its strongest presence in construction markets.

Regional chains had accounted for less than 20% of industry sales in 1970, but by 1980, 314 chains (including the national distributors) represented about 35% of sales. Many local independent distributors had grown through acquisition into multilocation firms. Several foreign firms, moreover, had acquired some multilocation U.S. distributors as a way of aiding their market-entry strategies.

The strength of local *independents* varied from city to city. Many independents had "grown up" in their areas, and had close relationships with customers in their areas. Further, the independents aggressively pursued and attracted some of the best salespeople from the chains. Many independents were essentially specialty distributors, targeting either a particular type of customer or group of products (e.g., electrical apparatus for the mining industry, or lighting supplies for commercial/industrial/residential uses, or, increasingly, a focus on certain high-technology products).

Within given markets, local distributors were often WESCO's toughest competition. One local independent distributor noted that:

> Some suppliers shun multilocation distributors, and especially a captive distributor, and look to build their distribution networks around independent, local distributors.
>
> These suppliers fear that a multilocation distributor will shift its products among branches and sell in areas where the supplier may have exclusive arrangements with a strong local distributor. These suppliers also often believe that a captive distributor will focus most of its primary efforts on selling its parent's products, and only its secondary efforts on the products of other manufacturers.
>
> Finally, some suppliers believe they can wield more power and control over a small, local distributor than over a large, nationwide chain.

A Westinghouse corporate manager argued that, "In general, WESCO is more efficient in distribution, but the local independents are sometimes a more effective channel":

> WESCO's number of branches allows them to achieve economies of scale, nationwide distribution, and the ability to attract and service larger, national accounts in our customer segments. In addition, their size can support the investments necessary for large computer systems. Finally, as a captive distributor, they have a stable banker, and that allows them to develop more long-term programs than an independent distributor can. The independent is tied to its operating cash flows and therefore often can't afford to make investments in programs or products (e.g., hi-tech products) that won't generate cash soon.
>
> On the other hand, branch managers at WESCO move around more than an independent does and so often can't develop sustained local relationships in an area. And those relationships make a difference in the distribution business in many small but crucial ways. At WESCO, moving from branch to district management or to a position at WESCO corporate headquarters is usually an important career objective.
>
> The independent also has more pricing flexibility than WESCO branch managers do. WESCO management sets margin guidelines. The independent can go after lower-price business on a "loss leader" basis, where the WESCO branch can't.
>
> The independent can also take more chances in other areas. For example, at WESCO branch managers have a great deal of autonomy, but there are also pur-

chasing policies that prevent "speculating" on certain products [i.e., buying a lot of a certain product at some point because the branch can get a good deal from a given supplier]. The independents don't have these constraints, and often speculate on both purchases and receivables [i.e., will take more chances with credit-risky customers than WESCO does]. The result is that, in general, the independent will hit more home runs *and* strike out more often than WESCO does in these areas.

Further, many of these "small" independent distributors are often important people in their local business communities, and they can move in areas where local WESCO branch managers can't. For example, in my market, the toughest competition for WESCO is a local distributor who semiannually invites the entire purchasing department of a big steel company up to his country estate for hunting, fishing, and general relationship-building activities. That fellow is a big wheel in this community, and that gives him an advantage on many orders in areas where product differentiation is harder to achieve.

Finally, the independent distributor is an entrepreneur working for himself or herself. That has to make a certain difference in terms of motivation and effort.

Captive Distribution: A Dual Mission

As a business unit within Westinghouse, WESCO had a dual mission: to maximize sales of Westinghouse products and to optimize its own return on investment. WESCO sold products manufactured by about 30 Westinghouse product divisions as well as those of about 600 non-Westinghouse suppliers. With few exceptions, WESCO did not sell brands that competed directly with the Westinghouse brand in a given product category.

WESCO's sales of Westinghouse product divisions' total sales varied significantly, depending upon the product category. For some Westinghouse product divisions, sales through WESCO accounted for more than half of that division's total sales. For other Westinghouse divisions, direct sales accounted for two-thirds or more of total divisional sales with the remainder sold through WESCO and independent distributors. These differences were attributed to factors such as the degree of technical applications support required to sell a given product line (the more applications support required, generally the more the product tended to be sold direct) versus the importance of local, off-the-shelf delivery (the more important local delivery, generally the more the product went through WESCO and/or independent distributors).

Within the amount sold through distributors, the proportion of sales through WESCO versus sales through independent distributors also varied significantly, depending on the product category. For some Westinghouse product divisions, independent distributors were a much bigger proportion of distributor sales; for others, WESCO accounted for the majority of sales through distributors.

Conversely, sales of Westinghouse products accounted for different proportions of WESCO's total sales in different product categories. WESCO, like most electrical distributors, assembled packages of product items in most product categories, such as industrial control equipment, load centers, meters, relays, and other types of electrical apparatus. In some product categories, Westinghouse equipment accounted for much of the total volume sold by WESCO; in other product categories, Westinghouse equipment accounted for relatively small proportions of the total volume sold by WESCO. In total, 10 Westinghouse product divisions accounted for nearly 80% of Westinghouse products sold via WESCO.

Compared to the industry average for electrical wholesalers, WESCO's profits had varied throughout the 1970s and early 1980s. However, WESCO's operating costs were estimated as less than the industry median due to scale economies for the national distributor, and its sales per employee were estimated as exceeding the industry median by a substantial amount. Management attributed the difference in sales per employee both to economies of scale enjoyed by WESCO versus smaller distributors, and to the larger proportion of big-project construction sales made by WESCO: these transactions were often large-volume sales drop-shipped from the manufacturer to the end user.

Captive Distribution: Dual Perspectives

Over the years, both the role and performance of WESCO had generated differing opinions throughout the corporation. One executive described the relationship between various Westinghouse product divisions and WESCO as "basically an informal tug-of-war."

Some product division managers believed WESCO's gross margins should exceed, rather than lag, the median for electrical wholesalers. They pointed to the strength of the Westinghouse brand name in many lines and the financial credibility of the Westinghouse corporation as competitive advantages for WESCO. One manager commented that "suppliers dealing with WESCO know they'll get paid—something they can't take for granted with many local distributors. And Westinghouse is a stable banker for WESCO. Those factors, plus the awareness and quality of Westinghouse products, are big advantages for WESCO."

Others questioned the extent of their reliance on WESCO outlets for market penetration. In total, Westinghouse product divisions sold through approximately 700 distributor locations, 243 of whom were WESCO branches. In some divisions, WESCO accounted for over half of divisional sales made through distributors. One manager noted that "the total for the four national distributors, including WESCO, is about 14% of the estimated $30 billion wholesale electrical apparatus market. We miss a substantial portion of the market if we ignore independent regional and local distributors, and we can't afford that."

Another manager, in a product division that manufactured products for OEMs, stressed that:

. . . historically, WESCO has been oriented toward construction, not industrial, markets. They have made significant progress in improving their penetration and expertise in industrial markets, but I can still find better local and regional distributors, especially in the more technical product areas. Frankly, I believe WESCO performs better when our products are also being sold through independent distributors. This sometimes creates conflicts between WESCO branches and local independent distributors in an area. But I believe you must manage those conflicts.

Finally, one product manager stated that she preferred working through independent distributors rather than WESCO. "The independents have often been in their areas for two or more generations. They have strong contacts in the local business community, and those relationships are very important in the product category we sell. By contrast, the turnover in WESCO branch personnel is often greater, and that tends to prevent the development of local relationships."

In response, other managers pointed out that many operating procedures in the relationship between WESCO and Westinghouse product divisions tended to understate the financial, as well as strategic, performance of WESCO. One WESCO manager cited the following:

> First, part of our mission is to sell Westinghouse products, and we rarely carry competing lines. Westinghouse products are high quality and well respected but not always the best, in price or performance terms, in a given product area. But unlike an independent distributor, we can't shop around for another supplier.
>
> Second, unlike an independent, we can't threaten to go elsewhere if a product division doesn't meet our requirements on payment terms or stocking levels. That decreases our negotiating leverage with the product divisions in comparison to independent distributors.
>
> Third, I believe those payment and inventory terms often overstate revenues and income at the manufacturing level, rather than at our level of distribution. For example, a Westinghouse division's product is often placed on WESCO's books at the time it is shipped rather than, as with independent distributors, when payment has been received by the division. Similarly, our payments to the product divisions are fixed and prompt, whereas payment terms with independent distributors tend to be more flexible. The same is true for our policies concerning stocking levels for Westinghouse products: we generally carry a deeper and broader inventory of division products than the independent does.

Other managers noted that, in addition to corporate accounting procedures, other practices tended to impact WESCO's financial performance. One WESCO manager noted:

> I feel we incur what you might call "good samaritan" costs as a captive distributor. For example, for many product divisions we gear our purchases to complement their manufacturing cycles, not market conditions. Therefore, we carry a higher average inventory on many Westinghouse lines in comparison to the independent, who can source more opportunistically from a number of suppliers.

We, however, are tied to the manufacturing cycle of the product division, which hurts our inventory levels even as it helps the product division's throughput.

I also believe some product divisions tend to take WESCO for granted, and give us less service support than they give to their independents. We provide more functions for the product division than the average independent distributor does, such as preparing a complete bill-of-materials on an order.

Another WESCO manager emphasized organizational issues:

In many product areas, the primary value added of an electrical distributor is providing a sensible *package* of products. That's what customers are often looking for, and that's where the margins are.

But Westinghouse's organization has many complementary products in separate P&L centers. For example, load centers and transformers—usually sold in one package—were historically separate profit centers with different market share objectives. This can make it more difficult for WESCO to combine such products into a competitive package, compared to the independent distributor who cherrypicks from a number of suppliers in these product categories.

Until relatively recently, moreover, the field salespeople at Westinghouse did not get credit for sales of their products made as part of a package by WESCO sales reps.

In addition, corporate policies affected WESCO. According to one WESCO manager:

Our employees are covered by the Westinghouse benefits package, which is more generous than the benefits offered by most independent distributors. In turn, the WESCO branch pays for the benefits. Up-front salary, however, is better at many independent distributors than at WESCO. We lose some younger reps, who are generally more concerned with the cash compensation than with longer-term benefits.

A Westinghouse corporate executive suggested the following:

Westinghouse investment in WESCO is largely investment in inventory and receivables. As a result, our investment in WESCO is more fluid than investments made in manufacturing divisions.

Overall, I believe the relevant numbers and criteria for judging WESCO's performance are different than the criteria usually employed to judge the performance of our manufacturing units. There are many "hidden economics" embedded in a captive distribution operation, an intricate mingling of costs and benefits. And any specific decision affecting the relationship between WESCO and the product divisions must be made within this context.

Conclusion

As part of his review of Industries Marketing distribution policies, Mr. Hawks had spoken with executives at WESCO, the Westinghouse product divisions, and Westinghouse corporate headquarters. Their various viewpoints could be categorized as follows:

Viewpoint #1.   WESCO was currently performing the proper functions for the product divisions in its traditional customer segment, electrical contractors. To increase sales of Westinghouse products to other segments, only improved coordination with WESCO branches was required.

Viewpoint #2.   Some managers questioned the profitability of WESCO which, while generally in the upper quartile for electrical distributors (see Exhibit 6), was lower than that of most Westinghouse product divisions. Similarly, WESCO's ROI was generally lower than that of the total corporation.

This lower return raised the question of whether Westinghouse funds could be better invested elsewhere. Some managers believed that distribution for Westinghouse products should be entirely through the direct sales force and independent distributors. Westinghouse would concentrate on manufacturing and marketing, but stay out of distribution.

Viewpoint #3.   Other managers argued that corporate accounting policies understated the "true" returns of WESCO to the corporation. Some believed that WESCO did not receive the same sales support from product divisions that independent distributors did. Others argued that increased purchases of Westinghouse products and faster payment terms by WESCO affected WESCO negatively.

These managers also argued that the fact that WESCO did not sell products that directly competed with Westinghouse products, WESCO's national network of branches capable of servicing large geographically dispersed customers better than local distributors, the scale economies implicit in WESCO's size, and the WESCO computer systems were all important advantages for Westinghouse when it sold through WESCO. These managers believed that independent distributors should be used by product divisions only when absolutely necessary, since both flexibility and service could be increased by expanding WESCO. Over time, according to this viewpoint, WESCO branches would replace independent distributors as the corporation's financial and managerial resources permitted.

Exhibit 1   Westinghouse Electric Corporation (A)

Financial Information

Financial Information by Segment (in millions)

	1985	1984	1983
Sales and Operating Revenues			
Energy and Advanced Technology	$ 4,407.8	$ 4,077.3	$3,835.3
Industrial	3,732.3	3,638.0	3,401.6
Commercial	1,750.8	1,843.7	1,643.2
Broadcasting and cable	1,069.2	984.9	852.4
Divested units and other	119.9	114.1	216.4
	11,080.0	10,658.0	9,948.9
Innersegment sales	(379.8)	(393.5)	(416.3)
Total Sales and Operating Revenues	$10,700.2	$10,264.5	$9,532.6
Operating Profit			
Energy and advanced technology	$ 417.8	$ 375.0	$ 328.1
Industrial	61.2	(3.7)	(19.3)
Commercial	134.7	194.0	144.0
Broadcasting and cable	138.7	71.2	47.8
Divested units and other	(10.3)	(26.5)	(22.8)
Operating profit	742.1	610.0	477.8
Equity in Income of Finance Subsidiary and Other Affiliates	120.8	105.2	72.8
Other Income, Net	118.0	123.6	59.1
Interest Expense	(185.0)	(176.6)	(151.1)
Income before Income Taxes and Minority Interest	$ 795.9	$ 662.2	$ 458.6
Segment Identifiable Assets			
Energy and advanced technology	$ 2,896.7	$ 2,392.9	$2,103.6
Industrial	1,875.9	1,850.1	1,798.2
Commercial	1,005.1	980.8	846.2
Broadcasting and cable	1,680.9	1,762.0	1,683.5
Divested units and other	318.5	298.6	302.2
Adjustments and eliminations	(120.2)	(118.1)	(148.1)
	7,656.9	7,166.3	6,585.6
Investments	762.3	694.8	605.1
Corporate Assets	1,262.4	1,289.3	1,378.3
Total Assets	$ 9,681.6	$ 9,150.4	$8,569.0

Segment sales and operating revenues include products which are transferred between segments generally at inventory cost plus a margin. Operating profit of the segments consists of sales and operating revenues, less segment operating expenses.

Assets not identified to segments principally include cash and marketable securities, deferred income taxes, investment in the nonconsolidated finance subsidiary and the prefunded pension contribution.

Adjustments and eliminations deducted from segment-identifiable assets represent the removal of intersegment operating profit from the identifiable assets.

(continued)

Exhibit 1   *(continued)*

Divested units and other includes miscellaneous Corporate operations, and for 1983, the divested lamp and lighting business units and WESA, the Spanish subsidiary. Revenues and operating profit of foreign manufacturing operations are included in the appropriate segments.

Other Financial Data (in millions)

	1985	1984	1983
Depreciation and Amortization			
Energy and advanced technology	$140	$122	$ 97
Industrial	87	91	79
Commercial	35	30	28
Broadcasting and cable	152	153	133
Divested units and other	35	30	46
	$449	$426	$383
Capital Expenditures			
Energy and advanced technology	$238	$204	$224
Industrial	116	111	117
Commercial	53	76	63
Broadcasting and cable	155	234	290
Divested units and other	6	37	22
	$568	$662	$716

The largest single customer of the Corporation is the United States Government and its agencies, whose purchases accounted for 20 percent of the consolidated sales and operating revenues in 1985, 17 percent in 1984 and 18 percent in 1983. Of these purchases, 95 percent in 1985, 94 percent in 1984 and 91 percent in 1983 were made from Energy and Advanced Technology. No other customer made purchases totaling 10 percent or more of consolidated sales and operating revenues.

Source: Westinghouse Annual Report.

Exhibit 2 Westinghouse Electric Corporation (A)

Industries Group: Corporate Organization

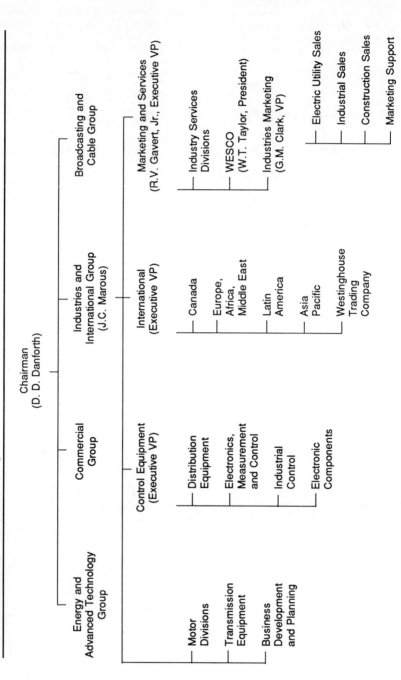

Exhibit 3   *Westinghouse Electric Corporation (A)*

Lead Salesman
Distributor Responsibilities

WESTINGHOUSE

Lead Salesman

DISTRIBUTOR RESPONSIBILITIES

1. Training
- Customize training for the distributor's needs –
  A prelude to specific sales effort.
- Train the distributor on catalog usage - pricing - Ⓦ products
- Make available training materials for distributor use
- Schedule training for annual requirements
- Encourage attendance at Ⓦ sponsored training schools
- Involve other Ⓦ personnel in training

2. Policy
- Communicate & interpret the Ⓦ distributor policy
- Ensure an understanding of division selling policies
- Ensure both Ⓦ & the distributor remain committed to FSD policies
- Communicate price policics - payment terms - warranties - minimum
  billings - freight, etc.

3. Inventory Management
- Review stock levels regularly
- Negotiate & write stock orders
- Process return authorizations to reduce excess stock
- Take inventory at least twice annually
- Communicate division stock requirements & return policies
- Ensure adequate inventory to serve customers
- Ensure distributor inventory commitment under FSD programs

4. Distributor Market
- Know the market served by distribution
- Evaluate the adequacy of Ⓦ distribution to reach the market
- Monitor Ⓦ distributor support to customers
- Know & communicate competitive distributor activity
- Recommend needs for additional Ⓦ distribution (full-line -
  limited line - specialized)
- Recommend cancellation of marginal distributors

(continued)

Exhibit 3 (continued)

5. Planning

- Formulate joint sales plans - be involved in co-direction
- Write target customer marketing plans in concert with the distributor
- Establish agreeable sales volume objectives that reflect growth
- Conduct regular performance reviews
- Strategize with the distributor

6. Division Programs

- Provide the distributor - division interface
- Administer stock sales rebate programs
- Promote division sponsored incentive programs
- Administer the Control Division modification program
- Communicate division / satellite service capabilities
- Communicate price changes

7. Coordination - Cooperation

- Coordinate the selling support provided by other Ⓦ salesmen
- Be the corporate interface
- Administer the stock sales allocation program
- Function as the liaison between the distributor and Ⓦ treasury - Ⓦ customer service
- Keep the distributor informed
- Monitor total Ⓦ support to the distributor and communicate with management any needs for improvement

8. Marketing Communications

- Conduct customer seminars
- Assist with local trade shows
- Introduce & promote new products
- Undertake direct mail programs
- Participate in open houses
- Ensure utilization of Ⓦ literature
- Maintain mail list forms for distributor people

Exhibit 4   Westinghouse Electric Corporation (A)

Product and Market Data for Electrical Distributors

Customer Mix
(for all types of electrical wholesalers)

Electrical contractors	40.8%
Non-electrical contractors	6.5%
Commercial/institutional accounts	7.9%
Industrials (for maintenance and repair)	18.4%
Industrials (for OEM)	6.9%
Utilities (private, REA, PUD, municipals)	3.9%
General public—retail	4.4%
Retailers for resale	4.5%
Government (federal, state, local)	3.5%
Other wholesalers	1.8%
Export	.8%
Others	.6%

Market Mix
(for full-line electrical wholesalers only)

Residential new construction	16.7%
Industrial new construction	13.6%
Commercial/office new construction	14.5%
Industrial maintenance and repair supplies	20.3%
Commercial/institutional customers	5.6%
Industrial or commercial renovation/retrofit	7.2%
OEMs (for use in the products they make)	7.1%
Utilities	5.0%
Government	2.3%
Retailers (for resale)	2.2%
Export	1.0%
Retail trade/lighting showroom/D-I-Y supplies	3.2%
Other wholesalers	1.0%
Other	.5%

Electrical Wholesalers' Sales ($ millions)

	Census 1982	EW Estimates 1983	EW Estimates 1984	EW Forecasts 1985	EW Forecasts 1986
Nation	**$24,502.3**	**$26,247.1**	**$30,587.5**	**$32,936.6**	**$34,718.4**
New England Region	1,208.8	1,373.0	1,640.4	1,780.5	1,867.9
Middle Atlantic Region	4,184.6	4,440.7	5,080.1	5,584.6	5,991.9
East North Central Region	3,732.6	3,992.0	4,956.0	5,408.8	5,668.9
West North Central Region	1,733.2	1,847.6	2,069.5	2,158.0	2,214.6
South Atlantic Region	3,897.1	4,338.4	5,213.4	5,777.6	6,158.8
East South Central Region	1,161.4	1,264.8	1,487.2	1,574.3	1,639.1
West South Central Region	3,725.9	3,771.4	4,201.9	4,314.8	4,535.2
Mountain Region	1,165.6	1,151.2	1,321.5	1,395.1	1,446.9
Pacific Region	3,692.9	4,067.9	4,617.2	4,942.8	5,195.2

(continued)

Exhibit 4 (continued)

Product Mix (for all types of electrical wholesalers)

Residential lighting fixtures	6.7%	Circuit breakers (includes GFI)	
C/I lighting fixtures	7.4%	and load centers	6.1%
Lamps	8.1%	Fuses	2.5%
Ballasts	2.7%	Transformers	1.7%
Building wire	8.1%	Busway	.6%
Flexible cord, cord sets	2.2%	Motor controls, starters and relays	5.1%
Power cable (includes service		Programmable controllers	1.0%
entrance)	2.4%	Motors and drives	2.2%
Lugs, connectors and terminations	1.3%	Instruments and test equipment	.8%
Fasteners	.8%	Tools (power and manual)	1.2%
Pole line hardware/utility supplies	1.8%	Electric heating equipment	1.9%
Electrical tape, insulating materials	1.3%	Air conditioners	.4%
Metal conduit and EMT	4.4%	Fans and ventilating equipment	1.5%
Nonmetallic conduit	2.0%	Sound, signal/alarm and	
Conduit fittings and bodies	3.2%	communication equipment	.7%
Wiring devices (includes GFI)	4.5%	Electric generator sets	.4%
Boxes and enclosures	3.0%	Electrical appliances, housewares,	
Panelboards and switchboards	3.8%	table lamps	.6%
Safety switches	2.7%	Electronic products	.6%

Source: Electrical Wholesaling, November, 1985

Exhibit 5 Westinghouse Electric Corporation (A)

WESCO Organization

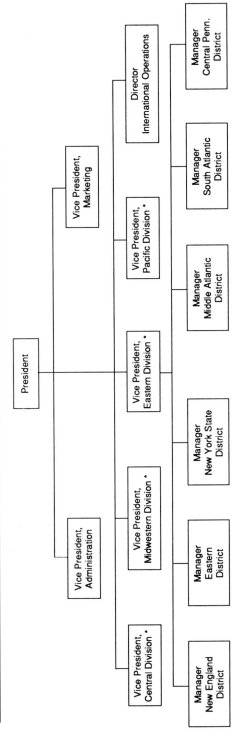

*Organization structures similar to Eastern Division.

Exhibit 6   *Westinghouse Electric Corporation (A)*

Financial Norms for Electrical Wholesalers

	1985	1984	1983	1982	1981	1980	1979
Cash[a]	4.00%	5.04%	5.5%	5.6%	2.1%	5.7%	3.4%
Receivables[a]	48.7%	46.1%	51.3%	49.0%	42.3%	44.4%	43.5%
Inventory[a]	47.3%	48.8%	43.2%	45.4%	55.6%	49.9%	53.0%
Current ratio	1.99	1.85	2.16	1.86	1.98	1.90	1.96
Quick ratio	1.04	.94	1.23	1.01	.88	.99	.91
Worth/debt ratio	.86	.80	1.16	.96	.93	1.01	.84
Gross profit	18.8%	19.2%	19.1%	21.3%	20.4%	19.9%	17.9%
Net profit before taxes	2.7%	3.1%	3.4%	2.9%	3.9%	3.6%	2.8%

Source: Electrical Manufacturers' Credit Bureau.

[a] = Data presented as % of current assets.

Current Ratio = Current Assets ÷ Current Liabilities.

Worth/Debt Ratio = Net Worth ÷ Total Liabilities.

Westinghouse Electric Corporation (B): Control House

Under the Control House program, a number of our branch managers will be very upset. They won't be selling the Westinghouse line of programmable controllers, and they won't be able to sell a competing line either. That will hurt them in their local markets during the coming years, and they know that.

Although specialty products today, programmable controllers will soon become standard items—items distributors must carry and be able to sell efficiently. My people must gain experience in this area and develop a strong local market position. But the Control House program prevents that for many WESCO branches.

WESCO has done a lot to support the Westinghouse control business during the past few years, and without the kinds of support being proposed for a Control House. Any WESCO branch not designated a Control House will have great difficulty maintaining its position in the industrial market.

—Mr. Tom McBride
Vice President, Marketing
WESCO

In late 1984, Mr. Chuck Hawks, manager of distribution for Industries Marketing at Westinghouse Electric Corporation, was reviewing a new distribution program proposed for programmable controllers (PCs) and certain other industrial control products manufactured by Westinghouse. A corporate task force had recently recommended establishing a limited number of specialized distributors, known as "control houses," to develop the market for Westing-

---

This case was prepared by Associate Professor Frank V. Cespedes as a basis for class discussion rather than to illustrate either effective or ineffective handling of an administrative situation. Certain company data, while useful for discussion purposes, have been disguised.

house's line of PCs and allied industrial control products—such as starters and relays—used by OEMs. Terms of the proposed agreement had been defined. Mr. Hawks, one of the task force members, had been asked to review the task force recommendations, suggest any modifications necessary for effective implementation of those recommendations, and then present the final recommendations to Westinghouse top management.

Westinghouse control products had traditionally been sold through all the branches of Westinghouse Electric Supply Corporation (WESCO), in addition to independent distributors and by Westinghouse's Industries Marketing sales forces. Under the Control House program, however, distribution for many control products in areas with high OEM potential was to be very selective, and in a few areas, independent distributors (rather than the local WESCO branch) might be chosen as the designated Control House. Of particular concern to Mr. Hawks was the impact of such a distribution program on WESCO and its relationship with the Westinghouse product divisions. Without a line of PCs to sell throughout its branches, WESCO's presence in the industrial market was likely to diminish.

Industrial Controls and Programmable Controllers

Industrial controls were used to regulate machining tasks, temperature, and pressure in various manufacturing applications. "Process control" systems were sold to companies with continuous production facilities as in the chemical, cement, paper, and food industries. "Discrete control" systems were used in batch manufacturing applications in all industries and for many specialized applications in industries such as fabricated metal, automobiles, and electrical products.

Programmable controllers were industrial logic controls used in both process and discrete systems to control machining tasks. PCs were initially developed in the mid-1960s to replace electromechanical control devices such as relay switches. PCs were generally a more versatile control system which also provided memory storage. Thus, users could access data such as the number of parts that passed through a machine, how long a machine had been operating, the time between tool changes, and other useful operating information. They could also change the sequence of operations by reprogramming.

A PC typically consisted of three basic components: a microprocessor memory, input/output devices, and a power supply. Important options included terminals to program the controllers and monitor machining operations, and network links to a central computer system. PC products differed in terms of memory size, programming devices, and in the number and types of input/output devices the unit could handle. By 1984, developments at the high end of the PC market indicated a trend toward networking applications in which PCs were linked to a central computer in order to provide greater coordination and control of a company's manufacturing process. Depending on options, a PC typically cost the user customer between $1,500 and $20,000 per unit.

Programmable Controller Market: Size and Competition

The worldwide PC market totalled about $1.5 billion in 1984 with the United States, Germany and Japan accounting for about 75% of sales. The U.S. market was an estimated $360 million with forecasted growth rates varying by industry sector as indicated in Exhibit 1. During the early 1980s, market growth had been relatively low as many industrial customers delayed capital spending programs during repeated recessions. But growth in the PC market had recovered along with the general economic recovery of 1983–84. Growth was expected to continue as PCs replaced older industrial control technology and as PC product families expanded downward to replace relays and upward to replace minicomputers in many applications.

Potential PC customers typically had to be educated about the product's capabilities, sold on the economics of replacing traditional control equipment, and often provided with specific applications support and software development assistance. PCs were generally not interchangeable, moreover, and most specifications work was done with users who were experimenting with their first orders.

In comparing the buying process for PCs with that for traditional control products, Mr. Hawks noted:

> Traditional control sales tend to focus on a single production process, and the product is then sold directly to the plant engineers responsible for that process. These engineers are also involved in the purchase of PCs, but the features of PCs bring other people into the buying process as well. Since the PC can transmit information to other computers owned by the customer, the plant manager, other engineers from other production processes, and often headquarters financial people are also involved in these purchases. Both the selling cycle and the sales efforts are greater due to the extensive testing and educational efforts involved.
>
> In addition, PCs are usually sold as part of a larger system, so a PC vendor must often be able to sell that system in order to make the PC sale.
>
> For a distributor, the PC is not an inherently attractive product. The distributor must make a lot of up-front investment in equipment and technical-selling capabilities, and the sales cycle means there are few short-term returns. In addition, the technology changes rapidly and that means the risk of carrying obsolete inventory is greater; and since the PC is sold as part of a total system, many other products are implicated in the obsolescence of a given PC line. But if you want to be a factor in industrial markets in coming years, you've got to be able to sell PCs.
>
> For Westinghouse, PCs represent a window of opportunity. Other firms, especially Allen-Bradley, have traditionally been stronger than us in the OEM segments for control products. Customers often have hundreds of specifications geared to our competitor's traditional control products, and so their switching costs have inhibited our penetration in the control market despite quality

products. But PCs represent a major technological change and so an opportunity to displace competitors if we move fast and effectively.

In 1984, the major suppliers of PCs in the U.S. market were:

Allen-Bradley: A-B had estimated 1984 sales of about $1.1 billion in all control products and a leading 37% share in PCs. In addition to PCs, A-B's chief products were electronic components, control equipment, and specialty plastics for manufacturing plants.

Modicon: a subsidiary of Gould, Modicon was the pioneer in the PC market and had been the market leader until the early 1970s. Its estimated 1984 market share in PCs was 25%.

Texas Instruments (TI): manufactured a range of electronic products and, through its Industrial Systems Division, PCs and related system products. With a 1984 PC share of about 9%, TI was strong in the low end of the PC market which it had dominated since the mid-1970s.

Industrial Solid State Controls (ISSC): previously a subsidiary of a German corporation before being acquired by Honeywell, ISSC was one of the original suppliers of PCs in Europe and had an estimated 4% of the U.S. market.

Square D: with 1984 total sales of about $1.5 billion, Square D was primarily a supplier of electrical control and distribution equipment. But the company had announced its intention of emphasizing electronic products, and its network-oriented PC system had an estimated 2.5% market share.

General Electric (GE): GE had been a later entrant in PCs, but its PC product line was considered an important part of GE's broader strategy to achieve worldwide leadership in factory automation. In 1984, GE had an estimated 8% of the U. S. PC market.

Other manufacturers, including Westinghouse whose market share was less than 5%, accounted for the remaining 10% of the U.S. market.

Distribution Channels for Programmable Controllers

The percentage of PC sales through independent distributors (versus direct through companies' sales forces) had increased to more than 80% in 1983, although there were important differences in the distribution strategies of major PC suppliers.

Allen-Bradley was considered by most observers to have the strongest distribution network for PCs. Long a major supplier of traditional control products, A-B had drawn its estimated 200 PC distributors from its existing industrial and contractor equipment distributors, where A-B's products usually accounted for a large percentage of these distributors' sales and profits. A-B had insisted that these distributors add expensive engineering and technical personnel who could understand PC technology and identify potential applications. In turn, A-B provided its PC distributors with educational training and sales support, 13 customer service centers with trained service people and extensive parts inventories, and exclusive distribution rights for A-B's PC products in a market area. In addition, A-B's sales force contained a number of application specialists who focused on getting A-B products, including PCs, specified by end users.

By contrast, Gould/Modicon relied almost entirely on its direct sales force, which included over 110 sales engineers focused exclusively on PCs. Modicon sold a higher-priced, broader product line than most competitors, and its sales force concentrated on getting these products specified for PC applications in areas such as machine tool automation.

TI relied on distributors to sell its PCs but, unlike A-B, TI's distributors had not been drawn from traditional industrial and contractor equipment organizations. Instead, TI had developed a new network of firms with software and engineering skills for hi-tech applications of PCs. These firms were known as systems houses.

GE marketed its PC line through independent distributors, some branches of GESCO (General Electric Supply Corporation, the captive distribution arm of GE), and in some industries its own direct sales forces. GE's distribution network for PCs consisted of approximately 100 distributors who, like A-B's distributors, were given exclusive rights to the GE line if they fulfilled certain requirements: a dedicated PC sales specialist, the carrying of fairly large inventories of GE's PC equipment, and on-site demonstration facilities. In a number of instances, independent distributors had been chosen over local GESCO branches. In addition, GE's direct salespeople were given credit for PC sales regardless of whether the sale was made direct or through a distributor. According to published estimates, GE's PC sales through distributors had increased from about $1 million in 1981, the first year of the program, to approximately $32 million by 1984.

Because of their growth potential in relation to mature electrical products, electronic products such as PCs had attracted increasing attention from traditional electrical distributors. These distributors had attempted to enter the electronics market in a variety of ways. Some had bought existing electronics distributorships, while others had focused on selected electronic product lines to be sold by their existing sales forces. Others had hired salespeople with electronics backgrounds or had started special marketing groups for electronic products.

According to most observers, however, sales of electronic products by traditional electrical distributors had generally yielded greatest success with small components (e.g., resistors, capacitors, diodes), where the products were near commodities usually sold from a catalog by quoting price and delivery terms. Less successful had been traditional electrical distributors attempting to sell products such as industrial control systems, which required more technical knowledge and involved longer selling cycles than electrical products.

Industrial Control Business at Westinghouse

A major supplier of electrical and electronic equipment, Westinghouse was organized into four operating groups in 1984 (see Westinghouse (A) for background information about the corporation). Within the Industries Group, a variety of businesses focused on products designed for industrial applications of electrical and electronic equipment. Each was a profit center.

Industrial controls were manufactured primarily by the Industrial Control business unit (IC). Westinghouse's traditional industrial control product line consisted primarily of motor control centers and enclosed starters (used for power distribution and control of motors) and components such as relays, open starters, push buttons and limit switches (used to open or close circuits after small changes in current or voltage). These products were generally purchased by machine-tool manufacturers. Westinghouse's market share in traditional control products was significantly less than the leaders in this market, Allen-Bradley and Square D.

Westinghouse sold its control products through the Industries Marketing sales forces and through more than 600 full-line electrical distributors, including all branches of WESCO. Product management believed these distributors served an essentially "captive" component business and sold generic, standard product lines. One manager commented:

> Most distributors' activity with Westinghouse control products has been in the "aftermarket" created by the large installed base of Westinghouse motor control centers where Westinghouse has long been a leader. They also do well in selling specification-intensive standard products, since these products are often pulled through by the control assemblies.
>
> Unfortunately, these broad-line electrical distributors have not done well in selling more technical or specialized control products. Many don't have the resources and expertise to sell these products, and those that do often felt they were competing with our own direct sales efforts. And there probably was an attitude here which tended to say, "The best customers will be sold direct and others through the distributors."

Westinghouse's PC line, "Numa-Logic" (see Exhibit 2), was manufactured by the Industry Electronics Division, which was a separate division from the industrial control business units. Numa-Logic was considered very competitive in price/performance terms and suitable for a variety of control logic applications in areas such as food, petroleum and chemical processing, automated assembly and testing, machine tool and robotics applications, material handling and pollution control. Numa-Logic was also sold direct and through distributors. Management was disappointed with Numa-Logic sales during the early 1980s and felt that its distribution policies were a major factor. Mr. Hawks commented:

> Numa-Logic is an excellent product and a clear opportunity for us to gain business. But the existing distribution strategy prevents establishing Westinghouse as

a major "presence" in the PC marketplace. Spread across different product groups, distribution programs tend to be short range and focused on price. We also miss opportunities for selling a package of control products which would include a PC.

WESCO PC Marketing Efforts

In 1982, WESCO sold a total of about $10 million worth of Numa-Logic PCs and other Westinghouse electronic products such as solid state motor starters. "In general," noted one WESCO manager, "our success with PCs was spotty, depending upon the initiative and technical competence of a local salesperson or manager." After meetings with managers from the Numa-Logic product group, WESCO agreed in 1983 to implement a series of actions designed to build sales.

First, each WESCO division, with funding from WESCO headquarters, hired four electronic product specialists who worked closely with potential PC customers. These specialists were responsible for developing sales plans for electronic products sold by WESCO to industrial customers, and for training WESCO salespeople. One WESCO manager noted:

> Hiring these specialists was a very new and expensive move for us. Most of these specialists were highly qualified in engineering or computers and were often considered "temperamental" by the branch manager who has lots of other things to focus on besides PCs. Also, this kind of selling effort does not generate big revenues for some time, and that's also a concern to a manager running a P&L center.

Second, WESCO agreed to place inventories of Westinghouse electronic products in selected locations within each WESCO division. These inventories included a large number of Numa-Logic PCs, as well as complementary items often sold with the PCs. These inventories were managed by the electronic product specialists in each district and were to be used by all branches within each district.

Third, a number of WESCO branches agreed to make investments in demonstration capabilities for Numa-Logic and other electronic and control products. Demonstration capabilities were considered important in selling Numa-Logic and required time, money, and a critical mass of inventory commitment by the branch. The initial investments could be considerable, and half of the investment was borne by WESCO headquarters and half by the branch.

WESCO spent a few million dollars in each of 1983 and 1984 on programs designed to sell Numa-Logic and related Westinghouse electronic control products. One WESCO manager described the expenditure as follows:

> We spent that money to improve Westinghouse's position, not WESCO's. There were plenty of other, higher-margin areas we could have invested that money. As it is, we do not expect to make a profit with PCs over the next several years.

Control House Task Force

Concerned about sales of Numa-Logic and other electronic industrial control products, Westinghouse corporate management appointed in late 1984 a task force to analyze the situation and make specific recommendations. Task force members included product managers from relevant control units as well as Mr. Hawks and Mr. McBride.

After repeated meetings, the task force agreed that a critical ingredient in building the industrial control business in the OEM market would be the establishment of a limited number of specialized distributors, designated as "Control Houses." In seeking to implement this concept, the task force focused on four major areas.

The first was to define the direct vs. distributor channel flow for products covered by a Control House agreement. The task force recommended that, as a general policy, all control products covered by the agreement be sold exclusively through distributors. Mr. Hawks explained that "we recognized that, in a few special cases, business would go direct for these products. But this would be discussed when a Control House agreement was signed with a distributor. The point was to emphasize that, in contrast to past practices, we were committed to distributor, not direct sales in these areas." The products covered by the Control House agreement were Westinghouse's Numa-Logic PCs manufactured by the Industry Electronics Division, Power Miser and Accutrol solid state motor controls manufactured by the Vectrol Division, and motor starters, contactors, relays, push buttons, and terminal blocks manufactured by the IC division (see Exhibit 2 for product information). A major reason for selecting these products as Control House products was that they were purchased primarily by OEMs.

Second, the task force considered whether, in contrast to the historical emphasis by Westinghouse on wide distribution, Westinghouse should focus its sales support for Control House products in a market area. Those arguing for highly selective or exclusive distribution stressed the improved distributor margins and consequent incentive for distributors to devote "up-front" investments in market development for these product lines. They also argued that highly selective distribution would focus Westinghouse product division resources and support for Control Houses as well as facilitate both planning and measurement. Those arguing against selective distribution stressed that it could limit customer coverage and risk losing parts of the traditional control business where availability and local distributor relationships were very important. They also pointed out that a highly selective approach was revolutionary in comparison to traditional policy, and would force a choice between a WESCO branch and an independent distributor in many areas.

The task force finally recommended the highly selective approach to franchising Control Houses in a given market area.

Third, the task force considered whether only WESCO branches should be Control Houses. The following advantages were cited: instant loyalty to and knowledge of the Westinghouse organization, easier administration and control, a nationwide network in place with advanced computer systems, and in-house retention of all margin dollars by the Westinghouse corporation. In response, other managers stressed that a given WESCO branch was not always the best candidate: independent distributors in many areas often had better customer knowledge and, especially in OEM segments, better relationships than a WESCO branch. Some independent distributors also had more experience and expertise with electronics products. In addition, some managers foresaw an adverse reaction from independent distributors, possibly affecting other Westinghouse products, if WESCO were given exclusive rights to Westinghouse control products. "Many independents already believe that we privilege WESCO over the local independent distributor," said one manager. "This would solidify that perception."

The task force concluded that all available distributor options should be utilized in selecting Control House distributors. In addition, the task force recommended that Westinghouse should consider offering Control House status to the most qualified distributor in a market even if that distributor did not presently carry the Westinghouse line.

Fourth, the task force specified the terms of the agreement between Westinghouse and distributor locations designated as Control Houses (see Exhibit 3). In specifying terms, the task force felt that product availability and demonstrations were critical in selling PCs, and that therefore a Control House must stock both a broad and deep line of the designated Westinghouse products. In addition, the Control House distributor had to agree to dedicate an outside salesperson to the OEM segment and to hire a new, technically trained control products specialist. In return, Westinghouse would have a no-fault return policy on unsold products and would help the Control House fund a portion of the initial required inventory. Westinghouse would also cover the distributor's out-of-pocket costs of adding a control-products specialist, training inside and outside salespeople, and providing equipment for the required demonstration room at the distributor's facility. The agreement also specified volume objectives and incentives for both Westinghouse field salespeople and distributors and provided for a three-year commitment on both sides.

Current Situation

Mr. Hawks had been asked to review the task force recommendations, suggest any modifications, and present the final recommendations to Westinghouse top management. Commenting on the proposed Control House program, Mr. Hawks said:

> The Control House concept could integrate the complementary distribution needs of a number of product divisions. It also simplifies the Westinghouse/distributor interface and improves our market development efforts in the control

area by focusing Industries Marketing salespeople efforts on a few distributors. It also allows for a coordinated, focused approach to the OEM control market, which has been a weakness for us.

A key issue here is that our PC line has only a limited window of opportunity. Westinghouse has been in the control business for years, but has lagged a market leader like Allen-Bradley. Numa-Logic PCs give us a potential edge in that market. It's also clear that over the coming years PCs will replace our electromechanical relays and other products that now comprise the core of our control business.

Therefore, for both offensive and defensive reasons, we must concentrate our sales efforts during the next few years as the market moves from electromechanical to electronic technology. The Control House is one way to do that.

As manager of distribution, responsibility for the success of the proposed program would fall primarily on Mr. Hawks, and he was concerned about its implementation and, in particular, the reaction of WESCO. What would be the key tasks in implementing the program? Would successful implementation require any changes in the task force's recommendation? Mr. Hawks recalled the strenuous statement made by Mr. McBride at the conclusion of the task force's final meeting: "Any WESCO branch not included as a Control House will be very angry indeed." Mr. McBride also pointed out that, in addition to the projected market growth for programmable controllers, PCs were attractive to distributors because they could be used as "lead items" to pull through sales of related products such as electronic sensing devices, switches, and cables. Further, given the forecasts for factory automation products in general, PCs would be a key items in broadening the mix of products carried by WESCO as electronic products gradually replaced electromechanical products at WESCO's customers. "But under the Control House program," noted Mr. McBride, "many WESCO branches won't be selling Numa-Logic or other important electronic control products, and they won't be able to sell competing lines, either."

As he reviewed the task force recommendations, Mr. Hawks increasingly felt that, from the perspective of the corporation, the PC situation posed a dilemma.

> To survive in the industrial control marketplace, it's necessary that the product divisions have the best distribution outlet available whether it be a WESCO branch or an independent distributor in a given market. But each time an independent is chosen rather than the WESCO branch, that prevents WESCO from moving into the electronic marketplace, and this is a necessity for the future welfare of that organization.

Mr. Hawks' final recommendation and any implementation suggestions were due in one week.

Exhibit 1 *Westinghouse Electric Corporation (B): Control House*

U.S. Programmable Controller Market: Industry Estimates
($ in millions)

Industry Sector	1984	Estimated Growth Rate (1983–1986)
Food	$ 27	23%
Paper	14	21
Chemical	22	21
Petroleum & coal	10	19
Rubber & plastic	14	20
Cement & glass	9	20
Utility	17	25
Primary metal	18	15
Nonelectrical machinery	27	19
Electrical & electronic	46	20
Fabricated metals	23	18
Transportation	72	13
Other	61	15
Total	$360	

Total U.S. NEMA Programmable Control Market

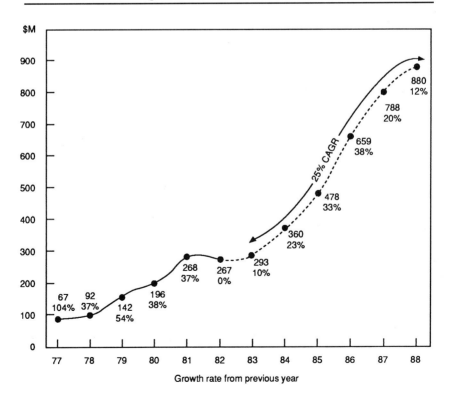

Growth rate from previous year

Exhibit 2 Westinghouse Electric Corporation (B): Control House

Numa-Logic 700, 900, 1100 Series Programmable Controllers

FUNCTIONS/APPLICATIONS

Westinghouse Numa-Logic 700, 900, and 1100 Series of programmable controllers combine the low cost and high performance of the microprocessor with the reliability of solid state engineering. The memory sizes of the PC-700 (up to 8192 sixteen-bit words) accommodate medium to large control needs. Designed for smaller applications, the memories of the PC-900 range from 256 to 2560 sixteen-bit words. The PC-1100 has been designed for the smallest of applications, and offers a memory range of from 512 to 3584 sixteen-bit words. Regardless of memory size, however, the PC-700, PC-900, and PC-1100 provide users with dependable control operations and sophisticated capabilities, including arithmetic, drum control, analog and digital conversions, distributed processing, and remote inputs and outputs (I O). The PC-700, PC-900, and PC-1100 belong to the Numa-Logic family of modular programmable controllers, and therefore, share common I O modules and peripherals.

Flexible and versatile, the PC-700, PC-900, and PC-1100 are ideal for a wide variety of control applications, including machine tool; robotics; automated assembly and testing; material handling; food, petroleum, and chemical processing; energy management; and pollution control.

SPECIAL FEATURES

The Numa-Logic PC-700 and PC-900 processors meet IEEE, ANSI, and NEMA noise immunity standards. Most I O modules meet IEEE surge withstand standards. Both the PC-700 and the PC-900 have remote I O capabilities which allow control over an area of up to 12.5 square miles. The PC-1100's Port Transmit feature can be used in remote I O applications. Distributed processing configurations are also possible over a maximum distance of two miles between processors. Numa-Logic's CRT program loader has a large 9" diagonal screen, yet is compact enough to fit under an airplane seat. (Actual dimensions of the CRT loader: 16" · 7½ · 13¾".) Numa-Logic's Mini Loader is a compact, hand-held or panel mounted program loader weighing only two pounds, and featuring message generation, assignable keys, pushbutton mode, and a tape capability. Numa-Logic's unique Memory Miser feature uses no memory words for branches, nodes, or unused contact positions, thus providing up to 36% more memory space than competitive units.

PC training classes are held at the Westinghouse Industry Electronics Division headquarters in Pittsburgh, PA. For further information contact the Marketing Department, Westinghouse Numa-Logic, Industry Electronics Division, 1521 Avis Drive, Madison Heights, MI (313) 588-1540.

PROCESS UNITS

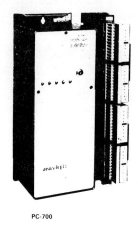

PC-700

PC-900

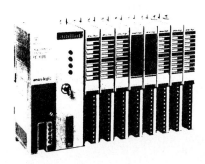

PC-1100

Exhibit 3   *Westinghouse Electric Corporation (B): Control House*

Overview of "Control House" Agreement

	Recommended Commitments	
	Distributor	Westinghouse
Channel	• Westinghouse their primary line	• Westinghouse's primary outlet
People	• Dedicated inside control specialists • Specialized outside OEM sales-person	• Dedicated OEM sales effort • Fund distributor inside person • Dedicated division inside support (direct Control House access) • Direct sales support: 　Lead Sales Engineer 　Solid State Specialist 　Division Product Specialist
Training	• Commit to initial concentrated training of inside and outside people • Commit to ongoing inhouse training • Division updates (minimum once a year)	• Provide training 　Product school 　Sales training 　Ongoing local training
Inventory	• Commit to maintaining: 　$100,000 of Control Division 　$35,000 of Numa-Logic 　$20,000 of Vectrol 　or 3 months supply whichever is greater	• Incremental growth stock above minimum to be funded by Westinghouse • Return/exchange policy • Provide analysis of additional purchases
Planning	• Agree to establish and have performance measured by mutually agreed-upon annual objectives, by providing sales records necessary to monitor performance quarterly	• Market & product analysis • Sales support based on plans
Facility	• Dedicated training and demonstration room • Keep current with up-to-date product	• Provide demonstrators and display package needed to initially equip room
Promotion	• Utilize Westinghouse designed Control House promotion 　Telemarketing　Customer seminars 　Direct mail　　　Displays	• Provide source material

Case 11
Alloy Rods Corporation

On Monday, July 1, 1985, Mr. D. Fred Bovie, president and chief operating officer of Alloy Rods brought important news to Mr. Philip Plotica, vice president of sales and marketing:

> Phil, the rumors are now fact. Lincoln Electric announced today a gas-shielded flux-cored product at a price considerably lower than ours. For 25 years Lincoln has stayed out of the gas-shielded segment. Now, they're taking a shot at our most profitable and fastest growing product line. I'm arranging a meeting with Bob Egan (chairman of Alloy Rods) and Eugene Sabel (general sales manager) for Friday, and I'd like you to get us started by presenting your recommendations and an action plan. What does Lincoln's move mean for our marketing programs in this product area? And how do we manage our programs in the face of this new competition?
>
> This can also be an opportunity to reevaluate our marketing system. Distributors account for the majority of our sales, and both Bob and Gene have raised questions about that. We've discussed these matters informally since we bought the company, and I think we're ready to make specific decisions. On Friday, let's be prepared to explain any changes we want to make in how we go to market as well as how we should respond to Lincoln's move.

Industry Background

"Welding may not make the world go around, but it does hold most of it together," noted Alloy Rods Chairman Bob Egan. In 1985, welding equipment and supplies was a $1.6 billion industry in the United States, providing the materials to hold together structures such as skyscrapers, ships, bridges, power

This case was prepared by Associate Professor Frank V. Cespedes and Research Assistant Ellen R. Hattemer as the basis for class discussion rather than to illustrate either effective or ineffective handling of an administrative situation.

plants, and pipelines. Alloy Rods competed in the consumable welding electrode, or "filler metal," segment where there were three major welding processes and five major product groups. (Exhibit 1 provides an overview of welding process and product types.)

Welding Processes

The predominant welding technique in 1985, electric arc welding, joined metals by passing voltage through an electrode (usually a metal rod, acting as a conductor) to maintain a current or arc between the electrode and the work piece. The electrical energy, converted to heat, caused the metals to melt and join. The temperature at the arc was about $10,000°$ F. In welding processes using consumable electrodes, the conductor itself also melted and became part of the weld. There were three major consumable electrode welding processes:

Shielded Metal Arc Welding (SMAW) was the original and still most widely used welding process. In this process, the welder used an electrode holder connected to a power source (see Figure 1). The electrode rod was coated with a material called flux which, as it burned, produced a gaseous shield for the molten weld. This shield prevented the weld from exposure to atmospheric oxygen and nitrogen which could harm the weld. The flux coating, available in hundreds of varieties, often also contained alloys to add durability, strength, or ductility to the weld. Mr. Plotica noted that, "At Alloy Rods we use proprietary formulations which we believe make our electrodes especially tough and useful in a number of applications."

Figure 1

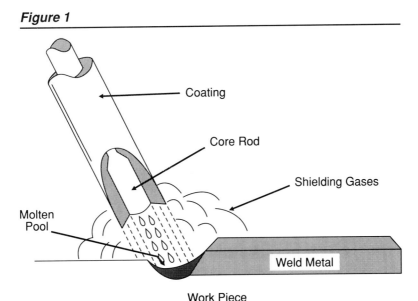

Shielded Metal Arc Welding

The equipment used in SMAW was simple and mobile (see Exhibit 1). In addition to the protective helmet and gloves standard for all welding processes, SMAW required a $1,500 outlay for an electrode holder, a power source, and various cables, connectors, and hand tools.

Gas Metal Arc Welding (GMAW) employed a continuous, solid wire electrode which was "fed" into the welding gun. Thus, GMAW was more efficient than SMAW where productivity losses occurred each time a welder stopped to replace a consumed electrode. Material losses also resulted since the stub of each electrode was thrown away.

However, GMAW sacrificed some of SMAW's simplicity and mobility in return for the productivity gains. A continuous wire could not be coated with flux as this material was too fragile to withstand winding and pulling. Thus, the use of wire electrodes necessitated an external gas source to shield the molten weld. The lack of flux coating also made it difficult to add alloys to the weld. Therefore, GMAW's use was concentrated in general-purpose, noncritical welding applications such as automobile fabrication.

In GMAW, the bare metal wire electrode, a shielding gas, and a power cable were fed separately into a welding gun (see Figure 2). Along with the gun, a welder needed a wire feeder and tanks of gas, as well as the cables, connectors, and tools used in SMAW (see Exhibit 1). The total equipment cost to set up for GMAW was about $2,800 in 1985.

Flux Cored Arc Welding (FCAW), introduced in the late 1950s, used a hollowed continuous electrode filled with a powder flux. Two types of flux-

Figure 2

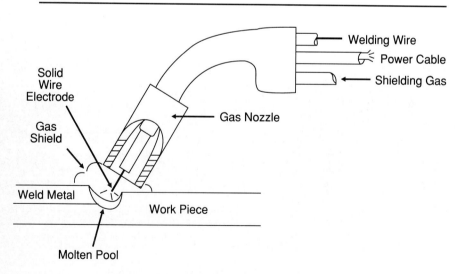

Gas Metal Arc Welding

cored arc welding developed: gas-shielded, which required an external gas source similar to GMAW, and self-shielded, which had gas-forming materials within the flux similar to the coated stick electrodes of SMAW (see Figure 3).

Gas-shielded flux-cored electrodes (the focus of Lincoln's recent move) combined the weld metal quality of coated stick electrodes with the high productivity of solid wires. The equipment required resembled that of GMAW, although a welder usually worked with a modified wire feeder to prevent flattening of the cored wire.

Self-shielded flux-cored electrodes, on the other hand, offered the welder the efficiency of solid wires and the mobility of stick electrodes. The self-shielded electrodes eliminated the need for gas tanks and hoses, and used a simpler welding gun than the gas-shielded method. However, materials within the flux core limited the weld quality. So, in comparison to gas-shielded flux-cored welding, self-shielded flux-cored welding was limited to less critical, general-purpose applications.

Consumable Welding Electrode Product Groups

Consumable welding electrodes were separated into five basic product groups:

1. *Flux-Cored Wire Electrodes*—Sales of gas-shielded and self-shielded flux-cored electrodes were $100 million in 1984, of which about two-thirds were gas-shielded wire. The average price per pound was $.79, but this price varied widely depending on the diameter of the electrode. Alloy projected the flux-cored segment to grow by 2% (in pounds) in 1985.
2. *Low Hydrogen Coated Stick Electrodes*—Low alloy steels for critical applications required an electrode with very low hydrogen content. These

Figure 3

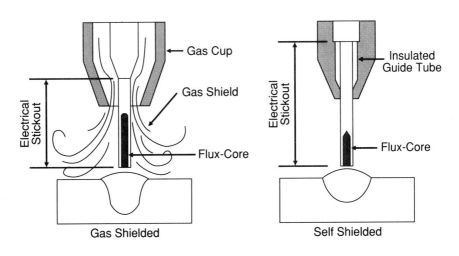

Gas Cup

Gas Shield

Electrical Stickout

Flux-Core

Gas Shielded

Insulated Guide Tube

Electrical Stickout

Flux-Core

Self Shielded

electrodes were manufactured and packaged to minimize exposure to moisture. Low hydrogen stick sales were $72 million in 1984 with no growth expected in 1985 and an average industry price of $.52 per pound.

3. *Stainless Steel Electrodes*—Stainless steel welding required different electrodes than "mild" or low alloy steels did, and the average price in 1984 was $2.65 per pound. Stainless steel electrodes, with 1984 sales of $51 million and a projected growth rate of 2%, were sold in three forms for each of the major welding processes.

4. *Mild Steel Coated Stick* (for SMAW), and 5. *Mild Steel Solid Wire Electrodes* (for GMAW) had combined sales of $204 million in 1984. Average industry prices were $.46 per pound for sticks and $.55 for wire; the projected growth rate was 1.0% in 1985 for solid wire and no growth for coated stick. Mild steel electrodes were low manufacturing value-added items in which it was difficult to achieve product differentiation.

Within each product group, electrodes were manufactured in a range of diameters. The diameter of the electrode often determined whether or not a given electrode was suitable for a given welding application. In general, it was harder to ensure consistent product quality in smaller-diameter electrodes, and so reputable smaller-diameter electrodes could usually command a higher price than larger-diameter electrodes of the same type. Alloy Rods produced more types of welding electrodes in more sizes and alloys than any other U.S. manufacturer.

Industry Trends

The welding consumables industry was hit hard in 1982 and 1983 by the economic recession (see Exhibit 2). In the United States, industry sales in pounds dropped by 30% in one year. Managers at Alloy expected much of this loss to be permanent since, to lower their labor costs, many heavy-equipment manufacturers and other major welding users had moved their operations overseas.

As the advantages of welding with continuous wire electrodes became better known, many users switched from coated stick electrodes to flux-cored and mild steel solid wires. The increased materials efficiency of the wires was part of the reason for the lower industry sales in pounds of metal. For example, for every pound of coated stick electrodes purchased, only 0.65 pounds became part of the actual weld, while the rest was discarded with the electrode "stub." The use of solid wire and flux-cored wire increased this efficiency rating to a range of 80–90%.

Although continuous wire electrodes could cost twice as much as stick electrodes per pound, conversion to wire was often economically justifiable. On a typical welding job, 2–5% of the total cost was power and equipment, 8–15% electrodes, and the remaining 80–85% labor and overhead. Including the purchase of the different equipment needed for wire use, conversion often offered a three-month payback because of labor productivity increases with continuous electrodes.

Customers: Purchase Process and End-Use Segments

Welding electrode end-users ranged from one-person mechanical contracting shops to major steel fabricators who used millions of pounds of electrodes annually. While end-users often ordered electrodes by specific brand, this product loyalty varied among end-user segments (see Exhibit 3).

The purchasing process also differed among companies. The owner, plant manager or welder of a small- or medium-size company made the electrode buying decision and placed the order. In large companies, a welding engineer often conferred with welders to designate a brand or define specifications. Then the purchasing department placed the order and often chose the specific electrode brand. Overall, end users ranked a supplier's product quality, line breadth, and delivery/availability as the most important criteria in their choice of electrodes.

In the welding supplies and equipment industry, over 70% of sales were made through distributors, although this varied by end-user segment (see Exhibit 3). Distributors' purchasing criteria were different from end users'. Distributors placed most importance on product quality, but they viewed "creation of demand," communications with the factory, and price as the next most important factors. Distributors estimated that 50% of their electrode sales to end users were dictated by customer brand preference, 30% by price, and 20% by product quality.

Welders and welding engineers often resisted switching welding processes despite the economics of stick versus continuous electrodes. The potential for liability if a weld failed made the change from a familiar to a new process risky. Conversion also required welding engineers to rewrite numerous specifications and procedures and to retrain welders. In unionized shops, established work rules often inhibited the adoption of new welding techniques. Additionally, the welders were often reluctant to switch, because welding with continuous electrodes required less operator skill. As one observer noted, "Welding is still enough of an art that welders can make a particular process look as bad or good as they want." Mr. Plotica added that the catalyst for a change in welding processes was often the adoption of a new process by an industry leader:

> For example, when Caterpillar adopted flux-cored welding for their construction equipment, they drove their competitors to adopt flux-cored as well. Nonetheless, in many industries, the welding procedures are built around sticks, and rewriting the procedures is a big job for welding engineers. They have a lot of pride in their established routines, and their attitude is usually, "if it's not broken, don't fix it." But sometimes you can find a young engineer at a company who's more receptive to change, and who can become a hero when management realizes the productivity potential of flux-cored. It's the same with distri-

butors: there are the old timers who don't want to convert users to new welding techniques, and there are the Young Turks.

Company Background

In 1940, Ed Brady, a welding engineer, founded Alloy Rods in Hanover, Pennsylvania. With seven workers, he began making stainless steel coated stick electrodes on two used extrusion presses. Demand for stainless steel welding soared during World War II and in the decade following the war. By 1960, Alloy Rods had seven sales offices, a network of distributors, and several company warehouses.

Chemetron Corporation bought Alloy in 1962 to add electrodes to its line of welding gases and equipment. Chemetron absorbed Alloy's sales and distribution network into its existing organization and, in a cost reduction measure, closed Alloy's regional warehouses, increasing delivery times for distributors and end users. Alloy soon saw its sales drop despite growth in industry sales during this period.

Allegheny Ludlum Industries acquired Chemetron in 1978 and made it part of Allegheny's Metal Products Group under Mr. Egan who had joined Allegheny in 1956 after graduating from Harvard Business School. Two years later, the Chemetron-appointed president of Alloy Rods was replaced by Mr. Bovie, a 27-year veteran of the welding industry.

In January 1985, Messrs. Egan, Bovie, and Plotica, along with several other managers and outside investors, bought the company from Allegheny. Typical "leveraged buy-out" capitalization was used to purchase the company with Messrs. Egan and Bovie as the largest shareholders. At the newly independent company, Mr. Egan was chairman, Mr. Bovie the president, and Mr. Plotica the vice president of sales and marketing (see Exhibit 4). Alloy Rods' business was defined by the new owners as follows:

> The primary business purpose of Alloy Rods is to develop, manufacture, and market high-quality, high-technology welding filler metal products on a world-wide basis, with emphasis on sales via distributor and wholesaler channels. Secondary business purposes include the sale of product and/or manufacturing technology via technical assistance, trademark license and joint-venture agreements.

In 1984, Alloy Rods' domestic operations had sales of approximately $65 million with an after-tax profit of between $1 and $2 million. Sales of flux-cored wire under the Dual Shield brand name accounted for nearly 40% of sales and over 40% of gross margin, while low hydrogen coated sticks under the Atom Arc name accounted for 15% of sales and over 20% of total gross margin. (See Exhibit 5 for domestic market shares by product type.) Most of Alloy's sales were to U.S. end users and distributors, although Alloy also sold electrodes to the U.S. government and in foreign countries. In addition to the Hanover plant, Alloy had a plant in Mexico and a maintenance and repair subsidiary in

Maryland. Mr. Egan noted, "The last thing this new L. B. O. needs is a major attack on its core business. I congratulate Lincoln on their timing, but we must not let them succeed."

Marketing at Alloy Rods

Product Policy

In a 1980 survey of welding distributors, Alloy Rods was ranked first among electrode suppliers in product quality, technical capabilities, and product innovativeness (see Exhibit 6).

In the welding industry, developing new products could take ten years from the initial concept to the actual application. Alloy devoted more dollars to R&D as a percent of sales than most of its competitors. One result was .035 inch diameter flux-cored wire. While many companies made flux-cored wire, Alloy Rods estimated that it had at least a one-year lead on its competitors in cored wire drawn to such a small diameter. This new .035 inch product, introduced in 1984, enabled welders to use flux-cored wire on jobs where they had previously been restricted to using solid wire. Management intended to develop more new products and believed the company's exclusive reliance on welding consumables would focus its R&D and support an emphasis on higher-margin technical innovations.

Under Chemetron, Alloy had sold welding equipment as well as electrodes, but the equipment business was unprofitable and was sold in 1978. In 1985, Alloy was the only major company in the industry to manufacture only welding electrodes, and had the broadest electrode line, listing 336 different items for flux-cored products alone with another 700 line items for the remaining four product groups. Mr. Bovie remarked,

> Any hold in our product line forces our distributors to shop at a competitor. We don't want to open that door, so we sell commodity items like mild steel solid wire even though the line is far less profitable than our higher-technology flux-cored products.

Pricing

In general, Alloy Rods' prices were higher than its competitors' in part because Alloy charged for freight while competitors absorbed freight expenses which comprised up to 10% of the total product cost (see Exhibit 7). Management believed the company's product quality and innovations enabled it to obtain this price premium in most cases. Like most electrode manufacturers, Alloy offered a volume discount and the broad array of available products enabled customers to take advantage of this pricing policy. Mr. Plotica noted:

> It's not our higher prices that distributors complain about as much as our Freight-On-Board (F. O. B.) policy. We believe pricing F. O. B. makes sense: A

major portion of the welding market is concentrated in six states (California, Michigan, Ohio, Pennsylvania, Texas and Illinois), and equalizing freight charges (as our competitors do) would essentially penalize our customers east of the Mississippi. F. O. B. pricing also helps to keep our prices down in real terms, since distributors and end users can save money by ordering in freight-load volumes.

However, there's no doubt that distributors generally dislike the F. O. B. policy; they say it complicates their bookkeeping and seems to result in a higher price. But we're not afraid to do something different if, in overall terms, it makes sense and makes us more competitive and more profitable.

Promotion

In 1984, Alloy spent about $500,000 on advertising, product literature, and sales promotions. Advertising in industry trade journals stressed Alloy's role as the leader in technology and the productivity benefits of flux-cored wire. Some ads reminded customers about Alloy's full product line. In total, however, Alloy did considerably less advertising than its competitors.

Most of Alloy's promotions were geared towards distributors because, as Mr. Plotica explained,

> We are in a constant battle for the distributor's time, attention and shelf space. Electrodes usually make up about 12% of the typical distributor's sales, and our products comprise about 70% of that at our major distributors. Compared to equipment and industrial gases, electrodes are a small part of a welding distributor's total business, and the margins also tend to be lower.

Most of the promotional budget went to product literature (see Exhibit 8), a home study course, field training seminars, newsletters, and trade shows. Alloy's product literature ranged from a one-page direct mail pamphlet to booklets detailing welding specifications and product characteristics. The company also offered literature that encouraged customers to perform cost comparisons that revealed the value of converting to flux-cored wire. In 1981, the company began offering a 10-month home study course on welding technology, designed for people with nontechnical backgrounds, especially distributors' salespeople. By 1985, over 4,000 people had enrolled in the course and more than 1,000 had completed it.

The remaining portion of the promotional budget was paid to distributors in the form of advertising and promotional allowances. Mr. Plotica believed that Alloy was the only company in the industry to offer this type of sales promotion support to its distributors.

Distribution Channels

Exhibit 9 provides an overview of Alloy's distribution channel structure. In 1984, 75% of Alloy's sales were to independent welding supply distributors: about 13% went direct to these distributors, while 41% went through independent wholesalers and 21% through company-owned wholesalers who then sold

Alloy's products to distributors. Another 13% of sales were made direct to end users, with the remainder sold to export, private label, and governmental markets. The company's field sales force called on both distributors and end users.

Throughout the electrode industry, the percentage of product sold through independent distributors had increased during the past decade. Mr. Bovie explained:

> Until a few years ago, the electrode business was tied to the welding equipment business, and the major players were companies that sold both equipment and electrodes direct to end users. But in recent years Federal Trade Commission rulings have prohibited formal tie-ins of welding equipment, gases and filler metal, and this provided an important window for companies like Alloy Rods, which sells only the electrodes, and Miller Electric, which sells only the equipment. Both rely heavily on distributors.

Mr. Bovie also explained that, over the years, Alloy's relations with its distributors had gone through different phases. For example, prior management policies had affected distributor relations:

> Chemetron's primary business was welding gases and equipment, and they saw electrodes as a way of spurring gas and equipment sales. When it bought Alloy Rods, Chemetron had about 400 distributors who had made big investments in tanks and other equipment necessary to sell the gas. If distributor overlap became a problem, then Chemetron usually cut the Alloy Rods distributors when it was forced to choose.
>
> In 1974, moreover, there was a shortage of welding electrodes. During the shortage, Chemetron chose to sell direct to end users (cutting out the distributors) at very high margins. The fallout from that move affected distributor relations for years afterwards.

In addition, distributor relations had been affected by individual personalities and management styles. According to Mr. Bovie,

> The person who ran Alloy under Chemetron and under Allegheny until 1980 had definite ideas about distributors: he felt they were at best a necessary evil. And in his interactions with distributors, he communicated that attitude. He lectured distributors about how they should run their businesses, but was not receptive to feedback from them. In addition, his policies and programs tended to change without any warning to or input from the distributors.
>
> I arrived at Alloy in 1980 and have spent most of the past five years working to regain distributors' trust and support. I met with each distributor, introduced feedback devices such as surveys, a distributor council, and co-op advertising and promotional programs. But most of all, I have been consistent in our distribution policies and programs: we do what we say we'll do, and we don't change our policies annually. If a change does become necessary, I try to explain the reasons behind our actions and give the distributors as much information as possible.
>
> None of this is magic. It's simply the kind of recurring, labor-intensive managerial work that must be done when you're working through distributors, but that unfortunately wasn't done in the past.

Welding Supply Distributors

In 1985 Alloy Rods used about 500 independent welding supply distributors (with a total of 1,500 locations) from a total of 2,200 welding supply distributors in the United States. "We prefer to be selective in our approach," noted Mr. Plotica, "looking for the best distributor in each market area." Electrodes were generally one among hundreds of products carried by these distributors, ranging from standard torches, welding guns, gloves, sweatbands and goggles to special devices for cutting and welding. According to one industry source, the average distributor's gross margin on welding materials was in the 21–28% range while the average distributor's gross margin on electrodes was in the 9–15% range. Additional information about the average welding distributor is provided below:

Annual sales (1984): $3.2 million
Number of locations: 2.5
Number of employees: 26
Number of customers: 4,439
Percentage of total sales derived from:
  Industrial gases (33%)
  Gas welding equipment and supplies (7%)
  Electrical welding equipment and supplies (13%)
  Medical gases and supplies (4%)
  Safety equipment (3%)
  Filler metals (16%)
  Cylinders (10%)
  Other products and services (14%)
Distributors offering welding equipment for purchase or rental: 75%

Alloy's managers estimated that their top 50 distributors accounted for 80% of the company's sales to distributors. Of these top 50 distributors, 20 also sold products manufactured by Lincoln Electric Company. In addition, almost all of Alloy's distributors had other suppliers for welding electrodes. Mr. Plotica noted:

> Distributors have long memories, and I think they still fear dependency on a single supplier because of the 1974 shortages. We in turn have moved away from exclusive distribution, although not nearly to the extent of many of our competitors. If a distributor has been especially effective, we'll try not to add a new distributor in the same area. But since distributors do business in large part through local personal relationships and often have certain accounts locked in, we feel we must work with rival distributors in some market areas to get access to each distributor's "captive" accounts, and maximize our market share.

Alloy's managers regularly reviewed their distributors in an effort to build a group with more technical expertise and thus more ability to sell Alloy products. In the past two years, the company had cancelled 100 distributor agreements and signed 80 new ones. Mr. Plotica explained,

We provide distributors' salespeople with training and target technically oriented promotions at them. Our aim is to have the distributor add or develop sales
engineering personnel capable of performing product demonstrations for customers and answering applications questions.

But we often run into two problems. One is that many distributors are reluctant to invest time and resources in this area. Another is that we may spend time
and money to train and support a distributor in selling our high-technology
electrodes only to lose the distributor to another supplier. A distributor's primary investment in selling a particular brand of electrodes is current inventory, so
the switching costs for a distributor are relatively low.

Some managers at Alloy Rods worried that the company might be too
dependent on its distributors. Mr. Egan commented:

A significant portion of direct sales is important in this business: such sales help
balance production schedules, especially during economic downturns when distributors cut their orders in order to draw down their inventories. Direct sales to
end users are usually made-to-order, customized products, and that helps to
garner higher margins as well.

Wholesalers

In addition to distributors, Alloy Rods had one company-owned and three
independent wholesalers with a total of six U.S. warehouse locations. The
wholesalers received product from Alloy at a specially discounted price and then
resold product to authorized distributors at Alloy's normal price to distributors,
which gave the distributors an average 15% gross margin on the suggested price
to end users.

Wholesalers were bound by two agreements. First, wholesalers were not
permitted to sell directly to end users, unlike the "master distributors" of other
companies in the industry who competed with the companies' own distributors.
Second, wholesalers could not sell competitive product lines, although they
were allowed to sell other welding products. "In the past five years, the concept
of wholesale warehouses has gained great acceptance among our distributors,"
Mr. Plotica asserted.

We first established this wholesaler warehouse network in 1979, and the percentage of product sold through these wholesalers has increased steadily since then.
I expect that the large majority of our U. S. sales will go through the wholesalers
in the future.

Basically, in exchange for the approximately 9% margin we give to the
wholesaler, Alloy Rods is relieved of performing the bulk of the routine, daily distributor service transactions, which require a lot of time and administrative support. The wholesalers take orders, ship products, and bill distributors. The
distributor and the end user, though, receive the real net benefits of the
wholesale operation. Especially for the smaller distributor, freight charges are
lower since the product is shipped in truckload quantities from our manufacturing plants to the regional warehouses of wholesalers. Distributors can also keep
lower inventories since delivery time from the wholesalers is typically one or two

days instead of nearly a month from our main manufacturing plant. And distributors can still purchase directly from Alloy if they desire, which gives them flexibility.

There have also been some unforeseen benefits. For example, in 1983, there was a 4 ½-month strike at our manufacturing plant. The field stock carried by the wholesalers allowed us to continue doing business during that period, thus minimizing market share loss.

However, other managers noted that, in a company with only 15% of its sales direct, the wholesalers became one more step between Alloy and the end user. These managers commented that when distributors had phoned their orders directly to Alloy headquarters, Alloy had received feedback about what was happening in the marketplace. But the wholesaler program cut back direct communication with distributors and end users. Alloy had recently begun a telemarketing program in an attempt to alleviate this problem. Mr. Plotica noted,

> The object of the program is not really to sell product but rather to reestablish communications with our distributors. We want to get feedback, and we also needed a better way to send them information. Not too long ago, we discovered that only half of our promotional materials ever reached the appropriate individual at our distributors.

Field Sales Organization

Alloy Rods employed 21 field salespeople responsible for distributor relations, direct accounts, and account development. Salespeople attended distributors' open houses, monitored service problems, and supplied technical assistance in the distributors' sales calls on end users. The field sales force was also responsible for calling on welding engineers and welders at direct accounts in order to promote Alloy's products. Their third duty was account development.

Mr. Sabel estimated that it required 6 to 18 months to convert an account from a competitor to Alloy Rods. He believed brand preference was sometimes a factor in a customer's reluctance to change, but loyalty to a given distributor was usually more significant. Typically, a salesperson only delivered 3 or 4 major new accounts per year.

Salespeople were paid incentive compensation equal to about 15% of their total compensation. Half of the incentive amount was based on gross margin dollars, one-fourth on sales dollars, and the remaining one-fourth on specific quarterly objectives. Alloy's salespeople received the industry average in total compensation, which was $37,300, and sold all product types to all customer segments. Because the salespeople were organized geographically and each had a large territory, there was little room for segment specialization. Management believed Alloy's annual sales per salesperson was far higher than the industry average.

Competition

In 1985 there were approximately 12 U. S. manufacturers of welding electrodes. But Alloy Rods primarily competed with 5 firms and, increasingly, with certain foreign companies.

- *Lincoln Electric Company* had been the world's largest manufacturer of welding electrodes and equipment for more than 40 years, with estimated 1984 sales of about $365 million. Alloy's management estimated that 50% of Lincoln's sales were welding electrodes, 45% welding equipment, and 5% electric motors. Lincoln had an estimated one-third of the total U. S. electrode market.

A 1975 Harvard Business School case study of Lincoln emphasized that "Lincoln's strategy had remained virtually unchanged for decades." [1] Lincoln's president noted: "We're not a marketing company, we're not an R&D company, and we're not a service company. We're a manufacturing company, and I believe we are the best manufacturing company in the world." Similarly, another executive emphasized that Lincoln had historically "limited research, development and manufacturing to a standard product line designed to meet the major needs of the welding industry." A Lincoln sales manager, describing the firm's marketing efforts, commented:

> Most competitors operate through distributors. We have our own top field sales force. We start out with engineering graduates and put them through our seven-month training program. They learn how to weld, and we teach them everything we can about equipment, metallurgy, and design.
>
> Our approach to the customer is to go in and learn what he is doing and show him how to do it better. For many companies our people become their experts in welding. They go in and talk to a foreman. They might say, "Let me put on a headshield and show you what I'm talking about." That's how we sell them.

In 1985, Mr. Bovie believed Lincoln continued to adhere to its traditional strategy, and he described Lincoln as concentrating on "making high-volume, established products at lower cost. They are much more vertically integrated than other electrode suppliers, sell both electrodes and welding equipment, and usually set the lowest market price in electrodes. Our perception is that, while their quality is satisfactory, customers buy Lincoln's products for the price rather than product features."

Alloy's management believed Lincoln was strongest in product lines like mild steel stick and mild steel solid wire electrodes, which Alloy managers characterized as "commodity items in the eyes of most end users," and in self-shielded flux-cored electrodes where Lincoln had pioneered in 1957. Alloy's managers had expected Lincoln to enter the gas-shielded segment eventually.

---

[1] "The Lincoln Electric Company," Harvard Business School case 376-028.

Mr. Bovie estimated Lincoln had more than 200 salespeople, 48 company-owned warehouses, and over 1,000 distributors and that about 60% of Lincoln's sales were made direct to end users. About 25% of Lincoln's distributors also sold.Alloy's products. "But Lincoln," Mr. Bovie believed, "has virtually no distributor support programs, and on most of its products doesn't even give its distributors a discount." Alloy's management estimated that the maximum Lincoln discount (from published list price) to its distributors was 5%. In addition, it was believed that Lincoln's salespeople and its distributors' salespeople frequently competed with each other at the end-user level since, according to Alloy's managers, Lincoln sold direct at much lower order quantities than many of its competitors. "Nonetheless," stressed Mr. Bovie, "distributors need Lincoln to provide the low-price end of the product spectrum. Also, Lincoln has name recognition among customers and a good reputation in welding equipment. In fact, I believe it's their equipment which drives their electrode sales at distributors. In addition, I think Lincoln's size and aggressiveness make many distributors feel they *must* carry the Lincoln electrode line."

- *Hobart* was a family-owned business with about $120 million in annual sales. Mr. Bovie viewed Hobart as "a smaller version of Lincoln," with 50% of its sales in electrodes, 45% in welding equipment, and 5% in generators. Hobart had an overall electrode market share of about 13%, similar to Alloy Rods. Hobart had about 100 salespeople, but a majority of its sales were through company-owned stores. Mr. Bovie believed Hobart's products, like Lincoln's, were of average quality but considered Hobart's new product development more aggressive than Lincoln's. In recent years, according to Mr. Plotica, Hobart's pricing had been inconsistent.

- *Airco,* owned by British Oxygen Company, sold industrial gases, medical equipment, and welding equipment in addition to electrodes. In late 1984, however, Airco discontinued production of its gas-shielded flux-cored product and reduced its electrode line to stick electrodes only. Most of Airco's electrode sales were through independent distributors.

- *McKay,* a division of Teledyne (a large conglomerate), had estimated 1984 sales of $30 million. According to Mr. Bovie, McKay had an excellent reputation for quality electrodes, but its distributors believed the company was not being fully supported by its corporate parent. McKay was strongest in stainless steel electrodes but also sold low hydrogen and gas-shielded flux-cored electrodes.

- *Tri-Mark,* with 1984 sales of about $16 million, only sold flux-cored electrodes. The company had been founded in the late 1970s by two former Hobart employees and, according to Mr. Plotica, "has been effective in product development and probably has, next to us, the highest quality flux-cored products. Tri-Mark targets a small number of quality-sensitive users, such as naval shipyards, where the margins can

support their investment in engineering and applications development." Most of Tri-Mark's sales were through independent distributors.

- *Foreign competition,* primarily from Japan, Korea, and Western Europe,
  had become a factor since 1982, especially in the stainless steel product category. A strong U.S. dollar had made imports increasingly
  price competitive with U.S. products. However, according to Alloy's
  managers, these firms had been unable to develop effective distribution because many U.S. welding distributors were wary of the long
  travel time for orders to reach the United States and were also concerned with unexpected pricing changes due to currency fluctuations.
  Management also believed there remained a "buy American" senti-
  ment among many welding distributors.

Alloy's managers believed the strongest potential foreign threat was Kobe
Steel, a large steel manufacturer in Japan and the largest electrode producer
in the Japanese market, which was about 80% as large as the U. S. market. Kobe
had established U.S. headquarters in Houston where it employed a few
Japanese salespeople who sold primarily to about 35 welding distributors. Mr.
Bovie believed that Kobe had high-quality products and a focus on the high-
technology end of the flux-cored segment.

Lincoln's New Product

During the week, Mr. Plotica received more information about Lincoln's new
gas-shielded flux-cored electrode line, labeled "Outershield," which would
compete directly with Alloy's "Dual Shield" product line. After conferring with
Mr. Sabel and a number of field salespeople, Mr. Bovie reported that:

> Lincoln's product is not state-of-the-art, but they do have a wide range of dia-
> meters available (down to .045 inches) and their prices—about 25% below our
> "Dual Shield" prices—will attract attention. However, initial reports indicate that
> Lincoln may be having some problems with the consistency of their product
> quality.
>
> In their distribution, Lincoln is following its standard procedures. Their large
> sales force is generally selling direct to end users, and they probably hope dis-
> tributors will carry the product if and when their customers start to ask for it. We
> believe the maximum distributor margin they're offering is about 7%, compared
> to 28% with our flux-cored products. Our salespeople report that distributors
> are upset but also fear Lincoln's potential ability to take an account direct if the
> distributor doesn't carry the line.

Conclusion

In reviewing the information about Lincoln's new gas-shielded product, Mr.
Plotica noted that, for the past decade, Lincoln's sales force had been selling
Lincoln's self-shielded product line on the premise that it was as effective as

gas-shielded electrodes while being easier and less expensive to use. "So how will they now explain their move into gas-shielded electrodes to their customers?" thought Mr. Plotica. "And will this move by Lincoln open up their self-shielded market to our gas-shielded products? How can we try to force that opportunity?"

Mr. Plotica also knew that, as Mr. Bovie had suggested, the Friday meeting would involve other matters about Alloy's marketing programs and, in particular, its distribution system. Since their purchase of the company 6 months earlier, Messrs. Bovie, Egan and Plotica had been discussing informally a number of issues that had a bearing on any response Alloy chose to make to Lincoln's new product.

Should Alloy Rods attempt to take a larger proportion of its business direct, and if so, how could this be accomplished with minimal disruption of its existing distributor relations? Conversely, how could Alloy Rods motivate its distributors to do more account-development work? Some in management felt that, "given the amount of support we give our distributors, we should receive more sales support of our products from them. But in some cases, our distributors are basically order takers rather than active sellers of our products." Would cutting back on the number of distributors and providing exclusive distribution agreements in more market areas provide such motivation?

Alloy's managers had also discussed whether to continue producing its line of mild steel solid wire electrodes. Some favored dropping the line since the margins were poor, and the low manufacturing value-added made increasing price pressures likely in that product segment. But other managers favored maintaining production so that Alloy could continue to provide its distributors with a full line of electrodes. In addition, mild steel electrodes were low-priced, high-volume products which, when ordered with other Alloy products, often allowed wholesalers and distributors to achieve freight-load quantities.

On Wednesday afternoon, Mr. Plotica was considering these questions when an Alloy salesperson brought him further news. In introducing its new "Outershield" product to its sales force, Lincoln had adopted the slogan, "Let's eat their lunch!" (see Exhibit 10).

Exhibit 1   *Alloy Rods Corporation*

Consumable Welding Process and Product Types

Consumable welding electrodes were categorized into five basic product types, according to the form of the electrode (e.g., flux cored and low hydrogen) and the type of steel to be welded. Different electrodes were used with different welding processes (with the exception of stainless steel electrodes, which were manufactured for use in all three major welding processes).

Electrode Product Type \ Welding Process	*Shielded Metal Arc Welding (SMAW)—Uses Stick Electrodes*	*Gas Metal Arc Welding (GMAW)—Uses Continuous Wire Electrodes*	*Flux-Cored Arc Welding (FCAW)*	
			Gas-Shielded	Self-Shielded
1) Flux-Cored Wire Electrodes			• 1984 industry sales—$67M • Projected 2% growth • Wide range of steel applications • See Note 1.	• 1984 sales = $33 million • See Note 2
2) Low hydrogen coated stick electrodes	• Used for low alloy steels in more critical applications • No growth projected in 1985 • 1984 industry sales = $72 million			
3) Stainless steel electrodes	• Stainless steel electrodes were sold in 3 forms, for each of the major welding processes • 1984 sales = $51 million • Projected growth of 2% in 1985			
4) Mild steel coated stick electrodes	• Used in less critical applications • Commodity item • 1984 sales = $84 million			
5) Mild steel solid wire electrodes		• Used in less critical applications • Commodity item • 1984 sales = $120 million • 1% growth projected		

Note 1: Lincoln Electric Company's new product would compete in this segment.

Note 2: Lincoln Electric Company's current products dominated in this segment; Alloy Rods had no product in this segment.

(continued)

Exhibit 1   (continued)

Equipment Set-Ups for Welding Processes

Shielded Metal Arc Welding Circuit

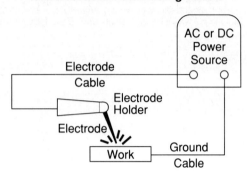

Gas Metal Arc Welding

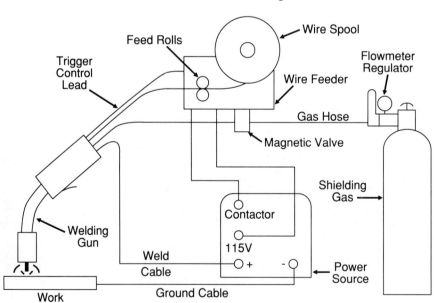

Exhibit 2   Alloy Rods Corporation

Industry Sales of Welding Electrodes
(thousands of pounds)

	Flux-Cored Wire	Low Hydrogen Coated Sticks	Stainless Steel	Mild Steel Coated Sticks	Mild Steel Solid Wire	Industry Total
1975	94,285	200,613	22,312	308,105	142,581	767,896
1976	100,283	170,877	21,145	269,572	162,908	724,785
1977	125,000	178,800	22,987	288,870	192,400	808,057
1978	146,870	201,066	26,485	296,568	218,784	889,773
1979	155,770	212,909	29,926	305,038	288,259	991,902
1980	141,406	198,704	23,353	282,006	190,672	836,141
1981	148,265	216,411	23,910	279,652	202,953	871,191
1982	97,586	154,844	19,263	191,935	150,172	613,800
1983	89,446	120,562	18,162	168,025	178,444	574,639
1984	126,146	137,486	19,233	179,801	218,767	681,433

Exhibit 3   Alloy Rods Corporation

Proportion of 1982 Sales of Welding Equipment and Supplies to Major End-User Industries

End-User Industry	
Machinery and equipment	27%
Fabricated metal products	17
Automotive and other transportation	13
Construction	8
Shipbuilding	6
Steel mills	5
Mining	4
Other	20

End-Use Segment	Percent Sold Through Distributors	Percent Ordering by Brand Name
Mechanical contractors	95%	65%
Steel fabricators	85	65
Construction contractors	90	35
Shipbuilding	25	75
Steel mills	85	35
Mining	80	85

Exhibit 4   Alloy Rods Corporation

Organization Chart

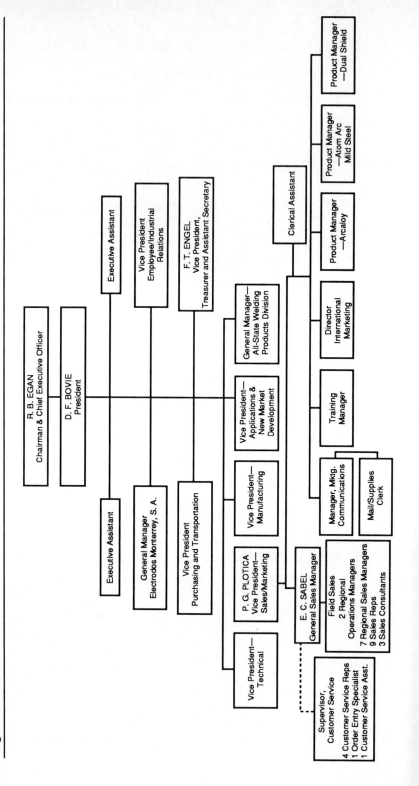

Exhibit 5   Alloy Rods Corporation

Estimated Domestic Market Shares—1984

	Flux-Cored Wire	Low-Hydrogen Coated Sticks	Stainless Steel (stick, wire, flux-cored)	Mild Steel Coated Sticks	Mild Steel Solid Wire
Alloy Rods	23%	22%	13%	7%	4%
Lincoln[a]	28	26	—	50	30
Hobart	13	16	—	16	7
Airco	12	17	10	16	—
McKay	—	8	16	—	—
TriMark	15	—	—	—	—
Sandvik	—	—	13	—	—
Techalloy	—	—	11	—	—
Oerlikon	—	—	5	—	—
National Standard	—	—	—	—	23
Linde	—	—	—	—	15
Page	—	—	—	—	7
All others	9	11	32	11	14
	100	100	100	100	100

[a]In 1984, Lincoln's flux-cored electrodes were entirely of the self-shielded type, not the gas-shielded type sold by Alloy Rods and some other manufacturers.

Exhibit 6 Alloy Rods Corporation

Distributor Survey—1980
Image/Positioning Rating: Distributors
(1–10 scale)

Supplier Selection Factors (Electrodes)	Relative Importance	Alloy Rods	Lincoln	McKay	Hobart	Others
Product quality	9.4	9.0	8.1	8.2	8.4	8.1
Creation of demand (pull)	9.2	6.5	7.2	6.1	7.1	6.0
Communications with factory	9.0	6.6	7.6	7.5	8.2	7.9
Prices	9.0	6.2	8.5	7.5	7.6	7.3
Deliveries/availability	8.8	7.3	7.8	7.7	8.0	7.7
Technical capabilities	8.6	9.1	7.5	8.4	8.0	7.5
Product innovativeness	8.4	8.7	7.7	8.5	7.9	7.5
Training	8.1	5.2	6.8	7.0	7.7	6.6
Quality of sales representation	7.9	6.8	7.2	7.4	7.3	6.5
Line breadth	7.9	8.5	7.2	7.7	7.4	6.6
Literature/catalogs	7.7	7.8	7.5	7.5	7.7	7.2
Terms	6.1	6.5	7.2	6.5	7.6	7.3
Furnish "other" welding products[a]	5.3	3.3	7.2	4.1	6.8	7.9
Overall reputation	—	8.2	7.7	8.0	7.9	7.5

[a]This referred primarily to equipment such as welding guns, helmets, gloves, etc.

Exhibit 7   Alloy Rods Corporation

Price Comparisons of Selected Products: Manufacturers' Prices to Distributors
(dollars/pound)

	Gas-Shielded Flux-Cored Wire		Low-Hydrogen Coated Sticks	Stainless Steel Coated Sticks	Mild Steel Coated Sticks	Mild Steel Solid Wire
	Large Diameter	Small Diameter				
Alloy Rods[a]	$.638	$.905	$.498	$2.38	$.506	$.571
Lincoln	.500	.730	.437	—	.465	.540
Hobart	.686	.957	.485	—	.500	.589
Airco	—	—	.535	—	.501	.451
McKay	.690	.990	.500	2.55	.530	—
TriMark	.625	.880	—	—	—	—
Sandvik	—	—	—	2.31	—	—
Techalloy	—	—	—	2.44	—	—
National Standard	—	—	—	—	—	.591
J. W. Harris	—	—	—	2.02	—	—

[a]All Alloy Rods distributor prices are quoted F. O. B. and do not include freight charges paid by the distributor. Average cost of freight per pound of electrodes in 1984 was $ .025 in truckload quantities, and significantly higher if shipped in less than truckload quantities.

Exhibit 8   Alloy Rods Corporation

Product Literature

WELDING SMARTER

A two-minute reminder

ARE YOU GETTING FULL VALUE FROM ALLOY RODS?

It's come to our attention that many people who use one or more of our products **are not aware of other Alloy Rods products that might save them money**—or otherwise meet some critical welding need.

Why don't you take two minutes and leaf through the reminders in this bulletin?

We do make more different varieties of top-quality welding electrodes than anyone else in America . . . to make sure you can get precisely what is best for your welding application.

Hanover, PA 17331
800-233-7070
(In PA: 800-692-7350)
An Allegheny International Company

WELDING SMARTER

IN LOW HYDROGEN STICK WELDING, THE BEST NEWS IS NO NEWS. IT'S STILL ATOM ARC®.

You see it so often on specs that it almost starts to get monotonous: "Atom Arc. No substitutes."

The reason is, a lot of critical welding jobs simply don't allow much room for doubt about quality. And ever since Atom Arc® electrodes were introduced in 1955—as the first low hydrogen, iron powder electrodes in the USA—they've produced the kind of results that make people keep asking for them.

Atom Arc® 7018 and low-alloy electrodes keep getting better, too. We are always refining them and updating to the latest spec requirements. (For instance, a new moisture-resistant coating lets you buy Atom Arc® 7018 in cartons as well as hermetically sealed cans—at a cost savings of about 5¢ a pound).

The one problem we have is that Atom Arc® electrodes are so well known, some people forget the name of the company that makes them. It's Alloy Rods.

Alloy Rods makes more different types of welding electrodes, in more sizes and alloys, than anyone else in the USA. See your Alloy Rods distributor. Or call us toll-free.

(continued)

Exhibit 8   (continued)

WELDING SMARTER

IF YOU WELD STAINLESS, OR CAST IRON, OR MILD STEEL, WE HAVE YOUR ELECTRODE.

For stainless, try Arcaloy stainless steel electrodes from Alloy Rods. You can get them in fabricated wires, solid wires, cut lengths, or covered stick electrodes (with a choice of three coatings)—in a wide variety of types and diameters.

For cast iron, you'll want our Nickel-Arc welding electrodes. You get a smooth, stable arc (with AC or DC) and clean, machinable welds. For manual mild steel welding, choose from Alloy Rods' full line of Mild Steel coated electrodes. For semi-automatic and robotic mild steel welding, try cost saving Dual Shield cored wires.

Got a high-speed welding job? Our Spoolarc copper-coated solid wires have the superior quality you need. Hardfacing? Try Wear-Arc coated electrodes or Wear-O-Matic open arc wires—both available in a number of alloys with different impact and abrasion resistance properties.

For special jobs, Alloy Rods will custom-design electrodes to your specs.

Alloy Rods makes more different types of welding electrodes, in more sizes and alloys, than anyone else in the USA. See your Alloy Rods distributor. Or call us toll-free.

WELDING SMARTER

IF YOU USE SOLID WIRE, TRY THIS INSTEAD FOR THIN-GAUGE STEELS.

It's the smallest-diameter flux cored wire yet made: just .035". This means you can now use cored wire to weld pipe and sheet as thin as 18 gauge without burn-through. It gives you better sidewall fusion in out-of-position work. And you can save money—because cored wire is faster, more efficient, and leaves a smoother, flatter bead than solid wire.

The new .035" cored wire is made by Alloy Rods, the company that pioneered gas-shielded flux cored wire. It's available in our Dual Shield 7000 series (for general use) . . . in the Dual Shield II 70 series (for low-hydrogen, high impact applications) . . . and in our Coreweld 70 line (metal cored and virtually slag-free).

Try .035" cored wire on your next thin-gauge welding job. Results are excellent on steel down to 18 gauge, and on heavy plate as well.

Alloy Rods makes more different types of welding electrodes, in more sizes and alloys, than anyone else in the USA. For application advice, see your Alloy Rods distributor. Or call us toll-free.

Exhibit 9   Alloy Rods Corporation

Percent of Sales $ by Distribution Channel for Alloy Rods

Distributor	1980	1981	1982	1983	1984
Direct to welding supply distributor	46.0	40.1	25.0	18.4	12.8
Via independent wholesaler	} 23.0[a]	33.0[a]	33.8	37.4	40.8
Via company-owned wholesaler	___	___	14.4	18.3	21.3
Subtotal	69.0	73.1	73.2	74.1	74.9
Direct to End-User	18.0	13.0	11.9	10.4	13.2
Private Label/Government	4.5	2.6	2.4	2.3	3.7
Export	8.5	11.3	12.5	13.2	8.2
	100.0	100.0	100.0	100.0	100.0

[a]Combined total for sales via independent and company-owned wholesalers.

Alloy Rods Distribution Channels

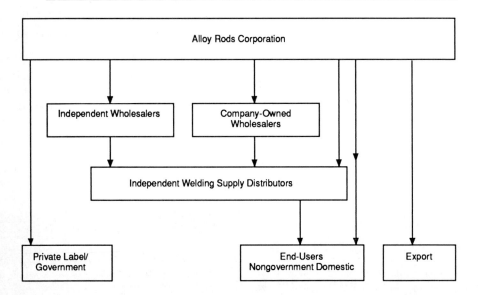

Exhibit 10

Alloy Rods Corporation

Case 12

Becton Dickinson & Company: VACUTAINER Systems Division

On Thursday, August 1, 1985, Mr. William Kozy, national sales director for Becton Dickinson VACUTAINER® Systems (BDVS), and Mr. Hank Smith, BDVS's vice president of marketing and sales, slumped into their seats on the evening flight from Chicago to Newark. They had just completed their fifth round of negotiations in as many months with the materials manager of Affiliated Purchasing Group (APG), a large hospital buying group. Historically, BDVS had supplied most blood collection products bought by individual APG-member hospitals. But in April, APG had announced its intention of initiating group purchasing of one brand of blood collection products for all member hospitals. Since then, Messrs. Kozy and Smith had represented BDVS in repeated negotiations with APG, while APG had also been negotiating with BDVS's competitors.

The subject of the negotiations was the pricing and delivery terms of a proposed purchasing agreement between APG and BDVS. Traditionally, all of BDVS's products had been sold through its distributors who also negotiated prices for those (and other) products directly with hospital customers. However, in recent years, BDVS had begun a new form of sales agreement, known as a "Z contract," in which BDVS negotiated prices and quantities directly with large accounts but supplied its products through one or more of its authorized distributors. Pricing decisions concerning specific Z contracts were made by a committee composed of Messrs. Kozy, Smith, and Ed Mehl, contracts administration manager. Mr. Alfred Battaglia, president of BDVS, was also involved in establishing the terms of such contracts with some large customers.

This case was prepared by Associate Professor Frank V. Cespedes and Associate Professor V. Kasturi Rangan as the basis for class discussion rather than to illustrate either effective or ineffective handling of an administrative situation. Certain company data, while useful for discussion purposes, have been disguised.

The August 1 meeting with APG had been an all-day session, at the end of which both sides agreed that BDVS would submit its final proposal by August 15. At issue were the specific prices and terms for BDVS's two major products. In addition, there were questions raised regarding which distributors would be used to service the contract, and APG negotiators had urged BDVS to consider manufacturing a private label for APG.

"They're bringing out the big guns this time," noted Mr. Kozy as the plane began to taxi down the runway. "They certainly are," agreed Mr. Smith, "and we'll have to decide what we do about that. Al Battaglia wants to meet with us tomorrow at 1 P.M. about the APG contract. Let's review the situation one more time, and make our recommendations."

Company Background

Becton Dickinson (BD) manufactured medical, diagnostic, and industrial safety products for health-care professionals, medical research institutions, industry and the general public. Sales in 1984 were $1.127 billion, 75% from U.S. operations (see Exhibit 1). The company had three business segments—Laboratory, Industrial Safety, and Medical Products—each a profit center with separate marketing responsibilities.

Medical Products had three divisions: 1) needles, syringes and diabetic products, 2) pharmaceutical systems, and 3) VACUTAINER blood collection systems which accounted for a significant portion of Medical Products' operating income.[1] In its 1984 annual report, BD management noted:

> Despite limited sales growth, BD maintained or increased its market share in every major medical product category. We attribute this to three factors: our strong reputation and brand identification, our ability to hold down production costs and thereby prices, and our continuing commitment to quality.

Management also outlined certain "core strategies to guide the company's activities in the marketplace," including "substantial improvements in research and the development of new technologies basic to the company's overall strategy. In a constantly changing industry such as ours, the successful development and introduction of new products are the company's lifeblood over the long run."

Becton Dickinson VACUTAINER® Systems Division (BDVS)

Mr. Alfred Battaglia was president of BDVS. Mr. Battaglia had previously served in various financial positions for BD. Mr. Hank Smith was vice president for marketing and sales. Reporting to Mr. Smith were three product managers, each responsible for one of the division's product groups, and a sales director, Mr. William Kozy, responsible for achieving sales targets through six regional

---

[1] Both VACUTAINER® and MICROTAINER® are registered trademarks of Becton Dickinson and Company.

managers who in turn managed 55 sales representatives. (See Exhibit 2 for BDVS organization chart.)

Products

BD introduced blood collection products in the late 1940s. BDVS was formed as a business unit in 1980 with three major product groups having total 1984 sales of $90 million: venous blood collection (about 70% of BDVS sales) consisting of VACUTAINER tubes and needles; capillary blood collection consisting of MICROTAINER® tubes and lancets; and microbiology systems consisting of culture tubes and specimen collectors. Each product group accounted for about 33% of BDVS's 1984 operating income.

Venous blood collection systems consisted of a needle and vacuum tube used for collecting blood from a patient's veins. VACUTAINER was the BD brand name for a broad line of tubes and needles designed to meet hundreds of differing needs in hospitals, medical laboratories, and physicians' offices. (See Exhibit 3 for sample products.)

In venous blood collection, the tubes were coated with reagents to preserve the integrity of the specimen (the stoppers on the tubes were color coded to indicate the specific reagent inside). The laboratory technician, known as a phlebotomist, collected blood in different tubes depending on the type of test required by the patient's doctor.

Evacuated-tube blood collection was considered superior to the older needle-and-syringe method in providing specimen integrity, convenience of use and lower costs. BD was the pioneer in converting the market to evacuated tubes and, according to industry sources, had an estimated 80% market share in the United States, where nearly 100% of venous blood collection had been converted to evacuated-tube methods (worldwide, evacuated tube methods accounted for less than 40% of blood collection).

Capillary blood collection systems consisted of a lancet for pricking the patient's finger and a tube (MICROTAINER was the BD brand name) used for blood collection and testing. MICROTAINER tubes used capillary action and gravity for collecting blood samples of smaller volumes than those generally collected by the venous method. MICROTAINER systems could be used for the same blood tests administered through VACUTAINER systems, but the common applications for MICROTAINER were in "single-tube" collections for infants, children, and geriatric patients.

The division marketed VACUTAINER and MICROTAINER systems as complete blood collection systems, but other suppliers' needles and lancets could be used on BD tubes and vice versa. On average, about two tubes were used per needle.

Microbiology systems provided a sterile environment for transferring blood specimens from the collection to the testing site. The division's microbiology tubes and collectors were all marketed under the VACUTAINER brand name.

BDVS had the broadest line of blood collection products in the industry. Mr. Peter Trow, sales representative for BDVS, noted:

> In this business, quality is not merely a function of needle sharpness or the integrity of the reagents. We also offer the widest range of tubes, and that's crucial. Big hospitals and labs run a multitude of tests, and they require product assortment and color coding schemes to make their jobs easier. That is part of their definition of quality.

Cost-containment pressures resulted in a 1.0% compounded annual decline in hospital blood testing between 1983 and 1985. Forecasts indicated hospital blood testing would decline through 1987, but an aging U.S. population should increase testing somewhat in subsequent years. Testing in commercial labs and physicians' offices was expected to be 40% of total blood testing by 1990.

Total microcollections were forecast to increase 5% annually through 1990 as less-expensive, easier-to-use equipment motivated physicians to do more testing in their offices rather than via a hospital or commercial lab. Mr. Battaglia also noted that blood-collection technology was changing rapidly:

> The clear technological trend is to enable end-users to do more of the diagnostic testing. This means more testing can be done in nonlaboratory settings such as doctors' offices. In turn, that has implications for our distribution network, which tends to be built around lab distributors rather than the medical/surgical distributors who sell to nonlab locations. The technological developments also place more technical selling demands on our sales force.

Industry Background

Blood collection products are used in hospitals, commercial laboratories, and many nonhospital health-care centers.

Hospitals

In 1985 approximately 7,000 U.S. hospitals performed 70% of all blood tests. Blood collection was generally performed at patients' bedsides and the sample then sent to a hospital laboratory for testing. The 1,800 largest hospitals (200 or more beds each) accounted for 50% of the market for medical equipment and supplies.

Within hospitals, the buying process for medical supplies, including blood collection products, was complex and changing. The primary contact of a BDVS salesperson varied, depending upon usage requirements and the purchasing process in an individual hospital. Mr. Robert Giardino, senior sales representative for BDVS, noted that:

> Blood collection tubes are a key product for a hospital lab: if the specimen is not collected properly, the lab has many problems. Hospitals order tubes frequently; most have a standing weekly order with one or more distributors for tubes.

The hospital's chief lab technician is usually the person responsible for the tests that are done, ordering supplies, and administrative matters. In a large teaching hospital, this person might have an MD or Ph.D.; in other hospitals, it would be someone who came up through the lab ranks. On average, there are 6 subsidiary lab departments, each headed by a supervisor who reports to the chief lab technician.

Purchasing influences vary, depending on the specific product. In general, the "bench people" (i.e., medical technicians in the lab) have product preferences, and these people tend to be concerned with the best quality and not price. Among the bench people, "VACUTAINER" is the best-known brand of blood collection tubes. But the department heads and chief lab technicians have budgets to meet. Increasingly, upper levels of hospital administration, and especially the materials managers (who perform a role analogous to that of purchasing agents in industrial concerns), are more influential. These people tend to come from different backgrounds than the lab people do, and they are always price sensitive.

In most hospitals, medical supplies accounted for 10–15% of a hospital's total costs, while the logistical expenses associated with supplies made up another 10–15%. Labor costs usually accounted for at least 70%. Blood collection products typically accounted for less than 5% of the total supplies purchased. A smaller, 100-bed hospital might purchase 40 cases of tubes (each case contained 1,000 tubes) and 20 cases of needles (each case contained 1,000 needles) annually, while a large 1,100-bed hospital such as Massachusetts General Hospital purchased about 1,700 cases of tubes and 800 cases of needles annually.

Commercial Laboratories

In 1985, 700 commercial labs in the United States performed about 25% of all blood tests. Larger, national labs had 15–20 lab locations for which the company purchased blood collection products centrally. In these labs, the purchase process for blood collection products was similar to that in large hospitals. Most commercial labs, however, were smaller, single-location companies where the owner-manager often supervised all purchases personally. In both large and small labs, according to Mr. Giardino, "The purchasers are cost conscious, because commercial labs compete with each other primarily on price."

Commercial labs analyzed blood samples sent to them by physicians or small health-care centers that had collected the blood from a patient but lacked either the equipment or expertise to perform tests. Many commercial labs also performed blood tests for hospitals for a fee. A significant percentage of a commercial lab's total revenues came from blood collection and testing.

Nonhospital Health-Care Centers

These centers accounted in 1985 for about 5% of blood collection and testing in the United States. But easier-to-use and less expensive technology, as well as changing patterns in health care, indicated that nonhospital centers would account for increased proportions of blood testing in coming years.

In 1985 there were approximately 250,000 physicians in 180,000 offices throughout the United States. A number of physicians—often, 50–60 per group—were affiliated with forms of group medical care. These physicians were increasingly performing in their offices many medical activities previously subcontracted to commercial labs or hospitals.

Other nonhospital sites—such as surgicenters, emergency centers and free-standing diagnostic centers—were also increasing in number and expected to perform a higher proportion of medical activities during the coming decade, including blood collection and testing.

Market Trends

Few industries have gone through such intense trauma in the past two years as the market for health care. New cost containment pressures have forced a wave of cutbacks: hospital use has dropped precipitously, hospitals have shaved their own costs dramatically, and an estimated 100,000 jobs have been lost in a range of health-care fields. Out of such chaos a new order seems destined to emerge.[2]

In 1983 a change in how the U.S. government reimbursed hospitals for Medicare patients (40% of all hospital patient days) affected the entire health-care industry. Previously, hospitals had been reimbursed for all costs incurred in serving those patients. Most observers agreed this cost-plus system did not reward hospitals for efficiency. Federal legislation in April 1983 provided for a change (over a four-year period) to a payment approach based on "diagnosis-related groups" (DRGs).

Under the new system, the payment to a hospital was based on national and regional costs for each DRG, not on the hospital's costs. Moreover, the national and regional averages were to be updated, so that if hospitals improved their cost performance, they would be subject to stricter DRG-related payment limits.

By 1985 the impact had been dramatic. In 1984, hospital admissions fell 4%, the largest drop on record according to the American Hospital Association; the average length of a patient's hospital stay fell 5% to 6.7 days, also the largest drop ever. For the first time, admission of people over the age of 65 fell. Nonhospital treatment—especially in-home treatment—was expected to account for larger proportions of health care. Conversely, estimates[3] indicated that the number of hospital beds would fall to 650,000 in 1990 from 1 million in 1983. In their place, it was expected that a variety of smaller, short-term health-care facilities would proliferate.

Another important development was increased concern among employers and insurers about the costs of health insurance. Many corporations began to

---

[2]*Newsweek* (15 April 1986): 79.

[3]Cited in "Hospital Suppliers Strike Back," *New York Times,* March 31, 1985.

adopt health-insurance plans that encouraged patients to shorten their hospital stays and to shun more expensive in-patient treatment in favor of outpatient care.

Thus, changes in health insurance were also expected to spur growth in nonhospital medical care. In 1985, many hospital administrators felt that, for the first time, they faced effective, increasing competition and a need to reduce costs. One response was the acceleration of a trend toward the formation of multihospital chains and multihospital buying groups. Both types of organization were intended to increase the purchasing power of hospitals for equipment and supplies. In 1985, about 45% of all U.S. hospitals were affiliated with multihospital chains, and it was predicted that 65% would be so affiliated by 1990. Similarly, in 1985 most hospitals were members of buying groups.

Multihospital chains were usually for-profit hospitals that purchased most supplies and equipment through centralized buying organizations. In these chains, individual hospitals submitted purchase requirements and preferences for specific products, but price and delivery terms were negotiated centrally. Buying groups were looser affiliations of not-for-profit hospitals. Like chains, purchases for buying groups were handled centrally; but individual hospitals were often free to accept or reject the terms negotiated on a specific item by the central buying group. Thus, if a given hospital's administration or lab personnel had a strong preference for a given brand, and the buying group had negotiated a volume discount for a different brand, that hospital might purchase its tubes separately while purchasing other items through the centralized buying group. In addition, many hospitals belonged to a number of buying groups, purchasing different items through different buying groups depending upon the product, specific prices, and other factors. One BD manager noted:

> The chains and buying groups structure negotiations on the premise that they can deliver so many thousands of beds to the manufacturer with the best price. But the actual strength of these groups varies. In some, all of their hospitals purchase through the centralized procedure. In others, a large percentage of the member hospitals do not adhere to the centralized procedure. The result is that the purchasing leverage differs from one group to the next.
>
> In addition, individual hospitals belong to a number of different buying groups, and often switch from one group to the next. The result is that the various buying-group headquarters organizations in effect compete actively with each other to attract and retain hospital clients. Nonetheless, there is no doubt that chains and buying groups have increased the pricing pressures on both manufacturers and distributors of health-care products in recent years.

Competition

Competition in the blood collection market was primarily among BD and two other firms. Terumo, a Japanese company, was a global competitor with a 1984 U. S. market share of about 18% in evacuated blood collection tubes and nearly 50% in blood collection needles. Sherwood Medical Corporation's

Monoject division was predominantly a U.S. competitor with a U.S. market share of about 2% in tubes and 15% in needles.

Over the past seven years, BDVS had maintained about an 80% share of the U.S. evacuated blood-collection tube market while increasing its average unit price from about 6 cents to 8 cents. During that time, Terumo had increased its share from 10% to 20% while maintaining its price at about 6.5 cents per unit. In blood collection needles, however, BDVS's share had dropped from 40% to 30% during this period, while Terumo had doubled its share from 25% to 50%. In needles, BDVS and Terumo charged approximately 7.5 cents per unit while Sherwood charged about 10 cents per unit.

A primary objective for BD in both tubes and needles was to maintain a leading market share. Management believed that Terumo was also committed to increasing its share in all segments and would continue to price aggressively. BD planned to combat such competition through accelerated new product developments and annual improvements in product quality, while using its strong market share to become the lowest cost producer in all product segments.

An important element in BD's marketing strategy was what one executive termed "quality aggression." Since BD had vertically integrated into the production of components such as glass tubes and rubber stoppers, it could keep a tight hold on quality. In addition, BD could process reagents and chemicals in its own plants at especially demanding specifications, and pioneer in new tube sterilization techniques which demanded large capital investments in radiation equipment. As one manager noted, "This raises our costs but also forces our competitors to raise their costs even more, since our higher volume allows us to amortize the capital investments over a larger base."

In the past, major companies including Corning Glass, Abbott Labs, and Johnson & Johnson had participated in the blood collection market but had withdrawn. However, BDVS management believed new technologies could provoke renewed competition from these firms as well as from companies that might enter the market from a base in computer equipment, other forms of medical diagnostic equipment, or biotechnology.

BDVS Marketing and Sales Programs

BD's blood collection products were initially sold through the Medical Products group pooled sales force. In 1980, however, separate sales forces were established for VACUTAINER products and a number of other medical products divisions. Mr. Battaglia explained:

> The basic reason for the reorganization was that the different products were
> sold to different buyers within hospitals, and had different selling requirements.
> Our division's products require our salespeople to speak with phlebotomists,
> nurses, physicians, and other technical people as well as the administrators and

materials managers at an account. The salespeople must also know a great deal about the people and procedures in the various hospital labs.

In addition, developments in blood collection technology also made our product line wider and required salespeople to learn more about more complex products. Our new product development plans also supported a move toward a separate VACUTAINER sales force.

In 1985 BDVS had 55 sales representatives organized into territories based on the number of hospital beds in a given area. Territories ranged from 10,000 to 20,000 beds. All hospital, commercial lab, and distributor accounts within a territory were the responsibility of that territory rep. Territory reps reported to one of six regional managers who in turn reported to Mr. Kozy, the national sales director.

Each BDVS sales rep had about 100 accounts and typically made five sales calls daily, four on hospital labs and one on either a distributor or nonhospital lab. A large metropolitan hospital might receive 2–3 calls monthly, while a small rural hospital might receive 1–2 calls annually. One rep noted:

> Our sales strategy has traditionally been to sell from the bottom up: we try to work with as many of the bench people as possible—that is, the lab technicians who actually use blood collection products, who care about the quality of what they use, and who will complain to the administrators if they do not get the product they want. BD has a reputation for being more responsive than other firms to end users.
>
> I think we've maintained our market share because of this philosophy. In recent years, I've seen a number of instances where materials managers wanted to standardize their purchases around a less expensive blood collection product, but the lab people complained and insisted on our product.

During the past year the division had introduced a new needle and had placed major emphasis on converting accounts from competing needle brands. Several sales promotions in 1985 for VACUTAINER needles gave sales reps cash awards for conversions. Results had been very positive, including the conversion of nearly 66,000 beds from competitive needles and a substantial increase in market share for VACUTAINER needles during the last 4-month promotion campaign (11/1/84 through 2/28/85).

Distribution

BDVS sold its products through 474 independent distributors who fell into two categories, laboratory-products distributors and medical-surgical products distributors. A laboratory-products distributor called on hospital and commercial labs and carried a range of items such as glassware, chemicals, spectrometers, lab coats and thousands of other supply items as well as tubes and needles. According to one BDVS executive, "Lab products distributors feel they must carry blood collection products, which hospitals order regularly, because hospitals often order the more expensive, higher-margin items along with those staple products." Medical-surgical products distributors called on physicians' offices and other nonhospital sites and carried items such as gowns, wheelchairs, examination tables and other products in addition to tubes and needles.

Mr. Battaglia noted that the distribution policies of BDVS and other BD divisions were developed and executed separately:

> We use many of the same distributors other BD divisions do, but the importance of various distributors to different divisions can vary significantly. For example, most of our sales are through lab products distributors, while other divisions sell more of their products through medical-surgical distributors. Those two types of distributors attend different conventions and speak different languages. In addition, we sell nearly all of our products through distributors, but some other BD divisions have a greater percentage of direct sales.

Nationally, there were over 1,000 distributors of hospital/medical supplies, but the 10 largest accounted for nearly 80% of hospital supply sales made through distributors. At BDVS, its six largest distributors accounted for more than 65% of division sales, the 50 largest for 85%, and 67 of the division's 474 dealers for nearly 95% of division sales.

BDVS's largest distributor was American Scientific Products (ASP), a division of American Hospital Supply Corporation (AHS) which in 1984 had total sales of $3.45 billion.[4] ASP was the largest lab products distributor in the United States, with an estimated 40% market share among distributors of products to hospital and commercial laboratories. In 1984, ASP accounted for a similar share of BDVS's sales.

ASP had 21 warehouse locations in the United States. In addition ASP had installed computer terminals in major hospitals and become an important part of their logistical system for purchasing supplies. According to ASP, for every dollar a hospital spent on a product, the hospital also spent nearly an additional dollar on acquiring and storing that item. Thus, less costly order entry and delivery could have a significant impact for supply items.

AHS also began in 1978 a Corporate Program for multilocation hospital accounts. Under this program, a hospital chain would agree to purchase from 50–75% of its supplies through ASP who, in return, would automate the hospital's inventory and materials-handling procedures, promising substantial reductions in overall costs. By 1985, other national distributors of hospital supplies also offered "Prime Vendor" programs analogous to AHS's Corporate Program. But it was estimated that AHS's program encompassed over 13% of the hospital beds in the United States with a total annual dollar volume in excess of $500 million covered by these agreements.

ASP paid higher commissions to its salespeople for selling AHS products. One AHS vice president was quoted as saying: "We manufacture 45% of what

---

[4]In 1985, American Hospital Supply merged with Baxter-Travenol, Inc., a manufacturer of medical equipment. The merged company was known as Baxter-Travenol and had 1985 sales of approximately $5 billion.

we distribute, but our manufactured products represented 70% of our profits last year. Before long, we hope to manufacture 65% of what we distribute." [5]

Terumo and Sherwood products were also distributed by ASP. Between 1979 and 1981, according to estimates by industry sources, over 70% of Terumo's U. S. sales went through ASP. Beginning in 1981, BDVS managers sought to build its relationship with ASP. BDVS managers held frequent meetings with ASP management and BDVS salespeople were encouraged to devote more time to sales meetings and product training sessions with ASP branches. In addition, as one BDVS manager noted, "We made clear to ASP our commitment to maintaining our market share and product leadership in blood collection systems and hoped they would support that objective." In 1985, BDVS was ASP's number one supplier of blood collection products. It was estimated that all BD products accounted for about 10% of ASP's sales (making BD one of ASP's top suppliers), and that BDVS products accounted for about 25% of the BD products sold by ASP.

Other major distributors for BDVS were Curtin-Matheson Scientific (CMS), which had 20 warehouse locations and sold primarily to hospital labs, and Fisher Scientific which had 20 warehouse locations and sold primarily to medical schools, research centers, and industrial labs.

In total, BDVS sold through 6 national distributors, with the remainder of its distribution network composed of regional chains and small local distributors. In most market areas, there were 4 or 5 different distributors selling BDVS products. One manager commented:

> Our relatively intensive distribution is a result of several factors. One is a legacy from when we were part of the BD division. Because BD sells syringes to a very fragmented physicians' market, intensive distribution is important there, and we retain many distributors which began selling VACUTAINER products when we were not a separate division. Another factor is that established relationships between a small local distributor and a lab have traditionally been important in the blood-collection products area. As a result, you sometimes must sell through a certain local distributor to break into an account.
>
> Also, since the DRG regulations, hospitals are more conscious of inventory carrying costs. As they cut stocking levels and order more frequently, some hospitals look more favorably on a supplier whose products are available from a number of different distributors in the area. If there is ever a problem with getting product from one distributor, the hospital knows there is back-up stock available at another in the area.

By contrast, Terumo sold its products primarily through ASP and CMS, the two largest national distributors. Terumo initially entered the U.S. market with needles in 1970 and tubes in 1972, selling through smaller West Coast distributors. In the mid-1970s, however, Terumo established a joint marketing agreement with Kimball Glass, one of ASP's major suppliers of lab products. Mr. Smith explained:

---

[5]"Hospital Suppliers Strike Back," *New York Times,* March 31, 1985.

Kimball opened the door for Terumo at ASP, which had been reluctant to take on an unknown line of blood collection products. ASP soon found, however, that Terumo's line provided them with an alternative to VACUTAINER. Terumo developed the relationship by focusing on individual ASP reps in individual branches: they worked closely with those reps to create a champion for their products in the branch.

Changing Buyer Behavior

During the 1980s, the distributor and end-user marketplace was changing significantly. According to a senior executive of one large national distributor of hospital supply products:

> In the past, our customer was the pathologist, chief technologist or lab manager. This person's responsibility was to produce quality diagnostic tests on specimens brought into the lab and to do it as fast as possible. A key was to ensure that an adequate supply of products was on hand at all times. It was also the element that these people were least prepared to deal with. Most lab managers and chief technologists had risen to their positions on the basis of their clinical skills, not their purchasing skills. In addition, they didn't particularly enjoy the purchasing part of their jobs.
>
> Thus, they tended to do business with a representative they liked and trusted, and who had a product line which encompassed most of their needs. They also wanted a company that would manage most of the purchasing job for them.
>
> Major national distributors flourished in this environment, with the distributor-served portion of the market growing at 10–17% annually throughout the 1970s. Also, distributors generally paid little attention to costs, because customers primarily wanted service and were willing to pay for it. After all, the lab was a true profit center then: hospital reimbursement procedures allowed any increased operating expenses to be passed on to customers.
>
> Those days are gone. First, the customer is different. Buying influence has moved out of the lab in most hospitals. Most decisions on products purchased from distributors are now made by professional purchasing people who require that traditional levels of service be provided along with lower costs. In addition, the buying influence is in many instances moving beyond the hospital purchasing department to the corporate purchasing department of national multihospital systems. Some distributors probably have over half of their total sales in these national accounts.
>
> Secondly, the distinction between manufacturers and distributors has become increasingly blurry. Currently, the three largest national distributors have manufacturing capabilities in important market segments such as hematology and therapeutic drug monitoring.
>
> Finally, while most distributors currently serve the hospital and commercial lab markets, little attention has been paid by distributors to the fastest growing customer segment, the physicians' market, which includes surgicenters, emergency centers, and diagnostic centers as well as the offices of individual doctors. All trends point toward more volume in these locations and less in the hospital.
>
> In this environment, distributors must lower costs. I believe many distributors will carry only two—or even one—vendors' brands in many product categories

in exchange for lower prices from those vendors. Moreover, distributors can reduce inventory, transportation, and some administrative costs through consolidation of their product lines.

In the early 1980s, moreover, larger hospitals and buying groups began to favor single-source, high-volume contracts with manufacturers of certain products rather than purchasing these products through distributors. One industry observer noted in early 1985:

> The once popular prime vendor contract, one of the distributor's favorite marketing tools to hospitals, seems to be undergoing an eclipse. Materials managers who eagerly embraced the program's convenience now want to take back much of the ordering and pricing responsibility they feel they have relinquished to the distributor. The new fashion is to use the purchasing power of committed volume to bargain down prices from individual manufacturers. . . . And to get the additional committed-volume business, manufacturers are perfectly willing to accept a portion of the distributor's responsibility, taking some of the cost of the product out of what was formerly the distributor's margin.[6]

Under direct buying contracts, a hospital or buying group negotiated a committed-volume contract directly with the manufacturer. The distributor would still deliver the product to the hospital for a commission from the manufacturer (and often in higher volumes than previously), but that distributor did not negotiate the initial purchase price directly with the hospital.

Further, by standardizing on purchases of certain products, buying groups could negotiate lower prices from the manufacturer *and* from the distributor: having negotiated a contract with a manufacturer, hospitals often held a second round of negotiations with distributors in order to lower their net purchase price further. The distributor, fearful of losing a big order, often relinquished a significant portion of the commission that distributor received from the manufacturer. As one distributor manager commented, "With the stroke of a pen, these multihospital systems can swing millions of dollars in revenues from one distributor to another. Having experienced both sides of this double-edged sword, I know what the sports announcers mean when they talk about the 'thrill of victory' and the 'agony of defeat'!"

Exhibit 4 indicates the difference in purchasing patterns under prime vendor contracts and the more recent, direct purchasing procedures.

BDVS Response

BDVS instituted a Z contract in which prices and order quantities were negotiated directly with hospitals but still delivered through distributors. Often Z contract prices with large buying groups were 30–40% lower than list prices.

---

[6] "The Devolution of Prime Vendor Contracts," *In Vivo: The Business and Medicine Report* (January–February 1985): 20.

Under a Z contract, as with other BDVS contracts, BDVS's distributors received a set commission from BDVS for stocking, shipping and billing the hospital.

One BDVS manager explained that "some hospitals negotiate with us and then shop among our distributors for the best price at that level of the chain. They force our distributors to compete away a portion of their commission on Z-contract orders." In response, BDVS offered its distributors periodic promotional cash incentives.

With Z-contract customers, a BDVS sales rep called on the buyer 30–60 days before the contract expiration date to gather information about the customer's product requirements and any competitive inroads at the account. This information was entered on a Critical Information Questionnaire, which suggested a selling price and which the rep submitted to the regional manager. One sales rep estimated he spent 25% of his time on contract negotiations:

> Until recent years, only 4 or 5 of my accounts were on Z contracts, but now almost all are. That means more paperwork and legwork. It also means less time spent with the bench people and more time with purchasing people. I've also been spending more time in negotiating seminars since these contract sessions can be difficult and tense. I've been in the business for nearly 15 years; selling in the health-care industry is more complicated, and less fun, than it used to be.

By 1985 most BDVS venous blood collection products, and approximately 20% of the division's capillary and microbiology products, were sold through Z contracts. Many of BDVS's hospital customers were affiliated with a number of different buying groups which had separate Z contracts with BDVS. While there were approximately 1 million hospital beds in the United States, Z contracts encompassed nearly 2.8 million hospital beds by 1985.

Affiliated Purchasing Group

Affiliated Purchasing Group (APG) was founded in 1975. A group of independent, not-for-profit hospitals were affiliated as shareholders with a central organization that provided various services for member hospitals, including purchasing programs. APG's motto was "In Unity There Is Strength," and the group sought to use the power of centralized purchasing while maintaining local autonomy among member hospitals.

APG headquarters personnel negotiated national purchasing agreements with suppliers, but member hospitals were free to make individual purchases separately with manufacturers or distributors of the products. APG purchasing staff monitored national and regional costs, and this data became the basis for their contract negotiations with manufacturers and distributors. The aim, according to one APG manager, was to "pay the lowest price available."

From a group of 20 hospitals in 1975, APG included more than 500 hospitals by 1985, accounting for more than 10% of all U.S. hospital beds and nearly 2 million annual admissions. Many large, prestigious hospitals affiliated with medical schools were APG members. In 1985, APG had national purchasing agreements with about 100 medical equipment suppliers, and the number of such agreements had grown consistently in recent years.

In addition to group purchasing, APG offered other services to member hospitals, especially for hospital administrative personnel. APG maintained a database on department administrators at APG-member hospitals, and this database was made available to APG hospitals seeking new managers; the intent was to offer administrators an opportunity to move among APG hospitals while retaining quality administrators within APG-affiliated hospitals. APG maintained a similar database on doctors. The group also coordinated a program which brought together doctors, nurses, and administrators from different APG-affiliated hospitals to discuss cost-reduction opportunities and develop specific action plans. The program allowed member hospitals to compare their costs by product line, therapy type, and department.

APG had been aggressive and innovative in other areas. It had recently established a private-label program in which it sought to have its suppliers use the APG trademark on products sold through APG purchasing agreements. By mid-1985, this private-label program encompassed a dozen product categories, and APG expected to add 30–40 additional products by 1986. According to Mr. James Wilson, APG's vice president for materials management and the person who had initiated many of APG's recent programs, APG eventually hoped to private-label "virtually all" products sold through APG purchasing agreements.

In early 1985, Mr. Wilson also announced APG's intention of establishing its own distribution network. Throughout 1985, APG negotiated with a number of smaller, regional medical-products distributors to provide warehousing, trucking, and related functions for hospitals that purchased under APG agreements. APG then sought to have its suppliers distribute their products to APG-affiliated distributors who, in return for a larger share of the high-volume APG contracts, distributed products for lower margins than hospital-supply distributors had traditionally received.

Mr. Wilson announced that the program would eventually involve a national order-entry system linking these distributors with APG-affiliated hospitals, and he expected that, if the system could achieve sufficient utilization by suppliers and APG member hospitals, it could lower the hospital's costs by 3–12% on most supply items.

By mid-1985, both the private label and distribution programs were being aggressively promoted by APG materials management. Some manufacturers had agreed to participate in these programs, while others had rejected participation. BDVS's management knew of at least two manufacturers that had not been awarded APG contracts after rejecting participation in these programs. At the same time, distributors not part of the APG distribution network, including the large national distributors of hospital supply products, were reportedly ready to stop supporting (and perhaps sever agreements with) manufacturers that agreed to the program.

Negotiations with APG

In 1982, APG had first sought to standardize its purchase of needles and tubes, and had demanded substantial price reductions from BDVS. BDVS had resisted negotiating prices and terms directly with APG headquarters and had continued dealing separately with individual hospitals. When APG established a national purchasing agreement with Terumo, BDVS's field salespeople had been able to retain most sales of BDVS tubes at individual APG-affiliated hospitals, in part by lowering prices when necessary on a hospital-by-hospital basis.

BDVS's success in retaining the business created a number of repercussions. One manager recalled:

> There was some ill-will between us and APG for some time afterwards. Their purchasing people had naturally worked hard to get the national contract in place, and felt our success tended to undermine them with administration at member hospitals. In addition, the experience made the whole issue of compliance by member hospitals with national purchasing agreements more visible and important for them.

APG subsequently established a group of field personnel charged with promoting the importance of compliance with APG-negotiated contracts at member hospitals. In turn, BDVS field salespeople soon reported that their relationships with many accounts in the APG system seemed to be suffering. One salesperson noted:

> There was a period in which I couldn't get phone calls returned from people I had done business with for years. This was especially true of certain administrators who had introduced APG programs in their hospitals. The word on the street was that APG personnel were bad-mouthing us with their members. I don't think this appreciably affected my actual volume with individual departments in hospitals, but it certainly made life uncomfortable.

In response, BDVS managers sought to "mend fences" with certain administrators and with APG headquarters personnel. One manager recalled:

> We held meetings with these people in different regions, and explained over dinner that our actions had been based on a reasonable business decision intended to retain our presence in those accounts, and nothing personal had been intended. There is definitely an emotional dimension to business situations like this, and it's important to establish lines of communications with important individuals.

Following this series of meetings, BDVS field salespeople reported a "better atmosphere" at certain hospitals.

In April 1985, Mr. Wilson announced his intention of establishing a new national purchasing agreement for blood-collection products. He asserted that the supplier awarded the contract would receive 90% of the business in these product lines from APG-affiliated hospitals. Informally, one APG manager also informed BDVS that APG considered the blood-collection agreement to be a "showcase program in which a high degree of compliance by member hospitals is important to us: we'll work for that." BDVS management estimated VACUTAINER products currently represented more than 80% of the venous blood-collection tubes and 40% of the needles purchased by APG hospitals, totaling about $6 million in 1984 purchases from BDVS.

In contrast to 1982, BDVS management in 1985 decided to negotiate directly with APG headquarters. Management felt that the APG system had grown considerably during the past three years, the central purchasing organization had increased its strength with member hospitals, and there was more risk in refusing to negotiate. Mr. Kozy recalled:

> These meetings with APG in Chicago were tense. At the first meeting, they dramatically announced that 90% of their business was available to the vendor with the right price. We then surveyed our sales force and, based on their contacts with users at APG affiliates, concluded that a substantial portion, but not 90%, of our business with these hospitals was at risk.
>
> At the next meeting, the APG manager pulled out a thick binder with the price of *every* item purchased by *every* member from *every* supplier. At the third meeting, out came another binder with their estimates of prices in our product category to all other hospital-buying groups in the United States. This is a difference from previous negotiations: they are very well prepared this time around.
>
> At a fourth meeting, they announced they had received bids from our competitor, and wanted to know if we would meet their prices, which were considerably lower than our list prices and, because of the volume involved, lower than our prices on other Z contract amounts.

Traditionally, BDVS products had been sold through its authorized distributors to APG-affiliated hospitals as to other BDVS accounts. At the start of the new negotiations with APG, Mr. Kozy noted that:

> We told our distributors we were negotiating a potential contract with APG and that the negotiations had the potential to be bloody: if we lost the contract, we would be very aggressive in seeking to retain business at end-user accounts and wanted their support, even if the contract went to another supplier whose products they also distributed. Since then, our distributors, who do lots of business with APG-member hospitals, have sought ongoing information about developments.

The Guns of August

At the fifth meeting on August 1st, Kozy and Smith proposed a Z contract with prices approximately 20% higher than competitors' proposals. The proposal required APG to deliver within 90 days of the initial contract date 95% of their member hospitals' purchases of venous blood-collection tubes and 90% of their purchases of blood-collection needles. If these targets were not achieved within 90 days, prices on BDVS products covered by the contract would automatically increase by 5% during the remaining 21 months of the proposed two-year contract agreement.

APG negotiators rejected this proposal, and gave BDVS until August 15th to submit a new proposal. They also announced that they wanted all blood-collection products covered by a national purchasing agreement to be part of the private-label program, and thus carry the APG logo. In addition, they wanted all products covered by the agreement to be supplied through distributors affiliated with APG, and provided a list of these distributors. The list did not include most of BDVS's major distributors. According to the APG negotiators, moreover, BDVS's competitors had maintained their original pricing proposals and had agreed to both the private-label and distribution demands.

Exhibit 1 **Becton Dickinson & Company**

Summary of Selected Financial Data
(thousands of dollars, except per share data)

	1984	*1983*	*1982*
	Years Ended September 30		
Operations			
Net sales	$1,126,845	$1,119,520	$1,113,921
Gross profit	498,128	469,077	478,291
Gross profit margin	44.2%	41.9%	42.9%
Interest income	23,824	18,211	15,147
Interest expense	22,757	32,511	32,336
Income before income taxes[a]	92,908	33,652	106,198
Income tax provision (credit)	29,505	(2,278)	29,506
Net income	63,403	35,930	76,692
Financial Position			
Current assets	$ 565,526	$ 553,281	$ 557,242
Current liabilities	245,794	190,222	229,523
Current ratio	2.3	2.9	2.4
Pretax income as a percent of sales	8.2%	3.0%	9.5%
Net income as a percent of sales	5.6%	3.2%	6.9%
Return on net operating assets	8.2%	5.8%	10.6%
Return on equity	10.5%	6.1%	13.3%
Additional Data			
Capital expenditures	82,324	91,031	130,008
Research and development expense	57,735	55,149	49,308
Number of employees	17,700	19,100	21,200

Summary by Business Segments			
	1984	*1983*	*1982*
Health Care			
Medical product sales	$ 668,757	$ 685,275	$ 685,553
Laboratory product sales	260,828	264,234	266,425
Total health-care sales	929,585	949,509	951,978
Segment operating income	108,178	100,069	130,342
% income to sales	11.6%	10.5%	13.7%
Industrial Safety			
Sales	197,260	170,011	161,943
Segment Operating Income	22,635	4,616	15,839
% of Income to Sales	11.5%	10.5%	13.7%

Source: Company annual reports.

[a] 1983 income was significantly affected by a one-time, nonrecurring charge.

Exhibit 2 Becton Dickinson & Company

Blood Collection Systems Division

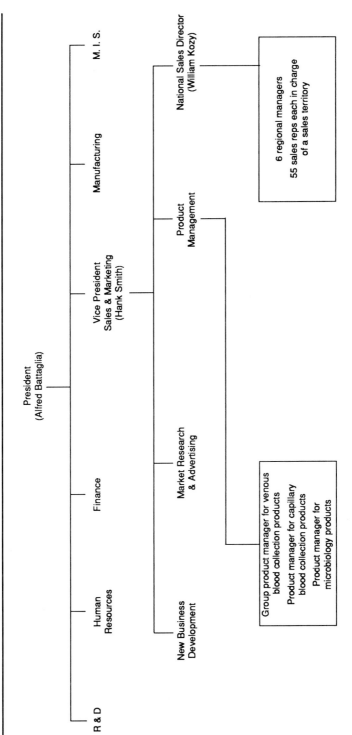

President
(Alfred Battaglia)

R & D

Human
Resources

Finance

Vice President
Sales & Marketing
(Hank Smith)

Manufacturing

M. I. S.

New Business
Development

Market Research
& Advertising

Product
Management

National Sales Director
(William Kozy)

Group product manager for venous
blood collection products

Product manager for capillary
blood collection products

Product manager for
microbiology products

6 regional managers

55 sales reps each in charge
of a sales territory

Advertising Sample

STERILE **VACUTAINER** BRAND EVACUATED TUBES

After 40 years, the goals and achievements of the VACUTAINER Brand Tube line are still unique. VACUTAINER Brand products offer unique benefits for the laboratory valuing the most extensive research and development program...an unequalled depth of product line...and an unrivaled commitment to specialized service. It's all here, exclusively with VACUTAINER Tubes.

Here is the most comprehensive line of evacuated blood collection tubes available today All sterile for safety. And featuring the widest array of tube sizes, draw and approved formulations...for chemistry, hematology, coagulation studies, special procedures and blood banking.

Here are the most extensively researched and documented tubes you'll find They have to be. That's the extra commitment we bring as the people who not only manufacture them, but pioneer their development as well. Every VACUTAINER Tube is backed by in-depth clinical and/or research studies. Data is available on request.

Here are the most significant tube introductions and improvements seen anywhere in recent years We improved blood collection tubes for trace element studies, therapeutic drug monitoring and coagulation studies. We've developed new tubes for special procedures like activated clotting time (ACT), LE cell preps and STAT tests. We've expanded our choice of tubes for serum preparation. Starting with our top-of-the-line SST™ (Serum Separator Tube with gel barrier material), we added our new CAT™ (Clot Activator Tube), and then improved our standard red-top tube with a new hemorepellent stopper. For laboratories that prefer their own labeling system, we now offer a new line of VACUTAINER Tubes with SeeThru labeling that provides all the essential information without impeding visibility of the specimen.

Here is the caliber of service support available only through VACUTAINER Systems...the company that stands behind every tube you use. Becton Dickinson VACUTAINER Systems is capable of meeting your special needs because we're not just a manufacturer, but researchers and originators ready to anticipate and respond to changes in your diagnostic procedures. Our sales representatives are accessible specialists in the laboratory field. Our nationwide distribution network is always ready to get you the supplies you need, when you need them. Our technical service team is available for immediate consultation (call toll free 800-631-0174). And, to help you train your staff for the best venous blood collection techniques, our educational materials—publications, films, and sound/slide programs—are at your disposal.

The following pages contain the latest information on our complete line of Sterile VACUTAINER Tubes and VACUTAINER Needles.

(continued)

Exhibit 3 (continued)

VACUTAINER BRAND NEEDLES AND ACCESSORIES

The VACUTAINER System offers a wide selection of blood collection needles and accessories that meet both demanding technical requirements and patient needs during venipuncture. Sterile needles are available for single sample or multiple sample collection, with standard or thin-wall cannulae, in peel-apart packages or plastic cases, and in lengths and gauges you require.

Improved VACUTAINER Multiple Sample Needles feature the most up-to-date improvements for sharpness and ease of use. A new point configuration, special polishing and a new lubrication process allow extra smooth vein entry and reduce "drag." Laser inspection of *every needle* detects even microscopic flaws for virtually flawless quality control. All needle hubs and shields are color-coded for quick identification of gauge. New tamper-evident labels protect against inadvertent use of an already opened needle.

There is a VACUTAINER Holder/Needle Combination designed to fit any VACUTAINER Blood Collection Tube or VACUTAINER Culture Tube. Available with choice of single sample or multiple sample needles, with standard or small diameter holder. VACUTAINER Holder/Needle Combinations are sterile, single-use units that assure protection of the sterile pathway from patient to blood collection tube. Preassembled, they offer the additional advantage of eliminating assembly and clean-up time requirements. Also available are VACUTAINER Reusable Holders in three sizes to meet any need. And sterile, single-use Luer Adapters—unique to the VACUTAINER System—that allow the use of a variety of attachments (needle holders, catheters) under a single venipuncture, sparing the patient unnecessary trauma.

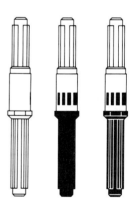

IMPROVED MULTIPLE SAMPLE NEEDLES
in Plastic Package with Tamper-Evident Label

Gauge	Length	Cannula Wall	Color Code	Reorder Number
20	1″	regular	Yellow	7214
20	1½″	regular	Yellow	7215
21	1″	thin-wall	Green	7212
21	1½″	thin-wall	Green	7213
22	1″	thin-wall	Black	7210
22	1½″	thin-wall	Black	7211

(continued)

Exhibit 3 (continued)

MULTIPLE SAMPLE NEEDLES, Peel-Apart Package

Gauge	Length	Cannula Wall	Color Code	Reorder Number
20	1"	regular	Yellow	7205
20	1½"	regular	Yellow	5749

SINGLE SAMPLE NEEDLES, Peel-Apart Package

Gauge	Length	Cannula Wall	Color Code	Reorder Number
18	1"	regular	Pink	5747
20	1"	regular	Yellow	5745
20	1½"	regular	Yellow	5746
21	1"	thin-wall	Green	5743
21	1½"	thin-wall	Green	5744
22	1"	regular	Black	5741
22	1½"	regular	Black	5742

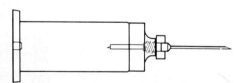

MULTIPLE SAMPLE HOLDER/NEEDLE COMBINATION
Peel-Apart Package

Holder Size	Needle Gauge	Needle Length	Color Code	Reorder Number
Standard	20	1½"	Yellow	7226
Small Diameter	22	1"	Black	7227

Exhibit 4   Becton Dickinson & Company

Figure 1
Prime Vendor Contract 1982

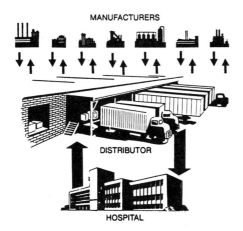

This figure illustrates the forces affecting prime vendor contracts and distributors. Under the older prime vendor contract (A), the distributor dealt more directly with many different suppliers, often negotiating the actual purchasing contracts for hospitals. As the suppliers' major conduit into the hospital, the distributor could drive a harder bargain. But as hospitals

Figure 2
Hospital Purchasing Today

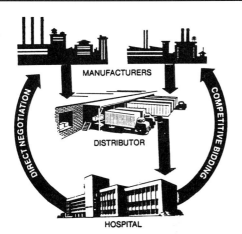

begin to cut back on the number of suppliers they deal with (B), standardizing their purchasing to increase buying power for their own direct negotiations with vendors, the distributor's role and power in the purchasing process are shrinking, as are the distributor's margins. The distributor becomes less the product broker and more of a product warehouser.

Source: IN VIVO: The Business and Medicine Report (January/February 1985): 22–23.

## Chapter 6

Managing Major Accounts

For most companies, all customers are *not* equal in that some customers account for disproportionately large shares of a company's sales volume and/or margins. Some managers refer to this as the 80/20 rule, meaning that, in many instances, approximately 20% of the accounts in a customer base may generate as much as 80% of the company's sales. This chapter focuses on issues encountered in the selling and management of these major accounts.

Major Accounts

The terms *national* and *major account* are often used interchangeably when referring to selling efforts directed at a company's largest potential customers. In this text, the term *major account* is preferred for a number of reasons. First, changes in the competitive environment increasingly require firms to take an international view of their largest customers. Hence, viewing customers as "national" accounts may limit thinking about the implications of such selling efforts for organizing and implementing the company's marketing effort. Second, beyond geographical dispersion, the term *major account* more accurately captures the special status such customers occupy in the revenue stream (and, often, product-development plans) of the selling company.

In line with others,[1] we define a major account as a customer that typically does the following:

- Purchases a significant volume, both in absolute dollars and as a percent of a supplier's total sales
- Involves several people (perhaps several different functional areas) in the purchasing process

- Buys for a number of geographically dispersed organizational units (e.g., stores, branches, manufacturing plants)
- Expects specialized attention and services (e.g., logistical support, inventory management, price discounts, customized applications, ongoing information, and reports about product usage)
- Because of these characteristics, requires a long-term cooperative relationship between buyer and seller as a means to effective and profitable exchange

A number of factors have made such accounts increasingly important to companies. Mergers, acquisitions, and other changes in the general business environment are forcing vendors in many industries to put greater emphasis on large customers with equally large and complex purchasing requirements. In consumer packaged-goods marketing, for example, conventional supermarkets accounted for about 75% of U.S. food retail sales in 1980 but only an estimated 25% by 1990. So-called super stores, combination stores, and warehouse stores account for dramatically increased proportions of total sales volume. These large chain customers possess the buying power and sophisticated information systems required to insist on better service, lower prices, and a coordinated approach from their suppliers, many of whom sell them multiple products through different sales forces. Similar trends are evident in industrial goods categories, where the increased concentration and automation of industrial resellers has generated new selling requirements for many suppliers.

Internationally, the emergence of more multinational (often, global) customers places new account-management demands on many sales organizations. Especially in industrial product categories, suppliers are increasingly called upon to provide coordinated sales and service at customer locations that may be scattered throughout the world. In these situations, moreover, the supplier's field marketing efforts are often made more complex due to the impact of physical distances, currency fluctuations in different countries, and many cultural differences—both within the vendor's sales force and among the customer's purchase and use locations.

Finally, the increased adoption of just-in-time materials management approaches has affected buying behavior for many large companies in many product categories.[2] Instead of maintaining multiple suppliers to assure competitive bids, many purchasers have reduced their list of potential vendors dramatically and sought to develop longer-term agreements that provide the vendor with the likelihood of high-volume sales over time in exchange for a variety of specialized sales, service, and support procedures. This, in turn, places more importance on a supplier's ability to organize and execute sales efforts aimed at achieving and maintaining preferred-vendor status at these major accounts.

To meet the increasingly complex requirements of a small number of important customers, many companies have had to reexamine their account management policies and practices. The term *account management* refers not only to the process of selling (i.e., turning prospects into customers) but also to the entire process of initiating and developing buyer-seller relationships over time. Major-account management is especially important in business-to-business selling situations, where problem solving of different sorts is often at the core of large sales transactions and requires significant applications engineering, installation or operating assistance, and, often, ongoing support services. Further, since the purchases are often critical components in the buyer's finished product and because in many markets the same buyers meet the same sellers repeatedly, long-term relationships (rather than one-time opportunistic transactions) are often the goal of account-management practices.

Managing major accounts requires the marketer to: (1) clarify account selection criteria; (2) analyze the human factors that typically affect selling and buying processes in these situations; (3) understand the dynamics of buyer-seller relations over time; and (4) diagnose and manage the formidable coordination requirements posed by major accounts.

Account Selection

Because of their buying power and complexity, major accounts typically require a large, long-term commitment of often-specialized resources from their suppliers. Delivery systems, the terms and conditions of the purchase contract, product applications, and the vendor's products themselves may well be changed (or developed from scratch) in these marketing situations. Further, the selling cycle can often mean years of effort and many costly sales calls before a contract is signed and revenues generated. The following example is representative:[3]

> Late-night travelers at the Philadelphia airport were startled one evening as they passed a well-dressed man shouting and jumping at a pay telephone on the concourse. Another stressed-out executive gone round the bend? No, just Frank Perry celebrating a hard-fought victory for Pilot Air Freight.
>
> Perry, who heads a fledgling national accounts program at the $85 million freight forwarder, had just called the Kansas City hotel room of his closest contact on GTE's traffic council, a 25-member body that had spent three days hearing proposals from more than a dozen suppliers. The GTE man had good news: after nearly three years and more than 100 sales calls on GTE plants and offices, Pilot had won a three-year contract from the huge corporation.

Such efforts mean a sizeable opportunity cost for the vendor: A selling effort encompassing more than 100 sales calls represents time and attention not allocated elsewhere, and a multiyear selling cycle is a formidable barrier for any marketing organization still held accountable for the generation of quarterly and annual sales revenues. Nonetheless, such efforts are usually required in major-account management. As one marketing manager notes, "No one's really interested in waiting three or four years for a sale. But few companies have discretionary accounts that allow a single manager to buy a million-dollar system tomorrow."

Clearly, because of the resources required, not every current customer or potential prospect can be treated as a major account. Account selection is a crucial decision for the selling company, and clarifying account-selection criteria a necessary component of effective account-management tactics. Depending upon the vendor's marketing strategy and competitive situation, a number of factors are relevant account-selection criteria.

Order size is probably the most common criterion used by companies in judging which customers merit major-account attention. A key reason is that, in most businesses, large orders are less expensive to fulfill than smaller orders due to scale economies and learning-curve effects inherent in many production processes and delivery systems. Also, the extent of the vendor's sales efforts in these situations often requires large orders to amortize the selling expenses and justify the effort.

Nonetheless order size alone is only one potential account-selection criterion. Depending upon the vendor's business characteristics, moreover, it may not be the best criterion on which to base these decisions. For example, a high-service, premium-priced producer may find that buyers that generate the largest orders are also the most price sensitive, and because their purchase orders allow them to establish in-house service and support capabilities for the product, these companies are the least willing to pay for the vendor's support offerings.

Product mix purchased by an account is another important factor in determining whether or not a customer is a major account. The potential of selling across the vendor's product line is often a key consideration in account selection. This potential can be especially important in situations in which the selling company's cost-of-goods-sold is approximately equivalent across its product line, but customer price sensitivity varies considerably for some products and not others. This situation pertains in many service businesses, where a number of products often share the same delivery system but customer benefits and price elasticity vary from one service offering to the next. Similarly, the advent of flexible manufacturing systems in industrial markets means that, for many industrial producers, the economics of manufacturing operations are driven more by "scope" than "scale" considerations.[4] Computer technologies are creating factories that can produce a stream of different product designs at the same (or lower) costs as an equal-size stream of different product designs in the traditional factory geared to unit-cost economies of scale. In such situations, systems sales across the vendor's product line are often more profitable than a large order for any single product.

Customer maintenance costs are a third factor in account-selection decisions. Some accounts may seem relatively unattractive when viewed solely in terms of order size or product mix characteristics. But, account profitability patterns often vary considerably when one considers the longer-term costs of maintaining large customers' orders over time. Thus it is important to project the cumulative cash flow history of the relationship.[5] During the selling and development period, cash flows are negative and customer demands typically encourage these expenditures by the vendor. When the product is delivered and reorders begin to materialize, cumulative cash flows by the vendor finally become positive. The expenses required to maintain these orders after the sale differ significantly from one account to the next, making customer-maintenance costs an important criterion.

In addition, more qualitative criteria may legitimately affect a company's major-account decisions. Some companies are inherently prestige accounts that help to generate sales at other accounts with order patterns or customer-maintenance costs more appropriate to the vendor's capabilities. In other situations, a given company may be a strategic account in the sense that major-account attention and resources are required to preempt a competitor from building volume or other capabilities through its relationship with that customer.

The key point, however, is that a major account ultimately represents a stream of orders for the supplier. This stream of orders, in turn, affects the supplier's business through a series of interrelationships that must be balanced in account-selection decisions: The size of the account has implications for capacity utilization at the selling company, both in terms of the amount of capacity utilized (order size) and the type of capacity utilized (product mix); the nature of the account's bargaining power affects the net price and margins available to the supplier; and the service, support, and other customer-maintenance characteristics of the account affect the cumulative cash flow history of the account relationship. Figure A depicts this quadrant of concerns inherent in account selection decisions.

In practice, there is no easy alignment among the factors shown in Figure A. The accounts likely to generate the largest orders across the selling company's product line are also those that, due to their purchasing patterns, have the knowledge and bargaining power to demand lower prices and many

Figure A
Impact of Account-Selection Decisions

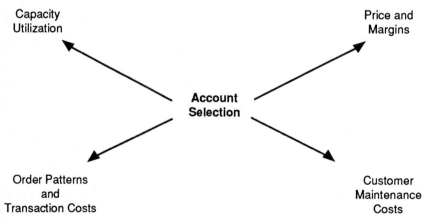

specialized services that increase the vendor's customer-maintenance costs. Yet these large and powerful buyers are also often those that occupy a particularly strategic position in the marketing plans of competitors in the relevant product category.

A useful way of beginning the trade-off analysis required in major account-selection decisions is to think of customers in terms of two key dimensions: net price realized and cost to serve.[6] This approach categorizes potential accounts into four categories for purposes of considering their implications for the seller.

1. "Carriage trade" customers cost a great deal to serve but are also willing to pay for such services, either because the seller's product is a critical component in their finished product or because they have little interest or ability in unbundling the product-service offering.

2. At the opposite extreme, "bargain basement" customers are price sensitive and relatively uninterested in service and support offerings. They can be sold and serviced less expensively than carriage trade but also generate lower net prices and margins.

3. A third category might be labeled "passive" accounts. In this category, the seller's net price realized is relatively high and the cost to serve is relatively low. These accounts generate highly profitable orders, and there may be any of a number of reasons for their purchasing behavior. In some instances, the seller's product may be perceived as not important enough to warrant the time and attention required by a tough negotiating stance over prices. Other customers are less price sensitive because the seller's product is crucial to their production processes, and quality or reputation are key considerations in sourcing the product. Over time, this creates a set of both economic and psychological switching costs. In still other situations, the vendor's capabilities are so well matched to buyer needs that the vendor's customer-maintenance costs are low even as the buyer continues to receive (and pay for) good service and quality.

4. A fourth category might be labeled "aggressive" customers. Their buying volume and repeat purchases in a product category give them the bargaining power required to demand both low prices and high service through price deals and customized programs.

Making appropriate account-selection decisions requires ongoing attention to these account characteristics: Customer purchasing patterns and purchasing criteria change over time as customers gain experience with a product category, as competition or product substitutes evolve, and as their own relationship with a vendor develops.

Analyzing the Buying Process

Once certain customers are targeted for major-account efforts, the decision-making unit (DMU) at the potential buyer must be analyzed. Because of the magnitude of the purchases involved and the specialized terms and conditions affecting multiple functions in both buying and selling companies, major sales usually involve a number of different personnel in the purchasing process, each of whom typically performs a set of distinct roles. Understanding the dynamics of such DMUs is essential.

The term *buying center* is commonly used in the marketing literature for designating the different roles that members of a DMU perform in a major purchase decision.[7] The more complex and involved the potential purchase, the larger the DMU and the more careful its decisions, thereby making the seller's ability to distinguish among different purchasing roles especially important. In analyzing the major account's buying center, it is useful to distinguish among six buying roles.

The *initiators* of the purchase process are those at the customer organization who perceive a problem or opportunity inherent in acquiring a particular product or service. Often, initiators are relatively lower-level managers concerned with reducing costs or increasing performance in a particular department or area of company operations. They may increase the buying company's awareness of the problem or opportunity but often lack the authority required to authorize expenditures.

The *gatekeepers* are those capable of acting as product or problem experts. They may be buyers or purchasing managers. Typically they are responsible for maintaining current knowledge of vendor offerings. In many industrial purchase decisions, gatekeepers develop purchase specifications and the short list of potential vendors capable of meeting these specifications. Influencing the development of specifications is a key goal of the selling company's account-management efforts because the specifications often determine who is on the approved-vendors list and, among those vendors, their relative attractiveness and capabilities for the particular order. Hence identifying the relevant gatekeepers early in the buying process is an important marketing task.

Influencers are those who have indirect authority or persuasive power. The number and type of influencers becomes particularly large in major purchases because so many areas are affected. For example, one survey found that, in the typical capital equipment purchase, an average of four departments (engineering and purchasing were always involved), three levels of company management (e.g., manager, regional manager, vice president), and seven different people at the buying company were involved in the purchase decision.[8] Depending upon the purchase, moreover, important influencers might include a board of directors committee (often involved in major construction or information services purchases) or shop-floor production personnel (often key influencers in many supplies and factory automation purchases).

Deciders are those who can say yes or no to the potential purchase and a prospective vendor. Often, the deciders may have little or no formal designation within the purchasing process. But, their status as product experts, managers from whose budget the purchase expenditures will come, or managers of functional areas whose operations will be heavily affected by the purchase decision gives them an important behind-the-scenes role in the buying center. Identifying the deciders is perhaps the most crucial and difficult task in selling to major accounts. An important motivation for forming major-account programs at many companies is the need facing the selling company to sell "higher and wider" in order to influence the purchase criteria adopted by deciders. Further, it is important to distinguish between deciders who can make (affirmative power) or break (veto power) a purchase decision, since their relative importance in the buying process can differ as the sale progresses.

Purchasers are those who formally sign the purchase agreement. A corporate purchasing manager often plays this role in many industrial buying decisions and often has the responsibility of negotiating price and specific terms and conditions. The important point here is that the purchaser may (but, in many cases, may not) also play the key roles of initiator, gatekeeper, influencer, and/or decider.

Users are those in the purchasing company who actually use the product or service being sold and hence must live with the decision. Depending upon the product or service and the nature of the buying process at a specific account, users may or may not have significant influence on the initial purchase decision. However, because major-account sales often involve years of effort aimed at establishing a long-term relationship, developing and maintaining efficient lines of communication with users is usually an important goal of the selling company's account team.

Note that the buying-center concept refers to behavioral roles performed by different members of a DMU. Thus depending upon the nature of the purchase, the same person might perform more than one role or, in some circumstances, all roles. What is important in applying this concept is not the particular jargon embedded in this approach but rather an understanding of the implied marketing realities. With these distinctions in mind, a useful way of analyzing major-account customers is to consider, for each person in the buying center, a set of questions focused on the "3 Ps" of Power, Perceptions, and Priorities:

- Power: What is each person's relative power in the purchase decision and to what extent does each person at the buying company have veto or affirmative power?
- Perceptions: What are each person's assumptions and perceptions concerning the purchase and the strengths and weaknesses of particular vendors? What are the key factors influencing these perceptions?
- Priorities: What are each person's major priorities in the purchase decision: Cost reduction? Performance improvement? Delivery? Convenience? Risk reduction?

"Companies don't buy; people do." The buying center concept, in tandem with intelligent application of the Power/Perceptions/Priorities distinction, can help to operationalize this fundamental fact about marketing and account management.

Developing Buyer-Seller Relationships

Account-selection decisions and the initial sale, however large, are often only the starting point in managing major accounts. A key goal is the development of a long-term relationship rather than a series of discrete transactions.

The distinction between transaction and relationship is more than semantic. The two can be distinguished along several important dimensions.[9] Most important is the fact that relationships transpire over time and reflect an ongoing process. Thus each particular purchase decision made as part of that relationship should be viewed in terms of its history and anticipated future. This contrasts with the nature of transactions in many other sales situations that have a distinct beginning, short duration, and a sharp ending, or close. Second, because of the duration of the relationship, exchange between buyer and seller in major-account situations often is characterized by the development of tacit norms and obligations aimed at satisfying changing goals and requirements. By contrast, standard sales transactions tend to focus on the price and other specifications relevant to the particular moment; little or no attention is paid to future requirements or performance obligations above and beyond the specifications of the current contract. Third, in long-term relationships, dependencies develop for both the buyer and seller, and discrete measurements of vendor performance are often difficult to make. These dependencies and uncertainties ideally lead to deeper communication and cooperative planning aimed at anticipating and resolving conflicts; and they usually mean that social, interpersonal, and noneconomic factors are important aspects of the exchange process. In contrast, transactions predominate in situations in which performance criteria are relatively obvious; dependencies (or switching costs) for the buyer and seller are minimal (thus facilitating price bargaining by the buyer); and personal relationships may not be important dimensions of the bargaining, problem solving, or setting of specifications required by the transaction.

These differences between exchange relationships and transactions have real implications for account analysis and tactics, ranging from pricing (e.g., penetration pricing in order to develop a relationship as opposed to skim pricing aimed at maximizing transaction revenues) to product policy (e.g., the relative willingness of seller to devote time and resources to product customization for an account and the relative willingness of buyer to share confidential information) and distribution (e.g., capabilities involving physical distribution or inventory management). In addition, these differences underscore the importance, in major-account situations, of understanding the dynamics of buyer-seller relations over time and the mechanisms that affect the transformation of transactions into exchange relationships. One perspective posits that buyer-seller relationships evolve through five phases: (1) awareness, (2) exploration, (3) expansion, (4) commitment, and (5) dissolution.[10] Each phase represents a major transition in how the parties involved regard each other.

Awareness refers to one party's recognition that another is a potential exchange partner. The account-selection process by the vendor is part of the awareness phase, as are the roles performed by initiators and compilers of approved-vendor lists in the buying center. In this phase, specific transactions may not take place although there may be positioning and bargaining by each party.

Exploration refers to a search and trial phase. In this phase, potential partners consider possible obligations, benefits, costs, and the overall feasibility of a long-term relationship. Depending upon the companies involved and the nature of the purchases, the exploration phase may be relatively brief or extended. Trial purchases may take place; the seller may give the buyer special introductory terms or special promotions; the buyer may give the seller special information about future capacity expansion or product development plans. But relationships in the exploratory phase are fragile in that minimal investments and interdependencies are involved, making termination relatively easy for each party.

Expansion refers to the continual increase in investments, interdependencies, and benefits obtained by the buyer and seller. The knowledge and trust accrued during the exploration stage now lead to increased risk-taking, financial exposure, and allocation of resources by each party. Within this stage, moreover, certain norms and standards of conduct by each party develop. These norms often specify how performance will be assessed. Depending upon the account relationship, it is not uncommon for third parties to get involved at this stage in both the process of the exchange and the adjudication of the conflicts that inevitably arise as each party's stakes increase.

Commitment refers to an implicit or explicit pledge of continuity in the relationship between the exchange partners. This may take the form of a long-term, multiyear contract. It may simply involve the informal but important recognition by each party that alternative sources of supply continue to be considered but that the past and future investments by buyer and seller make this relationship particularly efficient, effective, and (perhaps due to switching costs) hard to alter.

Dissolution is a fifth phase implicit in any buyer-seller relationship. Many forces can strain exchange, including increased costs of transaction, decreased obstacles associated with altering sources of supply or account-selection criteria, and changing goals and competitive requirements for buyer or seller. In major-account situations, precisely because of the magnitude and visibility of resources involved, the process of dissolution is more important than in other selling situations. For the seller, how such relationships are terminated often affects its ability to market effectively at other accounts as well as its ability to establish another long-term relationship (perhaps based around a different division's products or a new technology) at the same major account.

This view is a brief summary of how buyer-seller relationships develop. It does highlight major transitions and important characteristics at different phases, however. Also, for the seller it underscores an important objective in major-account management: To the extent that account relationships contribute to product or vendor differentiation and create barriers to switching, the task is to *manage* relationships with customers and encourage the profitable evolution of exchange from awareness to commitment.

Sales Coordination

A crucial aspect of developing the buyer-seller relationship is the seller's ability to coordinate the efforts of its different sales and support personnel working at the same account. In major-account situations, the salesperson remains a boundary-role person, responsible for managing (and aligning) the marketing strategy of the selling organization with the procurement strategy of the buying organization. Managing the major-account boundary inevitably adds layers of complexity to the salesperson's task because it involves the management of an interlocking set of internal as well as external relationships, as Figure B suggests.

Externally, the salesperson must analyze the buying process and manage a complex DMU with its array of gatekeepers, influencers, and decision makers. The task is (through customer education efforts and successful trials) to manage customer perceptions of needs in the relevant product category, the selling company's product and overall capabilities in relation to competition, and the benefits of working longer term with the sales team itself. To accomplish this, however, the salesperson must motivate and coordinate an array of internal personnel. This array includes: other salespeople and sales managers who also deal with that major account (perhaps in remote locations or different countries); corporate marketing managers who often have authority or influence in granting any special prices or customized terms and conditions requested by the account; technical support and administrative and operations personnel in areas such as product engineering (for special applications) or logistics (e.g., for just-in-time delivery procedures); and often top management itself when the potential of the contract (or the magnitude of the account's demands) reaches a certain point.

In these circumstances, selling often *is* the vendor's ability to marshal its internal resources effectively across a range of buying locations, buying influences, and internal organizational boundaries. Further, the coordination requirements affect the selling company's expense-to-revenue ratio, ability to retain current business or develop new business at these accounts, and sales force morale and management. Accordingly, surveys consistently find that among the most important factors affecting the success of major-account programs is coordination of the various field and headquarters activities conducted by the vendor.[11]

Figure B
Role of the Account Manager

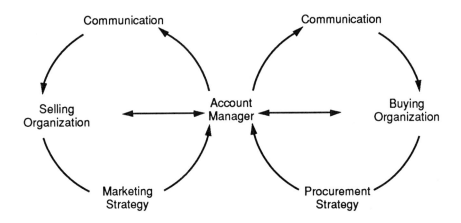

Managing the Major-Account Boundary
Involves Internal and External Relations

Internal	**External**

- Other Salespeople
- Sales Managers
- Corporate Marketing
- Technical Support
- Operations, Administration
- Top Management

- Gatekeepers
- Decision Influencers
- Decision Makers
- Customer Perceptions Of:
  Needs
  Our Company
  Our Product
  Sales Team
  Competition

In diagnosing the sales coordination requirements posed by major accounts, it is important to distinguish among three common situations.

Geographical

In this situation, different salespeople selling the same product line call on different locations of an important account. In industrial markets, this is typically the case in selling to large companies with multiple plants or to large multilocation distributors. In consumer-goods markets increasingly characterized by local marketing programs of different types, this is the case when a large retail chain is sold through different regional sales forces. In both industrial and consumer markets, geographical coordination is essential in selling to multinational or global accounts through multiple country sales organizations.

Across Product Lines

In this situation, different salespeople (perhaps different sales forces), selling different product lines, call on the same major account. This is often the case where the same vendor markets both capital equipment and supply items. Many large customers often want to coordinate their purchases of equipment and supplies because of the impact both have on their production processes. But, the vendor often sells these products through different sales organizations for a number of legitimate reasons: Equipment sales are usually higher-priced transactions than supply sales, occur much less often, and typically involve contact with more people from more functions in the customer's organization. Therefore such sales require more sales calls, a longer selling cycle, and different delivery and support requirements after the sale. At major accounts, coordinating these markedly different sales efforts (and sales skills) is often required. Similarly, in many multidivisional companies, achieving preferred-supplier status at major accounts means similar coordination requirements across divisional boundaries at the selling company.

Organizational

In this situation, one or more senior salespeople are responsible for coordinating a vendor's various efforts at an assigned account that is also sold and serviced by different field sales offices of the vendor. For example, a headquarters national account manager (NAM) or account executive (AE) must coordinate with field sales reps. The NAM or AE is usually dedicated to one or two major accounts, but these accounts are among dozens, or hundreds, in a field sales representative's territory.

These distinctions are important because each coordination situation poses different requirements and, in turn, different factors become more or less important. For example, when the coordination requirements involve different product lines, cross-product training may be particularly important in encouraging a shared understanding and coordinated efforts. When coordination means the spanning of geographical boundaries, more efficient means of communications among a dispersed sales effort usually is a priority. Finally, in the national-account situation described above, the ability of the NAM or AE to manage a host of dotted-line reporting relationships is often crucial.

In most sales coordination situations, however, research suggests that three internal areas are typically most influential: compensation systems, the goal-setting process, and staffing and training issues that typically arise when major accounts are an important part of the vendor's marketing plans.[12]

Compensation Systems

Where there are multiple salespeople calling on major accounts and coordination is important, a bonus based on total account sales often makes more sense than traditional, individually oriented incentives. Within any incentive arrangement, moreover, another important issue is the time frame. As noted earlier, sales efforts at major accounts often take years to develop. Most sales compensation plans, however, tie incentives to quarterly or annual snapshots of performance. The usual result is a focus on short-term sales efforts rather than on the more complex efforts required to develop the buyer-seller relationship at major accounts. Bonuses for multiple-year performance often can encourage coordination efforts.

A perennial and particularly complex compensation issue in these situations concerns the sharing of sales credit. Surveys of major account programs indicate that only a minority use credit splitting to help coordinate sales efforts. But in many instances, split credits among the different salespeople calling on the same account are often better than mutually exclusive credit decisions, which provide little incentive for collaborative efforts. At the same time, a common psychology often makes sharing of sales credit a nettlesome issue. As one sales manager notes, "Most salespeople feel that when the split is 50/50, they're losing 50% instead of gaining 50% of the incentive pay. A lot of time and energy is wasted arguing over splits."

This attitude may be unfortunate but it is common (e.g., consider the last time you worked on a group project); and the result often is increased resentment that hinders rather than helps teamwork. In many situations, however, companies can give those involved in major-account efforts full credit and still not (as many managers fear) "pay twice for the same sale." The key lies in having a good, up-to-date understanding of the sales tasks involved and an information system capable of tracking performance so that shared sales volume can be taken into account when setting the objectives and quotas of incentive programs.

Goal Setting

Another important factor affecting sales coordination appears to be the vendor's goal-setting process: in particular, defining individual salespeople's main responsibilities and desired accomplishments (e.g., opening new account locations vs. maximizing sales from current locations or selling new products). When goals are unclear, major-account selling efforts can be particularly frustrating because salespeople do not know where they stand in relation to some standard. Good performance may appear to be a random occurrence, independent of specific effort. This can discourage effort, especially in those sales opportunities that require working in concert with a number of other people.

Information, two-way communications, and ongoing feedback are important elements of the goal-setting process in major-account management. But, perhaps the key issue is the nature of the measurements used to define important goals for salespeople. Some companies respond to the more protracted and complicated nature of major-account sales efforts by ignoring quantitative measures. As one sales manager has noted, however, in most busy sales organizations, "That which is not measured does not happen." It is precisely *because* major-account sales demand sustained attention that measures are important. Without them, the pull in most sales organizations is toward the shorter-term, individually assigned accounts.

Note, however, that in major-account efforts sales volume is only one possible measure of performance. Profitability, cross-selling, or new product introductions are often more important goals and appropriate measures, depending on the vendor's marketing strategy.

Staffing and Training

These are particularly important issues in major-account management due to the nature of the boundary-role requirements described earlier. Major-account programs place salespeople in positions where they have little line authority over others in their company who affect their performance at important accounts. In such a situation, things often get done through persuasion, a knowledge of how the organization sets budgets and allocates resources, and a network of internal relationships cultivated over time. In these circumstances, what one manager calls "the ability to manage the white space on the organization chart" is important, and staffing of account teams must take this into account.

At the same time, many salespeople are initially attracted to a career in selling precisely because of its seemingly entrepreneurial characteristics. Salespeople are often uninterested in, and not particularly good at, the coordination requirements posed by major-account selling; thus training is important. In major-account management, product knowledge and generic selling skills (e.g., presentation skills and time management) remain important, but the coordination requirements make other skills also necessary. Because salespeople often must work across internal product organizations or geographical organizations with little line authority, team building is a crucial part of sales competence in these situations.

Changes in compensation, goal setting, staffing and training require much time, effort, and money from the vendor. They are only worth making when the returns are likely to be commensurate with the effort. This further underscores the initial point about the importance of account-selection criteria in major-account management. In seeking to obtain the coordination required by these selling efforts, it is also important to keep in mind a key distinction: Coordination—collaboration and coherence at the customer interface—does not necessarily mean consensus. As one experienced sales manager notes, "You cannot legislate teamwork. It's an attitude that comes over the long term, and it's essential in a well-run sales organization. Despite this, there still needs to be plenty of room for individual success and achievement. Otherwise, teamwork becomes an amorphous concept that can lead a group to underachieve in harmony."

Case Studies

The cases in this chapter concern managing major accounts. In dealing with the issues posed here, moreover, other dimensions of managing field marketing requirements considered previously—recruiting, training, and evaluating the individual salesperson; deploying and focusing the efforts of the sales force; and managing the give-and-take of reseller relations—will be relevant. Hence this chapter serves as a capstone to our study of customer encounters by illustrating the impact of these other dimensions at the major-account interface.

The Springs Industries case focuses on account selection and account management in an international context. The president of one of Springs' largest divisions is considering how to increase the division's international sales. Particularly important decisions concern the division's distribution channels overseas, management of the Marks & Spencer account in the United Kingdom, market selection and product mix choices in international markets, and a revised sourcing policy for the division in the face of increased global competition.

When you analyze the Springs case, consider these questions:

1. Evaluate the opportunities for Springs' Apparel Fabrics division to expand its European sales. Which is the best opportunity?
2. Evaluate the performance to date of the division's agent in the United Kingdom. What, if any, action would you take with regard to the agent? How would you implement this action?
3. What role, if any, should Marks & Spencer play in the division's marketing plans? What are the advantages and disadvantages of dealing with this account? Is it, given Apparel Fabrics' business characteristics, a good account?
4. Evaluate the duty drawback suggestion. What are the opportunities and risks inherent in this sourcing arrangement? How would it affect

the other decisions in this case and, in particular, the management of accounts such as Marks & Spencer?

The Springs case is particularly complex. It illustrates the intricate web of marketing decisions within which account selection decisions must typically be made.

The next case, Capital Cities/ABC, Inc.: Spot Sales, focuses on winning a major account's business. Where the Springs case raises issues of appropriate account-selection criteria, those issues are less relevant to the Spot Sales situation, if only because winning the business of the newly merged parent company is vital to the continued existence of the Spot Sales organization. The Spot Sales case also emphasizes a core requirement in account management—the development of a sales presentation—and the attendant skills in customer analysis required to perform this task effectively. The case outlines important industry trends and provides quantitative data about relevant sales, market share, and financial performance of Spot Sales and its major competitor for this account's business. But, the bulk of the case is essentially the differing views of several managers (who are scheduled to be at the presentation) about important aspects of this decision. Like the case protagonists, you must combine these quantitative and qualitative data in deciding "what do we say, how do we say it, and who should talk about what" at the climactic presentation to the parent company's management. In making these decisions, you must analyze the buying process, the history of the relevant buyer-seller relationships in this situation, and the coordination requirements posed by this account-management situation.

As you analyze the Spot Sales case, the following questions might be helpful:

1. How is advertising time bought and sold? What are the key selling tasks in this business?
2. What are the important economic characteristics of the television stations owned by Capital Cities/ABC? How do they make money, and what is the role of the sales channel in this process?
3. Who will be at the presentation discussed in this case? What is each attendee's decision-making power in this situation? What are their perceptions of the Spot Sales organization vs. an independent sales channel? Finally, what are their individual priorities concerning this purchase decision?
4. Who should represent Spot Sales at the presentation? What types of information should Spot Sales emphasize, and why? Who should speak about a given topic?

The next two cases in the chapter concern MCI, a telecommunications firm that has traditionally competed as a discount long-distance-voice provider for residential customers but finds it increasingly necessary to penetrate the market for advanced voice and data services among large corporate accounts. In this corporate market, AT&T is the dominant supplier of these services and MCI a relative newcomer. Each case, moreover, extends the analysis of account management issues explored in different industry contexts in the Springs and Spot Sales cases.

The MCI Communications Corporation: National Accounts Program case focuses on Mr. Jonathan Crane, vice president for a new national account program at MCI. After six months on the job, Mr. Crane is preparing for a review of the national accounts program with MCI's senior management and is also attempting to handle a variety of specific account problems. Among the issues are: (1) coordination of field sales efforts by MCI's divisions with headquarters' national accounts program efforts; (2) sales strategy for major accounts; and (3) management of resource-allocation procedures for the national accounts program efforts. Hence the MCI: National Accounts Program case builds on the themes introduced in the Springs case. A key issue concerns account-selection criteria, and how MCI should organize to sell and build effective relationships with selected major accounts. The case also illustrates the internal-coordination issues encountered in managing major accounts and the various sales management decisions implicated by these issues: who to select for major-account teams; how to demarcate account responsibilities between corporate and field units; compensation plans; training; and the importance of both formal and informal motivational tools in these situations.

In analyzing this case, consider the following:

1. What is a national account? What criteria should take priority in deciding which customers receive the priority status implied by this designation?
2. Who is MCI in the corporate account marketplace? How do customers perceive this vendor, and what are the strengths and weaknesses of MCI's competitive position?
3. What should Mr. Crane do about the specific account situations outlined toward the end of this case? Are these incidents a good or bad sign concerning MCI's new national account program? What policies are relevant in managing the issues raised by each account situation?

In the next case, MCI Telecommunications Corporation: Vnet (A), we move several levels down in the MCI organization to focus on a national account manager and her dealings with individuals at a particular major account. Ms. Barbara Voigt, a national account manager at MCI, is asked to prepare a proposal for Seaboard Insurance Company (SIC), a large insurance firm. Several of SIC's telecom staff have attended a presentation by MCI personnel about a product called Vnet, a networked information system that represents an important new market (and sales requirements) for MCI. The case provides information about the account team, the prospective customer, and the account team's presentation to this customer. You are asked to evaluate the presentation and to consider what Ms. Voigt should do next.

The Vnet case builds on themes introduced earlier in the chapter. As in the Springs case, account-selection criteria are important here and the question, "Was this a successful sales presentation?" extends the themes explored earlier in the Spot Sales case: analysis of the potential customer's economic characteristics, the perceptions and interactions of key DMU members, the consequent goals of a particular presentation, and the topics that should be emphasized. Further, the Vnet case looks at the individual manager who works within the structure and systems described in the preceding MCI: National Accounts Program case. You should consider this larger organizational context and marketing strategy in your analysis and recommendations.

The following questions may help you to analyze the MCI: Vnet case:

1. What are the important characteristics of SIC as a potential customer? How would you describe the key elements of its competitive situation, organizational structure, and buying process and purchase criteria for telecommunications services? In the final analysis, is SIC a good account for MCI? for the Vnet product in particular?

2. What are MCI's strengths and weaknesses in this product category and with this account? Given the history of this particular buyer-seller relationship and MCI's strengths and vulnerabilities, how fast or aggressively should Ms. Voigt pursue opportunities at SIC?

3. Evaluate the presentation made by MCI's account team to SIC managers. Given your analysis of this potential buyer and seller, were the right people from the selling organization talking to the right people at the buying organization about the right topics?

4. What should Ms. Voigt and the MCI account team do next?

In many ways, the Vnet case, with its focus on specific buyer-seller interactions, returns us to the opening chapter of the Managing Customer Encounters section of this book: the nature of the salesperson and the sales force as performing a crucial boundary role for a company and the many issues inherent in the management of field marketing requirements. As the final case study in this section, the Vnet case also underlines an important dimension of marketing worth considering throughout the next section of the book, which is concerned with how different structures, systems, and processes do (or do not) encourage behavior that supports the firm's marketing strategy.

Throughout the next section on marketing organization, the concerns illustrated in a case such as Vnet remain important: Salespeople's interactions with major accounts must inform any judgments about overall marketing organization. Whatever else a well-organized marketing operation involves, it should aid the accomplishment of the field salesperson's boundary role. In other words, any marketing organization that helps someone such as Ms. Voigt do her job more effectively must be doing something right—however much we may want to change and improve other facets of the organization. Conversely, any marketing organization that hinders someone such as Ms. Voigt from performing her job with customers (the ultimate sources of revenues, profits, and growth for any company) is inadequate—however elegant, logical, or theoretically compelling that organization may seem on paper.

References

1. See, for example, John Barrett, "Why Major Account Selling Works," *Industrial Marketing Management* 15 (1986): 63–73; Jerome Colletti and Gary S. Tubridy, "Effective Major Account Sales Management," *Journal of Personal Selling and Sales Management* 7 (August 1987): 1–11; Mack Hanan, *Key Account Selling* (New York: American Management Association, 1982); Linda C. Platzer, *Managing National Accounts* (New York: The Conference Board, 1984).

2. For more on this topic, see John H. Sheridan, "Betting on a Single Source," *Industry Week* (1 February 1988): 31–36; Robert E. Spekman, "Strategic Supplier Selection: Understanding Long-Term Buyer Relationships," *Business Horizons* (July-August 1988): 75–81; and Gary L. Frazier, Robert E. Spekman, and Charles R. O'Neal, "Just-in-Time Exchange Relationships in Industrial Markets," *Journal of Marketing* 52 (October 1988): 52–67.

3. The source of this example is Martin Everett, "This Is the Ultimate in Selling," *Sales & Marketing Management* (August 1989): 28.

4. See Marian Jelinek and Joel D. Goldhar, "The Strategic Implications of the Factory of the Future," *Sloan Management Review* (Summer 1984): 29–37; and Joel D. Goldhar and Marian Jelinek, "Computer Integrated Flexible Manufacturing: Organizational, Economic, and Strategic Implications," *Interfaces* 15 (May-June 1985): 94–115.

5. Theodore Levitt, "After the Sale Is Over . . . ," *Harvard Business Review* (September-October 1983): 87–93.

6. This approach to analyzing customers is discussed in more detail in Benson P. Shapiro, V. Kasturi Rangan, Rowland T. Moriarty, and Elliot B. Ross, "Manage Customers for Profits (Not Just Sales)," *Harvard Business Review* (September-October 1987): 11–18.

7. Seminal discussions of the buying center concept include Patrick J. Robinson, C. W. Faris, and Yoram Wind, *Industrial Buying and Creative Marketing* (Boston: Allyn and Bacon, 1967), and Frederick E. Webster, Jr. and Yoram Wind, *Organizational Buying Behavior* (Englewood Cliffs, N. J.: Prentice-Hall, 1972), pp. 75–87. An excellent review and application of these ideas is Thomas V. Bonoma, "Major Sales: Who Really Does the Buying?" *Harvard Business Review* (May-June 1982): 111–119.

8. Wesley J. Johnston and Thomas V. Bonoma, "Purchase Process for Capital Equipment and Services," *Industrial Marketing Management* 10 (October 1981): 253–264.

9. The source for these distinctions is the concept of relational exchange developed most fully by the legal scholar, Ian Macneil, *The New Social Contract: An Inquiry into Modern Contractual Relations* (New Haven: Yale University Press, 1980).

10. The source for this model of relationship development is J. Scanzoni, "Social Exchange and Behavioral Interdependence," in *Social Exchange in Developing Relationships*, ed. by R. L. Burgess and T. L. Huston (New York: Academic Press, Inc., 1979). The model in its present form is adapted from F. Robert Dwyer, Paul H. Schurr, and Sejo Oh, "Developing Buyer-Seller Relationships," *Journal of Marketing* 51 (April 1987): 11–27.

11. See, for example, Platzer, *op. cit.*, p. 14, and Colletti and Tubridy, *op. cit.*, p. 2.

12. For a more detailed discussion of these issues, see Frank V. Cespedes, Stephen X. Doyle, and Robert J. Freedman, "Teamwork for Today's Selling," *Harvard Business Review* (March-April 1989): 44–58.

Case 13
Springs Industries: Apparel Fabrics Division

In September 1983, Mr. Edward P. Harding, president of Springs Industries' Apparel Fabrics Division, faced decisions concerning international operations. Corporate goals targeted 15% to 20% of divisional sales outside the United States, but Apparel Fabrics was generating few sales outside the United States. Among the countries where the division sold fabrics, the United Kingdom seemed to offer the best potential for a sustainable sales increase. But expanding sales to the United Kingdom meant resolving issues concerning distribution channels, international pricing and sourcing policies, and the role of the U. K. market within a global marketing strategy for the Apparel Fabrics Division

Industry Background

Springs manufactured finished fabrics and home furnishings products. Finished fabrics, 54% of 1982 sales, were sold to manufacturers of men's, women's and children's apparel, bedspreads, draperies, and handkerchiefs and to home sewing markets. Fabrics were sold under private labels and under Springs trademarks.

Most of Springs' fabrics were blends of cotton and synthetic fibers such as polyester. Fibers, purchased from outside sources, were run through one of Springs' eleven spinning and weaving plants. Spinning converted raw fibers into continuous yarns, while weaving produced fabric by interlacing yarns. Finishing then changed colors, added patterns and introduced new physical properties. Spinning and weaving normally accounted for 80% of fabric production costs and finishing for 20%.

This case was prepared by Associate Professor Frank V. Cespedes as a basis for class discussion rather than to illustrate either effective or ineffective handling of an administrative situation.

As well as dyeing and printing, a common finish applied permanent press resins to cotton/polyester blends. But many other finishes were possible, such as soil-release, antistatic, flame retardants, water repellents, flannel and suede, and various shrinkage control finishes.

Springs' finishing plant in Lancaster, South Carolina, was the largest in the world. Ten to 12 million yards of fabric per week passed through the plant, and about 60% was made to order for Apparel Fabrics. The plant had significant scale economies and fixed costs. Mr. Harding explained that "within limits, an improperly woven fabric can still be sold at a discount. But with a finishing mistake—a grease spot or inconsistent shading, for example—the fabric loses most of its value. Our finishing operation is both high-quality and flexible. Compared to most textile firms, we make relatively few fabrics but try to differentiate them in finishing."

Cutting and Sewing: Buying and Selling

Apparel firms bought 40% of textile mills' output, with the remainder going to industrial fabricators and retailers. In 1983, there were 15,000 U. S. apparel firms with highly labor-intensive manufacturing. Smaller firms, located near major trade centers (especially New York City), generally produced fashion garments; the few large apparel firms, in the Southeast, produced items like work clothes, shirts, jeans, and sleepwear.

Fabric purchase criteria varied among apparel firms, often involving a unique combination of price, quality, and perceived fit with a planned line of garments. Providing colors and patterns "appropriate" for a given trade was important, since such factors distinguished bedspread fabrics from children's or women's wear fabrics. Similarly, purchase influences and decision makers varied, depending on the firm's size and fashion sensitivity of its retail customers and their consumers. At small apparel firms, the owner typically inspected and approved fabric purchases, often consulting with a stylist or designer. Such firms often bought on the basis of "just the right color (or print)," at a given price, and a manufacturer like Springs might be sole supplier for a given fabric and account for a large percentage of the firm's total fabric purchases.

At large apparel firms (e.g., Levi Strauss or Van Heusen), the purchase was typically made by a merchandise manager, consulting with a stylist and quality control personnel who established cloth specifications. The merchandise manager was responsible for product policy, pricing, and inventory control, and was generally assigned by end use rather than fabric type. Thus, a boys' wear merchandise manager might purchase many different fabrics. Some large apparel firms with limited lines meant for large retail chains also had centralized purchasing agents for fabric.

For large and small apparel firms, quality considerations included defect-free fabric and consistent color shading throughout an order. For smaller, fashion-oriented firms, service requirements included spot delivery of relatively small total yardage (1,000 to 25,000 yards) made up of several colors. For large apparel firms, delivery meant shipping by a promised date perhaps 15,000 to 75,000 yards each of three or four colors. Mr. Harding noted that, for large apparel firms, "the worst thing you can do is to keep their factories idle due to late delivery." Conversely, bulk orders meant production and selling economies for the fabric manufacturer, and volume discounts of 6% to 8% were common.

The sales cycle among fabric and apparel firms generally had the following pattern. Planning the spring 1985 season, for example, began in September 1983 when fabric manufacturers researched the types of finished fabrics to be produced by monitoring current sales trends and fashion developments and consulting with large buyers. By January 1984, the fabric manufacturer prepared fabric samples and promotional materials. Apparel firms supplying menswear to chains were generally the first to see fabrics, while firms supplying women's wear to fashionable outlets were the last. During spring 1984, the fabric manufacturer's sales force showed the fabric line to apparel firms via "color cards" (i.e., brochures containing fabric swatches in various colors and finishes). Listing fabric on a color card generally obligated the manufacturer to carry inventory for that product. At Springs, for example, the minimum order quantity for a line item was 500 yards, but the minimum production run was 10,000 yards.

By June 1984 apparel firms chose fabrics and, during the summer of 1984, prepared garment samples for their retail customers. By September 1984, orders were placed with the fabric manufacturer and orders peaked by December. Fabric orders continued through spring 1985, because the most fashion-sensitive apparel firms made product-line decisions as close as possible to the consumer buying season.

Fabric buying involved personal selling efforts between the fabric manufacturer's salesperson and some combination of owner, merchandise manager, stylist, and purchasing agent from the apparel firm. In New York City's garment district, where many apparel firms and most fabric manufacturers' sales offices were located, the buying season was fast-paced and competitive with many fabric manufacturers likely to call on an apparel firm in a given day. Many of the same buyers met many of the same sellers year after year, and information about new products or policies traveled quickly. When an apparel firm agreed to buy a quantity of fabric at a price for a specific delivery date, an oral commitment was made. The textile firm later sent a written contract confirming all details and asking the customer to sign and return a copy. Oral commitments for multimillion dollar orders were not uncommon.

During the early 1980s, a number of trends characterized the U. S. apparel industry. First, high interest rates and a recession motivated apparel firms to order in smaller quantities, demand stricter delivery terms, and rely heavily on fabric reorders. Second, apparel firms used more styles and colors. For example, Springs' line in 1962 had 800 colors, while in 1983 the line had 800 different fabrics in blue alone. Third, while fabric orders had always been sensitive to supply/demand conditions (with prices often changing from order to order), price volatility increased. Mr. Harding estimated that, during the mid-1960s, the average price of Springs fabric was about $.30 per yard and a change of $.005 per yard was significant, while by 1983 the average price was about $1.30 per yard and changes of $.10 per yard were common. Fourth, computers had altered production processes in some apparel firms, and the capital investments had caused a slight trend toward concentration.

International Trade and Global Competition

As Exhibit 1 illustrates, U.S. *apparel imports*—mainly from Japan, Hong Kong, Taiwan, South Korea, and increasingly, China—increased from 1970 to 1983. Especially affected were underwear, gloves and sweaters, and shirts, blouses, jackets, and coats at lower prices.

Several reasons were cited for the import surge, including Asian suppliers' lower labor costs and a strong U.S. dollar which made imports relatively cheaper and U.S. exports more expensive. (Exhibit 2 provides data about exchange rates.) Tougher U.S. environmental and worker-protection laws also raised costs for domestic producers. Further, foreign firms were often more export oriented than U.S. firms, which traditionally believed the U.S. market would absorb capacity. Some observers also believed smaller, offshore producers could more easily style apparel for the large and relatively homogeneous U.S. market than large U.S. apparel firms could style for smaller, segmented markets abroad. In addition, some countries' trading companies provided their firms with financing, an international sourcing network, contacts with importers, documentation, and the trading company's experience with international marketing issues. Finally, price competition led some large U.S. retailers to purchase fabric and apparel direct from foreign suppliers, often establishing buying offices abroad.

Throughout the world, apparel production was a major source of employment. Thus, no other major product group faced higher average tariffs or more quantity restrictions. Many countries also imposed garment specifications, inspection and labeling requirements, and other procedures that slowed or discouraged imports. Except for flammability and labeling requirements, the United States had fewer nontariff barriers than other countries. But the United States had higher apparel tariffs than most developed countries. Under the Multifiber Arrangement regulating textile and apparel imports between countries, the United States could further limit imports, and in late 1983 the government was considering such action.

As the domestic apparel industry weakened, U.S. fabric manufacturers altered their marketing strategies. Some emphasized nonapparel fabrics. Others increased advertising and emphasized brand-names versus lower-priced imported fabrics. Finally, some concentrated on long production runs of staple products and sought cost leadership. Nearly all firms sought increased exports, however, and from 1975 to 1982 U.S. *textile exports* doubled; 50% of exports were to Canada and Europe, 20% to Mexico and Hong Kong where low-wage workers sewed U. S. fabric into apparel for re-export to other countries (including the United States), and 30% was used locally in Asia, Africa and Latin America.

One reason for the export increase was improved productivity due to capital investments by U.S. textile firms. A 1982 study found U.S. spinning and weaving plants to be the world's most productive. West German plants were 73% as productive as the average for U. S. plants; France, 57%, and the United Kingdom less than 50% as high. Japan was the only Asian country with a textile productivity level greater than 50% of the U. S. average. Another reason seemed to be some U. S. companies' increased emphasis on fashion items and advertising abroad.

A 1983 study[1] concluded that global competition in textiles would increase in the future. The study noted that, especially in fabric manufacturing, the international spread of new technology had increased capital intensity and industry concentration levels as firms faced higher risks and costs in new product and process development. In sum, the study projected a more internationally competitive, but smaller (in terms of number of firms and workers) U.S. textile complex.

Nonetheless, in 1983 exports were less than 10% of U.S. textile sales. Many companies, including Springs, sought to increase exports by reevaluating target markets and channels in various countries.

Company Background

Springs was founded in 1887. Under the flamboyant leadership of Elliott White Springs (a World War I flying ace and novelist), Springs acquired other textile firms and integrated forward into finished fabrics. By 1982, Springs was the fourth largest U.S. textile firm (see Exhibit 3) and operated in two major segments: 1) Home furnishings and 2) finished fabrics, which included Apparel Fabrics. Each division's president reported to Mr. Walter Elisha, CEO of Springs.

In 1982, management set three goals. Using 1980 as the base year (when sales were $794 million and income from continuing operations was $32 million), management sought to double sales and earnings by the end of 1985 (a compound sales growth of about 15% over the five-year period and a return on sales of 4.4% in 1985).

A third goal was to become the low-cost producer. In 1983, Springs began a seven-year program to install new technology. The first phase replaced 6,600 older looms with 1,160 air-jet weaving machines, which were faster, quieter, and cleaner than the older looms and produced virtually defect-free cloth.

---

[1] *The Competitive Status of the U.S. Fibers, Textiles, and Apparel Complex* (Washington, D. C.: National Academy of Sciences, 1983).

Apparel Fabrics Division

In 1982, Apparel Fabrics generated 40% of Springs' sales (see Exhibit 4). Apparel firms comprised 80% of the division's sales, with the remainder sold to the home fabrics market for use in products such as curtains and bedspreads. The division had 3,300 customers; 37% in New York City accounted for nearly 50% of dollar sales. The ten largest customers accounted for 12.5% of sales, and the 50 largest for 37%.

The heads of finance, quality control and information services, and the vice presidents for manufacturing sales, and merchandising, reported to Mr. Harding (see Exhibit 5). The five Merchandise Groups were organized by type of fabric: (1) lightweight, cotton/polyester blends were the least expensive fabrics and were used in children's wear and home fashions; (2) lightweight combed cotton/polyester blends, used in men's shirts and women's blouses; (3) midweight fabrics such as poplins and twills, used for jackets and heavy work shirts; (4) prints, used in both apparel and home furnishings; and (5) a converted fabric group, which purchased unfinished fabrics from other mills and finished them. Merchandise managers were responsible for approving the colors and prints designed by stylists, scheduling production and finishing and, in Mr. Harding's words, for "having all the right inventory for a selling season and none at the end of that season."

The sales force was organized geographically, with about half the division's 45 salespeople in New York City. A salesperson typically had more than 100 accounts across the various end-uses of different fabrics, and could earn up to 40% of base salary in commission and bonuses. Salespeople visited major accounts as often as twice per week. These calls included demonstrations, follow-up to negotiate or clarify price and delivery, calls to promote new fabrics or designs, and "hello" calls to maintain visibility and gather market information. Small accounts were visited twice per year, during the spring and fall buying seasons. Sales force turnover was low, and the career path might include merchandise management and then a general management position. Mr. Harding explained that "everybody in our top management was a salesperson at some point; that experience is probably essential in this business."

Major customers included manufacturers for lines such as Blue Bell/Wrangler, Arrow Shirts, and J. C. Penney's sleepwear department. Mr. Harding explained that:

> The most important annual changes in our product line concern finishes, colors, and print designs. The good news is that we have many outlets for our fabrics. The bad news is that we have little control over those outlets. Manufacturers change their fabric mix frequently and will often shift toward fabrics we don't make.
>
> That volatility is important because we need to keep the mills humming. Our finishing plant operates five days per week, twenty-four hours per day, and produces cloth at thirty-four miles per hour. Therefore, our salespeople, work-

ing thirty-five hours per week (nine to five with an hour for lunch), must sell fabric at 116 miles per hour! The message is volume: sell it by the ton.

In product development, the division tried to work with apparel manufacturers to meet market requirements. During the 1970s, for example, flame-resistance became important in children's wear and sleepwear. Apparel Fabrics developed a flame-resistant fabric and won a large share of these two high-volume segments. The division's advertising relied on the trade press. Other promotional tools included trade shows and occasional cooperative advertising with fiber suppliers.

Competition varied since most textile firms focused on limited segments of the apparel fabrics market. In the United States, major competitors across a number of Springs' fabrics included Burlington Industries (the world's largest textile firm) and Greenwood Mills (which was about the size of Apparel Fabrics and had a similar product mix).

International Marketing at Springs

During the 1970s, Springs' export business was a separate division, international Sales (I. S.), staffed by people with knowledge of export procedures, tariff regulations and shipping protocols. Mr. Harding explained that "the 'internationalists' established the necessary paperwork for exports, but they didn't know either the textile or apparel business or how we merchandise products."

Springs' first exports were to Germany, France, South Africa, and the United Kingdom. Springs hired agents[2] in these countries who sold to distributors, who often bought in large quantities. But Mr. Harding noted,

> We had no control and no feedback concerning the market. Since the distributors resold our fabric to manufacturers at a mark-up, the price to the manufacturer was that much higher. Also, while a distributor might buy large quantities, it generally bought one type of fabric and might drop us without warning. The result was that we never developed our full line and often lost the real customer—the apparel manufacturer—without knowing the problem. In fact, we often didn't know which manufacturers bought our fabrics.
>
> We also lost opportunities to segment markets by creating fabrics for specific end uses. For example, a bra manufacturer gets many garments from a yard of cloth and, compared to labor, fabric is a small percentage of total costs. But a curtain manufacturer does little cutting and sewing, and fabric is a high percentage of costs. Pricing should differ between these markets. But our distributors basically stocked cloth and sold at one price.

---

[2] An international *agent* was similar to a manufacturer's representative in the United States. Working on commission, the agent used the manufacturer's product literature and samples to present the product to potential buyers. The agent did not take title or possession of the goods. The foreign *distributor* purchased merchandise from a U. S. manufacturer at a negotiated price and resold it, generally under the distributor's name.

Perhaps agents-to-distributors was a fast way to penetrate other countries. But our name, good deliveries, and other strengths weren't visible to manufacturers, and we didn't *build* our business by going through distributors.

Another problem was I. S.'s status as a profit center. I. S., not the supplying divisions, received credit for sales.

In 1978, I. S. functions were folded into other divisions. Mr. Leroy Close, VP for Merchandising in Apparel Fabrics, had been in I. S. and managing the division's exports became his responsibility.

United Kingdom Market

Mr. Harding and Mr. Close believed the United Kingdom offered the best immediate potential for expanding exports. Springs had relationships with some U.K. manufacturers, and nearly 50% of all fabric used in the United Kingdom was consumed in the apparel sector. In addition, management believed Springs' production costs were lower than those of U. K. textile firms and competitive with other suppliers of its types of fabrics.

Among British textile manufacturers, the market was fragmented but influenced by a few large corporations such as Courtaulds. Among retailers, several major retailers bought textiles on the world market and had the fabrics converted into products for their stores. Marks & Spencer (M & S) was an example of a retailer with centralized buying that had both the volume leverage and technical capability to buy competitively priced textiles made to its specifications and designs.

During the 1970s, imports reduced the number of U.K. apparel firms. By 1980, there were about 6,000 British apparel firms, of which 20 accounted for 25% of output and 500 for about 75%. Among British textile firms vertically integrated into retailing, the 14 largest companies accounted for 45% of total apparel sales.

Apparel buying practices among British retailers were like those of U.S. retailers. Most had central buying organizations organized along departmental lines. The schedule for buying and merchandise arrival (see Exhibit 6) was similar to the United States, but merchandise arrived in stores closer to the calendar season. (This helped the exporter, since it compensated somewhat for shipping time.) Similarly, buying practices among British apparel firms were like U. S. apparel firms, with a range of decision makers and purchase criteria depending upon the firm's size and fashion sensitivity.

According to a U.S. Commerce report, a factor inhibiting exports to the United Kingdom was "the British view of the U.S. textile exporter":

> Today, the United Kingdom buyer sees the Americans in a Jekyll and Hyde role—that is, as a producer of desirable, competitively priced, quality products; and as an on-again, off-again seller who disposes of seconds, quotes low prices when the U. S. market is slow, and disappears from the scene when U. S. business is good. Obviously, to increase exports it will be important to change that image.

Several U.S. textile firms had U.K. sales offices: Burlington, Dan River, J. P. Stevens, United Merchants and Manufacturers, and Fieldcrest.

Springs' Operations in the United Kingdom

Springs had exported to the United Kingdom since the early 1960s and in 1973 hired an agent. The agent had worked for another U. S. textile firm, and his knowledge of both the British market and a U.S. manufacturer's practices was attractive. This person remained the division's primary U.K. channel in 1983.

Initially, the agent carried Springs' fabrics and those of other noncompeting U.S. firms. As his Springs' business grew, he dropped other lines and, by 1977, carried only Springs' products. But the agreement was not exclusive: the agent could carry other lines, and Springs could terminate the agreement or supplement the agent. In 1983, he was 55 years old, had a London office, employed a salesperson and administrative assistant and received a 5% commission on sales.

During the mid-1970s, the agent emphasized a Springs' fabric suitable for M & S sleepwear products. The agent sold the idea to an M & S supplier, who in turn convinced M & S managers to specify Springs fabric for this product. Mr. Close noted that "the agent took the initiative, and got our foot in the door. Soon, we were an important supplier for this fabric in three colors. For some time thereafter, the agent sold several million yards of this fabric without doing much else for us."

Springs therefore assigned a U.S. salesperson to work in Britain with the agent. The salesperson remained on salary while the agent received a 1.5% commission on sales generated by the salesperson. "We divided our line between the agent and our salesperson," noted Mr. Close. "Frankly, one purpose was to light a fire under our agent and get wider distribution for our line. And it seemed to work well: this arrangement lasted for about two years until 1980, and our U.K. sales increased in volume, types of fabric sold, and number of accounts."

Mr. Close estimated the salesperson's salary and expenses at $100,000 per year. He believed most new accounts were attributable to the agent, but the salesperson's presence was probably an important motivating factor. "When U.K. sales increased and we had seemingly established a wider range of accounts," said Mr. Close, "we recalled our salesperson. The agent was making most incremental sales, the relationship was naturally a strained one, and the arrangement seemed to have done its job." Mr. Harding added that "another purpose was to educate our agent in the details of how our division works. Our salesperson was experienced, knowledgeable about the trade and our organization, and helped to educate our agent about our entire product line and merchandising approaches. After two years, that dimension of the arrangement also seemed to have served its purpose."

In 1980, Apparel Fabrics' international sales declined:

Export Sales: Apparel Fabrics Division
(000s omitted)

Year	Total		United Kingdom		Other Countries	
	Yards	Dollars	Yards	Dollars	Yards	Dollars
1976	6,795	$ 4,566	3,450	$ 2,420	3,345	$ 2,146
1977	4,927	3,616	1,473	1,179	3,454	2,437
1978	5,305	4,639	3,031	2,589	2,274	2,050
1979	16,047	16,085	8,641	8,773	7,406	7,312
1980	11,494	13,613	5,045	5,875	6,449	7,738
1981	8,539	11,028	4,064	5,287	4,475	5,741
1982	5,412	7,036	2,650	3,464	2,762	3,572
1983 (6 mo)	1,785	2,259	773	918	1,012	1,341

Mr. Close noted that by 1981, "our price abroad was raised by exchange rates. Meanwhile our U. S. market was strong, and we saw no reason to cut prices to maintain share abroad." Mr. Harding added that, "At that time, we did not have a full-time divisional export sales manager. So, when our domestic market absorbed attention, we may have let some international matters slip. Also, in good years, our agent makes the equivalent of a few hundred thousand dollars, and the British tax rate is very high."

At the height of its U. K. sales, Apparel Fabrics sold primarily two fabrics to British manufacturers: (a) polyester/cotton broadcloth for men's shirts, and (2) lightweight cotton/polyester blends for women's dresses and lingerie and for women's and children's sleepwear. In 1983, the latter fabrics remained the core of the division's U. K. sales, but during the preceding two years, the men's shirting market had been lost to Japanese suppliers. A 1980 shipment of defective fabric opened the door to alternative suppliers and, as Mr. Close explained, "since then, they've taken much of the business, and it will be a challenge taking it back. Their quality and price are good, and they stock some fabrics in England and have sales offices there."

Mr. Harding noted that trading companies gave Asian suppliers advantages in such situations:

> Fabric stocked in England by our Japanese competition is in the trading company's warehouse with motorcycles and other goods exported by Asian firms. Thus, inventory costs are spread over a number of products. The trading company also has worldwide sourcing, and thus a hedge against currency fluctuations: if fabric is expensive in one country due to exchange rates, they can source from a temporarily less-expensive country. Since they also have worldwide markets, they in effect can allocate quality by shipping higher-quality fabrics to a country like England and lower-quality fabrics to less-developed countries. We can't segregate our quality because we don't have markets for lower-quality cloth. Our standard quality must therefore be equal to their highest-quality fabrics.

Mr. Harding also saw competitive advantages for Springs in the U.K. market. Springs' long production runs meant Apparel Fabrics often had fabric in stock, and so could ship 5 to 10,000 yards immediately. Further, the Japanese competition stocked in the United Kingdom only a limited amount and range of fabrics, and shipping times gave Springs a three to four week delivery advantage over Asian suppliers on many orders. Springs also made more types of fabrics for a wider range of end uses and had a large U. S. market to support incremental U.K. sales. Similarities between the U.K. and U.S. markets also gave Springs important market knowledge: "We know how to style, color, and choose appropriate fabrics for that market," Mr. Harding said, "since we make those types of fabrics for the U.S." Finally, Springs finished fabrics in wider lots (sixty-inch vs. forty-five-inch for Asian and most other textile firms), thus offering more efficient fabric utilization to the apparel manufacturer. The cost savings for apparel firms could be especially significant in shirting and sleepwear.

Marks & Spencer. In evaluating the U.K. market, Mr. Harding and Mr. Close agreed that Marks & Spencer should receive high priority.

In 1983, M & S was the largest U.K. retailer with sales of 2.5 billion pounds sterling (about $3.9 billion at prevailing exchange rates). Thirteen million customers shopped weekly in M & S's 260 U.K. stores (M & S also had 209 stores in Canada and 8 in Europe), where some 700 food and 3,000 nonfood items were sold. In fiscal 1983, clothing generated 53% of M & S sales, food 36%, and general merchandise 11%. M & S accounted for nearly 12% of total British consumer expenditures on clothing and footwear, held one-third of the market in women's lingerie and men's underwear, and its London Marble Arch outlet was listed in the Guiness Book of World Records as the store with the most sales per square foot in the world.

M & S sold its merchandise only under the "St. Michael" label. Buying, merchandising, distribution, and quality control were centralized at headquarters in London. The company owned no production facilities, relying on a broad network of suppliers. M & S often accounted for 80% of a supplier's output and provided strict specifications. The firm maintained a small range of markups for merchandise, and with margins relatively standardized, M & S "selectors" (i.e., buyers) sought goods of acceptable quality that would turn over rapidly. M & S never held sales, required cash purchases, and reduced prices for clearance purposes only. It did little advertising besides new product announcements.

In 1982, the ten best-selling departments at M & S were (1) ladies' skirts and blazers, (2) produce, (3) ladies' blouses and lightweight skirts, (4) ladies' dresses, (5) poultry, (6) meat and bacon, (7) dairy products, (8) men's knitwear, (9) pies, and (10) men's shirts. According to a 1982 company publication, the trend in M & S's clothing departments was toward "younger, more fashionable styling":

> In ladies' wear, coordination was the main theme, in both color and fabric. A new "after six" range of coordinated tops and bottoms in light-weight crepe-de-

chine was an immediate sell-out. Prettier styling also led to very successful sales
in blouses. In menswear, leather and suede jackets were highly successful, as
were the new shirts styled to attract the younger customer. More use was made
of natural fibers and luxury fabrics.

The babywear department was extended to all stores and continues to grow; a
major exercise was started to improve the boys' wear range. And for the whole
family there was a move toward "stretch" fabrics in jeans and trousers, boosted
by a major ladies' wear promotion in magazines and stores.

Exhibit 7 indicates M & S's organization within its Textiles Division, which
had two subdivisions: (a) men's and boys' wear, home furnishings, footwear,
accessories, and new products; and (b) women's and girls' wear. Each subdivision had a *managing director,* to whom reported *senior executives* who managed
the subdivision's product lines. Each product line was divided into segments
managed by *junior executives,* who supervised *selectors* who developed merchandise ranges and *merchandisers* responsible for sales estimates, production, packaging, and distribution. Fabric decisions were usually made jointly by
merchandisers and selectors. M & S also employed scientists and technicians
on its *technical staff,* which worked with merchandising departments and suppliers to develop product specifications and monitor product quality. Mr.
Harding and Mr. Close visited M & S's headquarters semiannually, and had met
with a number of M & S senior executives and managing directors. Springs'
agent had long-established business relationships with M & S merchandisers
and selectors and knew many of the technical staff.

M & S annually bought nearly 20% of British apparel production and had
a generally "Buy British" policy. M & S's 1982 annual report stated:

> More than 90% of "St. Michael" clothing, household textiles, and footwear sold
> in Britain, Europe, and for exports is manufactured in the United Kingdom. We
> import when high quality goods representing special skills and good values are
> not available from home suppliers; regrettably, many fine quality woven fabrics
> are no longer made in the United Kingdom. These selective imports stimulate
> our British manufacturers.

M & S encouraged its foreign suppliers to establish plants in the United
Kingdom for processing or finishing, and a number of firms had complied.

Mr. Close recalled that when Apparel Fabrics learned of a shipment of
defective fabrics in 1980, "We immediately took back the fabric, reshipped, and
swallowed the costs. But M & S is uncompromising about quality, and that
shipment hurt us in their eyes." Mr. Harding noted that, in years when sales
were relatively strong in both the United States and United Kingdom, Apparel
Fabrics had "helped M & S out of a tight spot by shipping a large amount of a
needed fabric on very little notice. That increased our visibility among their
management."

In 1983, Springs supplied fabrics for M & S's women's nightwear and
children's sleepwear but, according to Mr. Harding, "We should also supply

fabrics for their men's shirts and slacks, and women's shirts and blouses. Our fabric fits their good-quality staple items, but we haven't penetrated those lines."

Mr. Harding explained that "M & S often orders 175,000 yards of fabric in a single print. With U. S. manufacturers, the average order per print run is about 15,000 yards. Sears might order 175,000 yards of a fabric but spread over 20 different items, and you won't receive the entire order up-front, as you do from M & S." Mr. Close added that M & S was an important account beyond the United Kingdom: "If you walk into an apparel manufacturer anywhere in Europe and it's known that you're an important supplier to Marks & Spencer, you have an advantage."

The Decisions Facing Mr. Harding

In reviewing the export sales situation, Mr. Harding believed certain decisions should be made soon.

First, a marketing plan was needed for the M & S account. What were Apparel Fabrics' strengths and weaknesses with this account, and what resources were required? Beyond its current business for women's nightwear and children's sleepwear, should Apparel Fabrics target a few or a broad range of other M & S lines? How should the effort be organized and what would be the impact on servicing other accounts?

As part of this decision, Mr. Harding believed the division's U.K. distribution should be reevaluated and saw the following alternatives to the current arrangement:

- Apparel Fabrics might again send a salesperson to work with the agent. As before, salary and expenses would be about $100,000 per year, not including the agent's 1.5% commission on sales made by the salesperson.

- The division might hire an additional agent for the United Kingdom. This would involve a complicated and potentially bitter allocation of either existing accounts or fabric types between the two agents. Either allocation could mean coordination problems. In addition, terminating an agent agreement in the United Kingdom (and most European countries) often involved a lengthy legal suit and the risk of an agent taking an account to another manufacturer.

- The division might establish a U. K. sales office. Costs would include $100,000 per salesperson for annual salary and expenses and fixed costs for office and support of $75,000. In addition, decisions would be necessary about staffing (salespeople from the United States or people hired in the United Kingdom?), timing (establish an office soon or later?), and relations with the agent during a transition. It was also unclear what level and type of sales would justify a United Kingdom office. Due to a strong dollar and declining U. K. sales, at least one U. S. textile firm was reportedly closing its U. K. sales office.

Second, Mr. Harding had to decide about potential European accounts beyond M & S. Mr. Close had recently visited some apparel firms in France and England and prepared a memorandum (see Exhibit 8). Mr. Harding had to consider which, if any, of these firms deserved attention, the resources required to service these accounts, and how such accounts fit into a coordinated strategy for Apparel Fabrics.

Third, Mr. Harding believed the division's international pricing and sourcing policies should be reevaluated. Exchange rates had traditionally determined whether Springs was price competitive in a country. Since currency fluctuations often pushed Springs below breakeven on many fabrics, the division had not met prices in countries where the dollar was strong. Most U. S. textile firms also followed this policy, but Mr. Harding wondered if pricing should be revised in any way.

Recent U.S. "duty drawback" legislation allowed firms to reclaim duty on imported goods that were later exported. For textile products, duty was often 20–25%. That is, when Springs bought fabrics overseas, it paid a 20–25% U. S. import tariff. But with duty drawback, Springs would receive a 99% rebate of duty paid if it later exported the cloth. Therefore, when the dollar was strong, export margins suffered, but Springs could also buy unfinished fabric from Asian suppliers more cheaply than it could manufacture the fabric in its U. S. plants.

To qualify for duty drawback, (1) the imported goods had to be of "the same kind and quality" as that manufactured by the U. S. firm; (2) the finished product had to be "a new and different article having a distinctive name, character, or use different from the original material"; (3) the value added by the U. S. firm had to involve substantial investment of capital and labor, thereby fulfilling the spirit of the drawback law which was to enhance employment while lowering export costs; (4) the finished product had to be produced within three years, and exported within five years, of the importation date; and (5) extensive documentation had to be kept of all these transactions.

During the past three years, Apparel Fabrics' imports, while a small percentage of divisional sales, exceeded exports. Most imports had been broadcloth and poplin used for shirts and sportswear. Mr. Harding believed overhead for additional recordkeeping would be negligible, and believed duty-drawback created potential to be more price competitive under certain currency conditions. The "same kind and quality" provision might also increase flexibility, since a manufacturer could export imported or domestic fabric (or some combination) and still reclaim duty (e.g., exported finished fabric could be produced solely with domestic raw materials and drawback claimed against similar imported raw materials used to produce other fabrics within the three-year period).

The current situation in shirting fabric provided an example. If Springs shipped to the United Kingdom fabric manufactured and finished in its U. S. plants, costs (including manufacturing, shipping, and 16% U. K. tariff on the selling price but not including commissions) were about $.98/yard, and selling price was about \$1.00/yard. Meanwhile, a Japanese firm sold the same fabric to M & S suppliers for \$.90/yard. However, with current exchange rates between the United States and some Asian countries, and with import duties refunded, Springs could buy unfinished fabric from an Asian supplier and finish it in the United States for a total cost of \$.74/yard. The additional U.K. import tariff would still allow Springs to meet its competitor's price.

Mr. Harding wondered if duty drawbacks should be used extensively by Apparel Fabrics. What were the short- and long-term risks and benefits, and the implications for market selection, product mix, and perhaps other aspects of the division's international marketing strategy?

Exhibit 1 Springs Industries: Apparel Fabrics Division

U.S. Apparel Imports-Exports
1970–1983/Q1

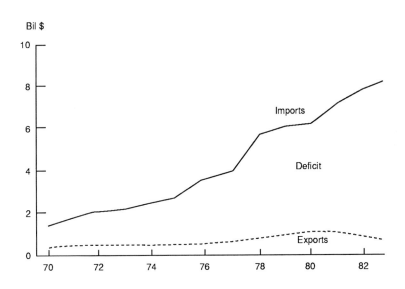

Exhibit 2 Springs Industries: Apparel Fabrics Division

Exchange Rates for U.S. Dollar for Selected Currencies
(period averages of exchange rates)

	1976	1977	1978	1979	1980	1981	1982	1983 I	1983 II
Brazil (Cruzeiros per U.S. Dollar):									
	10.7	14.1	18.1	26.9	52.7	93.1	179.5	326.4	475.9
Canada (Canadian Dollar per U.S. Dollar):									
	.99	1.06	1.14	1.17	1.17	1.10	1.23	1.23	1.23
China (Yuan per U.S. Dollar):									
	1.94	1.86	1.68	1.55	1.50	1.71	1.89	1.95	1.99
France (Francs per U.S. Dollar):									
	4.78	4.91	4.51	4.25	4.22	5.43	6.57	6.89	7.47
Germany (Deutsche Mark per U.S. Dollar):									
	2.52	2.32	2.01	1.83	1.82	2.26	2.43	2.41	2.49
Hong Kong (Hong Kong Dollar per U.S. Dollar):									
	4.67	4.61	4.79	4.91	5.13	5.68	6.48	6.72	7.15
Italy (Lire per U.S. Dollar):									
	832	882	849	831	856	1,137	1,353	1,399	1,478

(continued)

Exhibit 2 (continued)

	1976	1977	1978	1979	1980	1981	1982	1983 I	1983 II
Japan (Yen per U.S. Dollar):	296	268	210	219	227	221	249	236	238
Korea (Won per U.S. Dollar):	484	484	484	484	607	681	731	753	770
Spain (Pesetas per U.S. Dollar):	66.9	76.0	76.7	67.1	71.7	92.3	109.9	129.9	140.0
Taiwan (Taiwanese Dollar per U.S. Dollar):	38.00	37.04	35.10	35.10	35.10	38.00	38.12	38.12	39.97
United Kingdom (British Pound per U.S. Dollar):	.552	.571	.521	.472	.429	.493	.571	.654	.654

Exhibit 3   Springs Industries: Apparel Fabrics Division

Financial Data: Springs Industries, 1980–1982
(In thousands)

Springs Industries, Inc.
For the Fiscal Years Ended January 1, 1983,
January 2, 1982 and January 3, 1981 (53 weeks)

	1982	*1981*	*1980*
Income			
Net sales	**$874,512**	$917,042	$794,460
Cost and Expenses:			
Costs of goods sold	**731,090**	759,709	657,455
Selling, administrative and general expenses	**80,626**	79,219	70,508
Interest expense	**5,820**	8,996	8,203
Other (income)	**(6,102)**	(2,520)	(1,061)
Total	811,434	845,404	735,105
Income Before Income Taxes	**63,078**	71,638	59,355
Income Taxes	**25,621**	31,652	27,195
Income from Continuing Operations	**37,457**	39,986	32,160
Income (loss) from Discontinued Operations			
From operations, net			(7)
On disposition, net	**5,597**		(21,551)
Net Income	**$ 43,054**	$ 39,986	$ 10,602

Distribution of the 1982 Sales Dollar (in millions)	Amount	%
Raw Materials and Purchased Goods	$285.6	32.7%
Wages, Salaries, and Benefits	307.2	35.1
Other Manufacturing, Selling and General Admin. Expenses	218.6	25.0
Income Taxes	25.6	2.9
Cash Dividends and Retained Earnings	37.5	4.3
	$874.5	100.0%

(continued)

Exhibit 3 (continued)

Segment Information (in millions)	1982	1981	1980
Sales			
Finished fabrics	$472.3	$504.0	$409.7
Home furnishings	402.2	413.0	384.8
	$874.5	$917.0	$794.5
Profit from Operations*			
Finished fabrics	$ 50.9	$ 64.1	$ 42.9
Home furnishings	24.4	28.0	34.8
	$ 75.3	$ 92.1	$ 77.7
Net Income as % of Net Sales	1982	1981	1980
All manufacturing industries	3.5%	4.8%	4.9%
Textile Mill Products firms	2.0%	2.4%	2.2%

*Sales less operating expenses of the segments

Exhibit 4   Springs Industries: Apparel Fabrics Division

Percentages of Total Divisional Yardage and Dollar Sales by Product Group

	1982		1981		1980	
	Yards	Dollar Sales	Yards	Dollar Sales	Yards	Dollar Sales
Sleepwear, loungewear and intimate apparel	10.4	10.7	13.7	13.8	13.5	13.3
Children's wear	19.7	19.9	13.4	14.6	17.6	18.8
Home fabrics	17.6	15.9	21.7	19.9	19.5	17.0
International sales	1.9	2.1	2.7	3.2	3.7	4.6
Handkerchiefs and lightweight fabrics	2.9	2.3	4.2	3.2	4.2	3.4
Men's and boys' casual wear	4.8	7.3	12.5	14.7	11.2	13.1
Women's sportswear and dresses	15.7	18.3	12.4	13.6	9.9	11.1
Industrial services and shirting	14.3	16.2	9.2	11.7	8.9	11.9
Finished off-goods[1]	10.7	6.8	8.3	5.7	9.3	6.1
Unfinished off-goods	1.8	0.5	1.9	0.5	2.2	0.6
	100.0	100.0	100.0	100.0	100.0	100.0

[1] "Off-goods were fabrics which were either damaged or not produced to specifications.

Exhibit 5   Springs Industries: Apparel Fabrics Division

Organization Chart

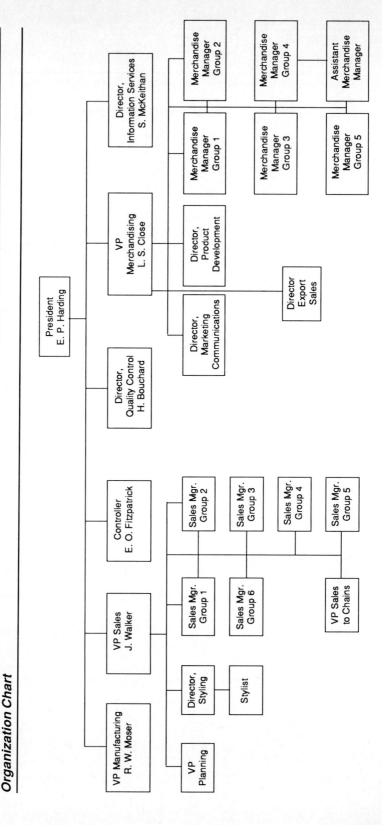

Exhibit 6 Springs Industries: Apparel Fabrics Division

Production and Merchandising Calendar—Textiles and Apparel—United Kingdom

ACTIVITY	MONTH J F M A M J J A S O N D
Fiber Producers	
Receive main orders	
Produce fiber/tops	
Spinners	
Yarn sampling	
Order fiber/tops	
Receive orders	
Spin bulk quantities	
Weavers	
Show cloth	
Order yarn	
Receive first orders	
Receive second orders and confirmations	
Manufacture cloth	
Deliver cloth	
Knitters	
Order yarns	
Show cloth	
Receive orders	
Deliver cloth	
Garment Manufacturers	
Place sample & bulk orders	
Confirm orders & order seasonal/fashion cloths	
Prepare ranges	
Selling	
Receive cloth	
Manufacture	
Retailers	
Chains & independents order garments abroad	
Department stores and independents order	
Chains look at cloth and book capacity	
Chains give color and make instructions	
Deliver to central warehouses	
Deliver to stores	
Selling to consumers	

Legend: ▓ Spring   ─── Fall   P = Promotions

Source: U. S. Department of Commerce, International Trade Administration.

Exhibit 7   Springs Industries: Apparel Fabrics Division

Marks & Spencer, Ltd.
Organization of the Textiles Division for Men's, Boys' Home Furnishings, Footwear, Accessories, and New Products, Including Detailed Organization for Men's Wear

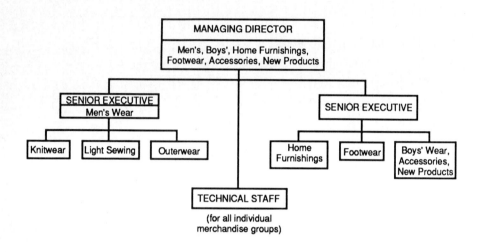

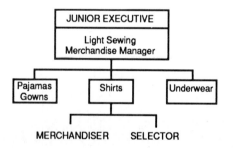

Exhibit 8   Springs Industries: Apparel Fabrics Division

Memorandum Concerning European Market

To: E. P. Harding
From: L. S. Close
Re: Europe, 1983

Attached are notes on my two weeks in France and the U.K. I returned with some ideas about how we should spend the next few years in the export business, and will discuss them with you at our meeting next week. Our goal should be to emerge from a difficult period (currency and demand-wise) with a solid customer base. It won't be easy or fun, but the European market is a key one for us.

France:

Odette's:	Total usage of 1 to 2 million yards annually. Sells to the major chains in France. Two possible problems: 1) timing: she begins product line presentations in May, so we must ship by late March, and there's no flexibility in her schedule; 2) the prices are very low, and there's no relief in sight.
Les Enfants du Paradis: (Children of Paradise)	Manufacturer of boys' and girls' gym shorts and pants, with total annual usage of 2 to 4 million yards. Monsieur Swann has owned the business about 5 years, and volume has tripled. Our current prices, with a 5–10% gross margin, are competitive.
Albertine's:	Manufactures ladies' blouses for large chains. Does not want large volumes of most fabrics. But might buy 100,000 yards of a fancy fabric since they put one fancy fabric in multiple styles. The owner reproached us for not changing styles more often. Small fry now, but growing.
La Rouge et le Noir: (Red and Black)	Largest uniform manufacturer in France, currently buys from [another U.S. textile firm]. The owner explained to me his policy of "picking one good house and sticking with it." I asked him to try us no matter how small the trial order. He admitted that having a second supplier would be to his benefit. We set appointment for December to pursue specifics.

United Kingdom:

Appleton House:	Met with Commercial Director and General Manager, and got an 80,000 yard print order (and "perhaps more in a few weeks").
Cents and Sensibility:	They have a 50,000 yard order for us, but want to iron out details of shipping.
Dombey and Son:	Discount clothing stores that buy their own piece goods and then style their own lines. They bought 300,000 yards from us in 1982, but currency will make our prices 15–20% higher this year. I doubt we'll get the order at those prices.
From Here to Maternity:	They are a big producer of ladies' wear and children's wear, and sell both in the U. K. and on the continent. Met with Managing Director. They're in the market for one of our types of fabric, but I expect trouble at current prices. We used to do more than 300,000 yards per year with these people.
Marks & Spencer:	Visited their flagship Marble Arch store and was especially sick to see the women's nightdress section. It seemed our kinds of fabrics as far as the eye could see, but little of it was our goods. Next year, their women's nightdress and children's wear departments should look like a Springs showroom.

(continued)

Exhibit 8 (continued)

Some general comments:

— In the U. K. our major competition is Asian suppliers of fabrics, not U.K. textile firms. In France, however, there is more effective competition from domestic fabric firms.

— None of these companies has the clout or long-term potential of a Marks & Spencer. Further, their stringent service and delivery requirements make it possible that, in some years, these European accounts could take some finishing time from some U.S. customers.

— Service (and price) will be the key to breaking into these accounts. That probably means losing money on such accounts for the next year or more. If we succeed, we could develop a good base of business on which to expand our efforts when economic conditions improve. But I repeat that the service requirements are stiff: generally, we will receive orders that must be shipped in four weeks, and our promptness won't be rewarded with volume in the near term.

Capital Cities/ABC, Inc.: Spot Sales

In June 1986, Mr. John Watkins, president of ABC-TV Spot Sales, was finalizing plans for a presentation to managers at Capital Cities/ABC. Mr. Watkins had worked at ABC over 14 years and had joined Spot Sales as president in February. Three managers joined him in developing the presentation: Mr. Philip Sweenie, Spot Sales' vice president; Mr. Keith Ritter, director of marketing and sales planning; and Ms. Christine McCaughey, director of research and market development. The four had met several times before to discuss the project and were now making their final decisions.

Capital Cities Communications had acquired the American Broadcasting Corporation in January; each company brought four television stations to the merger. Spot Sales, which had sold advertising nationally for the four ABC-owned stations, was to be considered for all eight. Blair Television, which had served the four Capital Cities stations in a similar capacity, was also being considered.

In April, Mr. James Keeley, the co-chair of the annual CC/ABC station sales management meeting and general sales manager of KTRK-TV (one of the original Capital Cities stations), had written to Mr. Watkins. The letter included the following paragraphs:

> The coming together of Capital Cities and ABC has created any number of situations which must be sorted through. High on our list of pressing matters is the issue of national sales representation for the owned television stations. Clearly our intent is to mount the most effective national sales effort possible. How that will be accomplished has yet to be determined.

Research Associate Jon E. King prepared this case under the supervision of Associate Professor Frank V. Cespedes, as the basis for class discussion rather than to illustrate either effective or ineffective handling of an administrative situation.

Station management has now been asked to participate in the representation review, and we ask that you present your thoughts at our annual Sales Management Meeting at the Arrowwood Conference Center on June 17.

Your presentation can take any form and cover any subject matter you feel germane to our review. We have scheduled Blair Television to present on Monday afternoon (6/16) and ABC Spot Sales to present on Tuesday afternoon. In addition to CC/ABC corporate personnel, we expect the general managers and sales management from all eight stations. We anticipate a lengthy Q&A at the conclusion of each formal presentation.

Television Stations

Television stations could be owned by a network, affiliated with a network, or operated independently. Each network provided up to 12 hours of daily programming to affiliated stations; each affiliate decided what part of the network package to air. Affiliate time not filled with a network program (and all independent airtime) would contain either locally produced programs (such as local news and sports), feature films, or programming contracted from syndicators.[1]

A station's major operating expense was programming, including fees for licensing syndicated programs. The networks paid their affiliates a nominal fee for broadcasting network programs and, in general, affiliates aired most network programming because the cost of producing programs was high. A typical affiliate might broadcast 10 hours of network programming daily, two hours of locally produced shows, and fill the rest of the broadcast day with syndicated programs. Most stations operated at least 18 hours daily.

The number of commercial minutes per hour of programming varied according to the time and type of program. In agreeing to air a network's or syndicator's program, a station agreed to air the included advertising but received no share of the revenues for that advertising. For a one-hour prime time[2] show, a network would sell about 12 minutes of advertising and leave 2–3 minutes for the local station to sell, while syndicators typically sold four minutes of ads and left eight minutes available to the station. Besides the ads carried for the network and syndicators, an individual station aired approximately 7,000 ads each month, which represented the bulk of the station's revenues.

Network shows typically drew higher audience shares than syndicated shows. High audience shares in turn drew higher advertising fees, which were a station's principal source of revenue. In setting ad fees, the station competed directly with other stations in the area, with the networks, and with other advertising media (print, radio, etc.).

---

[1]Syndicators owned the broadcast rights to one or more television series. Like television networks, they contracted with stations to broadcast their programs and the attached advertising. Unlike network programming, these programs were not run on a standardized schedule, were rarely debuts, and each series was contracted separately.

[2]"Prime" time was the most popular viewing period, usually 8–11 P.M.

Network Advertising vs. Station Advertising

To air a television commercial, an advertiser could purchase space either from a network for airing across the entire country or from an individual station for broadcast in that station's market. Network ads were sold by the network's sales force; this group was completely separate from any stations owned by the network's parent company. At CC/ABC, for instance, the ABC Television Network Group had its own sales force, which did not interact with the Broadcast Group which managed the eight television stations (see Exhibit 1).

Network advertisers were usually large consumer goods manufacturers desiring nationwide exposure. Mr. Daniel Burke, president of CC/ABC, estimated that there were only about 250 advertisers who bought network time, and only 150 bought regularly and in quantity. Station-specific advertisers focused on one or more individual markets either because the advertiser was a regional firm or because a market represented specific demographics the advertiser wished to target. Mr. Thomas Kane, general sales manager of WABC-TV in New York, pointed out:

> Network advertising is still fundamental for a national advertiser; advertising in individual markets is still secondary for most national firms. The majority of the budget will be spent on network ads in order to achieve the desired level of national exposure, and the remainder of the budget then used to increase exposure in certain target markets.

Advertising fees were traditionally measured as cost-per-thousand viewers (CPM). Rating companies monitored households to estimate the number of viewers tuned to each station and program and published their results monthly. A popular program might have a rating between 17 and 25 (out of a total of 100). CPM rates were typically set lower on networkwide ads than on single-market ads, since the network advertiser could not specify desired markets. For example, New York City's market[3] represented less than 8% of the national population, but a New York minute of air time consistently cost about 13% of a network-wide minute. A prime time minute on the network might cost $650,000, while a minute in the New York market alone would cost $80,000. Smaller markets drew even proportionally greater CPMs because those cities tended to have fewer stations, thus fewer competitors for the advertising dollars available.

Station Sales Representation

Market-specific ads were sold by the station's sales force to ad agencies located in the station's local area (approximately 75-mile radius). For sales to agencies in other cities, stations contracted sales representation firms ("reps")

---

[3]Media markets were defined as 209 "areas of dominant influence," or ADIs. Each ADI included population beyond the municipal borders of a city, reflecting the broadcast range of television and radio stations and the circulation range of metropolitan newspapers and magazines.

to represent them on commission. Although the products were identical, ads were distinguished by where they were sold: ads sold by the station's sales force were denoted "local" while those sold by a rep firm were "national." Typically, a station's general sales manager would divide responsibilities along these lines between a national sales manager and a local sales manager. The local sales manager was therefore in charge of the station's dedicated sales force, and the national sales manager was responsible for the performance of the contracted firm.

Truly "local" advertisers, such as the corner auto-body shop, were not a great percentage of a station's business; most revenues came from large advertisers who advertised in many markets. Although an advertiser might buy on a "national" scale, any stations located in the same city as the advertiser's agency would treat all revenues from that advertiser as "local." Therefore, stations in cities with many national-scale ad agencies tended to get most of their business through their local sales forces. WABC-TV in New York, for example, sold directly to all the ad agencies in New York City. Although those agencies represented the largest advertisers in the country, WABC counted that revenue as local, since it was sold by the station's own sales force (not by Spot Sales). Spot Sales' New York office, by contrast, sold advertising space for KABC-TV (Los Angeles), WLS-TV (Chicago), and KGO-TV (San Francisco) to ad agencies in New York City. That office did not sell space for WABC to New York agencies, since WABC's local sales force covered that area. Spot Sales' Detroit office, as another example, sold ads for all four ABC-owned stations.

National Representation

Broadcast sales firms were either independent organizations representing many stations (such as Blair Television), or in-house groups serving the stations owned by a single corporation (such as ABC Spot Sales). The independent rep firm could represent hundreds of stations, but only one per broadcast market; thus, none of the firm's clients were direct competitors. The network-owned rep firms were barred by law from representing stations not owned by the parent company. All rep firms were prohibited from bundling ads for more than one market.

In 1962, there had been 603 television stations in the country, and 20 national representation firms, for an average of 30 stations covered by each rep firm. By 1985, the number of stations had grown to 1,194, but the number of rep firms had shrunk to 12, for an average of 100 stations per rep firm. One reason was the large fixed cost of fielding a sales force across the country. Many broadcast groups had dissolved their in-house groups in order to reduce expenses and receive broader coverage. By 1986, only Westinghouse Broadcasting, Storer Communications, and the three network-owned station groups used in-house rep firms. However, some observers believed that with more stations to sell, independent sales reps were frequently unable to keep abreast of the important details about each station in their portfolio.

Several times during its history, Capital Cities had considered fielding its own national sales organization, dedicated to serving only its stations. Although plans were drawn up in detail, they were rejected each time.

Market Potential

Network advertising, about 50% of total television advertising in the 1960s, had declined to 40% by 1985, while local and spot ads were about 30% each of a total $20.5 billion television advertising marketing in 1985:

	Total TV[a]	% Change	Network	% Total	Spot	% Total	Local	% Total
1980	$11.416	12.4	$5.130	44.9	$3.269	28.6	$2.967	26.0
1981	12.764	11.8	5.575	43.7	3.746	29.3	3.368	26.5
1982	14.489	13.5	6.210	42.9	4.364	30.1	3.765	26.0
1983	16.489	13.8	7.017	42.6	4.827	29.3	4.345	26.4
1984	19.498	18.2	8.526	43.7	5.488	28.1	5.084	26.1
1985	20.533	5.3	8.285	40.3	6.004	29.2	5.714	27.8
1986E	22.085	7.6	8.535	38.6	6.485	29.4	6.455	29.2
1987E	24.116	9.2	9.065	37.6	7.105	29.5	7.238	30.0
1988E	27.284	13.1	10.220	37.5	8.020	29.4	8.217	30.1
1989E	29.931	9.7	11.055	36.9	8.740	29.2	9.180	30.7
1990E	33.430	11.7	12.135	36.3	9.775	29.2	10.430	31.2
1991E	35.930	7.5	12.850	35.8	10.530	29.3	11.330	31.5

Source: McCann-Erickson and Bernstein estimates.

[a]All figures in billions of dollars.

About half of all national spots were sold in New York City, due to the concentration of large ad firms. The total national and local sales figures for the 8 markets Capital Cities/ABC stations served were projected at $1.2 billion and $1.6 billion respectively for 1986. National sales at CC/ABC through ABC Spot Sales and Blair Television were expected to reach approximately $298 million in 1986, 25% of the available market for those 8 cities. Of this, Blair accounted for $127 million (32% share of the four CC stations' markets), and Spot Sales $171 million (22% share of the four ABC stations' markets). See Exhibit 2 for revenue projections for the CC/ABC stations.

National Spot Buying Process

Advertisers usually had ad agencies plan and execute their ad purchases. Agencies worked on a fee, typically 15% of the client's purchases, on top of any charges for "creative" work (campaign development, artwork, filming, etc.). For television ad sales, three people at the agency were important: the media buyer, the media planner, and possibly the assistant media director. Agency media planners averaged 26 years of age and salaries of $20,000. An advertising plan would specify markets targeted, time of day required, dates of the run, ad length, gross rating points demanded ("GRPs," the number of consumers exposed to the ad), CPM targeted, and names of rating services used for measurement. Plans were approved by the agency's clients before execution.

Once a plan had been set, an agency media buyer would contact the firms representing stations in the target markets and ask each for an "avail" (availability report). Most media buyers were recent college graduates; senior buyers averaged 25–27 years of age. The largest agencies had 10–15 buyers, each focused on specific geographic markets. The media buyer's list of details for the rep would include the name of the client and the product, the date the avail was due, and the plan's requirements. Each station was purchased separately; most buys were short term, averaging four weeks at a time, and consisting of 5 to 50 airings usually sold as "rotations" so that the ads were not run at the same point in the program each week.

The sales rep dealt primarily with the agency media buyer but could meet with the media planner to seek information or a change in the plan. The rep might meet with the assistant media director for a special sale that was not the result of a buyer's request. It was not typical for a sales rep to meet directly with the ad agency's client although it was not prohibited.

The spot salesperson would consult the rep firm's database and customize the avail proposal using the exact time slots available at the station in question. Stations set rates but it was possible to buy spots for less, depending on the competition for the spot, competing programming, and the number of spots in the purchase. Buyers wanted to place orders as close as possible to the start dates in order to obtain the best possible rate, but delaying risked sell-outs. The rep might alert the station's national sales manager (NSM) that the spots were being considered and to consult on strategy. The rep would also report to his or her own sales manager about expected revenues.

Several days after the avail was presented, the rep would discuss price with the media buyer. Most stations considered set prices to be somewhat flexible because unsold ad space would be wasted. Mr. Burke noted, "There is a lot of work to do to keep sales at the right pace; ads should never be sold out, because that means they went too cheaply. Yet inventory must be covered, and that demands dialogue." To close an important sale, the station's NSM might travel to the agency's offices.

A resulting order from the media buyer would often be taken over the telephone by a sales assistant. The sales rep would acknowledge it that day and confirm it within 48 hours. All sales were finalized by the stations, and payments went directly to them. Payments were made by the month, and only after the spots were run.

Mr. Kane (WABC's general sales manager) noted,

> The systems, philosophies, and avails for local sales and national spot sales look very similar. But local advertisers are much more in touch with the station. The local buyer has more emotional feel for the product since the ad can be seen on the set at home. The local sale is more spontaneous, since buyers watch their competitors' advertising as well. National spots, especially in the large markets, tend to sell later in the cycle because buyers try to bargain prices down.

Industry Trends

Several aspects of the national spot sales business were in flux in the mid-1980s, including television audiences, advertising agencies, and representation firms. Mr. Watkins was sure that any decision made at Arrowwood would take into account the changing face of the industry.

Since the 1970s, the three national television networks had been losing share of market to other video media: independent stations, cable systems, and home video cassettes. Since 1978 the number of VHF (high transmission quality) independent stations had doubled, the number of homes with cable TV had tripled to 45%, and homes with VCRs had grown to over 40%. Between 1978 and 1985 the three networks' share of the four ABC-owned stations' markets dropped from 68% to 53%; in the four CC stations' markets, that figure dropped from 79% to 62%.

In addition, media buying groups began forming in the 1970s; these firms performed the media purchasing tasks traditionally handled by ad agencies but charged a lower fee than the standard 15% and offered no "creative" work. Conversely, some agencies were moving away from media buying, concentrating more exclusively on campaign development.

The 1980s also saw some regionalization by major agencies. Essentially, this involved relocation of media buyers from the agency's home office to regional branch offices in order to put them in closer touch with their assigned areas. This allowed a "national" advertiser to buy as a local over many parts of the country and conversely, stations treated advertisers as local if the advertiser's agency had a regional office in the station's home city. Although total revenues were probably unchanged by such regionalization, a certain amount of revenues and sales responsibilities migrated from national to local status.

One result of the increasing competition for advertising dollars was that marketing, especially market research, was growing in importance to station sales managers. Ms. McCaughey commented:

> Market development—selling rather than order-taking—is more important now, but station sales managers aren't typically accustomed to looking at individual accounts; they will see someone spending money on ads in their market and then seek their share, but they usually do not hunt down new customers to enter their markets. Now that some advertisers are actually leaving TV and there are more competitors for the ad dollar, marketing services are essential to station growth.
>
> Selling a market as an ad target boils down to getting the market included in an advertiser's media plan. When you ask an advertiser to change its ad plan, you better be able to speak the planner's language. This demands demographic surveys comparing the market to those markets the advertiser is currently in or perhaps comparing the advertiser's presence in this market to its competitors'. Perhaps the client wants to target current customers or perhaps noncustomers matching customer demographics. At Spot Sales we emphasize CPM adjusted to target audience: the idea is that our higher gross CPM is actually cheaper if there is a higher concentration of target customers viewing the ad in our market than in someone else's.

At Spot Sales we use 34 different databases for compiling evidence for persuading buyers, planners, and advertisers that we can deliver the impact they require. By contrast, the agency has a limited incentive to change the set of markets covered in a media plan. Agencies get their 15% commission regardless; the less time they spend fiddling with a satisfactory plan, the more time they can spend making new money. They are judged on the efficiency of the buys; that is, the lowness of their CPMs. Few are judged on efficiency with respect to the target consumers, i.e., cost per thousand targets.

We'll try to sell to the agency ad planner; if we provide an advantageous change, the planner can take credit. But frequently we have to go to the client, because it's their money being wasted in a less-than-effective campaign. Sometimes you have to tell the emperor he's naked, not his tailor.

Few rep firms approach advertisers directly, and none as much as we do; few have many research resources, though it is on the rise, and no one else has what Spot has. I've done interviewing for new positions here and believe my junior analysts know more than top analysts at other firms.

Capital Cities/ABC, Inc.

Before acquiring ABC, Capital Cities Communications, Inc. was already a diversified media company with television, radio, cable and print operations. Decentralization was the cornerstone of Capital Cities' management philosophy. Most decisions, including station programming, were made at the local level with the stipulation that operations be consistent with the basic legal and moral responsibilities of corporate management. Budgets, which were set yearly and reviewed quarterly, originated with the local general managers who were responsible for them. Each station general manager was responsible for the daily operations of the station.

Capital Cities acquired ABC on January 3, 1986, for $3.37 billion. The merged company was expected to have revenues over $4 billion in 1986, derived from television and radio networks, stations, cable television services, newspapers, and specialized publications. Virtually all of the broadcast revenues and 70% of the publication revenues came from the sale of advertising space. Although the television network was not currently profitable, the "owned and operated" [4] television stations had tallied consistently high margins.

The corporation was divided into three groups: the ABC Television Network Group (54% of combined CC/ABC 1985 sales), responsible for national programming and network advertising sales; the Publishing Group (23%), which operated newspapers, shopping guides, and magazines; and the Broad-

---

[4] Television networks provided programming to affiliates around the country, but were limited by the Federal Communications Commission (FCC) in the number of such stations they could own. Regulations current in 1986 limited a network's holdings to twelve stations, which as a group could not reach more than 25% of the nation's total population. In 1986, CC/ABC's eight television stations reached a cumulative 24.4%. Through these eight stations and the other 207 affiliate stations, ABC's network reached over 99% of the television households in the United States.

cast Group (23%), comprised of the ABC Radio Network, 19 owned and operated radio stations, three cable television programming groups, the eight television stations (divided geographically into two groups), and ABC Spot Sales.

Mr. Michael Mallardi, president of the Broadcast Group, commented, "We have the largest network-owned station group in the country, including number one stations in the five biggest markets." Exhibit 4 provides information about the stations, including the percentage of ad revenues generated outside the local market.

Spot Sales and the ABC Station Group

Spot Sales was founded in 1961; before that, the ABC stations had been represented by Blair Television. Most current Spot Sales staff had previously worked for one or more of the ABC owned and operated stations; few reps in independent firms had station experience. Before the merger, Spot Sales represented five stations: ABC's Detroit station had been sold in order to meet FCC requirements.

Of the reps joining the New York office, 90% came from other Spot Sales branch offices; 10% came from the ABC stations. The average Spot Sales rep in the New York office was 31 with 9 years' experience in national or local sales or broadcasting. The typical tenure in the office was 2–5 years. Across the country in Spot Sales, the average age was 34 for an account executive (sales rep) and 38 for a sales manager.

The New York office was responsible for three stations in early 1986 and expected to account for over 50% of Spot Sales' revenues (see Exhibit 3). Besides New York City, it also handled all business out of Boston, Philadelphia, and Canada. The 12 account executives, each with a sales assistant, were split into two groups, each with a manager and a list of agencies to cover. New York Spot Sales' three sales managers also made a total of 20–25 calls per week with the reps. Sales managers' responsibilities also included (but were not limited to) training, sales contract review, business projection, business tracking, setting quotas and objectives, and communicating with station management. See Exhibit 5 for Spot Sales' organization chart.

Spot Sales used a compensation plan unique to the industry. Account executives were salaried at an average of $40,000, with an incentive divided between quota achievement and secondary objectives based on 3–5 specific tasks set by the sales manager. Average incentive compensation was $30,000 if the rep met 100% of goals, for a total compensation target of $70,000. Sales managers made $90,000 on average, though New York figures were slightly higher.

Total compensation targets were set close to the following ratio: 55% salary, 30% on billing quota, and 15% on secondary objectives. The sales manager reviewed the rep's performance on the assigned tasks and determined the percentage of target achieved (which could be lower or higher than 100%). For example, a typical rep would have a target of $10,000 incentive compensation for achieving secondary goals. One of the tasks assigned by the sales manager might be to sell three Olympics ad packages, with a stated bonus of $3,000 (the other tasks would account for the other $7,000 of secondary incentive). If the rep sold 2 packages (66% of target), $2,000 would be paid; $4,000 would be paid for 4 packages sold (133% of target).

Quota incentive was levered such that deviation from revenue target was doubled in calculating compensation. Thus, if the rep sold 20% over revenue target, quota compensation would be 40% above target, but if the rep was 10% below quota, the incentive would be 20% below target. (Therefore, if the rep met less than 50% of billing quota, there would be no quota compensation paid at all.)

All ABC station sales managers had worked at Spot Sales at some time. Station sales managers had all also worked in local sales. Mr. Kane had managed the New York Spot Sales office before taking over Mr. Watkins' job as general sales manager at WABC (when Mr. Watkins was made president of Spot Sales). He explained:

> It is a deliberate system which rotates and exposes salespeople to all the markets and all the stations. The New York Spot Sales office is the management pool from which most new sales managers are taken; three quarters of all ABC station sales management have worked there. This way no one will put up with lousy performance, because we all know what it takes to do each other's job.
>
> Some Cap Cities people criticize the system because they believe the movement rate has been too high: for example, the average stay in the Detroit office is only a year, and one person only stayed four months. On the other hand, Detroit customers now know many ABC people who remain ABC people, often running the stations they are buying from. They will always know who to complain to.

Blair Television

Blair Television was a division of John Blair & Company, a publicly held media company with other operations in television and radio station management, program production and syndication, and direct mail and coupon marketing services. In 1985, television/radio representation commissions accounted for about 11% of total John Blair revenues, and provided the highest operating margin of any of its businesses; commission rates averaged about 7.5% of gross billing. After a weak year in 1985, JB & C embarked on a major restructuring, including divesting printing and free-standing (newspaper coupon) insert operations (see Exhibit 8).

JB & C was founded in 1935, and the broadcast representation arm started in 1948. Blair Television was the first independent television rep company, and consistently led other rep firms in national billing figures; billing for television and radio stations in 1985 was about $900 million. Blair had 18 sales offices across the country, and represented 140 television stations, covering an aggregate 80% of the national population. In 1985 their account list numbered 6,600 spot advertisers using 2,153 advertising agencies and buying groups.

Blair employed 225 account executives and a 60-person research staff. Blair had added 34 new stations to its client list in the past three years, and the average length of representation for current clients was 12 years. One fourth of Blair's reps started their careers with Blair; the average rep had five years of industry experience; managers averaged 12 years' experience. See Exhibit 6 for Blair Television's organization chart.

Mr. Burke noted, "When we started working with Blair in 1958, they could pay their bills better than we could." However, Capital Cities had grown to become Blair's largest client, accounting for over 10% of Blair's total commissions from station representation. As Blair had diversified and brought on more stations in recent years, Capital Cities' share of Blair's total sales had declined, even as revenues rose. However, were the entire eight-station CC/ABC group to be represented by Blair, that group would account for at least 20% of Blair's national spot sales. Mr. Spinner, manager of CC's Philadelphia station, stated:

> Blair has generally been a very responsive representative for us. On the other hand, there are some differences of opinion. For two years we asked them to take one team manager off our business, but they kept stalling. Blair will also paint a gloomy picture of the market so that they can beat expectations. But there are also people there with whom we have had excellent long-term relationships and trust implicitly.

Mr. Larry Pollock declared:

> Blair is the best rep firm around; they've stood the test of time. And the Cap Cities group is a pearl for them: the stations are highly rated, and provide a rep with muscle at selling time. Blair's top people know the Cap Cities stations because they grew up in the business selling them. There is give and take, and I believe they're honest with us when they think we aren't making a good decision.

Blair charged 6%–15% commission to its clients. Smaller markets tended to be charged higher percentages because of their relative difficulty and the smaller size of the average sale. Independent stations (those not affiliated with a national network) also tended to be charged higher rates, reflecting lower demand for nonnetwork advertising. Capital Cities, as Blair's largest customer, was charged 5.75% on all sales up to 105% of the previous year's revenues and 6% on sales above that target. Remuneration was renegotiated each year, and Capital Cities had pared down the commission rate over many years as CC had grown to become Blair's largest client and as CC stations achieved high ratings in their markets.

Capital Cities/ABC Merger

One ABC manager commented:

> We thought the acronym CC meant "Capital Cities." We were wrong; it stands for "Cost Conscious." Cap Cities stations tallied 60% margins, while ours aver-

aged 32%, although we're improving fast. ABC had started cutbacks two years ago, but the pace has accelerated with the merger. There has been a certain degree of cultural assimilation already. Yet before the merger, the two corporations were very decentralized, so there are really few general policies.

Mr. Ritter noted differences between the CC and ABC station groups:

Many of the cultural differences between the two station groups stem from market demands. The four ABC stations cover four of the five largest ADIs. These are big cities, each with several high-quality VHF stations. Market share is hard to come by and hard to hold on to; one- or two-point advantages in the Nielsen ratings[5] are about the limit. The top station will have ratings in the high teens or low twenties.

ABC's big metropolitan sales often require entertaining, parties, football tickets, and suites in the hotel. Capital Cities people consider that wasteful, because they have never needed it: dominant stations in smaller markets are "must-buys" for an advertiser wishing to make a big splash in those markets, so the hand-holding isn't as important. Smaller markets tend to have more dominant leaders, because there are fewer competitors; in Raleigh/Durham, for example, there is only one other competitive station. The smaller markets charge premium CPMs because of the lack of competition: the advertiser has few alternatives if it decides to run in that ADI. And dominant leaders in small markets are even more highly priced, by extension.

ABC's owned stations are number one in each of their large metropolitan markets. These are old, industrial cities with very limited cable development (with the exception of San Francisco). But the late '70s and early '80s saw rapid growth of the metro independents as they professionalized and developed the Independent Television Association which helped them pool their skills. The Cap Cities stations' markets are generally not as mature.

Because of the level of competition in ABC's markets, Spot Sales uses a lot of statistical data to highlight our stations' advantages. But the personal relationships are also important. Between two groups with good figures supporting them, the relationship breaks the deadlock. Advertisers want their programs executed properly, and will remember if some station or rep did not.

Mr. Kane at WABC added: "The big markets need research resources because their ratings can shift literally overnight. Those last-minute sales require up-to-date data."

In-House and Independent Rep Firms

CC/ABC station managers had varied views on relationships with rep groups. Mr. Burke pointed out, "The Capital Cities stations have been happy

---

[5]Neilsen compiled statistics on television viewers. A program's rating of 19.1 meant that of all the televisions on during that hour in that market, 19.1% were tuned to the program; the rest could be tuned to other stations, cable services, or VCRs. A station's Nielsen rating could either be specified for a day-part (such as 8 to 9 P.M. Tuesday nights) or aggregated across the week, as used in this case.

to use the stick to motivate Blair sales reps, but that is not as appropriate with an in-house group." Mr. Pollock commented:

> Performance is best measured by the margin of share of billings over share of audience. Who's the better rep firm? The one that brings in the most sales. Commission rate is an important number but secondary to sales dollars.
>
> People make the difference in this operation, especially the station sales manager. A good manager with average reps will bring in more money than an average sales manager with good reps. I believe Blair is the best independent rep firm in the business and Spot Sales is the best in-house.

Mr. Spinner offered his point of view:

> Blair and other independents have 55-year-olds selling for them as well as 25-year-olds. It's a career for them. If they move, they move to another rep firm. An in-house firm has younger people and higher turnover; and when they move, they tend to go someplace besides national Spot Sales.
>
> Other rep firms have made a pitch for our business in the past, and we've reviewed the idea of in-house representation every few years. But one value in having an outside firm is that we can always fire them. And, besides, I don't want my national sales manager to go to work for Spot at some point.

Another Capital Cities manager explained:

> There is something to be said for having an outside "monitor." I am not saying that I definitely think we should stay with an outside firm, but there are certain advantages from a political standpoint that you can't put an exact dollar value on. Blair works for us on commission; that provides them with an impetus to sell to the best of their ability. We don't always think the reps do that, and we challenge them. But the fact that Blair does not report directly to anyone at Capital Cities provides us with a form of "checks and balances." There is a danger that an in-house rep will work hard to sell one station in particular to gain that station's favor and to enhance his or her employment opportunities.

Mr. Todd Wheeler, general sales manager at CC's WPVI station stated:

> Conflicts do arise, because our goals are not really the same as those of Blair. The reps at Blair want to get the job done quickly and easily. They have other stations to sell and sometimes work hard to sell us on a deal that may not be good for the station. They are on commission and only get paid after the spot is run. But I want to sell the largest number of commercials at the highest possible rate no matter how hard we work and how long it takes.

Mr. Richard Spinner, as general manager of WPVI-TV in Philadelphia, had the highest percentage of national revenues of the CC/ABC stations. He noted:

> I care about market development: new categories of business, individual accounts, and special problems. Capital Cities needs to improve its research resources. Blair has only one research person for all our stations, when in fact they need at least four. Cap Cities stations have virtually no market development/research staff. This is the way Capital Cities has always worked. Blair has seven people for business development for 180 stations. Spot has five people for four stations.

Mr. Kane of WABC commented:

The advantages of an in-house rep firm boil down to more attention paid to each individual station, since a salesperson's time is not divided among 180 stations, but 4–8. The average rep firm handles over a hundred clients. Cap Cities people do have to push Blair to focus on their stations, since there are so many other stations competing for the reps' time.

On the other hand, independent firms often organize in teams, so that each individual only has to cover a subset of stations. No media buyer will buy spots in a hundred markets anyway. But since each rep will not know details about each station (only those about the stations on his sublist) independents are not as coordinated: the effectiveness of the entire rep firm is limited by the ability of each individual sales rep to know the entire spectrum of stations repped by the company. In-house firms can know more about all their stations. A rep won't know the station very well if he or she only sells that station once in four months.

There is a difference in motivational levels: an independent rep can just hang up the phone when a conversation is over, but the in-house rep has his personal reputation on the line with peers. I'm not impressed with a system where the rep is motivated strictly by money; I want a rep motivated by career. I want the rep to know I represent the paycheck and the future. A good in-house rep will allow you to turn down an order that's against your best interests, even though the rep then loses the sale; an indy won't. The CC people are skeptical of this because they have never seen it themselves. ABC Spot Sales hires away good people from other rep firms. ABC represents a career, big markets, big stations; these are real talent draws.

The CC guys are procrastinating over the decision to go with Spot Sales. Here is the opportunity to have the internal system they have already looked at and rejected because of start-up costs. Besides, if the threat to leave Blair is supposed to be so serious, why has that threat never been carried out in 28 years? And if all eight stations go with Blair, we'll be locked in, because with only a limited number of rep firms, there is no one else who doesn't already have commitments with competing stations in our markets.

January to June 1986

Mr. Watkins recalled the situation at Spot Sales during the past six months:

At the first annual management meeting in January 1986, emphasis was placed on "the bottom line." I was approached there about taking on Spot Sales, and I took it because of the challenge. I knew well the sales managers at all the ABC stations and was confident of their support. However, at the February forecast presentation, Dan Burke was noncommittal about keeping Spot past the end of the year, but he did recommend that I "ignore bottom line and focus on boosting revenues."

We've had a lot to do other than just pitch for the new stations. Phil Sweenie and I have visited all the Spot offices to nail down operations, soothe worries about new ownership, new management and threatened existence, and encourage head-to-head competition against Blair's performance. By April, Spot Sales was 4.5% ahead of second-quarter pacing targets and 24.4% ahead of third-quarter goals. Christine meanwhile has been upgrading our Avail system. We're having trouble recruiting good people right now, because we can't guarantee they'll have a job next year.

We've also spent time with station managers from both Cap Cities and ABC, discussing philosophies and objectives and digging up facts about the new stations. This has impressed some, but not others: KFSN people told us, "Nobody ever came to visit Fresno before," but at KABC we heard, "Alright, don't oversell yourselves."

Both station group managers, Larry Pollock and Ken Johnson, have visited us in New York. These meetings had a major impact on our thinking. Ken Johnson explained that his concerns were our adaptability to the Cap Cities style of selling and our ability to accept policy from the station and group managers. He said Cap Cities' station managers were concerned that Spot Sales dictated sales strategy to ABC station sales managers, rather than vice-versa.

An example of Mr. Watkins' schedule in this period is shown below:

4/09	Philadelphia, WPVI-TV
4/10	Raleigh/Durham, WTVD-TV
4/11	12 noon lunch with Mike Mallardi (informal review of Spot Sales)
4/15	Larry Pollock at New York Spot Sales (all day)
4/16	Larre Barrett, head of ABC Sport Sales, presents 1988 Calgary Olympics pitch to New York Spot Sales (8:30 A.M.)
4/16	Los Angeles, L. A. Spot Sales—review of office
4/17	Los Angeles, KABC-TV
4/21	Fresno, KFSN-TV
4/22	Dallas, Dallas Spot Sales, 9:30 A.M. presentation of 1988 Olympics to American Airlines (all eight stations)
4/23	Houston, KTRK-TV, dinner with key clients

Mr. Ritter and Ms. McCaughey developed marketing materials for the Capital Cities stations along the lines of the materials they produced for ABC's. Mr. Ritter recalled:

When we developed our Olympics presentation books this spring, we were allowed to include market data on the four CC stations, with a footnote referring advertisers interested in those markets to Blair. We sent copies of the book to the Cap Cities national sales managers. The responses to the promotions were positive from people at the stations, but Larry Pollock looked at it and said, "This is interesting. How much does it cost?"

Our philosophy is: market the station, open up new advertisers, don't just wait for avail requests. Blair would never develop a special package for something like the Olympics or provide market data for individual stations. We used this opportunity to learn something about the four Cap Cities markets and got some practice using the available data.

Mr. Sweenie interpreted the results of the meetings with the Capital Cities station managers:

One concern of the CC people is what they call the "mentality" of in-house national reps: they think that in-house reps are good old boys who don't work hard and take care of their pals at the expense of the firm. One station manager told me, "The old story at Spot Sales is the buddy system: a rep will call the station manager and say, 'help me out and take this offer.'" I think that is a big misperception.

Another concern was that "the reps dictate decisions to the stations." This may be true of Group-W at Westinghouse or of NBC National Television Sales, but it's never been true of ABC Spot Sales. Some CC managers think that Spot management has set policies and terms of sale, which simply isn't true. All four of the ABC stations have separate pricing policies, and although we have to coordinate them, we make no attempt to homogenize them.

Mr. Mallardi, president of the Broadcast Group, stated:

I have my own opinions, but I'm not going to direct this decision. Both groups have fine reputations. The Arrowwood presentations are only the culmination of a long series of lobbying efforts from the two rep groups. There are no guidelines: we left it open in order to gain some insight into what the two management teams find important. An obvious priority is sales performance, but each market is different, so it is important to have confidence in the unit itself on some visceral level in order to be satisfied. There will unfortunately be significant transition demands for whichever station group switches.

Plans for Arrowwood

Mr. Watkins' managers had various ideas about what to present and emphasize at the June 17 presentation at Arrowwood. Mr. Sweenie was concerned about the negative feelings expressed at Capital Cities about personnel and policies at Spot Sales. He suggested a presentation strategy of highlighting the complete transformation of the organization: new management, new research resources, new availability reporting system. He recommended coining a new name for the organization in order to formalize the changes, and he prepared a profile of the top managers at Spot Sales to highlight their experience and counter the impression of constant turnover:

		Industry Years	ABC Years
Joe Cohen	Director of Eastern Sales	20	20
Michael Colleran	Eastern Sales Manager	13	4
Mary Webb Ellis	Eastern Sales Manager	11	7
Phil Sweenie	Vice President	17	12
Christine McCaughey	Director of Research	10	6
Keith Ritter	Director of Marketing	10	8
Mike Sullivan	Director of Finance	25	25
John Watkins	President	14	14

He also prepared statistics on account executives: averages of six years' television experience before joining Spot Sales, including three years of local sales, and two years with Spot Sales so far. Every sales manager at the four ABC stations had worked at Spot Sales.

Ms. McCaughey noted that in a 1984 market study conducted biannually by the Dyco Organization (an independent research firm), 200 buyers and supervisors from 100 ad agencies were polled about their most important demands of a station representation firm and how they rated various firms. In 9 of the 11 major concerns, ABC Spot Sales was rated highest in the cities where it had offices (see Exhibit 7). Similar surveys by Westinghouse and Telerep reported equivalent findings concerning the salient categories and Spot Sales' performance.

Mr. Ritter noted that although gross revenues (or gross revenues minus commissions) were important in evaluating a rep firm, other comparisons could be made. One was the level to which a firm outperformed its circumstances; that is, the level to which market share exceeded audience share. A chart of Spot Sales' performance in this regard is shown in Exhibit 9. Another possible comparison was Spot Sales' billings against those of CBS and NBC across the four markets covered. For instance, in Spot Sales' four ADIs, Spot outbilled CBS and NBC national spot sales by a percentage higher than audience shares could account for. The index of sales advantage to audience advantage was 183% in 1983, 310% in 1984, and 274% in 1985.

Closing

Mr. Watkins offered his thoughts to his colleagues as they met to determine the final structure and content for Spot Sales' Arrowwood presentation:

> Mike Mallardi's views seem plain to me: he wants to maximize corporate earnings but doesn't want to interfere with station managers or with Ken Johnson and Larry Pollock.
>
> Blair's commission rates are 5.75% until quota is reached, and then 6% for sales above quota. Spot Sales' commission is currently 6.5% flat, and I think we could operate efficiently at 5.5% if we get all eight stations. I might be willing to offer 5% if that's what's needed to survive. So far, Spot Sales has been measured on gross revenues and secondarily on market share. On the other hand, although Dan Burke said to concentrate on sales, I'm sure Mike Mallardi is paying attention to my bottom line. I think by going in-house, the corporation can get up to $2.5 million savings on commissions and up to $9.5 million in extra sales.
>
> If we do get the business, we've got four new stations to learn about quickly and thoroughly. We're expecting to sell $170 million this year for the four ABC stations. If we get the others, we'll need to reach $310 million next year; we'll need to expand our sales force by 50% by November to start selling the new stations for first quarter 1987.
>
> This is a live or die decision for Spot Sales. And Blair has an advantage in presenting: they do this all the time, but we've never made a pitch before, so we're inexperienced. We don't want to focus on Blair's shortcomings, because that would insult the CC people who have used them for 28 years and we want to stand on our own merits anyway. Besides, after 28 years of doing business

together, there must be personal relationships and friendships involved, and we don't want to criticize somebody's close friends.

No one ever disagreed that we have more thorough and powerful marketing and research than Blair. But the specifics we've presented are not as important as our specificity itself. That is, maybe the details can be argued, but the fact that there are details at all is an improvement over Blair. Throughout my canvassing, I've been trying to underscore the idea that "these ABC people pay attention to details."

Let's get down to work: what do we say at Arrowwood, how do we say it, and who should talk about what?

Exhibit 1 Capital Cities/ABC, Inc.: Spot Sales

Corporate Organization

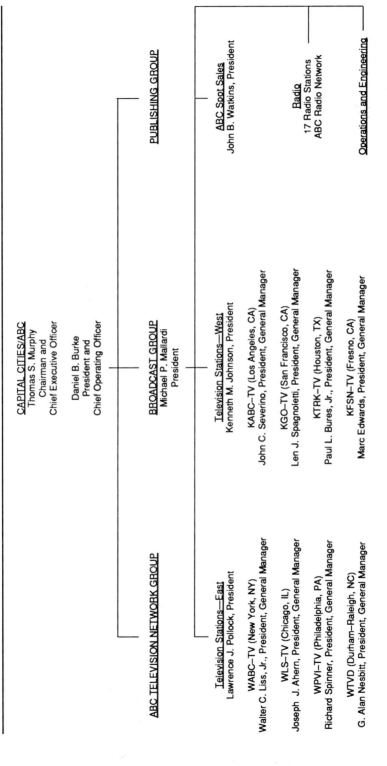

Exhibit 2   *Capital Cities/ABC, Inc.: Spot Sales*

Annual National Revenues by Station
(Projected-millions)

	1983	1984	1985	1986 (est.)	1987 (est.) Market	Revenue	Share %
WABC (SS)	$ 21.8	$ 31.3	$ 26.0	$ 28.3	$ 141.4	$ 30.7	21.7
KABC (SS)	53.6	60.4	49.6	54.6	286.5	59.3	20.6
WLD (SS)	33.7	41.7	44.7	49.0	177.6	51.5	29.0
WPVI (Blair)	50.3	58.3	61.6	65.6	212.0	69.5	32.7
KGO (SS)	37.4	45.1	39.9	38.8	192.4	41.8	21.7
KTRK (Blair)	44.9	50.1	48.9	44.1	145.0	43.5	30.0
WTVD (Blair)	9.1	9.6	12.6	12.8	35.0	14.3	40.9
KFSN (Blair)	4.7	5.0	4.8	4.8	21.0	5.6	26.6
	255.5	301.5	288.1	$298.0	$1,210.9	$316.2	26.1%

Note: SS = Represented by ABC Spot Sales.
Blair = Represented by Blair Television.

Exhibit 3   *Capital Cities/ABC, Inc.: Spot Sales*

Sales Forecasts by Office
(millions)

	1986	1987
New York	$ 95.8	$180.9
Chicago	20.8	33.4
Los Angeles	18.8	25.3
Detroit	14.4	21.7
Atlanta	8.2	15.7
Dallas	7.0	26.2
San Francisco	5.7	8.9
	$170.7	$312.1

Exhibit 4 Capital Cities/ABC: Spot Sales

Owned Television Stations

Station	City	Original Owner	Market Rank (of 209)	Percent of U. S. Homes	No. of Commercial Stations in Market	National Sales Percent of Station Revenue	Overall Station's	
							Nielsen Share	Percent of National Advertising Dollars in Market
WABC	New York	ABC	1	7.78	6	17	19	21
KABC	Los Angeles	ABC	2	5.17	8	32	18	20
WLS	Chicago	ABC	3	3.50	7	40	23	29
WPVI	Philadelphia	CC	4	3.01	6	70	26	35
KGO	San Francisco	ABC	5	2.37	7	35	19	22
KTRK	Houston	CC	10	1.66	6	65	25	30
WTVD	Raleigh/ Durham	CC	35	.71	5	60	26	39
KFSN	Fresno	CC	63	.46[a]	6	50	20	24
			Total 8-market sales (1986-projected) $1.2 billion national, $1.6 billion local			$298 million national sales (1986-projected)		26%

[a] UHF station; counted as .23% for FCC purposes.

Exhibit 5   Capital Cities/ABC, Inc.: Spot Sales

Spot Sales Organization

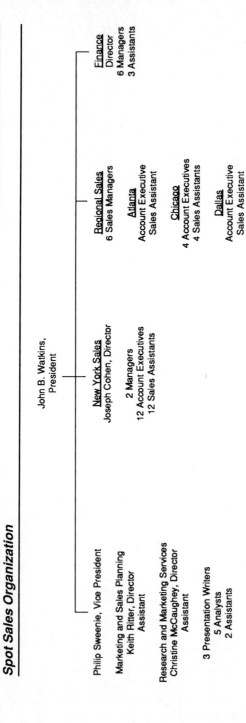

John B. Watkins,
President

Philip Sweenie, Vice President

Marketing and Sales Planning
Keith Ritter, Director
Assistant

Research and Marketing Services
Christine McCaughey, Director
Assistant

3 Presentation Writers
5 Analysts
2 Assistants

New York Sales
Joseph Cohen, Director

2 Managers
12 Account Executives
12 Sales Assistants

Regional Sales
6 Sales Managers

Atlanta
Account Executive
Sales Assistant

Chicago
4 Account Executives
4 Sales Assistants

Dallas
Account Executive
Sales Assistant

Detroit
2 Account Executives
2 Sales Assistants

Los Angeles
3 Account Executives
3 Sales Assistants

San Francisco
Account Executive
Sales Assistant

Finance
Director
6 Managers
3 Assistants

Exhibit 6 Capital Cities/ABC, Inc.: Spot Sales

Blair Television Organization

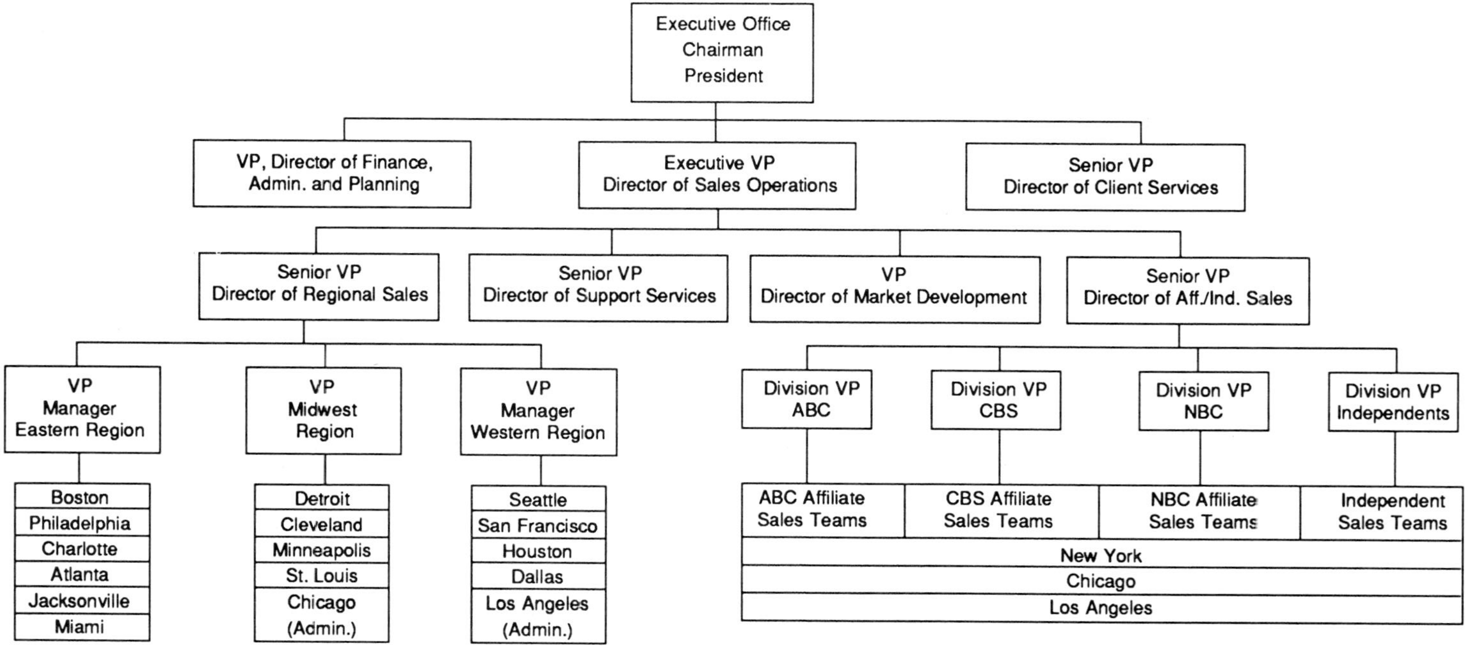

Executive Office
Chairman
President

Executive VP
Director of Sales Operations

VP, Director of Finance, Admin. and Planning

Senior VP
Director of Client Services

Senior VP
Director of Support Services

Senior VP
Director of Regional Sales

VP
Director of Market Development

Senior VP
Director of Aff./Ind. Sales

Regional Sales

VP
Manager Eastern Region
- Boston
- Philadelphia
- Charlotte
- Atlanta
- Jacksonville
- Miami

VP
Midwest Region
- Detroit
- Cleveland
- Minneapolis
- St. Louis
- Chicago
- (Admin.)

VP
Manager Western Region
- Seattle
- San Francisco
- Houston
- Dallas
- Los Angeles
- (Admin.)

Affiliate/Independent Sales

Division VP ABC — ABC Affiliate Sales Teams

Division VP CBS — CBS Affiliate Sales Teams

Division VP NBC — NBC Affiliate Sales Teams

Division VP Independents — Independent Sales Teams

New York
Chicago
Los Angeles

Exhibit 7   Capital Cities/ABC, Inc.: Spot Sales

Dyco Survey Results

Advertising Agency Buyers' Opinions on Sales Representation Firms (7 Cities)	Importance Rating[a]	ABC Spot Sales Rank
Accurate placement and telecast of schedules	99.2%	1
Accurate paperwork and billing	96.9	1
Accurate and complete information	96.7	1
Competent sales assistants	93.6	1
Flexibility to react to market conditions on the spot	86.3	2
Low salesperson turnover	79.6	4
Information on special programming	79.1	1
Rapport with salesperson	74.3	1
Market research information	70.9	1
Being future oriented	69.6	1
Rationale with avails	69.0	1

[a]Percent of respondents citing a given factor.

Exhibit 8 Capital Cities/ABC, Inc.: Spot Sales

John Blair & Co.
Results for Year
(000)

Revenues	1985	1984	1983	1982	1981
Marketing services	$449,878	$327,208	$ 15,744	$ —	$ —
Owned broadcasting stations	99,372	89,021	39,867	25,541	23,077
Broadcast representation	66,009	62,229	55,398	50,797	42,923
Other activities	15,288	8,788	4,355	1,687	1,155
Total Revenues	$630,547	$487,306	$115,364	$78,025	$67,155
Percent increase from prior year	29%	322%	48%	16%	21%
(Loss) Earnings from Continuing Operations					
Marketing services	$(30,681)	$ 10,454	$ 940	$ —	$ —
Owned broadcasting stations	14,301	15,688	5,526	2,667	2,259
Broadcast representation	12,604	11,751	11,732	12,322	11,023
Other activities	2,346	1,115	(3,507)	(8,185)	(6,589)
Corporate expenses	(13,637)	(7,931)	(6,056)	(3,714)	(2,674)
Total (Loss) Earnings from Continuing Operations	$(15,067)	$ 31,077	$ 8,635	$ 3,090	$ 4,019
Net (Loss) Earnings from Continuing Operations	$(30,820)	$ 607	$ (244)	$ 923	$ 676

Exhibit 9 Capital Cities/ABC, Inc.: Spot Sales

National Sales Performance Evaluation, 1985

	National Market Share (Advertising) [a]	Share Viewing[b]	Index
WABC—New York	22%	19%	120%
KABC—Los Angeles	20	18	111
WLS—Chicago	28	23	122
WPVI—Philadelphia	35	26	135
KGO—San Francisco	24	19	127
KTRK—Houston	32	25	128
WTVD—Raleigh/Durham	39	26	150
KFSN—Fresno	24	20	120
(All ABC—SS)	23	19.6	117
(All CC—Blair)	32	24.3	132

[a]Station's share of advertising dollars spent in that market, but originating outside that market.
[b]Average share of television households in that market viewing that station.

MCI Communications Corporation: National Accounts Program

In July 1986 Mr. Jonathan Crane, vice president for National Accounts at MCI, was preparing for a review of the program with MCI's top management. Since becoming head of the program six months earlier, Mr. Crane had helped to build a headquarters staff and revised the organization, training, and compensation plans for national account personnel. The review was to consider the program's progress toward the goal of increasing MCI's presence and business with large corporate customers and to consider any changes that might aid in achieving this goal.

Mr. Crane had recently confronted several problems in implementing the program. He was especially concerned about three areas. One was coordinating the impact on national accounts of field sales efforts in MCI's divisions. Another was the appropriate focus for the program: some managers believed MCI should focus on a few key accounts, while others argued that the market and competition required MCI to work more extensively and less "deeply" with a large number of key accounts. Finally, Mr. Crane wanted to develop a more effective approach for marshaling and directing the technical and sales talent necessary for making major sales to large, sophisticated customers.

Speaking to the casewriter, he noted that, "in the new competitive environment, it's essential that we shed our image as a discount long-distance carrier and establish ourselves as an industry leader in telecommunications. That's my program's primary mission. But we encounter a number of opportunities and problems in executing that mission."

This case was prepared by Associate Professor Frank V. Cespedes, with the assistance of Research Assistant Jon E. King, as the basis for class discussion rather than to illustrate either effective or ineffective handling of an administrative situation.

Company History

In 1963, Microwave Communications, Inc. sought FCC permission to construct a telephone system between Chicago and St. Louis. AT&T opposed the application. In 1986 Mr. William G. McGowan—son of a union organizer, graduate of Harvard Business School, and a successful entrepreneur—joined the original investors and formed an enterprise that sought to construct and operate a nationwide long-distance telephone system. At the time, the commercial segment of long-distance service represented a $5 billion market, and AT&T had a de facto monopoly position. In 1971, the FCC denied AT&T requests for additional hearings and granted construction permits to MCI, which thus became the first of the so-called Specialized Common Carriers (SCC) that built and operated their own intercity transmission networks or leased circuits from other carriers on certain routes.

The original MCI system between Chicago and St. Louis opened in January 1972. MCI had spent $10 million in legal costs to secure approval, while the actual facilities between St. Louis and Chicago cost less than $2 million. At that time, MCI expected to sell 37 million circuit miles with an average revenue of $1.00 per circuit mile excluding AT&T's interconnection charges (still under negotiation).

Within AT&T, there was considerable debate about the proper response to MCI. Notes from the Bell Presidents' Conference of May 1972 (later submitted as court evidence in suits initiated by MCI) indicate support for a direct price response:

> How many MCIs will proceed with construction plans if we file matching rates now? A big fat zero. . . . You bastards are not going to take away my business.
>
> —President, Northwestern Bell Telephone Company

> Shouldn't we act now rather than wait until they have going businesses which regulators might not permit us to dislodge?
>
> —President, Southern New England Telephone Company

> . . . large amount of revenues vulnerable which we can preserve if we choke off now. I think you have to hit the nails on the head.
>
> —President, Illinois Bell Telephone Company and later Chairman of AT&T

However, AT&T finally decided to defer pricing action for further study.

MCI's principal task at the time was securing adequate local interconnections from AT&T and Bell System companies. During 1972, MCI raised $110 million in venture capital funding. In September 1973, however, AT&T halted negotiations concerning interconnections and, according to Mr. McGowan, "the sky fell in on us. We were ready to go into business; had all the people on board hired; customers, orders were ready to go, and we just couldn't proceed at all." Layoffs totalling a third of MCI's employees began, and the company obtained an amended credit agreement permitting it to use loan proceeds as working capital in order to survive until interconnections could be obtained through legal proceedings.

When in 1974 the FCC ordered interconnections, MCI was deeply in debt and unable to complete its network. Moreover, MCI believed that AT&T practices degraded the quality of MCI's interconnections, causing needless expenditures of time and money. In March 1974, therefore, MCI charged AT&T and subsidiaries with "attempting and/or conspiring to monopolize, monopolizing, and unreasonably restraining trade in the business and data communications services market in violation of Federal antitrust laws." In June 1980, a district court awarded MCI $1.8 billion. AT&T appealed this ruling, and in May 1985 a verdict of $37.8 million in damages was returned and automatically trebled to $113.4 million.

In 1975, MCI began its "Execunet" service which allowed commercial customers to dial (at a substantial discount from AT&T rates) any number in a city served by MCI. With Execunet MCI was able to compete not only in a specialized segment of telecommunications—the private-line market[1]—but in the entire market for long-distance services. Thereafter, the company's sales and its ability to raise money and finance the expansion of its network increased sharply. The company's first profit was in 1977, and revenues increased steadily through 1985 (see Exhibit 1). Referring to the company's history, Mr. Mc-Gowan commented:

> MCI's history has encompassed four different "businesses." First, we had to learn the venture capital business. As a fledgling, capital-starved company in a capital-intensive industry, we had to raise enough money to convince the regulatory community that we really could construct and operate a long-distance network.
>
> Later, we moved into a second business: lobbying. Our industry was heavily regulated by the FCC, subject to congressional oversight, and dominated by AT&T, then a monopoly with enormous clout in Washington. To gain even a modest foothold in the market, we had to become as much a lobbying firm as we were a communications firm.
>
> Our next business was raising the money necessary to *build* a communications system. We were fortunate. We were able to raise $100 million without having generated one penny of revenue. At the time, this represented the largest start-up financing in Wall Street history.
>
> Our fourth business was litigation. We challenged AT&T in court with such fervor that someone once described MCI as "a law firm with an antenna on top."
>
> Some may argue that MCI wasn't *really* in all these other businesses along the way. I disagree. They engaged the primary energies of our senior managers; consumed a large chunk of our human and financial resources; and were the principal focus of our efforts each day.

---

[1]A private line linked two points and was leased by a customer from a telephone company. The line was specifically for that customer's use and was always available for the sole use of the leasing customer.

It was only in the 1980s that MCI was able to focus on its original mission. By then marketplace and technological changes had transformed the industry. Today, we answer the question "What business are we in?" by saying, "We are an integral part of the information technologies business. We help our customers make the most of these technologies."

Growth and Evolving Marketing Programs

MCI's marketing programs responded to changing regulatory and competitive constraints and opportunities. During the 1970s, moreover, these programs were developed within the context of a highly leveraged, cash-constrained company fighting for survival. Mr. Carl Vorder Bruegge joined MCI in 1972 after 15 years in sales management with IBM. He recalled that, when he joined MCI,

> . . . there were six people in the company, and we had not yet firmly focused our business. In fact, there was a strong feeling at the time that data, rather than voice communications, was the direction to head in. However, our debts and the money necessary to build towers and establish service indicated that, whatever we did, we had better generate revenues quickly.

McGowan and Vorder Bruegge focused on the top 75 users of private-line services in the United States. Their reasoning was that these users (and, in particular, financial managers at these companies) would most appreciate the cost differentials between MCI and AT&T, and thus be willing to work with a new type of phone service. "Our message," said Mr. Vorder Bruegge, "was basically, 'try us for 90 days and see what you save.' We wanted to get our feet in the door, and establish ourselves as an alternative to AT&T for large-volume users of long-distance services." The marketing program for private-line service kept MCI afloat during the 1970s. Mr. Vorder Bruegge noted, however, that "it was the recession of 1973–1974 that really started to turn things around for us. Companies were motivated to reduce costs; they began to look at items such as phone bills, and began calling us for long-distance service."

With the introduction of Execunet in 1975, MCI changed its sales strategy from one that emphasized large accounts to an organization focused on commissions and prospecting. Mr. Vorder Bruegge explained that,

> We hired 500 salespeople to sell Execunet on straight commission. The salespeople received one day of training, worked through telephones in a boiler-room atmosphere, and had a total corporate target of 500 sales per week. This sales organization generated revenue and thus allowed us to survive and expand the network. But we paid a price in terms of our image and reputation in the marketplace: under the straight-commission framework, some salespeople stole each other's leads and sometimes a half-dozen or more different MCI people were calling on the same company, and cancellations were high. Our cash needs, however, compelled us to work with this arrangement until November of 1976 when a court order halted Execunet service for 18 months.

The moratorium on Execunet sales was caused by an AT&T appeal, upheld by the FCC, that Execunet was illegal competition in the long-distance market. Execunet service was halted while MCI won a court reversal of the FCC decision. During the moratorium, MCI expanded its network and revised its sales force. According to Mr. Vorder Bruegge,

> We spent that time developing a more professional, salaried sales force with more extensive training and better promotional literature. We also restricted sales representatives to certain regions in order to avoid the problem of salespeople poaching each other's leads.

When Execunet service resumed in 1978, MCI had approximately 300 sales representatives, and the target for each was 25 sales per month.

In 1980, MCI began advertising to residential customers. Mr. Vorder Bruegge recalled:

> I was skeptical about selling our service to residential customers. The ad agency itself predicted we would generate about 20 sales per day. We were both wrong: almost from the start, we garnered about 200 sales per day through the advertising. After a few months, we cut our sales force from 300 to approximately 100 people and emphasized selling over the phone rather than through personal calls.

Throughout the early 1980s, MCI focused on residential customers in major cities on its network. Management considered its marketing to be a combination of "push" and "pull." The "pull" consisted of TV and print ads complemented by direct-mail. The ads compared MCI and AT&T prices in order to appeal to price sensitive heavy and medium users of long-distance services (see Exhibit 2). Potential customers were urged to call an 800 number to learn more about MCI's services. The "push" consisted of telemarketing to support MCI's advertising efforts.

MCI spent $15 million in media advertising in 1981, $25 million in 1982, $31 million in 1983, $70 million in 1984, and more than $80 million in 1985. By 1984, MCI's ads had begun to stress that the company was a large established corporation, rather than simply a provider of discount long-distance service. Management felt it was important to emphasize the credibility of the company as a whole in addition to its discount pricing.

MCI also conducted extensive promotional campaigns that were new to the telecommunications industry when MCI pioneered them. But, by 1986, these marketing programs had been imitated by most long-distance providers.

Customer Base and Services Offered

Business accounts had once represented MCI's total customer base. With residential service growth rates that approached 10,000 new customers weekly during the early 1980s, the customer mix changed. The following chart shows the number of MCI subscribers from 1981 through 1985:

	3/81	3/82	12/83	12/84	12/85
Commercial subscribers	95,000	176,000	315,000	363,000	608,000
Residential subscribers	225,000	558,000	1,238,000	1,810,000	2,879,000

Source: MCI Annual Reports.

MCI's principal service, its long-distance telephone services, permitted subscribers to make interstate calls anywhere in the United States. MCI also offered intrastate service in several states. By 1985, MCI was the second-largest provider of long-distance services with an estimated market share of 5%.

MCI's services were used by customers primarily for voice communications but could also be used to transmit data, facsimile, teleprinter, and other signals. *Dial Up Service* billed customers on the basis of the distance and duration of the call. A subscriber accessed this service from a push-button phone by first calling a 7-digit access number, a 5-digit code unique to each subscriber, and then the desired area code and telephone number. *Dial 1 Service* did not require inputting the access number and authorization code. Following the antitrust agreement between AT&T and the U.S. Justice Department in 1982 (see below), Dial 1 Service had expanded significantly.

Other long-distance services included *MCI WATS*, which provided a dedicated access line between the customer and MCI's nearest operations center and was used primarily by commercial customers with a large volume of communications. *Private Line Service* could be configured in a variety of ways to meet particular requirements and was billed at a flat monthly rate based on distance without regard to the extent of usage. In 1985, MCI had several hundred private-line accounts generating more than $150 million in revenues.

MCI International was begun in 1982 with the acquisition of Western Union International (WUI), one of the five largest data-transmitting firms, from Xerox. This acquisition provided MCI with access to 200 countries. The international market was the fastest growing segment of telecommunications (about 20% annually), with an estimated $4 billion in voice traffic from the United States to other countries by 1984.

In 1983, MCI introduced an electronic mail service known as *MCI Mail*, which permitted subscribers to send messages or documents instantly from a properly equipped terminal (e.g., computer, word processor, or telex machine) to the terminals of other subscribers. MCI Mail was later expanded to include international transmission capabilities. In 1985, there were approximately 75,000 subscribers to MCI Mail, generating more than $15 million in annual revenues.

Network Expansion

Historically, MCI had first leased facilities from AT&T, built volume, and after establishing a customer and revenue base in a region, had then installed its own microwave facilities. By 1981, MCI had established a coast-to-coast network. From 1981 to 1985, MCI invested nearly $4 billion in expanding and upgrading its network and planned to spend about $1 billion more during 1986. These investments, through the installation of digital technology, also allowed for more reliable data transmissions over the network. In 1986, in a comparison of six leading long-distance carriers, *Data Communications* magazine concluded that "on the whole, MCI's data transmission performance was the best," offering the lowest error rate on average of the companies tested.

MCI's biggest investments were in fiber optics, which transmitted voice or data via pulses of light generated along tiny strands of glass by lasers. Many observers believed fiber optics would replace other technologies in long-distance applications: fiber optics were almost unlimited in terms of potential capacity; there was no interference as could occur in traditional systems; and the fiber could handle both voice and data transmissions efficiently. Although the fiber material was significantly more expensive than copper cable, its capacity potential made fiber less expensive than cable at sufficiently high levels of utilization.

MCI did not invest in R&D to upgrade its network. Instead, it purchased the latest technology from what it considered to be the best sources, using several vendors to supply each line of equipment. "We are unique because we are not locked into our technology," one manager explained. "We have access to the best technology as soon as it's available, not as soon as we can develop it."

SBS Acquisition

Satellite Business Systems (SBS) was initially a joint venture among IBM, Comsat, and Aetna Life Insurance. By the early 1980s, IBM was the major owner of SBS and had invested significant amounts in the operation, which used satellites to provide voice and data transmission capabilities primarily for large-volume business customers.

In March 1985, MCI acquired SBS in exchange for 47 million shares of common stock, which gave IBM a 16.6% interest in MCI. In addition, IBM agreed to purchase about $400 million in MCI securities between September 1, 1986, and December 31, 1988. Mr. McGowan noted that, "with this money, MCI's ability to continue funding its capital needs remains strong. SBS also brings several major strengths to MCI, including approximately 200,000 customers, over $400 million in annual revenues, and experience in successfully marketing to large business accounts for major portions of their network needs." Throughout 1985, MCI awaited regulatory approval of the SBS acquisition (which was granted in February 1986), and also began integrating SBS's leased and private line traffic with MCI circuits.

As part of the acquisition, IBM also agreed to limit its interest in MCI to 30%, unless otherwise approved by MCI. In the 1985 Annual Report, Mr. McGowan commented:

> The convergence of telecommunications and computers is creating a competitive weapon that businesses will use to change the way they operate. . . . Forward-

looking companies already are starting to combine the planning and procurement of information technologies. This is an indication of where our relationship with IBM will manifest itself; at our customers' requests, we will be able to provide a total integrated communications solution, capitalizing on IBM's capabilities in data processing and office automation systems, and MCI's capabilities in long-distance digital transmission.

Market and Competitive Developments

In January 1982, AT&T agreed to divest its local Bell operating companies (BOCs) in exchange for the right to compete in all information-service markets. The former BOCs became independent regional telephone companies, which also had the right to compete in deregulated businesses. This agreement, implemented in January 1984, ended a seven-year antitrust suit against AT&T by the U.S. Justice Department and had important implications for the industry.

Post-Settlement Pricing. After the settlement, AT&T lowered its long-distance rates repeatedly. In response, MCI reduced its rates and eliminated both subscription fees and monthly charges for its service. MCI also introduced volume discounts for some of its services, effectively lowering prices for customers who placed more calls over MCI's network.

A comparison of WATS charges for major competitors in the U. S. long-distance market is shown in Exhibit 3. By the spring of 1986, MCI had lowered its rates an average of 22% since January 1, 1984, when the Bell System was broken up. Throughout that time, MCI kept its rates below AT&T's, but the difference had narrowed. By 1986, MCI's rates represented average discounts of 5–10% below AT&T rates, compared with rates 25–50% below AT&T before the settlement.

In 1985, moreover, AT&T began changing the pricing of its private-line services for large business customers. Before the settlement, AT&T had kept its fees for private-line installations low, while charging high monthly rates on the actual service. After the settlement, AT&T lost many private-line customers to other carriers who offered lower rates. In 1985, AT&T lowered its private-line monthly rates while increasing its installation fees from an average of $156 per line to $748. Private-line charges for the three largest carriers are indicated in Exhibit 3.

Before the settlement, a number of small companies entered the long-distance business by reselling circuits purchased from larger long-distance companies at a discount. Price competition forced many of these vendors out of the business. At the same time, larger companies announced merger and acquisition plans. In January 1986, for example, Sprint and U.S. Telecom, the long-distance units of GTE Corporation and United Telecommunications, Inc., merged. One observer, commenting on the long-distance industry in early 1986, predicted that "by the 1990s, we'll have only three or four very big companies competing with AT&T."

Access Charges. For MCI and other long-distance carriers, the AT&T settlement also meant significant increases in the "access charges" they paid to BOCs for connecting their long-distance networks to the local exchange systems. Before the settlement, SCCs had paid approximately 35% of the per-minute charge paid by AT&T. The assumption was that SCCs did not receive the same quality of connections as that provided to AT&T, since their customers had to input additional digits. The settlement stipulated that, as the revenues of long-distance carriers grew, so would the access charges paid by these firms to the independent BOCs. For "Dial 1" service, moreover, the access charges were equivalent to those paid by AT&T.

MCI's interconnection costs increased from $143 million in 1982 to $874 million in 1985. As a percentage of revenues this represented an increase from 15.8% in 1982 to 34.4% in 1985. Management expected access charges to increase further as MCI expanded its network for intrastate calls to complement its interstate, long-distance business: in many states, intrastate charges exceeded interstate access charges.

Along with increased price competition, higher access charges meant margin pressures for MCI and other long-distance carriers. As a result, MCI's stock, which reached a peak in 1983 of $28.50, was trading below $10 for most of 1986.

Equal Access. The AT&T settlement also represented a unique opportunity for MCI. Under the agreement, residential customers could choose which long-distance firm would be their preferred vendor; this firm's network would be accessible by simply dialing "1" on the telephone. So-called Dial 1 service (also referred to as "equal access") was implemented on a region-by-region basis throughout 1984–1986.

Equal access meant that millions of residential customers, most of whom had been using AT&T's long-distance service, were accessible to MCI and other carriers. Carriers concentrated promotions, contests, public relations events and extensive advertising on a given area as residents began the process of choosing a long-distance carrier. During 1985, it was estimated, AT&T spent over $170 million, GTE $60.5 million, and MCI over $30 million on television advertising alone. Mr. McGowan noted that, "The equal access fight is an historic one-time opportunity to gain substantial market share. We're aiming for a 10–15% share of the long-distance market by the end of 1986 and will focus most of our resources on that goal."

Current Organization and Marketing Programs

In 1986, MCI had three major operating units: MCI Telecommunications (long-distance telephone services), MCI Digital Information Services (which marketed MCI Mail and other data services), and MCI International (voice and data services worldwide). Each unit reported to Mr. Bert Roberts, president of MCI who, in turn, reported to Mr. McGowan (see Exhibit 4).

MCI Telecommunications was the largest business unit, accounting for over 90% of MCI's total revenues in 1985. Prior to the AT&T settlement, MCI's domestic long-distance business had been organized functionally with most marketing activities either performed or coordinated by a corporate organization. In January 1985, however, MCI was reorganized into 7 geographic divisions, which coincided geographically with the boundaries of the 7 regional telephone companies. Each was headed by a president who had profit-and-loss responsibility for that division and a separate sales, operations, and service organization. One executive explained:

> As MCI grew, it became harder to make daily operating decisions efficiently. Also, the seven BOCs became independent companies, each organized and operated differently. To succeed in the equal-access battles, we had to establish local relationships and work effectively with each.
>
> There was also some feeling in the chairman's office that our success ran the risk of making the organization less lean and agile than it had been. Divisionalization could allow MCI to work closer with the former BOCs, individual state legislatures, and customers during equal-access battles. Giving each division *absolute* P&L authority could also help to maintain our entrepreneurial spirit.

Field Sales Organization

Each division organized its selling efforts differently, but in all divisions, the sales force was composed of field sales reps who reported within the division and account managers and support staff who were part of MCI's National Accounts Program (NAP). In all divisions, sales reps sold the same products and services.

The New England region of the Northeast Division was representative of the kinds of selling efforts undertaken in all divisions. The region had four groups of sales people. (1) Telemarketing reps sold to small companies and individuals who billed up to $1,500/month in long-distance calls. (2) Equal Access reps worked primarily as an outside sales force, targeting companies that required three or more lines (monthly long-distance revenues of $500+). This group sold only Dial 1 service. (3) Full-Line sales reps sold long-distance and more advanced products to companies that generated at least $1,500/month in long-distance bills. (4) Some Full Line reps were further divided into a Major Accounts group, which sold to regional companies that generated between $500,000 and $1 million of annual revenues with MCI. The regional director of sales and marketing explained that:

> Major Account reps maintain and build their accounts, and do little prospecting. They have 25 accounts each, primarily large, single-location regional accounts such as universities or banks. These accounts do not generate sufficient

revenues to qualify as a "national account," and generally do not have locations outside New England. Some have branch offices outside this region, and those branches are serviced by other MCI divisions. But important decisions about the account are made in this region.

Major account reps sell mostly WATS and private-line services. Some of these accounts are potential customers for a network service, but most are not large enough or dispersed enough. There are also 13 NAP accounts in our region, but that is a separate sales organization.

All categories of field sales reps were compensated through a combination of base salary and commission in roughly 50:50 proportions. Commissions were based on the number of telephone lines sold. Telemarketing and Equal Access reps also received a percentage of the customer's first full month's usage revenues as commission. Full-Line and Major Account reps received commissions both for the number of lines installed at an account, and for the number of hours the line was used during the first full month of that account's usage. Lines in use under 25 hours/month paid $20 in commission, 25–40 hours about $65, 40–50 hours $85, and up to 200 hours $145 in commission per line. Major Account reps also received bonuses based on maintenance and service of their accounts, protecting an account from competitive inroads, and other specific goals established by the regional director of sales.

One regional sales manager noted:

> About 50% of our sales people have moved up through the organization. We aim to "trade-up" the skills in our sales force, moving a person over time from Telemarketing to Equal Access to Full-Line and/or Major Account sales rep.
>
> For Full-Line reps, at least two years of experience are necessary, and we prefer people who can close a sale daily or every other day. Our successful sales people have tended to come from backgrounds where they sold copiers, facsimile equipment, or business forms. We haven't had much luck with those who sold telecommunications equipment before joining us; they tend to be used to a much longer selling cycle and a different set of selling requirements.

National Accounts

A key account program was officially established at MCI in September 1984 with the title, "National Account Service Program" (NASP). Its aim was to provide, through NAP reps in each division, coordinated selling efforts to the largest users of telecommunications services. One study estimated that 1% of long-distance customers accounted for 40% of all long-distance revenues and 2% accounted for 60% of total revenues. In 1985, the *Fortune* 500 alone represented an $8 billion market of which AT&T controlled an estimated 95%. One observer noted that "AT&T is more dominant in corporate telecommunications than IBM is in corporate mainframes."

Large corporate customers were important for other reasons as well: they were typically located in major urban areas (where MCI had circuits and newer fiber optic capacity), and their traffic ran primarily during business hours (when rates were highest). Mr. William Conway, Jr., MCI's chief financial officer, noted that "we are counting on national accounts to fuel our growth after 1986." In early 1986 MCI switched advertising agencies and focused its ad campaign on large business customers (see Exhibit 5).

NASP was initially headed by Mr. Vorder Bruegge, who focused the group on providing the divisions with support in servicing 65 high-potential accounts. Mr. Vorder Bruegge noted:

> MCI has always sold to big corporations, but the emphasis was on discount long-distance and private-line services. Beginning in 1984, our aim was different. We recognized that MCI's level and depth of penetration in these influential corporations was relatively small: when you're the discount long-distance firm, you represent no switching costs or real commitment for these companies. At the same time, our capital investments were yielding an upgraded network, advanced technology products, and excellent network management capabilities. To capitalize on our investments, we needed a strengthened key-account emphasis.
>
> My job was to develop criteria for selecting accounts, develop our marketing thrust, and start hiring and training good people. At the same time, Bill McGowan emphasized that the divisional presidents were to run their own shows. So each division developed its own emphasis and approach to managing national accounts in its area, while NASP played an advisory role. At corporate headquarters, we viewed this as a learning process for the company. Perhaps NASP's biggest immediate contribution in 1985 was a training program for national account managers in each area. The divisions loved the training program, until they were charged for it.

In its first year, NASP accounts generated about $12 million in monthly recurring revenues (i.e., as opposed to one-time charges or sales). During 1985, NASP was expanded to reach 200 accounts, and 200 additional people became part of the program. Mr. Vorder Bruegge noted that, "while NASP had to approve all senior account manager hires, the divisions did the hiring and structured incentives for national account people as they wished." During 1985, moreover, NASP drafted a letter to be sent by account managers in each region to key accounts introducing the program and its objectives (see Exhibit 6).

National Accounts Program

In January 1986 Mr. Vorder Bruegge became senior vice president, Sales and Marketing (the position he had held before running NASP), and Jonathan Crane became vice president, National Accounts (the name was changed from "National Accounts Service Program" to "MCI National Accounts Program" shortly after Mr. Crane arrived). Mr. Crane had been the NASP vice president in the northeast region, and before that a national account director with Rolm Corporation for three years. Mr. Crane noted:

> When I arrived, NAP headquarters had six people, who helped to train account managers in each area and provided customer seminars and sales support mater-

ials. Carl said, "Your job is to build a National Accounts organization to market and support the full spectrum of MCI's services; establish account control at important customers; and increase account penetration and planning." In addition, NAP's mission is to increase revenues and profitability for the company.

By April, NAP headquarters had 70 people, 90% of them from SBS. We also reorganized and made changes in training and compensation.

Organization. By mid-1986 NAP was organized as indicated in Exhibit 7. Mr. Crane commented:

> We created three classic marketing organizations at NAP headquarters. Product management coordinates the introduction of new products and enhanced services and so strengthens our ability to be a full-spectrum provider to key accounts. MCI was traditionally a "piece-part" vendor, incapable of providing a total system; but the broadening of our product line enables us to provide a total network solution and work as a strategic partner with large customers. Market management is handled by the director of National Accounts; there, the job is to define customer needs by focusing on specific business segments. For example, MCI for years marketed successfully to financial services companies; we plan to analyze why we've been successful with that segment and disseminate that knowledge to our sales force. Marketing Services' functions include training required to sell and support our product line, internal promotions, sales support, and customer education.
>
> With this organization, we can provide the divisions with current information about industry trends, product developments by competitors, traffic analyses at key customers. This data, essential for packaging our products into a competitive bid for large network business, can help the divisions plan their strategies with national accounts.

Training. Where the NASP training program had concentrated on generic selling skills, Mr. Crane added a heavy emphasis on product knowledge. Carl Thomsen, director of Marketing Support, commented:

> Selling sophisticated telecommunications products requires an account team to make an array of complex business judgments that, in turn, require in-depth knowledge of the products and services, their potential applications, and the fit with an account's business needs. A focus on industrywide applications is useful here, because within an industry telecommunications applications are often similar.
>
> Initially, however, our salespeople were weak in diagnosing and selling solutions. They were still oriented to selling on price. So our training focuses on selling solutions, because eventually our cost structure will not be far below AT&T's costs of providing basic services.

Compensation. Before 1986, compensation of NAP salespeople, who reported through the divisions, was established by each division. Thus, the compensation plans differed significantly and, in most divisions, were heavily weighted toward short-term incentives based on revenue objectives.

In 1986, NAP salespeople continued to report through the divisions, but Messrs. Crane and Vorder Bruegge, with the cooperation of divisional NAP directors, established a uniform compensation plan for NAP personnel in each division. Under the plan, total compensation consisted of a base salary and incentive compensation as follows. Base salary (paid bi-weekly) comprised 80–85% of target total compensation. The "target" level was the amount paid if a NAP rep achieved all objectives, and it was set at or above the levels paid by competitors.

Incentive compensation, 15–20% of target total compensation, was paid for performance against specific, predefined objectives and had two components: 1) Revenue Incentives were tied to the maintenance and growth of assigned accounts and ranged from 25–60% of target total incentive, depending upon the nature of the position. Here, annual revenue goals for assigned accounts were established by the NAP directors in each division; these goals were based on prior-year data, NAP forecasts, and total account revenue potential in the judgment of both the NAP divisional director and the account team. The revenue incentive, if achieved, was paid quarterly. 2) Special Objectives Incentives were tied to actions that impacted customer satisfaction and so contributed to future revenue growth. Depending upon the position, this incentive ranged from 40–75% of target total incentive. Each NAP team member was assigned 4–6 special objectives which were weighted in terms of their importance as defined by the NAP team and the NAP divisional director. At the end of each quarter, the NAP director determined the level of performance achieved against each objective. These objectives included activities such as account planning, account penetration at executive levels, and sales of advanced products such as digital data services.

In 1986, the average age of NAP reps was about 33 years. Total compensation averaged about $75,000, with a low of $50,000 and a high of $90,000. Commenting on the new compensation plan, Mr. Crane noted that "there is less leverage to the incentive portion than in the past, and we've structured the revenue incentive so that it rewards for a long sales cycle and team effort. But there are also no automatic caps on each person's revenue incentive, so the better a person's performance in relation to a revenue goal, the more that person can earn."

Account Teams. MCI's national account teams typically had 3–10 members depending upon the account's revenue production; in general, there was one salesperson per $3 million in account revenue and one support person per $1.5 million in revenue. Sales revenues generated by national accounts were apportioned on the following basis: revenues from customers with locations in several divisions were credited to the division in which that customer was headquartered. Thus, some divisions were net importers of revenues (serving customers' headquarters locations), and some were net exporters (incurring expenses for supporting remote sites of national accounts headquartered in other divisions).

The account team was led by a National Account Manager (NAM), who was usually responsible for three national accounts. The NAM reported to a director of National Accounts in the division, who in turn reported to the division president and, on a dotted-line basis, to Mr. Crane's NAP headquarters organization. (In each division, there was also a director or vice president of sales who reported directly to the division president.)

Reporting to the NAM were 1) *account executive(s)* responsible for primary client contact, selling the appropriate spectrum of MCI services to the account and its subsidiaries, identifying account training needs, and general "troubleshooting" for the account; 2) *support personnel* handled installation, scheduling, billing, traffic reports, and coordination among services provided to the account; 3) *technical consultants* had expertise in areas such as digital switches, data communications, transmission alternatives, and customization of engineering plans with a given account.

In general, each team managed one or more accounts headquartered in its region as well as the remote sites in that region of accounts headquartered in different regions. Each of the 200 national accounts was assigned to a given NAM who determined strategy for that account, including sites located in a different region. Mr. Crane noted:

> Before NAP, the divisional vice presidents of sales had essentially sold to both large and small companies in the same way. The NAM's job was to acquire new customers, primarily through cold calls. And since there was not clear account responsibility, a number of MCI sales reps often called on the same headquarters accounts, stepping on each other's toes and sometimes delivering inconsistent messages to big accounts.
>
> In addition, the program was administered differently in each division, depending upon the division president's level of commitment and quarterly P&L as well as the chemistry between the divisional sales vice president and director of national accounts. Assigned account teams help to avoid some of these problems and ensure more consistency and sophistication in our dealings with important customers.

Wednesday, July 23, 1986

Speaking in his office with the casewriter late on a Wednesday afternoon, Mr. Crane pointed to a pile of phone messages on his desk and commented that "these calls are a good illustration of where NAP stands at the present time." Picking one message from the pile, he commented:

> This is a call from the telecom manager at a leading brokerage firm which is one of our national accounts. I helped to bring this account on board when I was in the Northeast region, and we've stayed in touch since then.
>
> On Monday he called me to say he couldn't get our divisional operations people to help with an important line-testing over the weekend. "I don't believe what I'm hearing," he told me. "I told the operations manager who I was, and she said, 'we've got thousands of customers and we treat them with equal care and attention. You'll have to wait until an engineer is available early in the

week.'" Of course, that's not just any customer. I think I've got this straightened out by now; but this sort of thing happens more often than I'd like.

Picking a different message from the pile, Mr. Crane explained:

This is one I've been going around with for almost a week now. One of our highest potential accounts is Zembla Corporation (a large, diversified *Fortune* 20 corporation). We now do about $3 million worth of business annually with them, and that's increased significantly over the past year; but it's still peanuts compared to the potential.

An important part of Zembla's telecommunications strategy is their private network, which they've built at great expense over the past decade. Much of their network traffic is data transmission, which requires a high degree of transmission reliability. We've been handling transmissions for larger chunks of their network in the past year.

Last week, their Information Systems czar called me to complain about our salespeople in two regions: those salespeople were trying to sell MCI's discount WATS service at two different divisions of Zembla, and they were succeeding. He wanted me to know this kind of sales effort was completely counter to his corporation's telecom strategy, which required high utilization of the private network for voice and data in order to operate efficiently. Attempts to sell some of his people off the private network cause a lot of internal friction in his organization. And in ours, too!

Lifting a third message, Mr. Crane noted:

This is from one of our divisional presidents, confirming our meeting in his office this Friday at 10 A.M. He called Monday to set up the meeting. "Every day now," he said, "I'm getting requests from the NAP director in this division for more money and more experienced salespeople to be allocated to NAP efforts in our division. I'd have to take that money and those people from the division's sales efforts; my vice president of sales is not happy about that, and I'm not convinced NAP gives me a better return on my selling expenses than he does. More importantly, I don't have the time to smooth all these ruffled feathers while I'm trying to fight the equal-access war in my division and improve my P&L. We've got some talking to do."

Settling back in his chair, Mr. Crane reflected on the past six months:

Considering that the company's been focused on equal-access marketing to residential and small-business customers, we've made good progress with NAP so far this year. But there are still many unresolved issues.

Each division president runs a $300–$800 million business, and those individuals are veterans of MCI's fights for survival. They're capable, competitive, and depending upon the region, more or less interested in national accounts. The precise relationship between NAP, each division, and the national account customer is still being clarified.

Another related issue is the appropriate focus for NAP's efforts. For example, should we aim for, say, 80% of the business at 50 key accounts, or a much smaller percentage at 200 accounts? When you're handling only a small percentage of a large company's telecom traffic, you're about as important as the envelope supplier. But when you're handling a large percentage, the customer's switching costs increase, and given good service, price sensitivity decreases. Also, from MCI's point of view, large accounts demand about the same expenses and overhead whether you're handling 10% or 80% of their traffic. Some here have argued for focusing NAP more selectively on fewer than 200 accounts. However, I believe the divisions won't support a program like this unless it has a broad reach that can make an impact on their revenue targets.

Finally, while we've made good progress, there's still a turf-fight going on: the divisional salesperson complains that "I sold 600 WATS lines last month and the NAP team sold three, but they seem to get the resources and the glory." The response in each division varies. Carl Vorder Bruegge believes that, sooner or later, we must develop a truly corporate national account program, rather than a series of divisional efforts; but that's not an easy decision to implement. One of my previous employers, for example, ran a completely separate and autonomous key-account program, and relations with the product divisions were terrible and counterproductive. I don't want to see that happen at MCI.

Standing up from his desk, Mr. Crane noted that he had to return phone calls and still had some work to do in preparation for Friday's review with MCI's senior management.

Exhibit 1   MCI Communication Corporation: National Accounts Program

Statement of Operations
(in thousands, except per share amounts)

Year Ended December 31,	1985	1984	1983
Revenue			
Sales of communications services	$2,542,271	$1,959,291	$1,521,468
Operating Expenses			
Local interconnection	873,979	479,658	262,012
Facilities leased from other common carriers	280,474	343,257	273,663
System, marketing, administrative and other	834,580	696,324	487,254
Depreciation	347,151	264,573	158,959
	$2,336,184	$1,783,812	$1,181,888
Income from Operations	$ 206,087	$ 175,479	$ 339,572
Interest (expense)	(201,083)	(188,545)	(134,277)
Interest income	85,546	114,644	76,708
Provision for decline in value of communications equipment	(153,750)	(48,800)	
Portion of antitrust settlements, net	206,626		
Gain on sale of land	18,213		
Other (expense) income, net	6,317	(1,244)	365
Income Before Income Taxes and Extraordinary Income	$ 167,956	$ 50,534	$ 282,368
Income tax provision (benefit)	28,345	(8,669)	79,456
Income before Extraordinary Item	$ 139,611	$ 59,203	$ 202,912
Extraordinary loss on early debt retirements, less applicable income taxes ($26,653)	26,314		
Net Income	$ 113,297	$ 59,203	$ 202,912
Earnings per Common Share			
Primary:			
Income before extraordinary item	$.59	$.25	$.89
Net income	$.48	$.25	$.89
Assuming full dilution:			
Income before extraordinary item	$.59	$.25	$.88
Net income	$.48	$.25	$.88

(continued)

Exhibit 1 (continued)

Balance Sheet
(in thousands)

December 31,	1985	1984
Assets		
Current assets:		
Cash and short-term investments	$ 852,841	$ 865,140
Receivables, net of allowance for uncollectibles of $43,687 and $46,887	422,304	305,190
Other	87,256	63,084
Total current assets	$1,362,401	$1,233,414
Communications system:		
System in service	3,220,623	2,259,019
Other property and equipment	651,196	515,877
	$3,871,819	$2,774,896
Accumulated depreciation	(1,119,048)	(656,138)
Construction in progress	291,931	495,400
Total communications system, net	$3,044,702	$2,614,158
Other assets and deferred charges	102,584	46,246
Total Assets	$4,509,687	$3,893,818
Liabilities and Stockholders' Equity		
Current liabilities:		
Accounts payable and accrued liabilities	$ 766,343	$ 500,713
Accrued interest payable	66,851	66,432
Accrued income taxes	18,367	12,940
Long-term debt due within one year	456,230	60,901
Total current liabilities	$1,307,791	$ 640,986
Deferred Income Taxes and Other	188,035	232,573
Long-term Debt	1,695,853	1,821,138
Stockholders' Equity:		
Preferred stock, 20,000,000 shares authorized, none issued		
Common stock, $.10 par value, authorized 400,000,000 shares, issued 235,628,757 and 234,686,378 shares	23,563	23,469
Capital in excess of par value	795,494	789,998
Retained earnings	498,951	385,654
Total stockholders' equity	$1,318,008	$1,199,121
Total liabilities and stockholders' equity	$4,509,687	$3,893,818

Exhibit 2   MCI Communications Corporation: National Accounts Program

Print Advertising in 1984

Savings were enough to convince nearly 2,000,000 people to use MCI.

This should convince the rest of you.

Introducing MCI DIAL"1" Service. Now MCI will be as easy to use as AT&T. And you save on your long distance calls.

Across the country, nearly 2,000,000 people are using MCI for their long distance calls.

These people are enjoying savings of up to 20, 30, even 40% on all their long distance calls.

The savings total hundreds of millions

LONG DISTANCE CALLS	MINS	AT&T	MCI	SAV- INGS
Indianapolis to Fresno*	1	$ .38	$ .19	50.0%
Indianapolis to Dallas**	2	1.05	.75	28.6%
Indianapolis to Chicago***	16	2.57	2.11	17.9%
Indianapolis to Lexington, KY**	6	2.53	2.05	19.0%
Indianapolis to Garden City, NY***	4	.76	.58	23.7%
Indianapolis to Daytona Beach*	11	2.95	2.05	30.5%

Illustrative rates as of May 24, 1984. Final rate authorities on all tariffed services are MCI Tariff FCC #1 and AT&T Tariff FCC #263. Both AT&T and MCI's rates are being changed. Rates for MCI are for interstate calls on MCI's own network. Rates are subject to change in accordance with FCC rules and regulations and are subject to excise tax.
*Evening rate. **Weekday rate. ***Night and Weekend rate.

of dollars.

And now Indiana Bell is making it easier than ever for many Indianapolis homes and businesses to use MCI.

No extra numbers to dial.

You dial every number exactly the way you have been dialing.

You simply dial 1, the area code and number. The same eleven numbers you've always dialed.

It's as simple as that.

But the big difference is that once you've signed up for MCI DIAL "1" Service, you'll start enjoying MCI's low long distance rates. **Use any phone, rotary or push-button.**

You use the same phone you're already using. It doesn't matter whether it's push-button or rotary.

Mickey Mouse or antique.

You don't need any special equipment or rewiring. In fact, nobody will even come to your home or business. Once you sign up for MCI DIAL "1" Service, you'll automatically be connected to MCI.

No monthly fees.

Your local phone company and MCI have made it possible for you to take advantage of MCI savings.

There's absolutely no monthly fee for MCI DIAL "1" Service. All you pay is the low, low cost of your long distance calls.

No installation charge. No surcharge. No nothing. So you start saving from your very first MCI DIAL "1" Service call.

Get MCI savings.

A quick look at our chart will show you how much people have been saving with MCI on their long distance calls.

Now with MCI DIAL "1" Service you can save money without doing anything differently. You use the same phone to make the same calls to the same places you're already calling. You save on your long distance calls to anywhere AT&T goes, coast to coast.

Use it to talk longer to friends or foes. Or use the money on life's necessities. If all you save is 50 cents a phone call, well, add it up. Isn't there something you can do with that money besides make AT&T happy?

Consider what it means to a business. It means profits. Your profits, not AT&T's. For years, companies looked at phone bills the way they looked at gas, electric or water bills. Namely, that they were utilities and every increase was unavoidable. Not anymore. You have a choice. A choice that's based on getting the same convenience that AT&T offers at a price that AT&T doesn't offer.

What's Burt Lancaster doing in this ad?

He's now appearing in MCI television commercials.

As a spokesman for this choice in long

Use any phone, rotary or push-button.

distance telephoning.

He's telling you about the benefits of free enterprise. The benefits that go to you who now have that great choice: whether to give AT&T your business and your money. Or to give MCI your business. And save some of your money.

How to sign up with MCI.

There's only one thing that can keep you from getting MCI savings.

Indecision.

Yet it should be a simple decision.

It doesn't cost anything to get the service. You dial the calls the same way you're already dialing. You use the same phone you're already using. And you save on your long distance calls anywhere that AT&T goes in the continental U.S.

If you can save on your calls without doing anything differently, why would you stay with AT&T?

Sign up directly with MCI and start saving right away by filling out the coupon below. Or call MCI today at 1-800-624-2222 while it's fresh in your mind, and find out more about how you can start saving up to 20, 30, even 40% on your long distance calls.

You have everything to gain. And nothing to lose.

MCI

DIAL "1" SERVICE
The nation's long distance phone company.

MCI Customer Service
101 W. Washington Street, Suite 1325
Indianapolis, IN 46204
1-800-624-2222

I'd like to sign up for MCI DIAL "1" Service
☐ For Business   ☐ For Home

Name_____

Address_____

City_____ State_____ Zip_____

Phone Number_____

Signature_____

1984 MCI Telecommunications Inc.

Exhibit 3   MCI Communications Corporation: National Accounts Program

The U. S. Long-Distance Industry[1]

Market Share
(by revenue, in percent)

	1984 [a]	1985 [a]	1986 [a]	1989 [a]
AT&T	69.3%	66.6%	62.8%	58.0%
MCI	2.8	4.7	6.6	10.3
GTE Sprint	1.9	1.9	2.8	5.6
Bell operating companies	16.9	17.8	16.9	16.9
Independent local telephone companies	6.3	6.2	6.3	6.4
Other long-distance companies	2.8	2.8	3.8	2.8
Total U.S. long-distance reveue (in billions of dollars)	$52.3	$57.6	$64.0	$78.0

WATS Rates [b] (cents per minute)

	1983	1984	1985
AT&T	33.4	31.4	29.6
MCI	29.8	30.2	30.2
GTE Sprint	30.2	32.8	31.1

Private Line Costs
(Monthly charge, New York to Los Angeles)

	1983	1984	1985
AT&T	$2,005	$2,005	$1,243
MCI	1,507	1,507	1,057
GTE Sprint	1,475	1,457	1,165

Number of Customers (1985)

	Business	Residential
AT&T	7 million	80 million
MCI	625,000	2.68 million
GTE Sprint	340,000	1.4 million
US Telecom	101,000	274,000

Call Minutes (1985)

AT&T	105 billion
MCI	11.75 billion
GTE Sprint	(Not available)
US Telecom	1.5 billion

(continued)

Exhibit 3 (continued)

Calling Cost
(A three-minute call from New York to Los
  Angeles during business hours)

	1983	1984	1985
AT&T	$1.72	$1.61	$1.49
MCI	1.30	1.41	1.36
GTE Sprint	1.30	1.31	1.39

Network Circuit Miles (1985)

AT&T	932 million[c]
MCI	320 million
GTE Sprint	170 million
US Telecom	48.6 million

Source: Wall Street Journal, February 24, 1986.

[1]MCI figures include Satellite Business Systems. GTE agreed to spin off its Sprint unit and merge the unit with US Telecom, pending regulatory approval.

[a]Estimated.

[b]Assumes average business use of 500 hours a month and national coverage.

[c]Estimated.

Exhibit 4 MCI Communications Corporation: National Accounts Program

MCI Communications Corporation

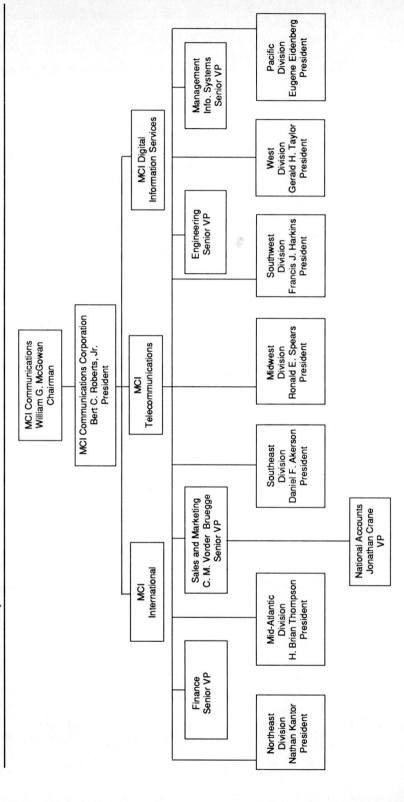

Exhibit 5 MCI Communications Corporation: National Accounts Program

Print Advertising in 1986

Foresight and Fiber Optics:

MCI® is committed to being first with the best.

Quality calling around the country or the world.

MCI pioneered the use of single-mode fiber optics considered today's standard for the clearest, cleanest connections. So, while others rush to build their fiber optic networks, MCI has fiber optics in place now.

MCI foresight doesn't end with hindsight. What have we done for you lately? This year alone, we'll add 90 million circuit miles of fiber optic capacity – enough for more than 180 round trips to the moon – to assure you of the most reliable transmission of your voice, data and video messages.

Anticipating your needs keeps us – and you – ahead. MCI invests a billion dollars a year in leading edge technology to give you innovative voice and data solutions. Like the unique MCI PRISM℠/ WATS family of products with international capabilities or MCI Mail.® Each brings flexibility that lets you control your communications – not the other way around.

Innovative engineering makes our network and your transmission superior.

MCI pioneered fiber optic technology now considered the industry standard.

Our commitment to your future. Thousands of MCI professionals use their special insight and creativity to make our products and network work harder for your business, anticipating your needs and developing the right solutions for you.

This competitive drive sets us apart. Because we compete, you win.

MCI

COMMUNICATIONS FOR THE NEXT 100 YEARS.℠

® MCI, the MCI logo, and MCI Mail are registered service marks of MCI Communications Corporation (MCIC).
℠ MCI PRISM and COMMUNICATIONS FOR THE NEXT 100 YEARS are service marks of MCIC. © MCIC. September 1986.

Exhibit 6   MCI Communications Corporation: National Accounts Program

Introductory Letter of NASP Program

Mr. Malcolm Murphy
Senior Vice President, Information Systems
Zembla Corporation
1492 15th Avenue
New York, NY

Dear Mr. Murphy:

In 1983, MCI invested $1,000,000,000 in new communications technology and increased capacity to meet the full spectrum of our customer's communication needs—voice, data, national, message, and personal communications device systems. In 1984 we invested another $1,000,000,000.

Now, we are delighted to tell you of our investment in a new National Account Service Program. This program is designed to serve you with professional support in utilizing what is generally recognized as "exploding" communications technology.

Highlights of the program include:

• commitment of a highly trained, professional sales team to work with your corporate staff in assuring availability of economic, efficient communications systems capacity for your nationwide needs.

• commitment of national account team members nationwide to assist your organization wherever and whenever the need arises.

• commitment of national account specialists in voice, data, international, message, and personal communication device systems to apply the full range of new technologies in assisting your efforts to improve your competitive position.

• commitment of MCI operations nationwide to provide a level of responsive service unequaled by any provided in our industry.

In order to inform you and your people of the details of MCI's full spectrum capability and of our new National Account Service Program, a one-day session is being scheduled in the near future.

I'll advise you of the time and place. I believe it will be an invaluable session for you and your key staff members.

Very truly yours,

Exhibit 7   MCI Communications Corporation: National Accounts Program

NAP Organization, 1986

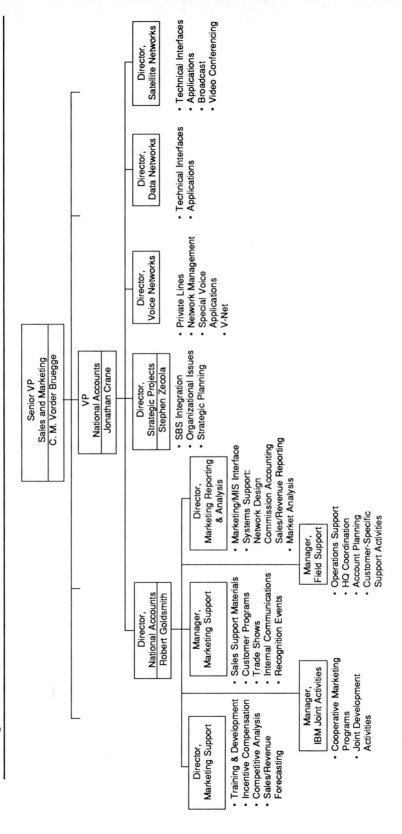

Case 16
MCI: Vnet (A)

In April 1987, Ms. Barbara Voigt, a National Accounts manager at MCI Pacific, was preparing a formal proposal for Mr. Brian Kelly, director of telecommunications at the Seaboard Insurance Company. The proposal was to sell to Seaboard MCI's new network product, Vnet. Mr. Kelly and several of his staff had recently attended a presentation of the product's capabilities at MCI, and he had requested a follow-up from Ms. Voigt.

Vnet had been introduced in September 1986. It was MCI's entry in a new category of network products which included AT&T's SDN and US Sprint's VPN, all introduced within the past year. These products shared the fundamental innovation that each reduced the customer's need for expensive equipment by using a sophisticated computer system to allocate the customer's traffic over the public carrier's lines; all the customer's traffic could be integrated in a single communications system without the customer owning or leasing expensive equipment on premises to handle the coordination. In addition, customers without existing networks could gain services previously unavailable to them.

Private Telecommunication Networks

In the 1950s, AT&T introduced a private-line service called Telpak which provided discounts to heavy users of long-distance transmissions. AT&T would provide a "trunk" (transmission cable) between two points for the exclusive use of a single institution. Price was based strictly on the length of the line, so the customer paid a flat rate each month, regardless of call volume. Private lines were typically leased between locations with very heavy telecommunications

---

This case was prepared by Research Associate Jon E. King, under the supervision of Associate Professor Frank V. Cespedes, as a basis for class discussion rather than to illustrate either effective or ineffective handling of an administrative situation.

Copyright © 1988 by the President and Fellows of Harvard College. Harvard Business School case 9-588-068.

traffic, since the flat fee made the costs very efficient: if the trunk was in constant use, the monthly charge was a fraction of the alternative per-minute pricing. However, customers soon needed communications engineers to optimize their systems: if a private line were overutilized, users would be annoyed by line noise or delayed by busy signals; if it were underutilized, the monthly charges might exceed the charge-per-minute alternatives.

As more locations in a given firm required interconnection, switching systems became necessary for integrating individual lines. Thus, private-line systems gradually became private-network systems. Customers were usually large institutions requiring extensive, continuous, and exclusive access to voice and/or data transmission facilities. The trend toward private networks increased in the 1960s and 1970s as more sophisticated switching hardware offered expanded network control capabilities such as automatic least-cost call routing and one-digit speed dialing for frequently used numbers. Network customers either purchased switching equipment or leased it from AT&T.

By the mid-1970s AT&T's private-line revenues were reportedly $1.2 billion annually, but for it and other long-distance companies, private-line services were not as profitable as standard switched services due to the heavy discounts involved. Private lines also required more expensive preventive maintenance by the vendor because if the line were to become inoperative, there was generally no back-up capacity for the customer; public-switched networks had enough capacity that they could easily compensate for a single line going down. In the 1970s, state utilities commissions also raised taxes on intrastate private lines, further depressing margins on private-line services.

In response, AT&T discontinued its Telpak pricing in 1981 and raised prices for private-line services. Consequently, many customers which had installed expensive switches for their private lines were actively looking for alternatives. Meanwhile, Satellite Business Systems and AT&T began offering integrated packages of lines and switches. These fixed-facility, private-network systems were sold at significantly higher rates than Telpak, even considering the inclusion of the switching hardware. One MCI manager noted, "AT&T wanted to own the customer's network business. By providing dedicated systems, they built up customers' aversion to risking everything on an untried competitor."

By 1984, AT&T's private-line/private-network annual revenues had reportedly grown to $2.4 billion, while the U. S. Bureau of Labor Statistics reported that interstate private-line charges had increased 68% from 1975 to 1985, with additional increases of 50% or more from 1985 to 1987.

Virtual Networks

In the mid-1980s, three long-distance companies announced the development of software-defined virtual networks. These virtual networks required no equipment leases or purchases by the customer because transmission and switching capacity was automatically partitioned from the vendor's public network. Rather than laying a physical trunk between two points (as with fixed networks), the carrier's computer system made transmission capacity available on demand. Exhibit 1 shows a simplified diagram of the hardware comprising and interacting with Vnet, not including the computer systems.

This type of a system required a carrier to establish a complex high-speed database. But since a carrier's public network was largely a fixed-cost system, more traffic over such a system would help to leverage the carrier's investment by utilizing existing capacity.

Beyond this basic similarity among the three virtual network offerings, there was significant divergence in design and strategy. Vnet, for example, utilized a centralized database system which stored all the customers' parameters in two computer banks, east and west. AT&T's SDN system included several separate databases, with each customer's data being stored on only one. In US Sprint's VPN architecture, every piece of data for every customer was stored in every switch. These and other design differences defined and limited the features which could be offered by each product. For instance, because of its centralized architecture, MCI offered customers immediate data updating, which US Sprint could not provide since there were too many databanks to revise in a short period of time.

One MCI manager involved in Vnet's development explained:

> Virtual networks can provide more flexibility and reliability than a fixed facility network. Private networks demand hardware; the owner must consider purchasing costs, obsolescence, demand fluctuation, operations, and maintenance. Staff requirements are extensive, and switching equipment requires space; if a building (or a subsidiary) housing the switches is sold, the entire network must be refit. Many corporations have certain branch offices too small or too remote to justify leasing cable for it; these remote locations would therefore not be integrated with the rest of the system and could only be reached through the public network. This becomes a serious concern as "intelligent" switches provide networks with advanced features that the remote sites cannot enjoy. Virtual networks can relieve these problems by eliminating hardware-oriented concerns and by integrating remote locations with the rest of the customer's system.

Each vendor also offered an array of customization options. Vendor engineers would work with the customer's telecommunications staff to design the system so that all locations were covered and desired services included. The net intended effect was to provide users with a service which duplicated or exceeded the sophistication of a fixed network, yet eliminated the operation's constraints.

An independent technical analyst reported on the value of virtual networks for various types of customers:

> For corporations without heavy, concentrated traffic, virtual network offerings are probably the only practical method of achieving a corporate network. Fixed facility overhead and fixed line rates just don't make sense for these customers.

Concentration is a big issue: if a customer's locations are dispersed, virtual networks are justifiable.

Corporations with significant evening and weekend traffic will generally justify more traditional fixed facilities; since demand will fluctuate less, capacity of private lines can be used very effectively. Conversely, customers with primarily business-hour traffic will more easily justify virtual networks, since they don't want to pay for round-the-clock availability when they're not using it.

Finally, single vendor responsibility for end-to-end network service is very desirable, since bookkeeping, service, and management are simplified for the customer; pinpointing the problem is the vendor's responsibility, not the customer's. This kind of arrangement is difficult to find in the post-divestiture environment.[1]

Prices and Services

MCI voluntarily followed AT&T's federally mandated practice of filing a public price schedule or "tariff" for each of its services. Tariffs were filed with the Federal Communications Commission and could only be changed with FCC approval. In the mid-1980s, tariffs for many products were lowered and refiled within a few months of the previous filing; this was true of virtual network services in 1986 and 1987. One reason was that the FCC limited AT&T profit levels, forcing prices down; another was the increase in industry competition. MCI often followed AT&T's format for its tariffs where applicable, so that competing services could be quickly compared by price. But one MCI manager noted, "This was only partially true of Vnet's tariff since it differed from AT&T's SDN product in many features, and also because MCI is determined to exhibit market leadership with this product. This is not a 'me-too' product, and we don't want to give any impression that it is."

Vnet was tariffed similarly to WATS-like[2] products in that calls were charged per-minute at five different rates, depending on the call's distance. These five bands, and the typical distribution of commercial long-distance calling in each band, were as follows:

---

[1] Single vendor responsibility meant having all telecommunications services provided by one firm; this was seen as an advantage by some analysts because it simplified interconnection and coordination. Others felt that using multiple vendors for different services was necessary in order to compile the exact set of services the customer desired. Some customers also valued having several vendors for the same reason many firms avoided single-sourcing an essential product: if one vendor failed, the customer would have a back-up, and each vendor might feel more pressure to perform better if there were an active competitor. Before its divestiture, AT&T had provided "end-to-end service" to its customers, including local calls.

[2] Dial 1 was basic, long-distance service available to commercial and residential customers; charges were per-minute and increased with the distance of the call. Wide-area telephone service (WATS) was similar to Dial 1 except that it was only for businesses, could be limited to a certain maximum distance, and had lower per-minute charges. There were many other services which were similar to WATS, referred to here as *WATS-like*.

Band	Distance (miles)	% of calls
1	0–292	41%
2	293–430	8%
3	431–925	21%
4	926–1990	16%
5	1991–3000	14%
		100%

Business hours	85%
Evenings	10%
Nights and weekends	5%
	100%

Intracompany, or "on-net" calling (the traffic that would be carried by a private network), typically accounted for 20% of a company's total telecom usage. For a company with a fixed network, off-net calls would be handled by a public commercial offering such as WATS or Dial 1. Virtual networks carried all calls on the vendor's public lines, and the product software merely billed the call differently if it terminated outside the customer's premises. Vnet ran approximately 20% lower than SDN for intracompany calls, and 8–12% less than SDN for off-net calls; the weighted average showed a 13% difference.

Per-minute rates for both Vnet and SDN increased as call mileage increased (see Exhibit 2). Per-minute rates also decreased as call duration increased. Assuming the typical mileage distribution above, average per-minute call costs were as follows:

Minutes	Vnet (MCI) On-Net/Off-Net	SDN (AT&T) On-Net/Off-Net
1	$0.1227/$0.1800	$0.2155/$0.2605
2	0.1186/ 0.1760	0.1679/ 0.2125
3	0.1173/ 0.1746	0.1520/ 0.1965
4	0.1166/ 0.1739	0.1440/ 0.1885

AT&T offered a 25% discount on calls outside business hours; MCI, 30%. MCI also offered a discount of up to 5% for high volume; AT&T had no volume discount. MCI charged a setup fee of $5,000 (which was waived until 9/87); AT&T's setup fee was $60,000, recently lowered from $105,000.[3] Special features were hard to compare without specific customer information, but MCI offered many that AT&T did not. Moreover, MCI sold most features as system-wide packages, while AT&T generally installed and charged for options individually at each customer location. Thus without knowing how many locations were being considered, and which options were needed where, total monthly service fees (not including per-minute charges) were impossible to compare. On standard features for which prices were easily compared, Vnet's rates were 10–20% below SDN's.

---

[3] US Sprint did not publish a tariff for VPN, so charges varied from customer to customer and might be adjusted dramatically from month to month. Although AT&T and MCI had published tariffs, each could offer limited promotions to individual customers.

Vnet Options

Vnet offered several service options and more were planned as demand for the product grew. Certain options were oriented toward end-users, such as single-digit dialing or credit-card calling from off-net. Other services, such as rerouting a call to avoid busy lines, were automatic, spanned only fractions of a second, and did not notify or interrupt the user although reports were generated for the telecom staff. One MCI technical manager noted, "Many of these features don't even come out in the sales process, but in fact end up impressing the customer after installation. On the other hand, customers without existing networks may not appreciate some of Vnet's features, since they have never had the problems those features solve."

Some of the MCI options not offered by AT&T were international calls, off-site access, dedicated trunks between the vendor's switches, and an automatic number conversion system which routed an on-net call cheaply, even if it were dialed as an off-net call (with 10 digits, rather than 7). MCI also provided a range of billing data broken down by location or operating unit; this allowed customers to allocate telecom expenditures to different profit centers. Previously, most companies' networks had operated as cost centers since it was difficult to pass financial responsibilities to the appropriate users.

An important Vnet design option was "hybridizing" with the customer's existing facilities. The customer could retain any part of its existing network, including all lines and numbering systems, and Vnet would provide the additional services the customer needed to fill out the system. While this was very demanding for Vnet engineers (since integrating with customer equipment was a detailed customization process), the customer could integrate every branch location with the network while utilizing existing facilities at full capacity. Ms. Peggy Knight, product manager for Vnet, noted:

> We designed Vnet with hybridizing in mind, so it is probably easier for us than for AT&T: they usually have a "rip-it-out" attitude toward existing networks. We realized that MCI does not have the clout in the business community to demand tearing out an existing system. We have succeeded by asking customers to try us out a little at a time and grow their Vnet usage as capacity needs increase and as existing fixed facilities obsolesce. The largest customers can justify fixed networks because they can use their equipment at capacity and because a fixed-facility network offers unparalleled security. So the 200 largest users will probably retain their existing networks for the time being.
>
> Since virtual networks are new services, AT&T will probably continue to add functions just as MCI will, though not necessarily the same ones. Thus, AT&T may include at some later date the functions we've included in Vnet.

Mr. Gene Eidenberg, president of MCI Pacific, commented:

> The telecom industry is fast-paced, and the advantages of technical innovations don't last long as competitors adopt those technologies. Therefore, lasting advantages will only be derived from customer service and problem solving.
>
> AT&T's position is very different from ours. They have no motivation to cannibalize their installed base of hardwired network services, which are annuities.

Selling SDN for them may entail large deconstruction and installation costs, only to replace a large current revenue stream with a smaller one. On the other hand, AT&T does not like to lose large national business and typically reacts immediately to inroads.

MCI does not have a big installed base of private network business and has been able to move aggressively. But MCI can't afford to damage its credibility with large accounts and therefore can't move too fast. One has to remember that telecom managers themselves are "vendors" to their internal users. The sales cycle for large customers can be two years; it requires good people, patience, and customer confidence.

MCI Organization

When AT&T divested its regional telephone companies in 1984, MCI decentralized its operations in order to work more closely with the seven newly independent regional telephone companies. Seven MCI divisions were set up to perform marketing, installation, and service within geographical regions. Concentrating on telco relations was important, since MCI needed hardwired interfacing with local telephone companies in order to provide customers with MCI's long-distance services. The years 1984–1986 were an especially crucial period because most residential phone customers in the nation were asked to decide on a long-distance carrier, and MCI focused most of its attention and resources on this opportunity. (See Exhibit 3 for financial information.)

The National Accounts Program (NAP) was started in late 1984 to coordinate selling efforts to the nation's largest users of telecommunications services. Although the program was managed at headquarters, each MCI division had a vice president of National Accounts responsible for dedicated NAP sales efforts. This person was responsible to the division president but also coordinated efforts with headquarters. Headquarters monitored account development, reviewed recommendations to add new accounts to the NAP list of about 225 firms, and coordinated interdivisional sales and service needs for these large, multilocation accounts. NAP headquarters organization in early 1987 is shown in Exhibit 4.

One headquarters manager pointed out that different divisions put different levels of emphasis on Vnet because of local conditions:

> Some divisions still have great growth potential in basic services and focus there. Eastern and central corporate customers often have widespread national network needs, but western networks are typically longitudinal down the coast, and comparatively few southeastern and southwestern companies have major branches outside their regions.

Mr. Bill Gallagher, MCI Pacific's VP of National Accounts, added:

> This division is three time zones away from headquarters in Washington, D. C., so we must be very independent here. The California Public Utilities Commission is one of the toughest in the country, so we have our own local constraints

and challenges. I wanted to make sure we had a full-service organization out here, because I knew we couldn't hope for frequent visits from East Coast product specialists. Further, AT&T has the resources to move mountains, so we must secure the mountains quickly before AT&T gets to them.

Since existing WATS lines can be converted to Vnet access lines, Vnet is a simple product to the user, perhaps too simple since it can be a threat to a corporation's telecom staff with obsolete jobs. In addition, customers like playing competitors off one another. It is therefore important to be positioned at all executive levels in the customer organization and to know top management at our National Account customers. But the telecom managers are the ones who make the decisions (even if they need board approval), and top-down selling can alienate these important middle managers. Brian Kelly, for instance, has reportedly been very unhappy about AT&T people going around him and dealing directly with business unit managers at Seaboard.

National Accounts did not have a dedicated technical operations staff, although individual accounts had dedicated operations personnel, and NAP headquarters did run a central service center to expedite work on account problems. National Accounts had a separate product management group responsible for product definition, development, implementation, and training. NAP also had a division sales support staff which developed sales tools, helped prepare proposals, and assisted NAMs during difficult stages of a sale.

An important event for MCI in 1986 was the acquisition of Satellite Business Systems (SBS) from IBM. SBS provided voice and data transmission primarily for businesses with large telecommunication volumes. Although SBS customers (and employees) were free to change vendors, many stayed with MCI. MCI and IBM also set up a limited set of joint marketing efforts.

MCI network operations (installation, maintenance, technical service) had been decentralized with the rest of the company in 1984, but was reorganized in early 1987 into three large units: east, central, and west. Responsibility for operations was moved out of the divisions and added to the engineering organization at headquarters.

Customers

Private lines used for voice transmission in the daytime were often used for data transmission at night. During the 1980s, as telecommunications devices incorporated more computing functions and computers demanded more communications facilities, the telecom and data processing groups in large corporations were brought closer together under the aegis of management information systems (MIS) departments. The telecom manager's role in many companies was changing into that of an information manager who had to assess the company's transmission requirements and sell significant investment decisions to top management. Conversely, as computers and software became more important in telecommunications, DP/MIS managers became more important in telecom purchase decisions. Whereas telecom managers' backgrounds generally involved dealing with the old Bell System (many were former Bell employees), DP managers were often computer programmers who had risen to managerial positions and came from environments dominated by IBM and other mainframe manufacturers. Exhibit 5 outlines the organization of the telecom unit at Seaboard.

MCI provided 5–10% of the telecommunications services of many *Fortune* 500 companies but had few deeply penetrated accounts. Mr. Jonathan Crane, vice president of National Accounts, stated:

> MCI could not expect serious commitment from National Account customers without a product such as Vnet. It is the flagship of our newly developed products and is aimed at convincing prestige accounts that MCI is innovative, responsive, and effective. It was designed for the largest, most widely dispersed users of telecom services; these are obviously targets of competition in the industry.
>
> It was also designed to be sold to headquarters: selling at headquarters requires fewer resources, less time, and headquarters staffs have the technocratic clout to impress branch locations with their expertise. So even in a decentralized company, selling to headquarters first has influence on branch decisions. MCI's tariffs reward consolidation of traffic, allowing corporate headquarters the benefit of volume discounts unavailable to an individual branch.

MCI sold Vnet through both its National Accounts and Major Accounts sales forces, although support staff at MCI headquarters focused on National Accounts. Every National Account received a brief presentation on Vnet sometime in 1986 or 1987, and about half were given hour-long introductions to the system. By April 1987, 12 customers had fully functioning Vnet systems, 15 more were in the process of installation, another dozen were in the final phases of their decision process. National Accounts headquarters staff formed a Vnet "swat team" for advanced presentations to customers at a National Account manager's (NAM) request. Sales of Vnet to major accounts were exceptions, usually initiated at the request of the customer.

Vnet Buying Process

Mr. Carl Vorder Bruegge, MCI's senior vice president of sales and marketing, stated:

> Vnet is not an easy product to sell: customers and this new product are both technologically sophisticated, and salespeople must understand both. Unlike most of MCI's products, Vnet requires extensive customer education, lengthy feasibility studies, and coordination within large multiregional accounts.

Some MCI managers were concerned that the traditional orientation of MCI's selling efforts would hinder Vnet's acceptance in the marketplace. One executive commented, "MCI will have to undergo a substantial change to sell Vnet; I think our salespeople are so accustomed to selling whatever AT&T sells, but at a lower price, that it will be hard for them to think and act differently."

Ms. Knight pointed out that, "Although MCI never marketed a network product before Vnet, SBS people sold only private network services; they are educating the rest of the sales force."

Mr. Vorder Bruegge distinguished between two types of customers:

At companies that don't presently have private networks, our most likely ally is the executive with financial responsibility for communications costs. This person probably has little or no communications staff and is likely confused about current communications costs at his company. There is probably decentralized decision making for telecom services at various locations, and some of the sites may already be using MCI long-distance service.

At companies that do have networks, the director of telecommunications is the decision maker. This person may not be a serious prospect for Vnet: a very large, sophisticated network which is already in place may be perfectly suited to the customer's needs.

We also run straight into an installed base of AT&T services; it has traditionally been much easier for telecom managers to buy AT&T services since most have never looked at the financial bottom line of their telecommunications. If there's a dial tone and the call goes through, most companies are satisfied and tend to ignore the costs. As a result, from the point of view of many telecom managers, "no one ever got fired for buying AT&T."

Ms. Knight offered another perspective:

The corporate telecom managers are the people to sell to; they want to hear about Vnet because they want to improve their private networks. These managers also have internal turf-fights to deal with: different site managers have different needs and cost levels. If we can help the VP of communications satisfy various local managers through Vnet, that VP will help us sell.

Vnet can't offer the best savings in a heavy-traffic area, but it can offer features across the entire system that would be prohibitive for a fixed network. For instance, Vnet can lower costs for a customer's remote location, but we can't improve costs for a central location with private trunks used at capacity 24 hours a day. Yet the headquarters manager wants a consistent system and consequently is looking for a package which will integrate all his locations. So if total costs can be lowered with Vnet, the HQ manager will likely subsidize a central location so that it will come onto Vnet instead of buying into a separate fixed-facility system.

We did not specifically target any accounts at the start: there was no standard profile or checklist circulated to highlight likely customers. A "typical" profile is a customer whose network has long, inefficient lines for several branches. The obvious alternative is shutting down those lines and signing those branches up for WATS service, but then those locations are lost from the network: WATS can't be integrated. This upsets the telecom manager who often is torn between the desire for control over one centralized system, and the need for cost-effective telecommunications.

It helps if the customer has confidence in MCI already, and dislikes AT&T for its perceived arrogance. It is also best if the telecom manager wants to aggressively manage the network to solve the company's problems; these people are the risk-takers.

MCI Pacific

The MCI National Account team for Seaboard consisted of Ms. Voigt, the National Account manager, Ms. Kathy Doll, National Account service specialist, and Mr. Joe Somerville, National Account technical specialist.

Ms. Voigt took over the Seaboard account in early 1987; before that, the account was managed by a NAM (National Account Manager) who also had responsibility for one of MCI Pacific's biggest accounts. Voigt had joined MCI in 1983 as a commercial sales rep and soon moved to major accounts. When National Accounts was founded at the end of 1984, she became a NAM. Besides Seaboard, Ms. Voigt had responsibility for another account which took up approximately two days of her time each week.

Since assuming responsibility for the Seaboard account, she had leased to Seaboard a new transatlantic trunk and sold a package of discount Dial 1 services called CAS (corporate accounts service). She was meanwhile trying to replace other vendors' WATS services with Prism[4] at several Seaboard locations.

Her immediate goal for Vnet was to convert some of the 16 Seaboard locations that MCI already served with Prism services, so Mr. Kelly (Seaboard's telecom director) could "try it out." Ms. Voigt's other account was already on Vnet, so she had experience with all stages of the sale; however, that firm had very little in common with Seaboard.

Ms. Doll has been with MCI for three years and had been on the Seaboard account since early 1986. As a service specialist, she was responsible for maintenance issues, billing, order taking, tracking implementation, expediting work orders, and general preventive precautions. Every several weeks she reported her findings to Mr. Kelly, including charts of Seaboard's continuing improvement in cost control. She developed a users' survey in 1987, which Ms. Paige Manning, Seaboard's voice services manager, distributed to the 16 locations MCI served. She also helped develop a database on Seaboard's customers. Ms. Doll also worked on another account but spent one or two days each week on-site at Seaboard.

Mr. Somerville, the account's technical specialist, also had responsibilities for another account but spent half his time at Seaboard. His tasks included technical specifications, engineering, and training the Seaboard telecom staff.

In addition to selling Vnet, Ms. Voigt had several other items on her agenda with the account. She had set up a presentation for higher management to consider subscribing to MCI Mail, an electronic mail service with which employees could send messages to one another (and to other subscribers) using their personal computers. She was also interested in selling data services (since Mr. Kelly was planning to modernize the data network) and was offering Seaboard a "co-location" service. This involved Seaboard placing its IBM data

---

[4]Prism was a WATS-like series of products offered by MCI which included more flexibility than the standard WATS service.

processing equipment at MCI switch sites, where MCI would contract to maintain the equipment. This would relieve Seaboard personnel from such operations. Ms. Voigt felt this would be hard for AT&T to counter, because it was their policy not to install competing (IBM) equipment on their premises. Through MCI's relationship with IBM, MCI was also considering joining a consortium of data processing vendors (called Insurance Value Added Network Systems) which provided data services at a discount to member insurance companies.

Seaboard Insurance Company

Seaboard was among the ten largest insurance companies in the United States, specializing in property and casualty insurance, predominantly for businesses. It had been owned by a larger financial services organization from 1968 until early 1985 when it was spun off as an independent company. At the time of the sale, property-casualty insurance was in a severe downturn, and Seaboard reported an $87 million loss for 1985. One industry observer reported, "Seaboard was trying to increase its share of the highly competitive U.S. commercial insurance market and, as a result, didn't charge enough for many policies." Yet, as recently as 1980, Seaboard had provided more than half of its parent's net income.

In 1987, Seaboard employed 12,000 people in 65 offices across the country. Additionally 9,000 independent insurance agents sold Seaboard policies, although most sold competing policies as well. Seaboard's president enumerated the following goals for the company: to be the largest provider of community, personal, and specialty insurance in the United States; to maintain profitability; and to improve distribution of services and create efficiencies through information systems.

At the end of 1985, Seaboard's three-year-old fixed voice services network (which had been leased from AT&T) was dismantled because of its high cost. Replacement long-distance services were then provided by different vendors at its 65 PBX locations across the nation.[5] MCI provided Seaboard with Prism services at 7 sites, and took over service at 9 more sites in 1986 after acquiring SBS. AT&T served the other 49 sites with WATS. Dial 1 services were provided by AT&T at all but 5 locations: those were contracted to MCI in 1987 as a test. MCI also installed a high-speed private line to London for Seaboard in 1987. All "800" (reverse-charge) lines and data lines were provided by AT&T, and all data processing equipment was IBM. For credit-card calling, Seaboard used American Express cards. MCI's 1986 revenues from Seaboard were $725,000 out of a total long-distance budget of about $6 million. (Seaboard's total telecommunications budget in 1986, including equipment and personnel, was

---

[5]A private branch exchange (PBX) was the electronic switchboard unit which coordinated all the telephone traffic at a single customer location.

$16 million.) Account revenues for 1987 were expected to reach $900,000 for MCI.

Mr. Kelly had responsibility for all voice and data communications at Seaboard. According to the previous NAM, Mr. Kelly's key criteria for selecting telecommunications services were cost, service, and transmission quality (lack of noise, etc.), and his current goals were a) to improve the efficiency of Seaboard's telecommunications system, b) to reduce operating expenses without sacrificing quality, and c) to enhance his staff's knowledge of the available range of products, services, and vendors in the telecommunications industry.

Mr. Kelly, 42, had joined Seaboard in 1985 after 6 years as telecom director at Arpac Corporation, a large West Coast conglomerate. In 1983, he had cancelled all MCI services at Arpac because of unsatisfactory service quality (notably call cut-offs). While at Arpac he had also cancelled a new product from AT&T which had performed poorly.

At Seaboard, he reported to Mr. Don Dowling, vice president of operations, and directed a staff of 14. Two recently hired senior analysts reported directly to him for special projects involving modernization, expansion, and "strategic design." Two managers ran voice and data services respectively. Ms. Paige Manning, 37, had recently joined Seaboard as manager of voice services, and coordinated 6 voice analysts. Her function was to allocate current work orders from the various Seaboard offices to the voice analysts. Ms. Doll noted, "Before Paige was hired, each analyst had covered a specific territory, and work flow tended to be high or low in different regions at different times. Brian felt that was wasteful, so he brought in Paige to coordinate."

The analysts' jobs were to make sure that the individual Seaboard locations had the facilities and services they needed: those offices had no one locally responsible for telecommunications. Analysts ranged in age from late twenties to late thirties.

Mr. Mike Carey headed the data services function and directed 4 analysts. Responsibilities were roughly parallel to those of the voice group, but the data group maintained a fixed facility data network which included high speed "backbone" circuits between the 6 major offices (San Francisco, Dallas, Los Angeles, Atlanta, Omaha, and Trenton), lower capacity links to the other 59 branches, and the data processing equipment linked by the network.

Depending on the service required, a telecom vendor decision at Seaboard could be made by an analyst or by the board of directors. For instance, WATS service had been primarily up to the analysts when they had set up each office's services. All purchases required Mr. Kelly's acquiescence. However, with the advent of Ms. Manning's position, vendor choices were increasingly brought to her. For corporatewide projects such as a network installation, the board would ultimately decide on the capital investments and vendors required. In such cases, Mr. Kelly would go to the board with a proposal for the project and present the vendors' alternatives. He would typically recommend one vendor over others.

Decision levels were harder to predict for decisions of medium scope. A pilot test of a new service which required expenditures would need to be reviewed by Mr. Kelly's superior, Mr. Dowling, and possibly by the executive vice president of systems and operations, Mr. Richard Cabell. However, if a trial or feasibility study required no significant outlay, Mr. Kelly could authorize such a test himself. The recent decisions for buying MCI's Dial 1 services and London cable were made by Mr. Kelly on his authority.

April 23 Presentation

On Thursday, April 23, Mr. Kelly, Ms. Manning, two voice services analysts, and two data services analysts visited MCI Pacific's headquarters in San Francisco for an in-depth presentation on Vnet from 1 P.M. to 4 P.M. (While the other Seaboard attendees arrived on time, Mr. Kelly arrived 40 minutes late.) Ms. Voigt had secured Mr. Roger Naff, senior manager of technical support at MCI Pacific, to lead the presentation; Mr. Naff had worked at Bell Labs and Western Electric before joining MCI in 1984. He brought two technical specialists with him from the Los Angeles office. Also present was Pacific's operations manager, Mr. Harry Sells, who had covered the Seaboard account when he had worked for AT&T. Ms. Linda Starek, an MCI senior sales manager, and Ms. Doll were also in attendance.

Mr. Naff started with an overview of current trends. Seaboard had been displeased with its previous network because of rising costs; high-capacity trunks were becoming more efficient due to new data compression and multiplexing technologies, as well as the widespread use of optical fiber; and local access charges were rising because of local telcos and state utilities commissions, especially California's. Average per-minute costs in 1987 ranged from 20 cents per minute for high-capacity digital trunks to 42 cents per minute for standard Dial 1 service.

He then covered the idea of network hybridization. He noted that an independent consultant had developed software for optimizing Vnet layout when integrated with an existing system. The current parameters of the customer's existing system were entered into the computer, which would analyze traffic patterns and any specifications the customer demanded. Mr. Kelly mentioned that he knew of the consultant and liked his work. Mr. Naff mentioned that most Vnet customers were hybrids but that AT&T resisted the notion of hybridization.

One Seaboard voice analyst noted that "although SeaNet, our private voice network, had been cost effective when set up in 1982, the cost structures changed so dramatically that in three years it was not competitive. What sort of fail-safe pricing is available with Vnet to insure that it is still economical for us in several years? You probably insist on a long-term contract to protect yourselves from falling prices." Mr. Naff responded, "MCI only asks for 30-day contracts, so the tariff can drop from month to month in a volatile market. We understand that customers aren't interested in an all-or-nothing commitment."

Mr. Naff then covered service options. Credit-card services could be integrated with Vnet, since they shared the same database, and Vnet could be accessed through dedicated trunks or through the local telcos. Seven-digit dialing was available for the entire network; one analyst mentioned, "That was the one significant feature lost when SeaNet was disassembled."

Mr. Naff outlined MCI Pacific's experience in designing and installing Vnet for customers and mentioned that the 16 Prism lines already being used at Seaboard could be immediately changed into Vnet lines without any adjustment required of the customer. MCI could also provide direct termination overflow so that if any access line was full, an incoming call would automatically be routed through the local telco, rather than meeting a busy signal. One- or two-digit speed calling would be available by December.

The next topic was Vnet's interactive features, none of which were currently being offered by competitors. The customer information manager allowed the customer's telecom staff direct and immediate access to the central memory bank of the Vnet system. Any changes the customer wished to make in range privileges, calling cards, ID numbers, etc., could be implemented by the customer in 15 minutes. Mr. Naff contrasted this system with US Sprint's VPN architecture, which required lengthy vendor updating of each switch, and with AT&T's system, which did not offer direct customer control.

Another interactive Vnet feature, the network information management system, would provide traffic-flow information to the customer for fine-tuning the design as the network grew. This included utilization figures, failure reports, call counts, and other statistics. IBM also offered a complementary system called Netview, which provided further network data. MCI could also provide multiple invoices, breaking down charges as the customer directed so they could be allocated to specific sites or individual operating units. One Seaboard analyst noted that several locations without "intelligent" PBXs could benefit from that information.

Discussion then moved on to pricing. SDN charged $60,000 for initial setup, while Vnet was only $5,000 and MCI charges were waived until autumn to encourage sampling. With maximum savings, a Vnet call could cost as little as 15 cents per minute, end-to-end; the average was 20 cents. A Seaboard analyst noted that their calls currently averaged 24 cents per minute. Mr. Naff mentioned that Vnet favored customers with short calls, since AT&T's charges were significantly higher in the early minutes of a call. Ms. Voigt noted that Vnet was slightly more expensive per minute than Prism, but the integrated features were incomparable.

Mr. Kelly stated, "We need more chats about voice-data integration, but for us, that's still far down the road. Our data network needs an overhaul, but that is separate from our consideration of Vnet." Mr. Naff noted that, "Vnet can be used to make the data net more efficient: excess capacity can be used for voice traffic, and data overflow could be handled by Vnet." A Seaboard data analyst pointed out that, "Only 7 or 8 of our locations have enough combined traffic to warrant that kind of piggybacking. And by the way, Seaboard is firmly entrenched with IBM, and therefore would demand compatibility." Mr. Naff responded, "We do business with IBM: they are our biggest customer, and our largest stockholder."

Mr. Kelly asked about including independent agents on the net and invoicing them the bills and then asked about putting agents on and allowing them to place free calls to Seaboard. Mr. Naff answered that either option could be worked into the hybridization program. Mr. Kelly then wrapped up the meeting:

> Seaboard has no established plan for network integration. For now, we in this room are just meter readers, not traffic managers. Our immediate concerns are grades of service, quality, features, and subsidization of smaller locations. For our next meeting, I'd first like to know, why does Seaboard need a network at all? Secondly, I'd like a detailed comparison with SDN; Sprint's VPN is not a consideration.
>
> The management tools in a network are worth something to us. We want to move away from cost considerations to strategic enhancements and modernization. This project won't fly if we're only saving money. How will you make us more effective in the marketplace? For example, airlines use their telecommunications systems to make themselves more competitive. Be creative: our habits can change. We want to be the innovator; everyone else will have to catch up. If you can do this, I'll be very happy, because I'll probably get a big raise.
>
> Barbara, let's set up an initial meeting for next week, and the full proposal can be presented next month.

After the Seaboard staff had left, the MCI team met to discuss the meeting and what the next steps should be.

Exhibit 1 MCI: Vnet (A)

Elements Involved in Vnet System, Including Off-Net Calls
(Diagrams simplified; typical systems would involve dozens of switches, access points, PBXs, etc.)

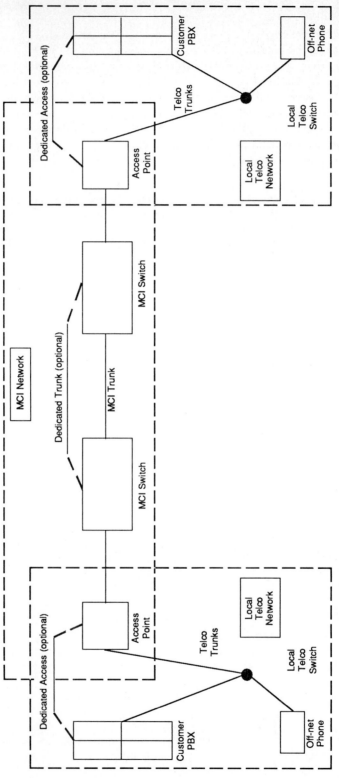

Dedicated lines were private lines integrated into Vnet's software, but leased separately, by MCI or the local telephone company. Such lines reduced or eliminated certain per-minute charges, and if used at capacity, could reduce total monthly costs.

Exhibit 2 MCI: Vnet (A)

ON-Vnet Call (7 Digits)

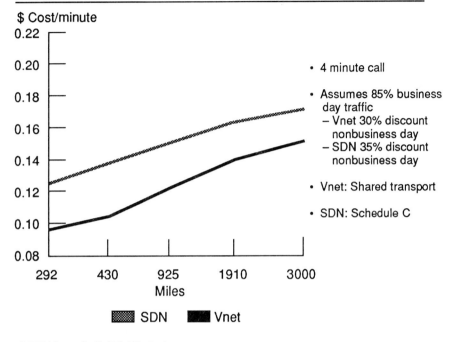

- 4 minute call
- Assumes 85% business day traffic
  - Vnet 30% discount nonbusiness day
  - SDN 35% discount nonbusiness day
- Vnet: Shared transport
- SDN: Schedule C

OFF-Vnet Call (10 Digits)

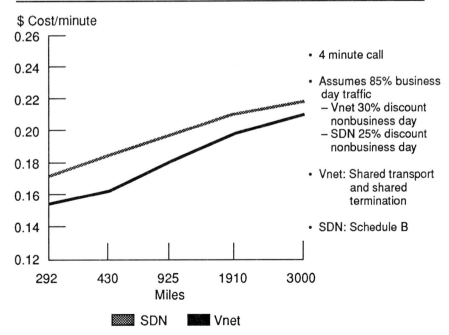

- 4 minute call
- Assumes 85% business day traffic
  - Vnet 30% discount nonbusiness day
  - SDN 25% discount nonbusiness day
- Vnet: Shared transport and shared termination
- SDN: Schedule B

Exhibit 3   MCI: Vnet (A)

Income Statement: MCI (1984–1986)

Year Ended December 31,	1986	1985	1984
	(In millions, except per share amounts)		
Revenue			
Sales of communications services	$3,592	$2,542	$1,959
Operating Expenses			
Local interconnection	1,636	874	480
Leased communications system	267	280	343
Sales, operations and general	1,097	835	696
Depreciation	451	347	265
Restructuring charges and asset write-downs	585	154	50
	$4,036	$2,490	$1,834
(Loss) Income from Operations	(444)	52	125
Interest expense	(187)	(201)	(189)
Interest income	63	86	115
Portion of antitrust settlements, net	39	207	
Gain on sale of assets	65	18	
Other income (expense), net	1	6	(1)
(loss) income before income taxes and extraordinary item	(463)	168	50
Income tax (benefit) provision	(32)	28	(9)
Extraordinary loss on early debt retirements, less applicable income tax benefits ($17 and $26)	17	27	
Net (loss) Income	($ 448)	$ 113	$ 59
(Loss) Earnings per Common Share			
Primary and assuming full dilution:			
(Loss) income before extraordinary item	($1.57)	$ .59	$ .25
Net (loss) income	($1.63)	$ .48	$ .25
Circuit Miles	485	322	198
Billable Calls	2,812	1,760	1,232
# of Employees	13,650	12,445	9,870
Average Revenue per Minute per Call	$.242	$.266	$.281
Local interconnection	.111	.91	.69
Leased communications system	.018	.029	.049
Gross margin	.113	.146	.163

Exhibit 4   MCI: Vnet (A)

National Accounts Organization
(April 1987)

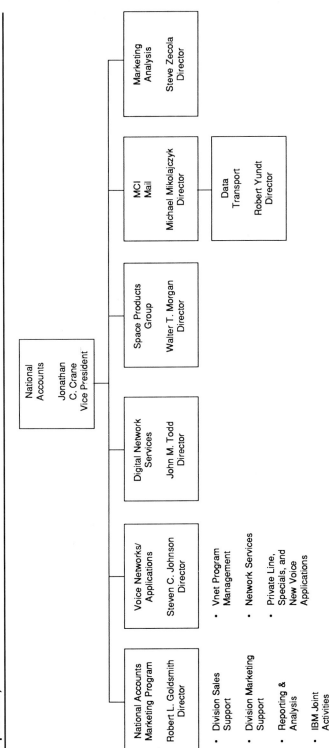

Exhibit 5   MCI: Vnet (A)

Seaboard Insurance Company Organization

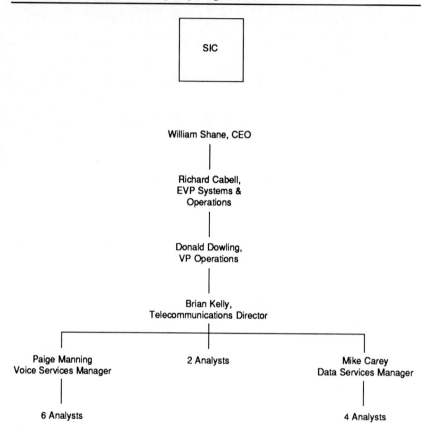

PART THREE 󠀠⃞⃞⃞⃞⃞

Managing Marketing Resources: Organization and Control

7. *Aspects of Marketing Organization: An Introduction*

8. *Key Interfaces*
   - Frito-Lay, Inc. (A)
   - Imperial Distributors, Inc. (A)
   - Peripheral Products Company: The Gray Market

9. *Customer Service*
   - Carolina Power & Light Company
   - General Electric: Customer Service

10. *Structure, Systems, and Process*

Marketing Organization at Leading Industrial and Consumer Goods Firms
   - IBM Marketing Organization (A): Changes in Structure
   - IBM Marketing Organization (B): Process
   - Procter & Gamble (A)
   - Pepsi-Cola Fountain Beverage Division: Marketing Organization

Centralization and Decentralization of Marketing Efforts
   - Turner Construction Company
   - Honeywell, Inc.: International Organization for Commercial Avionics (A)

Getting the Marketing Job Done
   - Imperial Distributors, Inc. (B)
   - Pepsi-Cola Fountain Beverage Division: Tea Breeze

Aspects of Marketing Organization: An Introduction

Organization charts do not make decisions; people do. But the facts of formal organization are vital to an understanding of how marketing tasks do (and do not) get accomplished in companies for at least three reasons. First, organizational structure affects not only the type and flow of information in a company but also the pattern of resource allocation. The structure is the terrain upon which managers' attempts at implementing policy occur. Second, the formal organization affects processes within a firm and functional area; structure affects who interacts with whom (and with what goals or interests in mind) and helps to determine the focus of attention for individual managers. Third, the way a company organizes its marketing activities determines over time the kinds of skills that are developed. This in turn affects the kinds of marketing strategies and people realistically available to the firm.

Part Two examined field marketing requirements in various company and competitive settings. Part Three will now look at broader organizational issues that affect the implementation of headquarters marketing and field sales activities. This chapter discusses the typical strengths, vulnerabilities, and key management skills associated with three common forms of headquarters marketing organization: a product-focused organization, a market-focused organization, and a functionally focused organization. The nature of marketing activities varies in each model.

Clearly, there are many hybrid forms as well as organizing principles other than product, market, or function. Certainly, matrix organizations—a large and complex topic in its own right—also could be discussed. But the three structures highlighted in this introductory survey are common, basic building blocks and so provide an overview of issues relevant to many other forms of marketing organization as well. Table 1 summarizes the major issues associated with each organization discussed.

Product-Focused Organization

Probably the most common method of organizing marketing is by product (see Figure A). The product management organization establishes product or brand managers who are responsible for a product's marketing plan, including coordinating its implementation and the achievement of volume, market share, and/or profit goals. Enlisting the support of sales, advertising, market research, manufacturing, and finance is a key task of the product manager, especially since the product manager rarely has direct authority over other departments vital to executing marketing plans.

Although this type of marketing organization is particularly characteristic of companies in packaged-goods industries, many industrial marketers also have adopted it. Product managers generally have been used in those situations in which a company has multiple products flowing through the same channels to the same (or related) customer groups. In these situations, the diverse requirements of taking different products to market are the focus of product management activities. Du Pont's Textile Fibers division long organized its marketing activities along product-focused lines, and the responsibilities of these product managers (known as Sales Programs managers) illustrate typical activities of product management:[1]

> Each Sales Programs manager was charged with looking after the "health" of a particular fiber and for serving as a clearing house for all information on it. The manager worked with the sales, research, and manufacturing organizations on scheduling production, allocating available supplies, planning new plant capacity, developing new products and applications, and promoting the use of fiber in the market.
>
> Each Programs manager met with production personnel monthly to work on schedules. For fibers in short supply, the Programs manager and plant personnel for that fiber established "grants" or "reserves" for each sales region.
>
> Each Programs manager also helped to plan new plant capacity by developing the long-range sales estimates on which plant investment decisions would be made. As new capacity was added, the Programs manager had the responsibility for determining the end-product markets in which efforts would be made to place the additional fiber output. These decisions were made in a way that would "build a sound market base" for the fiber. Programs managers were particularly interested, therefore, in building diverse end-product markets for their fibers and in avoiding excessive dependency on any one end-product application. In these activities, the Programs manager relied heavily on the recommendations of Merchandising and Regional Sales managers.
>
> In addition, Programs managers took an active part in the development of new fiber grades and new fabrics. They solicited ideas from field personnel, and estimated the potential sales volume for a proposed new fiber. New ideas were discussed with Coordination Committee members. If the response was favorable,

Table 1

Varieties of Marketing Organization

Product-Focused Organization

Strengths	Vulnerabilities	Key Success Factors
Puts one person in charge of making a business plan work for each major product Broad-based, cross-functional training and exposure; clear career path with increasing responsibilities Shortens response time between changes in strategy and changes in product plans and programs	Creates potential duplication in support functions "Marketing myopia": tends to focus attention on specific product requirements rather than market needs Complicates coordination of marketing activities if several products are sold to the same customer(s). Dilutes functional expertise	Process for ensuring that discrete product programs present a coherent message to customers Measurement and incentive system that encourages attention to broader market trends Ongoing vigilance concerning growth in overhead due to duplication of support functions

Market-Focused Organization

Strengths	Vulnerabilities	Key Success Factors
Concentrated focus on a defined group of customers Encourages attention to, and expertise in, the purchase and usage characteristics of certain industries Aids coordinated delivery of diverse products to a given customer segment and development of "systems"/"solutions"-oriented programs	Complicates interfaces with other parts of the company, such as manufacturing and R&D, which are generally product-focused. Creates potential inefficiencies in manufacturing and field operations "Market myopia": tends to focus attention on currently largest customer segments to relative exclusion of small but growing segments Dilutes focus on product management	Strong, ongoing analytical skills and information for purposes of clear market segmentation Measurement and communication systems that encourage coordination with other functional areas Human resource policies that prevent excessive specialization within the market management structure

Functionally Focused Organization

Strengths	Vulnerabilities	Key Success Factors
Marketing planning for the business centered in one position Increases efficiencies and expertise in selected marketing activities through specialization "Administrative simplicity": puts specific people and resources in place for key marketing functions	Tends to have a very high level of closure for the development and approval of integrated marketing programs Potential fragmentation and/or redundancy in the development of programs "Management myopia": Few marketing managers have responsibility for actual marketplace results and most tend to identify with a specific function within marketing.	Systems for maintaining complementary goals among different functional groups Measurements that drive coordination of distinct marketing activities in terms of marketplace results Human resource policies that develop management perspectives in terms of integrated marketing programs

Figure A
Example of Product Management Organization

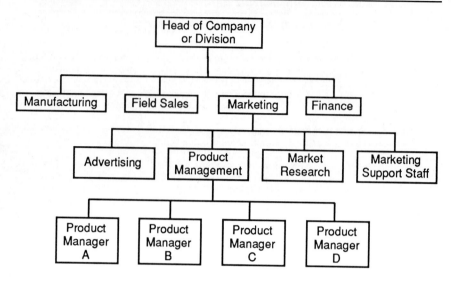

the Programs managers reviewed the idea with interested Merchandising managers and requested their help in promoting the new fiber in specific applications. Programs managers also recommended prices on new items in their line. Implementation of these recommendations required approval of the Sales Division director.

Each Programs manager had several assistants. The Development Assistant worked to coordinate Direct Sales, Technical Sales, and Merchandising effort in developing and launching new and modified fibers in the market. A Sales assistant maintained close direct contact with regional sales personnel and worked with them on any problems involving the sale of his particular fiber. The Merchandising Contact assistant was responsible for working with Merchandising managers to plan detailed actions to implement those programs which had been recommended for fiber.

The job of the product manager, then, is to coordinate among manufacturing, sales, and market programs in order to serve the "balanced best interests" of each. In practice, this means ongoing trade-offs between maintaining efficient production, satisfying fluctuating consumer demand in different market segments, and motivating the sales force to devote a "fair share" of its time to each product sold through a common channel. A fundamental concern of most product managers is to maximize the short-run return on investments in production facilities that are dedicated to a product and to maintain a cost-competitive product line that matches evolving customer demand. In many packaged-goods companies, a trend in recent years is to distinguish between the responsibilities of product managers and product group managers or category managers. The product manager tends to focus on issues of brand volume, brand share, and the marketing expenditures associated with a brand's profit-and-loss statement, whereas the product group manager or category manager deals with issues concerning capacity planning and asset management. Similarly, although new product development is not always separate from ongoing product management, the trend (especially among packaged-goods firms) is toward dividing the two functions, since the concerns of line extensions and ongoing product management tend to be different from those required for new product development. This is less the case in many industrial goods companies, in which new product development (including applications development) is often part of product management responsibilities.

In most product management organizations, the product manager acts as the crossroads, or clearinghouse, for marketing plans affecting his or her product (see Figure B). The job can be envisioned as involving a series of liaison roles within the organization.[2]

As a liaison among different groups over whom they rarely have line authority, product managers must maintain good relationships with managers in other areas and must optimize the attention and resources devoted to their particular product lines. Indeed, in many organizations, overt competition between product managers for limited sales, manufacturing, or other resources is an accepted part of "how we do things around here." In this type of situation, up-to-date information, skills in persuasion and influence-building, and a detailed knowledge of how budgets are set and of how resources are allocated within the company become important aspects of the product manager's ability to perform. As one brand manager has noted, "The way you sell an idea to management is what distinguishes a good product manager from a poor one. You gain authority here by what you recommend rather than by what you decide."

Figure B
Role of the Product Manager

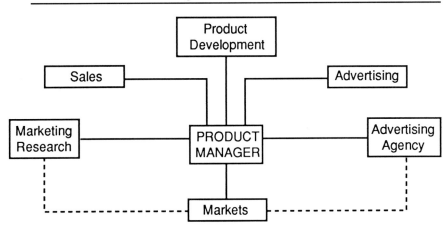

Strengths

A perceived strength of the product management organization is that it puts one person in charge of making a business plan work for each product and, due to the product manager's role as a central clearinghouse for product information, also shortens the response time between changes in strategy and changes in product plans and programs required to implement the strategy. Accountability and overall responsibility for managing the many tasks required to take a product to market are important goals in any organization. But these qualities are also often ephemeral—especially in the context of a large, complex organization. As a result, many general managers appreciate a structure in which "at least I know who to call if I have a question or problem concerning the marketing of a given product line."

Another perceived strength is the broad-based training and exposure individuals receive as they progress through the product management career path. The liaison role at the heart of the product manager's responsibilities traditionally has been viewed as good preparation for general management responsibilities. In consumer packaged-goods firms, especially, product management historically has been a career path that MBAs, entering as assistant product managers, can follow to associate product manager, product manager, product group manager, or category manager, before obtaining a possible appointment as general manager for a division. One manager has noted that the product management system traditionally has been like a pyramid in which individuals take on more responsibilities and brands with increased experience.

Vulnerabilities

The vulnerabilities of this structure involve overhead costs, ongoing coordination issues, and the kinds of skills and expertise that are (and are not) nurtured by this form of organization.

With each major product line supported by a panoply of brand assistants and associates, the product management structure creates potential duplication of support activities. As a result, this type of structure is most appropriate when a company markets multiple products, each with sales volume (or sales potential) sufficient to justify a separate line organization, and when the differences in marketing strategies among the products are great enough to warrant distinct attention by a specific marketing group. Traditionally, this has been the case among many, but not all, consumer goods firms. In situations in which a company markets multiple products, each with relatively modest sales volume, under an umbrella brand name (e.g., many cosmetics firms), or in situations in which one of the firm's brands dominates all others in volume and strategic importance (e.g., Coke, Pepsi, and other firms), the product management structure is often less appropriate, and brand managers in these organizations tend to have less responsibility and authority.

In many firms, moreover, the product management structure has been found to proliferate management layers, creating coordination problems among different groups. Remember that, despite prevailing stereotypes, "bureaucracy" is not specific to governmental agencies but potentially inherent in most organizations required to conduct complex tasks. During the 1980s, for example, product management structures at many leading packaged-goods firms were pruned considerably in an effort to reduce overhead and speed decision making in an increasingly competitive environment. A general manager at one firm explained:[3]

> Until last year, the Marketing function was overstaffed. We bent over to give good people career and salary advancement, and we could afford to do so. Our margins were so good that relatively small new product ideas seemed profitable enough to justify the expense of a separate product group. The problem was, however, that we had too many people chasing a finite level of decision-making responsibility. You distinguished yourself as an assistant by coming up with the big new promotion idea for the eastern region. Now, there is more work and task diversity for each person.
>
> With fewer people, the atmosphere is also less bureaucratic. There is less emphasis on formal written reports. Our annual product marketing plans are much shorter now. The depth of analysis may not be as great but the speed of decision making is faster. Our five advertising agencies appreciate not having to make presentations to as many levels of management and the support of our staff functions is more highly valued by the product groups. A leaner organization is more flexible. There are fewer turf issues.

Another vulnerability inherent in the product management structure is the complement to one of its strengths: Because the valued assignments are in terms of a particular product line, a myopic vision of the market in terms of current products and a corresponding decrease in attention and resources devoted to new ways of serving customer needs can occur. Customers, as the old adage notes, do not buy quarter-inch drill bits, they buy quarter-inch holes; people do not buy products, they buy the expectation of benefits derived through the use of products. But, a product manager typically is focused on the quarterly sales and profitability of an existing product line, and this orientation can lead to a short-term emphasis on pushing the drill bits while ignoring other innovative means of serving the market.

Finally, because it requires interacting with many functional groups, product management traditionally has developed individuals with a strong base of contacts and familiarity with issues in many areas of the firm. The term *little general manager* is often used to refer to this aspect of the skills developed in a product management position. In practice, however, this breadth of experience may be achieved at the expense of depth of expertise in any one area. Hence the little general manager may be a "jack-of-all-trades but master of none," especially since career advancement in many product management organizations entails rapid turnover in brand assignments and little time to master the details of the manufacturing, finance, physical distribution, or sales-related issues associated with a given product. The lack of breadth can become a liability if market changes make in-depth expertise in one or more areas vital to marketing success. In the past decade at many packaged-goods firms, for example, trade promotions have become an increasingly large part of marketing budgets and knowledge of in-store merchandising techniques have become a vital aspect of marketing programs. Similarly, a low-growth market and a battle for retail shelf space make product design and manufacturing issues that are aimed at reducing unit costs important in developing successful marketing programs. Unfortunately, the many interfunctional demands facing the typical brand manager often leave little time for developing expertise in each area.

Key Success Factors

Given the strengths and potential vulnerabilities inherent in the product management structure, there are at least three key success factors required to manage the product-focused organization:

1. A process for ensuring that discrete product-marketing programs present a coherent message to common trade and/or end-use customers.
2. A measurement and incentive system that encourages attention to market trends and opportunities that fall outside the scope of individual product managers.
3. Ongoing vigilance concerning "creeping overhead growth" and duplication of expensive, time-consuming support functions.

The last factor points to a broader issue in marketing organization. An organizational unit, once established, has a natural tendency toward self-sufficiency. The managers of those units become advocates for their role in the organization and often perceive dedicated staff reports and other support functions as necessary and perhaps evidence of the unit's importance and status. This dynamic seems inherent in most organizational structures. But, precisely because product-focused measures are more prevalent and easier to maintain in many organizations (e.g., financial measurements in most companies are generated by accounting systems that allocate costs by product categories),[4] this is a tension that the product management structure encounters repeatedly.

Market-Focused Organization

As the product management structure is intended to provide a single locus of responsibility for each significant product, the market management structure is intended to focus on significant market segments (see Figure C). In this context, the terms *market* and *market segment* are used synonymously to refer to a group of customers with homogeneous patterns of purchasing behavior and product use, not necessarily to a geographic market. In recent years, the phrase *vertical marketing*—a focus on an industry or occupational category with similar

Figure C
Example of Market Management Organization

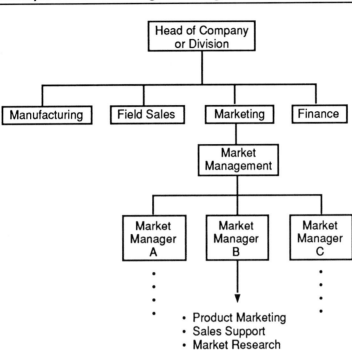

- Product Marketing
- Sales Support
- Market Research
- Applications Development

purchasing and usage patterns—has been used to refer to the type of market focus discussed here.

Whereas product managers have been prominent when a company has multiple products flowing through the same channel to the same (or closely related) customer groups, market managers are often prominent when the company needs to develop different markets for a single, or core, product line. In the latter case, a focus on developing discrete markets, rather than on taking different products to a common market, has been the primary objective.

Many companies sell the same or similar products to different markets through different distribution channels. A textile manufacturer, for example, may sell cloth through one channel to apparel firms and through other channels to furniture, bedspread, drapery, or home-sewing markets. In other cases, the same company may market branded and private-label goods, with significantly different demand characteristics, purchasing criteria, and product expectations inherent in each market. Industrial companies frequently sell the same products to two or more classes of companies, each with different application needs. In these situations, organizing by market often allows for more effective development of specialized marketing programs.

In the computer business, for example, there is significant diversity among market segments, especially in terms of end-use applications. Product development and manufacturing costs make a core product technology an important goal for a vendor. Hence ongoing attention to different market requirements is important. While the same hardware might be used across industry-defined markets, applications are often industry-specific and require extensive knowledge of the business procedures in each industry. The market-focused organization has been used by many computer firms to establish a focus on the evolving requirements of selected industry groups.

Market and product managers are not mutually exclusive choices. In the market-focused structure, however, market managers tend to focus on strategy development and the requirements of field execution in each market, whereas product managers are primarily concerned with line extensions and the administration of activities such as product seminars and delivery schedules. Since, in rapidly changing environments, it is often difficult for one product-focused person or group to know enough about the characteristics and requirements of different segments, it is likely that important opportunities will be missed. Furthermore, without an appropriate market focus, product development can lag behind rapidly changing user needs and product uses in a given segment.

Strengths

A strength of the market organization, then, is its concentrated attention to defined groups of customers. Market managers become coordinating points for information on their markets, providing a coherent perspective for evaluating market trends, long-range planning, and promotional and distribution programs in each market. Indeed, some have argued that this form or organization, which essentially works backward from a user group to the development of different market-specific programs, is synonymous with marketing: "There is no substitute for market orientation as the ultimate source of profitable growth. The only way to ensure being market-oriented is to put a company's organizational structure together so that its major markets become the centers around which its divisions are built." [5] This may be true when, as in sectors of the computer industry, the need for customer education and applications development is high yet varies significantly from one group to another.

Another perceived strength of the market-management structure is that it helps to focus on heavy users in a given market through the development of specific product applications and services. (Major account groups in sales often serve a similar function and often are aligned with market groups at headquarters.) This provides an opportunity for a vendor to become the preferred supplier to customers who, besides their high-volume purchasing patterns, are often prestige accounts that influence the purchasing patterns of other companies in the industry. Conversely, the market structure may be a means of defending a company's position when competitors have achieved sufficient product parity to deprive the leader of price/performance superiority. A focus on individual markets allows for the development of industry-specific expertise concerning delivery, service, and distribution needs.

Finally, this organization has often been used when a company that has been selling discrete products seeks to shift its marketing strategy to one that emphasizes "systems sales," "solutions," or "benefits, not features." While the terminology varies, the common notion is that the development of cross-selling opportunities among a company's product portfolio is often easier to manage through a market-focused organization. Whereas product managers concentrate on specific products that are their responsibility, market managers are likely to be more proactive in developing marketing programs that span individual product lines.

Vulnerabilities

The vulnerabilities of this structure involve the costs and scale required to maintain an efficient market organization, the potential complication of important interfaces with other parts of the company, and (again) the kinds of skills and expertise nurtured by this form or organization.

Where the product-management structure can create potential duplication of support activities for each product line (and hence escalating overhead costs in the form of staff assistants), the market-management structure often incurs increased costs in other forms. For one thing, in order to focus usefully on its designated customer group, market management generally requires its own market research activities and market-specific databases. For another, although a market-focused structure for marketing activities can be conducted independently of a market-focused organization in field sales, in practice the organization of marketing by market often leads to the same organization in field sales. Having established goals and performance measures by market/industry, the company may find that the management of each market lobbies hard for its own sales force, intensively schooled in the needs, buying patterns, and product requirements of a given customer group. In turn, industry or market specialization is an especially expensive form of field sales organization since it generally requires several separate programs for recruiting, training, deploying, and compensating field sales personnel, as well as increased travel and other field sales expenses when several different salespeople (each calling on a different group of customers) are deployed in the same geographical territory.

Beyond field sales, moreover, the market-management structure often involves some inefficiencies and increased costs for other functional areas, especially manufacturing and operations. For example, during the 1980s, the increased specialization and power of different classes of retail trade customers moved a number of national packaged-goods manufacturers to adopt various regional-market and channel-specific structures in their once strictly brand-focused marketing organizations. Whereas there are often good reasons for moving in this direction, a senior manager at one firm, in an interview with this author, bemoaned:

> the demise of one of the world's truly cost-efficient businesses. For years, we made one basic product (in this division), manufactured according to one core process and sold at one price and in one package, with big economies of scale. Now we have a diversity of sizes, prices, line extensions, and promotional programs for different regions and different classes of trade. Marketing points to the need to defend our market share position. But the proliferation of market programs plays hell with manufacturing variances, administrative expenses in field operations and our net product margins.

These costs in terms of information gathering, field operations, and potential inefficiencies in other functional areas underline the importance of scale for this organizational form. On the one hand, the markets chosen for discrete attention must be large and/or profitable enough to warrant the incremental costs. On the other hand, the requirement to choose a limited number of large and well-defined markets means consigning many customer groups to the "all other" category, where applications development and other important functions for these customers do not receive primary attention, leaving the door open to competition. In practice, this often results in a strategic Catch-22 for many companies. Today's large and attractive market is often tomorrow's mature and saturated market for the company's products whereas today's small but emerging markets require market-specific expertise that has not been developed by the firm precisely because it is focusing on the other, larger markets required to sustain its market-management structure. By contrast, a product-focused organization can often, less deeply but more efficiently, penetrate diverse customer groups, keeping the vendor in touch with a variety of market segments, large and small and mature and growing.

Finally, as well as creating opportunities, the focus and skills nurtured by the market-management structure also can create internal resource allocation problems for the firm. Because each market manager is focused on an assigned market, each manager may develop marketing programs without regard to the impact on the company's ability to sell to other markets with the same product line. For most companies, moreover, all markets are rarely equal: The currently largest market segments (or the more senior or persuasive market managers) tend to receive priority, which affects the company's position in other markets. Hence a tight focus on individual markets and the tendency in most organizations for the currently largest source of revenue to receive priority in resource allocations can threaten the development and implementation of a coherent, companywide strategy aimed at emerging as well as mature markets.

A related issue is the long-term impact on the allocation of human resources within the marketing organization. A market manager may know everything about the insurance industry, for example, but little about other customer groups for the company's products. As that market matures, the manager may lose flexibility and value for other, increasingly important assignments.

Key Success Factors

Given these strengths and potential vulnerabilities, then, there are at least three key factors required to manage the market-focused organization effectively. They are:

1. An ongoing data-gathering and analytical process that helps to ensure that the company's market-segmentation scheme generates clearly defined and mutually exclusive markets. Although market segmentation is a staple of good marketing practice in most situations, the market management structure places special pressures on management's abilities in this area. Since the point of this structure is to assemble interrelated market programs under a single management, market definition is crucial to the success of the market management structure.

2. Measurement, incentive, and management communication systems that encourage coordination with other functional areas. In many companies, there are good reasons for retaining a product focus in manufacturing and R&D, even if marketing organizes by market. This complicates the interface between marketing and other areas and requires measures and communications systems (e.g., planning processes) aimed at clarifying the trade-offs inherent in different market managers' requests of manufacturing and R&D.

3. Human resource policies (e.g., transfers, job rotation) that prevent excessive specialization within the market management structure. This danger is probably inherent in most forms of specialization and thus points to a broader issue in organization: Managers usually favor paths of business growth that use existing skills, and (as is often said about academic specialists) over time, they can easily "learn more and more about less and less." Hence a given market management team may champion the importance of its market despite better opportunities for the company in other areas. The result is that a company may devote inordinate resources to lower-return markets because the organization has in place a strong constituency whose professional interests are tied to those markets.

Functionally Focused Organization

In a functionally focused organization, a separate department is established for each major marketing function: for example, product management, advertising, sales promotion, or market research. These functional departments can report either directly to the president of the company or division or through a marketing vice president (see Figure D).

Organizing by function is common when certain marketing tasks warrant special attention, the development of sustained expertise, and centralized oversight and control in their planning and execution. In many consumer

Figure D
Example of Functional Organization

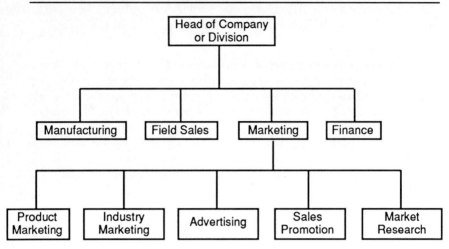

goods firms, for instance, advertising or trade promotions represent a high proportion of total marketing expenditures, and the coordination of these activities across product lines has important advantages. There are also often scale economies available in these activities: Television advertising rates, for example, have historically favored national volume buys. As a result, a number of firms maintain separate advertising or promotions departments with authority for developing campaigns and approving plans in these areas.

A common scenario is illustrated by the evolution of the marketing department at General Foods' Post Division during the 1950s and 1960s, where a product management structure became a functional organization as the product line grew from several cereals to 36 different food items by 1966. Certain specialized functions were created in order to relieve product managers of the necessity for being experts in promotion, packaging, and market research as well as strategy formulation:[6]

> At General Foods' Post Division, product managers, 1950s style, were versatile entrepreneurs. They negotiated with Operations (manufacturing) for supplies of product and with the field sales force for selling time, and they had their own advertising agencies. Their responsibility was simply to meet sales and profit objectives, and each had some skills in promotional planning, display design, package design, market research, and advertising.
>
> By comparison, product managers in the 1960s had to be team players, operating in a program management framework. Each was responsible for developing strategies and annual marketing plans for one or more products within a product group (such as Cereals or Pet Foods) for which there was a broad strategy framework. The product manager drew on the expertise of a Marketing Research Department, an Art Services Department, a Promotion Department, and a Marketing Accounting Services Department. These resources were used in studying a market, planning trade deals, in-store displays and premium promo-

tions, and monitoring the results in order to make quick, tactical adjustments in product plans.

The reasons for the change involved the proliferation of Post product lines, which created many more product management jobs, and the limited supply of broadly skilled product managers. The expanded ranks of new product managers needed support in technical areas such as market research, promotion, and art. Also, these functions required considerable expertise and were likely to be handled more efficiently by specialized resource units than by product managers who had to be "jacks of all trades." At the same time, annual planning and strategy formulation had to be integrated for the several product groups: Cereals, Pet Foods, and Beverages and Miscellaneous Products. Each group was a family of brands going to the same customers and often promoted together.

Hence, in the case of field sales, a sales development manager (who reported to the national sales manager) represented the sales force in meetings with individual product managers. Each product marketing plan called for various kinds of sales force support: introducing new products, selling a trade deal, modifying in-store shelving arrangements. Sales Development translated individual product marketing plans into an integrated set of objectives and sales plans for each district. Likewise, the Post Division's marketing research department worked with product managers to prepare plans for carrying out market studies. In effect, Marketing Research performed an interface function between product programs and outside market research organizations.

Strengths

Theoretically, then, the functional organization has certain advantages. First, marketing planning for the business is centered in the president or the marketing vice president, organizational levels that are often in a better position than down-the-line executives to make broad strategy evaluations and decisions. Second, as the Post Division example illustrates, the functional organization increases pools of expertise through specialization in key marketing activities of the business (e.g., advertising, product planning, promotions, or pricing). This can be especially important when state-of-the-art knowledge or technical skills are vital in the planning or execution of an activity. Third, this form of organization is often praised for its "administrative simplicity" because it seemingly defines responsibilities and puts specific resources and people in place for key marketing activities. For example, a leading industrial products company, initially organized by product and then by market, eventually adopted a functionally focused marketing organization. The reason, according to a senior manager interviewed by the author, is that "in the product and market organizations, something important always seemed to fall between the cracks: product management was good at product planning and product introductions, but weak in promotional programs in different markets; market management was good at applications development and market-focused programs, but product introductions were consistently late and over budget. Now, we have a specific person in charge of each of these activities, and I know who to call to get something done."

Vulnerabilities

The vulnerabilities of this structure involve the high level of closure required for the development of integrated marketing programs, the difficulties in achieving ongoing coordination among specialized functional units, and (as always) the kinds of skills that are (and are not) developed by a certain form or organization.

What seems "administratively simple" on paper is often not in practice. In many functionally focused marketing organizations, there is no mechanism for managers to resolve disagreements or make integrated decisions for a product or market below the level of marketing vice president or division top management. Hence constant meetings and ad hoc arrangements often characterize these organizations. Further while the senior managers of an organization may be in the best position to make cross-product strategy decisions, they are often *not* the best people to make specific judgments about a marketing program for a specific product or market. But the functional organization often requires these managers to become involved in these decisions, leading to a dysfunctional irony of organizational life: The senior manager bemoans the time spent in firefighting, whereas junior managers resent the senior manager's inability to delegate authority.

Because of its high level of closure, the functional organization is vulnerable to two different kinds of problems in the execution of marketing activities: fragmentation or redundancy. Because no one below the marketing vice president is assigned full responsibility for specific products or markets, there easily can be inadequate, fragmented planning for a given product or market. Products that are not familiar or favorites with various functional specialists may be neglected; or the necessity for constant negotiations with different functional specialists may lead to an excessively short-term orientation. At one beauty products firm, for example, the activities of sales, promotions, and advertising are delegated among different functional specialties, requiring constant interactions among various managers in the development of product marketing programs. One manager (echoing others) notes that "you find yourself in meetings from 9:00 to 5:00 and often willing to go along just to get the meeting over, not because the decision really makes sense. The result is usually a pale compromise among options, rather than a decision."

A related weakness is the difficulty of measuring the results of functionally organized work, since the individual function is concerned with a part of the marketing program, not with its whole. Objectives for each function tend to be set in terms of professional standards rather than in terms of the success of the product or entire marketing program. Because of this, functional organization often breeds levels of management that try to perform an integrating or coordinating role among functional specialties. Hence, despite the initial allocation of "different jobs to different people," the need to deliver an integrated marketing program can lead to the duplication and redundancy of these activities within the functionally focused organization.

Another vulnerability is inherent in the kinds of process and orientation that can easily characterize management in a functional organization. Functional specialists develop patterns of behavior and thought that are in tune with the demands of their jobs and their prior training. These specialists have different ideas and priorities when it comes to developing and executing a program. Also each group develops its own subgoals, which usually include gaining more budget and status vs. other functions. This tendency toward "empire building" often stems from laudable causes but has deplorable consequences for the development of managerial capabilities:[7]

> Every functional manager considers his function the most important one, tries to build it up and is prone to subordinate the welfare of the other functions, if not of the entire business, to the interests of his unit. There is no real remedy against this tendency in the functional organization. The lust for aggrandizement on the part of each function is a result of the laudable desire of each manager to do a good job. . . . Yet the functional specialist may become so narrow in his vision, his skills, and his loyalties as to be totally unfit for general management.

Key Success Factors

Given these strengths and vulnerabilities, the key factors in managing the functionally focused marketing organization revolve around the theme of coordination. These factors include:

1. Systems for ensuring that the goals of different functional groups are consistent and complementary.
2. Measurements that drive coordination of different marketing activities in terms of marketplace results and integrated marketing programs.
3. Human resource policies that encourage managers to develop broader perspectives than that available through a particular functional area of marketing.

Because of its high coordination needs, functionally focused marketing organizations usually have, at any one time, a number of cross-functional product planning committees, venture teams, and product or program integrators. These entities have essentially the same objectives: to perform a role aimed at making trade-offs among different functional goals and relieving top management from having to arbitrate day-to-day choices between one function's imperatives and another's.

This aspect of the functional structure illustrates a larger point about organization. The marketing department (like all organizational entities) faces simultaneous needs for differentiation and integration of its activities.[8] On the one hand, differentiated expertise in different activities is important for the achievement of in-depth knowledge, economies of scale, learning-curve effects, and ongoing efficiencies. In his famous chapter in *The Wealth of Nations* concerning the organization on pin-making factories, Adam Smith long ago emphasized these advantages of the division of labor. On the other hand, collaboration between specialized units or individuals—the integration of discrete activities in a single product or market program—also is essential.

This tension has led some to argue that the appropriateness of the functional structure depends upon the relative routinization vs. customization of the key tasks to be performed by the organization.[9] When the key tasks are relatively routine, repetitive, and hence codifiable, coordination often can be achieved by a centralized plan assembled at headquarters and managed through the hierarchy. If this is the nature of the marketing task facing the firm (or, to put it more accurately, if management and the company's strategy are satisfied with this definition of the marketing task), then the functional organization is often appropriate. In these circumstances, the functional organization encourages efficiencies in the performance of discrete marketing jobs. However, if the marketing task is of a problem-solving nature, requiring the collaboration and ongoing interaction of different groups within the marketing department, then the functional organization can impede necessary coordination. In these circumstances, developing integrated marketing programs (perhaps customized to the needs of different products or markets) is important. But the functional organization provides less incentive for marketing managers to develop skills in cross-functional programs and more incentive for them to maintain an orientation focused on their own specialties.

References

1. E. Raymond Corey and Steven H. Star, *Organization Strategy: A Marketing Approach* (Boston, MA: Harvard Business School Division of Research, 1971), pp. 187–196.
2. David J. Luck, "Interfaces of a Product Manager," *Journal of Marketing* 33 (October 1969): 32–36.
3. John A. Quelch and Paul W. Farris, "General Foods Corporation: The Product Management System" (Boston, MA: Harvard Business School Case Services, 9-586-057), p. 25.
4. See Robert S. Kaplan, "The Evolution of Management Accounting," *The Accounting Review* 54 (July 1984): 390–418; and H. Thomas Johnson and Robert S. Kaplan, *Relevance Lost: The Rise and Fall of Management Accounting* (Boston, MA: Harvard Business School Press, 1987).
5. Mack Hanan, "Reorganize Your Company Around Its Markets," *Harvard Business Review* (November-December 1974): 63.
6. Corey and Star, *op. cit.,* pp. 201–224.
7. Peter F. Drucker, *The Practice of Management* (New York: Harper & Brothers, 1954), p. 208.
8. See Paul R. Lawrence and Jay W. Lorsch, *Organization and Environment: Managing Differentiation and Integration* (Boston, MA: Harvard Business School, 1967, 1986) for the seminal statement of this issue.
9. Arthur H. Walker and Jay W. Lorsch, "Organizational Choice: Product vs. Function," *Harvard Business Review* (November-December 1968): 129–138.

## Chapter 8

Key Interfaces

This chapter considers the marketing organization in relation to the external environment confronting a firm and the internal company environment confronting individual marketing managers. It looks at the impact of different market conditions, a company's resource base, and important internal measurement systems on the organization and conduct of headquarters marketing and field sales, service, and distribution activities.

Boundary Spanning: Issues and Requirements

In Chapter 1, we discussed the boundary-spanning role of marketing in an organization. Marketing is responsible for managing customer encounters effectively. This means keeping the company's marketing strategy aligned with customers' changing buyer behavior, the nature and needs of distribution channels used to reach important customer segments, and threats and opportunities posed by competitors' changing product offerings and marketing strategies. Dealing with the external environment requires marketing managers to work toward the coordination of important inputs to marketing strategy: for example, manufacturing, product engineering, and various aspects of operations such as logistics, credit policies, or service terms. In performing this aspect of their jobs, marketing managers must often cross internal boundaries at their firms.

Indeed, a look at the daily calendars of various marketing managers would reveal that most of them spend more time with personnel in other areas of their own organizations than they do with customers. Further, in dealing with other parts of the company, marketing managers typically encounter an array of different measurement systems, established administrative procedures geared to a particular area's operating concerns, and different orientations and assumptions concerning "what's really important" about the company's business. As a result, in most situations organizing and implementing the marketing effort inevitably means addressing potential conflicts, political processes, resource-allocation battles, and honest disagreements between marketing and other functional areas of the firm.

Take, for example, the relationship between marketing and manufacturing. There are many areas in which cooperation is necessary, but potentially rife with conflict, in their dealings.[1]

Capacity Planning and Sales Forecasts

Partly because of the uncertainties inherent in forecasting and partly because the company personnel closest to the customer (field salespeople) often provide overly optimistic or overly pessimistic projections, capacity planning is a typical bone of contention between marketing and manufacturing. In many industrial firms, manufacturing people, measured primarily on reducing production variances and holding down costs, often second-guess the marketers and pare down sales forecasts. But, if capacity is too low, marketers are justifiably upset because they are losing sales.

Inventory and Physical Distribution

To provide rapid response and fulfillment of customer orders, marketing managers typically welcome a "deep" assortment of inventory in many field warehouse locations. By contrast, manufacturing managers, legitimately concerned with cost control and capacity throughput, seek to minimize "excess" inventory and smooth production runs. In the former situation, the result is often frequent and fast deliveries but higher costs and battered margins. In the latter situation, the result is often better inventory management and coordination with production scheduling but poorer customer service.

Breadth of Product Line and New Product Introductions

Marketing managers often welcome, and argue for, broader product lines and new product introductions in an effort to cover different market segments with a variety of product configurations (e.g., size, shape, and performance characteristics). But what may seem only a minor modification to a marketer often entails a major operating change in manufacturing, requiring new processes, employee training, different production equipment, and the "disruption" of established manufacturing procedures.

Different but analogous issues often generate contention between marketing and finance/accounting functions.[2] Marketers often argue for investments aimed at "opening up new market segments" or for penetration pricing strategies designed to "increase our share"—two typically salient goals of the marketing function in most firms. Meanwhile, finance people often evaluate a proposed investment in design, capacity, and/or selling expenses strictly according to its quantifiable net present value, whereas accounting affects the inputs to these calculations by allocating product overheads in ways that many marketers often consider wrong or "arbitrary."

In each instance the sources of the potential conflict are clear. People in different areas of a firm typically have distinctive skills, resources, capabilities, and short-term objectives. But at the same time, each area of the firm also depends on the performance of others, both for the accomplishment of tasks that serve as inputs for their own specialized functions (e.g., sales forecasts for production scheduling or product-costing data for marketing plan development) and for the attainment of common company goals. More than most areas, however, marketing is in the middle of this cross fire of necessary cooperation and potential conflict. To do their jobs efficiently and effectively, marketing managers must exchange information, resources, and technical expertise across a variety of areas. For this reason, the required interaction with other functional units is a key dimension of the marketing organization.

One way of thinking about the factors affecting marketing's interactions with other areas is outlined in Figure A.[3] In this framework, the important factors involve relationships among: (1) the environmental situation facing the firm and its marketing personnel; (2) the structural and process characteristics that help to channel interactions between marketing and other areas; and (3) the outcomes of these interactions.

The *situational dimension* refers to the context within which interaction between marketing personnel and individuals in other functional departments occurs. This can be further divided into internal and external environmental conditions. Externally, important factors involve the relative complexity and turbulence of the market environment due to changes in buying behavior, competitors' strategies and capabilities, or exogenous factors such as changes in relevant governmental regulations. Generally, more complex and turbulent market environments require a firm to be especially flexible and innovative; this, in turn, creates a greater need for people in different functional areas to interact.[4]

Internally, resource dependence and the company's marketing strategy are key factors affecting marketing's interactions with other functional areas. Because marketing managers do not have or control all the financial, informational, or human resources required to manage customer encounters, they must seek such resources from other functional areas. The extent of such resource dependence typically will be affected by the external environmental conditions just mentioned, creating a greater or lesser need for marketing organization to reflect ongoing transactions with other areas. Similarly, the company's marketing strategy is an important internal condition affecting interfunctional interaction. Organizations whose marketing strategies depend on extensive new product developments, for example, are likely to require greater interaction between marketing and R&D than those where competitive

Figure A
A Framework for Assessing Marketing's Interaction with Another Functional Area

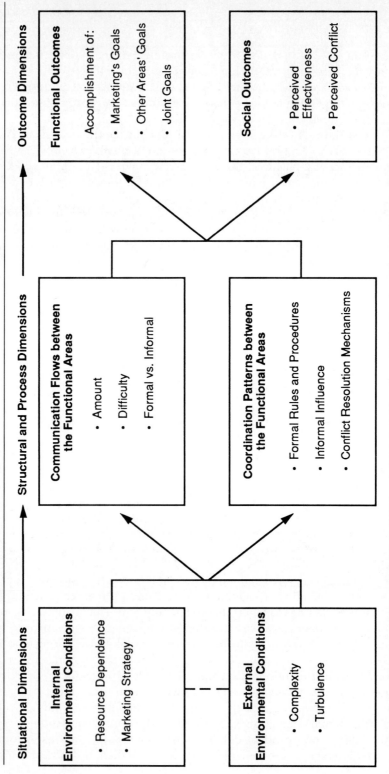

Source: Adapted from Robert W. Ruekert and Orville C. Walker, Jr., "Marketing's Interactions with Other Functions," *Journal of Marketing* 51 (January 1987): 1–19.

advantage is sought through cost reductions and aggressive pricing in mature product markets.

The two sets of situational factors influence the ways in which marketing personnel structure and execute their interactions with other functional areas. In turn, the *structural and process dimension* of interfunctional interaction can be divided into: (1) important communication flows between marketing and other areas, and (2) the coordination mechanisms used to manage these exchanges. Crossing boundaries involves a set of communications between marketing and other areas. Depending upon the nature of the external environment and the company's marketing strategy, such interfunctional communications will need to be more or less frequent, more or less formal or structured (e.g., written reports, memoranda, and financial justifications vs. telephone calls or group meetings), and more or less difficult (i.e., the relative effort required and problems involved in either getting into contact with or in persuading another party to one's point of view).

The coordination dimension involves formal working rules (e.g., who is required to sign off on a given marketing-related decision), the amount of influence a member of one unit can exert on a member of another, and the conflict resolution mechanisms typically used when either formal rules or informal influence fails. In any company, rules and standard operating procedures evolve to coordinate the flow of interactions among different functional areas. Typically the greater the formalization of such procedures, the less room there is for exceptions in the face of external changes and demands. As a result, such rules carry administrative costs and therefore are not used in all situations. The framework outlined here suggests that the relative formality and importance of these rules will be related to the extent of marketing's resource dependence on another functional area and the kinds of interactions implied by the external environment and the company's marketing strategy.

Also because formalized rules and procedures cannot be developed for every eventuality, informal influence over decisions made in other functional areas is also a salient aspect of a marketing organization. In some firms, for example, marketing managers wield considerable influence over the operating decisions of production or R&D managers, whereas in other firms marketing managers have less influence and are essentially the recipients of what the laboratories develop and the factories produce. Finally, the manner in which conflicts are resolved is another important aspect of the structural and process dimensions of interfunctional interactions. Organizational theorists have usefully distinguished among several typical conflict resolution mechanisms, including: (1) avoidance of the conflict; (2) smoothing over conflicts by focusing on common interests or adopting short-term "defensive routines," (3) openly confronting the issues and resolving the dispute through negotiations, and (4) resorting to higher authority to decide the issue unilaterally.[5] Each of these conflict resolution mechanisms may be appropriate in certain situations, but the effective use of each will be affected by the situational dimensions. In turn, each affects the performance outcomes of the marketing organization.

The final component of this framework refers to the outcomes that result from marketing's interactions with other functional units. The *outcome dimension* can be divided into: (1) the functional or performance outcomes for all parties involved, and (2) the social outcomes experienced by the participants. Functional outcomes include the degree to which marketing's goals, another area's goals, and any joint, companywide goals are accomplished. In practice, this often means which numbers (e.g., market share, sales volume, reduction of manufacturing variances, financial objectives, and/or earnings goals) take priority in the decision and its implementation. Social outcomes refer to important intangibles of these interactions: the extent to which the people involved in the interaction perceive the process itself as relatively effective and as involving a justifiable or unjustifiable amount of conflict. These aspects are important because marketing managers' interactions with another part of their companies almost always involve an ongoing series of requests, negotiations, and demands in the face of different customers' evolving needs. Making this quarter's numbers by persuading manufacturing to produce and carry inventory in excess of actual sales volume, for instance, often means sacrificing future influence over production's allocation of resources. As a result, marketing managers must pay attention to the social as well as performance aspects of their interactions with other functional areas.

This is clearly a very broad framework that requires a grounding in specific company and decision contexts. But, it is useful for directing our attention to the situational dimensions that affect marketing's interfaces with other functions. The case studies provide a grounding by focusing on important external and internal environmental conditions that affect key marketing tasks, the role of marketing personnel within the firm, and the design of the marketing organization itself.

Case Studies

The first case in this chapter focuses on Frito-Lay, a leader in snack foods, and particularly on the marketing structure and systems that support its "store door" field marketing activities. The organization described in this case study has been cited repeatedly as an example of marketing "excellence," and you should consider whether you agree with that evaluation.

The Frito-Lay case has no explicit decision or problem for you to solve, but it nonetheless poses challenging questions that directly affect marketing organization and implementation:

1. In your view, how valid or complete are the reasons cited by Frito-Lay's top management concerning the firm's historical growth and success in the salty snacks segment of the food market?
2. What are the important elements of consumer and channel behavior that affect marketing requirements in this business?

3. How do Frito-Lay's sales and distribution structures try to address these requirements?
4. In your view, what are the major strengths and potential vulnerabilities of the marketing organization described in this case?

The next case, Imperial Distributors, Inc. (A), concerns a regional service merchandiser. Changes in the firm's market environment have top management in this firm considering changes in the structure, compensation, logistics, and training of its marketing personnel. As well as requiring specific decisions, this case provides valuable information concerning an important type of channel intermediary for many package-goods firms that sell to supermarkets.

Like Frito-Lay, Imperial sells to various types of food stores through truck-driving salespeople who order selected products and provide shelf merchandising services. In analyzing this case, therefore, consider what lessons learned in the Frito-Lay case discussion might apply to the situation and decisions confronting Imperial's president. Consider, also, the following questions:

1. What functions does a service merchandiser perform, and how do changes in Imperial's marketplace affect the relative value of these functions for its suppliers and food store customers?
2. What can we learn from the case appendix about the essential field marketing requirements in this business?
3. What is "firefighting" in the service merchandising business? How would you distinguish firefighting from customer service?
4. What should the president of Imperial do about the possible changes concerning the firm's marketing organization outlined at the end of the case narrative?

The third case in this chapter, Peripheral Products Company (PPCo), concerns a marketing organization in a rapidly changing and technologically complex marketplace. PPCo manufactures and sells disk drives. In recent years, prices have fallen substantially, and new markets have emerged, raising various issues for PPCo management. In particular, the vice president of marketing, Mr. James Ousley, is concerned about the emergence of a "gray market" for PPCo's products and its impact on channel conflict, sales force management, and pricing policies.

This is a particularly complex case where an important dimension of analysis hinges on understanding the differing internal perspectives at PPCo on the gray market and the ensuing implications for Mr. Ousley who, as head of the marketing organization, is in the middle of these differing perspectives. In analyzing the case, consider the following questions:

1. What is the problem in this case? Whose problem is it? How "big" or "small" a problem is it for the PPCo division? For Mr. Ousley?
2. What are the important characteristics of the disk drive industry that affect the gray market situation? How would you characterize PPCo's strategy within the industry?

3. What is your evaluation of the alternatives being considered for dealing with the gray market? How will each functional area within the PPCo organization view each alternative?

4. What should Mr. Ousley do? How should any proposed changes in pricing, distribution, or sales management practices be implemented?

Thus, this chapter begins by focusing on two consumer goods firms (Frito-Lay and Imperial Distributors) that sell to the same group of customers through similar means but in different competitive environments and ends with a focus on an industrial, high-tech company and the issues facing the marketing organization in attempting to coordinate among manufacturing, product management, field sales, and other internal units of the company.

References

1. Benson P. Shapiro, "Can Marketing and Manufacturing Coexist?" *Harvard Business Review* 55 (September-October 1977): 121–132; and D. A. Clare and D. G. Sanford, "Cooperation and Conflict Between Industrial Sales and Production," *Industrial Marketing Management* 13 (1984): 163–169.

2. See Paul F. Anderson, "Marketing Investment Analysis," in *Research in Marketing*, ed. by J. N. Sheth, Vol. 4 (Greenwich, CT: JAI Press, Inc., 1981), pp. 1–37; and Patrick Barwise, Paul R. Marsh, and Robin Wensley, "Must Finance and Strategy Clash?" *Harvard Business Review* 67 (September-October 1989): 85–90.

3. This perspective on the factors affecting marketing's interfaces with other functions, and the framework presented in Figure A, is adapted from Robert W. Ruekert and Orville C. Walker, Jr., "Marketing's Interactions with Other Functional Units: A Conceptual Framework and Empirical Evidence," *Journal of Marketing* 51 (January 1987): 1–19.

4. See Paul R. Lawrence, "The Organization and Environment Perspective," in *Perspectives on Organization Design and Behavior*, ed. by A. Van de Ven and E. Joyce (New York: John Wiley & Sons, Inc.), pp. 311–345.

5. This typology of conflict-resolution mechanisms was introduced by R. R. Blake and J. R. Mouton, *The Managerial Grid* (Houston, TX: Gulf Publishing Company, 1964) and applied to interfunctional issues by Paul R. Lawrence and Jay W. Lorsch, "Differentiation and Integration in Complex Organizations," *Administrative Science Quarterly* 12 (June 1967): 1–47. See also, Chris Argyris, *Strategy, Change and Defensive Routines* (Boston: Pitman Publishing, Inc., 1985) for a discussion of conflict nonresolution mechanisms that often impede implementation.

Frito-Lay, Inc. (A)

Company and Industry Background

"The focus of this business is on execution and marketing control," said Mr. Willard C. Korn, senior vice president for marketing and sales for Frito-Lay, Incorporated (FLI). "But, if you look around my office, you'll see I have no files of any sort. I run my part of the business with only eight exhibits even though we make almost 170,000 sales calls per day, have 38 manufacturing plants, and a sales force of almost 9,000 people."

Mr. D. Wayne Calloway, president of Frito-Lay, Inc., replied:

> Yes, but controls aren't the whole story. The worst sin anyone can commit at Frito-Lay is to fail to communicate. You may have noticed that I have most of my vice presidents within "easy reach" on this floor—that's no accident.
>
> I think our primary business strengths are distribution and sales. However, the fact that these areas are subject to rapid change means top management must be involved in the details of the business. That's why we insist on weekly reporting at a minimum. Sales reports are distributed every Friday morning. Manufacturing variance reports arrive each Monday morning. This company is a paper generator, and management has to pick clear, simple measures or it will get buried.
>
> The heart of Frito-Lay is consistency. The Frito-Lay display in Joplin, Missouri, is identical to the one in Waltham, Massachusetts. In fact, the *way* the display is stocked in Joplin is the same as the way it is stocked in Waltham.

Mr. John Cranor, vice president of marketing, said:

> We have to be consistent. We're talking about a business where we served 300,000 outlets last year, an average of between 2 and 3 times per week. We move almost 4 billion product units annually.

This case was prepared by Professor Thomas V. Bonoma as the basis for class discussion rather than to illustrate either effective or ineffective handling of an administrative situation. Certain proprietary company data have been disguised.

The Frito-Lay section of a high volume supermarket exhausts its inventory, or "turns" more than 100 times a year. A particularly well-accepted brand might turn once a day in such a store. We manage all this with a maximum 35-day shelf life on our products, and sell half of our volume of goods for cash. You'd better have consistency and control in that kind of an environment, or the whole thing will get away from you in a week.

"No, no, no!" said Jack DeMarco, vice president of sales. "All our home office controls and consistency are great. But the *real* reason this place works so well is that we run our 9,000 route salespeople like an army. They're good, they're disciplined, and they're very effective on the street."

Frito-Lay, Incorporated

Frito-Lay, Incorporated was a division of PepsiCo, Incorporated, which had net sales of over $5.9 billion in 1980. PepsiCo, Incorporated was best known for its beverage products which had sales of approximately $2.3 billion in 1980 led by such brands as Pepsi Cola© and Mountain Dew® and for its Frito-Lay snack products which had sales of approximately $1.5 billion in 1980. PepsiCo also owned Pizza Hut and Taco Bell (1980 sales of $872 million), North American Van Lines and Lee Way Motor Freight ($673 million) and Wilson Sporting Goods Company ($230 million). Seventy-one percent of PepsiCo's 1980 operating profits were from its beverage and food products (not restaurants) business lines.

FLI, which had its first billion dollar sales year in 1978, was responsible for U.S. sales of Frito-Lay products. PepsiCo Foods International marketed snack products overseas. The foreign portion of PepsiCo's business, including all lines of business, generated over $1.3 billion for the company in 1980.

FLI was formed in 1961 by merger of the Frito Company and the H. W. Lay and Company. C. E. Doolin and Herman W. Lay started their respective companies in 1932. Both borrowed $100 for initial capitalization—Mr. Doolin to buy the recipe for a tasty Mexican product made from corn masa or dough; Mr. Lay to buy a distributorship for an Atlanta potato chip manufacturer.

In turn, PepsiCo, Incorporated was formed in 1965 through a merger of the Pepsi-Cola Company and Frito-Lay, Incorporated. "What we had in Frito-Lay, Incorporated in the early years," Mr. Calloway stated, "was a very decentralized business comprised of many small, regional potato chip companies. Even the manufacturing plants were managed on a regional level. During my first tour of duty at Frito-Lay during the late sixties and early seventies, one of my chief tasks was to help reorganize the company and to install planning and control systems." Mr. Calloway pointed out that Frito-Lay was organized into geographic sales centers, or zones. Each zone used to be run as a separate business. "The zones were autonomous financially then, but aren't anymore," Mr. Calloway said.

Today, we have seven functional departments here in Dallas which set policies for all the sales zones and the now separate manufacturing areas—manufacturing, quality control, sales, marketing, the finance area, employee relations, and the law department. For instance, our brand management marketing structure assures national consistency across the country, though there are some local variations. In addition, though much of our labor force isn't unionized, it is Dallas that sets the limits for bargaining with the unions in other parts of the country.

Exhibit 1 shows a partial FLI corporate organization chart.

The Snack Food Industry

The size of the snack food industry was somewhat ill-defined and tended to vary with the motivation of the reporter. The total snack industry was made up of a multiplicity of products ranging from beer, wine, and colas through ice cream and cookies to chips, gum, and candy. But, management felt that FLI could be best described as competing in the "dry snack" category of the snack food industry. One 1978 estimate of the "dry snack" category of the total snack food market yielded a $12.4 billion (in retail sales) category including the following:

	Retail Sales ($ billions)	%
Cookies	$ 2.5	20.0%
Potato chips	1.7	13.7
Bar candy goods	1.5	12.0
Savory crackers	1.4	11.0
Nut meats	1.2	9.6
Snack cakes and pies	1.0	8.0
Gum	0.8	6.0
Tortilla/corn chips	0.8	6.0
Pretzels	0.4	3.0
Meat snacks	0.2	1.6
Miscellaneous extruded snacks	0.2	1.6
Hard roll candy	0.2	1.6
Prepopped popcorn	0.2	0.8
Sweet crackers	0.2	0.8
Cereal bars	0.1	0.8
Toaster pastries	0.1	0.8
Frozen pastries	0.1	0.8
	$12.6	98.1%

Another 1978 study identified an estimated $8.6 billion retail sales category which included the following products:

	($ billions)	%
Salty snacks	$1.602	19%
Cookies	1.496	17
Candy	1.408	16
Cake	1.144	13
Crackers	0.792	9
Spreads	0.792	9
Other baked goods	0.704	8
Gum	0.352	4
Miscellaneous	0.352	4
	$8.642	99%

With the exception of some new business ventures, almost all of Frito-Lay's dollar sales came from potato chips (29%), tortilla chips (27%), pretzels (about 12%), corn chips (16%), cheese puffs (approximately 10%), and processed potato chips (about 3%). Exhibit 2 gives total salted snack segment dollar volumes by each product type from 1976 to 1980 inclusive, excepting processed potato chips, nuts, and other miscellaneous foods (e.g., bean dip). Exhibit 3 provides the same data in pounds of product sold.

The salted snack segment of the snack food market was served by three types of competitors. The first was manufacturers producing major national brands, such as Frito-Lay (Fritos® brand corn chips, Doritos® brand tortilla chips, Tostitos® brand crispy round tortilla chips, Rold Gold® brand pretzels, Lay's® brand potato chips, Ruffles® brand potato chips, and others), Bordens (Wise brand potato chips and pretzels, Guys brand potato and corn chips, Old London brand cheese crackers, and Cracker Jack brand caramel corn), Nabisco (several products such as pretzels and snack crackers sold under the Nabisco brand name), Standard Brands (Planters brand nuts, pretzels, cheese puffs, corn chips and Pinata brand tortilla chips) and Procter & Gamble (Pringles brand processed potato chips). These major branded manufacturers collectively sold slightly over 50% of the total pounds of salted snacks consumed in the United States in 1980.

Standard Brands and Procter & Gamble sold their products packaged in canisters and distributed them through food wholesalers' and retailers' warehouses. Frito-Lay, Nabisco, and Bordens packaged their products in flexible bags and had their own route salespeople deliver products directly to the retail outlets from which they would be resold.

Especially in the potato chip and pretzel product classes, a large number of strong regional manufacturers also produced branded goods. For example, in the northeast United States, both Snyder (potato chips and pretzels) and Bachman (potato chips and pretzels) were strong regional brands. In the western United States, Laura Scudder and Sunshine were regional manufacturers with almost 20% of salty snack sales between them. On national average, however, the regional branded manufacturers held approximately 35% of salty snack pound volume.

Finally, private label goods were usually produced on contract by regional or local manufacturers. The product was either labelled with the customer's own brand name, as when a major supermarket chain marketed its own "house" brand of salty snacks, or with a "captive" brand of the manufacturer which was granted exclusively to a given customer in a geographic area. Private label goods held about 14% of the salty snack poundage consumed in the United States in 1980.

FLI held about 16% of the $12.4 billion retail dry snack category, which included salty snacks. This 16% share was equivalent to over $1 billion at manufacturer's prices. Frito-Lay's products accounted for an estimated 46% of the overall poundage of the salty snacks consumed in 1980. However, Frito-Lay's share varied widely across the United States. In the Northeast, for example, Frito-Lay sold only 31% of the total salty snack poundage consumed there. In the southwestern United States, the company sold almost 80%.

Similarly, Frito-Lay's sales varied by salty snack product class. FLI products accounted for over 81% of both corn and tortilla chip pounds consumed, while accounting for only 32% of potato chip consumption and 14% of pretzel consumption. Exhibit 4 gives Frito-Lay's estimated dollar and pound percent of total salty snack sales by major product class for the years 1976–1980. Exhibit 5 shows the top five salty snack vendors' estimated percentage of pound sales by product category for the United States.

Frito-Lay Marketing

Mr. John M. Cranor, vice president of marketing for Frito-Lay, was 35 and a graduate of the Harvard Business School. He supervised a staff of six marketing directors. Five of the marketing directors in turn each supervised three or four product managers in a product category. For example, the marketing director for potato chips products supervised a product manager for Lay's® brand potato chips, one for Ruffles® brand potato chips, and one for new potato snacks. Each product manager was assisted by one or more associate product managers and one or more assistant product managers. The associate product manager usually assisted in managing the major brand and also managed a minor brand.

The sixth marketing director supervised brand support services, such as graphics services, consumer promotions, market information analysis and marketing research.

With the exception of the director of support services, product managers and marketing directors had profit accountability for their brands.

Frito-Lay Products and Accounts

Approximately 77% of Frito-Lay's revenue was generated from regular flex goods, 17% from small flex goods, and less than 6% from Go-B-Tweens®. Regular "flex" products (so named because the package was flexible) included family-sized bags of all Frito-Lay chip products, like $1.09 Doritos® brand tortilla chips. Small flex products included most of the same products packaged in individual-serve bags which were usually sold to complement a meal or as a separate snack. Go-B-Tweens® were a line of cookies, nuts, peanut butter crackers, processed beef sticks, and other snacks packaged in individual-serve sizes.

Frito-Lay sold its products in a large number of different outlets across the United States. For example, a typical geographic marketing area, one of Frito-Lay's six sales zones, included the following mix of business from five sales divisions (roughly corresponding to metropolitan areas) and 1,500 routes:

Type	Number	Average Weekly Sales	Calls/ Week
Supermarkets	5,500	$348	2.6
Convenience stores	5,200	108	1.7
Small groceries	13,000	50	1.2
Military commissaries	39	504	2.4
Liquor stores	2,700	57	1.2
Service stations	4,000	26	1.1
Nonfood stores	4,000	52	1.3
Schools	1,100	29	1.2
Colleges, universities	187	80	1.3
Vending and caterers	285	71	1.2
Eating places	5,000	19	1.1
Drinking places	5,100	68	1.1
Hospitals	241	51	1.2
Employee cafeterias	540	27	1.1
Hotels and motels	227	24	1.1
Government buildings	165	47	1.3
Penitentiaries	47	115	1.0

Accounts also could be categorized in other ways for analytic purposes. For example, much of the supermarket and convenience store business was comprised of many outlets owned by a single chain. Chain buyers decided whether Frito-Lay products would be authorized for sale in all outlets of a particular chain. Buyers also controlled, from a single chain headquarters location, how much space would be allocated to various product lines. Nonchain buyers made individual decisions for their separate outlets. Approximately 40% of Frito-Lay's business was generated from chain stores, which made up almost 20% of the total number of Frito-Lay accounts. Chain store sales calls and business reviews almost always required the participation of Frito-Lay division or zone management. Much of Frito-Lay's sales efforts went into securing shelf space for snacks in competition with sellers of paper products, cereals, pet foods, canned goods, and so on as well as making sure that FLI products received a fair share of the snack shelf space.

Accounts that did not require the participation of Frito-Lay sales management included "mom and pop" grocery stores, nonfood outlets, and, generally, any nonchain account where Frito-Lay route salespersons could gain display space and increase distribution. Route salespersons were expected to spend time as part of their route activities in selling these "Big [that is, important]/Little" accounts. "Big/Little" accounts were over 80% of Frito-Lay's total accounts, and represented almost 60% of its sales.

Supermarkets accounted for 35% of Frito-Lay's sales in 1980, and 11% of its 33,000 accounts. Convenience stores, making up 13% of its accounts, were responsible for 9% of sales. Nonfood stores, such as variety and discount stores, comprised 3% of sales and almost 6% of accounts. Military sales were 2% of 1980 totals, and less than 1% of accounts. Finally, all other accounts, which included service stations, liquor stores, small grocery stores, and a variety of institutional customers, were almost 70% of total accounts and accounted for over 50% of Frito-Lay's 1980 sales.

Frito-Lay Sales and Distribution

Frito-Lay's products were displayed in a number of ways in different types of outlets. In supermarkets, grocery stores, and other food outlets, its snacks might be placed on gondola shelving (regular aisle-type supermarket shelving), either in a primary display in the snack section or in a secondary display (a display in addition to the primary supermarket one, located perhaps on the end of an aisle). Where the retail outlet did not have standardized gondola shelving, Frito-Lay offered custom shelves to fit the customer's display space. Small flex products and Go-B-Tweens® were sold either from custom-made shelving, or from wire racks on which packets were clipped or hung. Often, stores would have a special wire-rack display near the cash register, called a check-out display. The amount of shelf space a manufacturer's product commanded in a retail outlet, the servicing of the manufacturer's space, the location of the space, the merchandising of the product, and the number of separate displays all had a relationship to the amount of product sold.

Frito-Lay used a store-door distribution system to get its products from the factory to the retail outlet. In a store-door system, the manufacturer performed the "wholesaling" function itself by delivering the product directly to the retail store-door and then servicing the manufacturer's allotted shelf space. Approximately 300,000 retail outlets were served in this manner by Frito-Lay's 9,000 route salespeople throughout the United States.

Frito-Lay sold its goods in six major geographical territories in the United States, which were serviced through a system of owned distribution centers, including warehouses, large distribution centers, and through what were called "bin warehouses." In distribution centers, route salespeople picked their own orders from the warehouse shelves before starting their selling/delivery day. In bin warehouses, which were located in areas where product volume was lower, the salesperson was responsible for stocking the warehouse bins, picking his/her own truckload, and then selling his/her route. Exhibit 6 shows Frito-Lay's major distribution centers, routes and bin routes (a route or bin route consisted of the activities of one salesperson), as well as Frito-Lay's field organization. Each zone was divided into several divisions, which in turn were subdivided into regions and districts. Exhibit 7 is a map of the Frito-Lay zones and divisions as of January 1980.

Sales administration was located in Frito-Lay headquarters in Dallas, where all policy setting occurred. Mr. Jack DeMarco, vice president of sales, supervised zone sales vice presidents of each of Frito-Lay's six geographic zones. In addition, Mr. DeMarco supervised two other administrative units, sales development and sales planning/administration. The sales development unit conducted research and set policy on vending sales, retail trade management, promotions, and space allocations. The unit also handled "special accounts," like military and export sales. The planning and administration unit concerned itself with management of Frito-Lay's over 10,000 unit fleet of trucks, its distribution facilities, and the company's report and control forms.

"In addition to achieving our volume objectives, controlling costs are crucial to our business," said Jack DeMarco. "With a store-door distribution system, we have to keep a close eye not only on route allocations and managing the paperwork, but on our selling expenses as well. For example, we provide most of the display shelving, called gondolas, for our customers. Frito-Lay owns most of the racks on which our products sit, both primary displays and stand-alone or end-displays. We monitor these costs, as well as our truck fleet expense which could be a money-eater." Exhibit 8 shows Frito-Lay's sales expenses by category for 1980.

Frito-Lay Field Sales—On the Truck

On Friday, January 23, Mr. Jess Pagluica started his day at 5:30 A.M. at Frito-Lay's Billerica, Massachusetts warehouse. Mr. Pagluica, 29, who had previously driven a truck for Pepsi-Cola Bottling Company in the Boston area, had worked for two years as a route salesperson for Frito-Lay. All salespeople in Mr. Pagluica's district were required to pick their own orders each day for delivery to their customers. Since many retail stores preferred that no vendor salespeople be in the store to service displays after 12 noon on most days, Mr. Pagluica had to get an early start in order to finish his day's quota of calls. As he filled out the Frito-Lay optical-scan order invoice to mark down how much product he was "buying" from the warehouse, Mr. Pagluica said, "From here on in, I am responsible for this product. If we're short at the end of the day, it's my responsibility. What we'll be doing today, after I load the truck, is to make a very easy round of five calls this morning. You know, everything we do, including packing goods on the truck, saving knocked-down product cartons, truck maintenance, and even the way I'm making these numbers on this invoice, is closely supervised and spelled out in the company's training program. But, we can talk along the way—let's get going."

Like all Frito-Lay route salespeople, Mr. Pagluica had undergone intensive training before being given a permanent route. This training included a 10-course, programmed learning route sales training program ("the Book"), field training with the Boston district manager, and several months as a relief salesperson filling in when regular route salespeople were ill or on vacation. "The Book" prescribed route sales activity from sales planning to postsale service. "Frito-Lay doesn't give exams," Mr. Pagluica said, "but you do things by 'the Book' not only to please your superiors but to maximize sales."

Mr. Pagluica's call activities were dictated by a set of five different route books, one for each day of the week. These small books were similar to appointment calendars. They were designed to slip into a larger metal binder on which the salesperson filled out orders. The route sales book contained customer contact information, scheduling frequency, and, most important, the store's "build-up" or normal full display of Frito-Lay products. Exhibit 9 shows the Frito-Lay route book, route card, and an explanation of this system extracted from the Frito-Lay route sales training program.

Mr. Pagluica's territory was a geographically small one in Arlington and Lexington, Massachusetts. He worked roughly within a 25-square-mile area, and serviced a total of 38 accounts requiring approximately 52 calls per week. Several of his accounts were serviced 3–5 times per week, though some "Big/Little" accounts only required weekly service and some chain supermarkets might have to be serviced twice in one day. Mr. Pagluica did not work Saturdays or Sundays.

Mr. Pagluica's first stop was the Foodmaster supermarket on Massachusetts Avenue in Arlington, Massachusetts. He arrived at 8:30 A.M., checked his route card for the "buildup" required, and went into the store to check the customer's display and inventory. As he straightened up the remaining stock in the gondola, Mr. Pagluica said, "This display is so far from good national pattern it's ridiculous. But, there's nothing I can do. I know how the display should look, since Frito-Lay has established national guidelines for pattern on all displays. But these guys have cut us back on space, and there's little I can do except neaten up the stock as best I can."

Mr. Pagluica was referring to Frito-Lay's Six-Point Space Management Program, a part of which deals with the "national pattern." This plan required the sales force to display Frito-Lay goods according to research-directed color, size, and price patterning in order to maximize customer response and purchase behavior. "At best," Mr. Pagluica said, "I've got something like two seconds to reach that consumer. The display had better be good."

After he greeted and conferred with the store manager about several opened or stale packages of Frito-Lay products he had removed from the display (the store would get full credit for the goods), Mr. Pagluica went back to his truck. As he loaded his handtruck with cartons of Frito-Lay products and checked them off on what would become the customer's bill, he said, "This store is tough. Frito-Lay district management and chain headquarters have been having a squabble, and these guys have cut me back on gondola space. I still have one primary gondola and an end cap [a secondary display on the end of a supermarket aisle] to work with, but the regionals have all the potato chip space. I'd better grab this roll of Fritos® brand corn chip price stickers here. Most stores expect us to specially price our promotional items ourselves. I'd also better get two extra cases of Fritos® brand corn chips. I won't be back till Monday. They can keep these in the back room for the weekend rush."

Back in the store, Mr. Pagluica opened every carton of incoming product in front of the store manager, carefully checking with the manager that the number of products marked on the invoice actually matched the number being brought into the store. Mr. Pagluica was always careful to do this checking, he said, even if the customer didn't care or didn't want to do it. "That way, they know I'm not inadvertently cheating them," he pointed out. "Frito-Lay management is committed to the integrity of the store-door system."

Back at the gondola display, Mr. Pagluica restocked the shelves with fresh product. He was careful to rotate his stock so that the packages with the oldest manufacturing dates were placed in front. He also took the time to "flex" every bag gently so that it was not wrinkled or folded. "These little things," he said, "don't seem like much, but they really help. Good attention to rotation keeps me from having to pull stale product as unsaleable when I'm restocking. Flexing and lacing the packages is another way to 'spiff up' the display, and to get the customer to buy. I'll even clean shelves if need be, because the stores don't do it anymore. People won't buy product from dirty shelves."

After making some small talk with the store manager, Mr. Pagluica left the manager the customer copy of the sales ticket, and left the store for his next call. The total bill was $145.10, minus $3.35 in promotional allowance for the Fritos® brand corn chips the store had bought and $.88 credit for spoiled product. Since Foodmaster was a charge account, no money changed hands. The time was 9:25 A.M.

"About half of my business is in cash, but the supermarkets are almost all charge accounts," Mr. Pagluica pointed out as he drove through the heavy morning traffic. "It is extremely important that the sales ticket be correct, and that there be no mistakes in the product I bring into the store. One good thing is that, despite the fact that I had to learn how to write numbers all over again, those computer tickets we use are great. They even have price extension tables on the back so I don't have to use my calculator." Exhibit 10 shows a front and reverse copy of the Frito-Lay route sales ticket.

The next stop, at 9:30 A.M. was D'Agustino's Deli in Arlington. This was a small delicatessen with both a primary and secondary display of Frito-Lay products. Very few of Frito-Lay's products had moved in the deli since Monday, so Mr. Pagluica spent several minutes talking to one of the two brothers who owned the store. He removed some stale product and straightened and minimally restocked the shelves. The order, which was paid in cash, totalled $20.53. As he drove to the next stop, Mr. Pagluica said, "That guy really doesn't need to carry so much of our product, but it makes him feel important. I've got to start cutting him back a little, though." Frito-Lay believed in trying to get as much space as it needed, but also in not taking more space than it could use.

Mr. Pagluica's third and fourth stops were in a small A&P supermarket in Lexington and a busy Stop & Shop in Arlington. Again, he checked his build-up card in the truck, visited the manager, removed stales and straightened up the display during his first visit in the store. Then, he went back to his truck, pulled and checked the order, closely checked it again with the "checker" in the store (a clerk charged with receiving merchandise), and restocked the display. He also put up some special promotional materials, flexed the bags and cleaned the display. The charge ticket came to $82.60 in the A&P, and $170 in the Stop & Shop.

Mr. Pagluica's final stop of the morning was at 11:40 A.M. at the Melrose Spa. The spa was located at a busy intersection in Arlington. Though it had only 1,500 square feet of selling space, it was one of Mr. Pagluica's major "Big/Little" accounts. As he checked the Frito-Lay displays (there were three of them) in the store, Mr. Pagluica found "cordwooded" product (i.e., potato chip bags laid horizontally on top of other bags) in violation of Frito-Lay's national pattern.

The Melrose Spa had a large amount of display space devoted to Frito-Lay products, especially Lay's® brand potato chips. It took Mr. Pagluica the better part of a half-hour to straighten out the displays. Still, he couldn't get all the product packed correctly. "These guys sell so much product that we don't get angry if they stock the shelves themselves," Mr. Pagluica noted as he walked back to the truck. "But, you see what would happen if we let everybody do their own stocking." Mr. Pagluica stocked several cases of Lay's® brand potato chips, Fritos® brand corn chips and Doritos® brand tortilla chips in Melrose Spa's basement after checking the order with one of the owners. He then collected $138 in cash.

As he sat drinking coffee and eating an English muffin, Mr. Pagluica said, "You've got to remember that I get to sell a product that in some ways sells itself. With a little attention to detail and the good plans out of district, you can make a good living at this job. But my goal is to be a first-level supervisor, so I've recently started college. It may take 10 years at night, but the company pays my educational expenses. I think this is the kind of company I want to stay with for a long time."

Exhibit 1 Frito-Lay, Inc. (A)

Partial Organization Chart

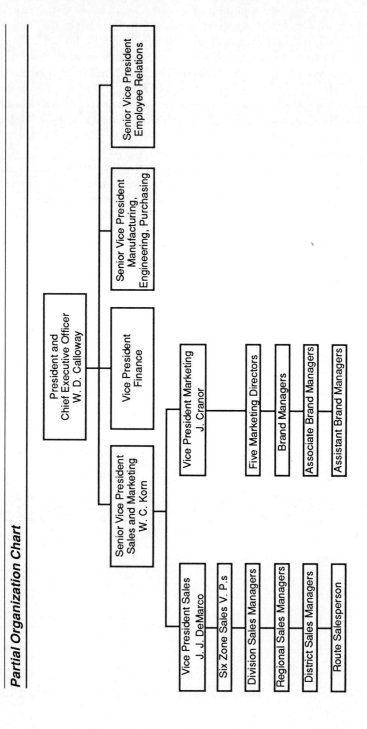

Exhibit 2 Frito-Lay, Inc. (A)

Manufacturers' Dollar Volumes—Salted Snack Segment Total U.S. (Food Store)
($000s omitted)

	1976	1977	1978	1979	1980
Total salty snacks* Index vs. Y/A	1,544,300 (107)	1,642,074 (106)	1,835,184 (112)	2,089,967 (114)	2,432,716 (116)
Total potato chips Index vs. Y/A	775,500 (111)	831,113 (107)	909,396 (109)	1,029,979 (113)	1,118,245 (115)
Total corn chips Index vs. Y/A	166,800 (106)	169,849 (102)	173,872 (102)	209,425 (120)	242,345 (116)
Total tortilla chips Index vs. Y/A	199,800 (133)	247,426 (124)	313,730 (127)	378,084 (121)	486,565 (129)
Total cheese puffs Index vs. Y/A	120,800 (99)	131,573 (109)	154,944 (118)	190,921 (123)	242,446 (127)
Total pretzels Index vs. Y/A	129,700 (101)	126,420 (97)	133,114 (105)	149,771 (113)	175,453 (117)
Total all other Index vs. Y/A	151,700 (81)	135,693 (89)	150,129 (117)	131,787 (88)	167,662 (127)
Total Frito-Lay Index vs. Y/A	619,900 (113)	693,481 (112)	794,171 (115)	977,433 (123)	1,222,290 (125)
Total competition Index vs. Y/A	924,400 (103)	948,593 (103)	1,041,013 (110)	1,112,534 (107)	1,210,426 (109)

* Y/A = year ago.

Exhibit 3 Frito-Lay, Inc. (A)

Pound Volumes—Salted Snack Segment Total U.S. (Food Store)
(in pounds, 000s omitted)

	1976	1977	1978	1979	1980
Total salty snacks*	1,039,700	1,071,569	1,118,071	1,146,878	1,212,725
Index vs. Y/A	(106)	(103)	(104)	(103)	(106)
Total potato chips	482,800	500,404	513,917	530,425	560,642
Index vs. Y/A	(110)	(104)	(103)	(103)	(106)
Total corn chips	132,900	133,758	128,369	133,454	139,521
Index vs. Y/A	(105)	(101)	(96)	(104)	(105)
Total tortilla chips	124,200	148,161	172,367	186,599	216,916
Index vs. Y/A	(129)	(119)	(116)	(108)	(116)
Total cheese puffs	78,100	83,697	92,267	102,248	115,488
Index vs. Y/A	(99)	(107)	(110)	(111)	(113)
Total pretzels	134,000	127,210	131,885	132,342	138,995
Index vs. Y/A	(97)	(95)	(104)	(100)	(105)
Total all other	87,700	78,340	79,265	61,810	41,162
Index vs. Y/A	(83)	(89)	(101)	(78)	(67)
Total Frito-Lay	395,600	428,677	453,451	489,630	555,150
Index vs. Y/A	(111)	(108)	(106)	(108)	(113)
All competition	644,100	642,892	664,620	657,248	657,575
Index vs. Y/A	(103)	(99)	(103)	(99)	(100)

* Y/A = year ago.

Exhibit 4 Frito-Lay, Inc. (A)

Frito-Lay Share of Salty Snack Segment
(data in %)

Dollars

	% Share of Total Salty Snacks	Potato Chips	Corn Chips	Tortilla Chips	Cheese Puffs	Pretzels
1976	40.1	27.3	81.6	88.3	52.6	13.7
1977	42.2	29.9	79.9	84.8	52.2	14.2
1978	43.3	30.9	81.5	59.0	51.8	14.4
1979	46.8	33.3	78.3	81.9	58.0	15.5
1980	50.2	36.7	79.4	84.7	57.8	15.8

Pounds

	% Share of Total Salty Snacks	Potato Chips	Corn Chips	Tortilla Chips	Cheese Puffs	Pretzels
1976	38.0	24.4	80.0	87.0	50.8	13.1
1977	40.0	26.8	78.5	83.9	51.0	13.4
1978	40.6	27.1	79.9	58.4	50.8	13.6
1979	42.7	28.4	78.0	80.2	55.3	13.9
1980	45.8	31.7	78.5	82.9	55.1	14.2

Exhibit 5 **Frito-Lay, Inc. (A)**

Top 5 Vendors by Product Class—Pound Share Total U.S.—1980

Total Salty Snacks			Potato Chips			Corn Chips		
Vendors		S. O. M.	Vendors		S. O. M.	Vendors		S. O. M.
1. Bordens		5.7	1. Laura Scudder		3.1	1. Nabisco		3.4
2. Nabisco		2.5	2. Bordens		3.0	2. Planters		1.7
3. Laura Scudder		2.2	3. Jay's		2.8	3. Laura Scudder		1.3
4. Bachman		2.0	4. Snyders		2.0	4. Blue/Bell		1.0
5. Snyders		1.7	5. Seyferts		1.8	5. Bachman		.8
Total		14.1%	**Total**		12.7%	**Total**		8.2%
Frito-Lay		45.8%	Frito-Lay		31.7%	Frito-Lay		78.5%

Tortilla Chips			Cheese Puffs			Pretzels		
Vendors		S. O. M.	Vendors		S. O. M.	Vendors		S. O. M.
1. Laura Scudder		1.7	1. Planters		5.4	1. Nabisco		12.4
2. Nabisco		1.4	2. Bachman		4.0	2. Snyders		6.5
3. Bordens		.6	3. Bordens		2.4	3. Bachman		6.2
4. Bachman		.5	4. Laura Scudder		2.2	4. Reisman		5.0
5. Granny Goose		.5	5. Nabisco		1.9	5. Keebler		3.9
Total		4.7%	**Total**		15.9%	**Total**		34.0%
Frito-Lay		82.9%	Frito-Lay		55.1%	Frito-Lay		14.2%

Exhibit 6 Frito-Lay, Inc. (A)

Frito-Lay Zones: Distribution Centers and Organization

	North Central Zone	Southwest Zone	Southeast Zone	West Zone	Mid Central Zone	Northeast Zone	Total
# Major distribution centers (D.C.)	35	18	32	31	24	29	169
# D.C. routes	1,017	754	832	1,061	592	833	5,089
# Bin routes	447	583	978	374	693	460	3,535
Total Routes	1,464	1,337	1,810	1,435	1,285	1,293	8,624
# Divisions	5	5	5	4	4	5	28
# Regions	25	20	26	21	22	22	136
# Districts	124	110	157	124	117	121	753

Exhibit 7 Frito-Lay, Inc. (A)

Frito-Lay Sales Boundaries
Effective: 1-1-80

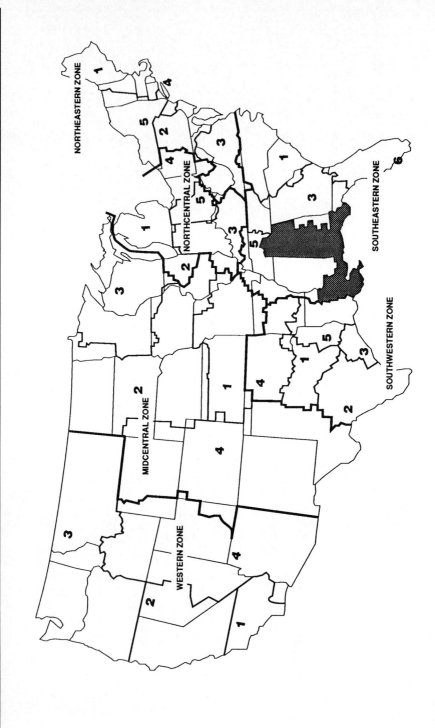

Exhibit 8   Frito-Lay, Inc. (A)

Summary of Sales-Related Expenses—1980

	$MM	*% Sales*	*% of Total*
Compensation, payroll, taxes, & benefits[*]	237.0	16.0	70
Fleet	33.9	2.3	10
Allowances, discounts, samples & stales	30.5	2.0	9
Display equipment	10.2	0.7	3
Facilities	10.0	0.7	3
Management & administration operating	10.2	0.7	3
General operating (salesmen-related)	3.4	0.2	1
All other	3.4	0.2	1
Total	338.6	22.8	100

[*] Includes sales commissions of 8%, on average, paid to route salespeople for net sales.

Exhibit 9   Frito-Lay, Inc. (A)

Your Route Book

Your Route Book

S-1   To be an effective Frito-Lay salesman, you must have an organized method of calling on your accounts.

You also need to know a number of facts about each account.

- Type of establishment
- Where it is located
- How often it is serviced
- What day(s) you service the account

Frito-Lay provides a tool to meet the above needs. It is called a *Route Book*.

Your District Sales Manager will provide you with a separate _____ _____ for each day of the week.

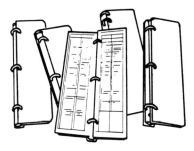

S-2   Each route book contains a number of *Route Cards.*

(continued)

Exhibit 9 (continued)

		The route cards are placed in the route book in the order of your calls. For each call you make on a particular day there is a _____ _____ .
R-2 Route Card	S-3	Let's look at a route card and take note of the information which it provides (see page A-3). Course 5 will go into detail regarding how the information entered on a route card is obtained. For now, just try to become familiar with the layout of the route card: (1) It provides information about the account and days of service. (2) It is a record of information about the products that an account uses. Note that the products are grouped by price. (3) It contains information about our display, important names, limitations and where to enter the account. (4) The salesman uses this section to enter any other necessary information about the account. (5) The back of the route card provides a sales history and action plans which need to be taken to build sales. It's quite clear that a _____ _____ is a valuable tool for the salesman.
R-3 Route Card	S-4	For each day of the week you will have a _____ _____ . Each route book will contain a _____ _____ for every account for each day serviced.
R-4 Route Book Route Card	S-5	**Big/Little Money Maker Route Cards** Each route book will also include special green-colored route cards used to solicit *inactive* Big/Little accounts. They are called Big/Little Money Maker route cards.

(continued)

Exhibit 9 (continued)

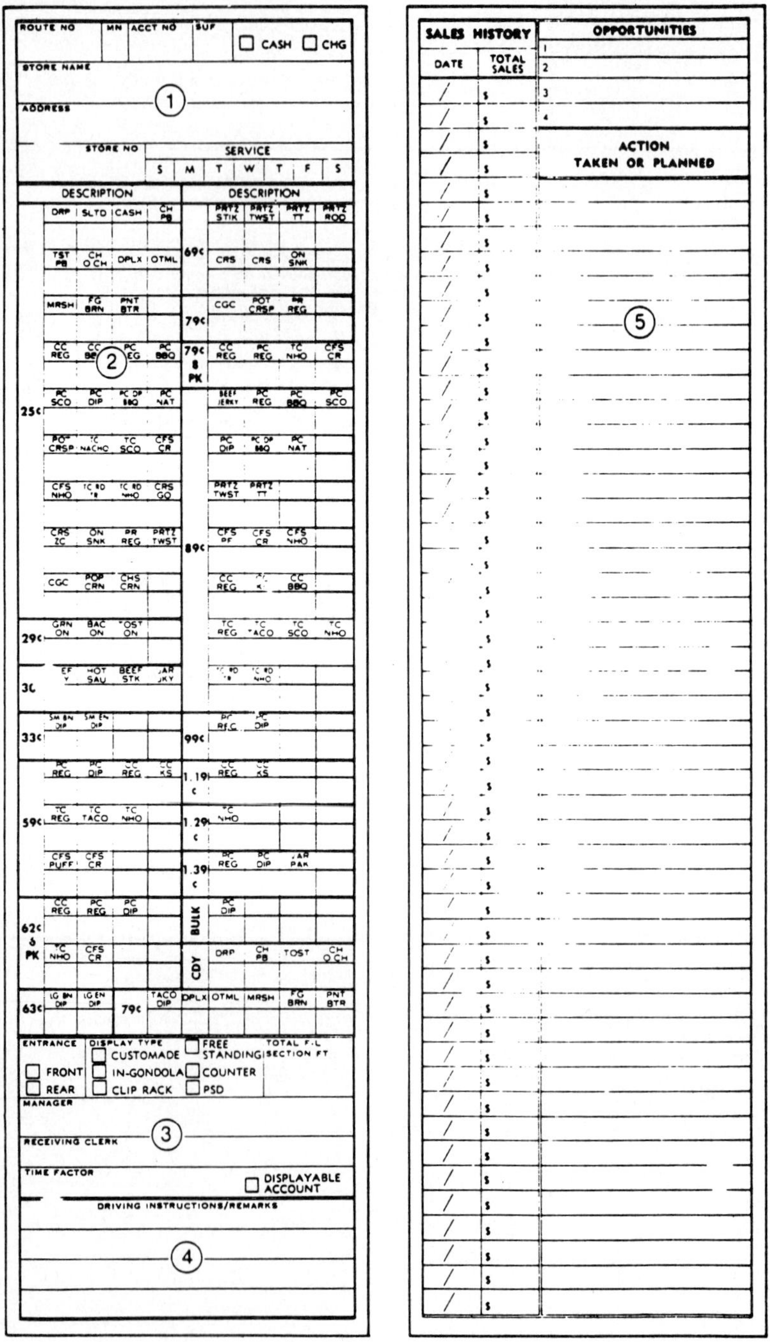

Exhibit 10 Frito-Lay, Inc. (A)

Sales Ticket

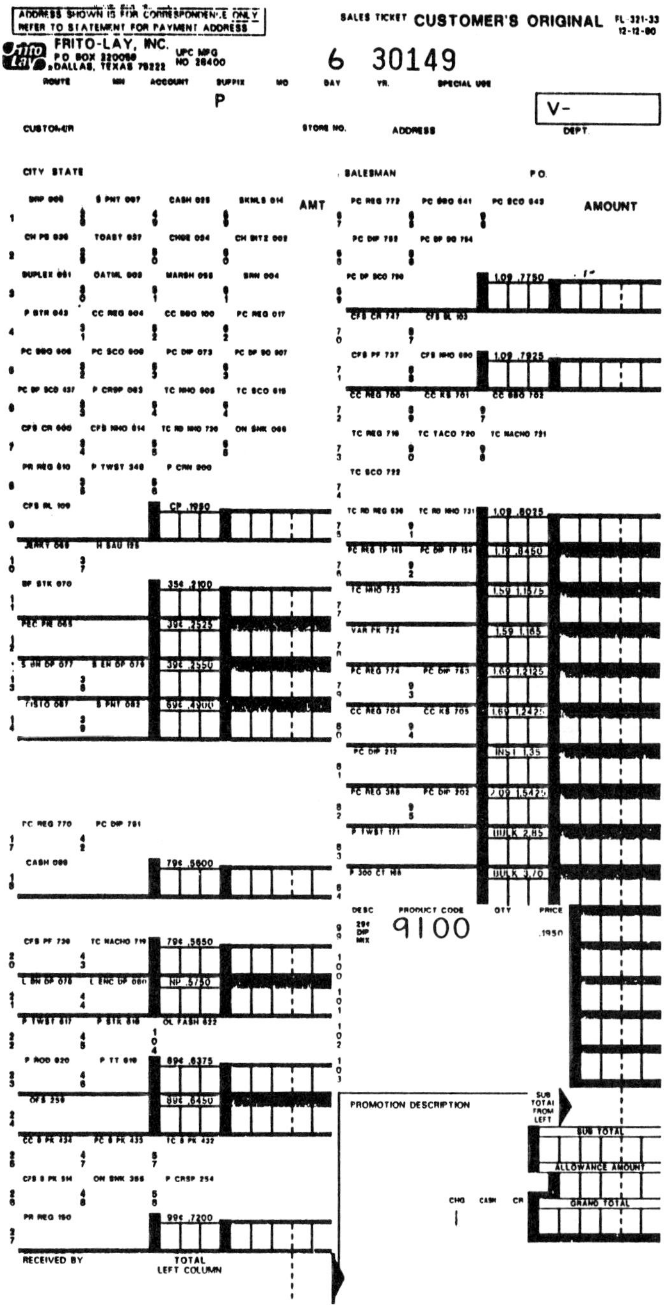

(continued)

Exhibit 10   (continued)

REGULAR PRICE EXTENSION TABLE

Q'TY	1950	2400	2975	3450	4900	4980	5000	5450	5750	6375	6450	7200	7750	7925	8025	8490	Q'TY
1	20	21	75	29	49	90	98	57	58	64	65	72	78	79	80	85	1
2	39	42	81	51	98	99	1 17	1 13	1 15	1 28	1 29	1 44	1 55	1 58	1 61	1 69	2
3	59	63	76	77	1 47	1 49	1 98	1 70	1 73	1 91	1 94	2 16	2 33	2 38	2 41	2 54	3
4	78	84	1 01	1 02	1 98	1 98	2 24	2 28	2 30	2 55	2 58	2 89	3 10	3 17	3 21	3 38	4
5	98	1 05	1 28	1 78	2 45	2 48	2 80	2 83	2 88	3 19	3 23	3 60	3 88	3 98	4 01	4 23	5
6	1 17	1 26	1 52	1 53	2 94	2 97	3 36	3 39	3 45	3 83	3 87	4 32	4 65	4 78	4 82	5 07	6
7	1 37	1 47	1 77	1 79	3 43	3 47	3 92	3 98	4 03	4 46	4 57	5 04	5 41	5 55	5 62	5 92	7
8	1 58	1 68	2 02	2 04	3 92	3 98	4 48	4 57	4 60	5 10	5 16	5 78	6 20	6 34	6 42	6 78	8
9	1 78	1 89	2 27	2 30	4 41	4 48	5 04	5 09	5 18	5 74	5 81	6 48	6 98	7 13	7 22	7 61	9
10	1 95	2 10	2 53	2 55	4 90	4 95	5 60	5 65	5 75	6 38	6 45	7 20	7 75	7 93	8 02	8 45	10
11	2 15	2 31	2 78	2 81	5 39	5 45	6 16	6 22	6 33	7 01	7 10	7 97	8 53	8 72	8 83	9 30	11
12	2 34	2 52	3 03	3 06	5 88	5 94	6 72	6 78	6 90	7 65	7 74	8 64	9 30	9 51	9 63	10 14	12
13	2 54	2 73	3 28	1 32	6 37	6 44	7 28	7 35	7 48	8 29	8 39	9 36	10 08	10 30	10 43	10 99	13
14	2 73	2 94	3 54	3 57	6 88	6 93	7 84	7 91	8 05	8 93	9 03	10 08	10 85	11 10	11 24	11 83	14
15	2 93	3 15	3 79	3 83	7 35	7 43	8 40	8 48	8 63	9 56	9 68	10 80	11 63	11 89	12 04	12 68	15
16	3 12	3 36	4 04	4 08	7 84	7 92	8 96	9 04	9 20	10 20	10 32	11 57	12 40	12 68	12 84	13 52	16
17	3 32	3 57	4 29	4 34	8 33	8 42	9 52	9 61	9 78	10 84	10 97	12 24	13 18	13 47	13 64	14 37	17
18	3 51	3 78	4 55	4 59	8 82	8 91	10 08	10 17	10 35	11 48	11 61	12 96	13 95	14 27	14 45	15 21	18
19	3 71	3 99	4 80	4 85	9 31	9 41	10 64	10 74	10 93	12 11	12 26	13 68	14 73	15 06	15 25	16 06	19
20	3 90	4 20	5 05	5 10	9 80	9 90	11 20	11 30	11 50	12 75	12 90	14 40	15 50	15 85	16 05	16 90	20

Q'TY	1950	2400	2975	3450	4900	4980	Q'TY
21	4 10	4 41	5 30	5 36	10 29		21
22	4 29	4 62	5 56	5 61	10 78		22
23	4 49	4 83	5 81	5 87	11 27		23
24	4 68	5 04	6 06	6 12	11 76		24
30	5 85	6 30	7 58	7 65	14 70		30
36	7 02	7 56	9 09	9 18	17 64		36
42	8 19	8 82	10 61	10 71	20 58		42
48	9 36	10 08	12 12	12 24	23 52		48
54	10 53	11 34	13 64	13 77	26 46		54
60	11 70	12 60	15 15	15 30	29 40		60
66	12 87	13 86	16 67	16 83	32 34		66
72	14 04	15 12	18 18	18 36	35 28		72
78	15 21	16 38	19 70	19 89	38 22		78
84	16 38	17 64	21 21	21 42	41 16		84
90	17 55	18 90	22 73	22 95	44 10		90
96	18 72	20 16	24 24	24 48	47 04		96
102	19 89	21 42	25 76	26 01	49 98		102
108	21 06	22 68	27 27	27 54	52 92		108
114	22 23	23 94	28 79	29 07	55 86		114
120	23 40	25 20	30 30	30 60	58 80		120

Q'TY	1475	1985	12125	17475	135	15425	2 85	3 70	Q'TY
1	1 18	1 17	1 21	1 24	1 35	1 54	2 85	3 70	1
2	2 37	2 33	2 43	2 49	2 70	3 09	5 70	7 40	2
3	3 47	3 50	3 64	3 73	4 05	4 63	8 55	11 10	3
4	4 63	4 66	4 85	4 97	5 40	6 17	11 40	14 80	4
5	5 79	5 83	6 06	6 21	6 75	7 71	14 25	18 50	5
6	6 95	6 99	7 28	7 46	8 10	9 28	17 10	22 20	6
7	8 10	8 16	8 49	8 70	9 45	10 80	19 95	75 90	7
8	9 26	9 32	9 70	9 94	10 80	12 34	22 80	29 60	8
9	10 42	10 49	10 91	11 18	12 15	13 88	75 65	33 30	9
10	11 58	11 65	12 13	12 43	13 50	15 43	28 50	37 00	10
11	12 73	12 82	13 34	13 67	14 85	16 97	31 35	40 70	11
12	13 89	13 98	14 55	14 91	16 20	18 51	34 20	44 40	12
13	15 05	15 15	15 76	16 15	17 55	20 05	37 05	48 10	13
14	16 21	16 31	16 98	17 40	18 90	21 80	39 90	51 80	14
15	17 38	17 48	18 19	18 64	20 25	23 14	42 75	55 50	15
16	18 52	18 64	19 40	19 88	21 60	24 68	45 60	59 20	16
17	19 68	19 81	20 61	21 17	22 95	26 22	48 45	62 90	17
18	20 89	20 97	21 83	22 37	24 30	27 77	51 30	66 60	18
19	21 99	22 14	23 04	23 61	25 65	29 31	54 15	70 30	19
20	23 15	23 30	24 25	24 85	27 00	30 85	57 00	74 00	20

Imperial Distributors, Inc. (A)

In November 1986, Mr. Michael Sleeper, president of Imperial Distributors, a
service merchandiser in the New England area, was considering changes in the
sales and service function at Imperial. During the past year, turnover among
the field force had increased, resulting in what Mr. Sleeper termed a "frustrating
rise in the firefighting necessary to maintain service levels in this business."

Mr. Sleeper was also concerned about the longer-term outlook for Imperial.
Fiscal 1986 (year ended March 31, 1986) had been unprofitable, and market
changes raised additional issues concerning Imperial's marketing operations.
Mr. Sleeper felt new business development should be a high priority and
encouraged by any changes in sales and service.

Industry Background

A service merchandiser was a nonfoods supplier to supermarkets and drug,
discount, and convenience stores. Service merchandisers generally bought
directly from manufacturers, stocked goods in their own warehouses, broke up
case lots and supplied products to stores in smaller quantities. In addition,
full-service merchandisers such as Imperial cleaned and straightened the shelf
displays and ordered merchandise for the stores.

Nonfoods merchandise was divided into two categories. Health and beauty
aids (HBA) included items such as shampoo, aspirin, after-shave lotions,
toothpaste, and mouthwash; general merchandise (GM) included housewares
and pet supplies, stationery, light bulbs, film, and seasonal merchandise.
Although HBA and GM each accounted for less than 5% of total supermarket
sales, retail margins on these items were generally much higher than for food
items, averaging 26% retail gross profit for HBA items in 1986 and 36% for GM.

This case was prepared by Associate Professor Frank V. Cespedes, with the assistance of
Research Associate Susan Gruber Vishner, as a basis for class discussion rather than to illustrate
either effective or ineffective handling of an administrative situation. Certain company data, while
useful for discussion purposes, have been disguised.

According to the National Association of Service Merchandising (NASM), 95% of supermarkets in 1985 were at least partially supplied by service merchandisers, 61% of discount/mass merchandisers, and 23% of drug stores. By class-of-trade, 73% of service merchandisers' sales volume went to food stores, 14% to drug stores, and 8% to discount stores. Overall sales were divided about 57% GM versus 43% HBA items.

During the 1980s, growth for service merchandisers had outpaced that of the retailers being supplied. NASM believed a trend toward "broader variety in retail presentations of HBA and GM into more specialized and slower moving products increased the relative advantage of less-than-case-lot distribution, compared to direct distribution." Within the supermarket segment, the "superstore" format (stores of more than 30,000 square feet) and "combination store" format (more than 33% nonfoods selling area) were increasingly common. One survey indicated that in conventional supermarkets about 11% of shelf space was devoted to GM and 6% to HBA, while in superstores it was 14% GM and 9% HBA, and in combination stores 30% GM and 11% HBA. On average, storage and distribution costs typically accounted for 3–5% of food retailers' sales revenues. As store size increased, there were often opportunities for a service merchandiser to provide more items but also a greater risk that the store's volume of purchases might move it toward direct buying from HBA or GM manufacturers.

Operations

Most service merchandisers were regional firms, with 300 miles as the average radius from a distribution center in 1985, although distance covered was also generally proportional to sales volume. Distribution centers averaged 114,000 square feet, with 30% of this space devoted to order selection, 14% to receiving/shipping, 34% to reserve storage, and 10% to office functions. The average number of SKUs was about 7,000 per firm in 1985 and the average order size was $546, up from $364 five years earlier. Sales per square foot at distribution centers were proportional to firm size: service merchandisers with sales of less than $5 million generated an average of less than $150 per square foot while firms with over $50 million in sales generated more than $400 per square foot, with an industry average of $294 in 1985.

According to trade association data, service merchandisers averaged a 19% gross margin on HBA and 29% on GM. Cash discounts often added another 1% in margin to each category. Average total gross margin (including cash discounts) was 26%. Operating costs averaged 24%, yielding an average after-tax profit of 2% in 1985 for service merchandisers.

More than 80% of service merchandiser volume was sold to retailers on guaranteed sales terms. If the product was not sold at retail, it could be returned for full credit to the service merchandiser who resold returns to other customers, returned them to manufacturers, or sold returns to companies specializing in discontinued goods. Returns amounted to 7% of service merchandiser sales in 1985, and estimated costs averaged about 11% of wholesale value. But Mr. Sleeper believed this underestimated the true costs to the service merchandiser:

> Processing returns is *very* labor-intensive and costs us 3–4 times more than the direct expenses of the initial servicing of the order; labels must be removed and changed, racks dismantled, and space utilized. A significant percentage of returns can wipe out the profits on a given sale, whether or not we resell the goods. Returns are generally higher on seasonal and promotional items.

Service merchandisers provided different levels of service. With full service, the merchandiser ordered product regularly for a section of the store; set up, cleaned, realigned and maintained displays; rotated stock, issued credits for returned items, and provided reports on items sold. Other arrangements were 1) retailers ordered products, the service merchandiser warehoused and shipped products to the store, and store employees stocked and maintained displays; or 2) products were bought by stores and stocked by store employees, with service merchandisers maintaining displays and planograms. Alternatively, some retailers performed all these functions with store employees.

Within supermarkets, HBA generally had a complete aisle, while GM tended to be integrated within grocery categories to encourage related sales (e.g., rubber gloves in the detergent aisle). For both retailers and service merchandisers, GM tended to have higher gross margins but lower unit prices and profitability than HBA. Less frequent purchasing, the seasonality of many items, and the relative lack of brand names among GM resulted in fewer inventory turns, while the irregular shapes, bulkiness and display requirements meant higher handling costs for GM in both the warehouse and the retail store. One Imperial manager noted:

> There are more opportunities for us in GM to select, display and package items differently than other service merchandisers do. HBA categories tend to be dominated at any given time by certain brands and driven by the amount of advertising a given manufacturer spends. GM suppliers tend to be smaller and have less brand identity among consumers.
>
> But even when we do merchandise products distinctively, our competitors are also in the store and, a number of times, they have simply introduced similar displays with similar selections of items some weeks after us.

Service Merchandiser vs. Direct Buying

According to NASM, retailers using service merchandisers,

> . . . draw upon the purchasing power and acumen, the warehousing capability, and field sales/service force of the service supplier for the successful execution of programs. The pulse of consumer purchasing patterns in GM and HBA categories is as different as night and day from those of much higher-velocity

food departments. The fast turnover and heavy tonnage needs for which a food retailer gears his total operation are far from the painstaking pick-and-price, "pack out three of this and six of that" requirements of nonfoods distribution. Over the years, service merchandisers have developed and adapted sophisticated material handling and computer-driven ordering, pricing, planogramming, delivery, and shelf-stocking systems and controls, which pass along their efficiencies and expertise to their customers.

The major alternatives to a service merchandiser were direct buying or using a wholesale grocer who ordered and delivered, but did not set up or maintain displays, for the supermarket. Among chain stores, direct buying had increased in recent years as mergers created organizations that could receive volume discounts directly from manufacturers. Other reasons for taking nonfoods buying and service in-house were stated by a supermarket executive in a trade journal:[1]

> With fewer outside vendors we reduce check-in interruptions to the store and the possibility of errors-or-worse in the order. . . . Then there is the point about profit. There's more of it for the retailer when you can eliminate the middleman. I'm sure the outside merchandisers are not packing in huge profits, but if they are in business there must be some profit. By eliminating the middleman we are in a position to keep those profits for ourselves or to provide lower price points for the customer—or a little of both.
>
> The profit side has also been augmented by picking up advertising and promotional allowances. . . . In addition, when you have full responsibility for buys you are more likely to be bold. It's your baby. Even taking a loss or breaking even is something you can act upon, if you feel it will pull in traffic for the store. It's difficult for an outside firm to suggest such an action, so there's a crimp in bold initiative.
>
> The do-it-yourself system also builds sales on an everyday basis . . . our nonfoods clerks are in the store every day. They fine-tune departments, face up the stock, control inventory and the planograms on a full-week basis. The outside merchandiser is on the premises less frequently.

A 1979 study[2] found that retailers using a service merchandiser had higher HBA and GM sales and contribution per linear foot of shelf space than direct-buying firms. One factor was that serviced firms could usually return unsold or slow-selling merchandise to the service merchandiser. Another factor was that direct-buying companies tended to dedicate more space to these items, while serviced companies tended to have smaller departments and limited merchandise selection in HBA and GM, thus increasing the relative sales per linear foot.

---

[1] Quoted in *Progressive Grocer* (November 1984).

[2] Walter J. Salmon, Robert D. Buzzell, and Ronald C. Curhan, *The Economics of HBA and GM Distribution Among Retailers and Service Merchandisers* (Cambridge, MA: Marketing Science Institute, 1979).

A development expected to impact service merchandiser versus direct-buying decisions was Direct Product Profit data (DPP). Traditionally, supermarkets and other retailers used an item's gross margin and turnover rate as the basis for merchandising decisions. But standard calculations of gross margin (selling price minus the product's purchase cost) ignored many handling costs incurred by the retailer. DPP was defined as the net profit contribution of a product after all trade allowances were added to gross margin and after all handling, shipping, warehousing and other costs attributable to the product were deducted. By 1986, check-out scanning information had stirred increasing interest in DPP among many manufacturers and retailers. Many service merchandisers believed DPP would highlight their economic value for retailers. However, one industry executive noted that "A major obstacle for DPP is the chain's buyer. He or she may know DPP is the way to go, but buyers are typically evaluated on gross margin contribution. And, if you use a service merchandiser, it generally lowers the gross."

Competition

Larger supermarkets generally used more than one service merchandiser. For example, one of Imperial's major accounts used three merchandisers and, according to one manager at Imperial, "that account is constantly comparing invoices item-by-item. Further, our competitors ask the store for copies of our invoices, and we do the same. The result is tough competition and, since in HBA we all tend to buy from the same suppliers, fairly transparent cost structures among service merchandisers."

While competition among service merchandisers was largely regional, there had been consolidation within the industry during the past few years, and distributors in areas such as drug wholesaling had entered nonfoods distribution. In 1986, the number of independent (unaffiliated) service merchandisers had decreased 50% compared to five years previously. Much of this consolidation was due to mergers aimed at increasing the available capital for expansion and/or warehouse improvements. In addition, the cost of warehouse construction often motivated service merchandisers to grow by acquiring an existing company rather than building from scratch. Moreover, some independent service merchandisers had been acquired by supermarket chains or wholesalers who operated these firms as in-house distribution arms specializing in GM and/or HBA.

In New England, Imperial's direct competition consisted of three other firms. *Millbrook*, with estimated 1985 revenues of $85 million, divided a department with Imperial in many accounts and (like Imperial) also carried a specialty foods line. In September 1986, Millbrook's management sold the firm to McKesson and Company, a $6.3 billion company whose primary business was drug wholesaling to pharmacies. McKesson had bought other service merchandisers in recent years, motivated in part by the increasing number of pharmacies in supermarkets and "superstores." Its 1986 annual report noted that "these acquisitions . . . have enabled us to create a truly national wholesale drug distribution system and to expand our reach to the huge market for HBA and other nonfood products sold by supermarkets and mass merchandisers." Management also noted that McKesson's "drug and service merchandising representatives are making joint calls on major food chains, taking advantage of McKesson's national presence and extending the market penetration of each unit. In a trial program, service merchandising is providing . . . general merchandise racks for distribution to druggists." Finally, management emphasized "the sharing of distribution, computer and transportation facilities; the combining of purchasing to maximize buying effectiveness; joint marketing programs and the expansion of private-label lines . . . to improve our position as a low-cost distributor."

Herman, with estimated 1985 revenues of $32 million, concentrated on convenience stores but also serviced supermarkets with HBA and GM. *Springfield Sugar,* with revenues of $1 billion, was primarily a food wholesaler that also offered service on HBA and some GM categories. Because receiving for food, GM, and HBA was usually done at the same time in supermarkets, Springfield could deliver GM and HBA with groceries. In contrast to competitors' logistics, Springfield delivered its goods to stores by truck, and the goods were held in receiving until Springfield service reps arrived separately to stock and service the items.

In addition, Imperial faced serious competition from customers who adopted direct buying. Any chain which "took the business direct" removed a significant portion of a regional market. During the past three years, some larger supermarket chains (including two former major customers of Imperial) had adopted direct buying after a merger, and some had established separate subsidiaries to act as service merchandisers for the merged corporation. Mr. Sleeper noted that, in these instances, "the new parent corporation wanted to go direct, and the local supermarket management had to fall in line. There's a 'control' mentality involved and, frankly, little we can do to affect decisions made in a chain headquarters by people we have not previously done business with."

Commenting on competitive developments, Mr. Sleeper noted:

> Service merchandisers have always lived or died on the basis of anticipating retailer needs. Our account bases are not captive, our leverage with both manufacturers and customers is minimal, and competition is fierce. We survive and grow, not by clout, but by expertise and willingness to experiment and innovate.

Company Background

Imperial was founded in 1937 by Mr. Frank Sleeper (father of Michael Sleeper) in Worcester, Massachusetts. At that time, there were about 400,000 U.S.

grocery stores, mostly small "mom-and-pop" stores. Frank Sleeper's original inventory consisted of 54 items and he personally serviced the stores. Imperial expanded during the 1940s by acquiring more space for HBA items when the stores could not stock all of their regular grocery items due to war rationing. In 1948, Imperial became a supplier to the first supermarket in Worcester. As supermarkets expanded, Imperial expanded beyond HBA into GM.

By 1986, Imperial's headquarters and central warehouse were located in Auburn, Mass. (a suburb of Worcester adjacent to the Massachusetts Turnpike). Imperial had 13 transfer depots throughout New England and serviced over 600 stores. Five supermarket chains represented about 50% of Imperial's service merchandise revenues, while its top 10 accounts represented about 70%. The average order was about $800, but larger accounts generated from $5,000 to $9,000 in weekly orders.

In April 1985, Imperial acquired the Jayson/Caron Company which distributed GM and HBA to over 2,000 stores in Maine and New Hampshire, mainly smaller stores where the average order size was about $50. In turn, Jayson/Caron operated a subsidiary, the Benson Sullivan Company, which specialized in candy and tobacco products distribution. Imperial also owned three retail stores called Luvs which sold HBA and GM in addition to over-the-counter drug supplies. The stores were located in shopping plazas not far from Imperial's headquarters.

Exhibit 1 provides financial data concerning Imperial; Exhibit 2 outlines Imperial's organization. Most of top management had worked for supermarkets and/or other service merchandisers before joining Imperial.

Mr. Sleeper was involved in most facets of daily operations. He commented that "this business is extremely fast-paced, with hundreds of stores serviced daily; and many customers demand speaking with the top person at their service merchandisers if something is not done exactly when it was supposed to be done." The following sections provide an overview of Imperial's operations including purchasing, warehousing, delivery service, and the organization and tasks of field personnel.

Purchasing

Imperial had three buyers (one for each of HBA, GM, and specialty foods which Imperial had started distributing in 1985) reporting to Mr. Kevin Howe, director of purchasing. Imperial bought products from about 500 vendors. The top 10 vendors accounted for 30% of Imperial's purchases, and included companies such as Procter & Gamble and Hartz Mountain. Many vendors, especially in GM, were small firms that produced a limited product line. According to Mr. Howe:

> A good vendor has merchandise available on deal throughout the year, enabling us to buy at lower cost. We look for off-invoice allowances (a cost reduction for buying in bulk), significant co-op advertising allowances, and good field support.

Some vendors' reps carry Imperial order forms which they fill out and send to the stores. Other vendors' reps check the facings of their products and the pricing. A good vendor will suggest ways to increase business for our customers, for us, and for themselves. Difficult vendors try to solicit direct business from our accounts, although they may end up selling less than through Imperial. Our sales reps make sure the product is displayed properly and the area is neat and clean. The supermarkets and manufacturers don't do as much as our reps do.

HBA companies are larger, national, and publicly held. There is not as much room for negotiation. Sometimes on promotional orders we can get an extra 30 days to pay the bill, which is worth about 1% discount. There are also truckload allowances. In GM, you start with list price and go from there. The companies are smaller, regional and privately held for the most part. There is more room for negotiation. At the end of the year there are also rebates on orders from some vendors. Payment terms are also negotiable.

Imperial must buy at the best terms, because our competitors buy from many of the same vendors. The pressure on margins is intense. Advertising rebates, showroom allowances and any other concession we can get from the manufacturers make a big difference in our profitability.

Imperial's buyers saw vendors' salespeople by appointment one day a week. On a full buying day, each buyer would see 10–12 sales reps. If the product was of interest, the sales rep would receive a scheduled appointment to present the item before Imperial's buying committee, which met every other week and discussed between 50–100 items at a 3-hour meeting. Over the past two years, Imperial's listing had increased from a total of 7,500 to over 10,000 SKUs.

The Warehouse

Purchased items were delivered to Imperial's warehouse in Auburn. In the warehouse, there were 9 lines for picking items for orders, which were placed in plastic totes that were then sent to Imperial's depots where the route sales reps delivered them to stores. Over 100,000 items were picked daily, with an expected error rate of less than 1/3 of 1%. Each morning, each line's previous day's hourly pick rate, the number of items picked, and the error rate were posted prominently in the warehouse.

At 6:30 A.M. the picking lines were stocked. The pickers arrived at 7:30 A.M. and began to fill orders. (The orders had been printed out in sequence by Imperial's computer during the night.) As each line picked an order, the totes arrived at the loading area in sequence to be loaded on trucks for delivery to the various depots. At 8:30 A.M. the loaders began to fill the trailer trucks, which left the Auburn warehouse every afternoon at 5:00 P.M. Trucks delivered the orders to the depots during the night and returned to the warehouse by 6:00 A.M. for reloading.

Most of the 90 people in the warehouse were women who were paid on an hourly basis. Depending upon the merchandise, each line had a "pick rate" with the average rate for all lines at 580 items an hour. Mr. Don Perry, director of distribution, stated:

Imperial has a reputation in the community for hard work and fairness. There are companies that pay better, but the working conditions, benefits, and atmosphere are better here. We encourage teamwork. For example, many of our warehouse employees have families and don't want to work overtime. When overtime is required, we have a policy of mandatory overtime, and no one leaves until all the work is done. Earlier this week, a flu epidemic meant no one was available to assemble racks so I did it. I expect my people to do the same.

The Depot

Each order was shipped to a transfer depot which had an assigned sales supervisor and route sales reps. The 13 depots were located just off major highways throughout New England and eastern New York State.

Each morning, route sales reps arrived at 7:00 A.M. (some as early as 5:00 A.M.) to load their vans. The sales supervisors arrived at 7:00 A.M. to handle any problems or questions. The regional managers were also available at the central depot for the area. Most merchandise in the depots had been packed in totes and in sequence for the day's deliveries at Imperial's central warehouse. A few bulk items, such as baby formula, were delivered to the stores in shipping boxes.

Each rep was assigned certain stores each day. After leaving the depot, the reps drove to the stores and began servicing Imperial's departments. Some customers were an hour's drive from the depots. Regional managers and sales supervisors remained at the depot to make telephone calls or do paperwork, but usually left by 9:00 or 10:00 A.M. to visit stores or customers' offices or fill in for a rep unable to work that day.

Field Sales and Service

Mr. Ray Patenaude was vice president of supermarket sales and service (see Exhibit 3). Reporting to him were account managers and regional managers for 1) Maine; 2) New Hampshire, Vermont, and eastern New York; 3) Worcester and Springfield Mass., and Connecticut; and 4) Boston. Nine sales supervisors reported to the regional managers. Depending on the number of trainees at a given point, about 70 route sales reps (who covered 63 routes) reported to the sales supervisors and account managers. Each region also had 2–4 merchandisers. Senior merchandisers physically reset the shelves in stores when the displays were changed ("Major Resets") and worked with store managers on merchandising strategies; junior merchandisers were trainees who covered routes during the sales reps' vacations and sick days. Mr. Patenaude commented: "Each rep gets two weeks vacation after the first year with Imperial. Many route reps and merchandisers have been with us for years and have amassed a lot of vacation time or sick leave. One region, for example, has 41 weeks of vacation time to cover annually, and the stores must be serviced on time no matter what the personnel situation on a given day. I don't believe absenteeism is a big problem, but vacations and turnover mean we need a certain number of 'extra' people to cover routes."

The Regional Managers

Each regional manager was responsible for sales and supervision in an area. Regional managers checked the stores for cleanliness, new product introductions, stock amounts, and the general look of the Imperial displays. Regional managers also made office visits to larger customers. One regional manager commented:

> When I visit a customer's office, I discuss store resets, promotional items, presells (floor stands and specials), new stores, market data and any problems the account is having. I bring in the 13-week reports which break out product movement and sales, and reports which look at the year-to-year and quarter-to-quarter figures.

Regional managers were also responsible for soliciting new business with current and new accounts. In some regions, most new business was with chain stores. In other regions, there were more independent, owner-operated stores. Each required a different sales approach. In independent stores, the regional manager could speak directly to the owner, presenting the costs and benefits of using Imperial. Often the manager built a personal relationship with the owner, meeting at industry events and calling on the store over a period of time.

Negotiating with chain stores usually required more time and meetings with more people. The regional manager or a supervisor would first speak to store managers to find out if they were pleased with the current service merchandiser. The regional manager would get the names of department buyers and an appointment at the chain store's headquarters office. The regional manager would then present the case for Imperial to the buyer, who could not make the decision to change suppliers but could recommend a change to a chain vice president. A recommendation to change usually resulted in meetings between Mr. Sleeper and the chain's executives where, if successful, terms would be negotiated and departments allocated. It typically took at least 6–12 meetings before a decision was reached. With many chains, the negotiating process continued for years.

Imperial paid a bonus to anyone in the company who brought in a new store, usually 10% of the first-year account gross profits and 5% of second-year profits. During fiscal 1986, bonuses totaled about $12,500 for new supermarket business, $1,500 for drug stores, and $450 for discount stores. Although the bonus could be split among employees, Mr. Sleeper had instituted the program primarily with the regional managers in mind: "They are the people with the level of access required to develop new business, and the bonus can mean substantial money on a new account. However, I'm disappointed with the level of new business development and am not sure it receives sufficient attention in the field."

Sales Supervision

Imperial had two additional levels of sales supervision.

One *account manager* had responsibility for all stores of one large account, while another serviced one main account and several smaller accounts. Account managers handled paperwork for their accounts (which included presells, checking replacement items, and price changes), supervised route salespeople, did store checks, and established schedules for resets performed by senior merchandisers. One account manager stated: "I show and tell my people what to do. I'll visit reps in the store and sometimes take them to lunch. I want them to feel they are not alone out in the field. This lets them know I'm watching and I care."

Account managers often spent 8–10 hours/week with buyers discussing price changes, new items, and promotional items. Each dealt with problems which ranged from technical problems with one chain's scanning systems to minor problems on invoices. The scanning problem made Imperial's weekly price changes difficult and created difficulties for route reps when the merchandise was received. The problems with invoices involved exact order amounts and prices. The account manager was able to expedite payments to Imperial by checking with his client's accounts payable department weekly. Depending on the chain, an account manager might meet with the vice president of merchandising periodically, or might accompany Mr. Sleeper in presentations to other chain executives.

Account managers also occasionally traveled with the chain personnel, touring stores and suggesting changes. In turn, the customer's personnel called the account manager if a store encountered service problems. Account managers tried to build rapport with store managers and chain supervisors so that problems could be handled before they reached the account's buyers and headquarters officials.

Account managers were also responsible for adding new business. Most chains had a formal approval process for adding new items, which could only be done through headquarters with the buyer's approval. Some account managers were able to solicit new departments within chains, but often Mr. Sleeper would be involved in bidding for major new business.

Sales supervisors did many of the same tasks as account managers. Their primary responsibilities were to supervise the route reps in servicing stores and to acquire two new accounts annually. They usually did not make headquarters calls but spoke to store managers, assistant store managers, and department managers. New accounts consisted of any store or department that was not currently serviced by Imperial.

Especially during the past two years, turnover among route reps had increased the time spent by sales management in field service. One account manager noted:

> My primary function should be helping the sales reps to obtain more shelf space in the stores, increasing their order volumes, and suggesting merchandising im-

provements. Instead, I'm constantly fighting fires and doing many resets myself because I don't have enough backup support. The problem started in the Boston area and has rippled throughout the territories. Six months ago I asked for another senior merchandiser, but I still don't have anybody and my account is getting unhappy about the pace of resets.

Similarly, a sales supervisor complained that too much of his time was spent "babysitting": "We have so many new sales reps who must be trained in the basics. I have little time to spend increasing sales and often have to fill in on routes due to turnover among the route reps."

The Route Sales Reps

Route reps were the backbone of Imperial's distribution system. The reps moved the merchandise from the depots to the stores via small vans. They stocked the store shelves, straightened and cleaned merchandise, reordered products, and wrote credits for returned merchandise. Mr. Patenaude stated: "The route salespeople have an average age of 25. We look for experience working in grocery or discount stores but try not to hire people from our customers because that can backfire. Our sales reps usually work more than 40 hours a week, 10–12 hours a day."

Most reps made 2–3 calls a day. The average sales per route per week was $8,000. A regional manager stated:

I look at the weekly route numbers, and if a route drops or shoots up, I want to know why. Some reps order lightly to have an easy week, but it catches up with them: the cleanliness of the shelves slips or the store may not be serviced correctly and there may be out-of-stocks. Overloading the stores with merchandise is also a problem. I want my reps to order steadily and keep the work steady, although we do see big changes in vacation areas during the summer.

To obtain more information about activities in the field, the casewriter spent a day with a route sales rep (see Appendix).

Compensation

At a number of service merchandisers, salespeople were paid entirely through commissions and covered their own expenses. Exhibit 4 outlines the compensation structure for Imperial's sales personnel. In addition to base salary, route reps received a commission based on sales volume, and Imperial paid the route reps' expenses for meals and miscellaneous items. In 1985 the average total compensation for reps who worked the full year was about $18,000, with an average of 65% in base salary and 35% in commissions. Total compensation for route reps in 1985 varied from $25,000 to $14,500. Sales management received bonuses for meeting quotas or booking new business, but not a commission.

About 50% of Imperial's sales was in HBA and 50% in GM. Average retail price per item was $1.80 in HBA, $1.25 in GM. Mr. Patenaude noted:

We pay higher percentage commissions on GM because there is generally more work there for the reps as well as higher gross margins and because lower unit prices for GM means it takes more time for a rep with a primarily GM store to amass the same dollars as a primarily HBA store. We also pay reps weekly, so they can see a cause-and-effect relationship between their efforts and wages. We have a cap on a rep's base salary but no cap on commissions.

In chain stores, all items were bought via an authorized list approved at headquarters. Individual stores could often only accept or reject items on this list. However, the Imperial sales rep could hang additional clip strips (a long plastic display with about 10 items attached) or J-hooks (metal hooks on which were hung various types of merchandise). An account manager noted, "Our reps can work for the best spots in the store for their displays, and try to convince a store manager to add a new section for certain merchandise. The store manager will need to ask upper management for permission, but the store manager's request is an important influence on that decision." Managers of independent stores had more autonomy, and so route reps had more opportunities to sell new items. However, one sales supervisor noted:

> Stocking the stores correctly is a time-consuming task, which takes most of the day for most reps. In addition, as supermarkets have become more automated, the amount of time our reps must devote to administrative tasks has increased, and the time required to get through receiving has increased to as much as 2 hours in many stores. The added work and hassle of getting a new item through receiving can outweigh the additional sales commission for some reps.

Each route rep had sales and returns goals set by the regional manager. Raises to base salary were based (according to one regional manager) about "35% on how well the sales goals were met, 35% on the returns goal, and 30% on qualitative factors. Returns for the company usually run at 7% of sales, and 5% is considered very good for a route rep. Lower returns indicate more accurate ordering and better display support for the merchandise ordered." In 1985, about 60% of Imperial's route reps attained their sales goals and about 70% attained returns goals.

Mr. Richard Dacri, director of human resources, noted:

> We survey competitive salaries annually, and that influences the range of salaries we offer. I am currently looking for a sales supervisor in the Boston area and, in the current employment market, will need to pay $26,000–30,000 for the right person.
>
> I see two potential problems with our compensation system. One is that new driver sales personnel often have difficulty dealing with commission compensation, which causes weekly fluctuations in pay. A second is salary compression. The need to increase starting rates to meet market demands means the spread in wages between new and experienced people is increasingly narrow. For example, a route rep recently refused a senior merchandiser position because his base salary plus commission exceeded the senior merchandiser rate, and this was not an isolated incident.

Sales Force Training

New route reps received on-the-job training over a number of weeks. The extent of the training varied by district and by the rep's previous experience. Those hired from other service merchandisers often needed only to learn Imperial's methods of ordering and crediting returns. An account manager described the training process he used with new reps:

> In the first week, I send the trainee out with my best salesperson. By the end of the week, the trainee should know how to check an order in and write a credit. In the second week, the trainee would learn how price changes are handled and be given an easy department to put up. In the third week, the trainee would start learning how to use the hand-held order entry computer. In subsequent weeks, the trainee would start servicing and ordering for a store, with the experienced person monitoring the trainee's work. After seven weeks, most trainees are ready for a route. If no route was available the trainee would cover vacations and sick days and help on routes with large orders.
>
> The ideal is to have time and people for this kind of training, but many managers complain about being shorthanded and move new reps into routes after one or two weeks.

Mr. Patenaude commented on new sales reps:

> Reps are not really effective for 3–4 months. They must learn the products and how to do the job efficiently. There are tricks of the trade and easy or hard ways to work a load. A rep has to learn what sells. This means looking at store location and assessing what people in that area will buy.

An Imperial regional manager stated:

> We hire people from diverse backgrounds. Many don't understand retail profitability and must learn what turns and what is profitable for them and the stores.

Sales Force Turnover

In 1985, turnover among all Imperial employees had been 64% while turnover among route reps had been 59%; the comparable figures for 1984 were 62% and 43%; for 1983, 55% and 41% and for 1982, 60% and 51%. Turnover among the field reps was higher in the Boston and Hartford areas and lower in northern New England. Mr. Patenaude said:

> In the metropolitan areas, the salespeople may leave for higher paying and less physically demanding jobs. The service merchandiser job has long hours and requires patience with the receivers. There is a career path, but it is not fast. In addition, the sales rep leaves the displays neat, but when he returns it is a mess and that's frustrating.
>
> In the past Imperial had a file of prospects, but not any more. We spent $25,000 in recruitment advertising, but it wasn't very effective. Experienced sales reps work 45–50 hours a week, but the new reps work 65 hours a week. Our

fringe benefits are excellent, but many new people never break through the initial frustration.

Other factors included low unemployment rates in New England, and the opening of many new service businesses that competed in the same labor markets as Imperial. In 1986, fast food franchises in the Boston area, for example, offered $5 or more per hour to entry-level employees.

Mr. Sleeper commented:

> Turnover inhibits our effectiveness since it takes time to learn the operations and needs of individual stores and department managers. We incur an opportunity cost in lost sales due to turnover and, if service levels are hurt, the danger of losing an account. Turnover also forces us to establish a "buffer" in the field: we have more reps than routes but, in part due to turnover, are constantly filling-in on routes. And our field organization can get bloated with the addition of junior merchandisers whose major function is to fill-in on routes. Finally, there's the time and money to find and train new people, and the cost of managerial frustration with the process.

Commenting on causes of turnover, Mr. Dacri noted:

> The tight labor market in this area is certainly a reason, but there are other factors as well. Many who leave complain about the "aggravation" of the job, and the "lack of supervision." Due to turnover, we must often push new reps into routes sooner than we'd like, and there's the danger of creating a vicious circle: without adequate supervision, new reps are less effective and more frustrated; but turnover places more demands on our sales supervisors, who have less time to spend with new reps as turnover increases.

A sales supervisor commented:

> In this business, a sales manager must be a cheerleader, platoon leader, and traffic cop. The field rep's job is very fast-paced, demands sustained attention to detail, and for hours at a time, requires the reps to work alone.

A regional manager stated:

> The sales job is harder than it was five years ago. The ordering is more complex, there are more promotional items, and Imperial has added many new departments. We have to be careful not to overload the reps. If Imperial adds more lines, then routes should be split, or HBA and GM lines split, or sales and service should be split. Or maybe we should consider reallocating tasks instead of keeping one person responsible for loading the van, driving to stores, unloading, checking-in through receiving, and then in-store service.

Market Environment

Mr. Sleeper believed any changes should recognize important aspects of the New England market and Imperial's business mix.

New England had many 2-worker households with more discretionary income than the national average. Over 70% of the $14 billion New England food store market in 1986 was held by 25 regional chains, up from 65% in 1985. Stop and Shop (115 stores) was the leader in market share, followed by Purity Supreme/Heartland/Angelo's (62 stores), Shaw's (47 stores) and DeMoulas (37 stores) (see Exhibit 5). A study found that consumers in Boston chose their primary supermarket on the basis of 1) location, 2) price, and 3) quality of perishables. The store's assortment, service, and environment were also important. In actual prices, the study found a range of 10% between the highest priced chain (Star Markets) and the lowest (Heartland) and suggested that prices were able to draw customers out of their usual shopping areas into Heartland warehouse stores.

Some New England supermarket chains were converting many of their traditional stores into superstores or warehouse stores. Since 1981, the total number of food stores in the region had declined slightly. Moreover, in mid-1986, there were many rumors of possible acquisitions and mergers among large supermarkets in the region.

In New England, according to the Nielsen Retail Index, 48% of HBA volume was in food stores, 26% in drug stores and 26% in discount/mass merchandising stores. National figures were 44% in food stores, 40% in drug stores and 16% in mass merchandisers. HBA volume was estimated at $1.145 billion in New England in 1985, of which about 20% was done through service merchandisers, wholesale grocers or other intermediaries. GM volume was difficult to estimate, due to the fragmented nature of the supplier market; but it was estimated that more than 20% reached retailers through service merchandisers and other intermediaries.

For Imperial, supermarkets represented about 80% of sales, drug stores 10%, and discount stores 10%. Of the three retail segments, Mr. Sleeper felt the potential for increased sales was greatest among supermarkets: "It only takes one supermarket chain to make a big difference in sales volume and throughput at the warehouse. Also, supermarkets tend to be full-service customers, while drug stores tend either to buy direct or use drug wholesalers." About 70% of Imperial's total business (and 75% of its supermarket business) was full-service, 15% nonservice (i.e., purchasing and delivery only), and 15% semi-service (i.e., Imperial reps wrote orders for stores but did not stock or maintain store shelves). Mr. Sleeper noted that the proportion of full-service business at Imperial had increased from less than 50% as recently as 1984: "This puts a premium on precise execution in the field and makes turnover a potentially bigger problem than formerly."

Conclusion

Mr. Sleeper was considering changes in three areas: logistics, compensation, and training.

Logistically, Imperial's reps loaded and drove vans to stores, checked goods through receiving, and then performed in-store service. Other firms separated field delivery and service. Mr. Sleeper had a leasing firm study the possibility of having trucks deliver goods from Imperial's depots to stores, while route reps arrived separately to perform check-in and service. This study focused on a 7-route area in Connecticut and, assuming a truck could make 11 stops per day and that route reps would be given company cars, found incremental costs to be $32,000 annually for the region studied (see Exhibit 6). Commenting on the study, Mr. Sleeper noted:

> I'm skeptical that a truck can make 11 stops daily: remember that goods must be through receiving at most supermarkets by 1 p.m. So that increases the number of trucks required to implement this change and the incremental costs. Also, the region studied tends to have its stores more geographically concentrated than some of our territories up north or in western Massachusetts.
>
> But I see other potential advantages to such a system. It would up-grade and make more pleasant the route rep's job. The rep would arrive in a company car, wouldn't be a truck driver, and could concentrate more time on ordering, merchandising, and servicing activities. Also, this change could also alter our potential labor pool for reps. We could use more part-timers, for one thing. And eliminating the loading and unloading of vans means the physical requirements of the job change, making more women eligible as route reps.

Current compensation for route reps was a base salary plus a commission based on sales of a given item. Within a product category and within a total order, the commission percentage did not vary by volume sold. Mr. Sleeper was considering a straight-commission compensation plan, in which commission percentages would vary by product category and would increase as the total volume of an order increased. In addition, there would be penalties incurred for returns over a stated amount and, conversely, reps would receive bonuses for surpassing previous year's performance on their routes. Using 1985 sales figures for each rep in one representative region, Mr. Sleeper calculated that a rep on an $8,500/week route would have earned about $2,000 more under the straight-commission option versus the current compensation system (this calculation did not include any estimate for a returns penalty). Mr. Sleeper commented:

> Once a rep is in the store, the effort involved in adding more items or another aisle is usually less than driving to and checking in an order at another store. But some people believe our current system doesn't provide enough incentive for reps to maximize sales per store: the more they sell, the harder they work since they must handle every item.
>
> A straight-commission plan, with appropriate percentages to handle the differences between GM and HBA prices and with an appropriate returns penalty, might provide the incentive necessary to improve sales performance. I'm also considering basing commissions on gross profit per item, but our people have become so attuned to thinking in terms of volume, I'm not sure that's practical. I also need to think through the potential impact of such a system on inventory management, service, and the reps' attitudes and motivations; for example, a straight-commission system doesn't reward people for seniority, and doesn't provide the security of a salary.

Mr. Sleeper was also considering changes in training of new route reps. "I'm concerned about our system of on-the-job training," he noted. "Perhaps a more formal training program is required." At issue were the focus of such a program, its costs, and the ability to sustain the program in the face of the needs created by current turnover levels.

Commenting on Imperial in 1986, Mr. Sleeper said:

> In five years, we've grown from $23 million to $52 million in sales, and my goal is a $100 million business. But lately we've run into a sort of "Bermuda triangle" in terms of continued growth and profitability. Important customers have merged and others may be acquired, new store formats and new types of retailers are impacting how HBA and GM are sold; a $6 billion corporation has acquired my major competitor, and I'm not sure what the fallout will be; and turnover puts pressure on us to stabilize our field activities.
>
> I'll consider fundamental changes if they address important problems and opportunities. What goals should guide any changes in our delivery, sales, compensation, or training programs, and what specific changes (if any) should be made? More generally, what will it take to continue growing the business, and given our resources and the current environment, what priorities should I set in our marketing operations?

Exhibit 1 Imperial Distributors, Inc. (A)

Operating Statement
(Year Ended March 29, 1986)

	Jayson/Carson	Imperial Distributors	Eliminations [a]	Consolidated
Sales	$18,387,120	$34,977,261	$(812,000)	$52,552,381
Cost of Sales	16,202,787	28,055,170	(812,000)	43,445,957
Gross Margin	2,184,333	6,922,091		9,106,424
Advertising				
Allowances	142,533	562,574		705,107
Purchase Discounts	376,277	460,689		836,966
Gross Profit (Loss)	2,703,143	7,945,354		10,648,497
Operating Expenses				
Selling	1,071,650	3,160,370		4,232,020
Warehouse and shipping	844,465	2,545,468		3,389,933
Office	397,445	1,256,148		1,653,593
General and administrative	610,501	1,461,760		2,072,261
	2,924,061	8,423,746		11,347,807
Other Income (Expenses) from Affiliated Divisions	—	23,496		23,496
Net Operating Income (Loss) Before Income Taxes	(220,918)	(454,896)		(675,814)

		5-Year Operating Data			
	1981	1982	1983	1984	1985
Sales	$17,293,149	$23,204,134	$30,953,431	$33,737,104	$34,680,617
Gross Profit	3,396,621	4,868,877	7,217,946	7,580,101	7,438,156
Net Income (Loss) Before Taxes	(62,925)	301,671	783,446	554,800	559,396

[a] "Eliminations" refer to intercompany transactions, which have been eliminated in the consolidated statement.

Exhibit 2 Imperial Distributors, Inc. (A)

Headquarters Organization

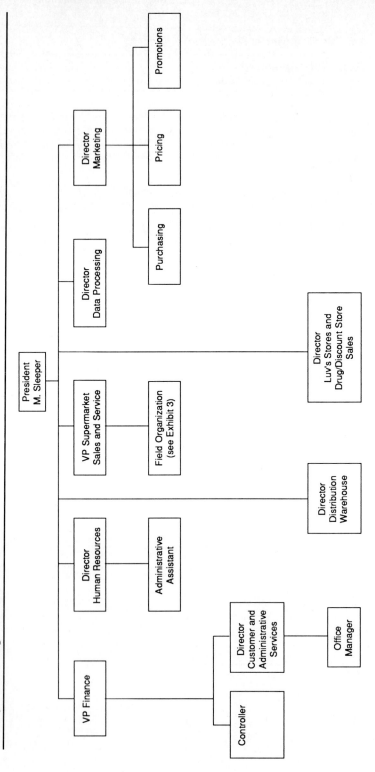

Exhibit 3 Imperial Distributors, Inc. (A)

Field Sales and Service Organization

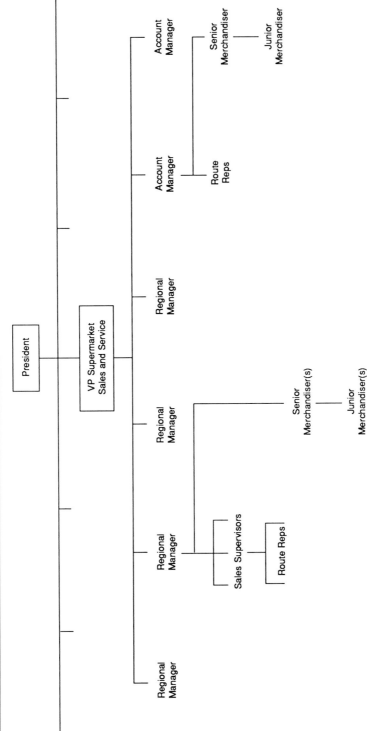

Company Totals: 4 Regional Managers, 2 Account Managers, 14 Merchandisers (9 Senior, 5 Junior), 9 Sales Supervisors, 70 Route Reps (63 Routes, and 7 Trainees).

Exhibit 4   Imperial Distributors, Inc. (A)

Sales Department Salary Grades
Effective 9-1-85

Labor Grade	Weekly Rate	Position
A	$148–270 (plus commission)	Driver Sales
21	$239–345	Jr. Merchandiser (Trainee)
23	$265–387	Jr. Key Account Rep.
25	$307–454	Sr. Merchandiser
26	$332–493	Sr. Key Account Rep. Drug Discount Coordinator
29	$418–637	Sales Supervisor Account Manager I
30	$454–694	Account Manager II Retail Manager Drug Discount Manager
31	$575–888	Regional

Commission Structure

Department	Commission Rate
HBA (01)	1%
Housewares (02)	2%
Plant (03)	2%
Panty hose (04)	1%
Stationery (05)	2%
Hair care (06)	4%
Soft goods (07)	2%
Toys (09)	4%
Auto (10)	1%
Film and other (11)	1%
Food (12)	1%
Floor stand (13)	2%
HBA promotional (98)	1%
Miscellaneous (99)	2%
Housewares promotional (97)	2%

Exhibit 5   Imperial Distributors, Inc. (A)

Leading New England Food Chains

Rank	Company	% of 1986 Market	1986 Avg. Store Sales in Thousands	% of 1985 Market	1985 Avg. Store Sales in Thousands	Imperial Customer
1.	Stop & Shop	13.58	$16,812	12.26	$14,486	No
2.	Purity Supreme/ Heartland/ Angelo's[a]	7.89	18,105	5.58	18,373	(until acquisition)
3.	Shaw's	6.81	20,617	5.43	17,463	Yes
4.	DeMoulas/ Market Basket	5.58	21,484	4.82	19,017	Yes
5.	Hannaford Bros.	4.86	10,985	4.56	9,559	No
6.	Finast/Edwards	4.42	11,434	4.31	10,635	Yes
7.	Star Market	3.60	11,386	3.75	11,527	Yes
8.	Waldbaum's/ Food Mart	2.99	12,529	2.65	10,776	No
9.	Almacs	2.70	9,867	2.84	9,809	No
10.	Grand Union	2.60	7,116	2.55	6,778	No
11.	A&P	2.47	4,952	2.47	4,808	No
12.	Mott's ShopRite	1.81	12,294	2.12	12,208	Yes
13.	Big Y	1.49	9,650	1.32	8,295	Yes
14.	Wonder Markets/ Big D	1.48	15,080	1.44	14,207	Yes
15.	Pathmark[a]	1.23	21,840	1.22	21,093	No

Source: Boston Globe, June 6, 1986.
[a]In 1985, Pathmark acquired Purity Supreme and its Heartland and Angelo's subsidiaries.

Exhibit 6   Imperial Distributors, Inc. (A)

Study of Revised Field Delivery System: Summary

TO: M. Sleeper

FROM: BNJ Leasing: Auto, Truck & Equipment

At your request the following study was completed:

Assignment: Can deliveries in 7-route area of Connecticut be made in trucks instead of mini vans? If so, at what cost in terms of service changes and dollars?

Conclusion: One large truck can deliver to stores on all 7 routes, averaging 11 stops per day. Production schedules from warehouse to depot would not change. Delivery schedules from depot to stores would change somewhat. Incremental cost for implementing this system of delivery would be approximately $32,000 annually for the 7 routes.

Summary: The present transportation cost of deliveries on these 7 routes is about $50,000 annually, using 7 vans. These vans could be replaced by one truck operating from the existing depot. The route representatives would be provided automobiles or mini vans (about equal in cost from BNJ). The net savings on this arrangement approximates $9,500 per year. Cost of leasing the large truck approximates $41,500 annually. Subtracting the $9,500 savings equals a net cost increase of $32,000 (or 64% higher than at present).

Comments: Under this system, the truck would deliver orders to 11 stores daily; and route reps would then drive to the stores in cars or mini vans to check in and service the orders. Delivery routes were constructed on the assumption that no change in production schedules was possible (i.e., a delivery had to be made after the order was picked at the warehouse, but no later than the day the store was next serviced). In some instances, we have assumed delivery times later than the customary 1 P.M. limit, but usually only for the smaller stores on these routes.

Alternatively, the truck might operate from the warehouse depot in Auburn, thereby eliminating the Connecticut depot. Or a private contractor might take responsibility for operating the truck and making the deliveries to stores. We have not attempted to quantify savings or costs from these alternatives.

Appendix
Imperial Distributors, Inc. (A)

The casewriter traveled with a route sales rep from the Boston area, Mr. George Todd, who was 29 and had a bachelor's degree in business management. After college, he worked at Star Market running "the front end" (i.e., the bundle boys and cashiers). He left Star and worked for Bradlees Discount Stores before joining Supermarket Distributors (SD), a service merchandiser. He was attracted to the job because the hours were better (no weekends) and it offered higher pay. In his three years with SD in New York State, Mr. Todd progressed to supervisor.

He decided to work for Imperial as a route rep in order to return to his home south of Boston. Mr. Todd commented: "I took a cut in pay, but there is no other way to learn how Imperial works. I've been here six months and am about to be promoted to senior merchandiser." Mr. Todd had spent two weeks as a trainee before taking over a route. He had trained mostly in Imperial's methods of ordering and paperwork.

Mr. Todd compared Imperial to his former employer, SD, which trucked merchandise to stores by private shippers and then the sales reps picked up and shelved the goods.

> In theory this was a good method, but the shipments were often late and service suffered. Imperial is more efficient at getting the orders out and stocked in the stores despite the fact that SD is much larger than Imperial.
>
> Imperial is more attractive despite the immediate cut in pay, because the long-term picture is more in keeping with the life I want. At Supermarket Distributors I was traveling all the time and never at home. Even with the long hours at Imperial, I still have weekends free. I don't mind the hours as long as there is a progression or a goal in sight.

Mr. Todd worked out of the Bridgewater depot (south of Boston) but on the day spent with the casewriter was filling in on a route from the Woburn depot (north of Boston). He left his home at 5:30 A.M. in order to reach the Woburn depot by 7:00 A.M. to load his van. He was scheduled to service three Purity Supreme supermarkets. The three supermarkets were less than 10 minutes apart and the first approximately a 30-minute drive from the depot. Each store had a 1:00 P.M. check-in time, which meant the supermarket

529

receivers left at that time and no other merchandise would normally be accepted. At 7:30 A.M. Mr. Todd left the Woburn depot.

At the first stop, at 8:00 A.M. in a Purity Supreme Superstore in Peabody, Mass., the receiver would not accept a number of items in the order and repeatedly interrupted the discussion with Mr. Todd to take other orders. After resolving differences with the receiver, Mr. Todd took until 11:30 A.M. to service the store because the store was big, the order large, and Mr. Todd had never before been in this particular store.

Mr. Todd next attempted to get the order accepted at Purity Supreme's other Peabody store, which was the third scheduled store on the route, before servicing Purity Supreme Danvers, the second scheduled stop. The Peabody store was an older supermarket and closer to the superstore, and Mr. Todd was trying to get all his orders through receiving before the 1:00 P.M. deadline. His intent was to "drop" the merchandise and then return later to service the shelves. However, at the Peabody store, the receiver insisted that Mr. Todd also service the store at the same time. As a result, Mr. Todd did not leave Peabody until 1:45 P.M.

Before leaving the store, Mr. Todd called his supervisor, explained the situation, and requested the supervisor to call store management in Danvers and try to arrange for a later check-in time.

Mr. Todd arrived at the Danvers supermarket at 2:00 and the receiving doors were locked. Entering through the front doors of the supermarket, he spoke to the store manager about receiving the order. The store manager denied having gotten a call and was short-tempered. He asked Mr. Todd, "Are you going to pay overtime for my receiver?" However, the store manager stated that Mr. Todd could wait for the grocery manager to return from lunch, and if the grocery manager felt like doing it, he would receive Imperial's order. The store manager offered no further information on the grocery manager's name or probable time of return. Mr. Todd commented to the casewriter that this was not unusual:

> To do the route job well you have to be a "rubber person" and just let comments from receivers and store managers roll by you. The receivers are a little like bouncers at a night club: they have power but only over a limited area and people. It is their job to look for shortages and incorrect product. Many receivers always assume that the route sales rep is trying to pull the wool over their eyes. There is no point in getting upset. The sales rep should concentrate on getting the merchandise in and writing the orders.
>
> Relationships are important. It takes time to build trust with the receivers. Part of the reason that I am having such a tough time with the receiver today is that they don't know me. On my own route, I often bring the receivers coffee in the morning and try to get to know them. If they trust you and like you, the job is a lot easier.

While waiting for the grocery manager, Mr. Todd decided to eat a quick lunch at a small restaurant in the shopping plaza. At 3:00 P.M. he returned to the store to find the grocery manager. At 3:15 the grocery manager agreed to receive the order if the store manager approved. The grocery manager said: "I'll do it, I'm already on time and a half." At 3:30, the grocery manager returned with permission to take the order. Mr. Todd brought in 10 totes from his van and opened the first and removed the invoice. The grocery manager received the invoice and checked amounts and prices as Mr. Todd picked up each item of the order (usually 3–6 pieces banded together) and read the information on the tag, which included the line number on the invoice, the item amount, product description and price (for example, "line 2, 3 red candles at $.99"). It took only 10 minutes to read through the two invoices for the small order.

Mr. Todd then asked the grocery manager to accept a promotional display ordered by Purity Supreme management for all the stores. The grocery manager stated that the general merchandise manager would have to approve the display, but that she was no longer in the store. None of the stores on the route had accepted the display.

At 3:40 Mr. Todd moved most of his totes into his van, having consolidated the order in two totes. Most of the order was J-hook merchandise with some candles, pet supplies and general housewares. At 3:50 he began to hang the J-hook merchandise, walking up and down the aisles, checking tags next to the J-hooks against the merchandise in his order. If the correct item was not in the order, Mr. Todd tried to fill the hooks with other merchandise that was appropriate or to reapportion the merchandise so that there would be no empty spots.

All of the pet supplies were in one end-cap display (a freestanding set of shelves at the end of an aisle). He straightened and rotated the products according to the dates on the price tags, removing other grocery items from the display and adding items from his order. Looking at the soft drink aisle, Mr. Todd commented that about 25 feet was clear of J-hooks. He stated that "other vendors' reps don't like the J-hooks because it makes their areas harder to service. Often the soft drink reps just move them." Mr. Todd found J-hooks on the floor and on the shelves and rehung them.

Mr. Todd finished putting up merchandise from the order at 5:00 P.M. He commented that, since this was the day's last stop, he had done the job in a leisurely fashion and that not knowing the layout of the store took more time. At this time, he also started ordering products for the store, using a hand-held computerized order-entry terminal. He went up and down every aisle quickly, entering the code number of products from the tags and the product amounts. In the baby care department he stated that he couldn't order the correct item to fill a hook, because the tag had not been changed when the item changed. The number on the tag was refused by the order-entry terminal as invalid because the item was discontinued.

As he ordered, Mr. Todd checked each of Imperial's departments, pulling product forward on some racks so that the racks would look neat and full. He commented:

> At least the store manager will know I've been here. I really don't know who or-
> dered for this store the last time it was serviced. Many things are missing, includ-

ing some of our high-volume items. It could have been somebody filling in the route like me, but the next person is going to have to go through the entire store and check it. I am ordering something from each department and J-hook area. I have to guess the amounts to order in many cases because I don't know what kind of volume this store does or what kind of things people buy here. That is another disadvantage of filling in on a route, especially in an area that I don't know.

At 5:35 P.M. Mr. Todd finished ordering. He took the remaining totes out to the van, and returned to dust the displays. Mr. Todd commented that normally he and the receiver would go through returns item by item and generate a credit slip. However, because the receiver had gone, this was not possible and so there would be more work for the next rep on the route. As he left, Mr. Todd estimated that in the rush hour traffic, it would take 90 minutes for him to get to his home south of Boston.

Imperial Route Sales Rep's Schedule

5:30 A.M. – 7:00 A.M.	Leave home and travel to Woburn depot
7:00 A.M. – 7:30 A.M.	Arrive depot, load orders into van
7:30 A.M. – 8:00 A.M.	Travel time to first stop
8:00 A.M. – 9:30 A.M.	Check in order with the receiver
9:30 A.M. – 11:00 A.M.	Hang and shelve merchandise
11:00 A.M. – 11:30 A.M.	Order merchandise, straighten displays
11:30 A.M. – 11:45 A.M.	Drive to older Purity Peabody store
11:45 A.M. – 12:30 P.M.	Check in order, attempt to leave order for later servicing
12:30 P.M. – 1:15 P.M.	Hang and shelve order
1:15 P.M. – 1:45 P.M.	Order merchandise, straighten displays
1:45 P.M. – 2:00 P.M.	Drive to Purity Supreme in Danvers
2:00 P.M. – 2:10 P.M.	Speak to store manager about receiving the order
2:10 P.M. – 3:00 P.M.	Lunch; wait for grocery manager
3:00 P.M. – 3:15 P.M.	Return to store, speak to grocery manager about receiving the order
3:15 P.M. – 3:30 P.M.	Grocery manager speaks to store manager, and is given permission to receive the order
3:30 P.M. – 3:40 P.M.	Order checked in
3:40 P.M. – 5:00 P.M.	Hang and shelve order, hang J-hooks
5:00 P.M. – 5:40 P.M.	Write order, straighten displays
5:40 P.M.	Drive home through rush hour traffic

Peripheral Products Company: The "Gray Market" for Disk Drives

In June 1985 James Ousley, vice president for OEM Marketing at Control Data Corporation's Peripheral Products Company division (PPCo), met with division management to review the performance of PPCo's disk-drive product line.[1] Prices for disk drives had fallen substantially during the past few years. Meanwhile, new markets had emerged and PPCo had added indirect distribution channels to reach these markets. PPCo increasingly found its various selling efforts not working as originally planned: channels often competed for the same customers, and a thriving "gray market" had emerged.[2]

This gray market had been the meeting's main topic. Top management at PPCo was concerned about the impact on prices and revenues, and Ousley had received complaints from PPCo's distributors, some sales managers, and some large OEM accounts. This morning's meeting was intended to reach decisions concerning the gray market, and thus representatives from sales and marketing, manufacturing, and the product lines were present. All agreed that PPCo's pricing policies on disk drives needed reexamination. During the meeting various proposals had been discussed, and the blackboard in the conference room was covered with diagrams and numbers offered by different participants.

As the meeting broke for lunch, Ousley felt the problem was being addressed directly. He was uneasy, however, with the focus of the morning's

---

Associate Professor Frank V. Cespedes prepared this case as the basis for class discussion rather than to illustrate either effective or ineffective handling of an administrative situation.

[1] *OEM* refers to an "original equipment manufacturer" (e.g., a computer company that uses a disk drive as a component in its system).

[2] A *gray market* refers to a situation in which a manufacturer encounters difficulties managing the flow of its products to market. Customers "divert" the flow by reselling the products in ways unintended and undesired by the manufacturer.

discussion: little attention had been paid to the impact of a pricing decision on PPCo's distribution network. As the participants began filing out the door, Ousley said, "We want to develop a pricing policy, but we should understand how we'll implement *any* pricing policy through our distribution channels and what the longer-term impact will be. Let's discuss that when we meet again this afternoon."

Industry and Technology Background

Disk drives—used in computers to record, store, and retrieve data—utilized either rigid or flexible ("floppy") disks (see Figure A). Floppy disks were removable from the drive mechanism. Rigid (or "Winchester") disks were fixed in place and sealed from the atmosphere. This eliminated contamination, allowing rigid drives greater storage capacity, reliability, and speed than floppy drives. By 1985 demand for rigid drives was growing much faster than for floppies to satisfy a need for higher-capacity, higher-performance storage systems for computers.

The disk drive was a large percentage of a computer's cost (often as much as 40% of the manufacturing cost of a microcomputer) and an important determinant of the computer's capabilities (i.e., its ability to process certain amounts of data at certain speeds, and thus its capability of running different software programs). As a result, selecting a disk-drive supplier was an important decision for a computer OEM, and the largest computer OEMs usually required more than one source of supply and a stringent qualification process. In addition, most large computer firms also manufactured their own disk drives for use in their computer systems.

Mass-storage technology was changing rapidly in 1985. Various companies had announced new technologies such as optical recording, which promised better performance than currently available drives. Simultaneously, the performance and costs of disk drives were improving. Product life cycles were short and, as one observer stated, "In this climate the ability to innovate and to understand rapidly evolving customer requirements is essential. A successful drive product is not so much a long-term franchise as it is a platform for the timely introduction of the next generation."

Products

Disk drives were manufactured in different diameters, ranging from 14 inches to 3.5 inches. The larger 14-, 9-, and 8-inch drives had been manufactured since the 1970s; the smaller 5.25- and 3.5-inch drives were introduced in the early 1980s. A drive's performance was generally measured in cost per megabyte (a *megabyte* is 1 million bytes, and a *byte* is 8 units or "bits" of information processed by a computer as a single unit). Cost per megabyte had decreased dramatically during the past decades and was expected to continue decreasing at least until 1990.

Figure A
Sample Disk Drive: 5.25-inch Winchester Model

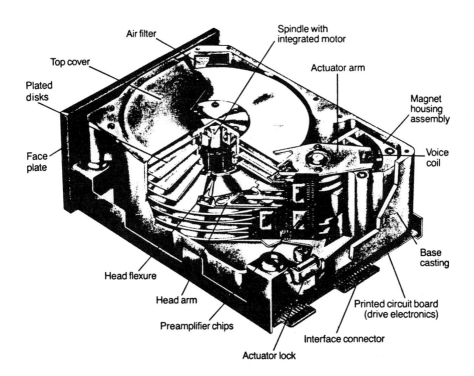

As drives were produced in smaller diameters, moreover, their capacity also increased. In industry parlance, "more activity on less real estate" was the objective in product policy for drive manufacturers due to the growth in the market for small computers. Thus, 5.25- and 3.5-inch rigid drives were replacing the 8- and 14-inch drives in some higher-capacity segments and had virtually eliminated the larger drives in the lower-capacity segments. Meanwhile, 8- and 14-inch drives were also growing in capacity to satisfy increasing storage requirements of mainframes and "super" minicomputers.

Pricing and purchase criteria for drive products differed depending upon the type of computer and end-user application. In 1985 most firms distinguished among three product types according to the drive's capacity: a low end (5–30 megabytes of capacity), medium performance (30–100 megabytes), and a high end (100 megabytes and above).

■ At the low end, in single-user desktop or portable computers, price was the dominant purchase criterion used by OEMs. In these systems, floppy drives and low-capacity 5.25- and 3.5-inch rigid drives were typically used. The low-capacity segment was expected to represent over 50% of total market growth for disk drives through 1989.

- Medium-performance drives were used in multi-user systems, where the drive's capacity increased in importance. Higher-capacity 5.25- and 8-inch drives were typically used, with smaller-diameter drives replacing larger-diameter drives in newer systems. This segment was expected to grow at 20% annually through 1989 and account for 20% of total market growth.

- High-performance drives were used in many minicomputers and mainframes where capacity and fast access time were critical. The price of the drive, while important, was often secondary. These systems generally used 14-inch and some higher-capacity 8-inch drives although, by 1985, newer 5.25-inch Winchester drives had reached comparable speeds and capacity. This segment was expected to account for 30% of market growth through 1989 with smaller products replacing 14-inch drives. In 1984 PPCo held over a 50% share in the 14-inch/>100 megabyte product category.

Markets

Disk drives were produced by computer firms for their own systems (captive production), by "plug-compatible" manufacturers (PCMs), and by various firms for sale to manufacturers and other suppliers of computer systems (the OEM market). IBM represented 50% of about $7 billion worth of captive drive production in 1984. PCM production referred to drives compatible with the computer systems of a given manufacturer such as IBM but manufactured by another firm and generally sold at a lower price. In 1984 PCM shipments of rigid drives were estimated at $300 million.

OEM markets included drives manufactured by computer and disk-drive firms for sale to computer manufacturers, systems houses (i.e., firms that combined components from different vendors to offer users complete computer systems), and "value-added resellers" (i.e., firms that bought computer hardware and added software or technical support for certain industries or applications). In 1984 the worldwide OEM market for rigid drives was about $2.8 billion and for floppy drives about $1.4 billion.

Especially in mainframes, captive production of drives was often very profitable for a computer OEM. A proprietary, high-performance drive allowed an OEM to charge a higher price for the computer system in which that drive was a necessary component. IBM, which had essentially founded the disk-drive industry with its pioneering work in drive technology, continued to dominate the mainframe drive business in 1985.

Historically, IBM had tended not to sell its drives to other OEMs. In addition, few other computer OEMs attempted to meet disk storage requirements internally because the technology changed rapidly and external sources of supply were often the locus of innovations. In products other than its mainframe computers, moreover, IBM also relied heavily upon external sources for disk drives. Thus, throughout the 1960s and 1970s a market emerged for supplying drives to OEMs. During this period, PPCo was the largest supplier to other OEMs, primarily at higher-capacity segments. However, first minicomputers and then microcomputers revolutionized the market. The size, as well as performance capacity, of the drive assumed new importance in these systems. Demand for more compact drives soon outstripped demand for the older and larger disk drives.

In 1984 worldwide disk-drive shipments grew 40% over 1983 shipments, with noncaptive production increasing faster than captive production. Annual growth in disk-drive revenues was forecasted to slow to about 20% during the 1985–1987 period, with a higher rate of unit shipments offset by a continuing decline in prices. Exhibit 1 provides historical and forecasted pricing trends for major drive product categories.

U. S. manufacturers held about 75% of the worldwide market, but Japanese firms were becoming competitive in several product groups, especially in the more price-sensitive, lower-performance drives. Across product groups, rigid drives were expected to replace lower-performance floppy drives in many applications.

Customers and Buying Behavior

In the disk-drive market, large customers dominated the landscape. In 1984, according to one estimate, the 10 largest computer manufacturers accounted for about 50% of disk-drive purchases, while the 50 largest OEMs represented over 80%. Frequently a disk-drive supplier would sell to just a few large customers. In addition, the customer base tended to be concentrated in areas such as Silicon Valley in California or Route 128 in New England, where several large firms were only a few miles from each other. This customer base was served primarily by the drive manufacturers' direct sales forces. In 1984 less than 10% of the drives sold to OEMs went through indirect channels such as distributors.

At larger computer OEMs, the buying process generally had the following characteristics. In the first stage, the OEM sent a request for information (RFI) to potential drive vendors. The RFI provided general information about a computer system being planned by the OEM, and requested information about the drive supplier's current or planned products that might be compatible with that system. The second stage was a request for quote, which requested technical specifics and a quantity price from the drive vendor. A third stage was a business proposal, where the drive vendor explained how it proposed to guarantee its supply of product as well as covering other matters such as a quality-assurance program and the contract agreement. Large OEMs generally contracted to buy a quantity of a specific drive product over some time frame, usually from one to two years.

Because there were significant scale economies and learning-curve effects in drive production, large orders were attractive to drive vendors despite the quantity discounts involved. In addition, larger computer OEMs often set standards for peripheral devices. Thus, selling to a large account often meant sales at other accounts as well as replacement sales for several years if the OEM's system was successful in the marketplace. The importance of large customers meant that, besides sales representatives and product engineers, the senior management of a drive firm often participated in these account-selling efforts. One executive of a drive firm referred to this as "head-of-state selling":

> The big sales in this business are closed at the summit conference level, when I and other senior managers from this firm meet with our counterparts at the OEM. That doesn't mean the field sales reps are not important: they must develop and maintain a strong relationship with those accounts, penetrating throughout a very decentralized and complex decision-making unit, because the product policy of a drive vendor is intimately dependent upon the product plans of the larger OEMs. Also, the field sales rep must negotiate the purchase through the technical specialists and purchasing people at the OEM. And the sales rep must, of course, try to influence the OEM's make-buy decision.
>
> But closing a major sale usually occurs at a face-to-face meeting between the senior managements of the firms involved. As well as a set of technical specifications, the OEM is buying a trusted supplier. Because the product is technically complex and so important to the ultimate performance of the OEM's system, [the] delivery, reliability, quality control, and other aspects of a good supplier are crucial.

As drives declined in price, many new, small customers had emerged, especially in the small business and personal computer segments. These newer customers often required specialized products, initially bought in relatively small quantities. To reach these newer customers and to act as a "buffer" for the inherent credit risks, many drive vendors began selling through industrial distributors during the early 1980s. One executive at a drive manufacturer noted:

> Distributors are often in a better position to identify and sell to emerging companies because they can leverage their current sales calls. They are often already calling on these small companies to sell semiconductors, controllers, power supplies, and other electronic equipment, and the purchase decision for drives at those companies is often made by the same people buying those other components.

Exhibit 2, based on a survey from an engineering journal, indicates various purchase criteria for rigid disk drives. Also, once an OEM had become familiar with a drive vendor's product, engineering team, production personnel, and top executives, this greatly improved the chances of the drive vendor winning contracts for new-generation products (assuming that the current drive met expectations). The OEM's costs of qualifying a new vendor were extensive, ranging from a battery of product tests to numerous plant visits, resolution of integration problems, and so on. If a new drive provided a means of upgrading both the OEM's current product and its installed base, the OEM often found it easier—from a time and cost perspective—to continue its current relationship with the drive vendor. In many instances, it was primarily an OEM's reluctance to become too dependent upon a single source of supply that opened the door to competing drive vendors. From the drive supplier's perspective, moreover, steady relationships with major computer OEMs provided the benefits of greater visibility for its products, focused selling efforts, and insights into the market's future drive requirements.

Competition

During the early 1980s dozens of firms entered the disk-drive industry. In 1985 there were over 50 U.S. drive manufacturers with another 20 overseas companies that had entered—or planned to enter—the U.S. market. Since the 50 largest U.S. computer OEMs accounted for most drive purchases, there was more than one drive supplier per major customer. A supplier that encountered production difficulties, fell below parity in product performance, or failed to meet delivery dates was vulnerable with these accounts.

Conversely, a drive manufacturer able to penetrate and hold large accounts often established a cost advantage over the competition. So-called experience curve pricing—where drive manufacturers added capacity and were committed to lower-priced, high-volume orders in anticipation of lower costs due to scale economies and learning-curve effects—was common in the industry. This applied especially to floppy and lower-capacity drives, where product differentiation proved harder to achieve and where the drives were components in small computers that were themselves coming under increasing price pressures.

To maximize their R&D efforts, most drive manufacturers traditionally targeted certain segments rather than attempting across-the-board competition. However, as computer OEMs broadened their product lines to include systems of varying capabilities, drive manufacturers also broadened their product lines to maintain and develop account relationships with these OEMs. The result was increased competition, higher R&D investments, and new marketing requirements as companies entered new segments or targeted new users and applications.

Company Background

With 1984 revenues of $5 billion, Control Data Corporation (CDC) had two business segments: Information Services and Products (75% of 1984 revenues) and Financial Services (see Exhibit 3). Within Information Services, CDC manufactured and sold computer systems and services. Through PPCo, CDC manufactured and sold "peripheral" equipment such as disk drives to other computer manufacturers, computer resellers, and some end users.

Peripheral Products Company

In 1962 CDC acquired a small firm that eventually became the PPCo division. In 1970 PPCo developed a 14-inch drive that became standard in many non-IBM mainframe systems. That product helped fuel a nearly 50% annual growth rate for PPCo through the 1970s. PPCo later introduced drives in 9-, 8-, and 5.25-inch diameters (see Exhibit 4). The division's goal was to maintain leadership in high-performance, high-capacity drives, starting with the 14-inch products and evolving down the product spectrum through smaller, high-performance drive segments.

High-performance, high-capacity disk drives accounted for about 60% of PPCo's 1984 revenues. These drives, used primarily in mainframes (including CDC products) and "super" minicomputers, included the 9-inch and 14-inch products. Products for the mid-range market, used in minicomputers and small business computer systems, represented about 15% of PPCo's revenues. Finally, 5.25-inch floppy and rigid disk drives for the fast-growing microcomputer market accounted for about 10% of revenues. PPCo also marketed related equipment such as disk packs, coated disks, and magnetic tapes, but disk drives made up about 85% of PPCo's $1.5 billion in revenues in 1984.

Organization

Exhibit 5 provides an overview of the PPCo organization, focusing on the marketing and operations functions. In OEM marketing, headed by Ousley, PPCo's products were sold in the United States through a field sales organization that reported to three regional managers who in turn managed 10 sales offices, each headed by a district manager.

Seventy-two OEM sales representatives provided sales and customer support in an assigned geographic territory. In OEM accounts, the salespeople generally met with both engineering and purchasing personnel. The salespeople reported to district managers, who established individual sales quotas. On average, each OEM sales rep generated 1984 sales revenues of $7 million with a high of $110 million and a low of $1 million. Compensation was a base salary of approximately $25,000 and a bonus based on achieving quota. In turn, the quota was based on achieving a target for orders booked and total revenue as well as on opening new accounts and selling new products.

Separate from the field sales organization was a national programs organization, which sold and serviced seven large accounts that, as a group, bought over 50% of PPCo's disk drives.

PPCo's disk drives were manufactured at two plants, Twin Cities Disk Drives (greater than 80-megabyte drives) and Oklahoma City (drives of 80 megabytes or less). Each operation had its own engineering and manufacturing division and a business management office (BMO). The BMO had profit-and-loss responsibility and pricing authority for all drives manufactured by the plant. Within the BMO, program and product managers worked with their counterparts in marketing and engineering on the technical design and applications aspects of product development and customer support.

Distribution Channels

PPCo had traditionally sold through a direct sales force only, but in 1979 the company signed agreements with two distributors of electronics components, Arrow Electronics and Kierulff Inc. One executive explained:

> Our main thrust is the 30 largest computer OEMs, where a single account can generate tens of millions of dollars in annual sales revenues. However, low-end peripherals became increasingly important and also experienced dramatic price reductions. Therefore, alternate channels became a way of making sales of these products more cost-efficient to all the many smaller customers that emerged as the price of peripherals and computer systems fell.

Both Arrow and Kierulff had branches throughout the United States and often in the same areas. Table A provides additional information.

Over 80% of PPCo's drives were sold to about 100 OEM customers, with each buying over one million dollars' worth a year; the remaining 20% were sold to over 600 direct accounts. Thus, while the average sales per account was more than $1 million, the median sales per account was less than $90,000 annually. One executive noted:

> With this customer base, the question becomes, "What's the most efficient way of serving those hundreds of customers who buy small but, in the aggregate, can add up to a significant figure?" In addition, turnover among accounts in this business is very high: new OEMs constantly emerge and often out of nowhere. We need a presence among those smaller customers who may grow big but initially buy small.

In 1983 James Phelps was named manager of a separate distributor sales program at PPCo. He described the situation as follows:

> In this business, we face an extreme version of the 80-20 rule, with the lower 50% of the customer base accounting for less than 10% of our total revenues. Our basic goal for distributor sales was to allow the direct sales force to provide more support to large OEM customers, while distributors focused on the many small accounts.

Table A
PPCo's Distributors

	Arrow	Kierulff
Total 1984 sales	$740 million	$400 million
Number of branches	44	30
1984 sales of PPCo products	$6 million	$12 million
Other disk-drive products carried by distributor	Quantum, Miniscribe, Seagate	Tandon, Qume

Phelps developed and managed seven dedicated distributor sales representatives, whose responsibilities were to train and make calls with the distributors' salespeople and to act as liaison between the OEM reps and the distributors' branches. According to Phelps, these distribution reps were placed in local PPCo sales offices both "to integrate them and distributor sales into our field sales organization, and because distribution is a local marketing effort. Relationships between individuals in a distributor's branch office and one of our local sales offices are often the key to selling through this channel." In fiscal 1984 sales to the two distributors represented about 1.4% of PPCo's total disk-drive sales; one of the distributors was among the top 10 accounts for PPCo drives.

In 1985 the distribution sales program was reorganized. Phelps was promoted to regional sales manager, and the distributors became part of the national programs organization in OEM marketing. The distribution reps reported to local OEM district managers and had primary responsibility for managing relationships with the corporate and regional managements of the two distributors.

Exhibit 6 provides an overview of PPCo's distribution channels. Besides direct sales to larger OEM accounts, systems houses, and value-added resellers and sales to its industrial distributors, PPCo also sold drives to computer retailers, to commercial distributors (who, in turn, sold to smaller computer dealers), and to some corporate end-user accounts. These latter groups usually purchased "subsystems" (i.e., the disk packaged with a controller and power supply) rather than the "raw" drive, as OEMs and industrial distributors did. The subsystem supplemented the capacity of a computer system, and the retail, commercial, and corporate segments had grown as users sought to increase the capabilities of their installed micro- or minicomputers.

Pricing

As Exhibit 7 indicates, PPCo's pricing of disk drives was structured so that as the order quantities increased, OEM customers received larger price discounts while distributors received drives at a constant price. On order quantities of less than 1,000 units, the distributor was sold the drives at a price intended to allow the distributor a 15% to 20% resale margin. On order quantities of 1,000 or more, the direct price to OEM accounts decreased, and as the order quantities increased, distributors were progressively priced out of the market.

This pricing structure had been established for two reasons. One reason was that, as an OEM purchased more, it generally demanded a volume discount that made selling through an intermediary economically unattractive for PPCo. Another reason was that the OEM also usually requested a more direct relationship with the drive manufacturers for technical service, information concerning the next generation of compatible products, and assurance concerning continuity of supply.

In tandem with this list-price structure, PPCo also maintained a price-exception program for competitive bids on certain orders. First, the OEM sales rep, or a distributor, submitted a price-exception report to the district sales manager, explaining why a lower price might be necessary to win a given order. The district manager could accept or reject the request. If accepted, the district manager submitted another request to the BMO at either Twin Cities or Oklahoma City. The BMO could accept or reject the request but often delegated the decision to divisional managers of pricing and contracts such as John Anderson.

Anderson noted that the frequency and extent of price exceptions differed at Twin Cities and Oklahoma City:

> From Twin Cities, which makes the higher-end drives where we have long had a presence and where the purchase criteria tend to be more technical, I receive only about six price-exception requests weekly. At Oklahoma City, which makes the lower-end floppy drive products, probably as much as 90% of their business goes through the price-exception process.

In past months several issues had arisen concerning PPCo's pricing policies and the implementation of those policies. First, many in sales felt the price-exception process took too long and was often unresponsive to market conditions. One sales rep commented:

> It can take four or five days for a request to filter up and back down the organization. Many customers go to another vendor during that time. Also, our book prices become increasingly meaningless as competition, especially from the Japanese, intensifies and prices fall throughout the industry.
>
> The BMO looks at each quarter's bottom line and is reluctant to lower prices. We have lost some major orders because of price—and sometimes to competition that will be hard to dislodge. For example, other companies also produce a full line of computer products in addition to drives. Therefore, if I lose a drive sale to such competition, I also jeopardize other peripherals I sell to that account.

Second, many in the BMO organizations felt the OEM and distributor salespeople often tried to compete on price when this was unnecessary and undesirable. One manager commented:

> At PPCo we have a broad product line, and it's difficult for a salesperson to be knowledgeable about every product in the line. And this problem is compounded by the pace of technological change and new-product introductions in this business. The result is that, in my opinion, some salespeople "cave in" on price when it's unnecessary.
>
> For example, last week I received a price-exception request from an OEM rep running into "X" [a company that produces drives and other computer products] for this particular order. The rep felt a lower price was necessary to compete. But, in fact, the technical specifications for the order suggested that the customer could not use the competitive product for the intended purpose.

Third, many in OEM marketing felt that pricing, and especially new-product pricing, was not aggressive enough. One manager noted:

> PPCo has been a leader in the 14-inch category. But we were a later entrant in the 5.25-inch category and don't have a large presence there. In 1983, however, PPCo developed an excellent 5.25-inch drive. We urged penetration pricing to develop a segment that's increasingly important. But the BMO decided to price about 25% higher than competing drives. In a business where product life cycles are short, customers waited for competitors to introduce analogous products. In my opinion, we lost a good chance to develop the 5.25-inch market for PPCo.

Fourth, PPCo's distributors had voiced concerns about the price-exception process and pricing policies. One distributor commented:

> Our business depends on availability and quick response. Taking days to respond to a price request can be the kiss of death on an order. The customer doesn't want to wait.
>
> Also, PPCo has probably the largest sales force of any company selling disk drives, and their order quantities for the direct vs. distributor cut-off point tend to be somewhat lower than the industry norm. The result is that we at the distributor may develop a small account into one that now orders at least a thousand units annually, but the fruits of that work go to the manufacturer. That's of course a generic issue in any manufacturer-distributor relationship. But my point is that we can keep an account "our account" longer with some other manufacturers, because of their pricing policies.

In 1985 industry demand for drives was not growing as forecasted and had even declined from 1984 levels in some segments. The result was a general weakening of prices. In addition, during the past five years many drive manufacturers (especially in the 5.25-inch segments) had added capacity to achieve scale economies. As competition intensified, many firms cut prices to keep volumes up. PPCo, despite superior quality in some products, also found itself cutting list prices to utilize high fixed-cost capacity. As one manufacturing manager commented, "Throughput is a very important dimension of this business: making money on drives often requires high volumes."

The Gray Market

The gray market referred to a situation in which some of PPCo's customers purchased drives at significant volume discounts but, rather than "adding technical value to the products" as required by Article 1 of CDC's OEM purchase agreements (see Exhibit 8), these firms resold the raw drives to major computer dealers, smaller systems houses, smaller OEMs, and some end users. These firms were often called "pseudo-OEMs," because they purchased under the terms of an OEM agreement. They typically operated on low gross margins (e.g., 5% to 10%), and usually undercut the prices of distributors and other resellers of PPCo's drives.

In recent years, gray markets had sprung up throughout the computer industry, affecting many products besides disk drives. In 1985 one trade journal reported:[3]

> In the fast-paced world of computer distribution, it's often every man for himself [sic]. What are supposed to be complementary relationships between manufacturers and dealers[4] frequently break down in territorial squabbles. All the confusion proved a hot topic in the aisles at Comdex/Fall.[5]
>
> "It's very disruptive and it's the fault of manufacturers," dealer Anthony Morris asserted before a Comdex group. Dealers in the audience nodded knowingly. Manufacturers, meanwhile, blame dealers for diverting the merchandise.
>
> Neither party is happy because the gray market threatens channel and pricing stability. Nonetheless, manufacturers continue to structure stepped dealer discount schedules in favor of large orders, particularly in a period of excess supply. To get the largest discounts, dealers buy more than they can sell, moving the rest "sideways" to unauthorized dealers who run more or less cash-and-carry operations. Dealers grow particularly miffed when they've tried to sell a walk-in customer, educate him, then watch him buy at a lower price from gray market operators.

A PPCo executive commented about the gray market:

> We first noticed these pseudo-OEMs cropping up a few years ago, when demand was strong and we had to put customers on allocation for drives. Some firms began buying in larger quantities and sold a percentage of the drives "raw" to other customers. They usually sold to mid-range accounts buying from about $100,000 to $1 million annually, and not to the major accounts who already received big volume discounts and naturally received high priority during allocation periods.
>
> When demand was strong, the pseudo-OEM resold the drives at a profitable premium, because customers were concerned about supply and faster delivery of product. That motivated the gray operator to purchase and sell more. And, frankly, we were not overly concerned: it was a small amount of total sales being diverted in this manner and, in those market conditions, we even felt the pseudo-OEM performed an indirect service by acting as a kind of "second source of supply" for our drives at some smaller accounts. When demand weakened suddenly in late 1984, the gray market became a bigger problem. Customers became more price sensitive and the pseudo-OEM, operating with low overhead and offering little or no credit, could offer lower prices than our distributors and still make money.

---

[3] "As Technology Matures . . . Computing's Highrollers Turn to Marketing," *Business Marketing,* January 1985, pp. 102–103.

[4] In this article, *dealer* refers to any independent selling organization, including retail "dealers."

[5] Comdex is a computer trade show for new-product announcements. Top managements of most computer firms usually attend Comdex.

This gray market grew gradually. It's difficult to know just how much is going through pseudo-OEMs, but we estimated that about $30 million of our total disk-drive sales are accounted for by pseudo-OEMs.

Other managers explained that "double bookings" and consequent price erosion were problems accelerated by the gray market. The pseudo-OEMs sold to many of the same customers served by PPCo's distributors. Therefore, both the distributor and the pseudo-OEM often ordered product for the same customer, somewhat like an airline traveler who books more than one flight and finally chooses one. PPCo ramped-up production to meet these orders but found itself with increased inventories and excess capacity when the end user bought from one source and then canceled orders placed with the other source. One manager described the resulting situation as "the pendulum effect," where PPCo found itself swinging between first putting customers on allocation due to the upsurge in demand and then having excess inventory that, in turn, often motivated price cuts to move the inventory and utilize excess capacity.

Concerns about the gray market were widespread throughout PPCo. A PPCo distributor sales representative labeled the gray market as "my number one problem and getting bigger":

When one of our distributors' branches loses a sale to a pseudo-OEM, two things happen. First, the branch manager lets me know about it in seven different languages. Second, that distributor is less motivated to push our product.

Selling through distributors often depends on establishing close relationships with key individuals in each branch. Our distributors sell hundreds of other products, and most of them are less technically complex than disk drives. A large part of my job is developing those relationships and, through training and support, motivating the distributor's salespeople to spend time on our products. Months of hard work can be shot to hell by these pseudo-OEMs.

An OEM sales rep emphasized the impact on pricing and account relationships:

I first encountered this when a customer showed me an invoice which offered our product—with exact specifications—for nearly $1,000 less per unit than the price I was offering. My first reaction was to suggest the invoice contained a typographical error: I thought a zero had been omitted! But I checked out the order and had to go back to the customer and offer an embarrassed apology and a lower price.

This problem is compounded because the price-exception process takes time, and the BMO doesn't want to grant an exception unless it absolutely has to. Meeting my sales quota this year is in jeopardy because of these pseudo-OEMs.

District sales managers (whose bonuses were based on total district sales volume) stressed the complexity of the situation and the effect on morale. One district manager commented:

I get different stories from salespeople about pseudo-OEMs, partly because some salespeople now depend on these resellers for a significant portion of their quotas and some do not. The result is some tension within the office, and often between people who share the same cubicle.

Also, there is a vicious cycle due to double bookings. When demand weakens and the bubble bursts, the excess inventory brings pressure down on the sales organization: in a business with short product life cycles, excess product can soon become a write-off if not sold. The result is that many salespeople then feel pressure to sell to anybody, including pseudo-OEMs, and this further erodes prices, fueling the entire cycle all over again.

I don't know how many of our district's sales go to the gray market. But if you factor out sales made by National Programs to major accounts, then our primary customer base in the field is those medium-sized accounts pseudo-OEMs also focus on.

A regional sales manager noted that the severity of the problem differed between regions:

Many of these pseudo-OEMs are on the West Coast, because that's where most drive manufacturers are located. But they sell nationwide. So often our western offices will book sales to the pseudo-OEMs, and we in the East will feel the brunt of the price competition. I sometimes feel I'm being shafted by my own people, and I don't like it one bit.

In OEM marketing, a manager explained that identifying a pseudo-OEM was not a straightforward task:

Some of these gray marketers are brokers who buy drives, stock them in a garage, and sell the lot to whomever they can find. But others are systems houses or value-added resellers who may be selling just 10% to 20% of their purchased drives without adding value. And in the current conditions of depressed demand in the computer industry, we've even seen some larger OEMs dumping excess drives on the gray market.

These pseudo-OEMs are a diverse group, and some are legitimate, important customers for our products. It's a tough situation. Short term, the gray market happens incrementally with good business and it moves product. But longer term, we wind up competing with ourselves at a lower price.

In operations, a BMO manager stated that "the gray market is a problem, but should be put in perspective":

First, when our salespeople encounter pseudo-OEM competition, they should emphasize to the customer that the gray marketer is not a reliable source of supply and that his units are not covered by our warranty agreements. Salespeople can also emphasize that CDC can sell the entire package of products the customer needs, whereas the pseudo-OEM cannot.

Second, much of the gray activity is in the 5.25-inch drive categories, and especially in the floppy drives. This is an area where product differentiation is hard to achieve and which is quickly being superseded by new-product technologies. Frankly, pseudo-OEM sales in that product category utilize capacity for products that, as far as major OEM customers are concerned, are near commodities.

Reflecting on the gray market, Anderson noted:

Ten years ago it was simple: we sold to a few customers and treated everybody as an OEM customer. But this market has fragmented as it has grown. Pricing is an important dimension of this problem. But I believe the underlying issue is, how should we define and manage the different types of customers out there and the different channels we deal with?

Alternatives Being Considered

During the morning, three alternatives had been considered.

First, some managers argued that PPCo should identify the pseudo-OEMs and refuse to sell to them. Serial numbers could be used to identify PPCo drives bought on the gray market, and the OEM purchase contract made shutting off sales to pseudo-OEMs legal. These managers also argued that if the pseudo-OEMs were cut off, PPCo might lose some sales in the short term but would probably sell more products via its distributors. In addition, a cut-off might mitigate the price erosion caused by the gray market and so perhaps increase profitability as well. They pointed to companies like Lotus Development Corporation in software and IBM in personal computers, which had also encountered gray markets for their products and had responded by refusing to sell to some resellers.

Against this course of action, other managers argued that "in this industry, there are many places to get product. These brokers will simply buy from another source." These managers also believed that, if cut off from PPCo's drives, the pseudo-OEMs would simply sell another vendor's drives, and PPCo would not recoup these lost sales. Others maintained that the time and costs of tracking down gray marketers would be burdensome.

Second, some managers argued that, as the current contracts with identifiable pseudo-OEMs expired, these customers should be reclassified as a new channel, "independent selling organizations," rather than OEMs. The price to these customers would be a higher price without volume discounts. These managers reasoned that, since it was the volume discounts that allowed pseudo-OEMs to compete with other channels, PPCo should price according to type of customer rather than size of purchase. In particular, they argued, if gray marketers were sold drives at the same price as PPCo's industrial distributors, then the pseudo-OEM's ability to compete with this legitimate channel should be lessened.

These managers also believed that the current market conditions of falling prices offered an opportunity to implement this policy smoothly. "When a gray marketer's contract is up for renewal," said one manager, "our salespeople can offer the new contract as an independent selling organization and point out that the new contract contains no price *increase* over the prices in the old contract signed a year or two ago."

Third, some managers argued that, rather than type of customer, purchase quantity should indeed be the sole criterion for determining PPCo's selling price. These managers wanted PPCo to sell its drives at the same price (for a given quantity) to all classes of customers—OEM, distributor, large retailers, and commercial distributors. These managers noted this was already the actual practice for some of PPCo's products where the gray market had been most intense. One manager commented, "In 5.25-inch floppy drives, price competition has effectively forced us, through the frequency and intensity of price exceptions, to sell these products to all customers at the same price." Another manager stated that this pricing tactic should benefit PPCo over the long term: "The channel that's most efficient, and that can sell our product at the lowest realizable gross margin, should gain strength over time. And that's the channel we want to use to get our products to market."

When the meeting reconvened after lunch, Ousley reminded participants that any pricing tactics had to be implemented through PPCo's sales force and current distribution channels. He also pointed out that many of PPCo's largest customers were affected by the gray market:

> Many computer manufacturers have long seen the drive, and especially add-on or replacement drives to current customers, as a way of marking up prices for their systems and as an important source of revenues. Important OEM customers are now complaining to me that the gray market cuts into these sales significantly. They complain that their sales forces do the legwork and incur the costs of selling and installing the computer system to a customer. But the customer then turns around and buys either the original drive, or replacement drives, from a lower-priced gray marketer who does not provide product support and service. In an industry like this, when those large OEM customers talk, I must listen: what should we do about the gray market for our drives?

Exhibit 1   Peripheral Products Company

Industry Pricing Data for Selected Disk-Drive Product Groups

Year	14-in. Rigid Drives (to OEM purchasing in 100-order quantities): [a]	
	80 Megabytes	300 Megabytes
1981	$7,000	$11,500
1982	6,200	11,000
1983	5,800	10,500
1984	5,400	10,000
1985	5,200	$9,500
1986 (est.)	5,100	$9,100

	9-in. Rigid Drives (to OEM purchasing in 100-order quantities): [a]		
	160 Megabytes	340 Megabytes	500 Megabytes
1981	—	—	—
1982	$5,300	—	—
1983	4,800	$7,200	$8,200
1984	4,400	6,600	7,600
1985	4,100	5,300	6,300
1986 (est.)	3,500	4,800	5,800

	8-in. Rigid Drives (to OEM purchasing in 100-order quantities): [a]	
	160 Megabytes	360 Megabytes
1981	—	—
1982	—	—
1983	—	—
1984	$3,500	—
1985	3,000	$4,500
1986 (est.)	2,500	4,000

	5.25-in. Rigid Drives (to OEM purchasing in 500-order quantities): [a]			
	10 Megabytes	20 Megabytes	30 Megabytes	80 Megabytes
1981	$1,250	—	—	—
1982	900	—	—	—
1983	450	$550	$1,400	$1,750
1984	300	400	950	1,450
1985	250	350	800	1,100
1986 (est.)	200	250	600	950

	3.5-in. Rigid Drives (to OEM purchasing in 500-order quantities): [a]		
	10 Megabytes	20 Megabytes	30 Megabytes
1981	—	—	—
1982	—	—	—
1983	$450	—	—
1984	400	—	—
1985	325	$450	$475
1986 (est.)	250	350	450

(continued)

Exhibit 1 (continued)

	5.25-in. Floppy Drives (to OEM purchasing in 1,000-order quantities): [a]	
	0.5 Megabytes (full-height)	0.5 Megabytes (half-height)
1981	$260	—
1982	240	—
1983	210	$230
1984	110	110
1985	85	50
1986 (est.)	70	45

[a]Prices are estimated average *unit* prices at manufacturer's selling price for the specified order quantity.

Note: Large computer OEMs often ordered in quantities much larger than those used in this exhibit's examples. Larger orders generally received volume discounts that made the average unit price of the drive significantly lower than the prices cited in these examples.

Exhibit 2   Peripheral Products Company

Importance of Factors Affecting the Selection of Winchester Disk Drives

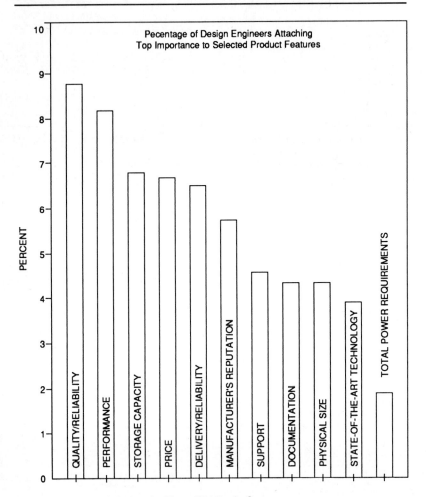

Pecentage of Design Engineers Attaching
Top Importance to Selected Product Features

Source: Electronic Engineering Times, 1984 Reader Survey.

Exhibit 3 Peripheral Products Company

Control Data Corporation: Financial Information, 1982–1984
($ in millions, except per share data)

	1984	1983	1982
Revenues			
Information services and products			
Net sales	$2,083.4	$1,915.7	$1,698.9
Services	1,401.4	1,251.0	1,239.0
Rentals	270.7	341.2	363.2
Total	3,755.5	3,507.9	3,301.1
Financial services			
Interest, discounts, and service charges	753.6	638.1	669.0
Insurance premiums	325.7	301.0	268.3
Investment and other income	192.1	135.8	101.9
Total	1,271.4	1,074.9	1,039.2
Total revenues	$5,026.9	$4,582.8	$4,340.3
Costs and Expenses			
Information services and products			
Cost of sales	1,514.0	1,356.6	1,188.6
Cost of services	798.1	711.5	724.2
Cost of rentals	82.6	113.4	127.4
Selling, general and administrative	790.5	711.9	693.0
Technical expenses	422.5	379.7	325.9
Interest expense	90.1	81.9	100.4
Total	3,697.8	3,355.0	3,159.5
Financial services			
Interest expense	493.1	368.3	358.6
Operating expenses	384.2	347.5	329.2
Provisions for credit losses	45.9	59.6	54.3
Insurance losses and reserves	266.4	238.8	209.4
Total	1,189.6	1,014.2	951.5
Total costs and expenses	$4,887.4	$4,369.2	$4,111.0
Earnings (loss) Before Income Taxes and			
Other Items			
Information services and products			
Before one-time charge	57.7	152.9	141.6
Loss from one-time charge	(130.2)	—	—
	(72.5)	152.9	141.6
Financial services	81.8	60.7	87.7
Total	9.3	213.6	229.3
Provision (credit) for income taxes	(36.4)	45.8	67.6
Earnings After Income Taxes and Before other			
Items	45.7	167.8	161.7
Minority Interests and Equity in Operations of			
Affiliates	(14.1)	(6.1)	(6.6)
Net Earnings	$ 31.6	$ 161.7	$ 155.1
Earnings per Share of Common Stock	$ .81	$ 4.20	$ 4.11

Source: Annual reports.

Exhibit 4   Peripheral Products Company

Selected Items from PPCo's Disk-Drive Product Line

Product	1984 List Price per Unit (in 100-quantity purchase orders)
Wren 5.25-inch Rigid Disk Drives	
21 megabytes	$ 1,410
36 megabytes	1,660
80 megabytes	2,555
Lark 8-inch Cartridge Disk Drives	
16 megabytes	2,600
50 megabytes	3,440
FSD 9-inch Fixed Storage Drives	
160 megabytes	5,305
340 megabytes	7,635
515 megabytes	8,875
RSK 9-inch Removable Drive	
80 megabytes	5,700
XMD 14-inch Disk Drive	
325 megabytes	10,660
Modular [a] 14-inch Disk Drives	
16 megabytes	5,315
48 megabytes	6,005
80 megabytes	$ 6,695

[a]Allowed combination of fixed and removable disk drives.

Exhibit 5 Peripheral Products Company

PPCo Organization Chart

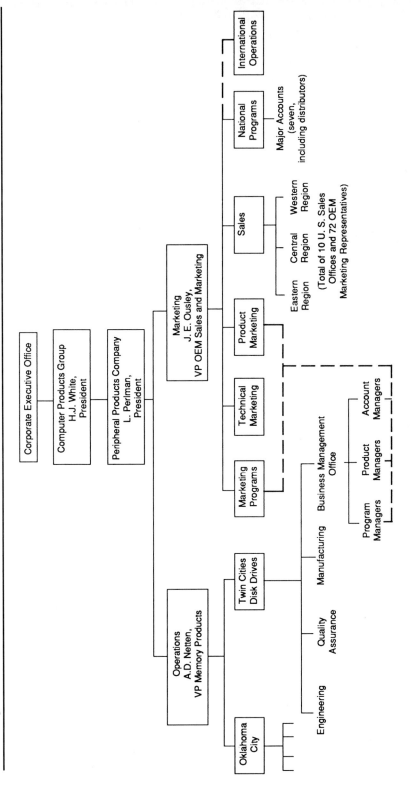

Exhibit 6 Peripheral Products Company

PPCo Distribution Channels

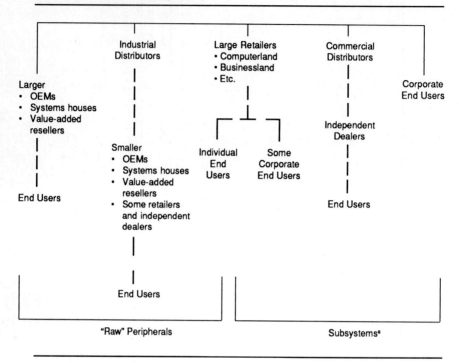

^a "Storage Master" was the brand name for PPCo subsystems manufactured for the commercial marketplace.

Exhibit 7 *Peripheral Products Company*

PPCo's Pricing Policy

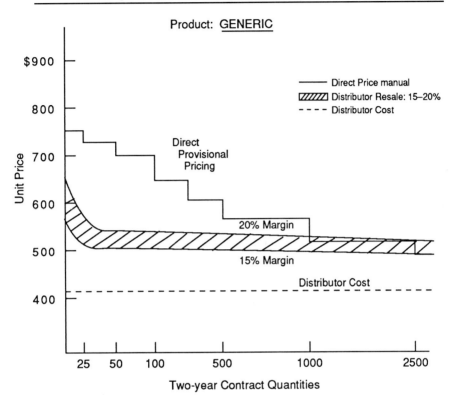

Exhibit 8   *Peripheral Products Company*

Agreement for Purchase of OEM Products (excerpts)

Check one:

☐ Provisional Pricing
☐ Staircase Pricing

TERMS AND CONDITIONS OF PURCHASE

ARTICLE 1   UTILIZATION OF PRODUCTS

To determine prices applicable to this Agreement, Customer certifies that the Products will be integrated, adding technical value to the Products, into the Customer's systems or subsystems which are sold or leased to others.

ARTICLE 2   PROVISIONAL PRICING

2.1 During the Order Term of this Agreement, Customer anticipates purchasing the quantity of Products (Provisional Quantity) specified on the OEM Product Exhibit. The price to be invoiced Customer for each Product is the price applicable to the stated Provisional Quantity (Provisional Price).

2.2 Six months after the effective date of this Agreement and periodically thereafter, Control Data will estimate the quantity of Products projected to be delivered during the Delivery Term of this Agreement (Projected Provisional Quantity).

ARTICLE 3   STAIRCASE PRICING

3.1 The price to be invoiced Customer for each Product will be the price applicable to the stated Quantity Range on the OEM Product Exhibit. To determine the applicable Quantity Range, each Product purchased under this Agreement will be added to the quantity of Products previously purchased under this Agreement.

3.2 Customer is not entitled to a reduction in price or any refund on Products purchased at a higher price (lower Quantity Range) than subsequent Products.

ARTICLE 6   CANCELLATION

6.1 Customer may cancel shipment of any Product provided Control Data receives written notice at its OEM Sales Office at least 15 days prior to the originally scheduled shipment date and Customer pays cancellation charges invoiced as follows:

Interval in Days Between the Notice Date and the Originally Scheduled Shipment Date	Cancellation Charge Expressed as a Percentage of the Price Per Product
15–45	40%
46–90	15%

6.2 Any termination of this Agreement by Customer prior to its expiration will be considered notice of cancellation of all unshipped Products and the applicable cancellation charges will be payable.

(continued)

Exhibit 8 (continued)

ARTICLE 11   INSPECTION AND ACCEPTANCE

11.1 Customer may conduct at its Acceptance Test Facility and at its expense, incoming acceptance tests to confirm that each Product conforms to the Control Data specifications referenced on the OEM Product Exhibit. Unless written notice of failure is provided to Control Data within 30 days of Product receipt, the Product is considered accepted.

11.2 Control Data will repair or, at its option, replace any Product which does not conform to the Control Data specifications during acceptance testing.

ARTICLE 12   WARRANTY

12.1 The Product warranty period is 12 months from date of shipment except for Media. The Spare Parts warranty period is 30 days from date of customer receipt.

12.2 The Product warranty for Media (disk packs and disk cartridges) which bear a Control Data logo is:

   a. 14-inch rigid disk removable Products—for the effective life of the Product;
   b. 8-inch rigid disk removable Products and single rigid disks purchases as components—90 days from date of shipment; and,
   c. flexible disk Products—1 year from date of shipment.

ARTICLE 13   DISCLAIMER OF WARRANTY AND LIMITATION OF REMEDIES

13.1 CUSTOMER AGREES THE ONLY WARRANTIES ARE THOSE STATED IN THIS AGREEMENT. ALL OTHER WARRANTIES, EXPRESS OR IMPLIED, INCLUDING ANY WARRANTIES OF MERCHANTABILITY OR FITNESS FOR A PARTICULAR PURPOSE, ARE DISCLAIMED. CONTROL DATA'S WARRANTIES ARE ONLY FOR THE BENEFIT OF CUSTOMER AND NOT FOR ANY THIRD PARTIES.

## Chapter 9

Customer Service

Most definitions of marketing cite "customer service" as central to the activity. In recent years, moreover, numerous books have emphasized the importance of service as a means to competitive advantage and market leadership. Yet these same books indicate that service seems to get short shrift in the ongoing resource-allocation patterns of many (if not most) companies.

This chapter considers organizational factors that affect customer service in most firms. Its purpose is *not* to illustrate techniques for developing a customer service program. That topic is the focus of many other books and articles.[1] Rather, its concern is with the interfunctional requirements inherent in the provision of customer service (an instance of the boundary-spanning theme examined in the previous chapter) and the kinds of issues that subsequently impact the marketing organization in its attempts to develop and maintain appropriate levels of customer service. This chapter discusses three topics: (1) a perspective on customer service; (2) the "internal marketing" tasks facing the marketing organization in its attempts to manage service levels; and (3) general organizational factors that typically affect the development and maintenance of customer service in many companies.

What Is Customer Service?

Many companies define customer service as product delivery and repair. As a result, they tend to focus on factors such as delivery time, order-fill rates, or the minimization of billing errors in deciding whether or not they are providing good service to customers.

But many factors determine the relative value of a purchase to a prospective buyer. The most obvious relate to the product itself: its price/performance characteristics, quality ratings in terms of industry standards or a respected rating agency (e.g., *Consumer Reports*), and the specifications of the product relative to the purchaser's particular requirements. Other factors, however, include various prepurchase and postpurchase elements that add value to the purchase. These nonproduct elements include any information and ordering costs, in-bound logistical costs, operation and maintenance costs, and (in many cases) disposal or trade-up costs. Customer service ultimately should refer to these broader elements of value creation and customer satisfaction: both the product and nonproduct elements of value added to the customer's operations from the purchase.

In line with this broader perspective on customer service, two key ideas are important. One is that the form of the product is a variable, not a given, in developing marketing strategy and in organizing the marketing effort. "The 'product' *is* what the product *does*";[2] it is the total package of benefits that customers receive when they buy. This includes the functional utility of the goods; the technical assistance provided before the sale in applications develop-ment; the training and/or repair services provided after the sale; assurances of timely delivery due to the manufacturer's distribution network; and any brand-name or reputation benefits that help the buyer in promoting its product or service to its customers. Benefits might also include the range of buyer-seller relationships discussed in Chapter 6, Managing Major Accounts. Especially in industrial markets, the technical and personal relationships that develop among people in buying and selling organizations have intangible, but real, value. Conversely, the package of benefits in some situations might include the absence of personal contact because reorders or other elements of the buyer-seller transaction are more easily and economically conducted through automated, online systems of different sorts.

The point is that customer service should not be conceived of narrowly in terms of purely product-related functions. Its meaning to the purchaser encom-passes the range of ways in which the vendor can contribute to that customer's business operations. A product or service might, in the narrow sense, be "undifferentiable" or a "commodity." But these various aspects of customer service often serve to differentiate and distinguish one vendor from the next in a product category.[3]

The second key concept is that customer service, in this broader sense, will inevitably have different meanings for different customers. Many books and managers often treat "service" as a constant quality between buyer and seller, rather than as a variable across settings. But critical elements of customer service will vary by type of customer and, for the same customer, across different phases of the order cycle and account relationship. For example, technical service may be an especially important dimension of customer service for smaller companies that have few or no R&D or in-house service organizations of their own. But technical service may have much less value for larger companies with extensive R&D and in-house service organizations, whereas ease of ordering and prompt delivery may have a correspondingly higher value for these customers.

These differences in customer valuation of service are important to recognize and manage in implementing marketing efforts. For one thing, these differences affect the relevant time frame for measuring service levels, the amount and kind of technical assistance or applications development inherent in providing good service to a customer group, and the degree and type of coordination with other internal and customer organizational units required to provide effective service. For another, these differences among customers are ultimately reflected in pricing and margin levels available to the supplier.

Customer Service and Internal Marketing

In the broader sense outlined here, customer service is inherently a multifunctional activity in a firm. In most businesses, the delivery of product and information to the customer inevitably involves a range of different areas.

The multifunctional aspect of service can be illustrated by considering the typical order cycle in most industrial businesses. As the order moves from a customer's request for specifications and quotation through to the purchase order and after-sale warranty service, the progress of a single order typically involves numerous functions at the selling company (see Figure A).

Figure A
Typical Order Cycle: Functions Involved

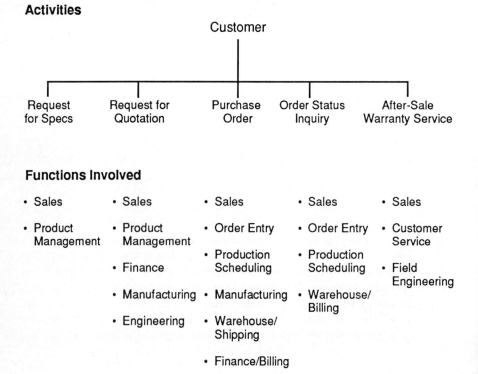

Activities

Customer

| Request for Specs | Request for Quotation | Purchase Order | Order Status Inquiry | After-Sale Warranty Service |

Functions Involved

• Sales	• Sales	• Sales	• Sales	• Sales
• Product Management	• Product Management	• Order Entry	• Order Entry	• Customer Service
	• Finance	• Production Scheduling	• Production Scheduling	• Field Engineering
	• Manufacturing	• Manufacturing	• Warehouse/ Billing	
	• Engineering	• Warehouse/ Shipping		
		• Finance/Billing		

In turn, this means that those responsible for managing customer encounters face a series of internal marketing tasks in developing and maintaining appropriate customer service levels. They must often persuade personnel in other functions, each of which typically has its own particular operating concerns and procedures (as illustrated in the cases in the previous chapter), to help customize an order and the attendant services. Service problems arise in part because those who do the selling, marketing, manufacturing, and financing in a firm typically have different incentives and therefore view "the customer" differently. As Theodore Levitt notes, "an organization necessarily internalizes itself, even though it may depend on externals (customers) for its fate":[4]

> "Inside" is where the work gets done, where the workplace is, where the penalties and incentives reside, where the budgets and plans are made, where engineering and manufacturing take place, where performance is measured, where one's friends and associates are, where things are managed and manageable, and outside is where "you can't change things."

At most companies, moreover, this situation is complicated by the fact that, while the nonproduct elements of customer value are often crucial, it is the product-related elements that typically receive the bulk of managerial time and attention. This contrast is striking in a number of important areas, as Figure B suggests.

In many companies, the product elements of customer value have focused management responsibility in the form of product or brand managers, whereas the various nonproduct elements have fragmented responsibilities. As noted earlier, for example, the different activities required to develop and process an order in an industrial business typically have no one function or manager responsible for all the required activities. Management responsibility, moreover, usually means the development of formal business strategies and plans, budgets and financial tracking of activities, and the cost/benefit trade-offs inherent in profit-and-loss responsibility. Again, companies often have such

Figure B
Product and Nonproduct Elements of Customer Value

Product	Nonproduct
Focused management responsibility	Fragmented responsibility
Formal business strategies and plans	No plans
Budgets and financial tracking	No financial tracking
Financial measurements (cost accounting system)	No internal financial measurements

Performance measurements
  Technical
  Quality
  Sales revenue
	Few performance measurements

Cost/benefit trade-off focus (e.g., profit-and-loss responsibility)	No cost/benefit trade-off

management controls in place for the product-related elements of value, but the nonproduct elements are managed on a more improvised basis, often without a planning process, financial controls, and a method for making inevitable trade-offs among different customer groups and different perspectives on service needs. Further, the cost accounting system in most companies (especially manufacturing firms) is set up to allocate costs by product; this in turn drives the salient financial and performance measurements at the firm. By contrast, the nonproduct elements often have no clear internal financial measurements and, as one manager sardonically notes, in most busy organizations "that which is not measured does not happen." Perhaps worse, in many companies, the absence of clear service measures means that the actual measures used to allocate resources to service-related activities tend to change from year to year (perhaps from quarter to quarter), depending upon the company's earnings or other elements of its financial performance.

As a result, in performing the internal marketing tasks required to provide effective service, those responsible for customer encounters must develop tools for managing these nonproduct areas that often *are* "service" in a business. A key task for marketing management is to make customer service needs tangible. In the absence of focused measures and management responsibilities, these needs are perceived as intangible (and therefore unimportant) by other functions in the organization.

Organizational Issues

Because customer service involves internal marketing, there are usually significant organizational issues at the heart of a company's customer service problems and opportunities. One way to begin analyzing these issues is to consider what, in many firms, is the typical internal context for the development and implementation of service initiatives. Figure C outlines some common organizational issues.

Figure C
Customer Service Organizational Issues

Customer service components are typically dispersed throughout a company.	Fragmented
Coordination is often complicated by business units using pooled service organizations.	Complicated
Service initiatives are driven by the most visible needs, e.g.,	
New product introduction	Reactive/Intermittent
New sales recruits	
Major customer complaints	
Few measurements relate customer-support expenses to profit-and-loss criteria.	Invisible/"Discretionary"
Service responsibilities are often "everybody's business" and therefore "nobody's business."	No ownership/"Champions"

Because customer service involves the product and nonproduct elements of customer value and because provision of these elements necessarily involves a cross-functional effort, the activities involved in providing service are typically dispersed throughout a company and, in this sense, fragmented rather than concentrated with one group or manager. As a result, accountability for service results is often diffuse. Conversely, coordination among the various people and functions that affect service often is complicated by different groups that use a shared service organization differently. Many companies have legitimate reasons for centralizing service even while they decentralize sales or product units. Especially in manufacturing firms, for instance, there are typically important scale economies in field service, and cost-effective service is often contingent on efficient use of dispersed field service locations and personnel. Because different sales or product organizations often face different service demands and patterns, however, the pooling of service units can often result in uncoordinated service provision at the customer that purchases across these units.

In many firms, service initiatives also are driven by the currently most pressing needs. For example, the importance of service is usually stressed when a new product is introduced, new salespeople are hired and initially trained, or a major customer complains. But the firm's ongoing procedures often do not reflect the continuing importance of service, and the result is an essentially reactive, intermittent emphasis characterized by periodic outbursts of programs aimed at "service excellence." In many instances, these programs unintentionally damage the firm's service reputation: They raise customers' expectations but do not deliver sustainably consistent levels of service quality, and the customer thus focuses on "lapses" from the promised threshold.[5]

One reason that service programs are hard to sustain, moreover, is that few managerial performance measures actually relate customer-support expenses to profit-and-loss criteria. Everyone may realize that service is important, but in the absence of specific measures (and the presence of continuing pressures to make quarterly and annual earnings objectives), service expenditures can easily become invisible and therefore "discretionary" (i.e., allocated when budgets allow and dropped when cost pressures increase). This is analogous with a typical cycle of advertising expenditures in many firms: The level of advertising spending in many firms is often the result, rather than the cause, of historical sales volumes. That is, firms tend to cut back on advertising expenditures when sales are flat or declining and cost pressures most intense. One can argue, however, that it is precisely at this juncture that advertising is most important.

Finally, in an effort to manage the multifunctional efforts required to provide good service, companies often define service as "all employees' responsibility." But at many large, complex organizations, that which is everybody's business tends in practice to be nobody's business. The result is an unintentional exacerbation of the lack-of-accountability syndrome that plagues service efforts at many firms.

Given these factors, it should not be surprising that "good service" seems more often the exception rather than the rule and the lack of service a frequent topic in the business press. But these organizational factors also indicate what a true emphasis on improving customer service must address in specific situations. Books and articles outlining the importance of customer service are usually "preaching to the converted": Most managers realize service is important but often don't provide what they know is important due to these organizational factors. An emphasis on "service culture" and a "service obsession" may help to galvanize the firm, but it won't help much if management preaches service without recognizing and managing the implications of these organizational systems and structures. These organizational dimensions of customer service illustrate what might be called the "paradox of a marketing orientation": "Keep close to your customer" is good advice but, by itself, is operationally meaningless. External responsiveness (the responsibility of the marketing organization) requires internal coordination and attention to matters such as performance measurements, the locus of profit-and-loss responsibility, and organizational structures that aid in the integration of service components. These are internal factors and negotiations that customers rarely see or care about but that ultimately motivate customer praise or customer complaints.

Case Studies

The two case studies in this chapter concern large, complex organizations facing significant changes in their external environments and consequent stresses on their internal organization of marketing- and service-related activities. Carolina Power & Light Company (CP&L) focuses on customer service at a public utility, whereas the General Electric case concerns service issues in the industrial business units of one of the world's largest and best-known corporations.

The CP&L case concerns the reorganization of the function responsible for the marketing and maintenance of CP&L's services. The reorganization of the Customer and Operating Services Group—designed to improve customer service for this utility—is still underway at the time of the case, raising issues concerning employee morale, dislocation of reporting relationships, and the fate of local offices. Hence as well as an examination of customer service, the CP&L case concerns marketing issues in a context (public utilities) not usually associated with marketing; it also raises issues concerning the potential role(s) and impact of reorganization in marketing.

As you analyze the CP&L case situation, consider the following questions:

1. As a public utility, CP&L is often referred to as a monopoly. What does the term *monopoly* mean in this context? Is it harder or easier to perform marketing and service activities in a public utility vs. a commercial business? How would you define the nature of the product being sold by CP&L, and what are the implications of that definition for good marketing and service practice at this organization?

2. Who are the major customer groups for CP&L? How does each customer group define service from CP&L? In turn, how should CP&L define and measure customer service?
3. Was the reorganization described in the case necessary? Useful? What further changes (if any) in the organization of the Customer and Operating Services Group would you recommend?
4. The final section of this case outlines a variety of issues raised by the recent reorganization. In your view, which of these issues are important and which are minor?
5. Should management retain or close the local offices? What view of customer service is implicit in your decision about this issue?

The GE case extends this brief chapter's analysis of customer service and the boundary-spanning nature of marketing activities. Where the CP&L case looks at a reorganization's attempts to deal with ingrained habits and assumptions concerning service, the GE case considers the mindset concerning service that accompanies an established set of structures, measurement systems, and evaluation criteria. Further, this is one of those case studies where you can learn a great deal before class discussion through attentive reading. The analyses of industrial customer service conducted by GE analysts are insightful and suggest concepts relevant to many other businesses.

Consider the following questions about the GE case study:

1. Why is the issue of customer service attracting so much attention at GE during the period covered by this case? What has been happening internally at GE and externally with customers and competitors during this period? What are the implications for service requirements in GE's industrial businesses?
2. Is the definition of customer service as total customer satisfaction a good definition? Is it actionable?
3. Review the pooled-sales study outlined in the case. What can you learn from this study about the factors that aid and hinder customer service in a large, diversified corporation?
4. Review the chronology of events outlined in the case, from 1981 through 1985. What happened in terms of improved service efforts during this period? Were the results worth the time and effort expended?
5. Review the comments from GE managers presented at the end of the case. In your view, which of these issues are important? What can you learn from these diverse comments about customer service? About how things do (or do not) get done in a large organization?

Although each firm operates in a different product/market environment, both the CP&L and GE cases concern large organizations' attempts to satisfy two often-conflicting requirements at the heart of service and marketing activities: provide close-to-the-customer decentralization and operating autonomy, while also integrating the many cross-functional and cross-business components of customer service. Further, good service must be a goal of any marketing organization and thus the issues, interactions, and tensions explored in these two cases are also pertinent to the following section on structures, systems, and processes used to organize and manage marketing in different consumer- and industrial-goods companies.

References

1. For discussions of customer service programs at various companies, see Karl Albrecht and Ron Zemke, *Service America* (Homewood, IL: Dow Jones-Irwin, 1985); Robert L. Desatnick, *Managing to Keep the Customer* (San Francisco: Jossey-Bass Publishers, 1987); or William H. Davidow and Bro Uttal, *Total Customer Service: The Ultimate Weapon* (New York: Harper & Row, 1989).

2. E. Raymond Corey, *Industrial Marketing: Cases and Concepts,* 3rd ed. (Englewood Cliffs, NJ: Prentice-Hall, Inc., 1983), p. 173.

3. Theodore Levitt, "Marketing Success Through Differentiation—of Anything," *Harvard Business Review* 58 (January-February 1980): 83–91.

4. Theodore Levitt, "Relationship Management," in *The Marketing Imagination* (New York: The Free Press, 1983), p. 117.

5. For a discussion of how consumers' perceptions of service quality are influenced by seller communications, see Valarie A. Zeithaml, Leonard L. Berry, and A. Parasuraman, "Communication and Control Processes in the Delivery of Service Quality," *Journal of Marketing* 52 (April 1988): 35–48.

Carolina Power & Light Company

Customer and Operating Services Group

Senior vice president Russell Lee, speaking in November 1985 at the annual plans and programs meeting for managers of the Customer and Operating Services (COS) Group of Carolina Power and Light (CP&L), commented:

> We are up to our elbows in change and doing our best to manage it well. And the time is here when we cannot take any customer for granted. We cannot simply supply electricity and assume that the customer will buy it. If the customer does not characterize us as affordable and reasonable, he or she will seek satisfaction elsewhere.
>
> I think we have already moved toward addressing this challenge. Within COS we have, in the past four years, created a Conservation and Load Management Department, reorganized the Group Services Department and, most recently, have begun a realignment of the field structure.
>
> We had several objectives with these moves. First, to improve efficiency and effectiveness. Secondly, to anticipate future customer needs. Thirdly, to reduce the level of supervision in COS so that day-to-day decision making takes place in the field. We also wanted to eliminate duplication of effort, encourage team work and create ownership in the geographic areas we serve so that the teams not only felt responsible, but were also held accountable.

Service Territory

CP&L was a publicly owned utility providing electricity to a 30,000-square-mile service territory covering the eastern half of North Carolina, a quarter of South

---

This case was prepared by J. E. P. Morrison, MBA '87, under the supervision of Associate Professor Frank V. Cespedes, as the basis for class discussion rather than to illustrate either effective or ineffective handling of an administrative situation.

Copyright © 1987 by the President and Fellows of Harvard College. Harvard Business School case 9-587-179.

Carolina, and a portion of the Great Smoky Mountains in western North Carolina (see Exhibit 1). The company served a primarily rural territory, and although both North and South Carolina were expected to be in the top 12 states in population growth through the end of the century, most of that growth was occurring in the cities and larger towns. Agriculture, particularly tobacco, was a mainstay of the economy, but the economic base was shifting as agriculture declined and the service sector expanded. Much of the economic growth was centered around Raleigh, the state capital, and one of three cities in an area known as the "Research Triangle." [1] Industries such as textiles, furniture, and agricultural processing were facing hard times, but other industries were growing as firms, both domestic and foreign, moved to the area.

Customers

At the end of 1985, 726,000 **residential** customers comprised 85% of the company's customer base and 31% of corporate revenue. The average rate charged residential customers was 7.2 cents per kWh, far above the rates for commercial, industrial, and wholesale customers. The cost to serve residential customers, however, was also the highest of any class. Energy sales per residential customer were relatively low, yet the company incurred fixed expenses similar to that for larger customers to connect the customer and meter usage. The residential class also had the lowest load factor,[2] which meant that generation capacity allocated to serve residential customers at peak was idle for long periods. Exhibit 2A indicates the residential class load shape (power demand over a 24-hour period).

Commercial customers such as farms, office buildings, stores, and shopping centers accounted for 14% of CP&L's customer base and 19% of revenue. The average commercial rate was 6.3 cents per kWh. The commercial class load shape was flatter than residential with a correspondingly higher load factor.

Industrial customers accounted for 0.5% of CP&L's customers and 29% of revenue. Even with rates of 5.0 cents per kWh, industrial customers were the most cost efficient to serve. The industrial load shape was virtually flat (Exhibit 2C) with a load factor of nearly one.

The **resale and military** segment included Energy Member Cooperatives (EMC), municipal utilities and military bases. These customers bought energy and distributed it to end users such as rural customers, city residents and military personnel. Some EMCs and municipal utilities also invested in CP&L generating facilities. Resale and military customers were 21% of revenue and 0.3% of the company's customers.

---

[1]Durham and Chapel Hill, the other two cities in the triangle, were served by a neighboring utility.

[2]A customer class load factor is the ratio of actual energy used to the energy that would have been used if the customer class operated at its peak load all of the time.

Customer expectations of the quality of service were increasing due to the widespread use of electronic devices which were less tolerant of power surges and micro-outages. A digital electronic clock, for example, must be reset after even the briefest power interruption. Some electrical anomalies resulted from difficulties in power generation and transmission, but the majority were traced to local distribution system operations (e.g., downed lines or faulty automatic fault protection devices).

Customers also had come to expect nonelectrical services from CP&L, including new customer connects, bill inquiries, answers to questions about service, and information on issues such as conservation, alternate energy (e.g., solar, wind), and new technology (e.g., heat pumps, electrification of industrial processes, cogeneration).

Customers also had more energy choices. Natural gas competed with electricity for residential and commercial space and water heating. In a typical home, these were the two largest uses of energy. This competition was greatest in the Raleigh area, where the network of gas distribution pipelines was most extensive.[3] Due to the recent drop in oil prices, many industrial customers switched from electricity to natural gas and fuel oil. CP&L also faced competition for large customers, who were wooed by neighboring utilities and had numerous choices when choosing a site for a plant.

Generating Capacity

With 9,316 employees and $1.9 billion in revenue in 1985, CP&L was a mid-sized public utility. The company served its 853,000 customers with generating plants that had a total capacity of 8.8 million kilowatts (kW).[4] Sixty percent of capacity was provided by 7 coal-fired plants, 26% by 3 nuclear units, 12% by 33 turbine generators burning oil, natural gas or propane, and 2% by 4 hydroelectric plants. During 1985, CP&L generated 37.3 billion kilowatt-hours of electricity.[5] Of this, the coal plants generated 66%, the nuclear plants supplied 33%, and turbines and hydro plants the remaining 1%.

Utility Economics

CP&L's generating facilities accounted for 90% of company assets. Per kilowatt of capacity nuclear power plants were the most expensive to build. Turbine generators were the least capital intensive but more expensive to operate. Operating costs generally followed an inverse relation with capital costs:

---

[3]Residential gas service was not available in many areas of the service territory where the pipeline distribution system did not exist. In 1985 bottled gas and other means of distribution were too costly to compete effectively with electricity.

[4]A kilowatt (kW) is a unit of electrical power equal to approximately 1-1/3 horsepower.

[5]A kilowatt-hour (kWh) is a unit of energy defined as 1 kilowatt (kW) of power used for 1 hour. For example, ten 100 watt light bulbs (1 kW) burning for 1 hour would consume 1 kilowatt-hour.

	Year Most Recent Plant Brought On-Line	Capital Cost (Nominal $000)	Capacity (MW)	$/KW	1985 Operating Cost ($/kWh)
Nuclear [a]	1977	$343,672	790	$435	$ 1.76
Coal	1983	$535,085	705	$759	$ 2.31
Turbine	1974	$ 53,142	572	$ 93	$55.35
Hydro	1930	$ 12,261	105	$120	$ 0.32

[a] The Harris nuclear plant with a capacity of 900 MW was forecast to cost approximately $3.8 billion or $4,222/kW when completed in 1987.

Given operating costs, CP&L tried to maximize generation from the nuclear plants and minimize generation from turbines. However, customers used electricity at different rates throughout the day and year (see Exhibits 2 and 3), and the level at which a large nuclear or coal plant generates electricity cannot be rapidly changed or easily cycled (turned on and off). Therefore, during extreme peaks in demand (e.g., a hot summer afternoon when many customers turn on air conditioners) or during a rapid ramp-up in demand (e.g., a winter morning when customers heat their homes and industry begins to operate), the utility must rely on sources of energy which, although more costly to operate, can track demand (e.g., turbines and hydro) (see Exhibit 4).

A utility's load curve determined which generating plants could be used to meet demand and what generating capacity must be built to meet peak demands.[6] A utility with a low load factor (the ratio of energy sales to total energy generating capacity) would be forced to idle plants built to meet demand during relatively short peak periods. A utility could improve its load factor by lowering its peak (i.e., reducing the need for little used plants) or by increasing its off-peak sales (i.e., increasing the generation and revenue from previously idle plants).

Revenue

Utilities are regulated monopolies mandated to serve a defined geographical territory with oversight by state and federal regulatory commissions. These commissions determined the rates CP&L could charge customers, based on an allowable return to the utility. Each commission determined the assets used by CP&L to serve the area under the commission's jurisdiction (the "rate base") and then determined the cost of service for various classes of customers.

State commissions regulated retail rates while the Federal Energy Regulatory Commission (FERC) regulated wholesale energy sales. Retail included residential, commercial, and industrial customers; wholesale included neighboring utilities, municipal utilities, military bases, and EMCs within the

---

[6]CP&L maintained generating capacity for 115% of peak demand to ensure reliable supply in the event of unplanned outages of generating facilities or in case demand exceeded forecasted peaks.

CP&L service territory. FERC also regulated transactions between CP&L and its suppliers which included neighboring utilities, cogenerators,[7] and small independent energy suppliers. CP&L was therefore subject to three commissions. The North Carolina state commission was the most important, regulating 68% of the company's revenue. The South Carolina state commission regulated 16%, and FERC 16%.

The rate of return allowed by the commissions was not guaranteed. It was a ceiling, and if the company exceeded this ceiling, the regulators would require a rebate to CP&L's customers. The company's 1985 annual report indicated that in the years 1983–1985 returns on equity were "consistently below the levels allowed by regulatory authorities." The company, however, faced increasing resistance to its rate hike requests. Consumer groups testified at rate hearings against any increase and exerted indirect political pressure on the utility commission since the commissioners were appointed by the governor.

Utility regulation faced potential changes. Although no explicit proposals had been put forth, deregulation of telecommunications was a precedent. Regulation of utilities and AT&T was based on the concept of "natural monopolies," and the pre-deregulation structure of AT&T was analogous to that of many utilities. Many within CP&L felt similar "deregulation" would eventually occur in the electrical utility industry.

CP&L Organization

CP&L was divided into three groups: generation and transmission; customer, regulatory, and public affairs; and corporate services.

Generation and transmission constructed the company's generating plants and transmission lines and coordinated plant generation from a central control center.

Customer, regulatory and public affairs oversaw relations with the company's external constituencies. This area included: Corporate Communications (media relations and advertising), Public Affairs (relations with federal and state elected officials), Rate and Service Practices (relations with utility regulatory bodies), Customer and Operating Services (customer service), and the Legal Department.

Corporate services included many internal staff functions such as accounting, audit, treasury, information services, employee relations, planning and coordination, and total quality.

Planning and coordination forecasted future electrical demand and planned the timing of future generating capacity expansion to meet demand. Poor forecasting could leave the utility either short of capacity to meet demand or with idle capacity straining corporate profitability. Forecasting and capacity

---

[7]Cogenerators were companies which produced both steam and electricity. Some were manufacturing firms which used the steam and some or all of the electricity for their own use. Others were companies specifically established to produce energy (steam and electricity) for sale.

expansion planning, however, were becoming increasingly difficult for at least two reasons. First, since the mid-1970s energy growth was no longer clearly correlated with economic growth. Planners could not rely solely on macroeconomic forecasting models to predict future energy demand but had to turn to new and as yet unproven models. Second, construction times and costs for new plants were increasingly difficult to predict. Public opposition to new plant construction and the greater size, complexity, and risk of modern plants slowed the regulatory decision-making process and increased the uncertainty of approval for new generating capacity.

Total Quality was a recent addition to the organization. In CP&L's 1985 annual report, Chairman Sherwood H. Smith explained:

> Our Total Quality effort is based on three important objectives of our Company: first, to provide electric service in a highly reliable way at the lowest reasonable cost; second, to work even more closely with our customers to help them make the best use of electricity and get the greatest value for their electricity dollar; and third, to improve our own teamwork and to enable all employees to work more effectively together, so every employee can make a maximum contribution to the success of the organization. Total Quality will be a dynamic, changing activity. Its goal is continuous improvement in everything we do.

Several managers described Total Quality as a vehicle for cultural change within CP&L. The purpose was to create "common sense management, treating people like people," and a "new breed of manager" who was "open and receptive." Quality teams were created to "encourage ideas to flow up in the organization" and to establish a "team approach" which would "utilize the full abilities and resources of all CP&L personnel." Total Quality was initiated by Mr. Smith and met with a positive reception within the company. Complete implementation, however, was expected to take several years.

Customer and Operating Services Group

In 1985, COS consisted of five geographic divisions with 2,440 employees in 52 offices throughout the service territory along with 296 employees in 2 headquarters staff departments. CP&L's 1987 business plan indicated that COS's mission was "to provide and maintain appropriate services associated with the delivery of electrical energy, promote energy management, and positively influence CP&L's public image" via programs for "meeting competition, reducing peak load, increasing off-peak sales, maintaining market share, and rebuilding ally relationships."

COS had four major functions: 1) Accounting, 2) Marketing, 3) Operations, and 4) Engineering.

Accounting was customer billing and revenue collection. The process started with the company's meter readers who, on a regular schedule, visited each customer location and recorded energy usage since the last visit. This information was entered into CP&L's corporate computers. Accounting clerks responded to customer inquiries concerning their monthly bills which were mailed to customers from central billing in Raleigh. Most revenue came in by mail to the central office, but customers could also pay in person at any of CP&L's 52 local offices.

Marketing consisted of Public Relations, Economic Development, and Conservation and Load Management.

Public relations were conducted at the local level by COS field managers who were often asked to speak before various local civic organizations. This effort was aimed at the grass roots level as opposed to relations with federal and state officials carried on elsewhere in the CP&L organization.

Economic development sought to maintain the economic well-being of the CP&L service territory through rural development and industry retention. Economic development worked to create and retain jobs in the area with the State Development agencies of both North and South Carolina. CP&L also extended service and advice to existing customers, helping them make more efficient use of their energy purchases. Economic development also assisted CP&L's public affairs and community relations effort.

Conservation and Load Management (CLM) sought to influence energy usage and consumption patterns in order to help customers manage their energy expenditures and improve the utility's load shape and load factor. Many CLM programs provided incentives in the form of lower rates or rebates and were grouped into five categories depending on the load shape objective (see Exhibit 5). Appendix 1 describes the CLM programs.

CLM was a refinement of previous marketing efforts. During the 1960s the company concentrated on building load. This was a period of declining marginal costs due to falling fuel prices and efficiency improvements in new plants. Any incremental energy sale, on- or off-peak, meant additional profit. During the 1970s CP&L focused on conservation as marginal costs rose and the "energy crisis" caught the public's attention. In the early 1980s load management or peak load reduction was the major marketing drive as CP&L faced rapidly escalating costs for new plant construction due primarily to regulatory delays in the construction and licensing of a plant. In the late 1980s with major construction programs winding down, CP&L's marketing included a combination of conservation, load management, and off-peak load building to match the company's load profile to existing capacity and maximize revenue from that capacity.

Operations, the third function of COS, was responsible for connecting customers to the company's distribution system and for the operation and maintenance of that system. The distribution system was distinct from the high-voltage transmission system that was the responsibility of the generation and transmission organization within CP&L. COS distribution was a lower voltage network designed to distribute energy from utility substations to customers. Substation transformers stepped the electricity down from 230,000 volts on the transmissions lines to 23 kV on the distribution system (see Exhibit 6). Additional transformers, such as the pole-mounted units on many residential streets, then stepped the voltage down further for customer use, typically 240 or 120 volts.

Operations included line crews, the most visible embodiment of the company, who worked throughout the system, erecting new lines, connecting new customers, and repairing downed portions of the system.

Engineering included the design of lines and transformer stations, acquisition of new rights-of-way, and ensuring the quality of service supplied from the distribution system to the customers.

COS Organization

The COS **field organization** was divided into five geographic regions (see Exhibit 1): the Northern, Central, and Eastern divisions covered eastern North Carolina; the Western division covered CPL's service territory in the mountains; and the Southern division covered the company's territory in South Carolina. Reporting to each division vice president were an engineering manager, operations manager, and 1–3 district managers[8] (see Exhibit 7). Each district was subdivided into 3–6 areas, each with an area office and area manager. In all, there were 10 district and 42 area offices providing customer service and contact.[9]

District managers were responsible for accounting, marketing, and engineering. The meter readers and accounting clerks were supervised by a district accounting manager who reported to the district manager. The marketing function was performed by the following personnel:

Customer Service Representatives (CSRs)	Primarily served residential and commercial customers. CSR responsibilities included responding to customer requests for new service and inquiries regarding existing service, promoting CLM programs, and enrolling customers in those programs.
Energy Services Engineers (ESEs)	Primarily served residential and commercial customers. Responsibilities included providing assistance to customers in heating, cooling, and lighting design for new construction and developing relationships with architects and engineers. There was generally only one ESE in each district.

---

[8]The Eastern, Southern, and Central divisions were divided into two districts. The Western division contained only one district, while the Northern division, which was the fastest growing, had three districts.

[9]Division offices were separate from district and area offices, but had no facilities or personnel to respond directly to customer inquiries.

Industrial Power Engineers (IPEs)	Primarily served industrial customers with responsibilities similar to CSRs. Serving industrial customers, however, called for greater technical expertise and training since service was often tailored to specific customer needs. CLM programs also often called for custom application. In addition, IPEs were the "eyes and ears" of CP&L's economic development effort, involved in expanding and retaining industry in the company's service territory. There were generally two IPEs in each district.
Equipment Service Representatives (ESRs)	Primarily served commercial and residential customers. ESRs provided technical assistance to customers with equipment problems (e.g., air conditioners, heat pumps on refrigeration equipment). ESRs also developed relationships with contractors and electrical equipment dealers. (They supported a network of allies providing service to customers who used and purchased electrical equipment.) There was generally one ESR in each district.

The CSR, ESE, IPE, and ESR in the district office all reported to a customer service manager who reported to the district manager. CSRs in area offices reported to the area manager who reported to the district manager. The area, customer service, and district managers all shared public relations responsibility, maintaining relations with local elected officials and speaking before civic and professional groups.

A district engineer was the final direct report to the district manager. This staff person coordinated engineering activities in the district. Area engineers, reporting to the area managers, also provided engineering services in each area.

The district manager shared responsibility for the engineering function with the division engineering manager. Direct reports to the division engineering manager were the following:

Right-of-Way Agent	Purchased land and right-of-way for new distribution lines and substations.
Project Engineers	Designed distribution lines and substations.
Line Inspection Supervisor	Inspected new and existing distribution lines. Approved the work of the line and service crews (see operations below).

The operations manager, responsible for construction and maintenance, had four direct reports: a line and service manager, a division forester, a superintendent of stores, and a superintendent of services.

Line and Service Manager	Supervised the line and service crews that worked on the division distribution system. CP&L maintained company crews for routine construction and maintenance and minor emergency repair but relied on contract crews to augment this force for major new construction and repair efforts.
Division Forester	Responsible for maintenance of company property along the distribution system, including clearing and trimming trees along the distribution right-of-way and substations.
Superintendent of Stores	Supervised the division warehouse and maintained divisional supplies.
Superintendent of Services	Responsible for the division truck and car fleet, communication network, meter shop, and substation crew.

Responsibility for new customer connects, an operations function, was shared by a number of company personnel. A new service request might come in to a CSR, ESE, or IPE. For any nonroutine request (e.g., underground residential service and most commercial and industrial requests), engineering provided design assistance at the area, district, or division level. If the customer was not located near the distribution system or requested a higher voltage service than was available at the location, the right-of-way agent secured new right-of-way. The line and service crews then built the new line. Then the facilities were inspected by line inspectors to assure conformance to standards and specifications, and appropriate metering devices were installed.

COS **staff** was divided into two departments. *Group Services* provided support to divisions, established uniform standards and practices across divisions, provided a liaison to corporate information services and corporate generation and transmission, conducted distribution R&D, and operated a central shop to purchase, test, and repair metering equipment. *Conservation and Load Management* created marketing programs to help customers control energy expenditures and thus slow the growth of CP&L's peak load. The department was divided along customer lines (residential, commercial, industrial, and resale and military) with managers in each area developing programs and monitoring implementation in the field.

COS Field Reorganization

In July 1985 at the annual senior management retreat, Russell Lee presented a plan for reorganizing the COS field structure. That plan was approved by the executives present and announced corporatewide in September.

Four factors prompted the decision to reorganize. First, despite CP&L's geographic monopoly to provide electric power, the utility faced competition. For example, in Raleigh, where over 60% of existing houses used electric heat, less than 54% of new houses were installed with electric heating. Natural gas was taking share in that market. CP&L also competed with other utilities. Santee Cooper, a small South Carolina utility, offered attractive rates to new industries.[10] Jim Massengill, formerly CP&L's Raleigh district manager, commented:

> The day of the **electric company** is coming to a close. Our environment has changed. Our customers, who are demanding a higher quality of service, have changed, and also our elected officials. Deregulation [of electric utilities] is possible. We have to become an **energy** company.

Another manager characterized the required change as one from a construction company (building power plants) to a company providing energy services.

Second, CLM programs, after several years of success, appeared to be stalling. Efforts to sign up customers for the programs, particularly in commercial and residential sectors, were behind plan (see Exhibit 8). The problem was particularly acute in the Northern division around Raleigh where, according to Massengill, "the high growth rate [calling for new customer connects] usurped CLM goals. Other divisions did better than Northern, but in general CSRs were too busy to do both CLM and service."

Third, there were too many levels of supervision and middle management in COS. In 1983, there were 2,615 COS employees but 2,842 by 1986. Employee feedback indicated discontent with bureaucracy and supervision. Furthermore, division vice presidents found themselves increasingly called upon to resolve day-to-day problems and decisions. One division vice president commented, "My subordinates find it necessary to get me involved [in decision making], and one reason is that the bureaucratic processes do not encourage appropriate delegation of decision-making. Therefore, a go-between is necessary to resolve staff and line authority." Throughout COS, moreover, the distinction between staff and line was often obscured. In engineering, for example, responsibilities of area engineers (line) often conflicted with those of district engineers (staff) and division project engineers (staff). Industrial Power engineers (line) and Energy Service engineers (line) often also contributed to the engineering effort. One manager noted, "The areas, districts and even the division often were managed as separate fiefdoms. Effective communication was sometimes difficult between managers."

---

[10]Santee Cooper's incentive industrial rate was 2.9 cents/kWh compared to CP&L's average for industrial customers of 5.03 cents/kWh.

Fourth, feedback indicated the customer had to deal with too many different CP&L employees and that it took too much time to satisfy a customer request.

Several managers commented on the need for change. Bill Smith, manager of CLM planning and support, indicated:

> Electricity is a commodity. If we're to stay in business we must keep rates as low as possible, and distinguish our services so customers and potential customers do it electrically and do it in the CP&L service territory.

Russell Lee added:

> We modify and upgrade our distribution system regularly, and there is every reason to pay as much attention to our management systems. The management structure had been in place [with only minor modifications] for decades. We're in a totally different ball game now, and if we don't recognize it, we'll get blown away.

New Organization

By August 1986 the 5 division vice presidents were the only familiar faces in familiar spaces in the COS field organization. The responsibilities of virtually every other manager had been redefined. The new structure (see Exhibit 9) separated the 4 COS functions (accounting, marketing, operations, and engineering), clarified distinctions between line and staff, realigned boundaries to make the divisions more equal in size. Each new division served 100,000 to 150,000 customers. Northern division was large enough to be divided into Northeast and Northwest.

Three to five managers reported directly to the division vice president. The **services manager** acted as staff to the vice president and provided many of the support services previously handled by the operations manager (e.g., fleet maintenance, communications, forestry, substations, and meter shop).

The **commercial manager** was responsible for divisional accounting and marketing functions. Reporting to each commercial manager were 2–5 area business managers (ABM) serving 20,000 to 40,000 customers. In each area were up to 3 local office managers as well as an accounting manager and a marketing manager. Also reporting to the commercial manager were two staff managers, an accounting support manager, and a marketing support manager, who coordinated the accounting and marketing functions across the areas in the division.

The **operating and engineering (O&E) manager** was responsible for 2–5 area distribution managers (ADM). In each area one or more line and service supervisors and an engineering manager reported to the ADM. The O&E manager also had one to two staff personnel, a division contractor support manager and an engineering support manager.

Implementation

The plan Russell Lee presented in July 1985 included a few preliminary recommendations from a consultant's study. Following senior management endorsement and the completion of the consultant's report, Lee assembled a team of division vice presidents to define the responsibilities of the new commercial, O&E, and services managers and to choose individuals for those positions. Those changes were announced in November 1985. Other positions were not filled at that time, nor was the organization structure below the commercial, O&E, and services managers fully defined. This was left to a task force of commercial, O&E, and services managers under close supervision of the division vice presidents. The task force met for several months and, in March 1986, announced the selection of the next level of management. The process continued in this manner until all levels of management were identified and selected.

The slow pace of the reorganization created some tension within COS, particularly among customer contact personnel and first line supervisors. Their new responsibilities had not been defined and, a year after the first reorganization announcement, there was fear, uncertainty, and doubt in the lower ranks. One area manager commented that despite the company's informal "no lay-off" policy there was a great deal of resentment among first-line supervisors and their subordinates. Senior managers in COS, however, viewed the process more positively, appreciating the opportunity to indicate their desires and influence the reorganization.

By July 1986, responsibilities and selection of front-line personnel was one of several unresolved issues. In the new organization, the engineering manager was accountable for much of customer service (e.g., new connects) yet the customer contact personnel (CSRs, ESEs, and IPEs) reported to marketing managers and the right-of-way agents reported to the engineering manager. The customer contact personnel also had marketing responsibilities and were unsure of the relative priority of their service and marketing duties. A proposed solution for this problem was the single point of contact (SPOC) program. The idea was that customers only had to deal with one CP&L employee who coordinated service for that customer. A pilot SPOC was being run in one area; however, numerous questions about the exact nature of the program remained.

The role of the IPE (Industrial Power Engineer) was also a concern. IPEs were trained engineers, yet much of their time was spent handling service/administrative matters and other activities (e.g., right-of-way, street lighting, nonindustrial accounts) that could be handled by CSRs or other less highly paid personnel. Greg Pittillo, the CLM industrial section manager, indicated:

> The engineering and technical skills of IPEs are not fully utilized. The job content, time allocation, priorities, and expectations of IPEs should be analyzed and redefined. The job should allow for a greater emphasis on CLM, marketing and utilization of their technical skills. That may mean new customer assignments.

Currently there are over 4,200 industrial accounts, but only 1,500 are over 200 kW,[11] and only 800 greater than 500 kW. There could be some reallocation of account responsibility between IPEs and CSRs.

Many managers also questioned the need for local offices, which were expensive to staff and maintain. Customers increasingly phoned the company when requesting service and paid their bills by mail, particularly in the larger cities and towns where most growth in the CP&L service territory occurred. Others pointed out that customers in smaller, rural communities still maintained the habit of paying bills in person on their visits to town. Also, there were political consequences to closing the offices since they were a very visible embodiment of CP&L's support for the many small communities in its service territory. CP&L could not endanger that relationship, particularly with the new Harris nuclear power plant coming up for regulatory review.

A related issue concerned customer records, which were kept in area offices and customers had to call that particular office for service. Customers, however, had little idea (nor did they particularly care) which office served them. Area boundaries were defined by the distribution system, not necessarily by geographical or political boundaries. Thus, customers often had to call several offices before they could get a response to their inquiry. Area offices often had to staff the phones beyond the normal business day to handle inquiries.

Central telephones were proposed as a way to improve service and reduce staffing needs. The proposal was to establish one or more central numbers a customer could call for service. The operators would have access to customer records and handle most inquiries. Requests for service would be forwarded to the appropriate area office. Many managers questioned the need to centralize phone service since one emphasis of the reorganization was to place more responsibility with area managers. Others agreed with the concept but questioned whether one central telephone service was adequate or whether each division needed a separate service.

The new structure of the COS group itself raised an issue. Several managers questioned the relationship between the commercial and O&E managers and the relationship between the ABM and ADM. These sets of managers shared many joint accountabilities and had to coordinate to serve their area or division. In their official descriptions each manager was to "ensure and promote the development and maintenance of customer satisfaction." Wilson Craig, a division vice president, described the two sets of managers as "handcuffed" together and "equally responsible for the same geographic area." One commercial manager, however, saw the potential for tremendous stress if the managers could not work together. To date that had not occurred, but it was a potential problem.

---

[11]The size of an account was defined by the customer's peak demand, which determined the size and complexity of equipment needed to provide service.

Many COS managers wondered whether the new structure was but a transition organization. Several noted that there would be considerable turn-over in COS in the next few years. By one count over 100 managers out of a total of approximately 700 were due for retirement in the next four years. Russell Lee often spoke of the need for a "lean" organization, but with that attrition it was not clear where new managers would come from or how the organization would respond.

Exhibit 1   Carolina Power & Light

CP&L Service Area

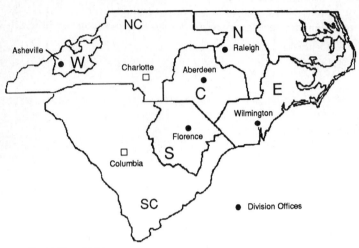

N = Northern Division
C = Central Division
S = Southern Division
E = Eastern Division
W = Western Division

Exhibit 2   Carolina Power & Light

A. Residential Load Shape
(Winter Peak Day)

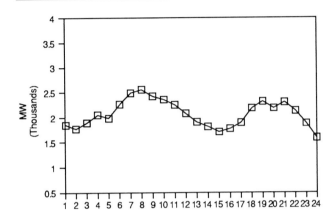

B. Commercial Load Shape
(Winter Peak Day)

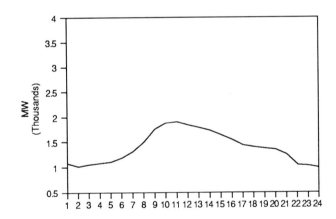

(continued)

Exhibit 2   (continued)
C. Industrial Load Shape
(Winter Peak Day)

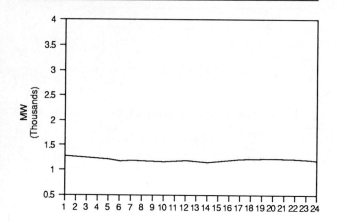

Exhibit 3   ***Carolina Power & Light***

A. System Load Shape
(Winter Peak Day)

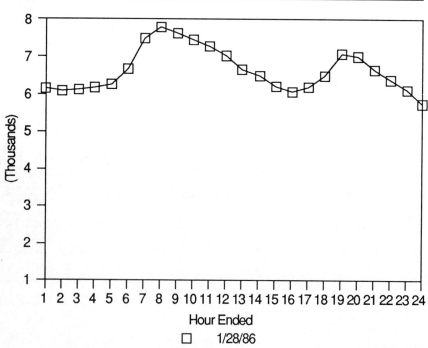

Hour Ended

☐   1/28/86

(continued)

Exhibit 3   (continued)

B. System Load Shape
(Summer Peak Days)

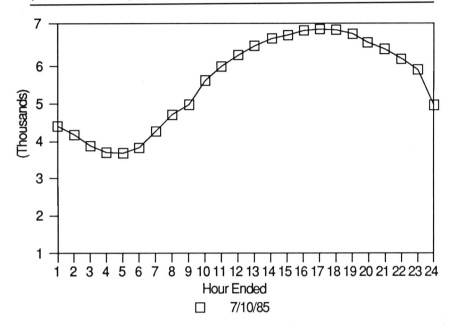

Hour Ended

□   7/10/85

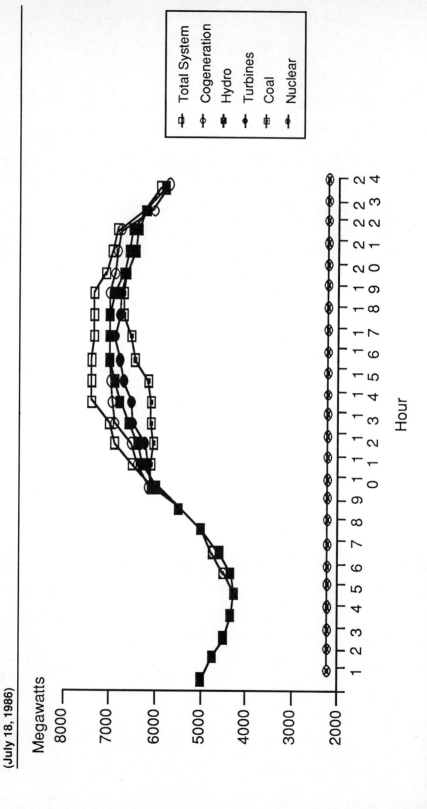

Exhibit 4 Carolina Power & Light

Generation Mix
(July 18, 1986)

Exhibit 5 Carolina Power & Light

Load Shape Objectives

	Loading Shifting	Valley Filling	Strategic Load Growth	Peak Clipping	Strategic Conservation
Picture					
Definition	Moving existing load from peak to off-peak periods	Adding load in off-peak periods	Adding load in both peak and off-peak periods with majority off-peak	Reducing specific loads intermittently according to system operator's needs	Reducing load in peak and off-peak periods mostly on-peak
Advantages to the company	Increased use of lower cost generation Builds load factor Holds down growth in peak load	Adds sales Builds load factor Does not contribute to growth in peak load	Adds sales Builds load factor	Reduces peak load Avoids use of high-cost fuels for peaking	Holds down growth in peak load
Examples	Time-of-use rates Thermal energy storage for water heating, space conditioning	Outdoor lighting Off-peak electrification of industrial preocesses	Appliance control Economic development Industrial electrification	Commonsense homes Standby generators Industrial curtailable loads	Low interest loans for home insulation

Exhibit 6   Carolina Power & Light

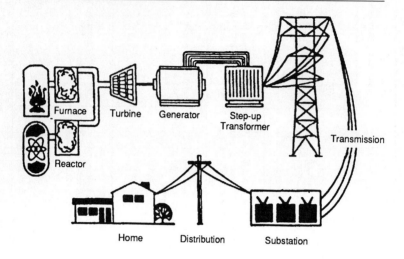

Furnace   Turbine   Generator   Step-up Transformer   Transmission

Reactor

Home   Distribution   Substation

Exhibit 7 Carolina Power & Light

Typical Division Structure Prior to Reorganization

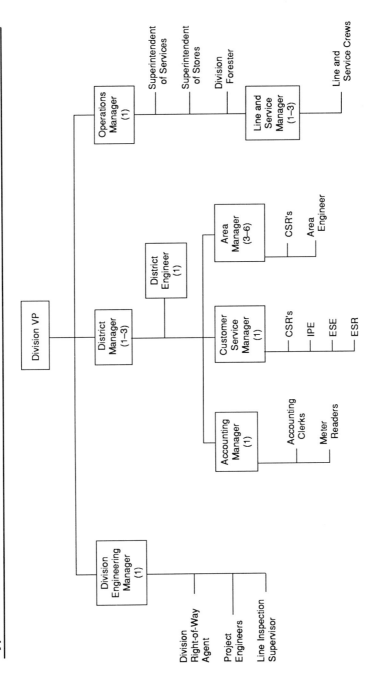

Numbers in parentheses indicate the number of managers reporting to the next level of management.

Exhibit 8   Carolina Power & Light

CLM Load Reduction Goals

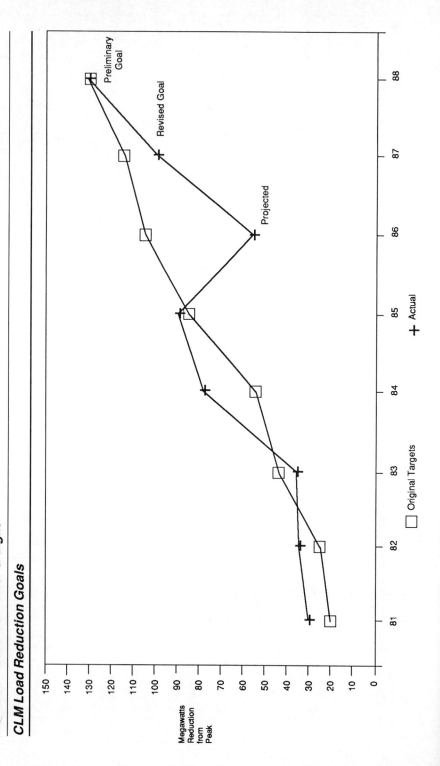

Exhibit 9   Carolina Power & Light

Typical Division Structure After Reorganization

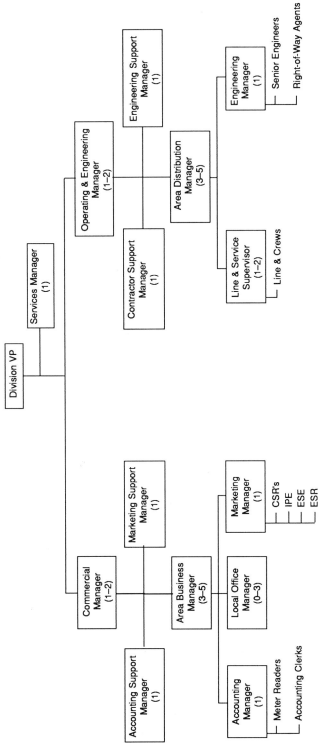

Numbers in parentheses indicate the number of managers reporting to the next level of management. The Northern Division had two Commercial and O&E managers, one each for the Northeast and Northwest Divisions. In some divisions the IPEs reported to the Marketing Support Manager.

Appendix
Carolina Power & Light

Conservation & Load Management Programs

Residential Customer Options

Option	Load Shape Objective *	Description	1995 Goal		Results Through 1985	
			Customers	MW	Customers	MW
Solar water heating	C	Company encourages new and existing customers to install solar hot water systems; may include a control device to enhance peak load reductions and customer's savings.	72,500	29	—	—
Passive solar design	C	Company encourages homebuilders to use solar design features that will reduce energy consumption and peak load.	31,500	38	—	—
Tune-up	C	Company services customer HVAC equipment to increase efficiency, lower customer cost, and lower peak load.	13,300	4	—	—
Apartment audit	C	Company analyzes energy usage and recommends low cost/no cost practices for apartment dweller.		4	—	—

(continued)

Residential Customer Options   (continued)

Option	Load Shape Objective*	Description	1995 Goal		Results Through 1985	
			Customers	MW	Customers	MW
High SEER	C	Company influences purchasers of new or replacement heat pumps and air conditioners to choose high efficiency models.	186,000	93	—	—
Efficient appliances	C	Company increases awareness and wise use of efficient appliances to save energy.		46	—	—
		TOTAL	N/A	630	N/A	131.5

Residential Customer Options

Option	Load Shape Objective*	Description	1995 Goal		Results Through 1985	
			Customers	MW	Customers	MW
Water heater control	PC	Customer allows Company to turn off water heater up to 4 hours per weekday and receives $2 per month credit.	172,500	69	33,400	13.3
Air conditioner control	PC	Customer allows Company to turn off central air conditioner up to 4 hours per weekday and receives $10/month credit, June-September.	40,000	100	16,950	42.4
Common sense	C	Company encourages energy efficient construction standards for houses, apartments, and mobile homes.	123,800	99	73,300	55.3
Time of use rates	LS	Company uses financial incentives, through rate design, to encourage customers to shift usage to off-peak times.	38,700	31	2,150	1.4

(continued)

Residential Customer Options   (continued)

Option	Load Shape Objective*	Description	1995 Goal		Results Through 1985	
			Customers	MW	Customers	MW
Low interest loans	C	Company lends up to $600 to customer at 6% interest for 3 years to finance approved conservation measures such as insulation and storm doors.	167,500	67	5,500	1.9
Home audits Residential conservation service and wrap-up	C	Company analyzes customer's home and makes recommendations for energy conserving measures and practices.	166,700	50	57,300	17.2

Industrial Customer Options

Option	Load Shape Objective*	Description	1985 Goal MW	Results Through 1985–MW
Time of use rates	LS	Company uses financial incentives, through rate design, to encourage customers to shift usage to off-peak times.	126	66.6
Audit	C	Company conducts detailed on-site energy surveys to develop conservation and load management opportunities.	90	64.6
Cogeneration	C	Company identifies and promotes customer generation potential among large users of process steam.	480	289.4
Hydroelectric generation	C	Company assists entrepreneurs in developing hydro sites in CP&L service area.	18	8.8
Standby generation	PC	Customer uses his standby generation capacity to reduce system demand during peak load periods.	10	—
Energy-efficient plants	C	Company encourages appropriate conservation and load management techniques in new plant construction.	29	—
Large load curtailable	PC	Customer agrees to curtail load on request in return for reduced demand charge.	40	—
Cooperative curtailable	PC	Company develops co-ops of plants that agree to reduce load upon request in return for an incentive.	38	—

(continued)

Industrial Customer Options (continued)

Option	Load Shape Objective [*]	Description	1985 Goal MW	Results Through 1985–MW
Reschedule plant shut- downs	PC	Customers reschedule July 4 week shutdowns to achieve sustained reduction in system peak loads.	12	—
HVAC optimization	C	Company assists customers in fine- tuning their heating and cooling systems.	14	—
Thermal energy storage	LS	Company promotes installation of thermal energy storage systems to lower customer energy cost and shift usage off peak.	13	—
		TOTAL	870	429.4

Commercial Customer Options

Option	Load Shape Objective [*]	Description	1985 Goal MW	Results Through 1985–MW
Energy manage- ment development	C	Company advises customers on energy management practices and provides on-site recommen- dations.	75	37.3
Time of use rates	LS	Company uses financial incentives through rate designs to en- courage customers to shift usage to off-peak times.	43	6.2
Thermal ener- gy storage	LS	Company promotes installation of thermal energy storage systems to lower customer energy cost and shift usage off peak.	51	1.0
Audit	C	Company provides computer-as- sisted energy analysis for larger commercial customers to shift usage, reduce peak demand, and improve energy efficiency.	36	0.5
Standby generation	PC	Customer uses his standby genera- tion capacity to reduce system demand during peak load periods.	35	—
Field facilities	C	Company demonstrates energy- saving measures in its new build- ings.	1	—
Agricultural services	PC	Company assists in research and field testing of conservation and load management techniques in agricultural sector.	5	—
Cooperative curtailable	PC	Company develops co-ops of cus- tomers that agree to reduce load upon request in return for an in- centive.	4	—
		TOTAL	250	45.0

[*]C = Conservation; PC = Peak Clipping; LS = Load Shifting. (See Exhibit 5 for definitions.)

Case 21

General Electric: Customer Service

In early 1985, two letters circulated throughout top management offices at General Electric. One was a letter from a customer to John F. Welch, Jr., GE's chairman and CEO:

Dear Mr. Welch:

When you are at the top of the company, it might be that you do not hear much about your day-to-day business. This letter is not intended to cause a major shake-up or even a response to us, but it is to let you know that General Electric seems to have a very serious problem with intercompany communications.

My company placed an order in June 1984 for an expensive system. The product was shipped partially in November and December 1984. Without a doubt, we have since made over thirty phone calls to your plants trying to get answers, and we are still working on the solution. The biggest problem is that nobody has control over the complete system, and apparently several GE divisions are involved. This has become a pass-the-buck situation. Just to find names and addresses of GE people is a big task. Most of your offices do not have a listing of plants, offices, personnel, and phone numbers.

Thanks for taking the time to read this.

— A Frustrated Customer

The other letter was from Lawrence A. Bossidy, a GE vice chairman, to senior vice presidents heading a number of GE's business units:

January 23, 1985

Gentlemen:

Jack and I receive a number of customer complaints during the course of a year. Most center on GE's lack of interest, attention, or follow-up of product or service problems our customers have encountered.

This case was prepared by Associate Professor Frank V. Cespedes as the basis for class discussion rather than to illustrate either effective or ineffective handling of an administrative situation.

Copyright © 1988 by the President and Fellows of Harvard College. Harvard Business School case 9-588-059.

When we follow up these complaints, we find that our people transfer some responsibility for the problem to the customer. They generally admit they did not handle the complaining customer properly, but then add that they might have, had the customer behaved differently. In other words, we don't review the complaint from the customer's perspective and, as a consequence, we don't establish the appropriate standard to eliminate these deficiencies.

I intend to follow each complaint I receive this year and, in this connection, I would appreciate your reviewing with your organization the need to concentrate on providing better products and service every day. Complaints about neglect, disinterest, and failure to perform are embarrassing and demonstrate an arrogance towards customers which we can ill afford.

Let's fix this problem.

Very truly yours,

L.A. Bossidy
Vice Chairman of the Board

In subsequent months, the topic of customer service received a great deal of attention at GE. An analysis of customer service in GE businesses was performed by Corporate Marketing and GE's corporate Audit Staff; a task force was formed to identify and rectify customer service problems in particular businesses; and specific goals and actions were developed. The focus of these efforts in 1985 was GE's industrial businesses, because it was felt by many in management that customer service was an increasingly important issue in the industrial businesses and an area of potential competitive advantage for GE. Mr. Bossidy commented:

> This company has a huge investment in large, mature, profitable businesses that have several striking characteristics in common. Most have few major technical advantages over the competition; they have high labor costs and seldom have a cost advantage over competitors; many have been targeted by low-cost, high-quality, foreign competitors who will do anything to gain market share.
>
> If we are to win in this environment, we are going to have to begin playing on a much broader keyboard of value, tapping the resources, talent, and experience that this company has in staggering quantities. That is our unfair advantage. We're a service station. We can't compete with gas stations.

This case study focuses on GE corporate efforts concerning customer service. It describes the analyses performed by corporate units during 1985, the actions taken, and the issues raised by those analyses and actions.

Background

In different contexts, customer service had been an area of attention at GE for some time. Shortly after becoming chairman, Mr. Welch delivered a speech to the Conference Board entitled, "Where Is Marketing Now That We Really Need It?" In that speech, he distinguished marketing from strategic planning (an important emphasis at GE and many other corporations during the 1970s) and concluded:

> Let's face it: the news of the 1970s was the absolutely devastating way the Japanese managed to decode the U. S. market—from cars to fishing gear, from copiers to textile machinery, from videocassette recorders to motorcycles. With hindsight, it was incredible that a foreign country, with such a different culture and language, could crack the riddle of the U. S. market so much better than we could. The Japanese used the same dealers and distributors that we did. They hadn't invented new ways to sell. But they had embraced marketing as the primary purpose of their business.
>
> They undermined us on marketing fundamentals—innovation—while we were polishing technique. Their focus on ends, not means, led them, *forced* them, to do a better job of figuring out what society was valuing, how people were living, what customers really wanted.
>
> Where was *our* marketing? Twenty-five years after the U. S. came up with marketing as a comprehensive management concept, for many American companies it was still largely a theory in search of execution. We had mouthed the words, but the Japanese had heard the music.
>
> (In the 1980s) megamarkets are emerging: the so-called office of the future, factory of the future, home of the future. The winners in these megamarkets (will be) those who deliver solutions from a user point of view. That's a big part of marketing's job. Innovation—the marriage of technology and market insight—won't hinge on discrete products, but on entire systems solutions.

Following this speech, GE instituted two studies that had direct implications for customer service: a review of GE's industrial businesses in 1984 and a review of GE's pooled sales efforts in 1984–1985.

"Go-to-Market" Study

In 1984, Corporate Marketing studied how a number of GE industrial businesses moved products from the factory to end users. This "Go-to-Market" study was motivated by the fact that market conditions for many of the businesses involved had been changing significantly in recent years, perhaps requiring a realignment of the GE product unit/sales channel/customer configuration.

At the time, GE's industrial and power businesses had approximately 40 product departments (see Exhibit 1), selling through four pooled sales forces. Each product department had profit-and-loss responsibility. The sales forces were organized by: 1) distributor customers, 2) OEM (Original Equipment Manufacturing) customers, 3) large end users, and 4) utilities. For the businesses involved, this organization of sales efforts had been in place for years and reflected (in the words of one manager) "historical differences in what and how each type of customer bought from GE, different skills traditionally required to sell and service each customer type, the force of 'that's how we've always done it here,' and a GE tradition of P&L autonomy for the product departments."

By the early 1980s, however, there were many overlaps among the customers served by these four sales forces and, consequently, complaints from customers who received competing proposals from multiple GE salespeople. Further, many felt the current organization did not optimize opportunities to sell systems, exploit potential interrelationships among the products manufactured by GE, or keep GE product departments in touch with evolving customer requirements in fast-changing markets. One manager commented:

> In that organization, the sales force represented the customer, but the product department controlled the P&L and the resources. Sales and Product often saw the world differently: a customer might be interested in a system or semicustomized package of products from GE, but the product departments weren't particularly interested in systems selling or the best package; each was primarily interested in its particular product line and was resistant to altering price or terms and conditions for the sake of the system or package.
>
> This is a problem, because in much of U. S. industry in the 1980s, industrial customers are not adding big chunks of capacity. Instead, they're looking primarily for productivity and cost improvements. As a vendor to these customers, you provide those improvements with a system, not simply individual product components. And GE is, in many ways, ideally suited to provide this value: our products flow into a multitude of markets, and the overlaps (and therefore the potential combinations) are enormous.
>
> The product departments recognized the problem and the opportunity, but no one was willing to compromise their autonomy or quarterly results to address a specific problem or build an opportunity. One result was a consistent message from big, important customers that "GE is difficult to do business with." In addition, this organization tended to focus people's attention on factories, not markets, because that's where the resources and responsibility resided. But a focus on markets is crucial for effective marketing and service in these businesses.

One result of the "Go-to-Market" study was a 1984 reorganization which created four business units: Motors, Construction Equipment, Factory Automation, and Power Systems. These units aggregated many formerly separate product departments. Another result was the creation of an Industrial Market Board (IMB) which included the senior sales and marketing managers of the industrial businesses. The IMB was chaired by Paul Van Orden and met regularly to review issues concerning GE's industrial businesses, including the issue of customer service.

Pooled Sales Review

The intent of the 1984 reorganization was to focus a number of previously separate product departments on certain major markets. Commenting on the reorganization, one manager noted:

> The reorganization brought together product departments that should have been working more closely together. But each product department had its own particular order-entry system, information system, terms and conditions, and

long-established policies and procedures. Systems sales opportunities multiplied under the new organization, but so did problems with customer responsiveness due to the multiplicity of procedures that had to be integrated.

In late 1984, GE's Corporate Audit Staff examined the sales activities of GE industrial businesses. By March 1985, the Audit Staff's "Pooled Sales Review" was completed, and a memorandum outlining the results was submitted by GE's Corporate Auditor (see Exhibit 2). In addition, members of the Corporate Audit Staff made a presentation to the IMB summarizing the results and emphasizing the following:

a) Effective marketing requires effective commercial service routines (i.e., efficient quotation processing, order entry, order tracking, and delivery) and strong support systems in areas like information systems, measurements, and training.
b) Acceptance of the status quo has perpetuated inefficiencies in these areas, a lack of coordination among product components, and an internal (rather than customer) focus within individual product components.
c) These factors have significantly impaired sales effectiveness.
d) "Corrective action must begin by establishing ownership for commercial service responsibilities. Most concerns identified cannot be addressed adequately by any single organization, because responsibility cannot be clearly assigned and ownership established."

The Audit Staff's presentation generated considerable discussion at the March meeting of the IMB, which Mr. Welch attended as a visitor. One executive present recalled: "Jack Welch was very concerned about the implications, and at the end of the meeting, he turned to Paul Van Orden and said, 'Paul, you're in charge of Marketing; can you and your group find out more about the causes and help to start fixing things?' "

Customer Service Project

In the weeks following the March 1985 IMB meeting, Mr. Van Orden, Leonard Vickers (vice president of Corporate Marketing), and members of GE's Corporate Marketing staff interviewed managers in various GE businesses in order to gather more specific information about customer service, the nature of the problem, managers' perspectives on the issues, and practical first steps in addressing the issues. This review, noted one manager, "made a few things very clear."

First, the issue of industrial customer service was not new, and had been studied several times at GE since the mid-1970s. As one manager noted, "the basic issues are understood, but solutions are elusive." Second, customer service was defined differently by each GE organization, reflecting the nature of the products sold (e.g., components vs. highly technical complete systems). Accordingly, support systems and improvements were usually confined within each business, while many customer transactions cut across organizational boundaries. " The only consensus," recalled one manager, "was that coordination was essential and very difficult to achieve since each business wanted to control and optimize its own particular solution."

Third, "customer service" involved multiple functions within a business (see Exhibit 3). Fourth, the nature of customer service issues varied depending upon the kind of transaction involved. One manager involved in the review explained:

> We found it useful to distinguish between flow products (standard, high-volume products where distributors were typically the customers, and where stocking levels were critical) and custom products (special-order items that could be either high volume or one-of-a-kind). We also found it important to recognize where GE's involvement with the customer was limited to a single business and where our involvement cut across a number of GE businesses. The relative time frames, complexity, and coordination involved in providing good service differed with each combination of these factors (see Exhibit 4). And we found that GE's industrial businesses tended to be in those areas where customer transactions are most complex: custom orders often involving a number of GE businesses.

The complexity was increased due to the relationship between the product departments and the pooled sales channels. Some product departments sold most of their business through a given sales force, but that product department still might not be a big percentage of that sales force's business. The result was that Sales and Product might view the importance of a given order very differently.

Fifth, problem-solving was often at the heart of industrial transactions, requiring significant applications engineering, installation or operating assistance, and on-going support. Since the purchases were often critically important to a customer's business, relationships between buyer and seller had to be continuous rather than transitory. One manager in Corporate Marketing commented:

> In many businesses, there is less technology and performance difference between GE and other major suppliers. Competitors are increasingly global in scope, markets are maturing, and customers are often seeking fewer, more valuable suppliers to act as "strategic partners." When product performance is relatively equal, customers place more importance on vendor performance, and service becomes the major area of differentiation between suppliers.

In considering these factors, Van Orden, Vickers, and others were especially struck by the lack of "ownership" for customer service issues at the business-unit level. "There was no one person responsible for these matters in the businesses," said one executive, "and thus often no champion to raise awareness of the issues involved." The first action taken was to have each business designate one person to be responsible for identifying and addressing customer service issues within that business. In early May, Mr. Van Orden sent letters to Mr. Welch outlining the initial proposed steps and to various GE vice presidents requiring them to appoint a Customer Service manager (see Exhibits 5A and 5B).

Customer Service Task Force

By late May, Customer Service managers had been appointed for 20 industrial businesses with representatives for both product departments and pooled sales organizations. One manager recalled:

> . . . with the letters and jawboning from people like Van Orden and Bossidy, and the blessing of the IMB, this had become a very visible issue for business-unit managers, and the quality of their appointees reflected that. The Customer Service managers tended to be veteran GE managers, highly regarded in their businesses, with lots of field experience so they understood the issues involved, and with a reputation for being "zealots" in the area of service.

These managers were constituted as a task force which had the following charter:

> Reps should represent their business's total perspective on customer service and, in most cases, will have assigned responsibility for customer service quality in their business.
>
> The reps will work on two fronts to address issues which negatively impact customer service:
>
> —Work individually within their businesses to improve customer service.
> —Work together to address broad customer service issues which require inter-SBU cooperation to resolve.
>
> The task force solutions to these issues may include changes in systems and procedures, and the addition or expansion of measurements to ensure quality performance of service activities.

The first meeting of the Task Force was in late July 1985 at GE headquarters in Fairfield, Connecticut. The meeting had three objectives: 1) to identify shared obstacles to good customer service and the approach to overcome these obstacles; 2) to share best practices across the business units; and 3) to develop a common language and establish informal communication networks to enhance cross-business teamwork concerning customer service. At the meeting, Mr. Van Orden outlined the history of the customer service issue at GE; Mr. Bossidy emphasized top management's commitment to solving the problem; Mr. Vickers explained the importance of shifting many of the industrial businesses from a transaction to a relationship orientation with customers. One manager present explained:

> Given the people at this meeting, much of this was "preaching to the converted," but very important. Customer service is an "optics issue"; it has to remain visible. When we went back and told our general managers that Bossidy and Van Orden were there, it focused attention.

In addition, the 20 Customer Service reps were formed into 4 teams where, in workshops, they analyzed customer service issues in specific businesses and then presented their findings and recommendations to the IMB on August 1. In their presentations, the reps emphasized that management had to broaden its definition of customer service from "order service" to "total customer satisfaction." The latter involved all facets of customer contact, including transaction services (e.g., delivery time, order fill rates, billing errors) as well as customer support activities in areas such as sales personnel effectiveness, responsiveness, inquiry handling, and technical assistance.

The reps also emphasized that critical elements of customer service varied according to the phase of the order cycle and whether the transaction involved "flow goods" (i.e., standardized products ordered frequently from stock) or "project" business (i.e., semicustomized orders involving a variety of products manufactured and sold by different GE business units); see Exhibit 6.

At the close of the meeting on August 1, the representatives were asked to return to their businesses and prepare individual action plans to improve customer service. Although improving service and funding any changes were emphasized as individual business unit responsibilities, the representatives were reminded that help was available from corporate Marketing and Information Systems groups. Action plans were due by September 30.

Conclusion

In the months following the Fairfield meeting, actions were implemented in a number of areas. Intercompany communications began to focus on customer service. Customers were surveyed in order to establish more accurate measures of customer service quality. In many businesses, there was increased use and accuracy of order-tracking systems; customer service contact directories were established; policies for order changes and customer claims resolutions were specified and clarified; and training was upgraded. In addition, at the annual Corporate Officers meeting in October 1985, customer service was the major topic on the agenda, and Messrs. Bossidy and Van Orden reported to GE officers on the obstacles identified by the customer service managers at the Fairfield meeting.

In December 1985, one GE executive commented that "I've seen more concrete action to improve customer service during the past five months than at any time during the past five years." Nonetheless, by the end of 1985, many in top management raised a number of issues concerning the company's renewed emphasis on customer service. One manager remarked:

> Customer service has traditionally been the most studied, least engaged issue in General Electric. How do we prevent the recent attention from becoming a fad— an important issue that engages people's energies for a while but then dissipates? This must be viewed as the first step in a process, not a one-time event.

A manager in Corporate Marketing commented:

> We at headquarters can't really "do" anything concrete about this issue. But we can provide a spotlight, aircover, and a support network for the service doers in the operating groups. The issue is complex, but the first step is to elevate the functions involved which, at GE, have been relatively low-level functions that don't always get their calls returned from a busy manager seeking to make next quarter's numbers. The key is appointing accountable business representatives that have visibility and lines of communication to the top.

A customer service manager commented:

> The key issue is mindset. Many business unit managers don't really care about the issue of customer service. They're more concerned about financial performance near term and respond to customer service as a "motherhood" issue. Ultimately, the issue is listening to and responding to customers' needs, and that's a function of mindset.

A business unit manager commented:

> The key issue is measurements. So many aspects of customer service are typically fragmented in a business, not measured, and thus relatively invisible. It's tough for a manager to trade off a tangible addition to this quarter's bottom line in return for some intangible benefits in service that are not reflected in measurement criteria. As a company, we live on our measurements. If we don't measure customer service appropriately and continuously, the issue won't get sustained attention.

A senior corporate executive reflected:

> The question is, how can you embed true customer service in the culture of the business? How quickly can you get started and realistically proceed? How can the general managers help most effectively? And how can we do all this in an environment that requires GE to respond to constant cost pressures from aggressive competition? We cannot interpret a necessity to cut costs as a license to ignore customers, but we also can't reverse the downsizing of overhead costs undertaken during the past few years.
>
> The Customer Service project has done a lot of good in a short period of time. But it's a delicate beginning. In one sense, appointing Customer Service managers means that responsibility has been placed on their shoulders to patch up and save relationships that the whole organization should be nurturing. I hope the Customer Service task force has begun that process without, unintentionally, diluting the sense of responsibility and opportunity that every employee here, not just the Customer Service reps, should feel in this area.

Exhibit 1   General Electric: Customer Service

General Electric: 1984 Organization Chart

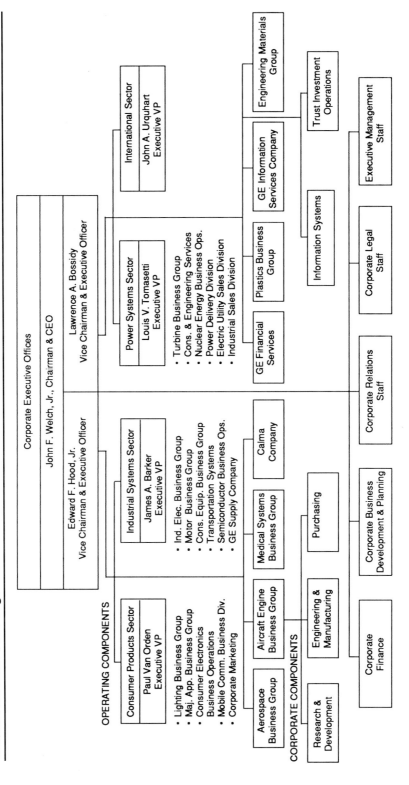

Exhibit 2   General Electric: Customer Service

Audit Memorandum

June 16, 1985
J. W. Hickling; Corporate Auditor

Audit Memorandum—Company Pooled Sales Activities

Summarized in this memorandum are the results of my review of the Company's pooled sales activities. To the extent feasible, management has agreed to implement corrective action; however, many of the issues can only be addressed at the Company level.

Quotation Processing Routines

Sales personnel generally solicited customer business in the following manner:

Quotation processing routines

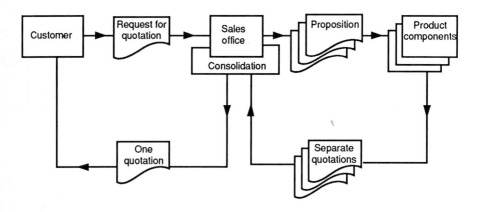

1. Sales representative prepares requests for quotation (RFQ) and identifies the various components (three in the hypothetical example) required to supply portions of the customer quotations.
2. Each product component analyzes the proposition independently and returns its portion to the sales representative.
3. The sales representative compiles the information, strategizes based upon the competitive environment, makes appropriate adjustments, and forwards the quotation to the customer.

   In this process, coordination between sales and product components is critical. I found that sales personnel often failed to provide sufficient data with which to prepare quotations (RFQs frequently were returned repeatedly for additional information); lead times to prepare quotations were inadequate; RFQs generally were mailed (as opposed to using

(continued)

Exhibit 2 (continued)

Rapifax or electronic mail), thereby increasing processing time an average of four days; and at several product components, recent personnel reductions in proposition support contributed to processing delays.

It is recommended that, where feasible, processing should be mechanized to improve the quality, promptitude, and accuracy of quotations.

Order Entry Routing

The ways customer orders are communicated to product components vary significantly. It appears that no standard modes of order entry have been established. The impact of order entry inefficiencies is significant. Comparison of manufacturing cycle times in one unit for orders transmitted electronically versus manually indicated an opportunity to reduce manufacturing cycle time approximately five days (20%) by processing orders electronically.

Suggested corrective action principally relates to mechanization opportunities. Consider integrating order entry and quotation processing into one system. In the absence of a mechanized order entry system, standard modes of entry should be established, responsibilities clearly defined, and appropriate measurements formulated.

Order Tracking

Although sales personnel have a mechanized system (CS&DO system) for tracking the status of customer orders, the system has been rendered virtually useless because most product components have established autonomous tracking systems. Components that maintained an internal system generally had not input data to the CS&DO system and, those that did, failed to maintain CS&DO data currently. As a result, sales personnel generally were unable to advise customers of order status and, therefore, devoted significant time (approximately 7% of available time) attempting to track order status manually.

It is difficult to assess the total impact of these conditions but they appear to be a cause of chronic customer complaints. Corrective action should begin with the establishment of one system which will serve the needs of both sales and product components. Secondly, procedures and measurements should be established to ensure timely and accurate submission of data.

Late deliveries also appear to contribute significantly to customer dissatisfaction. In this connection, I noted that measurements typically were based on production schedules (i.e., when the item was scheduled to be manufactured) rather than delivery dates originally promised to customers. I also found different causes of late deliveries at each audited location, including material unavailability; factory loading delays resulting from recent personnel reallocations; and inconsistencies between actual manufacturing cycle times and marketing commitments (i.e., promised delivery dates). Several sales representatives stated that poor delivery performance is adversely affecting the Company's ability to price aggressively in the marketplace and has resulted in lost orders.

Underlying Support

Information Systems: To date, systems development has not been viewed on a companywide basis, but confined within CS&DO and product components. In essence, current systems represent autonomous "islands of automation."

Office Services: The entire communications network which serves pooled sales requires attention. Virtually every transaction required oral communication between sales representatives and product components. I noted that sales and product personnel spent an inordinate amount of time just attempting to contact each other. Electronic mail

(continued)

Exhibit 2 (continued)

generally was not utilized, and phone switching systems generally were not in place to avoid busy signals or unanswered calls. At one plant, I noted that 44% of incoming calls were on hold over sixty seconds, of which 33% were eventually abandoned; calls in the customer support area routinely went unanswered, principally because sales specialists had been instructed to answer only their own telephones.

Training: With recent headcount reductions (13% reduction in three years), responsibilities of sales personnel have increased significantly. In addition to their traditional responsibilities, sales representatives generally are now required to perform the former duties of application engineers and sales assistants. However, it appears that training has not kept pace with these expanded responsibilities.

Time Allocation Survey

A time allocation survey conducted during my review demonstrates the cumulative effect that the conditions discussed in this memorandum have had upon selling effectiveness.

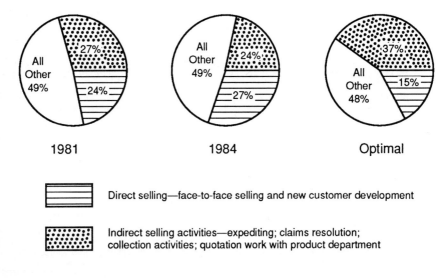

Direct selling—face-to-face selling and new customer development

Indirect selling activities—expediting; claims resolution; collection activities; quotation work with product department

The implication appears clear: pooled sales representatives are devoting as much time compensating for procedural inefficiencies as they are selling. For comparative purposes, I contacted representatives of Major Appliance and Plastics Business Groups (MABG and PBG). MABG informed me that, based upon a 1981 study, retail salesmen devoted 47% of their time to direct selling and PBG estimated direct selling time to be 50%. Significantly, both groups have integrated customer service operations.

(continued)

Exhibit 2   (continued)

Conclusion

Most of the concerns identified cannot be addressed adequately by any single organization. Implementing corrective action will require a companywide approach. Corrective action must also begin by establishing ownership for service responsibilities. Once ownership is established, a comprehensive plan should be prepared documenting (1) the flow of information between and within organizations, (2) procedures and systems necessary to facilitate the process, (3) measurements which will highlight performance trends, and (4) training required to perform new responsibilities.

I wish to express appreciation for the courtesies and cooperation extended during the audit by the management and employees of the components who participated in the review.

Exhibit 3 General Electric: Customer Service

Order Cycle and Customer Service

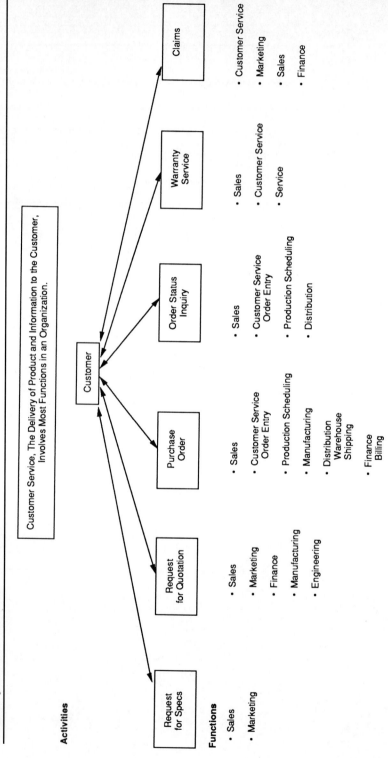

Activities

Customer Service, The Delivery of Product and Information to the Customer, Involves Most Functions in an Organization.

Customer

| Request for Specs | Request for Quotation | Purchase Order | Order Status Inquiry | Warranty Service | Claims |

Functions

- Sales
- Marketing

- Sales
- Marketing
- Finance
- Manufacturing
- Engineering

- Sales
- Customer Service
  Order Entry
- Production Scheduling
- Manufacturing
- Distribution
  Warehouse
  Shipping
- Finance
  Billing

- Sales
- Customer Service
  Order Entry
- Production Scheduling
- Distribution

- Sales
- Customer Service
- Service

- Customer Service
- Marketing
- Sales
- Finance

Exhibit 4 General Electric: Customer Service

Customer Service Issues Vary Depending on the Nature of the Transaction

Type of Product

	Flow	Custom
GE Involvement		
Single Business	• Stock-item • Standard, high-volume products • Typically distributors as customers	• Special order items • May be High-Volume or one-of-a-kind
Multi-Business	• Distributor business • Customer is systems integrator	• Projects • Long lead times • High engineering content • GE is integrator

Increasing time →
• More engineering content
• Increasing scheduling difficulty
• More customer coordination

Increasing complexity →
• More internal coordination
• More handoffs

Exhibit 5a   General Electric: Customer Service

Internal Memorandum

May 8, 1985

Mr. J. F. Welch
E3E Fairfield

Dear Jack:

Progress report on Industrial Customer Service issue.

- Issue has been "studied" since mid-'70s. The Marketing Consulting files coughed up several. Apparently easy to delineate the problem . . . tough to solve.
- Attempt to find key customer service people didn't produce names . . . no *one* person responsible . . . highly fragmented.
- Comparison of "customer service" and "quality" may be a good one in that both are mind-set issues.
  - At present, everyone sees it as a problem.
  - No one has ownership.
  - The answer isn't "fix it," the answer is build it in.
- Our approach will be similar to that used on "quality":
  1) Package the story . . . to get *attention* and *education.*
  2) Get SBU Manager to designate one person to be responsible for Customer Service.
  3) Get the responsible people together.
     - Surface the problems.
     - Get suggested approaches.
     - Set up a continuing task force.
     - Establish goals.

Desired Outcome
  - Issue recognized as important
  - Key people appointed in each SBU
  - SBU Managers committed
  - Measurements in place
  - A continuing action team in place

The attached is the beginning.

P. W. Van Orden

lcf

Attachment

Cc: E. E. Hood
Cc: L. Vickers

Exhibit 5b General Electric: Customer Service

Internal Memorandum

May 8, 1985

Messrs.
G. B. Cox   J. D. Opie
D. M. Engelman   M. S. Richardson
C. D. Keaton   H. J. Singer
E. J. Kovarik   J. Tenzer
H. T. Luedke   T. L. Williams
D. E. Momot   V. W. Williams

Gentlemen:

As most of you know, the Industrial Market Board is a coordinating group appointed by the CEO to follow up on issues identified by the Go-to-Market team.

This group has become increasingly concerned about the quality of customer service in our businesses. An Audit Staff report to the Industrial Market Board on March 26 (and subsequently to the CEO) brought this issue to a head.

Because of our responsibility for Corporate Marketing, Len Vickers and I have been asked to coordinate an effort to improve our customer service performance . . . and we need your help.

The complexity of the customer service issue for GE is clear from the attached charts.

You'll see from the charts that the complexity is based on the fact that the term "customer service" covers a multitude of activities that together add up to customer satisfaction. And usually no single individual is responsible for managing or coordinating these activities.

I've also discovered that customer service is not a new issue. It has been studied several times . . . dating back to the mid-'70s, at least. Clearly, we don't need another study. What we do need is a coordinated action plan to improve.

As a first step, it seems to me we should capitalize on many excellent activities already underway in individual businesses, and pool the smarts of involved managers from each business. We are working on the agenda for a meeting of these managers, tentatively planned for mid-July.

Please drop me a note with your selection for attending. Independent of current title, the person you send should be the individual you want to be responsible to you for all facets of customer service. For example, John Opie will be sending Bill Teague, his Manager of Marketing Services.

Thanks for your help.

P. W. Van Orden

lcf

Attachment

cc: J. A. Baker
R. D. Benveniste
L. V. Tomasetti
L. Vickers

Exhibit 6 General Electric: Customer Service

Critical Elements of Customer Service

	Pre-Order	Order-To-Shipment	Post-Shipment
"Flow" Business	• Accurate, timely quotations • Knowledgeable sales force	• On-time, complete, accurate shipments • Accurate, timely order tracking/status reports	• Timely, responsive complaint resolution • Quality, timely in-warranty and out-of-warranty service
"Project" Business	• Accessibility and responsiveness of personnel • Quality, timely application support • Product availability information	• Flexibility to react to customer changes to the order • Experienced project managers • Ownership/authority for multi-product department orders	• Competent installation support • Accurate, timely billing • Effective spare parts support

Critical Elements Varied By Phase Of The Order Cycle And By Type Of Business—Project Vs. Flow

Chapter 10 ⬛⬛⬛⬛⬛

Structure, Systems, and Process

This chapter considers some of the common structures used to organize marketing and sales activities and the issues within each structure involved in coordinating customers' purchasing and service requirements, channel management demands, and internal management systems. The chapter also looks at the processes that characterize marketing decision making within each type of organization studied. Hence this final chapter gives a unified look at issues that were considered separately in the previous chapters and stimulates your thinking about the interactions among structures, systems, and management processes in marketing decision making. Further, the variety of companies in this chapter helps you consider the kinds of conceptual and interpersonal skills required to be an effective marketing manager in a given organization.

Strategy, Structure, Systems, and Process

The meaning of the term *strategy* has been "stretched" in myriad directions in recent years. But an enduring, sound, and useful definition of strategy is "the determination of the basic long-term goals and objectives of the enterprise and the adoption of courses of action and allocation of resources necessary for carrying out these goals." [1]

The term *structure* typically refers to the formal reporting relationships (and hence formal lines of authority and influence) in an organization. Structure helps to determine the characteristics of the organization's division of labor, whether it is centralized or decentralized, functional, matrixed, or takes some other form.

The term *systems* refers to the formal and informal devices intended to inform and control marketing decision making. Thus systems include measurement, evaluation, compensation, and budgeting criteria in an organization.

Finally, the term *process* is used here to refer to the important tasks that must be accomplished by marketing and sales managers in a given structure, given the marketing organization's strategy and systems. Thus process indicates both the kinds of managerial interactions that characterize an organization and the kinds of skills (both conceptual and interpersonal) that must be developed by successful managers in that organization.

Most organizations engage in an ongoing procedure of evaluating, modifying, and refining the linkages among their marketing strategies, structures, systems, and processes. A common relationship among these factors is illustrated by Figure A.

It is often argued that "strategy drives structure" and that the structure, in turn, helps to determine the kinds of management systems and processes that take root in an organization. In his study of 100 U.S. companies (including an intensive investigation of the development of four large firms in the first half of the twentieth century: General Motors, Du Pont, Sears, and Standard Oil), Alfred Chandler provided a seminal discussion of the impact of strategy on organizational structures and processes. He found that "a new strategy required a new or at least refashioned structure if the enlarged enterprise was to be operated efficiently." [2] It is clear from Chandler's work, however, that there is no simple, causal link among strategy, structure, and process. The companies Chandler studied typically spent years developing, clarifying, and modifying the structures and processes required to implement their strategies. Moreover, in a series of empirical studies of marketing organizations, Corey and Star found

Figure A
Strategy, Structure, Systems, and Processes

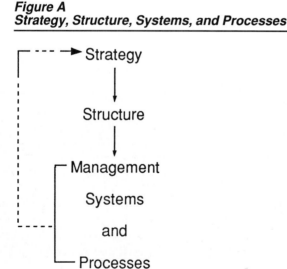

that strategy is also a function (as well as a contributing cause) of "the kind of organization which produces it and the balance of power within the structure. Today's organization is an important influence in molding tomorrow's strategy which, in turn, shapes tomorrow's organization."[3] Hence there is an iterative relationship among these factors: As well as being influenced by strategy, structure and process also influence (and, typically, constrain) strategy. What seems clear, however, is that effective organizations establish a congruence among these dimensions. By contrast, ineffective organizations struggle with conflicting demands placed on their personnel by incongruent strategic goals, formal structures, key measurement systems, and various managerial processes.

A classic study of organizations and decision making provides relevant perspectives on strategy-structure-systems-process interactions and tensions, especially in marketing activities. March and Simon[4] argued persuasively that because human beings are limited in their ability to make completely rational decisions, organizational structures and processes evolve to prevent uncertainty, or too much information, from overwhelming these limited capacities (what March and Simon called "bounded rationality"). Thus the development of rules, programs, measures, and other standard operating procedures serve to break down large, and often intractably complex, problems into more manageable units for decision makers. In reducing uncertainty in this manner, however, organizational procedures also reduce the scope of decision makers' attention and the focus of their skills. Over time, this focus often becomes routinized in an organization, so that the organization can do some things very well (e.g., develop marketing programs and field sales efforts for current types of products, channels, or customer groups) but lacks capabilities in other important areas (e.g., develop marketing programs and field sales efforts for new products, channels, or customer groups).

Thus on the one hand, any organization needs congruence and focus among strategy, structure, systems, and process. On the other hand, it needs to adapt to changing market conditions, and this very congruence among key organizational dimensions often inhibits the development and execution of new and more appropriate strategies.

This tension is particularly central to many issues in marketing organization. Because of their boundary role in the firm, marketing managers usually face two often conflicting goals.

The first goal is the need to be predictable and consistent. Because capacity planning, production scheduling, bank borrowing requirements, operating cash flow estimates, and hiring patterns throughout the firm are often contingent on annual estimated sales revenues, the marketing organization is typically under pressure to "deliver the numbers": that is, achieve the sales quota established in the annual plan. Hence consistency and predictability in marketing operations ("no surprises") are valued by top management and by other functions in the firm.

The second goal for marketing managers is to make it new. At the same time, marketing management typically faces the requirement of increasing annual sales and generating new sources of revenue through new products, new channels, new customer groups, and so forth. But, new products or new channels usually mean learning about new technologies, establishing relationships with different decision makers in reseller or customer organizations, and confronting different buying processes and purchase criteria. In short, "newness" means developing new ways of selling and marketing that are often perceived as "alien" to established and proven revenue-generation routines.

In practice at many companies, therefore, the imperatives of the first goal (to be predictable and to make quota) often overshadow the longer-term and necessarily risky requirements of the second (to make it new), leading to "marketing myopia" [5]: a focus on current products and channels, and an actual business definition that ignores product substitutes.

This tension (and its often unfortunate outcome) has been implicitly illustrated in earlier case studies in this book. In this final section, we consider a variety of marketing organizations and their relative abilities in dealing with these cross-cutting requirements that typically face marketing managers. Hence in analyzing decisions and evaluating the marketing organizations encountered in these case studies, consider how well each organization's structure, systems, and process achieve five key goals:

- To allocate available marketing resources efficiently
- To focus marketing managers' attention on appropriate markets
- To develop and maintain an appropriate process among field and corporate marketing personnel
- To execute marketing strategies effectively in the field
- To do the above while still building skills appropriate for future growth

Marketing Organization: Components and Functions

Most marketing organizations are composed of three generic types of positions, each performing a distinct set of functions that must be coordinated with each other. We can categorize these components of marketing organization as program managers, resource managers, and marketing support managers.[6]

A program is a total plan for serving a particular market segment. It provides for product design, pricing, channels of distribution, advertising, promotion, and field-selling goals and priorities. It may also include specifications for product supply and customer service. Program managers are responsible for the development and management of such programs. They include personnel such as product management or, depending upon the marketing strategy, various market or industry managers. No matter how the company's segmentation scheme ultimately defines its targeted customer groups, the core task of program management is to provide the framework for planning and tailoring the firm's overall business strategy to individual market segments. In performing this task, program managers typically have substantial influence on the allocation of available marketing resources to various segments. Of the three types of management roles discussed here, program management typically has the highest proportion of "strategy formulation" responsibilities, as distinct from field implementation responsibilities.

Resource managers have responsibility for deploying and managing various kinds of company resources (e.g., field sales personnel; customer service facilities; telemarketing units; advertising or promotional expenditures) that have been allocated to the marketing organization and its various programs. Resource managers must assess the various demands on the marketing organization imposed by program managers' plans, coordinate and arbitrate among these demands, and manage the allocation and use of specific marketing resources. Of the three types of management roles discussed here, resource management typically has the highest proportion of hands-on managerial responsibilities. A key task facing resource managers is to maintain in their respective areas the appropriate level of skills and motivation required to use important marketing resources effectively. Resource managers typically must work with a number of external parties as well. For example, the field sales manager must work both internally at his or her own company and externally with customers and, often, the community. Similarly, advertising and promotion managers typically are responsible for developing various communication programs by working both internally with product managers and externally with advertising agency personnel, direct-mail institutions, and various radio, television, or print media.

Support services in a marketing organization include activities such as market research, sales training, sales analysis, pricing analyses, and general marketing education. In companies in which indirect channels of distribution are important, there may also be marketing support managers for the development and monitoring of different distribution-related activities such as co-op advertising, promotion, inventory, and delivery management. Managers of these various forms of marketing support are responsible for keeping their activities in touch with best practice in a given area and for providing timely, cost-effective information on each activity to program and resource management. Of the three types of management roles discussed here, support management typically has the highest proportion of "project-driven" work, since activities here are generally defined by evolving needs from program and/or resource management. To take advantage of scale economies in research and training, support managers also tend to be based at headquarters rather than in field units at many corporations. Like resource managers, moreover, support managers usually work both with internal company personnel and with external resources such as market research firms or training organizations.

Program, resource, and support management refers to the generic functions performed by marketing managers, not to specific job titles. Many marketing jobs are a combination of program, resource, and support functions. The particular alignment of program, resource, and support-management activities will vary with the firm's marketing strategy and, in particular, with the extent to which this strategy implies a relatively more centralized or decentralized emphasis in the marketing organization (see the following section). Most marketing organizations—however they title specific activities—must perform and coordinate these functions.

Centralization and Decentralization of Marketing Efforts

A perennial issue in organization concerns the extent to which activities are organized and managed on a headquarters-centralized basis, or a field-decentralized basis. Years ago, Alfred P. Sloan expressed the issues involved (if not the "solution") as well as anyone, and in terms particularly relevant to the typical concerns of marketing managers:[7]

> Good management rests on a reconciliation of centralization and decentralization. Each of the conflicting elements has its unique results in the operation of a business.
>
> From decentralization we get initiative, responsibility, development of personnel, decisions close to the fact, flexibility—in short, all the qualities necessary to adapt to new conditions. From coordination, we get efficiencies and economies. It must be apparent that "coordinated centralization" is not an easy concept to apply. There is no hard and fast rule for sorting out the various responsibilities and the best way to assign them. The balance . . . varies according to what is being decided, the circumstances of the time, past experience, and the temperaments and skills of the executives involved.

Centralization vs. decentralization is a particularly important organizational issue in marketing for a number of reasons. First, as a boundary function responsible for keeping the firm in alignment with customers and market conditions, effective marketing depends on the marketing organization's ability to keep "decisions close to the facts" of the marketplace and to "adapt to new conditions." Getting "close to the customer" means, for many marketing organizations, decentralization of important activities. But in fact many key marketing functions are characterized by substantial scale economies that can only be realized through relative centralization of these functions; in turn, capturing these scale economies is vital to maintaining a competitive cost structure and competitive prices.

Second, developments in both the external macro-environment and the larger organizational environment at many firms make the tensions outlined by Sloan particularly relevant to marketing management. The international dimensions of marketing have increased dramatically during the past two decades. This means that marketing managers can face an ongoing series of decisions that revolve around the relative extent of standardization/centralization of major marketing programs such as product lines, prices, distribution, and communications vs. the customization/decentralization of these programs to reflect local country differences in culture, regulations, or other factors.[8] Similarly, many companies have decentralized their various operating groups into separate business units, each with profit-and-loss responsibility and operating autonomy, while also seeking to achieve synergies (or various forms of interrelationships) among those autonomous business units. Some observers believe that these developments make "horizontal" strategies and tactics—a coordinated set of goals and policies across distinct but interrelated business units—"perhaps the most critical item on the strategic agenda" for many firms.[9] The centralization/decentralization tensions inherent in this agenda often are most salient in marketing activities, since the task is to develop and implement companywide marketing programs in a context in which important resources and marketing skills are decentralized in local operating units.

All of these factors, then, make centralization vs. decentralization a key organizational issue in marketing. As Sloan correctly emphasized, there are important benefits inherent in each mode of organization whereas the ideal ("coordinated decentralization") is not an easy concept to apply. What seems clear, however, is that the desired extent of centralization vs. decentralization in marketing will depend upon the factors noted by Sloan and on the particular kinds of activities in the context of the firm's marketing strategy and skills. Analyzing these activities, in turn, will draw heavily on the kinds of knowledge and experience relevant to topics examined earlier in this book: analysis of the sales tasks and other field marketing requirements inherent in managing customer encounters; recognition of the key interfaces (both internal and external) that should influence the organization and control of marketing efforts; analysis of the sources of buyer value in a marketplace; and diagnosis of the organizational factors that typically affect customer service, and thus buyer value, in a firm.

Case Studies

The case studies in this final chapter fall into three groups. The first category includes cases about IBM, Procter & Gamble, and Pepsi-Cola, three companies viewed by many as especially effective at organizing and implementing marketing efforts. These cases look at different ways of structuring product management and field marketing operations and the role of various systems and processes. The second category, the cases about Turner Construction Company and Honeywell's Commercial Avionics division, concerns the issues involved in developing and implementing corporatewide marketing programs within traditionally decentralized organizations. Finally, the concluding cases about Imperial Distributors and Pepsi-Cola provide consumer-goods contexts and decisions that require integrated consideration of many of the organizational and implementation issues considered in previous cases throughout this book.

The two IBM case studies describe IBM's U. S. field marketing organization over a twenty-year period. Neither case focuses on a decision or problem that must be solved. The (A) case concerns structure: It describes some major changes in the formal organization of IBM's field marketing efforts between 1966 and 1986 and briefly describes a major corporate reorganization in early

1988. The (B) case concerns systems and process: It discusses aspects of field marketing that remained constant throughout the changes described in the (A) case.

For the IBM (A) case, consider the following questions:

1. Many people believe IBM is an "excellent" marketing company. Based on what you see in this case history, do you agree?
2. At various times between 1966 and 1986, IBM's marketing efforts were organized by product category, by customer categories, and by geographical location. Which organization of marketing makes the most sense for this company in its product/market environment? What are the important issues involved in managing each type of organization?
3. Has IBM been well organized in marketing during the period covered by this case? Be sure to clarify what you mean by "well-organized" before rendering a judgment.

For the IBM (B) case, consider the following questions:

1. Much of this case describes certain aspects of field marketing at IBM: branch operations, how sales quotas are set, and incentive and recognition events. As a marketing manager, what would you seek to avoid or emulate in the way IBM conducts these activities?
2. In particular, consider the following topics:

   - "IBM had long operated by rotating line personnel across sales regions, and into and out of marketing staff positions at corporate headquarters." What is the impact of such a policy on branch operations? On continuity at the customer interface? On the individuals involved?

   - In its compensation and quota-setting process for marketing reps, IBM follows a procedure that one senior manager describes as "a top-down plan with bottom-up input." Does this make sense? What purposes (if any) are served by the manner in which IBM establishes annual quotas for business units, marketing managers, and individual marketing reps?

   - In its nonfinancial incentive systems, IBM sponsors a series of events. What, if anything, seems noteworthy about this company's use of awards and recognition events to motivate field personnel?

   - At the end of the (B) case, IBM's CEO exhorts company personnel to "put yourself in the customer's shoes. Look at their problems the way they do. And then solve those problems." This is standard advice and a staple of good marketing. In your view is the CEO's speech a good or a bad sign concerning IBM's marketing organization?

3. Has IBM been well organized during the period covered by the (A) and (B) cases? Be sure to clarify what you mean by "well organized" before rendering judgment.

The Procter & Gamble case study returns us to a specific decision-making context. This case concerns the options facing an associate advertising manager in Procter & Gamble's Packaged Soap and Detergent Division as he seeks to develop and implement a marketing strategy aimed at increasing the division's share in the light duty liquid detergent (LDL) category. The case also provides a detailed look at a classical brand management system, including its strengths, potential vulnerabilities, and the skills it requires of marketing managers.

In studying the Procter & Gamble case, consider these questions:

1. Why has Procter & Gamble been so successful in this product category? What is the logic underlying the positioning of Procter & Gamble's existing brands in the LDL category?
2. How do consumers buy and use LDLs? What are the implications of consumer behavior for product positioning and market segmentation in this frequently purchased product category?
3. Should Procter & Gamble introduce a fourth LDL brand? What criteria should guide any decision concerning new-product introductions vs. investments in existing brands in this category?
4. The first half of this case study details the marketing organization in a brand management system. What are the strengths and weaknesses of this type of marketing organization? How applicable is this organization to other product-market contexts (e.g., IBM, Frito-Lay)? Aside from brand management, what can you learn about marketing planning and marketing programming from Procter & Gamble's conduct of these activities?
5. During the 1980s, the packaged-goods environment underwent many significant changes. Some of the more important changes include a number of trends covered in some detail in the Actmedia case study (see Case 6): more heterogeneity among consumer segments; more impulse purchasing by consumers; increased information and power of the retail trade; many new products and line extensions in a mature market; and increased prevalence of two-career families. What are the implications of such market changes for the marketing organization described in this case study?

The next case study is the first of two cases in this final chapter about Pepsi-Cola's Fountain Beverage Division, that portion of Pepsi which markets its soft-drink products to restaurants, institutions, and other fountain outlets. Thus the case concerns consumer-goods marketing but of a different sort than that investigated in the Procter & Gamble case. In this case, the president of the Fountain Beverage Division (FBD) is considering what kinds of skills are required to conduct marketing effectively in this product-market environment and the kind of marketing organization likely to develop and sustain those skills.

Consider these questions as you analyze the case:

1. What are the key sales and marketing tasks in the fountain business? How do FBD's products go to market and what are the implications, in particular, for motivating and managing the bottler network for FBD?

2. What is the competitive significance of the fountain business in the "cola wars" described in the case?
3. Consider the history of FBD within the larger Pepsi organization. What has been FBD's traditional role and status at Pepsi? How would you describe the relationship between marketing operations at FBD and those at the larger Bottle-and-Can organization?
4. What are the stated goals of the proposed "channel marketing" organization discussed in the case? Is this proposed marketing organization the only, or best, way of accomplishing these goals? What are the implications of this proposed organization for FBD's hiring criteria in marketing? For its relationship with Bottle-and-Can? For its ability to perform important marketing and sales tasks with its bottler network and fountain customers?

The next two case studies in the chapter—Turner Construction Company and Honeywell's Commercial Avionics—concern the interaction of corporate and field perspectives on marketing decisions. In different ways, these cases raise a range of issues inherent in the centralization/decentralization tension at the heart of many marketing-organization decisions. The cases also illustrate the context in which managers usually confront important issues in marketing organization: a context marked by resource-allocation battles among different parts of the organization, limited time frames for analysis and implementation, diverse constituencies, and a situation in which (as one of the managers in these cases notes) "whatever organization we recommend must be capable of winning the commitment of the different parties involved. And nearly every option has the potential of disappointing people who will be key in implementing it."

Turner Construction Company operates in 16 territories in the United States, each territory headed by a general manager (GM) with profit-and-loss responsibilities. One GM has requested approval to pursue a commercial-building project in his territory while ignoring a lead concerning a hospital-building project. Mr. Robert Kupfer, an executive vice president at Turner, is responsible for approving all such project requests. He must decide whether to approve use of territory resources for the commercial project and whether (and how) to urge the territory GM to allocate resources to the hospital project.

In analyzing the Turner case, consider these questions:

1. How would you characterize the important marketing tasks in the construction business? Within Turner Construction Company, what level of the organization—local territory, regional management, or corporate headquarters—should be responsible for each task?
2. What are the major responsibilities, problems, and rewards of a territory general manager at Turner?
3. How would you segment the construction market from Turner's point of view? What are the attractive market segments? What are the important market trends? Who is Turner's major competition in each segment?

4. What should Mr. Kupfer do about the commercial building and hospital-building project proposals on his desk? How should he try to implement any course of action with regard to these projects?

Many of the issues raised by the Turner case appear in an international context in the Honeywell case, which concerns the implications for organizational structures and process of a global vs. multinational approach to international marketing and many factors that affect proposed reorganizations in marketing. In 1986, Honeywell acquired Sperry's avionics business, whose product line complements Honeywell's avionics business. To integrate the two groups, a task force has been established to recommend an organizational structure and measurement systems. However, Sperry and Honeywell have long followed different marketing and organizational strategies in their international markets. The task force must make several decisions: whether avionics is a global or multinational business; how to structure a combined international avionics business unit; and how to implement any recommendations in a complex, contentious organizational context.

The following questions may be useful in analyzing this situation:

1. What are the important product, market, and buying factors in the avionics business that should be considered in making these organizational decisions?

2. What are the important differences in Honeywell's vs. Sperry's traditional approach to the commercial avionics business? Why has each company historically pursued such a different approach?

3. What are the skills required to manage marketing programs effectively in the two marketing organizations described in this case study? Which set of skills seems relatively more important in the context of the international avionics business? In the context of the larger Honeywell organizations?

4. What specific recommendations should the task force make with regard to the options outlined in the final pages of the case narrative?

The final two case studies return us to organizations studied earlier in the book. Hence each case provides an opportunity to look in depth at organizational decisions in firms where we are already familiar with important business dynamics. In addition, each case introduces other issues that influence marketing organization. Since one case concerns a small privately held firm and the other a division of a large multibillion dollar corporation, an instructive contrast emerges as well.

In Imperial Distributors (B), the president of this service merchandiser is considering a specific proposal for reorganizing the company's marketing, sales, and service operations. Through a consultant, the president has studied the organizations of other service merchandisers in different parts of the country and must decide whether or not to adopt a revised structure and altered measurement and compensation systems at Imperial. If these recommendations are adopted, the president must also consider how to implement them at his company.

The following questions may help you analyze the complex decisions facing the president of Imperial Distributors:

1. Review the larger facts of the business as described in the Imperial Distributors (A) case. Given your evaluation, what are the key success factors in the service-merchandising business and thus the key criteria that any reorganization should try to address?

2. Consider the organizations of other service merchandisers described in the case. Explain the rationale for each firm's marketing, sales, and service activities. What measures seem appropriate in evaluating marketing productivity at each firm? What can we learn about marketing organization from these varied structures, systems, and performance results?

3. Consider the consultant's specific recommendations. Do the stated goals of these recommendations seem valid, given your evaluation of industry forces and Imperial's specific competitive situation? Do you agree with the assumptions behind these recommendations concerning the roles of profit-and-loss responsibility, shorter spans of control, sales supervision, and revised compensation systems in this marketing reorganization? Which of these recommendations seem to be easier or harder to implement and more or less important for improved organizational effectiveness?

4. Toward the end of the case, the president of Imperial Distributors outlines a number of concerns about the proposed recommendations and argues for the importance of "incentives" and process rather than "structure" in reorganizing marketing activities. How valid or important is each concern? How would you describe the relationship between the changes in structure and systems advocated by the consultant and the emphasis on incentives and process stressed by the president?

Our final case study, Pepsi-Cola Fountain Beverage Division: Tea Breeze, moves several levels down in the FBD organization studied earlier in this chapter. Among other things, this case illustrates the implications for the individual brand manager who works within the structure and systems described in the earlier case. Further, while pricing is the immediate issue in the Tea Breeze case, most other elements of the marketing mix are also implicated in this decision and so, in its required quantitative and qualitative analyses, the case is a capstone to our investigations concerning marketing implementation.

Consider these questions as you analyze the decisions facing Mr. John Knight, director of new product development and Tea Breeze:

1. What are the important elements of consumer behavior in this marketing situation? Of channel concerns and support? Of fountain-outlet criteria with respect to the proposed iced-tea product?
2. What is your evaluation of both the form and substance of the test-market procedures concerning Tea Breeze? What can, and cannot, be learned from the market data and test-market experience?
3. Consider the entire new-product development and introduction process described in this case and outlined in Exhibit 7. Should anything about the process itself, and management's expectations concerning that process, affect Mr. Knight's decisions about Tea Breeze?
4. Should Mr. Knight recommend a national roll-out of Tea Breeze? If so, what arguments should he make to convince the management review committee to support this course of action with the required resources? If not, what arguments should he make to the management committee to explain the cessation of a two-year effort on this project?

The Tea Breeze case places many issues we've studied previously in a context where marketing decisions must take into account the structures and process of marketing decision making in the organization. If you are studying this material in an MBA program, this case can make more relevant the many issues concerning marketing organization that previous cases have illustrated. The Tea Breeze case focuses on a young product manager whose decisions are like those that many MBA students can expect to encounter within a few years after graduation. These decisions must be informed by broad, industry-level, big picture analysis. But, these decisions are ultimately the relatively humble and crucial ones in marketing management: What price should we charge for this product? How do we motivate our salespeople and distribution channels to notice and support this product? What elements of buyer behavior will affect how we allocate our limited marketing and managerial resources? How do we convince others, both in marketing and other functional areas, that whatever recommendations we make should be funded and supported? Answering these questions—and making implicit career commitments on the basis of one's answers and actions regarding these questions—are at the heart of organizing and implementing the marketing effort.

References

1. Alfred D. Chandler, Jr., *Strategy and Structure* (New York: Doubleday, 1962), p. 13.
2. Ibid., p. 15.
3. E. Raymond Corey and Steven H. Star, *Organization Strategy: A Marketing Approach* (Boston, MA: Harvard Business School, Division of Research, 1971), p. 35.
4. James G. March and Herbert A. Simon, *Organizations* (New York: John Wiley & Sons, Inc., 1958).

5. Theodore Levitt, "Marketing Myopia," *Harvard Business Review* (July-August 1960): 24–47.

6. This categorization of marketing functions is based on Corey and Star, *Organization Strategy: A Marketing Approach,* passim.

7. Alfred P. Sloan, *My Years with General Motors* (New York: Doubleday, 1963), p. 505.

8. For important discussions of the organizational aspects of international marketing, see Robert D. Buzzell, "Can You Standardize Multinational Marketing?" *Harvard Business Review* (November-December 1968); Theodore Levitt, "The Globalization of Markets," *Harvard Business Review* (May-June 1983); Christopher A. Bartlett, "MNCs: Get Off the Reorganization Merry-Go-Round," *Harvard Business Review* (March-April 1983); and John A. Quelch and Edward J. Hoff, "Customizing Global Marketing," *Harvard Business Review* (May-June 1986).

9. See Michael E. Porter, *Competitive Advantage* (New York: The Free Press, 1985), pp. 317–363.

Marketing Organization in Leading Industrial and Consumer Goods Firms

Case 22
IBM Marketing Organization (A): Changes in Structure

IBM's growth is an exciting chapter in business history. Fired as sales manager of National Cash Register Company, Thomas Watson, Sr. in 1914 became head of the Computing-Tabulating-Recording Company, which produced butcher scales, meat slicers, coffee grinders, time clocks, and a limited line of punched-card tabulating machines. By 1924, when the company changed its name to International Business Machines, it was the leading manufacturer of punched card equipment, but sales were only $53 million by 1939.

During World War II, IBM developed concepts for computers, but management believed the sales potential of the computer was limited. In the early 1950s, several competitors moved into the lead. After 1952, IBM came from behind to achieve a leading position in commercial computers. The 1960s were marked by the development and marketing of IBM's System/360 line, which consolidated IBM's leading position in large commercial computers.

During the 1970s, new competitors arose in the minicomputer segments of the industry; the cost/performance ratios of computers continued to improve dramatically, and many new customers entered the market; IBM's own product lines grew increasingly complex and diverse; and the company's sales and profits grew rapidly. The early 1980s were marked by a continuation of these trends, especially changes in technology, customers, and marketing requirements brought on by the development of microcomputers. (See Exhibit 1 for selected financial data.)

IBM's management made a series of changes in the company's U.S. marketing organization between 1966 and 1986. This case describes the major reorganizations in the U.S. marketing organization and the reasons for each change. A subsequent case discusses processes in the field sales organization.

Organizational Structure

Before 1956, IBM was organized as a single business with time equipment, electric typewriters, and accounting machines as its major product lines. In 1956, however, the company was reorganized into four separate groups, one of which was made responsible for the design, manufacture, and sale and service of data processing (DP) equipment and programming. Self-contained and having a separate identity, the DP business grew rapidly, and by 1959, its sales exceeded total corporate sales for 1955 of $500 million.

In 1962, IBM decided to produce a new family of computers, the System/360. *Fortune* magazine called the S/360 decision "the most crucial and portentous—as well as perhaps the riskiest—business judgment of recent times."[1]

> The new System/360 was intended to obsolete virtually all other existing computers—including those being offered by IBM itself. Thus, the first and most extraordinary point to note about this decision is that it involved a challenge to the marketing structure of the computing industry—an industry the challenger itself had dominated overwhelmingly for nearly a decade. It was roughly as though General Motors had decided to scrap its existing makes and models and offer in their place one new line of cars, covering the entire spectrum of demand, with a radically redesigned engine and an exotic fuel.
>
> The effort involved in the program had been enormous. No company had ever introduced, in one swoop, six computer models of a totally new design, in a technology never tested in the marketplace, and with programming abilities of the greatest complexity. IBM spent over half a billion dollars on research and development programs associated with the 360. This involved a tremendous hunt for talent: by the end of this year [1966], one-third of IBM's 190,000 employees will have been hired since the new program was announced. Between April 1964 and the end of 1967, the company will have opened five new plants and budgeted a total of $4.5 billion for rental machines, plant and equipment. Not even the Manhattan Project, which produced the atomic bomb in World War II, cost so much (the government's costs up to Hiroshima are reckoned at $2 billion), nor, probably, has any other privately financed commercial project in history.

These investments were made by a company with total revenues of $3.5 billion in 1965, and what industry observers estimated to be the leading market share in worldwide computer sales at the time. One reason was that management perceived a risk in "doing nothing." Certain IBM managers believed that

---

[1] "IBM's $5,000,000,000 Gamble," *Fortune* (September 1966).

a move away from record keeping toward more sophisticated business applications was needed.

For IBM, the significance of the 360 decision was fivefold. First, the line depended on a new technology, integrated circuitry. Second, the line provided for systems compatibility so that as users' computational requirements grew, customers could trade up from one machine to another without having to discard existing software programs and peripheral equipment. Third, all major 360 products were introduced simultaneously, so that customers would perceive the full impact of the new line. This meant that all parts of the Data Processing Group had to adhere to a meticulous schedule.

Fourth, IBM, which had essentially been a developer and assembler of computer components and a sales-service organization, became a vertically integrated manufacturer of computers and soon the world's largest producer of integrated circuits and many associated computer components and peripheral products. Fifth, in order to spread these expenses over a sufficiently wide sales base, IBM effectively committed itself to a single worldwide product line. The company's World Trade subsidiary halted development of its own line of computers and became the company's international manufacturing and marketing organization.

Organization for the System/360

Commitment to a single worldwide DP product line necessitated centralized development. IBM entered new fields of manufacturing as it vertically integrated, so economies and expertise were important there as well, especially since a major goal was quick delivery—a challenging task for a company with large, customized, complex products. Finally, a dynamic marketplace made rapid operating decisions necessary, and this required closer coordination among dispersed units.

In 1966, IBM's Data Processing Group (DPG) was organized around the System/360 products with divisions separated by function: Systems Development, Components, Systems Manufacturing, Data Processing Division (DPD, marketing), and Field Engineering (service) (see Exhibit 2). Other operating units included the Office Products Division (OPD), which manufactured and marketed typewriters and associated equipment, and the Federal Systems Division (FSD), which developed and sold products to the U.S. government. DPD staff and field marketing units were oriented toward individual industries, as they had been since 1960.

By the early 1970s, however, two developments impacted the company. First, the success of the S/360 line encouraged the growth of "plug-compatible manufacturers" (PCMs), which found it profitable to copy IBM's products and "plug" their machines into the standard interfaces and software developed by IBM. Without development costs of the computer hardware or software, these companies were often able to sell their products at substantially lower prices.

Second, although IBM had continuing competition from other mainframe manufacturers, minicomputers[2] had emerged as a growing market by the early 1970s. Certain IBM senior managers also believed that the System/360 (and its compatible successor, the System/370), while an undeniable success, had been too great a risk. As a result, IBM formed divisions throughout the 1970s to design smaller products with an emphasis on certain market segments rather than on compatibility with the 360/370 lines. In addition, technology advances and improved price/performance allowed for development of different systems for a broad base of businesses.

Development of Product Marketing Organizations (1969–1975)

The decision to give small systems more emphasis and to increase the customer base drove reorganization throughout the 1970s. In 1969, IBM established the General Systems Division within the Data Processing Group to manufacture and develop low-cost information systems. This was the first step toward creating a fully integrated low-end product group. IBM also began to place more emphasis on applications development in the early 1970s. It was decided that marketing should have the opportunity and ability to assess advanced applications software, since its development was driven by the customer as well as technology. Also, more industry specialists were added at the local branch level to maintain applications expertise as IBM developed more specific product families. Meanwhile, it became clear that semiconductor technology required more integration of manufacturing and product development.

In 1972, IBM Chairman T. V. Learson explained the reasons for IBM's next major organizational change:

> In any given period in as fast-moving a business as this, we have a given set of problems to manage, a given set of opportunities to exploit. In 1966, when the Data Processing Group was established, there was an overriding need for integration and control in the production and marketing of our first compatible system of computers, the System/360.
>
> Six years have passed and we have come to a couple of important turning points in the business. First, there is the need for greater responsiveness in the marketplace; we want to deal more effectively with increasing competition and accelerate the development of new and advanced marketing opportunities. And second, there is the need for closer technological integration in the design and manufacture of systems to meet those market demands.

---

[2]Mainframes were large, multi-user computer systems appropriate for general commercial applications in big businesses; prices were typically several hundred thousand dollars or more. Minicomputers could be loosely defined as small mainframes: they were intended to interact with several users at once, yet would generally average less than a quarter of the size and price of mainframes. Microcomputers were desktop machines meant to interact with one user at a time; prices during the 1980s ranged from a few hundred dollars to a few thousand.

In 1972, Data Processing Group was broken into two new groups: DP Product Group and DP Marketing Group (see Exhibit 3). A third group, General Business Group, managed IBM's other domestic operating units.

DP Marketing Group had responsibility for the Data Processing Division (DPD, sales) and Field Engineering Division (service), as well as the Advanced Systems Development Division for applications development. DPD concentrated on developing more product expertise in the field, and consolidated certain branches in order to concentrate those resources. Marketing Representatives in field branches were generally organized by system size and/or industry. This was the start of the product-oriented marketing programs developed in the 1970s.

The DP Product Group set up its operations by product line, with divisions having full development and manufacturing responsibility for their respective products. The Systems Development Division was responsible for systems architecture and programming, the Systems Products Division built central processors and memory and logic circuitry, and the General Products Division manufactured peripheral equipment such as magnetic memory storage units and printers.

In 1974, the General Systems Division (GSD) was given full marketing and service responsibility for the smaller computers it manufactured and developed. The purpose of this move was to complete the integration of functions and resources needed to compete in the market against minicomputer manufacturers. GSD sales and service units were set up in the United States and abroad.

At the same time, the General Business Group (GBG) was reoriented to manage all of IBM's small systems and office products. The Federal Systems Division was moved into the DP Marketing Group, and GBG took over the General Systems Division, the Office Products Division (OPD), which sold typewriters, copiers, dictation equipment and word processors, and the Information Records Division, which produced business forms and magnetic storage media. The major objective was to give a low-end product group its own resources to compete independently. Finally, in 1975, GSD's international marketing units were consolidated in GBG under the General Business Group/International Division (GBGI). This completed the integration task begun in 1969 (see Exhibit 4).

New Concerns in the 1970s

Although GSD started out selling small systems to small customers, larger customers were beginning to distribute their data processing functions and were therefore also interested in smaller systems. So by the mid-1970s when GSD sold its small systems to a customer which also used a competing vendor's mainframe, GSD would assign an account manager to be responsible for all IBM sales to that account, including attempts at replacing the customer's non-IBM mainframe with a DPD system. Likewise, if a current IBM mainframe customer wanted to add small systems to its network, the DPD account manager would be responsible for selling GSD equipment. However, GSD representatives did not have expertise in the larger equipment sold by DPD, and vice-versa. Meanwhile, systems developed by the DP and General Business Products Groups began to overlap in terms of functions performed. Large-systems were becoming multi-stationed for flexibility (so that data could be coordinated among a customer's various units or branches), and small systems were becoming more powerful because of technological and price/performance improvements.

Increasingly, field marketing reps from DPD and GSD were calling on many of the same customers. One manager recalled that, "Customers needed help putting systems together, and heard competing proposals instead. As a consequence, customers began complaining to management. On top of this, salespeople from GSD complained of second-class status compared to DPD reps, and GSD management complained of resource preferences given to DPD." In addition, it became harder to assign development and marketing responsibilities for new intermediate-sized systems.

Headquarters management soon perceived that product policy decisions as well as field morale were at stake. Yet immediate changes were not made for several reasons. First, many believed that not enough time had been given for the recent organizational changes to settle and produce results. Second, it was hard to determine if the problems were due to organization or to a rapidly changing product/market environment. IBM's product lines were becoming increasingly diverse and complex, and different market segments required substantially different approaches and solutions. The office products market, for example, was expanding into diverse environments as traditional office products became increasingly computerized. Between 1974 and 1979, moreover, IBM's revenues had nearly doubled, and management systems were inevitably taxed. But growth required diversity to meet customers' needs as technology advanced rapidly.

By 1979, IBM was marketing a number of product families which used different software operating systems. Further, new business opportunities were appearing quickly and without any single unit clearly responsible for addressing them. Finally, IBM's technical resources were spread out organizationally so that transfer of technological expertise among product groups was hampered.

IBM's mainframe competition in this era was known as "the BUNCH" (*B*urroughs, Sperry/*U*nivac, *N*ational Cash Register, *C*ontrol Data Corporation, and *H*oneywell Information Systems). Throughout the 1970s IBM's sales exceeded total sales of these competitors. By the later 1970s, minicomputer manufacturers such as DEC, Data General, and Hewlett-Packard had grown dramatically and achieved strong positions in certain segments such as universities and scientific/engineering environments. But none of these competitors had achieved more than a few percent of the revenues IBM had annually throughout this period.

Issues for the 1980s

IBM's 1980 Annual Report stated:

> Not only do we see growth in traditional computer systems, we also see an important expansion in applications that use communications to tie together parts of an enterprise. Another major growth area is the sale of information products to small businesses and individual users. Our studies indicate that only a small percentage of those who can economically justify a computer actually have installations today. In all these areas of IBM's business, we are finding significant market elasticity. As technical innovation lowers the price of information processing, the lower price attracts new users. It also produces greater use by present customers and stimulates the development of entirely new applications.
>
> To ensure superior products, we are investing heavily in the several dozen key technologies that drive the information processing industry ahead. Our emphasis is not only on speed, capacity and performance, but also on making products easier to use. Our product development includes improvements in software, so that the users of our machines will require less training in data processing.

In IBM's 1983 Annual Report, moreover, Chairman John Opel emphasized that the company's strategy for the 1980s "was established back in the mid-1970s with a program of sizable investments in plant, equipment, research and development." Opel noted:

> Central to IBM's strategy are four key business goals—growth, product leadership, efficiency and profitability. To attain these goals in today's highly competitive environment, we have placed increased emphasis on innovative programs in the design, manufacture and distribution of our products and services. . . . We are moving higher volumes of products through our organization and into our customers' offices.

Growth was defined as "growing with the industry." According to one industry source, this translated into a target of 15% annual average revenue growth through 1994. Meeting this objective, moreover, effectively required IBM's U. S. operating units to achieve better than 15% annual revenue growth, since exchange rates and other economic factors hampered growth of the corporation's international business at the time. Similarly, "efficiency" was defined in the chairman's letter as "achieving maximum productivity in every area of our business." In manufacturing, this included "more standardization and coordination among our plants . . . helping us control costs while we increase production." But beyond manufacturing, the efficiency goal included "the introduction of many new ways to market and service our products . . . to reach more customers economically."

Financially, IBM's strategy implied a revised pattern of resource allocations for the corporation. IBM reduced the amount of cash invested in rental machines, and redirected those funds into three areas: plant and property (primarily new and upgraded manufacturing facilities), program products (i.e., software development), and various investments. From 1977 to 1986, IBM's investments in the above three categories increased, while its investments in rental machines decreased. (See Table 1.)

The decreased investment in rental machines was also encouraged by changes in IBM's pricing policies during this period: for much of its product line, the purchase/lease ratios for IBM equipment were altered to favor purchase. John Akers, chairman of IBM, explained:

> Product life cycles have become shorter and shorter. You can't expect to design a machine, put a rental price on it, and expect it to maintain its rental price for 3, 4, or 5 years. A competitor will come out with a comparable machine in 3 or 4 months, and we will have to cut our price. And it became very difficult to implement price decreases when you've got all of that rental inventory out there.[3]

This revised pricing policy impacted IBM's cash flow in two ways: with purchase customers paid "up front" rather than over a stated rental term, and purchase required less working capital on the part of IBM than rentals. In effect, the cash released by the decreased investments in rental machines was utilized to help fund the billions invested in plant and property during this period. Conversely, rental revenues declined. (See Table 2.)

In turn, these changes in resource and revenue streams had marketing implications. Given its investments in manufacturing and R&D, IBM's corporate management was naturally concerned with managing marketing functions as efficiently as possible. In practice, this meant an increased concern with marketing expense-to-revenue ratios and more emphasis on reducing sales and support costs associated with direct sales of many products, especially the lower-margin, "low-end" products. As one marketing manager commented:

> At IBM, profit-and-loss responsibilities have traditionally been lodged with the product divisions, and not the marketing organization. Expense/revenue ratios then become a fundamental measure in marketing, since we don't set prices or terms-and-conditions for the products we sell. E/R is easy to compute, easy to understand, and an influential management tool.

In addition, decreased rental revenues placed additional emphasis on maximizing market coverage in order to encourage as much sales growth as possible on an annual basis. As an IBM manager noted:

> Decreased rental revenues mean the corporation is potentially more vulnerable to cyclical swings in demand. For years, the installed base of rental machines insulated us from those swings. It also means that forecasting demand is more important, since manufacturing output is based on those forecasts. For the product divisions, it means a primary concern is to move product and a secondary concern is through which channel it moves. And for marketing, it means that achieving quota has more than the usual importance, and more outlets for a product become more important.

---

[3] *The Harbus News* (April 13, 1987), p. 8.

Table 1

IBM Funds Flow: Cash Utilization
($ millions)

	1977	1978	1979	1980	1981	1982	1983	1984	1985	1986
Investments In:										
Rental machines	2,475	2,723	4,212	4,334	4,610	3,293	1,412	858	313	(128)[a]
Plant & property	920	1,322	1,779	2,258	2,235	3,392	3,518	4,615	6,117	4,748
Program products	—	—	—	—	348	468	588	803	785	907
Increase (decrease) in investments & other assets	176	132	338	275	105	(320)	1,887	1,764	454	1,678
Total Utilization	3,571	4,177	6,329	6,867	7,298	6,833	7,405	8,040	7,669	7,205
Total Utilization Minus Rental Machines Investments	1,096	1,454	2,117	2,533	2,688	3,540	5,993	7,182	7,356	7,333

Source: Annual reports.

Table 2

IBM Revenues: Sales, Service and Rentals
($ millions)

	1977	1978	1979	1980	1981	1982	1983	1984	1985	1986
Sales	$ 7,090	$ 8,755	$ 9,473	$10,919	$12,901	$16,815	$23,274	$29,753	$34,584	$34,276
Services	11,043	2,540	3,321	4,425	5,330	6,428	7,676	9,605	11,356	14,301
Rentals		9,781	10,069	10,869	10,839	11,121	9,230	6,579	4,116	2,673
	$18,133	$21,076	$22,863	$26,213	$29,070	$34,364	$40,180	$45,937	$50,056	$51,250

[a] Investment in rental machines is a composite of two amounts: the dollar value of rental machines capitalized in the year and the change in rental machine inventory. In 1986, the change to rental machine inventory was negative and exceeded the amount being capitalized.

IBM's manufacturing strategy also impacted marketing goals. Much of IBM's manufacturing investments during this period were made in highly automated capital-intensive facilities that depended on high volumes and high capacity utilization to achieve scale economies and reduced per-unit manufacturing costs. The need for volume was, in turn, reflected in the quota-setting process for marketing.

Emergence of Customer-Size Organization (1980–1984)

In 1980, the General Business Group (GBG) was restructured to create a single profit center from two fully integrated divisions (General Systems Division [GSD] and Office Products Division [OPD]) whose activities were beginning to overlap. All GBG development and manufacturing were consolidated in one division called the Information Systems Division and service units for GSD and OPD were consolidated as the Customer Service Division. Meanwhile, GBG's components unit was merged with DPPG's corresponding unit. In 1981, the three computer systems groups (the DP Marketing Group, the DP Product Group, and the General Business Group) were eliminated and three new ones formed: the Information Systems Group, the Information Systems & Communications Group, and the Information Systems & Technology Group. The Information Systems Group (ISG) took over all of IBM's marketing functions, including the three domestic sales divisions (DPD, GSD, and OPD), and the two service divisions: the Customer Service Division (small systems) and Field Engineering Division (large systems). GBG/International was gradually folded back into IBM's World Trade Corporation (the arm responsible for all international marketing).

IBM's development and manufacturing divisions were now organized into two new groups, the Information Systems & Communications Group (smaller systems, communications, and office products) and the Information Systems & Technology Group (larger systems, data storage, and components). IBM's chairman John Opel announced at that time:

> The restructuring of our manufacturing and development divisions into two new groups will put similar or related products under common management. This will allow us to take greater advantage of rapid changes taking place in technology and to coordinate long-range product plans more effectively.
>
> The new marketing group structure is the first step toward our objective of offering the broad array of IBM's products through individual marketing units that retain within them the degree of product, system, and industry specialization necessary to bring the best service to each customer. To achieve that objective, we will combine, early in 1982, the resources of the Data Processing, General Systems, and Office Products divisions into two new divisions. Each division will market the full product line to a specific set of customers.

In 1982, two new marketing divisions were established: the National Accounts Division (NAD), assigned to IBM's 2400 largest customers, and the National Marketing Division (NMD), serving all other accounts. The Field

Engineering Division continued to service large systems, and the Customer Service Division serviced small systems, no matter which division had originally installed the products (see Exhibit 5). Additionally, IBM's various supplies units were joined under the Systems Supplies Division, which marketed consumable products to all U.S. customers. Finally, IBM's various customer financing programs were consolidated under the IBM Credit Corporation. In 1983, Chairman Opel noted, "We have reshaped our organization as necessary to adapt to a changing environment marked by a significant growth of our industry. Our strategy has focused on ensuring our full participation in that growth."

Personal Computers and Indirect Channels of Distribution

By the early 1980s, technological developments had made computers economical for individual users. For many users, minicomputers, and soon microcomputers, could be more economical than mainframes. Organizationally, the user of a smaller computer had more independence and control over processing than did someone who shared a mainframe. And technically, hardware and software maintenance could be distributed to the end users, simplifying an organization's central MIS responsibilities.

By August 1981, when IBM introduced its first personal computer (PC), the market had already been entered by manufacturers such as Apple and Tandy/Radio Shack. IBM set up an independent business unit called Entry Systems for PC development, manufacturing, and marketing. The unit was outside mainstream IBM operations and free to develop whatever systems and strategies seemed best suited for the new product line. Entry Systems management decided to develop an "open-architecture" which encouraged third-party development of applications software and peripheral equipment. To sell this lower-priced equipment, the unit also set up a retail distribution network through independent dealers. This was significant since IBM had traditionally sold all of its products through its direct sales force. Entry Systems also used components (including the central processor) from third parties rather than proprietary sources, since development schedules were short and budgets tight. Finally, the PC's operating system software was developed outside IBM, and the developer was free to sell the system independently of IBM.

Demand for the IBM PC far outstripped management's expectations. Entry Systems' manufacturing capacity was unprepared for such volumes, so by 1982 competitors were already manufacturing compatible machines, dubbed "clones." It wasn't until 1984 that IBM's plants got up to full speed, and by then several clone manufacturers were well entrenched. But the IBM architecture and operating system had become the industry standard, and by 1986, there were an estimated 350 IBM-compatible PC manufacturers.

In 1983, Entry Systems was integrated into IBM's main structure: under IS&CG, the Entry Systems Division retained only development and manufacturing functions. But the unit had developed a strong nucleus of dealer-marketing skills particularly appropriate for relatively low unit-price items. It was considered uneconomical for IBM sales reps to work on selling single units of $2000 machines when they could be selling larger multiples of personal computers or larger systems that sold for hundreds of thousands of dollars or more.

Other IBM units had also developed their own mass-marketing distribution in order to lower selling expenses on lower-price products. The Systems Supplies Division sold paper, printer ribbons, business forms, and other consumable commodities through dealers. Typewriters had been sold through dealers for several years, and Retail Centers (showrooms) had been set up in the early 1980s for office products and small systems. IBM Direct had been organized to mail flyers to potential customers of small systems, and for several years IBM had used Value Added Resellers (VARs) to sell its minicomputers as "turnkey" (ready to use) systems with applications software.

All of these channels selling to remarketers were joined under the National Distribution division (NDD) within ISG in 1983. NDD tasks included advertising, dealer selection, demand creation, sales training for VARs, and integrating "alternate" (i.e., indirect) channels into marketing efforts. By 1984, NDD had contracts with over 3,600 dealers in 7 programs: 2,200 PC dealers, 600 typewriter dealers (plus selected wholesalers who supplied remote dealers), 600 "value-added dealers," 200 "dealer-associated VARs," 15 industrial distributors, and 20 special and miscellaneous outlets. NDD also managed IBM's product center showrooms. One manager emphasized that IBM's objective in using third-party channels was primarily coverage of a growing, increasingly diverse customer base.

In NDD branch offices, Dealer Account Managers (DAMs) each covered 10–20 outlets (1–3 dealers). Their functions were to support the dealers and "promote revenue": volume was the focus rather than account development. Half the DAM's time was spent managing inventory issues (receivables, expense, logistics). In 1982 IBM defined a single ticket price of $25,000 as the efficient minimum for direct sales effort, but that estimate soon rose to $50,000. By 1985 the average NDD salesperson generated 50 times the revenue of a person in direct sales. Third-party revenues for IBM rose from an estimated $600 million in 1981 to $4 billion by 1984.

While sales through indirect channels increased significantly, adding these channels raised a number of issues for IBM. As computing costs declined, larger machines became candidates for indirect distribution, and thus demarcation points between direct and indirect channels were fluid and sometimes overlapping. Many direct salespeople at IBM resisted the addition of indirect channels. Direct sales reps began to receive commission and measurement credit for sales made in their territories by resellers, and each year IBM attempted to refine the tracking of installation by indirect channels. But, according to management, the process remained "cumbersome." In addition, the sales force often complained that coordinating with resellers was difficult and time consuming. Further, a large order of low-end equipment was often a bone of contention between direct and indirect channels: while larger corporate customers of PCs could arrange volume pricing through their IBM account managers, they could take delivery from either IBM or a reseller, and typically a reseller would deliver faster from stock. Finally, the addition of indirect channels involved issues that one executive explained as follows: "For a company like IBM that has grown up on deeply held ideas about customer service and account control, working with intermediaries can be a culture shock in the field. These people sell competitors' equipment, they talk differently, have other selling objectives, and respond to very different incentives and goals."

Emergence of Geographical Marketing Organization (1985–1987)

Commenting on the NAD/NMD organization, one manager noted:

> From an information systems point of view, General Motors and the U.S. Army often have more in common than GM and American Motors. Organizing by size of account helps to focus these needs and is also useful when basic systems transitions are required. In addition, IBM's own size and product history have traditionally given the company a natural affinity for large accounts, and that orientation endured throughout the various reorganizations of the seventies.

At the same time, coordination between NAD and NMD field marketing units soon became an issue. Although the NAD large-customer list was gradually cut from approximately 2,400 to 1,800 accounts, the boundary between NAD and NMD accounts was a constant source of contention. A number of conflicts arose over which organization had ongoing sales and service for all locations of a given account. One problem was that, throughout this period, corporate MIS managers were often not the primary decision makers for products such as personal computers in many large organizations.

In addition, many IBM managers became concerned about the resource utilization implications of the customer-size organization. Although NAD and NMD sales, engineering, and service resources might share the same building, they were infrequently brought together at the customer interface because they were separate administratively. The lowest-level manager shared by NAD and NMD was the ISG Group Executive, who reported directly to a Corporate Management Board executive. Consequently, local and regional managers in NAD and NMD complained about the time taken to make decisions that impacted both marketing organizations.

In 1984, therefore, ISG's service divisions were combined into the National Service Division to act as a central service resource for both NAD and NMD. In early 1986, NAD and NMD were reorganized into two new marketing divisions (see Exhibit 6): the North/Central Marketing Division and the South/West Marketing Division. Account responsibilities were determined by the location of a customer's headquarters. Each division was organized into six or seven areas, and each area into two regions that covered a total of 240 local branches, each marketing the full line of IBM products, about 2,000 line items in total.

However, by 1986, according to one manager, "The desired simplicity in organization was stressed by the increasing complexity of the product lines.

With thousands of different products to sell, a given marketing rep was less likely to develop expertise in either the full range of technologies available or the possible applications for a given set of customers." Therefore, IBM put renewed emphasis on industry application knowledge and systems integration support for its field force through a new market development/customer sector organization. Each sector focused on a specific industry (e.g., financial services, transportation) or a sophisticated computer application (e.g., networking). Customers had access to these staff groups through the geographical marketing divisions.

Thus, between 1966 and 1986, IBM's field marketing efforts were organized, first, with a product orientation, then in terms of customer size, and then geographically. Commenting on IBM's reorganizations during this period, one observer noted "the apparent paradox that the industry's largest company is also one of its most agile":[4]

> Few companies organize as frequently or as radically as IBM. . . . IBM's competitive edge has been in fast and effective organizational response. IBM is no better than anyone else at identifying trends or recognizing problems. Nor is the average IBM manager or planner better than anyone else's. What IBM is uncommonly good at is shuffling its organization structure around to deploy management, capital and technical resources to exploit an opportunity or address a problem.
>
> A technique that helps IBM's organizational shuffle succeed is contention management. This involves setting objectives for the divisions that in some cases create product and marketing overlap. The practice produces competitive and incompatible products, and is bound to upset one or more sales organizations. . . . IBM differs considerably from those vendors who are careful to coordinate product strategies and manage interchannel conflict. Those vendors have fewer problems to resolve. They also typically have smaller market shares.

Current Events

At year-end 1985, IBM's worldwide market position in various computer categories was estimated as follows:

Large Systems (more than $350,000)		Small Systems ($12,000–$349,999)		Microsystems (less than $12,000)	
IBM	62.6%	IBM	20.0%	IBM	27.7%
Burroughs	6.5	DEC	12.7	Apple	9.0
Sperry	2.8	Nixdorf	6.0	Commodore	4.2
DEC	2.8	Hewlett-Packard	5.8	Hewlett-Packard	4.2
Fujitsu	2.8	Wang	4.3	NEC	3.6
Hitachi	2.6	Burroughs	2.8	AT&T	3.5
Control Data	2.6	NCR	2.7	Tandy	3.1
Amdahl	2.5	AT&T	2.4	Wang	2.7
Other	11.7	Other	36.1	Other	42.0

Source: Wall Street Journal, April 7, 1986.

---

[4]Brian Jeffrey, "IBM's Protean Ways," *Datamation* (January 1, 1986), pp. 65–68.

In 1986, IBM's revenues were $51 billion and net income was nearly $4.8 billion, but the latter figure represented a 27 percent decline from 1985 and the second straight year earnings had dropped (the first time this had happened at IBM in 50 years). By early 1986, the company had begun efforts to reduce costs. It imposed limitations on hiring, cut discretionary spending, reduced overtime and began encouraging employees to take vacations and use deferred vacation time. IBM also began shifting more than 5,000 headquarters staff and plant and lab personnel into field marketing positions.

In September 1986, IBM consolidated the headquarters staffs of its direct sales divisions and the Information Systems Group (ISG) into a single national support organization. "This is a significant step in the evolution of our direct sales organization," said Mr. Edward Lucente, head of ISG. "A single support staff will eliminate duplication of services and allow us to shift additional resources to our sales offices across the country."

In December 1986, IBM announced an early retirement program. By mid-1987 more than 13,000 IBM U.S. employees had opted for an early retirement incentive, and another 15,000 had been redeployed into new jobs, primarily sales. Headquarters staffs everywhere had been either trimmed or eliminated and critical areas such as marketing and programming substantially reinforced.

In January 1988, IBM announced a major restructuring (see Exhibit 7) which included the establishment of five new, highly independent businesses, the creation of a new organization ("IBM United States"), and transfer from corporate headquarters to the new businesses and IBM United States the responsibility for many daily operating decisions. The five new businesses were responsible for worldwide product development (including product line revenue and profitability) and marketing planning, as well as U. S. manufacturing. The new lines of business were: 1) IBM Enterprise Systems, responsible for mainframe products and software; 2) IBM Application Business Systems, responsible for low-end products and software; 3) IBM Personal Systems, responsible for PCs, most printers, typewriters, copiers, and other consumer products and software; 4) IBM Communication Systems, responsible for communications products and software; 5) IBM Technology Products, responsible for semiconductors and packaging for systems and technology products. Each line-of-business general manager had an IBM Management Committee member in the role of "review executive" to assist with responsibilities, with primary focus on product-line excellence. IBM's Management Committee continued to establish corporate policy and the fundamental strategic direction of the business.

IBM United States was responsible for U.S. revenue and profit. It also oversaw the new businesses with responsibility for worldwide marketplace requirements and interconnectivity between systems. Chairman John Akers noted that this restructuring "builds upon the actions we have taken over the last two years to streamline our business and enhance our partnership with customers. Having a general manager with responsibility for U.S. revenue, profit and day-to-day operations, permits key decisions to be made lower in the company, quicker and closer to customers than was possible before."

As of early 1988, the restructuring did not affect the organization of IBM's U. S. field marketing operations, which continued to be organized as depicted in Exhibit 6 into three major units: a full-line sales force organized geographically into North-Central and South-West divisions and the National Distribution Division with responsibility for indirect channels utilized by IBM.

Exhibit 1   IBM Marketing Organization (A): Changes in Structure

Financial Information, 1950–1986
(dollars in millions except per share data)

	1950	1960	1970	1976	1980	1981	1982	1983	1984	1985	1986
Operating Statement											
Gross revenues											
Domestic	215	1,436	4,571	8,150	12,426	15,088	19,028	23,127	27,371	28,511	25,362
Foreign	51	381	2,933	8,154	13,787	13,982	15,336	17,053	18,566	21,545	25,888
Total	266	1,817	7,504	16,304	26,213	29,070	34,364	40,180	45,937	50,056	51,250
Net Earnings (after tax)	37	205	1,018	2,398	3,562	3,610	4,409	5,485	6,582	6,555	4,789
Percent of revenues	31.91%	11.28%	13.60%	14.70%	13.60%	12.40%	12.80%	13.70%	14.33%	13.10%	9.57%
Per Share Data											
Earnings	0.08	0.39	1.78	3.99	6.10	6.14	7.39	9.04	10.77	10.67	7.81
Dividends	0.02	0.10	0.96	2.00	3.44	3.44	3.44	3.71	4.10	4.40	4.40
Balance Sheet											
Cash and marketable securities	29	320	1,339	6,156	2,112	2,029	3,300	5,536	4,362	5,622	7,257
Other current assets	40	252	2,050	3,764	7,813	8,274	9,714	11,734	16,013	20,448	20,492
Fixed assets and other	231	964	5,150	7,803	16,703	19,283	19,527	19,973	22,433	26,564	30,065
Total	300	1,536	8,539	17,723	26,703	29,586	32,541	37,243	42,808	52,634	57,814
Current liabilities	45	138	1,877	4,082	6,526	7,320	8,209	9,507	9,640	11,433	12,743
Pension reserves, deferred taxes and other liabilities	6	—	142	617	1,625	1,436	1,521	1,843	3,410	5,256	6,528
Long-term debt	85	425	573	275	2,099	2,669	2,851	2,674	3,269	3,955	4,169
Stockholders' equity	164	973	5,947	12,749	16,453	18,161	19,960	23,219	26,489	31,990	34,374
Total	300	1,536	8,539	17,723	26,703	29,586	32,541	37,243	42,808	52,634	57,814
Ratio and Other Information											
Return on equity	22.6%	21.1%	17.1%	18.8%	21.6%	21.1%	23.4%	25.4%	26.5%	22.4%	14.4%
Long-term debt percent of equity	51.8%	43.7%	9.6%	2.2%	12.8%	15.1%	14.3%	11.5%	12.3%	12.4%	12.1%
Number of employees (000s)	30	104	269	292	341	355	365	370	395	406	404
Number of shareholders (000s)	17	127	587	577	737	742	726	770	793	798	793

Exhibit 2 IBM Marketing Organization (A): Changes in Structure

IBM Organization, 1966

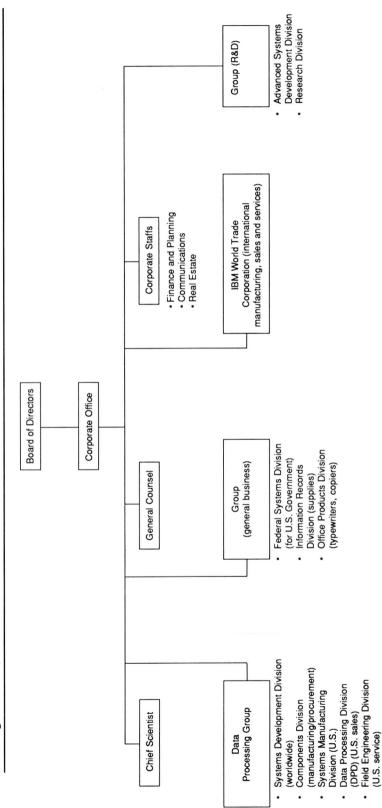

Exhibit 3   IBM Marketing Organization (A): Changes in Structure

IBM Organization, 1972

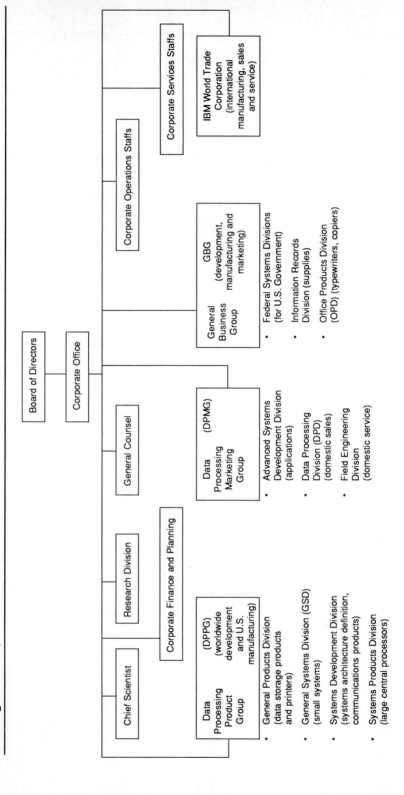

Exhibit 4   IBM Marketing Organization (A): Changes in Structure

IBM Organization, 1975

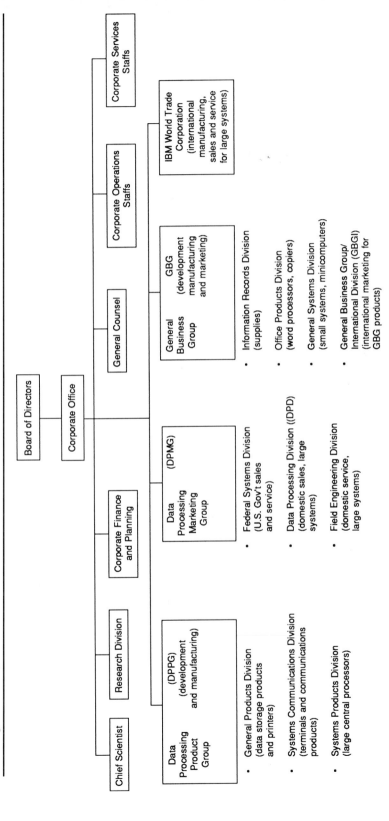

Exhibit 5 IBM Marketing Organization (A): Changes in Structure

IBM Organization, 1982

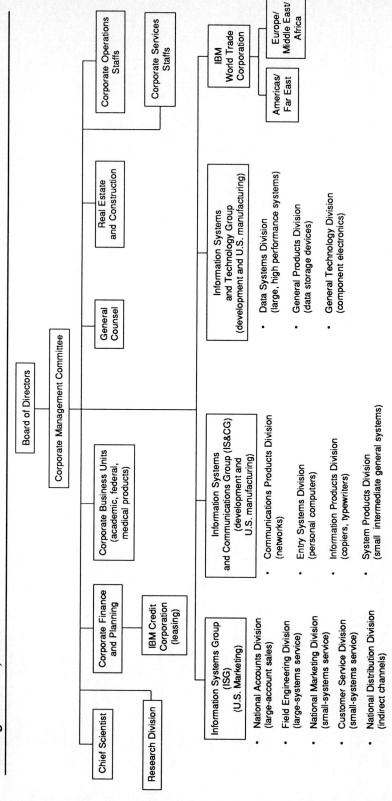

Exhibit 6 IBM Marketing Organization (A): Changes in Structure

IBM Organization, 1986

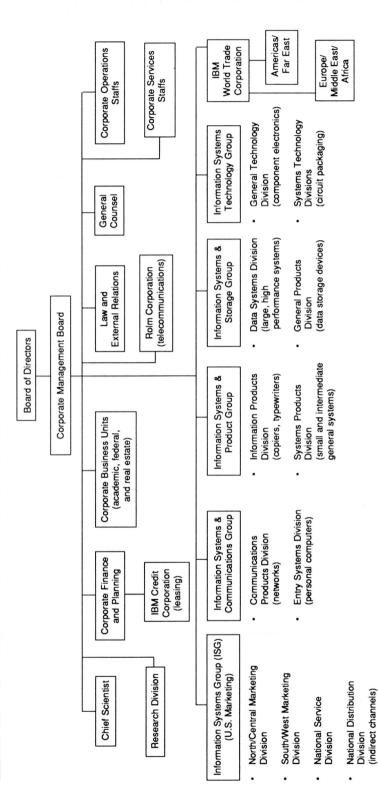

Exhibit 7 *IBM Marketing Organization (A): Changes in Structure*

Corporate Organization, January 28, 1988

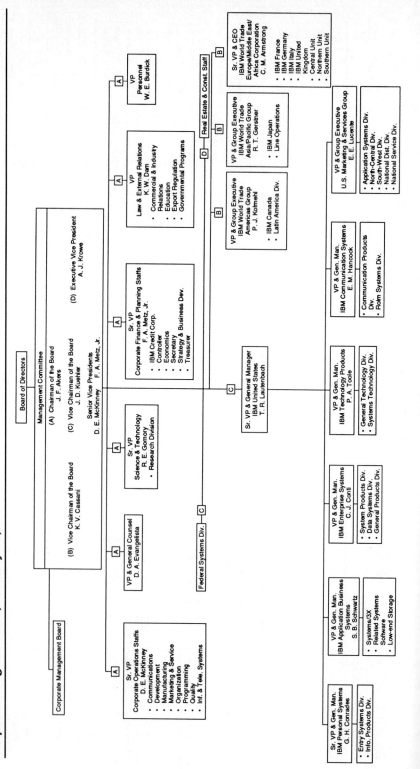

Case 23
IBM Marketing Organization (B): Process

Throughout the changes in structure described in the IBM Marketing Organization (A) case, certain field processes and systems remained relatively constant features of IBM's marketing programs. These include the role of the branch manager in the field sales organization, the compensation and recognition systems for field marketing representatives, an emphasis on industry specialization, and attention to "leadership" and new accounts.

Branch Management

Throughout the 1960s, IBM's field organization had three levels: regions, districts, and branches. As the business grew and branches became larger, the regional offices gradually took over functions performed by the districts. Regional managers served as reporting and performance review points for branch managers. Approximately 8–15 branch managers reported to each regional manager, making it possible for the latter to maintain close surveillance of branch operations and to advise, counsel, and appraise branch managers. Regional offices also developed and consolidated detailed sales and financial plans and budgets. In the other direction, they translated overall quotas and sales objectives into goals for field branches. Some regional offices also served as the locus for certain specialized resources such as education centers for training IBM and customer personnel. Finally, regional management participated directly in selling efforts, providing "high level" contacts with key customers and working on critical competitive situations. One regional

---

Associate Professor Frank V. Cespedes and Research Associate Jon E. King prepared this case as the basis for class discussion rather than to illustrate either effective or ineffective handling of an administrative situation.

manager noted that he spent time each week reviewing a "hot five" list with his staff.

Below the regions, the branch was the key unit, and its basic structure changed little throughout the period covered by this case (although individual branches differed considerably in their particular assignments depending upon the business in a given area). Reporting to the Branch Manager were Marketing Managers, who each directed 5–12 Marketing Reps, and Systems Engineering Managers, who each directed 7–12 Systems Engineers (see the Exhibit 1). Whereas the Marketing Rep's responsibility was to identify customer needs, Systems Engineers were technical staff who worked in developing viable product solutions through customization, programming, and installation of equipment. A typical branch was responsible for 100 account relationships, although branches focused by customer size might have as many as 4,000 or as few as 12. An "active" account required assignment of at least one salesperson assisted as necessary by systems engineering staff. On average, a marketing rep serviced 10 existing accounts and also sought out new business as appropriate.

Also reporting to the branch manager were several Administrative Managers responsible for the branch's clerical and administrative staff. A branch might also have a specialist systems engineering unit for certain advanced systems applications. A branch manager with responsibility for particularly large accounts usually had one or more Account Executives in the branch who, in turn, managed marketing and systems engineering managers. One branch manager noted:

> A number of Account Executives have VIP status at IBM. Their relations with important accounts have often lasted for years, and they've become confidants to top managers at those accounts and often on issues that range beyond DP. At those accounts, everyone at IBM checks with the Account Executive before approaching the account for *any* reason.

Within the branch marketing line hierarchy, IBM generally recognized five levels. Working upward from the entry position of the marketing trainee, these were: Associate Marketing Representative, Marketing Representative, Advisory Marketing Representative, Senior Marketing Representative, and Consulting Marketing Representative. Most of top management had come up through this hierarchy during their careers, and had spent time managing one or more branch offices. Further, IBM had long operated by rotating line personnel across sales regions and into and out of marketing staff positions at corporate headquarters. One manager noted that "In many companies, moving from line to staff is usually considered a demotion, but this is not the case at IBM . . . as long as you move back into the field at the appropriate time in your career."

Marketing Trainees spent 12–14 months in a combination of field and classroom training programs before being assigned a sales quota and thus qualifying for promotion to the Associate level. In a branch, these junior marketing reps were usually paired with more experienced reps on account assignments. With the senior rep as "team leader," the two would work on coordinating marketing activities and maintaining day-to-day contact with accounts. It was the branch manager's primary responsibility to organize his or her sales personnel and systems engineering staff into marketing teams and to monitor their progress.

Many of IBM's branch managers were so-called "high-potential" employees, considered candidates for top management positions at some point in the future. However, a significant number had opted for a career in branch management, where they might manage a number of different branches during their careers with IBM. One executive referred to this latter group as "the wise ones: they get the assignment if there's a particularly important turnaround situation in a given branch, and they often have developed long-term relationships with certain accounts. Also, since they have a history of solid field performance, they run their own shows as they see fit and implicitly win most arguments with division staff." One such branch manager commented:

> Branch manager is the best job at IBM. You manage the customer interface, can become a big shot in your community, and have direct responsibility for 100–200 people and associated resources. Also, while controls and procedures are highly centralized at IBM, branch managers who consistently deliver their numbers have a great deal of operating autonomy.
>
> Despite the changes in technology, competition, and organization, my job has been basically the same for the past 15 years: keep the customers happy, manage and develop my personnel, and maximize revenues for IBM. When a problem arises with an account, or if a change in account personnel becomes necessary, it's my job to soothe the customer, provide my personal guarantee of satisfaction, and then persuade, cajole, or crack whips until we deliver.

Branch managers annually reviewed account plans with the team responsible for each account. The branch manager's appraisal of these plans, and subsequent account performance, were key aspects in raises, promotions, and evaluations of branch marketing personnel. Conversely, IBM conducted an opinion survey bi-annually among all branch employees, and the results of this survey, reviewed by IBM's upper management, were a key factor in evaluations of branch managers. Throughout the period of this case, the number of IBM branches varied but was always between 225 and 250 individual branch offices in the United States.

Compensation

IBM compensated marketing representatives serving commercial accounts on a salary-plus-commission-plus-bonus basis. An important determinant of compensation was the salesperson's success in meeting assigned sales quotas. The quota system had been important at IBM since the days of founder Thomas J. Watson, who once noted that "One of the most significant words in the English language is 'quota.' From the cradle to the grave, quotas are the measure of our possibilities, the gauge of our progress, the test of our fitness for life itself.

Quotas, when set up for us by others, are challenges which goad us on to surpass ourselves." Similarly, years later, one observer noted that:[1]

> Everything (at IBM) is quantified and measured. Performances are rated on a 1–5 scale each year; only 8% get a top-notch 1. Salespeople must sell so many computers; a production manager must turn out so many terminals . . . IBM reps can earn more than $100,000 a year, but half their pay relies on meeting strict sales quotas. Many branches post charts that rank each rep. Says [one IBM rep]: "There were times when I had sleepless nights. There is a lot of pressure when your name and your life—not your life but you feel like it's your life—your salary, are on the line."

The quota setting process was driven by the Corporate Planning process, which began with Corporate goals set by the Management Committee. These were translated into specific growth and profitability targets for the operating units. As part of this process, the profit centers negotiated with the marketing organizations to agree or "interlock" on the volumes to be sold for major products/services. Marketing management's commitment to achieve the agreed upon volumes set the base for quota assignments.

Divisional marketing management then established quotas for each marketing unit, partly through discussions and partly through forecasting models which considered factors such as the size and potential of accounts in an area, customer requirements, the number of salespeople available, and desired staffing levels within the framework of IBM's full-employment practice. At each level of management, moreover, a "buffer" of approximately 1–5% was built into the quota figures as a "safety net" in the face of unforeseen conditions that might occur during the coming year. In turn, this buffer was available to management to use at their discretion if economic or other circumstances warranted altering quotas during the course of the year.

At the field level, the quota process was described by F. G. "Buck" Rodgers, who for a decade was IBM's vice president of marketing:[2]

> Each year, IBM wants to present an incentive package that will treat everyone evenhandedly and will do its job—that is, motivate. In a nutshell, it works like this: every regional manager begins the fiscal year with a new quota and a set of goals to achieve. His quota is split up among his branch managers. Each branch manager then divides his quota among the marketing managers who report to him. The marketing managers make the final quota allocations, determining the bogey for each marketing rep. If this sounds a little like the Abbott and Costello "Who's on first" routine, believe me, it's worse. We have tens of thousands of territories, and no two are alike.
>
> There is a lot to factor into each quota: the size of the territory, the types of customers, their potential to expand, the kind of systems they can use, their ser-

---

[1] Dennis Kneale, "Working at IBM," *Wall Street Journal* (April 7, 1986).

[2] F. G. Rodgers, *The IBM Way* (New York: Harper & Row, 1986), pp. 187–190.

vice requirements, the rep's involvement in team projects, the conditions affecting the marketplace, and product availability. There's more, but you get the idea. To complicate matters, no one is simply handed his quota. At each level, the factors and sometimes the numbers are debated. Think of this as a tops-down plan with bottoms-up input. The key philosophical point is that each individual, regardless of job level, is being measured against the same set of factors.

What about the service the company is proud of? Where is the dollar incentive for all that hard work? . . . First, it's part of the salary, and the true payback comes from having a satisfied customer. But there is also a take back provision. Specifically, when a customer cancels or discontinues any IBM equipment, all previously paid commissions are charged back to the marketing rep presently handling the account. While this sounds harsh, it serves as a key factor in making sure field people are paying attention to their customers, even during periods when little selling or installation is taking place.

IBM simply doesn't want to lose any business, and when it does, it investigates why. Monthly win-loss reports were prepared by the domestic and international marketing divisions from information supplied by their branch managers. . . . They are signed by division presidents and sent to IBM's top line management, with copies distributed to other high-ranking executives. It is distasteful, besides being embarrassing, to report a key loss, knowing that it will be reviewed, analyzed and evaluated by upper management. The idea is not to "headhunt" but to understand the problems and take whatever action is necessary to prevent a pattern of losses from developing.

At the beginning of each year, everybody complains that the quotas are too high. It's the natural thing to do and I did it too when I was a rep. However, when the year's over and all the numbers are in, management looks pretty smart. . . . Historically, 65 to 75 percent of IBM's people go over the top each year. Five to 10 percent usually break the bank. Of those who don't make 100 percent of their quota, only a few are in trouble. Most make it the next year and do okay. Under 4 percent of IBM's marketing people are asked to leave involuntarily each year, and unsatisfactory sales performance is only one of the causes. . . .

Changes in the quotas, though necessary at times, are not made easily or frequently. IBM wants its people to believe in and respect the sales package they receive. It doesn't want them to think that the numbers delivered at the beginning of the year are just a starting point and that they'll fluctuate throughout the next twelve months. IBM plays hardball, but plays it equitably.

Throughout the period covered by this case, key quota targets for field reps were 1) Sales Record Performance, which established the target for incremental equipment to be sold to existing and new customers during the year; and 2) Installed Record Performance, which established the target for equipment actually installed net of removals in IBM's customers' facilities during the year. The latter was thus a measure of incremental revenues generated by a marketing rep.

Awarded over and above salary and commission, bonuses were typically of two kinds. A bonus might be tied to sales of a specific product. More commonly, however, bonuses were tied to branch management's estimation of a rep's achievement of the qualitative objectives in his or her account plan, as established at that branch.

Sales compensation was reviewed annually by a panel of 6–8 branch managers. This panel made recommendations to the manager of sales planning, who was also the focus of product division managers' efforts to tie specific components of sales compensation to sales of a given product line. In turn, the manager of sales planning, who traditionally reported through IBM's personnel function and not through the marketing or product organizations, could establish or alter elements of future compensation programs.

Nonfinancial Incentives and Recognition

Historically, more than 70% of IBM employees were hired straight from college and turnover was lower than the industry average. Throughout the organization, moreover, awards and recognition events were sponsored frequently. One article commented:[3]

> IBM uses rewards and recognition (merit raises, bonuses, IBM-logoed luggage, or simply dinner for two and bulletin board praise) . . . nowhere more effectively or more effusively than in the IBM sales force. "Reps" are first among equals in IBM. Every man who ever ran the company rose through their ranks, beginning with Thomas Watson, Sr. . . . IBM treats them accordingly, motivating this army of politely aggressive blue suits with tons of cash, intense peer pressure and enough rah-rah rallies to rival a college fraternity.
>
> The rewards begin in IBM's 250 U.S. sales branches, where size is limited to 100 to 200 people to instill a small-team spirit. Each January, branches stage glitzy "kickoff" meetings replete with slogans, skits and mascots. Monthly meetings often close with a dramatic tale about an unnamed rep; finally, the person is named and comes forward to accept an award amid crackling applause. "It takes your breath away, it really does," says Diana Ingram, a Chicago rep who has received four awards in less than four years at IBM. . . . [Another rep] says, to him, IBM is only as big as his own Branch No. 088 and that, to customers, he *is* IBM.

A particularly important event was membership in the Hundred Percent Club, awarded to every rep who achieved annual quota. According to Mr. Rodgers, "There's no doubt in my mind that a survey of new reps would show that their first goal, after being assigned a territory, is not to make 'a lot of money' but to achieve membership in the Hundred Percent Club. A rep who has failed to make it for three years probably won't get a chance to go for it in the fourth."[4] Hundred Percent Club activities were generally three-day "recog-

---

[3] "Working at IBM," p. 27.

[4] *The IBM Way,* p. 194.

nition events" including banquets, entertainment and speeches from top executives. According to one observer:[5]

> Recognition events are staged for other IBMers: system engineers have IBM Symposiums; customer engineers have IBM Means Service awards; product developers have technical conferences. But those events aren't as lavish, and fewer people are invited. "That's mainly because (others) don't have their skin in the game the way the marketing rep does," says an IBM director of systems engineering.

Membership in the Hundred Percent Club was well-publicized throughout the company each year, and as one manager commented, "Those who make it are treated as celebrities."

Industry Marketing Programs

Industry specialization was, in the words of one IBM manager, "A sub-theme running throughout the changes in field organization." IBM had stressed such specialization earlier and more extensively than its competitors. Beginning in the late 1950s, IBM established industry marketing managers at headquarters in the Data Processing Division, while certain members of the field sales force began to specialize in industries such as utilities, financial institutions and manufacturing. The reasons for such specialization were several. First, while the same hardware might be used across industries, applications were often industry-specific. Second, a focus on certain industries served to place emphasis on certain critical markets where a relatively few customers represented a large volume of sales. Third, salespeople's knowledge of equipment and applications could be enhanced by an industry orientation. Mr. Rodgers noted:[6]

> IBM's customer list covers many different industries, and because a number of its products and programs can be tailored to handle specific tasks, it's imperative to build a sales force of industry specialists . . . if the intention is to run a solution-minded business. A salesperson can't be expected to be an authority on the automobile industry and the textile industry and the shipping industry. No matter how competent, he or she simply cannot call on a bank and talk about demand deposits, and then meet with an industrial company across the street to discuss an inventory or engineering problem.

Throughout the 1960s and 1970s, IBM used 15 major industry classifications with subdivisions within each (e.g., airlines, motor freight, and railroads within the transportation classification, or department store and supermarket specialists within the retail classification). In certain geographic areas branch offices were entirely focussed on a given industry. More commonly, however,

---

[5]"Working at IBM," p. 27.

[6]*The IBM Way,* p. 130.

only certain marketing reps were industry specialists, while headquarters personnel developed industry marketing programs, suggested the amount of sales and systems engineering effort required, and scheduled educational events for IBM and customer personnel.

Headquarters industry specialists did not have direct line authority over field marketing personnel and often complained that it was difficult to get branch managers to take a marketing rep out of the field to attend meetings concerned with specific industries. The headquarters industry specialists usually wanted to use such meetings to disseminate information and increase reps' interest in particular applications, whereas the branch manager was more interested in receiving industry-specific assistance only after a specific sales opportunity had been identified. Nevertheless, headquarters industry specialists often had strong influence over field sales activities because many branches had large portions of their quotas assigned by industry.

"Leadership Accounts"

One IBM manager noted that "IBM has always had a natural affinity for big customers. It comes with our mainframe heritage and the emphasis on account management in the field." For larger accounts, IBM conducted annual account-planning sessions in which both field sales and customer support people spent 3–5 days reviewing the account. With a major customer, as many as 50 IBM personnel, as well as customer personnel, could be involved. At these meetings, the customer's business conditions were discussed, and a review was conducted of all applications, installations, backlog, and maintenance issues concerning the account. The immediate objective was a detailed account plan for the coming year. An ancillary benefit, according to some IBM marketing reps, was the participation and coordination of the many support personnel involved with a given account. Mr. Rodgers noted:

> I could visit an IBM branch anywhere . . . and ask: "What can you tell me about your top accounts?" I would then be shown an extensive up-to-date file on every one of them. There'd be a booklet containing data ranging from current systems installed to the education programs in effect. These documents are kept current to make sure the needs of each customer are understood, and if there's a change in the sales force, new people can be informed quickly on the status of the account.
>
> The short- and long-term plans for major customers were always available not only to me but to all senior management, including the president and chairman of the board. Every business should keep similar data on its top accounts . . . what I call "leadership" accounts, those that are the most prestigious and make the greatest impact on their industry.

Another IBM executive commented: "Changing a computer vendor is not a trivial decision for a customer. But during the past 20 years, the technology has gone through repeated revolutions, new competitors have emerged, and thousands of companies have made important computer-purchase decisions in entirely new areas of their businesses. Yet turnover among our top accounts has been remarkably low during that period."

Finally, commenting on IBM's organizational changes during the period covered in this case, one senior IBM manager noted:

> Throughout this period, IBM was built around a small number of large profit centers. You should envision the corporation as a series of high pyramids which, because of technological and manufacturing considerations, have always been interdependent.
>
> In marketing, IBM's management has maintained a fairly transparent organization no matter how the field was organized. Senior managers call directly on branch managers, and every chairman came from the field, where they knew many managers and their big customers. As a result, customer complaints are meaningful at IBM: they get top management's attention. That's the important component of marketing organization for this firm, not the arrangement of the boxes.

Current Events

In 1986, IBM's revenues were $51 billion, and net income was nearly $4.8 billion, but the latter figure represented a 27 percent decline from 1985 and the second straight year earnings had dropped (the first time this had happened at IBM in 50 years). By early 1986, the company had begun efforts to improve competitiveness by reducing costs and balancing resources. It imposed limitations on hiring, cut discretionary spending, reduced overtime, and began encouraging employees to take vacations and use deferred vacation time. IBM also began shifting more than 5,000 headquarters staff and plant and lab personnel into field marketing positions.

In December 1986, IBM announced an early retirement program. By mid-1987 more than 13,000 IBM U.S. employees had opted for an early retirement incentive, and another 15,000 had been redeployed into new jobs, primarily sales. Headquarters staffs everywhere had been either trimmed or eliminated and critical areas such as marketing and programming substantially reinforced.

By year-end 1987, there were approximately 16,000 fewer employees at IBM than in 1985, and some 45,000 employees had been retrained (primarily for programming and field marketing positions) since 1985. One publication described these actions as "probably the most massive redeployment by a company in decades—all without firing a single employee."[7] In 1987, IBM's U.S. field marketing operation consisted of more than 28,000 people in 284 offices, a 22% increase in personnel from 1986.

---

[7] "Big Changes at Big Blue," *Business Week* (February 15, 1988), p. 93.

Chairman John Akers christened 1987 "the year of the customer." *THINK,* an IBM internal publication, commented:[8]

> For almost two years now, a slowdown in overall economic growth in the United States has taken its toll on many of IBM's customers and, hence, on IBM as well.
>
> . . . The company is taking some dramatic steps to better communicate to customers what it has to offer [them.] Short of disclosing information about future product announcements and other proprietary information, IBM is taking its strategy directions in products and technology—call it the "big picture"—directly to its customers. . . .
>
> As IBM Chairman John Akers said to his management team . . . "Put yourself in the customer's shoes. Look at their problems the way they do. And then solve those problems."

---

[8]"Days of Decisions—for IBM and Its Customers," *THINK,* Number 1 (1987), pp. 17–18.

Exhibit 1   IBM Marketing Organization (B): Process

IBM Branch Organization

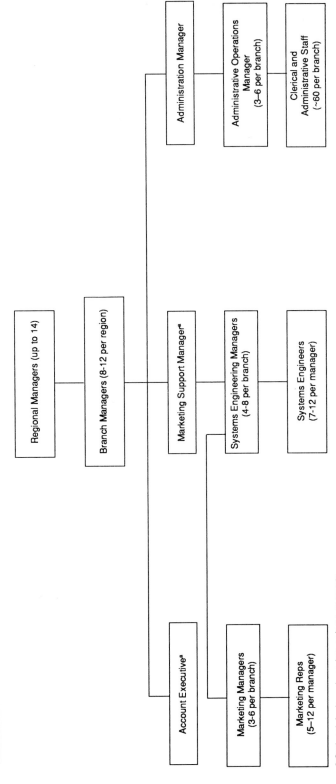

Regional Managers (up to 14)

Branch Managers (8-12 per region)

Administration Manager

Administrative Operations Manager (3–6 per branch)

Clerical and Administrative Staff (~60 per branch)

Marketing Support Manager[a]

Systems Engineering Managers (4-8 per branch)

Systems Engineers (7-12 per manager)

Account Executive[a]

Marketing Managers (3-6 per branch)

Marketing Reps (5-12 per manager)

a Optional; for large branches or large accounts.

Case 24

Procter & Gamble Co. (A)

In November 1981, Mr. Chris Wright, associate advertising manager of the Packaged Soap & Detergent Division (PS&D) of the Procter & Gamble Co. (P&G), was evaluating how the division could increase volume of its light-duty liquid detergents (LDLs).[1] The excellent growth of Dawn dishwashing liquid since its national introduction in 1976 meant that P&G now manufactured and sold three leading LDL brands and held a 42% share (by weight) of the industry's $850 million in factory sales.

Based on input from the three LDL brand managers who reported to him, as well as his own knowledge of the LDL category, Wright believed there were three major opportunities for volume growth: (1) the introduction of a new brand, (2) a product improvement on an existing brand, and/or (3) increased marketing expenditures on existing brands. In preparation for an upcoming meeting with Bruce Demill, PS&D advertising manager, Wright began evaluating the volume and profit potential of the three options.

Company Background

In 1837, William Procter and James Gamble formed a partnership in Cincinnati, Ohio, so that they could buy more efficiently the animal fats essential to the manufacture of their respective products, candles and soaps. The Procter & Gamble Company, which emerged from this partnership, quickly gained a reputation as a highly principled manufacturer of quality goods. As James

---

[1]LDLs are defined as all mild liquid soaps and detergents designed primarily for washing dishes.

Gamble said: "If you cannot make pure goods and full weight, go to something else that is honest, even if it is breaking stone."

In 1890, the Procter & Gamble Company was incorporated with a capital stock value of $4,500,000. This capital allowed P&G to build additional plants, buy new equipment, and develop and introduce new products. Sales volume more than doubled every 10 years following incorporation, largely as a result of new product introductions. By 1981, P&G operated in 26 countries. As indicated in Exhibit 1, sales totalled $11.4 billion, of which 70% were made in the United States. P&G manufactured 90 consumer and industrial products in the United States and sold the leading brand in 14 of the 24 consumer product categories in which the company competed (see Exhibit 2). One or more of P&G's products were used in 95% of homes in the United States—a penetration unequalled by any other manufacturer. P&G had historically grown both by developing products internally and by acquiring companies to which P&G's technological expertise was applied.[2]

P&G executives attributed the company's success in the marketplace to a variety of factors: (i) dedicated and talented human resources, (ii) a reputation for honesty that won them the trust and respect of their suppliers and customers, (iii) prudent and conservative management that encouraged thorough analysis prior to decision making, (iv) innovative products offering superior benefits at competitive prices, and (v) substantial marketing expertise. The following quotes from company executives and outside analysts emphasize these factors:

> If you leave the company (P&G) its money, its buildings and its brands, but take away its people, the business will be in real jeopardy—but, if you take away the money, the buildings and the brands, but leave the people here, we will build a comparable new business in as little as a decade.

> Richard R. Deupree, Chairman of the Board, P&G, 1948–1958

> Our predecessors were wise enough to know that profitability and growth go hand in hand with fair treatment of employees, of customers, of consumers and of the communities in which we operate.[3]

> Edward G. Harness, Chairman of the Board, P&G, 1974–1981

> There is no potential business gain, no matter how great, which can be used to justify a dishonest act. The ends cannot justify the means because unethical

---

[2] P&G acquired the Duncan Hines Companies (manufacturers of prepared cake, cookie, and muffin mixes) in 1956; Charmin Paper Mills (manufacturers of toilet and facial tissues, paper towels, and paper napkins) in 1957; the Folger Coffee Company (manufacturers of ground, flaked, and instant coffee) in 1963; the Crush Companies (manufacturers of Crush, Sun Drop, and Hires Root beer soft drinks) in 1980; the Ben Hill Griffin Citrus Company (manufacturers of concentrated fruit juices) in 1981; and Morton Norwich (manufacturers of pharmaceuticals) in 1982.

[3] As quoted by Oscar Schisgall in *Eyes on Tomorrow* (Chicago: J. G. Ferguson Publishing, 1981). All other quotations are drawn from P&G recruitment literature.

means, in and of themselves, can and will destroy an organization. . . . The total dedication to integrity in every aspect of the business, and the restless, driving spirit of exploration have already been vital to the company's past, and are critical to the company's future.

> Owen B. Butler, Chairman of
> the Board, P&G, 1981–

. . . Key to Procter & Gamble's continued growth is the importance we attach to research and development . . . if anything, research and development will take on even greater importance to us in the future.

> John Smale, President,
> P&G, 1981–

Disciplined and consistent. P&G people plan, minimize risk, and adhere to proven principles.

> Ogilvy and Mather
> Advertising agency

The secret, in a word, is thoroughness. P&G manages every element of its business with a painstaking precision that most organizations fail to approach.

> *Fortune*

Company Organization

The company comprised eight major operating divisions organized by type of product: Packaged Soap & Detergents, Bar Soap & Household Cleaning Products, Toilet Goods, Paper Products, Food Products, Coffee, Food Service & Lodging Products, and Special Products. As Exhibit 3 shows, each division had its own brand management (called Advertising), Sales, Finance, Manufacturing, and Product Development line management groups. These groups reported directly to the division manager, typically a vice president who held overall profit and loss responsibility. The divisions used centralized corporate staff groups for advertising services,[4] distribution, and purchasing.

The Advertising Department was formed in 1930 when P&G initiated its brand management system. This system allowed P&G to market aggressively several brands in the same product category by assigning the marketing responsibility for each brand to a single brand manager. He or she led a brand group that included an assistant brand manager, and depending on the dollar volume and marketing complexity of the product, one or two brand assistants. This group planned, developed, and directed the total marketing effort for its brand.

---

[4]Advertising services included the following specialized staff departments: TV Commercial Production, Media, Copy Services, Art and Package Design, Market Research, Field Advertising, Marketing Systems and Computer Services, and Promotion and Marketing Services.

It was expected to manage aggressively the marketing of the brand and to know more about the brand's business than anyone else in the organization.

One of the most important responsibilities of the brand group was the development of the annual marketing plan, which established volume objectives, marketing support levels, strategies, and tactics for the coming year. This plan took approximately three months to develop. It reflected substantial analysis of previous business results by the brand group. Additionally, the brand group solicited input from 6 to 12 internal staff departments and an outside advertising agency. The brand group then recommended a marketing plan, which was reviewed by three levels of management—the associate advertising manager, the advertising manager, and the division general manager. Since the planning process established the marketing plans and volume expectations for the coming year, it was regarded as a key determinant of brand progress. In addition, this process offered the brand groups substantial opportunity to interact with upper management. Details of the planning process are presented in Exhibit 4.

Promotion was based entirely on performance, and all promotions were from within the organization. In addition to their ability to build brand business, brand managers were evaluated on their ability to develop their people. A brand manager who demonstrated excellent management ability was promoted to associate advertising manager, as indicated in Exhibit 3. Associate advertising managers used the skills they had developed as brand managers to guide the marketing efforts of several brands within a division, as well as to further the development of their brand managers. Associates also became involved in broader divisional and corporate issues. For example, the associate responsible for coordinating division personnel policy would evaluate future personnel needs, coordinate recruitment efforts, insure consistent evaluation methods, analyze training needs, develop a training budget, and work with the Personnel Department to implement training programs.

Each associate advertising manager reported to an advertising manager, who was responsible for the total marketing effort of all of a division's brands. The advertising manager played a significant role in the general management of the division, as he or she was responsible for approving the brand's recommendations for volume objectives, marketing plans, and expenditures. In addition, the advertising manager had responsibility for approving each of the brands' advertising plans, as recommended by the brand groups and their advertising agencies. [5]

All new advertising required the approval of the associate advertising manager and the advertising manager, while significant changes in advertising direction required division manager approval.

---

[5] P&G retained 10 leading advertising agencies to work with the brand groups on advertising issues, of which seven worked on the PS&D Division's products. Each LDL was handled by a separate agency. P&G's relationship with most of its agencies was long-standing, and many of the brands had been handled by the same agency since their introduction.

Historically, brands competing in the same product category were assigned to different associate advertising managers within a division to assure maximum interbrand competition. Each of the associates promoted the interests of his or her own brand to the advertising manager who then coordinated the most effective and efficient use of limited divisional resources. However, in the fall of 1981, the PS&D Division was reorganized such that each associate advertising manager became responsible for all the brands within a single product category, as shown in Exhibit 5. This change focused authority for key decisions within category groups (e.g., LDLs) at the associate advertising manager level, thus allowing the advertising manager to spend more time on divisional issues. The brand manager promoted the interests of his brand while the associate advertising manager assumed responsibility for building the business of all P&G brands in his or her category.

Advertising's Relations with Other Line Departments

The brand groups worked closely with the following four line departments in both the development and the implementation of their marketing plans:

Sales

P&G's consumer divisions employed 2,310 sales representatives and 574 sales managers, who serviced an estimated 40% of grocery, drug, and mass merchandise retail and wholesale outlets, accounting for an estimated 80% of all grocery and health and beauty aid sales volume.[6] The PS&D Division employed 408 sales representatives and 102 sales managers, who serviced 27% of grocery outlets accounting for 75% of grocery sales volume. The PS&D sales force did not directly service drug and mass merchandise outlets because of their modest sales potential.

P&G sales representatives were well trained and regarded by the trade as consistently professional. Richard Penner, district sales manager, said:

> Our sales representatives must be experts and professionals in their field. Our customers know that our sales representatives are well-trained professionals whose objective is not only to sell a good, quality product, but whose expertise can show them how to improve overall productivity; people who will bring them business-building merchandising ideas for the next feature or drive, which will reach present as well as new customers, thus increasing overall turnover and profit for the store.

The brand groups and sales force frequently interacted. While the brand groups managed categories and brands, the sales force managed markets and accounts. As such, the sales force provided important perspective and counsel

---

[6]Small convenience and corner stores accounted for most of the remaining 60% of retail outlets. P&G did not directly service these stores, as they accounted for only 20% of all commodity volume (ACV). These stores could, however, obtain P&G products through wholesalers.

on trade and consumer promotion acceptance, stock requirements to support promotions, competitive pricing and promotion activity, and new product activity. Each brand group worked closely with the sales force to develop the optimal sales promotion plan for their brand together with appropriate merchandising aids. An understanding of the sales function was considered so important to successful marketing planning that each brand assistant was trained as a sales representative and spent three to five months in the field sales force.

Product Development Department (PDD)

Since superior product performance was key to the success of P&G products, each brand group worked closely with PDD to ensure continued improvement of their brand's quality. Fifteen professionals worked exclusively on research and development for LDLs. The PDD continually strove to upgrade product quality or explore new product formulations. If a potential new product was developed, it was extensively tested in consumer and laboratory tests before any test marketing began.

In 1981, P&G spent $200 million on research and development. This spending supported the efforts of about 3,500 employees. Approximately 1,200 were professionally trained staff, and nearly one-third of these held doctoral degrees. P&G had six major research centers, four of which were located in the United States. The PS&D Division spent $30 million on research and development in 1981, which supported the efforts of about 500 employees.

Manufacturing Department

P&G operated 40 manufacturing plants in 24 states. The PS&D Division utilized 10 of these facilities to manufacture its products. The brand group provided the Manufacturing Department with detailed brand volume estimates (by month, by size, and by form/flavor) to facilitate efficient production, as well as five-year volume base forecasts for capacity planning. In addition, the brand group discussed promotions requiring label or packaging changes with Manufacturing to determine the most efficient production methods. Manufacturing informed brand groups about ongoing manufacturing costs and provided potential cost savings ideas. Interaction between the Advertising and Manufacturing departments was particularly frequent during any new product development process and included discussions on manufacturing requirements, custom packing options for test markets, and critical paths for production.

Finance Department

P&G's Finance Department was divided into three major functional areas: Divisional Financial/Cost Analysis, Treasury, and Taxation. Both Treasury and Taxation were centralized groups, while Financial/Cost Analysis was divisionalized and reported to the division manager, as shown in Exhibit 3. Based on volume and marketing expenditure forecasts provided by the brand groups, Financial/Cost analysts developed and fed back brand profit and pricing analyses, as well as profit and rate of return forecasts on new products and promotions. This information was key in helping the brand groups to recommend action which would maximize volume and profit growth.

Advertising Services Department

Within the department, there were nine staff groups which serviced the Advertising Department. These were Market Research, Art and Package Design, TV Commercial Production, Media, Copy Services, Field Advertising, Marketing Systems and Computer Services, Promotion and Marketing Services, and Advertising Personnel.

P&G's extraordinary depth of staff resources was considered a key competitive advantage. For example, P&G invested an average of $20 million annually on consumer and market research,[7] 10% of which was spent on PS&D Division projects. PS&D market research included:

(i) Market Analysis—Including bimonthly syndicated market data that P&G purchased from A. C. Nielsen Co.,[8] as well as selected data purchased from Nielsen, Selling Areas Marketing, Inc. (SAMI), and other suppliers for test markets.

(ii) Consumer Research—Including studies to:

- Monitor how consumers used products and track consumer usage of, attitude toward, and image of P&G and competitive brands.

- Test the performance of current products and possible product modifications under in-home usage conditions.

- Evaluate the advertising, packaging, promotion, and pricing of P&G brands. Also, to evaluate the potential of new product ideas using such techniques as concept research and simulated test markets.

The major strength of P&G's consumer research was the quality of interviewing and consistent methodology among projects. This provided P&G with large data bases of comparable research over several years from which they could establish norms and accurately track changing consumer perceptions and habits. Only a limited amount of the research was actually conducted by P&G employees—most was conducted by outside suppliers but was closely supervised by P&G market researchers.

---

[7]This $20 million was part of the $200 million the company spent on research and development.

[8]The A. C. Nielsen package that the LDL brands purchased included data on retail shelf movement and share, distribution penetration, retailer feature advertising, special displays, regular and feature prices, out-of-stocks, retail inventories and percent of brands sold in special packs.

Light-Duty Liquid Detergents

During the 1940s, most U.S. consumers used powdered laundry detergents to wash their dishes. Research indicated, however, that consumers found these detergents harsh on hands. In response to these concerns, P&G designed a mild, light-duty liquid in 1949. By 1981, the LDL industry recorded factory sales of $850 million and volume of 59 million cases.[9] The average U. S. consumer had 1.5 LDL brands at home at any one time, used 0.6 fluid ounces of product per sinkful of dishes, and washed an average of 12 sinksful each week. The average purchase cycle was 3–4 weeks and an average household would use over one case of product each year. As Table 1 shows, the most popular sizes in the category were 32 oz. and 22 oz.

Table 2 suggests that LDL consumption increases, resulting from the growing number of U.S. households,[10] were partly offset by increased penetration of automatic dishwashers (ADWs), as ADW households used one half as much LDL as non-ADW households.[11] Based on these trends, the LDL brand groups projected category volume growth of 1% per year over the next 5 years.

LDLs could be conceptually divided on the basis of product benefit into three major segments. The performance segment, accounting for 35% of category volume, included brands providing primarily a cleaning benefit; the mildness segment, accounting for 37% of category volume, included brands providing primarily the benefit of being gentle to hands; and the price segment, accounting for 28% of category volume, included brands whose primary benefit was low cost.[12] As Exhibit 6 indicates, the performance segment had experienced the greatest growth in the past 10 years. Some LDL brand managers expected the performance segment to continue to grow at the expense of the

Table 1

Sizes of Dishwashing Liquid Used in Past Seven Days

	Size			
	48 oz.	32 oz.	22 oz.	12 oz.
% Respondents	13	30	42	15

Source: Company research.

---

[9]Volume is measured in P&G statistical cases, each containing 310 ounces.

[10]Household growth was a better indicator of LDL volume than population growth, as research indicated LDL household consumption varied only slightly with the number of people in the household.

[11]ADW households still used LDL for pots and pans and small cleanups.

[12]Price brands were sold to retailers for an average of $7.50/statistical case versus $17.00/statistical case for the premium-priced mildness and performance brands.

Table 2

U.S. LDL Market Influences

	Year			
	1960	1970	1980	1990*
% LDL household penetration	53	83	90	92
% ADW household penetration	5	18	36	44
Total Households (millions)	53	63	79	91

*Company estimate.

mildness segment since market research indicated that more consumers rated performance attributes (such as grease cutting and long-lasting suds) as the most important (see Exhibit 7). The price segment had been in decline but was expected to stabilize at its current share level due to increasing consumer price sensitivity resulting from the depressed state of the economy. The LDL brand managers did not expect this segment to grow because most price brands were not a good value, requiring two or three times as much volume to create the same amount of suds as a premium brand. P&G's Ivory Liquid, the market leader, used this comparison in its advertising to persuade consumers that Ivory was a better value.

The LDL market was relatively stable with one new premium brand introduced every two and one half years, and an average of two price brands introduced and discontinued per year. As Exhibit 8 shows, 3 companies sold almost 75% of LDLs, with P&G holding a 42% share[13] of the market, Colgate-Palmolive Company a 24% share, and Lever Brothers, the U.S. subsidiary of Unilever, a 7% share.[14] The remaining 27% of the market consisted mainly of generic and private label brands.

Total advertising and promotion spending in the category in 1981 was $150 million, over half of which was spent by the P&G LDLs, the balance being spent primarily by Lever and Colgate-Palmolive.

Slightly over half of the marketing budgets of the P&G LDLs was allocated to advertising, versus only about 40% for both Colgate and Lever LDLs. Colgate and Lever sold an estimated 75% of their LDL volume to the trade on deal, compared to about half for P&G. Both Lever and Colgate had introduced a single, new brand in the past 10 years. Dermassage, introduced in 1974 by Colgate, offered a similar benefit to Ivory, mildness to hands. The brand held only a 2% share in 1981. Sunlight, introduced by Lever into Phoenix test market in 1980, offered benefits similar to Joy, as a good cleaning, lemon-fresh LDL. The brand had achieved a 10% share in the test region after 12 months.

---

[13] Share of market is defined as share of statistical case volume.

[14] In 1981, U. S. sales of Colgate-Palmolive Company were $5.3 billion and U. S. sales of Lever Brothers were $2.1 billion.

Procter & Gamble's LDL Brands

P&G's three brands in the LDL category, Ivory Liquid, Joy, and Dawn, together accounted for 30% of the dollar sales volume and profit of the PS&D Division. While each of the three brands was a different formulation which offered a distinct benefit to appeal to separate consumer needs, they were all marketed similarly. All three brands were sized and priced in line with major premium-priced competition, as indicated in Table 3. Price increases occurred, on average, every 18 months.

In general, the brand managers spent over half of each LDL's marketing budget on advertising, of which 85–90% was spent on television media and commercial production, and the balance on print. (Exhibit 9 indicates the typical cost structure for an established LDL brand.) Brands typically held four to six major promotion events each year, each lasting four weeks. Promotions primarily included coupons, price packs, bonus packs, and trade allowances. Consumer promotions typically accounted for at least 75% of promotion dollars, while trade allowances made up the balance.

P&G's LDL brands held strongly established market positions as company research results reported in Exhibit 10 reveal. Neither Ivory Liquid nor Dawn had changed its basic product benefits or basic advertising claims since introduction. Joy, however, had undergone two basic changes. It was first introduced as a performance brand, but during the 1960s, as the mildness segment of the market began to grow, it was restaged with a mildness benefit. By the 1970s, Ivory Liquid was clearly established as the major mildness brand, and as research revealed that a consumer need existed for a good cleaning brand, Joy was reformulated to provide a performance benefit and restaged.

The brand's individual market positions are discussed below.

Ivory

Ivory Liquid was introduced in 1957 as an excellent dishwashing liquid that provided the additional benefit of hand care. Its mildness positioning was supported by the heritage of Ivory bar soap, a patented mildness formula, and unique product aesthetics—its creamy-white color and mild scent. In 1981, it was the leading brand with a market share of 15.5%. Although Ivory's share had

Table 3

Ivory, Dawn and Joy Pricing

Size	Items/Case	Manufacturer's Carload Case Price	Manufacturer's Carload Item Price	Average Retail Price
48 oz.	9	$22.77	$2.53	$2.99
32 oz.	12	21.24	1.77	2.04
22 oz.	16	19.20	1.20	1.46
12 oz.	24	16.08	.67	.84

declined slightly over the previous five years, it was expected to remain stable over the next five years. Ivory advertising copy featured a mother/daughter comparison to demonstrate its benefit of "young-looking hands." In 1968, the brand added a value claim which stressed the fact that Ivory washed more dishes per penny of product than price brands because of its higher sudsing formula. During 1981, Ivory allocated two-thirds of its advertising budget to the mildness message and the remaining one-third to the value advertising copy. Television advertising storyboards for these two campaigns are presented as Exhibits 11 and 12. The brand was perceived by consumers as the mildest and highest sudsing brand and had the highest ever-tried level in the category. For this reason, the principal objective of Ivory's consumer promotions was to encourage continuity of purchase rather than to stimulate trial.

Dawn

Dawn was introduced in 1976 as a performance brand. In two years, it rose to the #2 position in the LDL category, and by 1981, held a 14.1% market share. Dawn captured about 70% of its volume from non-P&G brands, with the remaining 30% cannibalized equally from Ivory and Joy. Dawn's rapid growth was attributed to its unique position as the superior grease-cutting LDL in the category—a claim that was supported by its patented formula which consumer research proved cut grease better than other formulas. The advertising claim, "Dawn takes grease out of your way," was supported by a powerful product demonstration, as shown in the storyboard presented as Exhibit 13. Consumer research reported in Exhibit 14 indicated that Dawn had the highest conversion rate of all the P&G LDL brands.[15] Dawn's promotion plan emphasized trial with most of the budget allocated to consumer coupons. Its share was projected to increase to 16.5% over the next five years. It was expected to take over the leading share position from Ivory by 1985.

Joy

Joy, introduced in 1949, was the first LDL. Since 1970, it had been formulated to provide a performance benefit, and it was positioned in advertising to deliver "beautiful dishes that get noticed and appreciated." Joy's lemon-based formula, lemon fragrance, and yellow package supported this image. Joy advertising (see Exhibit 15) claimed that it "cleans dishes right down to the shine and isn't that a nice reflection on you." Although Joy's image in the marketplace was good by category standards, it was not as strong as Ivory or Dawn. As Exhibit 14 indicates, it had the lowest trial level of P&G's three LDLs. As a result, its promotion plan was trial-oriented with particular emphasis on couponing. Joy's share of 12.1% was expected to increase by only 1% per year over the next 5 years.

---

[15] The conversion rate was the number of people citing a brand as their usual brand divided by total triers of the brand.

Exhibit 16 reports factory shipments and market shares for each of the three brands over the past five years, as well as the brands' estimates for the next five years. Exhibit 17 provides a demographic profile of users of each of the three P&G brands, illustrating how each brand appeals to a different consumer segment.

New Growth Opportunities

Wright considered the following three options in evaluating the opportunities for further volume growth on P&G LDLs:

New Brand Introduction

The success of Dawn led Wright to wonder if another new brand with a distinctive benefit could further increase P&G's LDL volume. Based on the impact of Dawn's introduction and the current strength of P&G's LDL brands, he estimated that a well-positioned new brand could capture at least 60% of its share from competitive brands. However, after talking with Manufacturing and PDD, he estimated that a new brand would require $20 million in capital investment to cover additional production capacity and bottle molds.[16] Further, based on input from the Dawn brand manager, he estimated a new LDL brand would need at least $60 million for first-year introductory marketing expenditures.[17]

Wright saw new product potential in all three market segments. First, PDD had invented a new technology for a high-performance product. The formula, called H-80, combined suspended nonabrasive scrubbers[18] with a highly effective detergent system to provide superior cleaning versus other LDLs when used full strength on tough, baked-on foods and parity cleaning versus other LDLs when diluted with water for general dishwashing. Wright believed that such a product could fulfill a clear consumer need, based on consumer research. Since market research indicated that 80% of U. S. households scour and scrub their dishes at least once a week, with an average household scouring four times a week, he believed that this product would be valued by a significant percentage of consumers.[19] In addition, the results of blind, in-home use tests, reported in Exhibit 18, were positive.

---

[16] This capital investment per case of estimated LDL volume was lower than the average for new P&G products, since substantial LDL manufacturing facilities already existed.

[17] This estimate was based on Dawn's 12-month introductory marketing plan. Using updated costs, a new brand would require $18 million for media support, $37 million for consumer and trade promotion support, and $5 million for miscellaneous marketing expenses.

[18] The scrubbers were made from the biodegradable shells of microscopic sea organisms.

[19] Many consumers used soap-filled scouring-pads such as Purex Industries' Brillo pads and Miles Laboratories' S. O. S. pads. Retail sales of such pads approached $100 million in 1980.

Second, Wright wondered if he could capitalize on P&G's expertise in the mildness segment to introduce another mildness brand. While the segment was currently declining, he believed there might be potential for a new brand if the mildness benefit could be further differentiated—just as had been done in the performance segment. As Exhibit 19 shows, research indicated that when consumers were asked what improvement they wanted most in their current LDL, more stated "milder to hands" than any other product benefit.

Third, P&G could introduce a price brand. PDD and Manufacturing had told Wright that they could produce a brand with parity performance benefits to existing price brand competition at a cost that would allow them to maintain a reasonable profit. Specifically, the percentage of sales available for marketing expenditures and profit would fall to 14% of sales versus the 32% of sales available from P&G's current LDL brands. Wright noted that P&G did not currently have an LDL entry in this fragmented segment of the market, characterized by low-share brands with little brand loyalty and substantially lower product quality than the LDL brands P&G currently marketed. He wondered if P&G's marketing expertise could enable the company to capture a significant portion of the price segment with a parity product.

Product Improvement on an Existing Brand

A product improvement on a current brand represented considerably less investment than a new brand and Wright wondered if he would be wiser to introduce the H-80 formula as a product improvement to one of the current LDL brands. While he estimated that the capital costs associated with a product improvement would be about the same as introducing a new product ($20 million), incremental marketing expenditures over and above the existing brand budget would be only $10 million. He wondered which, if any, of his brands would most benefit from this change.

Separately, the Joy brand group was eager to restage the brand with a new "no-spot" formula. The formula, considered a technological breakthrough, caused water to "sheet" off dishes when they were air-dried, leaving fewer spots than other brands. In addition, the formula reduced Joy's cost of goods sold by about $3 million per year. The brand estimated this relaunch would cost $10 million in marketing expenses but would require no capital investment.

Increase Marketing Expenditures on Existing Brands

Finally, given the low-growth potential of the LDL category, Wright wondered if his overall profits might be higher if he avoided the capital investment and introductory marketing expenses of a new brand or product improvement and simply increased the marketing expenditures behind the existing brands in an effort to build volume. In particular, the brand manager on Ivory Liquid had submitted a request for an additional $4 million to support extra advertising and promotion. Half of the funds were to be used to achieve leadership media levels for Ivory by increasing its current media level from 300

GRPs,[20] which was the average level for major advertised LDL brands, to 365 GRPs. The remaining funds would be used to finance an incremental 20 cents off price pack promotion on the 32 oz. size.

Conclusion

As Wright considered the various options available, he wondered about the time frame for implementation of each option. He knew that he could gain approval for increased marketing expenditures almost immediately if the plan was financially attractive, unless a test market was required, which would delay national approval by six to twelve months. Implementing a product improvement on an existing brand would take about a year, or two years if a test market was necessary, and the introduction of a new brand would require two years plus a year in a test market before it could be expanded nationally. Could he undertake more than one option? What effect would each option have on each of the existing LDL brands? What competitive response could he expect? What were the long- and short-term profit and volume implications of each of the options?

---

[20]A GRP (Gross Rating Point) is a measure of media delivery. Gross rating points equal the percent of viewers reached over a specific period of time (usually four weeks) times the average number of occasions on which they are reached.

Exhibit 1   *Procter & Gamble Co. (A)*

Consolidated Statement of Earnings
(millions of dollars except per share amounts)

	Year Ending June 30	
	1981	1980
Income		
Net sales	$11,416	$10,772
Interest and other income	83	52
	11,499	10,824
Costs and Expenses		
Cost of products sold	7,854	7,471
Marketing, administrative, and other expenses	2,361	2,178
Interest expense	98	97
	10,313	9,746
Earnings from Operations Before Income Taxes	1,186	1,078
Income Taxes	518	438
Net Earnings from Operations		
(before extraordinary charge)	668	640
Extraordinary Charge: costs associated with the suspension of sale of Rely tampons (less applicable tax relief of $58)	(75)	—
Net Earnings	$ 593	$ 640
Per Common Share		
Net earnings from operations	$8.08	$7.74
Extraordinary charge	(.91)	—
Net earnings	$7.17	$7.74
Average shares outstanding:		
1981—82,720,858		
1980—82,659,861		
Dividends	$3.80	$3.40

Source: Company records.

Exhibit 2   Procter & Gamble Co. (A)

Established U.S. Brands by Product Category—1981

A. Consumer

Laundry & Cleaning

All Fabric Bleach
Biz (1967)*

Cleaners and Cleansers
#1-Comet (1956)**
Comet Liquid (1976)
Mr. Clean (1958)
Spic and Span (1945)
Top Job (1963)

Detergents/Soaps
Bold 3 (1976)   Gain (1966)
Cheer (1950)   Ivory Snow (1930)
Dash (1954)   Oxydol (1952)
Dreft (1933)   Solo (1979)
Era (1972)   #1-Tide (1946)

Dishwashing Detergents
Cascade (1955)
Dawn (1972)
#1-Ivory Liquid (1957)
Joy (1949)

Fabric Softeners
Bounce (1972)
#1-Downy (1960)

Food

Coffee
#1-Folger's (vacuum packed &
   instant, 1963; flaked, 1977)
Instant High Point (1975)

Oil/Shortening
#1-Crisco (shortening, 1911)
Crisco (oil, 1960)
Fluffo (shortening, 1953)
Puritan Oil (1976)

*Orange Juice and Other Citrus
Products*

Peanut Butter
#1-Jif (1956)

Potato Chips
Pringles (1968)

Soft Drinks
Crush (1980)
Hires Root Beer (1980)
Sun-Drop (1980)

Prepared Mixes
#1-Duncan Hines (cake, 1956;
   brownie, 1956; snack cake,
   1974; pudding recipe cake,
   1977; cookie, 1978; bran
   muffin, 1979)

Personal Care

Mouthwash
Scope (1965)

Paper Tissue Products
Charmin (bathroom, 1957)
#1-Puffs (facial, 1960)
White Cloud (bathroom, 1958)

Paper Towel
#1-Bounty (1965)

Prescription Drugs

Shampoos
Head & Shoulders (1961)
Pert (1979)
Prell (1946)

Toothpastes
#1-Crest (1955)
Gleem

Bar Soaps
Camay (1927)
Coast (1974)
#1-Ivory (1879)
Kirk's (1930)
Lava (1928)
Safeguard (1963)
Zest (1952)

Deodorants/Anti-Perspirants
Secret (1956)
Sure (1972)

Disposable Diapers
#1-Pampers (1961)
Luvs (1976)

Disposable Incontinent Briefs
Attends (1978)

Hand and Body Lotion
Wondra (1977)

Home Permanent
#1-Lilt (1949)

(continued)

Exhibit 2 (continued)

B. *Industrial*

Finished Industrial Goods	*Unfinished Industrial Goods*

All-purpose cleaning products   Animal feed ingredients
Floor and hard surface cleaning   Cellulose pulp
   products   Fatty acids
Pot and pan washing products   Fatty alcohols
Cleansers   Glycerine
Commercial laundry products   Methyl esters
Coin-vended laundry products
Hand washing products
Institutional bar soaps
Coffee
Shortenings and oils
Surgical drapes & gowns

*The date the brand became part of the P&G line is in parentheses.

**#1 brands in the category are marked.

Note: Test market brands have been excluded.

Exhibit 3   Procter & Gamble Co. (A)

Divisional Line Management Organization

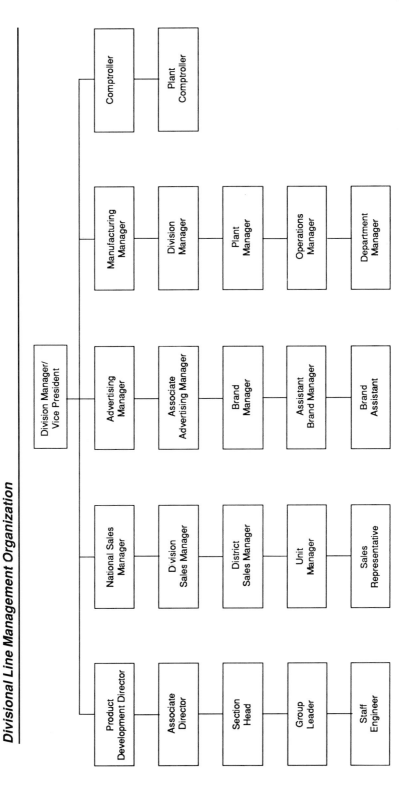

Exhibit 4 Procter & Gamble Co. (A)

Marketing Plan Development Process

Appropriate Number of Weeks Before Plan Approved	Activity or Event	Purpose
12	*Business Review.* Assistant Brand Manager thoroughly reviews brand's and major competition's past 12-month shipment and share results by region, by size and by form. Key lessons learned and indicated actions for the brand are developed by analyzing influences on brand share, including advertising copy, media weight, promotion, trade merchandising (display, co-op advertising and temporary price reduction), pricing and distribution.	To determine what elements of the marketing mix are affecting the brand's business and to develop clear guidelines and actions to improve business results.
8	*Competitive Forecast.* Brand Group forecasts competitive volume and marketing expenditures for coming year, using input from Sales and advertising agency.	To allow brands to gauge level of expenditures necessary to compete effectively.
6	*Preliminary Forecast.* Brand Manager forecasts brand's volume and share for the coming year and preliminarily recommends advertising and promotion expenditures.	To allow division and P&G management to preliminarily forecast total P&G volume, expenditures and profits for the coming year, and the brand to get preliminary agreement to volume objectives and marketing plans.
4	*Promotion Review.* Brand Assistant thoroughly reviews results of past 12-month promotion plan by region, event, promoted size and total brand. The document incorporates Sales comments, competitive brand activity and available research to explain possible reasons for success and failure. Plan includes broadscale effort and testing activities.	To gain preliminary agreement from Advertising and Sales management to the proposed promotion plan for the coming year.
4	*Media Plan.* Advertising agency develops detailed media plan, working with Brand Manager and Assistant Brand Manager. Plan includes broadscale media effort and testing activities.	To develop media plan for inclusion in budget proposal.
1	*Budget Proposal.* Brand group prepares document detailing proposed volume, share, and marketing plan for coming year. Marketing plan includes detailed media and promotion plans, both broadscale effort and testing activities.	To provide a written record of the proposed plan.
0 (March)	*Budget Meeting.* Brand group and advertising agency present the proposed plan to P&G management. The plan can either be approved in full, conditionally accepted provided certain issues raised in the meeting are addressed, or not approved.	To gain Management input and agreement to the proposed plans.

Exhibit 5   Procter & Gamble Co. (A)

PS&D Division Organizational Chart—Fall 1981

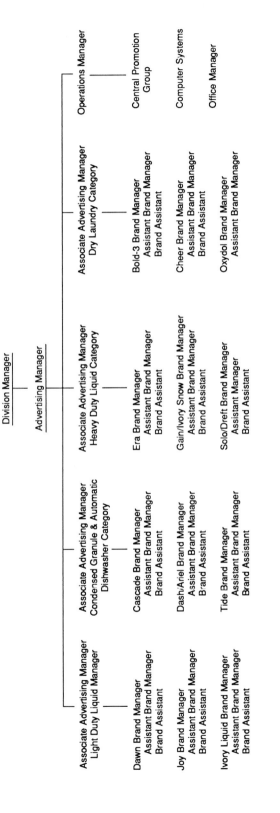

Division Manager

Advertising Manager

Associate Advertising Manager
Light Duty Liquid Manager

Dawn Brand Manager
Assistant Brand Manager
Brand Assistant

Joy Brand Manager
Assistant Brand Manager
Brand Assistant

Ivory Liquid Brand Manager
Assistant Brand Manager
Brand Assistant

Associate Advertising Manager
Condensed Granule & Automatic
Dishwasher Category

Cascade Brand Manager
Assistant Brand Manager
Brand Assistant

Dash/Ariel Brand Manager
Assistant Brand Manager
Brand Assistant

Tide Brand Manager
Assistant Brand Manager
Brand Assistant

Associate Advertising Manager
Heavy Duty Liquid Category

Era Brand Manager
Assistant Brand Manager
Brand Assistant

Gain/Ivory Snow Brand Manager
Assistant Brand Manager
Brand Assistant

Solo/Dreft Brand Manager
Assistant Manager
Brand Assistant

Associate Advertising Manager
Dry Laundry Category

Bold-3 Brand Manager
Assistant Brand Manager
Brand Assistant

Cheer Brand Manager
Assistant Brand Manager
Brand Assistant

Oxydol Brand Manager
Assistant Brand Manager

Operations Manager

Central Promotion
Group

Computer Systems

Office Manager

Exhibit 6   Procter & Gamble Co. (A)

LDL Market Historic Growth Trends and Projections

Fiscal Year Ending June 30		Volume (000,000 cases)	% of Category Volume		
			Mildness	Performance	Price
Actual	1973	56.4	44	19	37
	1974	57.0	45	20	35
	1975	56.4	44	21	35
	1976	56.8	43	22	35
	1977	56.1	40	28	32
	1978	57.8	40	30	30
	1979	57.0	39	32	29
	1980	58.7	38	33	29
	1981	59.0	37	35	28
Projected	1982	59.4	37	35	28
	1983	59.8	36	35	29
	1984	60.1	36	35	29
	1985	60.8	35	36	29
	1986	61.1	35	36	29

Source: Company records. Classification and projections were based on collective brand manager judgment.

Exhibit 7   Procter & Gamble Co. (A)

Attribute Importance Ratings

METHODOLOGY: Respondents were asked to rate the importance to them of LDL attributes on a 6-point scale, with 6 being "want the most" and 1 being "want the least." For example, chart below to be read: 64% of respondents claimed "Makes dishes shine" as one of the attributes they wanted most in a dishwashing liquid, while 2% of respondents claimed this attribute as the one they wanted least.

Attribute	% of Respondents						No Answer	Average Rating
	6	5	4	3	2	1		
Makes dishes shine	64	16	7	6	2	2	3	5.3
Pleasant odor or perfume	40	17	11	10	7	10	5	4.2
Don't have to use much	70	13	6	5	1	2	3	5.5
Doesn't make skin rough	65	12	7	5	4	3	4	5.0
Is low-priced	50	19	10	9	3	4	5	5.0
Good for hand-washing laundry	29	14	9	11	9	23	5	3.7
Does a good job on pots and pans	75	13	4	2	1	1	4	5.6
Does not spot or streak glasses or dishes	67	15	8	3	2	2	3	5.4
Is mild to hands	68	13	5	5	3	3	3	5.2
Makes long-lasting suds	83	12	7	2	2	2	2	5.5
Cuts grease	87	6	2	1	—	1	3	5.8
Is economical to use	72	13	6	4	1	1	3	5.5
Soaks off baked-on or burnt-on food	60	17	7	5	2	4	5	5.2
Good for tough cleaning jobs	52	13	8	9	4	9	5	4.8

Source: Company research.

Exhibit 8   Procter & Gamble Co. (A)

LDL Market Shares by Brand and Company
(shares of statistical cases)

		Year		
Brand	*Segment*	1961	1971	1981
Joy	Performance	14.9%	12.0%	12.1%
Ivory	Mildness	17.5	14.9	15.5
Dawn	Performance	—	—	14.1
Thrill*	Mildness/Performance	—	2.9	—
P&G		32.4	29.8	41.7
Lux	Mildness	17.3	7.3	3.1
Dove	Mildness	—	4.8	3.1
Sunlight	Performance	—	—	0.7
All Other	Price	5.9	1.0	—
Lever Brothers		23.2	13.1	6.9
Palmolive Liquid	Mildness	—	11.7	11.8
Dermassage	Mildness	—	—	3.5
All Other	Price/Performance	5.5	9.6	8.3
Colgate-Palmolive		5.5	21.3	23.6
All Other LDL's	Mainly Price-Generics and Private Labels	38.9	35.8	27.8
Total LDL's		100.0	100.0	100.0

Source: Company records.

*Thrill was introduced by P&G in 1969. The brand ultimately proved not to provide a needed product benefit and was discontinued in 1975 because of faltering volume.

Exhibit 9   Proctor & Gamble Co. (A)

Cost Structure for an Established LDL Brand

Cost of goods	51%
Distribution	7
Selling and general administration	10
Marketing expenditures	20*
Profit	12
Total	100

Source: Company records.

*Includes advertising, trade and consumer promotion expenditures.

Exhibit 10 Procter & Gamble Co. (A)

LDL User/Non-User[*] Attribute Association %

Respondents Were Asked to Indicate Which One Brand Was Best Described by Each Attribute Phrase.	Ivory Liquid		Joy		Dawn		Palmolive		Price Brands	
Usual Brand[*]:	Yes	No	Yes	No	Yes	No	Yes	No	Yes	No
Best for mildness	89	51	53	12	41	7	71	27	13	2
Best overall for getting dishes clean	64	9	78	14	88	15	61	5	18	1
Best for cutting grease	41	6	49	7	96	45	35	4	16	1
Best for removing tough, cooked-on foods	47	7	55	10	88	28	41	6	19	2
Best for leaving dishes shiny	44	10	81	45	59	5	40	4	14	1
Gives the best value for your money	74	24	60	4	65	6	55	5	40	7
Makes the longest lasting suds	79	29	60	10	67	11	50	5	12	1
Has the most pleasant fragrance	43	11	64	35	39	9	35	11	14	1

Source: Company research.

Note: To be read, for example: 89% of respondents who claimed Ivory Liquid as their usual brand indicated that it was best for being mild to your hands. 51% of people who did not claim Ivory Liquid as their usual brand indicated it was best for being mild to your hands.

[*] A brand user was defined as a respondent who reported that brand as her usual brand over the past three month period.

Exhibit 11   Procter & Gamble Co. (A)

1981 "Mildness" Ivory TV Storyboard

COMPTON ADVERTISING, INC.
625 Madison Avenue, New York, N.Y. 10022

Telephone: PLaza 4-1100

CLIENT: PROCTER & GAMBLE CO.
PRODUCT: IVORY LIQUID
TITLE: "STOKES"
COMML. # PGIL 5713   TIMING: 30 SECONDS
DATE: 10/22/80

1. (SFX: MUSIC)
ANNCR: (VO) Can you pick Jean Stokes' hands from her two daughters?

2. LISA: Mom's hands are as young-looking as ours!

3. KATHY: We sing together for charity --

4. MOM: Strictly amateur -- but your hands get noticed.

5. ANNCR: (VO) And Jean does a lot of dishes. What's her secret?

6. LISA: Ivory Liquid!
MOM: And I've told my girls how mild it is.

7. ANNCR: (VO) Lab tests show Ivory Liquid's

8. mildest of all leading brands.

9. And nothing gets dishes cleaner.

10. LISA: I'm going to stay with Ivory Liquid.

11. GROUP SINGS: Ivory Liquid.

12. ANNCR: (VO) Because young-looking hands are worth holding on to.

Exhibit 12   Procter & Gamble Co. (A)

1981 "Value" Ivory TV Storyboard

COMPTON ADVERTISING, INC.
625 Madison Avenue, New York, N.Y. 10022
Telephone: PLaza 4-1100

CLIENT: PROCTER & GAMBLE CO.
PRODUCT: IVORY LIQUID
TITLE: "THE KIPPERS"
COMML. #   PGIL 5573   TIMING: 30 SECONDS
DATE: 4/1/80

1. ANNCR: (VO) Is the Kippers' "bargain" brand a better buy than mild Ivory Liquid? Let's see...

2. INT: Let's test your brand against Ivory Liquid with a penny's worth of each.

3. Let's wash some dishes.

4. How are your suds? BOB: I don't have any suds now.

5. INT: How about the Ivory Liquid Mrs. Kipper? BEV: I still have a tubful.

6. INT: Let's scoop some up and compare.

7. Okay what happened? BEV: I did a lot more dishes.

8. What I thought was a bargain isn't really a bargain at all. INT: What's the bargain?

9. INT: What's the bargain? BEV: Ivory is the bargain.

10. It's gentle to my hands, and I can save money.

11. ANNCR: (VO) You don't have to give up

12. mild Ivory Liquid to save money.

Exhibit 13   Procter & Gamble Co. (A)

1981 Dawn Advertising Storyboard

| B&B | BENTON & BOWLES
909 THIRD AVENUE
NEW YORK, N.Y.
(212) 758-6200 | Client: **PROCTER & GAMBLE CO.**
Product: **DAWN**
Length: **45 SECONDS (PGDN 6105)**
Title: **"SLEEPOVER REV/FP"** |

1. (SFX: KIDS TALKING)
MOM: Lasagna? For break-
fast? DAUGHTER: Oh,
Mom! FRIEND: It's a
slumber party!

2. MOM: O.K. But you <u>will</u>
clean up.

3. DAUGHTER: All that
grease! Yuck!!! Gross!

4. MOM: No, Dawn.

5. DAUGHTER: Ah,
finished!

6. FRIEND #1: Uh-uh, forgot
a glass. DAUGHTER: You
forgot it. You wash it.
FRIEND: After that greasy
pan?

7. DAUGHTER: Try it.
Dawn'll handle it.

8. FRIEND #1: The water
doesn't feel greasy...and
neither do my hands.

9. And this glass looks as good
as the first one <u>you</u> washed.

10. ANNCR: (VO) Look. Add
a half cup of grease to
Dawn dishwater.

11. Dawn breaks up grease,
takes it out of your way.
Helps keep it away.

12. So dishes come out clean.

13. FRIEND: Dawn's great!

14. MOM: So, if lasagna's
breakfast, what's dinner?
DAUGHTER: Corn flakes.
(GIRLS LAUGH)

15. ANNCR: (VO) Dawn takes
grease

16. (SFX) out of your way.

Exhibit 14   Procter & Gamble Co. (A)

Current Product Usage

	Ivory	Joy	Dawn
Usual Brand	23	13	25
Past 12-month Trial	35	30	29
Ever-Tried	58	43	54

Source: Company research.

An estimated 60%–80% of total brand volume was consumed by usual brand users for each brand.

Exhibit 15   Procter & Gamble Co. (A)

1981 Joy Advertising Storyboard

Radio TV Reports

41 East 42nd Street New York N.Y. 10017
(212) 697-5100

PRODUCT:	JOY DISHWASHING LIQUID	758077
PROGRAM:	AS THE WORLD TURNS	60 SEC.
	WCBS-TV	1:35PM

1. MAN: Sam. MAN: Joe. It's been too long.

2. MAN: It sure has. Come on in. Honey, Sam's here. WOMAN: How do you do Captain Randall.

3. MAN: Major Randall now I hope my phone call didn't catch you two off guard. But Joe said, Sam if you're ever in town --

4. WOMAN: Well of course. And I hope you stay for dinner Major Randall. That is if you don't mind pot luck.

5. MAN: Oh, don't apologize. MAN: Sam. Make yourself at home. Honey, shouldn't we get out the good dishes?

6. WOMAN: Never mind the dishes. Ours here look fine. What about my dress? MAN: It's just fine.

7. ANNCR: When unexpected guests drop in one thing you don't have to worry about is the way your table looks when you use Joy.

8. Joy cleans every day dishes clear down to the shine. And smells fresh like lemons.

9. Keeps dishes ready for company, even if you're not.

10. MAN: Sure is nice to get home cooking.

11. And look at that shine. Looks like you were expecting company all the time.

12. ANNCR: Lemon fresh Joy cleans down to the shine.

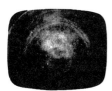

13. And that's a nice reflection on you.

Exhibit 16   Procter & Gamble Co. (A)

Shipment and Share Data for LDL Brands

		Shipments Millions of Cases			Share % of LDL Category		
		Ivory	Dawn	Joy	Ivory	Dawn	Joy
Actual	1977	9.1	6.7	6.7	16.3	11.9	11.9
	1978	9.0	7.3	6.7	15.5	12.7	11.6
	1979	9.1	7.5	6.8	16.0	13.2	12.0
	1980	9.1	8.2	6.9	15.5	14.0	11.7
	1981	9.1	8.3	7.1	15.5	14.1	12.1
Estimated	1982	9.2	8.7	7.2	15.5	14.7	12.2
	1983	9.3	9.0	7.4	15.5	15.0	12.3
	1984	9.3	9.3	7.5	15.5	15.5	12.4
	1985	9.4	9.7	7.6	15.5	15.9	12.5
	1986	9.5	10.1	7.8	15.5	16.5	12.7

Source: Company records. Projections are based on brand managers' judgment.

Exhibit 17 Procter & Gamble Co. (A)

LDL User Demographic Profile
(% of total responding households)

	Total LDL Households	Heavy LDL Users*	Usual Brand				
			Ivory Liquid	Joy	Dawn	Palmolive	No Name/ Plain Label
ADW Usage—Past 7 Days							
Yes	36	9	48	49	51	48	47
No	64	90	51	51	49	42	53
Yearly Income							
Under $15M	32	46	28	32	35	30	36
$15M–$25M	27	29	27	26	29	27	29
Over $25M	41	25	45	42	36	43	35
Population Density (000/sq. mile)							
Under 50	32	39	30	33	38	28	20
50–1999	45	40	45	44	43	46	48
2000 and over	23	21	25	23	19	26	32
Geographic Area							
Northeast	22	26	22	23	19	24	36
North Central	28	28	26	27	31	27	31
South	33	35	34	37	35	33	16
West	17	11	18	13	15	16	17
*Employment**							
Employed	48	37	48	50	49	49	55
Not Employed	52	63	52	59	51	51	45

(continued)

Exhibit 17 (continued)

	Total LDL Households	Heavy LDL Users*	Usual Brand				
			Ivory Liquid	Joy	Dawn	Palmolive	No Name/ Plain Label
*Age**							
Under 35	33	39	31	34	38	39	35
35–50	30	25	29	31	30	30	37
51–59	16	15	17	16	15	16	12
60+	21	30***	23	19	17	24	16
Number in Family							
1–2	40	41	43	38	38	42	28
3–4	44	41	42	45	46	44	50
5+	16	18	15	17	16	14	22

Source: Company research.

Note: To be read, for example: 48% of respondents who claimed Ivory Liquid as their usual brand had used an automatic dishwasher in the past seven days.

* Defined as +15 sinksful per week.

** Female head of household.

*** The heavy LDL user skew towards older respondents may be misleading. Management at P&G believed that, though they washed a large number of small sinkloads, they used a lesser amount of product per sinkload because they tended to live in smaller households.

Exhibit 18 **Procter & Gamble Co. (A)**

LDL Category Assessment
4-Week Blind In-Home Use Test of H-80

	H-80 with Scrubbing Instructions	Established Competitive LDL with Scrubbing Instructions
Attribute Rating (%)		
Overall	77	71
Cleaning	79	73
Removing baked/burned/dried-on food	73	61
Grease removal	77	72
Amount of suds made	73	69
Mildness	55	63
Odor of product	70	68
Color of product	72	69
Favorable Comments (%)		
Unduplicated cleaning	73	65
Cleans well	36	29
Cleans hard-to-remove food	25	15
Cuts grease	34	32
Unduplicated sudsing	49	45
Product color	6	5
Mildness	25	34
Unduplicated odor	45	40
Unduplicated cap/container	8	2
Unduplicated consistency	12	2
Like scrubbing particles/abrasives	12	—
Unfavorable Comments (%)		
Unduplicated cleaning	4	9
Not clean well	—	1
Not clean hard-to-remove food	1	5
Not cut grease	3	8
Unduplicated sudsing	9	17
Product color	1	3
Mildness	16	14
Unduplicated odor	10	9
Unduplicated cap/container	2	2
Unduplicated consistency	12	1
Not like abrasive/gritty feel	11	1
Dishwashing Information		
Used product full strength for scrubbing	61	52
Used scrubbing implement for tough jobs	79	85

Source: Company research. Unmarked bottles of H-80 were given to one of two representative samples of LDL users. The other sample group received unmarked bottles of an established competitive brand. Both brands were accompanied by instructions suggesting the product be diluted for general dishwashing but used full strength for tough dishwashing jobs.

Note: To be read, for example, 77% of the 425 households who used H-80 rated it as 4 or above on a 5-point scale on overall performance.

Exhibit 19   Procter & Gamble Co. (A)

Selected Research Data: Personal Feelings Concerning Dishwashing

	% of Consumers
1. *What Is the Worst Thing About Doing Dishes?*	
The time it takes	24
Having to do them	22
Cleaning pots and pans	15
Scrubbing/scouring	14
Cleaning greasy items	6
Hard on hands	4
2. *What Is the Toughest Dishwashing Job?*	
Removal of baked/burnt/fried/cooked foods	39
Removal of greasy foods	32
Cleaning of pots and pans	22
Cleaning of skillets	16
Cleaning of casseroles	7
Cleaning of dishes	3
3. *What Is Most Disappointing About Your Current Dishwashing Liquid?*	
Nothing	51
Suds disappear	12
Leaves grease	8
Odor	6
Hard on hands	2
Price/expensive	4
Have to use too much	4
4. *What Improvement Do You Want the Most in a Dishwashing Liquid?*	
Milder to hands	11
Do it by magic/itself	10
Eliminate scouring or soaking	9
Cut grease	9
Soak dishes clean	9
Suds never vanish	6
Nothing/satisfied	9

Source: Company research.

Pepsi-Cola Fountain Beverage Division: Marketing Organization

In November 1986, Mr. John Cranor, president of Pepsi-Cola's Fountain Beverage Division (FBD), was considering reorganizing the division's marketing efforts. Although FBD had been growing rapidly, Mr. Cranor believed the fountain business differed in several ways from the bottle-and-can business that dominated Pepsi's operations and which was organized along brand-management lines.

FBD was responsible for sales of soft drink syrup to fountain outlets—i.e., any location where a consumer purchased a soft drink not in a bottle or can. Industry conventional wisdom and some preliminary analysis established these categories of outlets: quick serve restaurants (QSRs),[1] sit-down restaurants, cup-vending machines, convenience stores, institutional feeders,[2] movie theaters, sports arenas, hotels, and cafeterias. These categories varied in size, volume, market, range, and number of beverages carried, and in other ways. At issue was whether these differences affected Pepsi's success in each class of outlets, and consequently should be focused on in order to allocate marketing resources most effectively. Should FBD's marketing be organized by channel (rather then brand); and, if so, what would this mean for the division's structure and for the skills required to operate within a new organization of marketing activities?

Associate Professor Frank V. Cespedes and Research Associate Jon E. King prepared this case as the basis for class discussion rather than to illustrate either effective or ineffective handling of an administrative situation.

[1]"Quick serve" in the food service industry was equivalent to the widely recognized term, "fast-food."

[2]Also called manual feeders or contract feeders, these were service companies which operated food services on the premises of their customers such as universities or corporations.

Pepsi-Cola

The Pepsi-Cola Company was founded in 1902 in North Carolina by Mr. Caleb Bradham, a pharmacist who developed the soft drink after several years of experimentation at his pharmacy soda fountain. By 1910 he had franchised 280 independent bottlers in 24 states to make and sell syrup and bottled Pepsi-Cola. Sugar price fluctuations after World War I bankrupted the company in 1923, and after another attempt, the Pepsi-Cola Company was declared bankrupt a second time in 1931. The dominant competitor in the industry was the Coca-Cola Company; although founded under similar circumstances in 1886, Coca-Cola was a $40 million company in 1931, selling one of the most advertised and profitable products in the country.

Throughout this period, Coke and Pepsi bottling franchises were sold in perpetuity: the franchisee had exclusive and permanent rights to bottle and sell the cola in a geographical area. Only a bottler's "gross negligence" could invalidate this contract, but the franchise could be resold. Although the franchised bottler was prohibited from selling any other cola, other flavors of soft-drinks were permitted. However, while Pepsi's franchises included rights to all sales (bottle or fountain) Coke franchised only bottling rights, and sold fountain syrup through distributors. Coca-Cola's focus had long been on the fountain market; in fact, its first bottling franchise was sold for only $1 because it was not expected to thrive. In contrast, Pepsi, beginning in the 1930s, focused on retail outlets. As one manager noted:

> Bottlers have large investments in plant, machinery, inventory, transportation equipment, and a field force that services accounts, opens new accounts, places ads, coolers, vending machines and other items in the place of purchase, and sees to it that customer inventory is maintained appropriately. Historically, the bottlers were even more important to Pepsi than Coke, because in Pepsi's system they have responsibility for distribution to fountain operations in addition to managing the bottling operation itself.

Loft, Inc., a chain of 200 candy stores with soda fountains, bought the bankrupt Pepsi-Cola Company in 1931. Loft had been a Coca-Cola account, and its president felt that Loft could reduce cola costs 40% with Pepsi. In 1933, in the midst of the Great Depression, a Loft candy salesman recommended selling 12-ounce Pepsi bottles at the same retail price as Coca-Cola's 6-ounce bottles. Sales suddenly jumped in an economy-minded marketplace, and the company started an aggressive campaign of signing up more bottlers. By 1937, the company was running 5 concentrate[3] plants, and 313 bottlers operated across the country. By 1941, Pepsi had enfranchised 469 bottlers and began to offer loans to bottlers to make capital investments.

---

[3]Pepsi-Cola sold beverage concentrate to bottlers, who added carbon dioxide, sweetener, and water to make beverages and beverage syrup.

However, trouble hit Pepsi again after World War II, and again due to sugar prices. Attempts to raise retail prices crippled sales. In 1949, Pepsi hired from Coca-Cola a new president, Mr. Alfred Steele, who focused on several policies: emphasis on quality control and product research, training programs, and a commitment to "partnership" with the Pepsi bottlers. Mr. Steele commented that, "Our job was not to sell the bottler something in the hope that he could sell it, but rather our true forte was to help him to move more goods at a profit." He told the bottlers, "You can save your way to bankruptcy or spend your way to prosperity." Marketing programs were developed area by area, concentrating on the cola battlegrounds one at a time.

Mr. Steele also repositioned the product; it was reformulated as a lighter, less caloric soft drink. Mr. Steele's wife, actress Joan Crawford, became the glamorous ideal of the Pepsi drinker. Instead of pursuing Coca-Cola's customers with a lower price, Pepsi now aimed the theme of "light refreshment" at young, middle-class, American women and the home market. This demanded focusing on grocery stores rather than fountains. One observer commented:

> Efforts were increased in the fountain area in the 1950s, but Coca-Cola had always been very strong there. Long before Pepsi, Coca-Cola had been installing equipment with its logo in soda fountains and luncheonettes all over the country. That equipment came with contractual obligations that the distributor put only Coca-Cola in it. First-mover advantage was very real in that channel. Less so in retail groceries where many different brands competed for limited shelf space. Here, a better deal offered by a more flexible Pepsi could result in more prominent retail display, of great importance for a low-ticket impulse item.

Pepsi's image in the 1960s shifted with the "Pepsi Generation" campaign, but the same marketing style remained. Mr. Alan Pottasch, in charge of Pepsi's advertising in that era, commented, "We stopped talking about the product and started talking about the user, and that is a major difference. What you drank said something about who you were. We painted an image of our consumer as active, vital, and young at heart."

By 1975, Pepsi had drawn ahead of Coke in grocery store sales, but Coca-Cola led in the overall market through its position in fountain accounts, including large fast food chains such as McDonald's. Fountain and vending accounted for two-thirds of Coca-Cola's revenues at the time.

Advertising increasingly became the battleground for the "cola wars," but Coca-Cola began to cut prices selectively in critical geographical areas. By 1980, approximately 50% of nationwide wholesale grocery sales of Coke and Pepsi were discounted, and the average cost of Coke was slightly lower. Operating margins for both companies dropped from the mid 1970s to the mid-1980s.

The 1980s also saw efforts by both companies to exert greater control over their franchised bottlers, especially those with substandard performance. This included encouraging franchise buy-outs and even direct purchase. By 1986,

Pepsi owned 32% of its bottler franchises, responsible for 40% of its retail volume. The other bottlers were split about evenly between multibottler conglomerates (owned by companies such as General Bottlers, General Cinema, and RKO) and independent single franchisees.

PepsiCo, Inc.

Pepsi-Cola had begun to expand its product line in 1963 with the introduction of Diet Pepsi. By 1986 the company sold a range of colas and other carbonated soft drinks (CSDs) with and without sugar, caffeine, and fruit juice in over a hundred countries. In 1965, Pepsi had started to diversify by merging with Frito Lay, Inc., a snackfood manufacturer, and later added restaurant chains including Pizza Hut, Taco Bell, and Kentucky Fried Chicken.

PepsiCo, Inc. had net sales of $9.3 billion in 1986, separated among soft drinks (39%), snack foods (32%) and restaurants (29%). (See Exhibit 1 for financial data.) Eighty-one percent of Pepsi's $3.6 billion soft drink business was domestic, representing approximately $12 billion in domestic retail sales (31% of the U.S. market). Pepsi's CSD 5-year growth rate was 6.5% annually: 30% faster than the industry; the flagship Pepsi-Cola brand was the best selling brand of any kind in supermarkets. The PepsiCo Annual Report noted, "Americans consume more soft drinks than water—about 42 gallons a year for every man, woman and child. More soft drinks [are consumed] than milk, wine, juice, tea, and liquor combined."

The domestic market for soft drinks was split into 3 major channels: retail (primarily grocery) stores (62%), can-vending machines (13%), and fountain (25%). Pepsi's business was divided among those three channels at approximately 55%, 30%, and 15% respectively. The company's strategy for growth in the soft drink industry was enumerated in its Annual Report:

1. Emphasize brand Pepsi.
2. Build a strong portfolio of brands.
3. Increase fountain syrup and vending sales.
4. Leverage the company-owned bottling system.
5. Focus on high-potential, underdeveloped international markets.

At the end of 1986, PepsiCo was divided into two major groups: beverages (Pepsi-Cola Company) and foods (Frito-Lay and restaurant chains). Pepsi-Cola Company was divided into 3 operating groups: Pepsi-Cola Company (U. S. soft drink operations), Pepsi-Cola International (international soft drink operations), and PepsiCo Wines and Spirits. The U.S. soft drink operations were further divided into three divisions: Pepsi-Cola Bottling Group (PBG) was responsible for all company-owned bottling franchises, Pepsi-Cola Bottle & Can (B&C) marketed all nonfountain soft drinks to franchised bottlers, and Pepsi-Cola Fountain Beverage Division (FBD) marketed syrup to fountain outlets. (See Exhibit 2 for organizational chart.) PBG managed each of its owned bottling franchises separately, but manufacturing managers reported to head-quarters manufacturing as well as to franchise management.

Colas dominated the U. S. CSD market with 69% of retail sales; lemon-lime was 11.3%, juice-added (various flavors) 5.3%, "pepper-type" 4.6%, root beer 2.7%, orange 1.5%, and all others 5.6%. Estimated 1986 market shares for each of Pepsi's CSDs are shown below.

Pepsi-Cola	18.6
Diet Pepsi	4.4
Mountain Dew (lemon-lime)	3.0
Pepsi Free (no caffeine, regular and diet)	2.0
Slice (10% fruit juice in several flavors)	1.5
Diet Slice	1.0
Others	0.1

Fountain Beverage Operations

Pepsi-Cola sold concentrate to its bottlers; bottlers then mixed concentrate with water and sweetener to make syrup. Syrup was either sold directly to fountain accounts or was combined with carbonated water for bottling.[4] FBD marketed fountain syrup but the local bottlers manufactured it, delivered it, and then either collected revenues from retailers on a cash-on-delivery basis and forwarded the appropriate portion of these revenues to FBD or, if the account was a "charge" customer, ensured that the account paid FBD directly. At the fountain itself, syrup canisters were attached to a dispenser and pressurized with carbon dioxide tanks. The dispenser had a fixed number of nozzles (usually 4 or 5); each nozzle could dispense one flavor. Few outlets served both Coke and Pepsi for several reasons. First, many retailers considered cola a commodity; second, since dispenser nozzles were limited, offering two colas would limit alternative flavors; and third, neither manufacturer was likely to provide superior market support for an outlet which also promoted the competing cola.

Coca-Cola generally did not sell concentrate to bottlers: instead, it sold the presweetened syrup, thus retaining the sweetener margin (which in Pepsi's case was split between the bottler and the sweetener supplier). Coke also used distributors to deliver syrup and paid them about 25¢ per gallon. These factors gave Coke an estimated 80¢-per-gallon margin over the price Pepsi could retain, since much of the difference went to the local Pepsi bottler who produced and distributed the syrup to outlets. A Pepsi manager pointed out that there were, however, advantages to Pepsi's situation:

> A good Pepsi bottler can bury the competition: Coke's third- and fourth-party distributors and service people are hard to coordinate. Coke also charges big

---

[4]For the purposes of this case study, "bottling" will refer to both bottling and canning.

premiums to local accounts, yet has no field sales force; they can't cover all those accounts as well as our bottlers can.

Developing new fountain business requires capital and staff that the bottler doesn't have and won't consider at the margin Coke offers. It requires delivery vehicles, drivers, sales reps, trained service mechanics, and production facilities; few bottlers will do that for the 25¢ per gallon that Coke pays its distributors. So Coke has started to buy out their distributors.

Mr. William Hober, FBD's sales vice-president, added:

Coke has, however, national standards and a consistent product line since their distributors are hired on that basis. In contrast, our bottlers may carry only brand Pepsi and few or none of our other flavors; they may even carry a competing flavor instead of ours in the lemon-lime or orange category. Unfortunately, if we were to try to get a different bottler in the area to carry Slice, our main bottler would get upset, endangering our primary business.

Fountain Beverage Division (FBD)

FBD was established in 1978 to market Pepsi brands to large national quick serve restaurant (QSR) chains, the biggest customers of fountain syrup. This group included companies such as McDonald's, Burger King, and Wendy's. Initially, FBD was comprised of only 5 headquarters personnel. One FBD manager noted:

Supermarkets and vending machines require of the established bottler less service or capital and produce terrific returns. For example, vending machines are simple to run, provide depreciation cash flow, investment tax credit, and lots of business. Bottle & can business generally provides an 80% gross margin for the bottler. Fountain, in contrast, involves a variety of customer-owned dispensers demanding of the bottler higher maintenance, training, and quality control measures, and requiring integration with the customer's personnel and operations. Delivery routes add complications to the bottler's existing system, and he has a lot to learn to make his operations in this area efficient, because fountain has been virtually ignored for so long.

We have to point out to bottlers the advantage of adding fountain as a complement to their existing business: fountain represents a quarter of the entire CSD beverage market, a huge market for incremental volume increase. We also have to educate bottlers that the ROI in fountain can be as high or higher than in bottle-and-can, *if* the initial investment is made.

Pepsi had 10% of the fountain market in 1978, and Coca-Cola carried most of the rest. Mr. Cranor's predecessor at FBD (and current president of Pepsi USA), Mr. Ronald Tidmore, pointed out to Pepsi-Cola top management that the $2 per gallon margin Coke reaped from its 20 million concentrate gallons of fountain business equaled an extra $40 million that Coke could invest back into fierce bottle & can competition. He asserted, "If we're going to stop Coke from subsidizing grocery sales from profits made in fountain, we have to develop our own fountain business. This means building up our fountain field force." In the late 1970s, a sales force was gradually established by temporarily assigning personnel from other Pepsi-Cola divisions to FBD.

Early on, bottlers remained disinterested in fountain because of the low volume: the 250 million retail gallons nationally in 1978 was not enough to draw attention, compared to Pepsi's 2 billion retail gallon bottle & can business. FBD's mission became to sign up new fountain accounts in order to boost volume. FBD contracted with bottlers to split sales responsibility between large and small accounts: the line was drawn such that FBD retained sales management of any account with two or more outlets in two or more bottlers' territories. FBD would approach the headquarters of such accounts to arrange a contract (including setting a price). FBD also established a special national accounts sales force to manage the 14 largest Pepsi fountain accounts. (See Exhibit 3 for a chart of sales responsibilities.) Just before moving into the presidency of Pepsi-Cola USA, Mr. Tidmore arranged to double the number of district sales managers (account reps) in FBD in 1986 to a total of 83.

Current Position and Organization

By 1986, FBD had increased its market share to 29% of the $10 billion retail fountain market, and some bottlers had set up their own fountain sales forces for local accounts. That year, FBD sold $210 million in concentrate to bottlers who in turn sold $472 million in syrup to fountain outlets; this represented $25 million profit after tax to Pepsi-Cola. Revenues had increased 12% over 1985, volume 8%, market share 1.4 points, and profit 21%. (See Exhibit 4.)

In 1986, 69% of Pepsi's fountain volume was national business, the rest locally sold accounts managed by the bottlers. However, only 35% of operating profit was attributable to national business. Mr. David Weinberg, FBD's vice president for New Business Development, noted, "Selling to national accounts is not as proportionately profitable as selling to smaller accounts because it is more competitive. It demands marketing services, co-op advertising, and low prices. But it does provide high volume and credibility, it gets consumers sampling and it is highly visible to smaller accounts."

Mr. Cranor had joined FBD in early 1986. He had been with PepsiCo for 10 years, mostly in Frito-Lay. Mr. William Hober, VP of Sales for Fountain, was also new in his job but had been in field sales at Pepsi-Cola for 25 years. Mr. John Swanhaus had been FBD's VP of Marketing for 2 years and had been at Pepsi-Cola for 10 years in Bottle & Can and Wines & Spirits. Top managers at FBD usually stayed in the division for 2–3 years before moving to another division.

The unit was staffed by 300 people in sales, marketing, finance and control, and systems operations (see Exhibit 5). Brand marketing involved 16 people; another 4 people were dedicated to regional marketing. Sales was divided into 4 geographic divisions plus National Accounts. National Accounts headquarters personnel included a 4-person new business development group and 10 account managers for managing sales to the 14 largest customers' headquarters (not outlets). Each field sales division had 3 or 4 regions, 2 division development managers (DDMs), and 3 National Account sales managers (NASMs). NASMs were responsible for National Account outlets in their areas; DDMs acted as consultants to the bottlers. Each sales region was divided into 5–7 districts run by district sales managers (DSMs: account reps). This geographic organization had been in place since FBD acquired a sales force.

Sales

In 1986, the FBD field sales force had added 40 new positions; one manager pointed out that this level of expansion was unheard of at Pepsi because of its "lean" operating style. This expansion raised the number of district managers to 83, each with a discretionary budget of $250 thousand for motivating the 1–10 bottlers in his or her district toward fountain accounts. Specific uses included local advertising and merchandising incentives and sometimes capital investment. Mr. Hober characterized this amount of cash as "not a lot," but more was available at the divisional sales managers' discretion.

DSMs were 26–30 years old and were paid a base salary of $45 thousand; bonuses ranged from $3–8 thousand. This compensation was considered very competitive. Entry level salespeople had 3–5 years of experience in consumer packaged goods sales, or 5–7 years in advertising/promotions. New DSMs received 4 weeks of formal training in their first year, as well as up to 4 weeks on the job training with the regional sales manager, other DSMs, NASMs, and development managers. Each DSM reported in detail on every bottler in the district three times a year, including evaluations of outfitting (i.e., appropriate production and distribution equipment), commitment and the area's fountain market.

The DSM was responsible for every bottler in that district, as well as all accounts not established as National Accounts (the 150 largest) or bottler-managed (local). FBD field sales reps made about two-thirds of their calls on bottlers and one-third on retail fountain accounts; before Mr. Hober took over sales in 1986, much less of the rep's time was spent on the bottler. Mr. Hober had considered and rejected the option of splitting the sales force in two (bottler/retailer):

> A function-oriented division concentrates on analysis and loses local market sensitivity: managers start caring about what "bottlers" think rather than what "the bottler in Baton Rouge" thinks. Success in this business comes from negotiating, developing relationships, nurturing accounts, and dealing with problems one by one. A rep can't fully serve a bottler unless he or she knows the local fountain market *better* than the bottler.
>
> Since our reps are responsible for bottlers and accounts, they can keep on top of all the important details about the area's market. The DSM who works in Baton Rouge knows what the bottler faces in Baton Rouge, and when he sells a new account he has something tangible to offer the bottler in return for the bottler's commitment of time and money to the fountain market.

Mr. Swanhaus added, "Account problems tend to take place on the local, not national level, so we want people where they're needed." Mr. Swanhaus had originated a field marketing program at Bottle & Can when he was VP of marketing operations there. The theory was that national programs were often too unwieldy to solve local problems. He established a similar organization at FBD by placing 12 managers in charge of programs tailored to their geographical areas (in addition to the 16 managers in brand development at FBD headquarters). Mr. Hober liked the idea and was interested in taking Mr. Swanhaus' organizational strategy even further by moving more of the available finances for development and promotion into the districts and placing NASMs and DDMs into the regions (they were currently at the divisional level). This combination would move toward putting profit & loss responsibility at the regional manager level.

Bottlers

One division sales manager pointed out,

> Before we started getting involved with bottler operations, most bottlers didn't know if their few fountain accounts were profitable or not. Analysis found they typically were, or could be with more effort. But if the bottler is not interested and committed, nothing happens. The division development manager will do an "infrastructure study" which entails separating fountain accounts and operations into a sub-unit of the bottler's organization. Then we can study volume and profitability, making recommendations where necessary, and offering cash flow subsidies to get the fountain business going. The idea is to get the bottler to understand the fountain market in terms of investment economics and focus resources on fountain business. There are three necessary steps: establish an operating unit dedicated to fountain accounts, add fountain complements such as cups, other equipment, and routes; and then quadruple sales.

Infrastructure studies took 8 weeks and had the objective of developing a strategy for growing fountain business 15% annually. Pepsi FBD offered bottlers financial incentives for making required asset investments which varied depending upon the size of the bottler's market area and the aggressiveness of the bottler's business plan. Fountain dispensing equipment constituted the bulk of the incremental asset requirements, and this ranged in price from $800 to $3,200 per unit (depending upon the type of fountain equipment appropriate for a given retail outlet) with an average of about $1,500 per unit. The plan would present a defined goal and included evaluation of pricing, merchandising, staffing control, delivery operations, fixed costs, contribution, and ROI for the bottler's market. Comparisons were made with historical performance, market potential, local B&C results, national fountain results, and committed bottlers in similar markets. Where time permitted, analysis was made of specific accounts in the area. In general, an entire business plan was developed for the bottler's fountain operations.

Bottlers were dealt with individually, even if they were owned by Pepsi Bottling Group. One division sales manager commented, "Bottlers are 'rugged individualists' and very tough negotiators: they never want us to think we're doing enough for them."

Customers

One FBD manager noted:

In our business, it always takes at least two sales to make one: we must sell to the outlet and also convince the bottler to make the changes required to keep selling and servicing that account. If the customer is a decentralized chain, moreover, each outlet must often be sold individually even if chain headquarters has established a contract with us.

Mr. Hober commented, "It takes price competition to get new accounts, but it takes a service record to renew an account. However, the most important thing in selling is account knowledge, or 'system savvy.'" Mr. Cranor's objective for FBD was to attain the leading market share in fountain business by 1994; a New Business Development unit (NBD) was created in June 1986. Before that, new customers had been secondary to increasing volume in existing outlets because of route economics: it was cheaper and simpler to ship more product to an existing route stop than to add another location. NBD was set up to deal with large, complex accounts which required time and depth to understand and sell. The group was given complete flexibility on where to focus but was not intended to manage an account once it was established: National Account Managers would become more and more involved as the sale progressed and assume account responsibility after the original sale. NBD was also not intended to become directly involved with local accounts.

Ms. Burden noted that bottlers were being more strongly encouraged to establish their own sales forces for fountain business:

FBD's focus has been so far on large accounts because those are legally defined as Pepsi's customers. However, we now want to get the bottlers more involved because our bottler service system has more potential than Coke's distributors, who are essentially delivery people. The bottler is important regardless of account ownership: if we want to capitalize on our advantage, the bottler must feel ownership of the fountain business.

Mr. Cranor had commissioned a study of "buyer values" (i.e., the issues most important to fountain syrup buyers). The study confirmed many perceptions but also established some differences in needs and preferences among retailers in various categories. Across categories, the five most important issues in general were (in order of decreasing importance) price/economic incentives, equipment and service, account management, product quality, and marketing support (the report broke these issues into numerous details). Mr. Cranor commented, "We were somewhat surprised to find that equipment and service advantages are almost as important as spending and allowance support in the selection of a soft drink supplier. This finding further encouraged our efforts to build our bottler service support into a leadership advantage." (See Exhibit 6 for an outline of the report's findings.)

Marketing

FBD had the highest growth rate of any part of PepsiCo; however, fountain industry growth was slowing. For example, QSR growth was expected to be down to 2% from the 7.7% rate of the past few years. Mr. Cranor was concerned with how to maintain a high growth level as the remaining (non-Pepsi) market shrunk and as Coca-Cola increased its attention to the threat FBD posed. He established three strategies for 1987: first, retain and grow national accounts; second, grow local business rapidly; and third, focus resources for maximum impact. Ms. Burden commented:

> FBD has grown for many years without any organized channel analysis; this is a very action-oriented company and fountain is not Pepsi's traditional business. But by 1985 all the biggest customers were covered, and those that were still Coke customers were committed for some time. Now growth must come from two areas: building current accounts in size, and bringing in smaller national and local customers.
>
> FBD needed little focus at first because the market was so untouched. But now Coke is becoming more aware and consequently tougher to compete with, and only 10% of the market is sold by anyone other than Coke and Pepsi. For example, only one of the top 25 restaurant chains serves a third competitor, and that's because the beverage company owns the chain. So to get new accounts now we have to go head to head with Coke, and we want to pick the best way to do that.

FBD had traditionally stressed to fountain customers that soft drinks were traffic builders for their stores and offered advertising support, point-of-sale promotions, and other services which would help increase store traffic. Mr. Cranor noted that brand marketing at FBD was dwarfed by Bottle & Can (which spent $130 million in 1986 on advertising alone), and had therefore traditionally supported B&C's focus on the consumer:

> We therefore studied each market and its soft drink consumers in order to develop a brand portfolio for each region, trying to convince fountain customers that our brands would enhance their images. Many of these vendors weren't interested.

Mr. Weinberg added:

> Many fountain customers don't take soft drinks seriously as a marketing tool. Many believe their soft drink business is "captive" in the sense that their customers aren't going to walk in or out of the establishment because of the beverage selection. Consequently, brand isn't as important as service and support (technical, sales, and marketing), and image isn't as important as understanding the fountain customer's business.

Frustration with this situation had in part motivated Mr. Cranor to consider an emphasis on channel marketing, rather than brand marketing, at FBD. He suspected that image enhancement would be important in some fountain channels but not in others, and marketing effectiveness might be improved by focusing on these differences. However, Mr. Cranor also noted some potential difficulties in reorienting FBD's marketing activities:

> It's hard to legitimize a sales-oriented division in a brand-oriented company. It goes against the grain here to dwell on channel processes. But many fountain customers are indifferent to brand advertising expenditures. In fact, I suspect FBD could simply stop spending money on advertising because the people down the hall at Pepsi Bottle & Can spend so much on consumer ads and promotions.
>
> In this business, volume is volume: what's the difference if the fountain outlet sells Pepsi or Slice? What's important is that Pepsi products are at the fountain and that competitors' brands are not. But we're now in only 70,000 out of a total of 220,000 chain fountain outlets, and we clearly can't go after 150,000 new outlets at once. We should focus on a few major segments, and there are several criteria we can use to focus: size, growth, our historical success with a fountain channel, and the nature of our competitive advantage.

Channels

During the winter of 1985–86, FBD unexpectedly achieved success with convenience stores because of an idea called "Dual Cola." 7-11 convenience stores started offering a choice between Coke and Pepsi, and other stores imitated the practice. Pepsi encouraged the trend in an effort to gain share in many chains. Although there were many successes, it became clear to sales managers that different sales strategies were effective in different channels. Mr. Swanhaus noted, "When our QSR tactics were extended to other restaurants, they met with little enthusiasm. Convenience stores run a very different kind of business from their point of view, and they did not respond well to being talked to as if they were QSRs. They wanted features we hadn't yet thought about such as joint can/fountain programs, since they sell both."

Ms. Burden added,

> Unfortunately there is not much information available in the fountain industry on volume and behavior patterns. We have long seen differences among quick serve restaurants, theaters, and convenience stores. But in the past, someone would have an idea, assign someone else to analyze it, and work from there ad hoc. Now we must develop tighter analysis, parallel points of comparison, and a marketing framework.

During the summer of 1986, nine channel categories (listed on page 699 and Exhibit 7) were established. Mr. Weinberg commented on the process:

> Understanding different channels means understanding different criteria. We broke outlets down into categories based on overall similarities and differences in buying criteria. This separation was necessarily somewhat arbitrary for the sake of making clean lines and not too many subclassifications. It's not been based on any sophisticated template or checklist: there are many opportunities out there, so we are still opportunistic.

Mr. Cranor commented,

Other manufacturers may have QSRs and convenience stores isolated, but that's all. We can also target low-competition, high-margin channels that the others are ignoring. The demand is to understand the channel, its mechanisms, consumers, and history, and develop a strategy, test it, and roll it out fast. I want to know how the buyer makes decisions, what's important, and how soft-drinks can help him achieve his goals.

For example, hotels do 10 million gallons of syrup business each year; what can FBD do for hotels that Coke can't? Hotels want simple operations, and Pepsi's bottlers can serve all the restaurants, bars, banquet halls, and can vending machines, while Coke has various bottlers and distributors driving in and out. That's the kind of competitive advantage we need to exploit. Sit-down restaurants also seem to respond to one-stop service: they will likely buy from the supplier who delivers everything they need without complication. Even supermarkets are now starting to serve fountain drinks at deli counters.

Marketing collected available estimates of volume in each channel as well as collective judgments about potential economic returns for FBD and its bottlers in each channel (see Exhibit 7). QSRs were the largest channel, accounting for over half the total volume. The largest QSR, McDonald's (a Coca-Cola customer), made up 23% of the QSR segment, or 8% of total national business. QSRs had also led growth trends, closely followed by convenience stores. Although FBD had contracts with Burger King and had been very effective in the QSR channel, national volume had declined in five of the other eight channels in the past four years.

Channel profitability for FBD was based primarily on the level of marketing spending required to support accounts in a channel; QSRs and other restaurants provided only adequate returns compared to other categories. Cup vending accounts required little support from FBD, but heavy equipment investments made these accounts prohibitive to bottlers and older technology made them inconvenient (to bottlers and consumers) compared to can vending. Many cup vending accounts were actually operations run by institutional feeders. Sports arenas demanded huge promotional spending and in fact were only considered national business so that both Pepsi and the bottler could share the expenses.

Ms. Burden also prepared a listing of the top 25 fountain accounts in the nation as well as a matrix comparing channel growth and market size with Pepsi's share of that channel (Exhibit 8).

Conclusion

Mr. Cranor reviewed FBD's current position and data about fountain channels with the following questions in mind. Should FBD focus its marketing activities on channel distinctions and, if so, how and according to what criteria and priorities? What restructuring within FBD would be required to put any new programs in place, and what were the implications of any changes for current marketing managers, the sales force, bottlers, and the place of FBD within PepsiCo? Finally, if marketing were reoriented to focus on channels, how should any changes best proceed for a smooth transition and maximum effectiveness?

Exhibit 1 Pepsi-Cola Fountain Beverage Division: Marketing Organization

Selected Financial Data: PepsiCo, Inc.
($ millions)

	1986	1985	1984
Net Sales			
Soft drinks	$3,588.4	$2,725.1	$2,565.0
Snack foods	3,018.4	2,847.1	2,709.2
Restaurants	2,684.0	2,081.2	1,833.4
Total continuing operations	$9,290.8	$7,653.4	$7,107.6
Foreign portion	$1,225.8	$ 951.9	$ 963.9
Operating Profits			
Soft drinks	$ 348.6	$ 283.4	$ 86.6
Snack foods	342.8	392.5	393.9
Restaurants	210.1	198.1	183.8
Corporate expenses, net	(221.2)	(202.4)	(213.5)
Income from continuing operations			
before income taxes	$ 680.3	$ 671.6	$ 450.8
Foreign portion	$ 64.7	$ 70.0	$ (139.9)
Capital Spending			
Soft drinks	$ 193.9	$ 160.7	$ 83.6
Snack foods	298.6	286.3	188.9
Restaurants	384.6	331.0	252.5
Corporate	9.2	7.9	30.8
Total continuing operations	$ 886.3	$ 785.9	$ 555.8
Foreign portion	$ 81.4	$ 67.3	$ 36.4
Identifiable Assets			
Soft drinks	$2,617.7	$1,318.6	$1,038.9
Snack foods	1,603.8	1,487.1	1,254.5
Restaurants	2,659.5	1,326.7	1,020.7
Corporate	1,147.6	1,760.5	1,277.0
Total continuing operations	$8,028.6	$5,892.9	$4,591.1
Foreign portion	$2,275.0	$1,054.3	$ 687.5
Statistics and Ratios			
Return on average shareholders' equity	23.5%	22.8%	15.1%
Return on net sales	4.9	5.5	3.9
Total debt to total capital employed	47.5	34.4	26.5
Employees	214,000	150,000	150,000

Exhibit 2   Pepsi-Cola Fountain Beverage Division: Marketing Organization

Corporate Organization

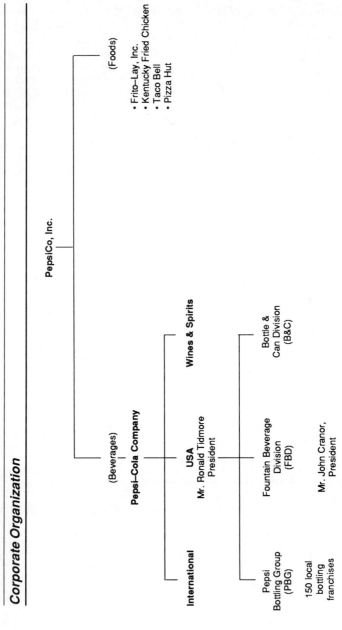

Exhibit 3 Pepsi-Cola Fountain Beverage Division: Marketing Organization

Product Flow Chart

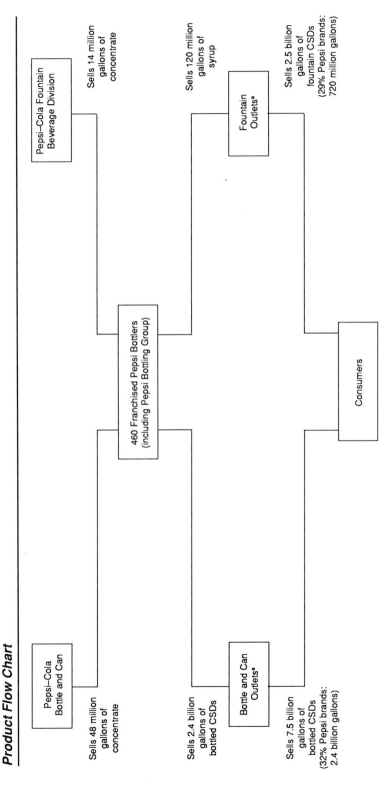

aSome outlets, such as convenience stores, sold both fountain and bottled beverages.

Exhibit 4 Pepsi-Cola Fountain Beverage Division:
Marketing Organization

FBD Syrup Gallonage Sold to Fountain Accounts
(millions)

	1986		1987 Goal	
	Volume	Increase over 1985	Volume	Increase over 1986
National business[a]	65.8 gal.	5.6%	69.7 gal.	6.0%
Local business	29.5	14.0	34.0	15.0
Total	95.3 gal.	8.1%	103.7 gal.	8.8%
National S. O. M.	28.9 share points	0.4 share points		
Local S. O. M.	29.4	3.4		
Total S. O. M.	29.1	1.4		

[a]Any account with two or more outlets in each of two or more bottlers' territories.

Exhibit 5   Pepsi-Cola Fountain Beverage Division: Marketing Organization

FBD Organization

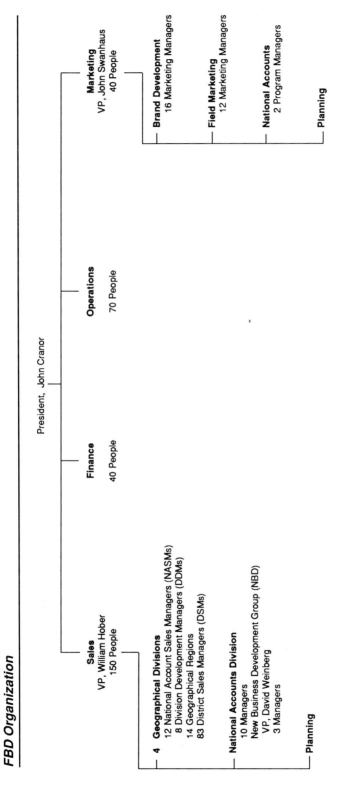

President, John Cranor

Sales
VP, William Hober
150 People

Finance
40 People

Operations
70 People

Marketing
VP, John Swanhaus
40 People

4   **Geographical Divisions**
12 National Account Sales Managers (NASMs)
8 Division Development Managers (DDMs)
14 Geographical Regions
83 District Sales Managers (DSMs)

National Accounts Division
10 Managers
New Business Development Group (NBD)
VP, David Weinberg
3 Managers

Planning

Brand Development
16 Marketing Managers

Field Marketing
12 Marketing Managers

National Accounts
2 Program Managers

Planning

(continued)

Exhibit 6 Pepsi-Cola Fountain Beverage Division: Marketing Organization

Customer Values by Category
(Check mark indicates "very important")

Buyer Values	Cafeterias	Contract Feeders	Hotels	Convenience Stores	Theaters	Chain Restaurants
Customized, individualized marketing programs	✓	✓	✓	✓	✓	✓
Marketing programs that are appropriate to our segment	✓	✓	✓	✓	✓	
Joint vending and food service programs		✓	✓	✓		
Market share/customer reference	✓	✓		✓		
Proven industry leadership and expertise	✓	✓		✓		
Proven profitability of selling soft drinks	✓	✓	✓	✓	✓	✓
Billing and rebate flexibility to ease use of marketing support	✓		✓		✓	
Innovations to improve our operating efficiency/capacity	✓	✓	✓	✓	✓	✓
Guaranteed high service levels	✓	✓	✓		✓	✓

Exhibit 6 (continued)

Comparing Images of Pepsi and Coke: The Customer's Viewpoint

Pepsi		*Coke*	
Most Frequent		*Most Frequent*	
Aggressive		Arrogant	
Frequent		*Frequent*	
Unorganized		Established	Conservative
A regional company		Autocratic	Marketing oriented
Marketing oriented		Aggressive	Professional
Quality company		Innovative	Quality company
			The Cadillac
Less Frequent		*Less Frequent*	
Entrepreneurial	Stronger sales organization	More personnel resources	Relying on past reputation
Solid	Going through the motions	Better structure & organization	Domineering
Competitive	Better attuned to corporate relationships	More marketing support	Promotional
Operational & service oriented	Ethical	More capable people	Game player
Better commercials	Reactionary	Motherhood	Docile
Turnover	Systemically flexible	More adaptable	Insensitive
Spotty service	Followers	Not adaptable	Inflexible
Lagging in marketing programs	Daring	Traditional	Leaders
Quality	Upstart	Stable	The "Big Blue" of soft drinks
Wrapped up in themselves	High energy	Consistent	Nonfinancial
Retail-oriented	Ready-aim-fire	"Coke Is It"	Diversification to the max
Midwestern	More interested in the business	The big company	Stodgy
Great marketing company	More able & willing to work with you	Vacillating	Resting on laurels
The Avis role		Wrapped up in themselves	Not as aggressive
		Popular	Bureaucratic
		National	Renewed

Exhibit 7 Pepsi-Cola Fountain Beverage Division: Marketing Organization

FBD Performance by Channel

Channel	1986 National Volume	1986 % of National Volume	1986 Pepsi National Share	1986 Non-Pepsi National Volume	1982–86 National Volume Growth Rate	1982–86 Pepsi Volume Growth Rate	Economic Returns Pepsi/Bottler	1986 Local Volume[a]
Quick service restaurant	118 MM gals.	51.9%	37.7%	73.5 MM gals.	7.7%	16.1%	Marginal/Good	6 MM gals.
Sit-down restaurant	29	12.7	7.4	26.9	1.2	1.2	Marginal/Good	34
Cup vending	25	11.0	23.5	19.1	0.7	(1.0)	Good/Negative	19
Convenience stores	22	9.9	37.8	13.7	7.4	6.8	Good/Good	1
Institutional feeders	10	4.5	12.6	8.6	1.2	(1.7)	Good/Good	5
Theaters	8	3.7	13.0	6.9	2.3	(1.1)	Good/Good	1
Sports arenas	7	3.0	11.7	6.2	4.5	(13.5)	Negative/ Negative	2
Hotels	5	2.0	12.2	4.4	(3.6)	2.7	Good/Good	4
Cafeterias	3	1.4	4.0	2.9	3.5	(7.1)	Good/Good	3
Totals	227 MM gals.	100%	28.5%	162.2 MM gals.	5.0%	10.6%		75 MM gals.

a Volume available to local, bottler-managed accounts.

Exhibit 8   Pepsi-Cola Fountain Beverage Division: Marketing Organization

Fountain Beverage Account Prospects

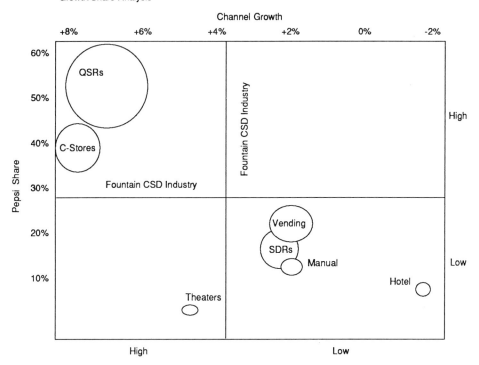

Fountain Beverage Division
Growth/Share Analysis

Top Restaurant Chains

Chain	1985 Revenues (millions)	Outlets	Cola Served
McDonald's	$11,000.9	8,901	Coca-Cola
Burger King	4,290.0	4,534	Pepsi-Cola
Kentucky Fried Chicken	3,368.0	7,106	Pepsi-Cola
Wendy's	2,664.0	3,442	Coca-Cola
Pizza Hut	2,580.8	4,845	Pepsi-Cola
Hardee's	1,890.0	2,562	Coca-Cola
Dairy Queen	1,572.0	4,805	Coca-Cola/Pepsi-Cola
Domino's Pizza	1,084.0	2,891	Coca-Cola
Taco Bell	1,065.0	2,328	Pepsi-Cola
Denny's	1,043.2	1,121	Coca-Cola
Big Boy	946.0	810	Coca-Cola
Red Lobster	869.4	386	Coca-Cola
Arby's	811.0	1,550	Royal Crown
Long John Silver's	667.0	1,369	Coca-Cola

(continued)

Exhibit 8 (continued)

Chain	1985 Revenues (millions)	Outlets	Cola Served
Church's Fried Chicken	639.9	1,549	Coca-Cola
Ponderosa	639.1	637	Coca-Cola
Jack-In-The-Box	597.0	800	Coca-Cola
Dunkin Donuts	476.7	1,447	Pepsi-Cola
Shoney's	570.0	497	Coca-Cola
Sizzler	500.0	475	Coca-Cola
Baskin-Robbins	484.1	3,217	Coca-Cola
Roy Rogers	471.8	543	Coca-Cola
Friendly	471.4	750	Coca-Cola
Western Sizzlin'	436.0	574	Coca-Cola
Bonanza	421.0	552	Coca-Cola/Pepsi-Cola

Centralization and Decentralization of Marketing Efforts

Case 26
Turner Construction Company

For much of Wednesday, June 20, 1984, Mr. Robert Kupfer, Executive Vice President of Turner Construction Company, had studied two pieces of that morning's mail. One was a memorandum from the manager of Turner's new Hospital Facilities Group, explaining that a lead concerning a major hospital chain was not being pursued in Territory A. The other was a standard form submitted by Territory A's general manager, requesting approval to pursue a commercial-building project in that territory.

A project of the size being considered in Territory A was normally sent to his office for corporate approval, and the Hospital Facilities Group reported directly to Mr. Kupfer. He knew that either the commercial building or the hospital would absorb Territory A's current capacity of available staff for at least several months. In addition, Mr. Kupfer believed these projects illustrated problems and opportunities he had been considering since assuming responsibility in May 1983 for corporate sales and marketing, strategic planning, and public relations/corporate communications. Like many situations in the construction business, moreover, time was important: he would have to make his decisions by the end of the week.

Turner Construction Company

Turner was founded in New York City in 1902. The company built the concrete station stairways for the city's first subway line and soon became well-known within the city's building trades. Turner later expanded geographically, generally following trends in building types and materials while pioneering in cost control, estimating, and construction management techniques. Its projects included the U.N. Building, Madison Square Garden, and Lincoln Center in

N.Y.C., numerous office buildings and headquarters (e.g., U.S. Steel and IBM), major manufacturing facilities, stadiums at the Universities of Pennsylvania, Pittsburgh, Brown, and Cornell, and Aldrich and Kresge Halls at Harvard Business School.

From its early years, Turner aimed for continuous employment for its personnel. This was unusual in the cyclical and uncertain construction environment, where firms generally maintained minimum organizations, hired additional people after contracts were obtained, then laid off personnel when jobs were completed. Turner also stressed promotion-from-within, doing most hiring at introductory levels (primarily from undergraduate civil engineering programs) while emphasizing training and cross-functional experience during an employee's years with the firm.

In 1983, Turner led building contractors in the value of contracts booked (see Exhibit 1). Management was especially proud of the percentage of repeat business (about 60% in 1983). Mr. Douglas Bennett, Manager of Corporate Contracts and Marketing, noted that "every building has unique structural and economic factors, and our marketing practices reflect that. But there's a learning curve for all participants in a building contract: pre-construction negotiations and job planning move faster among participants who have worked together in the past."

Construction Services

Turner operated as a general contractor and/or construction manager (CM). A contractor agreed to deliver (and built a portion of) a finished product to an owner,[1] while a CM acted as the owner's agent and advisor, providing pre-construction services and monitoring the firms that actually built the project.

Contracts were "lump-sum" or "negotiated." In lump-sum, an owner's architect completed plans and specifications and then contractors bid on the project. The contractors competed primarily on price, and their incentive was to meet specifications at minimal cost because their remuneration was the lump-sum price minus their final cost of materials and construction. If specifications changed during building, or if ground or weather conditions were "abnormal," the contractor usually sought further compensation from the owner.

In a negotiated contract, contractor and owner worked together from the planning stage, negotiating specifications, cost estimates, a guaranteed maximum price, and the contractor's fee. Depending upon a project's size and complexity, these pre-construction services could cost from $10,000 to $50,000 and, perhaps more importantly for the contractor, significant staff time. Sometimes the contractor was reimbursed for these services.

---

[1] In the construction industry, "owner" referred to a real estate development firm, manufacturing firm, or other entity purchasing a contractor's services. It was generally synonymous with "customer" from the contractor's point of view.

Most construction was awarded lump-sum, but Turner performed most of its work through negotiated fee contracts where it acted as both general contractor and CM. Turned planned and scheduled the project, procured materials, marshalled the different personnel required, awarded and supervised subcontracts, and assumed responsibility for on-time completion at a guaranteed maximum price. Turner relied heavily on local subcontractors,[2] generally limiting its own construction to foundations and concrete, masonry and carpentry.

For negotiated contracts, Turner first estimated the project's direct costs, primarily materials and subcontracting costs.[3] Indirect job-management costs were generally 5 to 7% of direct costs. Turner's fee (or operating profit) was 2 to 5% of the guaranteed maximum price, depending on size, complexity, personnel required, and the anticipated risks (e.g., uncertain ground conditions, availability of proven local subs, or the "predictability" of an owner or architect).

A contingency provision (usually 3% of direct costs) covered unexpected matters during construction (e.g., extreme weather). If the completed project exceeded the guaranteed maximum price, Turner absorbed the difference (aside from items covered by the contingency fee); savings after returning contingency fees were shared between the owner and Turner, with Turner generally receiving 25% of the difference between guaranteed price and actual costs.

Mr. Ed Clarke, Senior Vice President, explained that "our business is a combination of consulting and underwriting: we buy risk and sell predictability":

> We buy the risk inherent in completing a project on time and for a guaranteed price, and then subcontract pieces of that risk to local tradespeople. We manage all the project's details for the owner and, because we're involved early, we can guarantee a price earlier than the lump-sum bidder. Thus, the owner can begin arranging financing earlier and construction (and occupancy) can begin sooner. Time is money in construction. We provide the owner with some confidence about the time, costs and management involved.

Mr. Bennett added, "in the construction phase, our primary value-added is operations management":

> On-time completion and savings are affected by scheduling, improved construction techniques, selection and management of subs, and the project manager's

---

[2] "Subs" (as they were called in the industry) were independent organizations which performed work in specific trades such as electrical, masonry, etc. for the general contractor under lump-sum agreements. A performance bond protected the general contractor against a sub's default on contract terms, but "reputation" often exceeded "bid price" in selecting a sub.

[3] Costs and fees were normally paid to the contractor monthly during construction; thus relatively little contractor funding was required.

handling of weather, labor and delivery matters. We're organized to provide depth in these areas.

In 1983, Turner handled 216 construction projects (excluding small renovation projects handled by a special-project division), including 93 new contract awards. Of the projects, 124 were negotiated fee contracts (accounting for 60% of earnings), 68 were lump-sum (26% of earnings), and 21 were CM (6% of earnings). Of the new contracts, the construction value was less than $1 million for 12, more than $50 million for 7, while the median project value was about $7 million. Turner had 2,200 employees of which 210 were officers, project executives, or project managers; 1,600 were engineers, superintendents, purchasing agents, estimators, business development, or other professional staff; and the remaining were support or clerical personnel. In addition, the company averaged 2,500 craftsmen on the payroll for work not subcontracted by Turner. The open shop companies had staffings of 286 and 400, respectively. Most of Turner's competitors were smaller regional firms, generally with lower overhead.

Major Markets and Buyers

Turner built primarily in commercial, hospital/health care, public facilities, and hotel/residential construction (see Exhibit 2). Technical requirements and buyer behavior differed among these markets.

Commercial. Since the later 1970s, commercial construction had become a larger proportion of Turner's annual business. Accelerated depreciation rates made office buildings profitable at lower occupancy rates, thus spurring commercial building. However, Mr. Kupfer had recently heard at a trade association meeting the following figures: since 1980, U.S. commercial building had averaged about 350 million square feet annually, while projected demand through 1990 was about 225 million square feet per year. In 1984, an estimated 200 million square feet of U.S. office space was vacant. Commercial building was affected by factors such as interest rates, foreign investors seeking to put money in tangible U.S. assets, changes in depreciation rates, and regional differences. But less building was a likely forecast in the commercial market.

Within the commercial market, there were two types of buyers. The predominant buyer was a real estate developer who performed three roles: deal-maker in putting together the necessary financing; nuts-and-bolts coordinator in overseeing design and construction personnel; and marketer in leasing the office space. A contractor was often expected to be involved in each activity. Mr. Bennett described most developers as "tough, sophisticated buyers who know what they want."

> They look at the staff the contractor puts on the job and details of costing and scheduling. They're entrepreneurs who have a target rent-per-square-foot in mind, and then back into desired construction costs from that figure. So they're looking for a guaranteed maximum price before construction begins because, with that price, they can get construction financing earlier, start work in the

field sooner, and so start generating rental revenues as soon as possible. There's also a certain amount of ego and pizazz among the buyers: they expect to interact with top executives, and close personal treatment is an aspect of selling in this market.

The other commercial buyer was a corporation building a new headquarters. Mr. Roger Lang, Business Development Manager in New York, described this buyer as "concerned with the building's image and quality":

> The CEO usually gets very involved. In fact, some almost develop an "edifice complex": it's their building, their monument for the company, and these buildings involve lots of money and risks. Many companies acquire additional debt to finance a new headquarters, so the board and investors watch closely. During construction, moreover, there are lots of changes in this kind of building, so the ongoing relationship with the contractor is a big factor.

Health Care.   This market was relatively recession proof and, due to financing through municipal bond offerings, somewhat counter-cyclical to the commercial market. According to the Department of Commerce, total hospital construction expenditures were expected to continue increasing:

Year	1981	1982	1983	(Forecast) 1984	(Forecast) 1985
$ in Millions	$6,990	7,782	8,560	9,398	10,328

The hospital market varied by region. In older Eastern and Midwestern cities, the market was largely private, "not for profit" hospitals like Mt. Sinai in N.Y.C. The Southeast was largely "for profit" chains run by corporations like National Medical Enterprises, who also managed "not for profit" hospitals for a fee. The West was dominated by multi-hospital groups. Growth also varied, with more health care construction in the West and Southeast and less in the East and Midwest.

In all regions, gaining state regulatory approval for a new hospital facility took 6 to 24 months. A key step was the Certificate of Need which required the hospital to outline a construction program, including square footage for each component and a detailed breakdown of costs. This program was usually developed by hospital planning consultants, who were hired before architects or contractors and helped to select architects and contractors for a project.

In the "for profit" hospital chains, the decision-maker was normally the head of a facilities-design or construction department at chain headquarters. In private hospitals, the decision-maker was generally the hospital's Chief Administrator, influenced by consultants, hospital board members, peers (other hospital administrators), architects, and the contractor's references. Mr. Bennett classified administrators as either "movers" or "stayers":

> The "movers" are hired to manage a capital expansion program. They look for a contractor's cost and scheduling ability and have an excellent network in reviewing a contractor's references.

The "stayers" are administrators who remain at one hospital and usually have one building program in their careers. They are relatively unsophisticated in this area, rely heavily on the architect for guidance, and want to avoid trouble since they answer to the community-at-large if there is dissatisfaction with the building. They require much support during the selling process.

Consultants are increasingly important in health care construction, since they essentially formulate the package of "needs" which eventually becomes the building program. Technological advances in health care have altered construction, and consultants are often seen as necessary in managing this complexity. When a short list of contractors perceived as relatively equal is assembled, consultants will focus on preconstruction abilities in choosing among them.

Identifying a prospect in the health care market was easy, since the number of existing health care entities in an area was relatively fixed, and the approval process made plans public well before actual construction. This contrasted with the commercial market where entry barriers for developers were less complex, and the development process remained private for a longer period.

Public. In this category, correctional facilities (i.e., prisons and jails) were the fastest growing market. The trend in this market was toward negotiated CM contracts, which were attractive to Turner.

In the correctional market, local statutes often determined procurement procedures. In the Northeast, Midwest, and West, negotiated CM contracts were common. Lump sum was the rule in the South. In negotiated correctional projects, the builder was selected on a combination of fee, staffing, and previous experience. Besides other large contractors, Turner encountered in this market offshoots of architectural firms that focused on correctional facilities and provided some CM services. For lump-sum correctional projects, competition was primarily local contractors.

In designing correctional facilities, various theories and methods of rehabilitation were important. Further, flexibility of design to allow compliance with changing court decisions, state-of-the-art security systems, exterior appearances compatible with the surrounding environment, and more attention to the internal environment for inmates and staff had increased the technical complexity of building. In addition, the financial constraints of local governments made new financing methods—involving joint ventures among the contractor, the architectural firm, and an investment or commercial bank—more common.

The buyer of correctional facilities was typically a government official, knowledgeable about rehabilitation procedures but a novice at purchasing construction services. Mr. Bennett explained that

This buyer is a technical buyer from a performance standpoint, but generally a naive buyer in terms of analyzing construction services. During the early stages, the buyer is concerned with—and often confused by—such items as site selection, financing, and programming. Thus, we must offer these services and be perceived as competent in the functional aspects of corrections: you have to demonstrate that you know their business in order to get involved early, and that means keeping up with the factors impacting rehabilitation.

Announced federal and state correctional projects from 1984 to 1986 varied by region:

Northeast:	$910 million
Southeast:	690 million
Central:	2.02 billion
Western:	1.83 billion
	$5.4 billion

County and municipal projects could increase that total by 40%.

Hotel/Residential. Hotel and multi-unit residential building included a range of projects for a variety of owners. Their technical and buying characteristics resembled the developer segment of the office building market. Fast, reliable, on-time completion was crucial, since the owner sought quick occupancy of the building.

Forecasts for this market were positive, although demand was expected to vary considerably from city to city. In the hotel industry, large national chains such as Howard Johnson, Marriott, and Holiday Inn were expanding either above or below their current price points, offering opportunities for new construction and renovation.

The Selling Process

Winning a contract involved several activities.

A first step was to locate prospects and create awareness of Turner's capabilities in that building category. This aspect of business development varied among regions and markets. In hospital construction, potential building was public knowledge and presentations at hospital associations were a common means of maintaining awareness of Turner's services. In commercial construction, according to Mr. Lang, "you rely more heavily on the jungle telegraph. By the time you read about a project, it's too late. Contacts at developers and architects are crucial." In all markets, noted Mr. Ned Johns, Business Development Manager for the Boston Territory,

> Being part of the business community is probably the key marketing effort. That means having a presence with local planning boards, construction organizations, architects, and business leaders. In Boston, we've been a contractor for sixty years and do lots of repeat business with institutional clients; in some other, newer territories, Turner may not be as well known.

A next step was to meet with the decision makers, usually through referral from another architect or owner. At this meeting, the territory's Business Development Manager sought information about both the specifications and people involved in a project. Mr. Johns explained,

In this business, there are many strong personalities who don't forget: it's important to arrange the proper chemistry since we will work closely with the owners during construction. Judging who can work with whom is important and often determines the client's perception of whether a job was performed "well" or "poorly."

A third step was to send a proposal and references. Mr. Johns explained that "references and word of mouth are crucial and hard to manage since many factors determine a client's satisfaction with a job. But one poorly perceived job is worth ten excellent performances, and can affect business throughout the territory."

A fourth step was a 30 to 45 minute presentation to a board or development committee. Mr. Frank Basius, Vice President and General Manager of the Boston territory, explained that "I am there to explain our organization and be 'Mr. Turner' in the owner's eyes, since our competitors generally include local contractors where the top person interacts personally with the owner. For many projects, moreover, public relations factors come into play: it's often important that the contractor be perceived as a local contractor employing local people."

This presentation also covered pre-construction services such as cost estimates and scheduling. Mr. Bennett explained,

> We consider estimating to be an art and a science, like surgery. Unlike some firms, we've avoided cookbook, automated estimating procedures. Our estimators are trained to look at the unique situation and place it within a larger market context in order to make realistic judgments that we can make happen.

Turner was usually considered with 3 to 5 contractors, and Mr. Johns emphasized that "the presentation can cover just so much. A large factor is the general impression you make relative to the other contractors."

A fifth step involved pricing, where lump-sum versus a negotiated fee contract was often a key issue. Mr. Basius explained,

> Buildings are customized products with thousands of components. We believe a contractor should work with the owner and architect, and that's not likely with a lump-sum contract where the contractor must save every penny because it's primarily price competition. Also, scheduling and quality control are improved with the negotiated contract.
>
> An owner might go lump-sum if there are no time pressures, or for a simple building where quality control and customization are not issues, or if depressed building conditions might net a lower price through lump-sum bidding.
>
> We prefer negotiated fee contracts, and in setting a fee "return on staff" is our prime criterion: our price depends on how many and what kind of people are necessary to complete the project on time and for the guaranteed price.

Project Selection

Many factors affected the relative attractiveness of projects for Turner. Mr. Basius explained that while large projects were sometimes more profitable, "it's important to have some smaller, simpler projects for staff development. Also, small jobs start and complete more quickly and that has cash-flow implications. Finally, some big jobs don't materialize and you can't rely on those projects to utilize capacity."

Selecting a project meant judging future demand and potential opportunity costs. Construction generally lagged the economy by some months and in mid-1984 was recovering from recessionary conditions. Prices seemed firmer and potential contracts more plentiful in many territories. If a territory committed to a project, it might lose opportunities to pursue projects later when margins might be higher. But if the economy slowed or faltered, margins on future projects might suffer as construction firms sought to utilize excess capacity.

In considering criteria for project selection, Mr. Basius listed the following, in order of importance:

> First, type of contract: lump-sum or negotiated says a lot about the margins and if it's our style of business.
>
> Second, the job's size. Bigger can be better, but large projects take years and carry risks concerning the availability and performance of subs during that time.
>
> Third, the owner: some developers will chisel away your margin, and some existing relationships take precedence over the other criteria mentioned.
>
> Fourth, required staffing: is it a good fit for us? are the right people available? will it develop younger staff?
>
> Fifth, the level of business in the territory often determines whether we commit to pursuing a job.
>
> Sixth, whether it's a client we want to get to know. For example, in New England, growing high-tech firms will do more building in the future, and we want to establish relationships and track records with them.

Any proposal for a project whose estimated total cost was from $5 to $15 million was submitted by the territory to the regional office for approval; proposals for projects of from $15 to $50 million were submitted to Mr. Kupfer, and projects of greater than $50 million needed the approval of Turner's executive committee. The territory submitted a standard "Proposal Authorization Form," which provided information about the owner and architect, the type of contract, estimated volume and earnings, and any special risks involved in the project. Submitting a proposal to an owner meant committing resources to develop detailed estimates and a guaranteed maximum price. And if accepted by an owner, a proposal was binding.

Project Management

Managing construction projects was complex, entailing the range of operations management tasks such as purchasing, scheduling, fabrication at the job site, inventory control, shipping, and coordinating and supervising a network of subcontractors. The key Turner person during construction was the project executive, and depending upon the project's complexity and an office's level of business, seasoned project executives were the firm's scarcest resource. Territory managers at Turner typically had spent years as project executives.

During construction, Mr. Basius explained, "local knowledge is fundamental":

> We're uncomfortable going outside our network of proven subs and suppliers. It's always risky and, in the owner's eyes, our responsibility. To get a project completed on time and on budget, our purchasing agent monitors daily the financial and staff conditions of all suppliers and subs.

Most projects required changes during construction. "In hospitals," noted Mr. Basius, "new equipment develops rapidly and must be accommodated during construction. In other areas, owners may simply change their minds about something and expect you to make those changes. Accommodating changes smoothly is a big factor in gathering repeat business."

During construction, the project executive met almost daily with the owner's staff, and other Turner project members interacted closely with owner and subcontractors. Mr. Harold Parmelee, New York Territory General Manager, emphasized that "this is a 100% service business where good work can be perceived as lousy if you don't manage the owner properly."

Commenting on the process from business development to project completion, Mr. Bennett noted that "there are networks at each phase":

> In most markets, contacts at architectural firms, real estate developers, and the business community are means of prospecting. During pre-construction, good relations with local banks can finance large projects. During construction, reliable suppliers and subs are crucial. After construction, the project executive and business development staff maintain contact with the owner, and good references develop future business.

Organization

Until 1973, Turner was organized around a "home office/branch offices" concept. The branches handled most operating matters, but executive selling and (for large jobs) estimating and purchasing were handled by headquarters. In 1973, a reorganization decentralized the company into regions and, within regions, territories run by General Managers (GMs) with P&L responsibilities and project resources. During the 1970s, Turner also established new offices and subsidiaries. (Exhibits 3, 4, and 5 indicate Turner's organization in 1984 at the corporate, territory, and project levels; Exhibit 6 indicates each territory's 1983 performance.)

Territory GMs had been with Turner for 20 to 25 years and had experience in most functional positions such as estimating, purchasing, and project management. While transfers between territories were not uncommon, most GMs spent a number of years within a given territory. GMs reported to Regional Vice Presidents who reported to Mr. Kupfer for new business and strategic planning items. Both management groups were measured on annual sales and earning goals, and noted Mr. Kupfer, "these are tangible and visible measures which can account for up to 30% of a manager's compensation."

Turner's management believed an important aspect of its marketing depended on the company's career orientation for staff. "Everybody knows everybody at Turner," said Mr. Kupfer, "and they're trained in our operating methods. That makes for easier communication and a system of checks and balances as people move among functions within the firm. Of course, it's harder to assure consistency as we grow and open new offices, but a career orientation also means we must continually seek growth opportunities to utilize and challenge staff."

Recent Developments

Mr. Kupfer became Executive Vice President in May 1983, having been President of Turner International Industries and, prior to that, Senior Vice President for the eastern region. At that time, he assumed responsibility for company-wide sales and marketing, contract administration, and strategic planning. He believed two developments had potentially long-term significance.

Product Specialization. In the hospital market, Turner had lost share in recent years to a new company, Park, which billed itself as a "hospital construction specialist." Park operated from a central headquarters and emphasized its ability to bring national resources to a hospital project. Park also adopted different sales techniques. Mr. Bennett explained that "the core of their pre-construction services is software that provides a fancy checklist of cost and design estimates":

> They do "checklist" estimating, but it seems to impress the less sophisticated buyers. Also, Park's presentations are very professional, and they'll fly a hospital board to a previous job. Hospital planning consultants look nationally for architects and contractors, and Park has convinced some consultants it has unique expertise in hospital construction.

Similar competition had arisen in the correctional and high-tech industrial markets. In response, Turner established in 1983 a "Management Consulting Service Group" (MCS) reporting to Mr. Kupfer, which included Health Facilities and Correctional Facilities groups. Mr. Bennett noted:

> Some hospital consultants perceived variations in service among our territories. So we established this corporate group to coordinate our approach to these markets and augment the estimating and pre-construction capabilities of the local offices. In the Health Facilities group, for example, there are five people who prospect hospital accounts, contact architects and consultants in that market, and work with the territories during pre-construction and project management.

During the past year, response to the new marketing groups had been mixed. Some GMs welcomed these groups, while others considered their involvement redundant and potentially confusing to customers. "I'm not sure what their mandate is," said one GM. "And I'm uncomfortable not controlling the total process in my territory. If, for whatever reason, the customer is not satisfied with a job executed by an MCS group, it reflects on the territory."

Mr. Kupfer noted that in many territories office building had been strong in 1983 and thus far in 1984, and some GMs might be wary of assigning resources that could otherwise be used for commercial projects.

National Accounts. During the past decades, various factors had increased the national scope of much construction work. Large regional developers had expanded and sought to develop projects nationwide. Similarly, major architectural firms increasingly operated nationwide. Because of the cost of money, developers and national insurance companies had jointly financed projects, and the insurance firms were beginning to assume development as well as financing tasks. Finally, many large retailers and manufacturers had expanded into national companies.

In 1978, Turner established a National Account Program (NAP) aimed at selected firms. Mr. Bennett commented:

> We've done lots of business in the Northeast with national firms, but many seemed unsure or unaware of our capabilities in other areas. The NAP objectives are to develop a network for early detection of new business opportunities, and to avoid confusion and duplication of effort when a firm that's always done business with one territory begins to build in other territories.

At the territory level a NAP Representative (usually the Territory GM or Manager of Business Development) was assigned as a collateral responsibility to a few large firms. The representative's duties included understanding (and communicating to people in other territories) the account's decision-making process and its plans for capital improvement programs and, if needed, assisting other territories in the selling effort for a specific prospect. Within each territory, the Business Development Manager coordinated the program and handled certain accounts.

One Turner territory seeking to approach a NAP firm assigned to another Turner territory had first to speak with the Business Development Manager in the NAP's territory. At corporate headquarters, NAP was managed by Mr. Bennett who, as well as having certain accounts, coordinated information about prospects among the territories.

Although by 1984 NAP had established clearer points of contact within Turner for national accounts, corporate management was disappointed with the program. "By and large, we still aren't selling Turner's national capabilities," said Mr. Bennett.

> National firms are not pursued aggressively or proactively. Some NAP reps seem reluctant to call on an account in their area when that account is only building

elsewhere. Also, if a national account wants a national building program developed by Turner, a local office must commit people and time. Depending upon the situation, that can raise resource-allocation tensions for Territory GMs. The result is that sometimes a territory might keep its "A" team for a long-standing local account.

Mr. Kupfer believed that "our people are superb at operations, but less motivated by concepts. But it's important to build for tomorrow's growth, and that means getting people to think and act in terms of company-wide opportunities." He had asked for recommendations concerning NAP and the competition from specialty contractors. These included: a) granting a territory some percentage of the operating fee if one territory performed "work of substance" in generating a project for another territory; b) placing one or two senior business-development managers as full-time NAP reps at the corporate level; and c) developing Turner's product-specific capabilities beyond the MCS stage by establishing national groups (with dedicated pre-construction and project-management resources) for hospitals, correctional facilities, and perhaps other markets.

Today's Decisions

In considering the proposal request by Territory A (see Exhibit 7), Mr. Kupfer noted that the proposed project's owner had been described (by the territory GM) as "a savvy, growing developer who is a tough but fair negotiator." Turner had not previously worked with this owner.

The project's architectural firm, "Design Associates" (DA), was based in the Northeast but had a national practice. Turner and DA had worked together for nearly 30 years on various projects, and like Turner, DA's practice had tended to focus on corporate and higher-quality office buildings. DA generally provided complete, well-coordinated construction drawings and (unlike some major architects) was usually receptive to a contractor's design suggestions. Mr. Kupfer knew that Territory A's Business Development Manager had a good working relationship with DA's Marketing Manager and that the Marketing Manager had introduced Turner to this owner. Competing contractors for the project were strong, local firms who had also not worked with this owner.

Mr. Kupfer believed that while the proposal request indicated "all key staff available in territory," the actual situation was more complex. Territory A's commercial building market had been strong and, within the previous six weeks alone, Mr. Kupfer had authorized Territory A to pursue three large office projects. If all of these proposals were successful, Territory A would not have staff available for this project. While it might be possible to transfer staff from another territory, Mr. Kupfer did not welcome this move: such staff would not be familiar with local subs and codes, and a project of this size required continuity of staff for months. During the office building boom of the late 1970s, for example, Turner had lost money on some big jobs due to inexperienced staff on those projects. In addition, Mr. Kupfer noted that subsurface conditions had been especially complex in other Turner projects in that area, and the project's starting date suggested a tight schedule.

Alongside the Proposal Authorization form lay the memorandum from the manager of the Hospital Facilities Group (HFG). Mr. Kupfer had asked for a monthly report on prospects and developments in the hospital market, and in this report he noted the section concerning Territory A (see Exhibit 8). Mr. Kupfer knew Territory A had not built a hospital facility in more than a decade and had not worked previously with HFG. Pursuing the project outlined in the memo would probably mean dealing with some new subcontractors and estimating for a building-type where that territory's personnel had little previous experience. HFG could augment, but not replace, the territory's resources in this area.

Mr. Kupfer believed the hospital market would be increasingly important and that the commercial-building market, while currently strong, was vulnerable to overcapacity in the near future. "It's one thing to recognize the need to plan and make long-term decisions," he reflected, "but another to implement a marketing strategy through the local organizations." In addition, he believed these decisions might be affected by a phone conversation of the previous day. The Business Development Manager of Territory B had reported that a Senior Vice President of Goodnight Hotels, a large national chain, had spoken to him about a major renovation program. Goodnight Hotels would expect a uniform standard of service and fees throughout the United States. from the contractor of those renovations. This would entail coordination among a number of Turner's territories. "Nationally," the Business Development Manager said, "this renovation contract will probably be $50 million."

Exhibit 1 **Turner Construction Company**

Top 20 General Building Contractors: 1983

Rank	Firm	Value of 1983 Contracts ($ Millions)
1.	Turner Const. Co., New York, N.Y.	$1,500.0
2.	The Austin Co., Cleveland, Ohio	893.2
3.	Kellogg Rust, Inc., Houston, Tex.	875.0
4.	Centex-Bateson-Rooney-Golden, Dallas, Tex.	819.8
5.	Blount Int'l., Ltd., Montgomery, Ala.	813.1
6.	J. A. Jones Const. Co., Charlotte, N.C.	709.7
7.	HCB Contractors, Dallas, Tex.	664.0
8.	CEI Const., Inc., Bethesda, Md.	574.3
9.	McDevitt & Street Co., Charlotte, N.C.	461.0
10.	Rodgers Const., Inc., Nashville, Tenn.	426.2
11.	Swinerton & Walberg Co., San Francisco, Calif.	424.2
12.	HBE Corp., St. Louis, Mo.	423.5
13.	Mellon Stuart Co., Pittsburgh, Pa.	411.1
14.	Perini Corp., Framingham, Mass.	354.6
15.	Charles Pankow, Inc., Altadena, Calif.	347.0
16.	C. L. Peck Contractor, Los Angeles, Calif.	320.0
17.	Gilbane Building Co., Providence, R.I.	318.9
18.	Morrison-Knudsen Co., Inc., Boise, Idaho	307.5
19.	Fluor Corp., Irvine, Calif.	304.0
20.	Dillingham Const. Inc., San Francisco	302.9

Source: Engineering News Record, April 19, 1984.

Note: Rankings are by value of U.S. contracts, excluding construction management contracts, for general building and manufacturing plants. In 1982, Turner ranked second in this survey, with U.S. contracts of approximately $1.124 billion.

Exhibit 2 Turner Construction Company

Value of Construction Completed by Turner 1980–1983
($ in Millions; Figures in Parentheses Refer to Estimated U. S. Market Share)

Building Type	1980		1981		1982		1983	
Non-residential								
Commercial	$ 806	(4.9%)	$1,016	(4.8%)	$1,400	(2.6%)	$1,053	(2.3%)
Manufacturing	60	(.93)	59	(.38)	77	(.67)	58	(.84)
Hospital/health	287	(4.1)	301	(4.2)	331	(3.6)	278	(3.0)
Education/science	72	(.96)	70	(.68)	60	(1.7)	82	(.87)
Public	80	—	98	(1.7)	113	(.94)	37	(.82)
Other (Amusement/recreation)	124	(.34)	121	(.33)	43	(.34)	35	(1.63)
Residential								
Hotel/multi-unit	180	(.29)	159	(1.37)	171	(.55)	156	(.36)
Non-Building								
Miscellaneous projects	180	(.58)	129	(.14)	41	(.01)	11	(.70)
	$1,789	(2.06)	$1,953	(2.4)	$2,236	(1.52)	$1,710	(1.67)
Earnings From								
Construction contracts	$36.0		$46.7		$55.3		$60.5	
Real estate operations	1.2		2.3		2.5		1.7	
Other income	5.4		5.1		5.9		5.7	
Gross earnings	$42.6		$54.1		$63.7		$67.9	
General and Admin. Expenses	$30.4		$36.9		$45.0		$48.1	
Income Taxes	5.2		7.5		8.0		8.4	
Extraordinary Item	1.3		—		—		—	
Net Income	$ 8.3		$ 9.7		$10.7		$11.4	

Note: Value of construction completed represented the cost of the work put in place and materials fabricated during the year plus earnings from construction management contracts. It was essentially a measure of construction activity during the year rather than "sales" or "revenues" in the sense typically used in manufacturing companies. For general contractors, however, it was a key measure of a firm's business volume.

These figures were consolidated to include six small "open-shop" subsidiaries operating primarily in southern areas of the U.S.

Exhibit 3 *Turner Construction Company*

Turner Corporate Organization

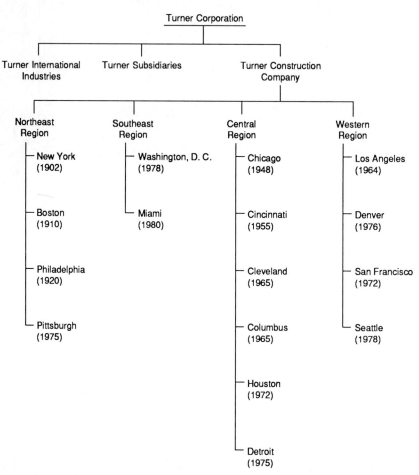

Note: The dates in parentheses indicate when that territory office was established.

The Turner Corporation was formed in the Spring of 1984 as a holding company to separate the open shop (non-union) subsidiaries from Turner Construction Company which operated primarily as a union contractor. Most executive officers had dual roles in both the parent and the subsidiaries.

Exhibit 4   Turner Construction Company

Turner Territory Organization

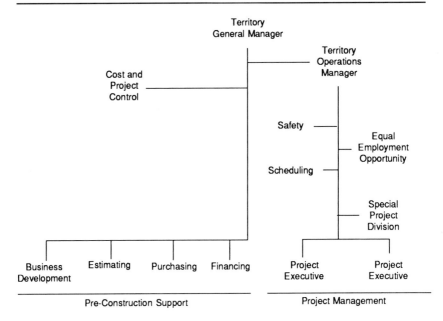

Exhibit 5   Turner Construction Company

Turner Typical Project Staffing

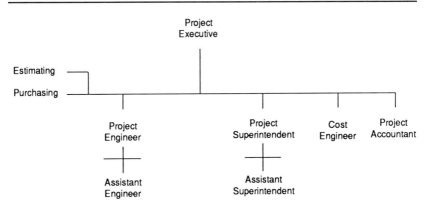

Exhibit 6   Turner Construction Company

Turner Territory Performance:
Sales and Earnings Goals vs. Actual, 1983

	Sales Volume		Earnings	
	% of Goal	% of Total	% of Goal	% of Total
Boston	111%	10%	101%	10%
New York	85	15	81	13
Philadelphia	104	7	125	8
Pittsburgh	69	2	44	2
Northeast Region	93	34	90	33
Miami	(-)	(-)	1	—
Washington, D. C.	43	2	74	3
Southeast Region	21	2	33	3
Chicago	222	18	90	7
Cincinnati	65	4	48	4
Cleveland	86	7	73	6
Columbus	69	3	100	4
Detroit	56	2	67	2
Houston	40	4	6	—
Central Region	95	38	59	23
Denver	—	—	—	—
Los Angeles	42	8	53	9
Seattle	—	—	—	—
San Francisco	37	3	43	3
Western Region	40	11	50	12
Total Territories	74	85	65	71
Total Subsidiaries	77	9	94	14
Total International	54	6	68	14
Grand Total	73%	100%	69%	100%

Note: Denver and Seattle statistics were consolidated into Los Angeles and San Francisco, respectively.

Exhibit 7 Turner Construction Company

Proposal Authorization

OFFICE: (Territory A)
DATE: 6/18/84

PROJECT NAME: "One Bond Place"   PROJECT TYPE: 40-story speculative office
                                                       building

OWNER: Dewey Properties, Inc.
OWNER'S REPRESENTATIVE: T. R. Dewey

ARCHITECT/ENGINEER: Design Associates
REPRESENTATIVE: Jim Phelps (Manager, Sales)

TYPE OF PROPOSAL & INFORMATION REQUESTED: Estimate of general conditions; project
staffing and qualifications; guaranteed maximum price to be prepared by time of presentation.

EXPECTED TYPE OF CONTRACT: Negotiated Contract; maximum price guaranteed, with
30% of contingency fee returned to contractor if savings; details to follow standard American
Institute of Architects contract form.
TO WHOM SUBMITTED: Owner   DATE AND TIME: 6/27/84, by 10 a.m.

FINANCIAL DATA: Estimated Volume: $40,000,000   Estimated Gross Earnings: $1,000,000

 Financial Status of Owner: Owner is a well-known local developer, in business here since
 1974. Financial history at bank to be checked.

 Projected Financing Method: Construction loan expected to be made by major regional
                                bank.

ESTIMATED START: Preconstruction: 7/5/84   Construction: 10/1/84   Completion: 7/1/86

COMPETITION: BCE; Blain; Morgan-Henry

DOCUMENTS FURNISHED: Schematic drawings, outline specifications

SPECIAL RISKS OR REQUIREMENTS: Contract will probably include specification that contractor be levied per-diem rate if project not completed on time. Also, owner wants contractor to
assume all risks of costs and delay due to subsurface conditions.

STAFF AVAILABILITY: ___x___ All key staff available in Territory
                      _____Key Staff required as follows:

APPROVED BY: _____

APPROVAL WITHHELD PENDING RESOLUTION OF THE
FOLLOWING QUALIFICATION: _____

DATE: _____

Exhibit 8   Turner Construction Company

Internal Memorandum

To: R. D. Kupfer

From: J. R. Newport; Manager, Hospital Facilities Group

Re: Business Development

Date: June 19, 1984

. . . (in Territory A): Sidney Hospital is planning a replacement facility, which would entail a 10-floor addition to one of two existing buildings (addition to include laboratory and bed space). The estimated volume on this project is $35 million and gross earnings would be about $1 million.

Sidney is a not-for-profit, private, inner-city hospital. Preconstruction on the addition would begin on 7/10/84, construction on 3/1/85, and completion by 4/1/87. The contract would be a negotiated, guaranteed-maximum-price. Financing would be through a public bond offering.

The architect for this project is Harley Associates: they're a large, mid-western firm which specializes in health care facilities. Turner has not done business with them before and, due to their prominence in the healthcare construction field, I and others in the Hospital Facilities Group have been spending lots of time with their people. In the past, Harley has worked primarily with Park, and our goal has been to convince Harley that Turner is preferable to Park in the hospital field. I believe we've made substantial progress on that count.

There's also a hospital consultant, Ms. Bonnie Moore, involved in this project. She has a national reputation and is very well-respected among hospital administrators. Moore has done a number of jobs with Harley Associates over the past five years. I've personally met with Moore and have at least increased her awareness of Turner in the hospital-construction market.

The competition on this project is Park and two strong local firms, Carraway Construction and Morgan-Henry.

I gave this information three weeks ago to Mark Ward (General Manager of Territory A), urged him to contact Moore and Joseph Fernandez (Chairman of the Sidney Hospital Board), and pledged our group's assistance in pre-construction services. But nothing has happened. If we're interested, we must submit a proposal by June 30. Should you talk to Mark Ward about this?

Honeywell, Inc.: International Organization for Commercial Avionics (A)

In June 1987 Mr. James J. Verrant, senior vice president of Honeywell International, was developing recommendations concerning the integration of international units of Sperry Aerospace and Honeywell. In late 1986, Honeywell had acquired Sperry's aerospace business. More than half of Sperry's $686 million aerospace business was attributable to its Flight Systems Group (FSG), which produced commercial aviation electronics ("avionics"); this unit's product line complemented Honeywell's $125 million Commercial Aviation Division (CAvD), making the combined operation potentially the world's largest supplier of commercial avionics.

Since the merger, both groups' international units had operated independently. But management was eager to integrate the groups in order to achieve important scale economies and marketing benefits. Mr. Verrant headed a task force charged with providing detailed recommendations by July 1987. However, this required resolving issues of international organizational structure and process which differed greatly between the two divisions. Sperry had consistently followed a centralized, global approach to the international avionics market, while Honeywell had adopted a matrixed, multinational approach. The first question in Mr. Verrant's mind was whether the commercial avionics market was "global," and the marketing implications of that analysis. The second was how to structure a combined international avionics operation. The third was how to implement any recommendations in the current organizational context.

Associate Professor Frank V. Cespedes and Research Associate Jon King prepared this case as the basis for class discussion rather than to illustrate either effective or ineffective handling of an administrative situation.

The Commercial Avionics Industry

Avionics, the electronic instruments in the airplane cockpit and associated systems throughout the aircraft, grew out of military development during World War II; by 1986 many of these instruments had evolved into complex digital computing systems. Avionics were bought by airframe manufacturers for installation into new aircraft, and by airlines as spares, replacements, or upgrades for existing instruments.

Commercial avionics represented a $1.15 billion industry in 1986. The market was commonly segmented by the type of aircraft in which the avionics would be installed:

1. Air transport (commercial jets with 50 seats or more) was a $900 million avionics market in 1986, forecast to grow 10% annually through 1992. Avionics totaled about $1 million per plane, or about 2.5% of the average $40 million price of the aircraft. In this segment, airframe manufacturers and airlines determined product specifications for new avionics systems. Historically, airframe manufacturers had been the systems integrators and had not allowed any avionics manufacturer to attain a major share of any one aircraft program. But technological and economic developments were changing this practice. Due to increasing fare competition among airlines, air transport avionics purchases were shifting, with an increased emphasis on the integration and standardization of avionics systems and comprehensive product support from the avionics supplier.

    Honeywell/Sperry had a combined 40% share of air transport avionics, with about 55% of revenues coming from sales to airframe manufacturers, 30% from spares and retrofits, and 15% from product support. Major customers included Boeing, McDonnell Douglas, and Airbus, with about 75% of revenues booked from U. S. customers and 25% internationally. During the past 10 years, Boeing and McDonnell Douglas (U. S. companies) had accounted for more than 50% of air-transport manufacture, but Airbus (a European consortium) was expected to account for a growing proportion during the coming decade. One manager noted that, "The air transport avionics market has always been competitive and is getting more so. The key success factors are formidable: recognized advanced technology in hardware and software; demonstrated product quality and reliability; worldwide customer support; competitive pricing; aggressive marketing; a broad product base; and a general reputation for dependability and credibility."

2. Commuter Turboprops were propeller-augmented jets with less than 50 seats. This was a $70 million avionics market in 1986, and Honeywell/Sperry had a 40% share.

3. Business Aviation (jets and turboprops) were smaller, nonrecreational aircraft typically operated by companies for internal use. Although

the airframes were smaller than large commercial jets, the average $400,000 avionics package represented approximately 10% of the $4 million price of the aircraft. This was a $150 million market in 1986, and Honeywell/Sperry had a 60% share.

Increased airport congestion was expected to keep the business and commuter markets flat through 1992. In both segments, the avionics manufacturer had determined specifications and, in contrast to air transport, had traditionally performed systems integration functions. As in air transport, however, there was a growing trend toward more factory standard avionics systems. One manager noted that, "Business and commuter aviation customers buy few spares, which is a big source of revenues in the air transport market. As a result, the avionics supplier assumes more inventory risks in what is a relatively low-volume, custom business that's hard to forecast." In business and commuter avionics systems, about 60% of Honeywell/Sperry's revenues came from aircraft manufacturers such as Gulfstream, Dassault, and Cessna, 17% from product support, 15% from airplane dealers, and 8% from "completion centers" (i.e., companies that integrated avionics and airframes for certain types of aircraft). About 60% of revenues were booked from U. S. customers and 40% internationally.

4. Civil helicopters (nonmilitary helicopters for commercial uses) were a $30 million avionics market in 1986, and Honeywell/Sperry had a 60% share of this segment.

Airframe manufacturers frequently focused on one aircraft category. For example, in 1986 of five major air transport manufacturers, the three largest were exclusively in this segment: Boeing (U. S.), McDonnell Douglas (U. S.), and Airbus Industrie (European consortium). The other two, Fokker (Holland) and British Aerospace (U. K .), had broad lines but separate purchasing groups for each class of aircraft.

Commuter aircraft manufacturers included DeHavilland (owned by Boeing), Aerospatiale (France), Saab (Sweden), British Aerospace (U. K.), Fokker (Netherlands), Embraer (Brazil), and Messerschmitt Boelkow Blohm (Germany). Helicopter manufacturers included Sikorsky (U. S.), Bell (U. S.), Aerospatiale, and Agusta (Italy). There were eight major business jet manufacturers in 1986: Learjet (U. S.), Cessna (General Dynamics, U. S.) Gulfstream (Chrysler, U. S.), Canadair (Canada), Dassault (France), British Aerospace (U. K.), Israeli Aircraft Industries (Israel), and Beech (Raytheon, U. S.).

Avionics Products

Avionics products were separated into seven categories (see Exhibit 1):

1. Auto-pilots directed the aircraft over long open stretches. Sperry had sold auto-pilots for many years and held 65% of the market.

2. Displays were dials and video screens. Sperry held a 31% share of market.
3. Flight Management Computers (guidance systems and monitors) relayed information to the pilot or the auto-pilot. Sperry had entered this line relatively recently and held a 51% share.
4. Flight Reference Systems (air data computers) were sensors which monitored location, altitude, and speed. They fed the flight management computers. Honeywell (with proprietary technology) was strong in this category, and Sperry also had a line. Together they held a 92% share.
5. Surveillance and Warning Systems included weather radar, collision avoidance computers, and identification transponders. Sperry, a recent entrant, had 17% of the market.
6. Inertial Navigation Systems (gyroscopes). Honeywell's laser gyroscope revolutionized this segment and held a 74% share of market by 1986.
7. Radios included communication and beacon navigation. Sperry had just entered product development for this segment.

Navigation and flight reference systems, based on technology originally developed for Honeywell's military aerospace-and-defense business, were CAvD's major products. By contrast, Sperry was a major supplier in a number of product segments and had begun development of a radio line before the merger with Honeywell. Together, management believed the operations represented a full-line supplier with resulting manufacturing, service, and distribution economies, as well as enhanced capabilities in developing and marketing integrated systems.

The latter was increasingly important, and it was easier for a broad-line supplier to perform this function. A narrower product line required working out complicated bids and joint ventures with manufacturers of complementary avionics. Further, due to the increasing importance of software, avionics were increasingly airframe specific, and entailed major certification costs; hence, while it might cost an avionics supplier $10 million to tailor an existing product to a new airframe, the airframe manufacturer could easily spend an additional $20 million to certify the system with the Federal Aviation Administration (FAA). Finally, technological developments allowed for increasing integration of all cockpit avionics, with major decreases in the space and weight devoted to these systems in the aircraft. As a result, R&D demands were growing, and avionics was growing as a percentage of the cost of an airplane. As one CAvD manager noted:

> The good news is that the avionics market is growing faster than the aircraft market, not even including spares and replacements which are more profitable than original sales and sell better as airlines keep their planes in operation longer. The bad news is that the avionics market is increasingly competitive and complex, both in terms of technology and marketing. The Honeywell/Sperry merger represents a genuine synergy—if we implement it correctly.

Competition

Honeywell/Sperry, Rockwell/Collins, and King/Bendix accounted for 85% of worldwide commercial avionics sales. One marketing manager explained: "This is a business where word travels fast about product developments and bids, and both Collins and Bendix treat the market as a global one."

Collins Aviation, a division of Rockwell International, had about 30% of the worldwide avionics market. CAvD managers described Collins as having "historically the broadest product line, including all major categories except inertial reference systems where Honeywell has dominated and flight management systems where Sperry dominated and Collins was not a competitor. They are investing heavily in new technologies for all product areas, are focused on becoming the dominant supplier to Boeing, and we believe they are targeting Honeywell for this purpose." A Sperry manager noted that Collins maintained "separate marketing and customer support organizations for its air transport and commuter/business avionics operations, and provided worldwide coverage of all customers, both domestic and foreign." (Exhibit 2 is an organization chart of Collins Air Transport division, based on information available to managers at Sperry Aerospace.)

Bendix Corporation had recently merged with Allied-Signal, a large diversified manufacturer. In turn, Bendix, which had an avionics division focused on the air transport market, had recently acquired King Radio Corporation, which focused on the general aviation avionics markets. A CAvD manager noted that "Bendix/King has a market share buy-in strategy. They are willing to price aggressively, and are targeting new technologies in flight controls and displays." Together, King/Bendix sold about $200 million in avionics annually. A Sperry manager noted, "When Bendix acquired King, Allied-signal management hired a big consulting firm to recommend an organizational structure. I could have saved them time and money. The resulting recommendation was to organize the way Sperry has traditionally organized its avionics business, with separate, dedicated marketing groups for the air transport and commuter/business aviation markets." (See Exhibit 3 for King Radio organization chart, based on information available to managers at Sperry Aerospace.)

Other competitors included SFENA and Thomson-CSF, European companies having close ties with each other and Airbus members. Litton Industries had been strong in the inertial navigation (gyroscope) category but had not recovered in the commercial avionics market after Honeywell took over this segment with new technology. Smiths/Lear-Siegler, a British-American firm, had a small avionics unit, as did General Electric (U.K.). As recently as 1980, there had been several $20 million businesses in the industry, but few had survived. Those operating in 1986 included Global Avionics, Universal Aviation Navigation, Delco (General Motors,) 3-M Avionics, and Safe Flight.

Buying and Selling Avionics

Avionics customers included over 30 airframe manufacturers, more than 350 large airlines and 150 regional airlines, 450 business aviation dealers, and some 8,000 corporate users.

Airframe Customers

Commercial airframe manufacturers (AFMs) faced long time horizons and substantial risks before production began or revenues were realized.[1] Launch investment costs typically involved five years and fell into three categories: 40% for development, 20% for tooling, and 40% for work-in-process. Hence, AFMs tried to book as many launch orders as possible, but no commercial aircraft had ever booked enough to break even before its launch date. As a measure of investment risk, Boeing's combined investment in the 1970s for its new 757 and 767 aircraft totaled more than the company's net worth at the time, while in the 1980s Airbus's A-320 had estimated launch costs of about $20 million per seat.

The development period began with the aircraft design known as the "paper airplane," a model with estimates of performance and operating costs intended to demonstrate new technology and assess the response of potential buyers. Typical was an interactive process between the manufacturer and key airlines as adaptations were made and options incorporated into the prototype. The reputation of these launch customers was important for subsequent sales. Once sufficient backing was achieved, either in the form of orders received from airlines or financial commitments from governmental bodies (in the case of nationally subsidized aircraft manufacturers such as Airbus), full-scale development began. The development phase faced costs such as regulatory approval and expensive, time-consuming flight tests, in addition to aircraft development and assembly costs.

The selling price of an aircraft typically included purchased parts, direct expenses (labor and supplies), and a 25% gross margin. The breakeven to recover launch costs was often 12–14 years. The AFM's sales force and designers worked closely with airlines throughout design, development, and launch. The AFM also found it critical to provide service worldwide, with minimum delay and a full stock of spare parts. Further, since operating and maintenance efficiencies dictated that airlines focus on certain types of aircraft in their fleets, an initial order tended to establish an airline's fleet composition for a decade or more. With an aircraft's normal service life of 15–20 years, therefore, a lost sale could easily have a ripple effect for up to two decades.

Avionics suppliers sought to work closely with AFMs throughout design, development, and launch, and faced similar requirements. AFMs had traditionally not multisourced avionics products because of the high certification costs to test and document each system. However, AFMs sought from their avionics suppliers reliability, service, competitive pricing, and (in air transport) had not traditionally allowed any one supplier to establish a dominant share of the avionics within an aircraft. Hence, avionics suppliers sold to AFMs at close to cost; profits were made in the large aftermarket for replacements, upgrades and

---

[1] Some information in this section is based on "Turbulent Skies: Airbus Versus Boeing," Harvard Business School Case Services, #9-386-193.

maintenance-and-repair services for airlines and other user customers. One Honeywell/Sperry manager noted:

> In air transport, purchasing departments are involved, but airframe engineering departments are strong and provide detailed specifications. In most cases, a high-level committee is used to select a given supplier, and successful suppliers develop good relationships at all organization levels. A key is carefully selected on-site technically oriented marketing personnel with the experience and ability to influence different functional groups at all levels.
>
> In the business and commuter aviation markets, it's possible to compete for the total avionics system in the aircraft. The final decision is usually made by top management at these airframe manufacturers, and supplier success is often dependent on established relationships.

There were few airframe development projects at any one time, and an avionics supplier might be involved for 36 months between first discussion of avionics needs and final decision of which systems would be installed. For this kind of sale, noted one manager, "90% of the effort goes toward the airframe manufacturer, and 10% to the launch customers. Many avionics sales reps are dedicated full time to a single AFM in order to keep abreast of new projects and influence the design specifications: the closer these specifications are to their existing products, the less expensive and more effective the supplier's own development process."

Once specifications were set, the AFM would send a request for proposal (RFP) for each system to avionics manufacturers; it included about seven full binders of specifications for each system. A vendor's response to an RFP also consisted of about seven volumes covering technical support, quality control, program management, terms of business, pricing, and product support. Developing this response took months. The next step in the sales process required the avionics bidder to convince the AFM of the product's quality and of the supplier's ability to support the product through the airframe's 15–20 year expected life cycle. Reps had to reach the AFM's designers, engineers, purchasing staff, and top management. One manager noted:

> It's impossible to say where the turning point is; you work each day to achieve inches. As well as dynamic technology and big capital investments, this industry has big customers with big egos; they want to see how much attention they can get from their suppliers. Consequently, success is based on individual attention as well as product and support.

Aircraft manufacture had a significant effect on a country's merchandise trade account, the technology developed, and employment. In the United States, for instance, aircraft engines and parts typically represented more than 10% of all U.S. manufacturing exports; in some European countries nearly 50% of the trade balance was derived from aircraft exports. Also significant was the prestige and political benefits to supplier countries of aircraft sales abroad. As a result, there was frequent government involvement in the commercial aircraft industry.

By the mid-1980s, moreover, multinational joint ventures and alliances were common in the industry. Airbus Industrie, for example, was a joint venture among Aerospatiale (France, 18%), Deutsche Airbus (Germany, 38%), British Aerospace (U.K ., 20%), and Construcciones Aero-Nauticas-CASA (Spain, 4%). Engineering and manufacturing were handled by member companies, but systems integration, testing, and marketing was done by Airbus. Japan Commercial Aircraft Corporation and Aeritalia (Italy) were strategic allies acting as joint subcontractors to Boeing for its 767 aircraft. Each manufactured airframe structures accounting for 15% of the airplane's cost, while Boeing handled basic design and marketing, supervised the engineering, and performed final assembly. Japan Aircraft was itself a government-sponsored partnership of Mitsubishi, Kawasaki, and Fuji.

Such collaboration shared the risks of technological and market uncertainties. Multinational joint ventures and alliances also served a political purpose. For example, some European governments in the Airbus program pursued foreign policies that some countries found more congenial than America's. Consequently, some Arab nations and Brazil had switched their airplane purchases from Boeing to Airbus during the early 1980s. Ambassadors from all the countries involved were often sent to promote a given manufacturer when potential contracts reached the governmental level.

Airline Customers

Airlines were involved in avionics purchases in two ways. First, as launch customers, they worked closely with AFMs and avionics suppliers in developing specifications and operating characteristics. Second, they made direct purchases of some avionics for their aircraft. Airlines had for many years exercised a "freedom of choice" concept for many categories of avionics. AFMs certified more than one supplier in a category, and airlines would then buy their avionics from the supplier of choice and have it sent to the AFM for installation prior to delivery of new aircraft. Airlines also made direct purchases of avionics for upgrades or for installation of new types of avionics systems in their existing fleets.

The airlines' roles as launch customers and direct purchasers made it necessary for avionics suppliers to market to airlines as well as AFMs. In the 1970s, Airbus, by giving its customers a choice of engines and avionics, had increased the requirement for more intense and persistent marketing to airlines by avionics suppliers.

The rate of aircraft replacement was determined by the airlines' ability to pay for new equipment versus the costs of keeping older equipment in service. Other factors included the obsolescence of some equipment, noise reduction regulations, fuel costs, safety issues, the resale value of old aircraft, availability of funds, and routes to be served. All of this implied a gradual, evolutionary process in which a successful airplane would typically outlast the technology of a specific avionics system. To maintain airframe sales through airframe retrofit and modernization programs, the AFM would often request proposals from avionics suppliers for upgrades, or airlines might directly seek to upgrade avionics systems in their existing fleets.

Projections for worldwide air travel growth were about 5% through the year 2000, slightly faster for non-U.S. carriers. The growth regions were in Asia, Latin America, and the Middle East. Between 1971 and 1984 non-U.S. carriers represented 61% of aircraft deliveries compared to 37% between 1958 and 1970. Of these, many were ordered by smaller airlines, most of which were government owned and tended to place smaller orders.

Except for the United States, nearly all airlines were owned by governments. Typically, airline management were civilians (and, in many countries, former military pilots and officers), while important board members were government officials (e.g., Minister of Transportation or Finance). Not unusual were negotiations for other purchases (energy-related, military, etc.) while discussions were held about aircraft sales. However, in avionics, purchase criteria differed for military versus commercial customers. One Sperry manager noted:

> Product knowledge can be traded across some military and commercial lines, but the items must meet very different specifications. Commercial avionics are opened frequently for overhaul or repair, while military avionics tend to be miniaturized and too "high-tech" for airline repair personnel.
>
> Also, the military is naturally a multinational market, each government having specific needs and concerns, while commercial avionics spans national boundaries. Military buyers do their own repairs or contract strictly in-country for security reasons; no foreign organization can be relied on in a crisis. Commercial customers need service available wherever they fly, and increasingly, international airlines are spreading farther around the world, rather than concentrating on certain hubs.

Honeywell's Aerospace and Defense division was a major supplier to the military market, selling many of its commercial and military products through the same sales force. By contrast, Sperry had traditionally separated its considerably smaller military avionics business from its commercial business, in manufacturing as well as in marketing and sales.

Customer Service

Customer service in the avionics business included timely delivery of replacements, quick repairs, and free support such as product documentation, field engineering personnel, formal training of customer technicians, in-flight training of flight crews, and extensive testing equipment. The key factor was quick turnaround: keeping the aircraft in the air was essential to an airline's efficient use of expensive capital equipment. Sperry ran the industry's fastest spares organization: any part could be shipped within six hours.

Service was recognized as a major selling tool to airframe manufacturers and airlines alike. AFMs typically required suppliers to establish permanent engineering resources at the AFM's production facility. Large airlines had set up their own repair shops for their aircraft, including the avionics. But new digital components in avionics required new service capabilities, while airline service departments were still electro-mechanically oriented.

As a result, the establishment of repair centers in international locations was increasingly important for successful marketing of avionics. These centers stocked a wide array of parts, kept trained personnel on site, and had the capability of providing quick repair and delivery to airline locations in a region. For the avionics supplier, the capital equipment and inventory investments required to establish a repair center were substantial, and it was typically 3–5 years before the repair center became profitable. Before their merger, Honeywell CAvD had established international repair centers in Britain and Australia while Sperry had repair centers in Britain, France, Singapore, and Australia. Mr. Verrant commented:

> Commercial avionics probably has the longest investment cycle of any business at Honeywell. It typically takes five to ten years to make money on a project, and there are heavy development costs. Each new aircraft requires us to provide test equipment and parts inventory at the internationally based repair centers, repre-senting another significant upfront cost necessary to the overall success of the aircraft introduction. As a result, the centers cannot perform as typical, high return-on-investment service businesses early in the life cycle of even the most successful commercial aircraft. When a number of new aircraft are being simul-taneously introduced worldwide, the short-term impact on the balance sheet and P&L of the individual service center is disastrous. Commercial avionics is profitable but requires a long-term perspective, one that includes all aspects of the business including the development of the avionics, the selling cycle, product maintenance, and eventual avionics modernization or replacement.

Honeywell, Inc.

Honeywell was a $5.4 billion corporation in 1986, comprised of three business groups: Industrial Automation and Control (22% of 1986 sales and $52 million in operating profit before a nonrecurring loss), Home and Building Automa-tion and Control (32% of sales and $145 million in operating profit before nonrecurring items), and Aerospace and Defense (A&D, 46% of sales and $241 million in operating profit). Honeywell had recently signed an agreement to divest its computer business and had also restructured the company, taking a $175 million loss from write-downs and other charges.

The three business groups were further divided into product divisions. In the United States, the Industrial and Building Automation groups had dedi-cated sales personnel at both the group and product-division levels, whereas A&D (which included the commercial avionics division) only had sales person-nel at the group level for both the military and commercial portions of the business. A fourth group, Honeywell International, handled international business for products of all groups through an organization in which autonomous affiliate companies in each country had operational authority for all marketing, accepting strategic input from the product division headquarters in Minneapolis.

Individual product divisions within A&D utilized product marketing managers who worked with the business group's field sales force in the United States, but for international sales, they worked through the appropriate affiliate. For example, CAvD marketed its commercial aviation products domestically through the Honeywell A&D field sales force, which was also responsible for sales of military avionics, space systems, torpedoes, and other products for military applications. For sales to British Aerospace as another example, CAvD sold through the Honeywell British affiliate company, with help from the A&D group marketing reps at Honeywell Europe.

Mr. Warde Wheaton was executive vice president of Honeywell A&D. About 40% of A&D's revenues in 1986 came from avionics, with the remainder coming from the Defense and Marine Systems divisions. About 85% of avionics revenue was military and 15% commercial. A&D had 80 U. S. salespeople and another 20 abroad. These reps focused on market intelligence, contacts, and relationship building. Product expertise came from marketing representatives and engineers at headquarters, who assisted reps in the sales process as needed. Salespeople at Honeywell tended not to be product specialists: they had local knowledge to offer and were expected to understand their accounts intimately. Many AFMs sold to military and commercial customers, so the A&D sales force had never been divided between commercial and military products; it was thought that reps could enhance the corporation's position across markets by handling all A&D product lines.

Commercial Aviation Division (CAvD)

Honeywell had been involved in commercial avionics since its inception, but until the mid-1970s, A&D marketing organizations had not coordinated sales efforts for avionics product lines to commercial aircraft customers. In 1973, Boeing approached Honeywell about using its technology in new airframe projects; Boeing was especially interested in ring laser gyroscopes and digital flight control computers, technologies originally developed by Honeywell for the U.S. Navy. Mr. Verrant was put in charge of commercial aviation and military business ventures for introducing the laser gyro technology in 1977 and soon organized the various commercial avionics products into a single venture. He noted that:

> Managers from the commercial avionics venture had to make the most of a very small budget. The new venture was expected to lose money in the near term, and was supported by the Military Aviation Division (MAvD). It was run on the idea that military technology would be transferred to commercial applications with as little investment as possible. It started with about 50 people, including three in marketing; A&D field salespeople were barely utilized. Everyone was initially focused on the Boeing sale.

In 1980, the commercial avionics venture became a separate operation within MAvD and in 1985 a full division (CAvD) within the Avionic Systems Group, which had four other divisions: Military Avionics; Space & Strategic Avionics; Electro-Optics; and Defense Communications. Prior to the merger with Sperry, CAvD was the only commercial business in A&D, and shared its buildings with the Military Avionics Division. By 1986, CAvD had become the leading supplier of laser-based inertial reference systems, with customers such as Boeing jet transports, the Airbus A-300 series, and all major business jets. CAvD had 1986 revenues of approximately $125 million and 700 employees, about 80 of which were in Marketing which included contracts, product requirements, support, pricing, promotion, advertising, and public relations. Sales were conducted through A&D and the international affiliates. One CAvD manager noted:

> A few A&D salespeople spend up to 80% of their time on CAvD products, but few other A&D reps focus on us. They've grown up on the military business, not the commercial. And our selling process is a complicated one; you have to understand pilots, airlines, AFM decision-making processes, and assorted national customs. CAvD is profitable and fun, but it's complex and only one relatively small part of what the A&D sales representative can concentrate on.

Honeywell International

For over two decades, Honeywell had adopted a "One Honeywell" policy, in which all operations in a country were the responsibility of a single executive. Consolidating operations through autonomous subsidiaries was intended to consolidate the company's influence in each country. Each affiliate had total sales responsibilities for all Honeywell products sold within its borders and, depending upon the level of Honeywell's presence, might also have manufacturing and service facilities. Sales personnel in each affiliate sold the full line of Honeywell products.

Honeywell International, headquartered in Minneapolis, provided administrative and marketing support to the affiliates. Mr. Michael Bonsignore, executive vice president for International, noted that "Honeywell has always distinguished between centralized 'what-to-do' decisions and decentralized 'how-to-do-it' decisions in the international area. The philosophy is to have a tight 'what' and loose 'how' because Danes will know the business in Denmark better than the Minnesotans do. This has been an important tenet in the company for years." Mr. Verrant added, "Throughout Honeywell, the culture emphasizes getting things done through collaborative bargaining and discussions. You don't kick a decision upstairs to a higher, more centralized level unless it's absolutely necessary."

Honeywell International affiliates were divided into four operating units: Honeywell Europe (headquartered in Brussels), Honeywell Asia/Pacific (Hong Kong), Honeywell Canada (Toronto), and Honeywell Latin America (Minneapolis). At this level, the three business groups were represented by specialized marketing reps; for example, A&D fielded four marketing people in

Brussels for Honeywell Europe. These business-group reps supported the full-line sales reps in each country (or "affiliate") organization. (See Exhibit 4.) One CAvD manager commented:

> Internationally, our organization is spaghetti: lots of dotted lines. Success in this organization is based on personal relationships with people in other units. It demands getting salespeople interested and excited about your products. And it requires stoking the interests of affiliate managers, too. CAvD is a relatively small business with long payback horizons, and it does not automatically motivate the time, attention and resources of an affiliate general manager measured on annual sales and earnings.

Affiliate general managers had full legal and profit-and-loss responsibilities for their organizations and typically stayed in these positions for 5–15 years. Up to 35% of a general manager's annual compensation was a bonus based on that affiliate's P&L and ROI performance over the preceding year. Country managers had wide autonomy, allocating resources as they saw fit in their markets and accepting primarily broad product strategies from headquarters managers. One affiliate general manager noted:

> Honeywell early recognized the importance of local autonomy in doing business overseas, and especially in Europe. This is needed to develop local knowledge, continuity with customers, and a sense of ownership and responsibility for the business. Especially in our controls business, local codes, regulations, and building practices make each country different. Honeywell had the right sense for this business; when I joined this office 15 years ago, there was only one American in the affiliate and he left within a year.

Affiliates received "markups" for sales of imported Honeywell products with the markup percentage depending upon the affiliate's "value added" and local market conditions. In the case of countries where no A&D expertise was available and value-added was negligible, out-of-pocket costs were reimbursed and a commission system was established. Countries with manufacturing operations for a product line received total value for the products. In some lines, there were necessary adaptations of U.S.-based products (or totally locally developed products), depending upon the region or country. Domestic heating controls, for example, depended upon the types of heating systems used in a country and various electrical codes. Responding to these local requirements was key to the success of the affiliate. By contrast, commercial avionics did not require country-specific alterations, although military avionics often did due to countries' national security regulations. The affiliates provided some other key benefits. Mr. Douglas Snure, CAvD Director of Marketing, noted:

> One advantage of the decentralized Honeywell system is that the affiliate general manager can take care of governmental bureaucratic demands more easily than any American manager. For example, it took only a day of my time to establish CAvD's British service center and only a week of my time to establish the Australian one. By contrast, setting up a service center at Boeing in Seattle took me a year: I had to deal with real estate, capital equipment, personnel, the

customers, and the government. The British and Australian managers handled those headaches abroad; all I had to provide was test equipment and inventory.

CAvD used two A&D people in Europe "to open doors," but these reps spent almost all of their time on military sales; there was one field support person in Europe dedicated to CAvD. The division was not very visible in Europe until 1982, when the French affiliate hired a well-known industry professional to pursue Airbus business. Mr. Snure commented:

> The Honeywell international organization has worked especially well for CAvD on recent Airbus business; I attribute the exceptional results to the personal abilities of the French affiliate account manager. He has close relationships with CAvD headquarters marketing management, and keeps up constant communications among the various country units. Because of the international makeup of the Airbus consortium, all five governments (and five affiliates) are involved in the purchasing process. European buying is typically very political because the AFMs and airlines are mostly nationalized. We at headquarters focused on being demonstrably better in technology, and he focused on responsiveness.

However, another manager noted:

> Internationally, CAvD must go through individual country managers to sell to foreign airlines and manufacturers. We are accompanied, monitored, and billed for the time. But since large airlines are each located in more than one country, it is difficult to provide consistent attention across borders and still satisfy each country manager with his share of revenues: purchases do not necessarily take place at customer headquarters, and service frequently doesn't.

The aftermarket was a major aspect of the avionics business, and affiliates were sometimes reluctant to make the initial capital and personnel investments in repair centers (resulting in CAvD directly subsidizing the centers and not transferring capital costs and inventory to the affiliate balance sheet). But the affiliates also often claimed "ownership" of airline accounts headquartered in their countries and pressed CAvD to relinquish to them all sales of avionics not already installed in an airframe. A CAvD manager commented:

> Any commissions or markups on products that a country manager can get from CAvD sales go directly to his bottom line, since he does not have to allocate much in the way of sales resources. Therefore, spares represent a way to increase profits and ROI quickly. So, many country managers have insisted that their account management skills deserve such consideration. While affiliate reps might have local knowledge and relationships, the value of these "relationships" to us is a question.
>
> For CAvD, there are some downsides to the traditional Honeywell organization; mostly, it is headquarters loss of control over worldwide business. For instance, since airlines frequently cover the globe, they can make purchases in the country offering the best price on specific equipment. Since Honeywell country managers have pricing freedom, they started fighting over business and cut prices to encourage buyers from outside the country. Not only did this damage corporate profit, but airlines were unimpressed with account coordination.

At the other extreme, one manager decided that if he raised prices, he would make more money, but in fact he only lost business to other suppliers. On a case by case basis, CAvD will occasionally give an affiliate a special transfer-price deal in order to encourage a big sale, but sometimes the country manager, concerned with making annual numbers, will not pass the savings on to the buyer, consequently losing the sale altogether.

In 1985 CAvD arranged for the British general manager to become the agent for CAvD with other European country managers. The U.K. manager represented CAvD interests for a fee. He took on avionics sales responsibilities for all of Europe, and in turn made the necessary arrangements with other European general managers. The Australian manager soon took on the same role in the Pacific. CAvD reimbursed Australia and U.K. for all warranty repairs. Non-warranty repairs were at affiliate discretion: there were guidelines, but some variation. CAvD managers stated that this "improved" the situation, but it was "still difficult to implement strategies consistently."

Sperry Organization

Sperry Aerospace had been an independent business group at Sperry Corporation (see Exhibit 5), with dedicated manufacturing, marketing, and sales operations for each of its divisions, including the Commercial Flight Systems Group headed by Dr. Larry Moore. Each division had profit-and-loss responsibilities for worldwide sales of its products. Dr. Moore noted: "As long as business goals were met, Aerospace management rarely had more than a half-day quarterly review meeting with Sperry's corporate management. The Aerospace Group and Commercial Flight Systems were both very successful for years, building a leading position in many product categories."

Sperry's Commercial Flight Systems Group (FSG) was divided into two business units, Air Transport and Business/Commuter Aviation, each an independent operating unit focused on a market segment. Dr. Moore emphasized that this market orientation "reflected the organizational philosophy throughout the Aerospace Group and, in my opinion, this philosophy was a key factor in the group's success: focus on the unique needs of each market and put in place a marketing organization empowered to respond to each market on a worldwide basis." The average age of managers within FSG's marketing groups was 44, each with an average of 21 years' experience in aviation, including experience as commercial pilots, flight test engineers, aircraft marketing, or military aviation. Sixty percent of FSG's marketing personnel had pilot's licenses, and the average tenure with FSG was 13 years. Dr. Moore noted that "Their backgrounds give our marketing people the ability to provide strong inputs to product planning and account management throughout the world. We also stress continuity of assignments, so they can establish relationships with key customer personnel and develop a detailed knowledge of people and organization both at customers and within our own locations overseas."

FSG International Organization

Within FSG's Air Transport group, there were marketing groups dedicated to Boeing, McDonnell Douglas, Airlines, and International. Similarly, within FSG's Business/Commuter Aviation group, there were marketing groups dedicated to OEM Marketing, Product Marketing, Field Marketing (to commuter airlines and dealers), and International Marketing. FSG had grown its worldwide business under a "global" approach: all sales, support, and field engineering reported to FSG's Phoenix headquarters, which set strategic, pricing, and resource allocation policies worldwide. Mr. William Pollak, FSG's Manager of International Marketing for Air Transport, explained:

> Customers generally get to know people at Phoenix headquarters as well as they know their local reps. Local and headquarters marketers trade information constantly; the core marketing people at FSG talk to customers, engineers, and overseas sales reps each day. For example, I typically spend 3 hours each morning on the phone with Europe, 1 hour with Asia/Pacific in the afternoon, and 1 hour with Air Transport marketers in between. I also take about 9 world tours each year. Turf trouble has never been apparent.

In FSG's International operations, the Basingstoke, England, office covered airframe manufacturers and airlines headquartered in the U.K., Holland, Scandinavia, and English-speaking Africa. The Paris office covered France, Spain, Portugal, Belgium, French-speaking Africa, the Arab Middle East, and India. The Munich office covered Germany, Switzerland, Austria, Yugoslavia, and the few sales to Eastern Europe. The Rome office was responsible for Italy, Cyprus, Malta, and Israel; the Singapore office covered Southeast Asia. The Pacific basin was covered out of the Melbourne office, and the Chinas from Hong Kong. Canada had a separate office as well, but South America was handled by Phoenix headquarters.

Each Sperry office reported to Phoenix. The major business of the office managers was marketing new products and repair services. Each had P&L measures, but prices for service and repairs were set at headquarters to avoid competition between centers. Offices were free to solicit business from new customers (not currently using Sperry repair services). Service centers were located in Basingstoke, Toulouse, Singapore, and Melbourne. Management tried not to duplicate all repair capabilities at all centers; although each center covered territorial customers, certain capabilities were too rarely needed to cover at each center. In those cases, the customer would approach a center, and then the item would be transferred to the center with the appropriate capability. Almost all parts inventory ($80 million) was carried on Phoenix headquarters' books. This was a large amount compared to other suppliers and considered a powerful illustration of FSG's commitment to customer service.

Each office manager was often in Phoenix, and regularly accompanied local customers visiting FSG headquarters. Conversely, Phoenix marketers by policy spent a day at the local office with managers and reps before calling directly on a local customer. Dr. Moore commented, "Our organization has allowed for rapid, coordinated responses in a business that demands speed and consistency at the customer interface and a long-term perspective on resource allocations." Mr. Pollak noted:

> After the merger, when we first started reviewing each other's organizations, managers at CAvD and FSG were both very surprised at how different the two organizations were. We at FSG perceived nothing but dotted lines in Honeywell's international organization for avionics and were certain that a multilayered matrix couldn't work in this business. For their part, CAvD managers were amazed, and generally envious, at the level of centralized control in our organization.

Organizational Issues

Soon after Honeywell acquired Sperry Aerospace, according to one manager, "Honeywell affiliates tried to absorb Sperry people and revenues, while the Sperry people tried just as hard not to be absorbed. As well as the uncertainties and turf issues that accompany any merging of organizations, there are also strong opinions and strong personalities involved in this one." A policy was soon announced from Honeywell's corporate headquarters that the separate organizations would be retained until a task force could decide upon the proper organization for the combined avionics businesses.

Mr. Wheaton, president of A&D, recommended Mr. Verrant to head the task force. Mr. Verrant had been with Honeywell for 25 years; in addition to handling aviation business ventures in the late 1970s, he had managed industrial process control business units, had been vice president of Marketing for Honeywell's A&D group, and had most recently returned to Honeywell International after helping to divest Honeywell's computer business. A colleague described Mr. Verrant as "one of the broadest international figures at Honeywell, and credible with the whole company. He has stature, no alignment with either organization, and people at all levels will listen closely to any recommendations he makes." Others on the task force were Dr. Moore and Mr. Pollak from Sperry FSG, Mr. John Dewane (general manager of CAvD), Mr. Gerald Jacobs from A&D International, and Mr. Lawrence Hallfin from A&D headquarters. The goal was to present a plan to Mr. Wheaton and Mr. Bonsignore, both of whom would have to approve and implement any recommendations.

Mr. Verrant's initial steps were to meet repeatedly with FSG managers at Phoenix and with various affiliate managers in order to understand the concerns and issues involved. He soon became aware of divergent views, some of which are represented below:

> There is no more global business than commercial avionics. Pursuing a country-by-country approach in this market will fragment our position with customers. (Sperry FSG manager.)

> Sales are made by people in an affiliate talking with customers who buy, or influence purchases for, other things besides avionics. There are important syner-

gies between military and commercial avionics that require a multidomestic approach. (Honeywell International manager.)

Sperry people are starting to call on my customers and that's generating confusion. I'm responsible for what happens in this country, and I don't like having people here whom I don't control. (Honeywell affiliate general manager.)

We're organized to move quickly and in a worldwide, coordinated manner, whereas the Honeywell International organizations stop abruptly at each border. We've always approached the avionics market as a global business, and that's why we've been so successful. I just hope any reorganization doesn't neutralize an important source of our competitive advantage. (Sperry FSG manager.)

There are really three "cultures" at work here. One is represented by the affiliates, who deal with annual P&L numbers, sell the whole Honeywell line, and have a long tradition of autonomy. Another is corporate Honeywell, which takes a hands-off approach to its international businesses and understands the importance of relationships for getting things done in a multinational organization. At Honeywell International, you *always* call on the affiliate manager even if you're just passing through the country on a stopover between flights. It's a sign of respect and part of the culture. At Sperry FSG they've been very successful as a stand-alone business and, being centralized, they're not used to touching base with a variety of other managers in a matrixed organization. But Honeywell's affiliates contact high levels in many organizations in countries, and they can help a now full-line avionics supplier if they're not alienated. (Honeywell corporate manager.)

After these meetings, Mr. Verrant concluded that "Speed and clarity of decision-making will be very important here. The longer we wait to resolve these issues, the more potential for emotions getting in the way of what can be done and the more potential for customer confusion." He therefore aimed for a joint memo from Messrs. Bonsignore and Wheaton outlining recommendations no later than July 1987 (six months after the establishment of the task force), and proceeded to focus the task force on three related issues: a) Was avionics a "global" business? b) What should be the organizational relationship between a merged avionics organization and Honeywell's affiliate organizations? c) What issues should be recognized and managed in any implementation of the final recommendations?

Global Business? Concerning this issue, Sperry FSG management prepared a memo outlining points they had stressed in conversations with Mr. Verrant (see Exhibit 6). This memo argued that Honeywell should approach the commercial avionics business as a global one, both because of the nature of major customers and how business was typically conducted.

Relations with Honeywell Affiliates? Mr. Verrant believed that any decision would have to consider a number of issues concerning Honeywell's affiliate organizations. First, the international affiliates had legal and tax responsibilities for all operations in their countries, and therefore affiliate general managers were concerned about any arrangement where they did not have line control over personnel operating in their countries. In at least two countries, both FSG and affiliate managers were pressing for quick resolution of where key avionics people should report: to FSG headquarters in Phoenix or to the local affiliate general manager.

Second, while commercial avionics represented about 10% of the restructured Honeywell's revenues, the proportions differed significantly among affiliates. Further, many affiliate managers believed that having the commercial avionics business as part of their product portfolios strengthened their image and revenue streams, and they argued that, in turn, it was more efficient and effective to sell avionics through the various Honeywell affiliates rather than through a centralized avionics organization. "It's efficient," noted one affiliate manager, "because my salespeople can sell both commercial and military avionics, thereby spreading the selling costs over a broader line. And it's effective because as a manager in this country for two decades, I know the senior people at airlines and various top governmental officials influential in aircraft and avionics purchases. And I deal with these latter people regularly for large governmental and state-influenced purchases of our automation and control product lines." Other managers, however, questioned whether the different buying processes between commercial and military avionics and between avionics and other Honeywell products effectively negated the benefits of these affiliate relationships for purposes of commercial avionics marketing.

Third, both affiliate and Honeywell corporate managers were strong believers in autonomous country organizations. One affiliate manager had stated to Mr. Verrant that "so-called 'global' businesses are a fad. Sales are made in countries by in-country personnel." A Honeywell corporate executive had mentioned that, "with the merged Sperry/Honeywell commercial avionics business, we may well be dealing with our first truly global business. But it will still account for just 10% of corporate revenues. And it's a real question whether we upset our historical multinational, autonomous-affiliate organization for a business that's not a big part of Honeywell in total terms."

Other Issues. Mr. Verrant viewed Honeywell's affiliate managers as "broad portfolio managers of Honeywell's various product lines. The incentive system encourages them to make resource allocations so as to optimize their annual ROI performances. This works well for many other Honeywell businesses, but it doesn't necessarily fit the longer time horizons and investment requirements of the commercial avionics business." Others on the task force had argued that only a centralized organization could take the longer-term strategic view necessary to make investments such as FSG's $80 million spare parts inventory and network of international service centers.

At the same time, Mr. Verrant noted that "local, in-country manufacturing is getting more important in other Honeywell product lines. For example, we increasingly encounter many state-owned companies that will buy certain products from us only on the condition that we place a certain amount of business in their country. This trend drives us toward even more integrated operations in our affiliates, and an autonomous commercial avionics operation could be isolated. Affiliate managers could adopt an 'out of sight, out of mind attitude' toward avionics, and we could lose potentially important synergies."

Conclusion

By June 1987, the task force was considering three basic organizational options. One was to establish the merged commercial avionics business as a separate business unit, headquartered in Phoenix, with its own sales and support resources throughout the world. In this approach, the responsibilities of Phoenix would include establishing global objectives and strategies, overall P&L and product responsibility, worldwide resource allocations for the avionics business, and pricing. Commercial avionics personnel would receive ongoing operational direction from Phoenix, but many would be located in affiliate offices where, in the words of one task force member, they would receive "bed and board from the host affiliate organizations." As a result of their hosting function, the affiliates would have legal responsibility for any contracts or actions executed by avionics personnel but would be reimbursed for expenses (including payroll, operating expenses, telecommunications support, and officing) and receive a commission on avionics sales in which the affiliate participated. Similarly, avionics service centers would become part of the Honeywell affiliate's legal responsibilities, but Phoenix would establish operating policies, annual operating plans (P&L and balance sheet), and day-to-day management authority for the centers. Further, the inventory and other assets would be carried on the books at Phoenix, and the location of and expenses involved in establishing new service centers would be the responsibility of Phoenix.

A second option was to have all commercial avionics sales and marketing personnel—and their assignments, measures, and operating directions—managed centrally by Phoenix, while the service centers continued to be managed by the appropriate affiliate organizations. The reasoning here, according to one task force member, was that "while avionics marketing may be global, the support functions at service centers are performed at specific locations. Also, some of our Honeywell affiliate general managers—for example in the U.K. and Australia—have made significant people and capital investments in service centers in their countries, and option 1 would be taking away from them a source of revenue growth that they've been nurturing."

A third option was to retain the multinational approach to the avionics business adopted historically by Honeywell. In this approach, Phoenix would provide "broad strategic direction" for commercial avionics (including pricing guidelines, marketing support, and product policy), but sales, service centers, and support would be managed, booked, and directed by individual affiliate organizations. One task force member noted that "25 years of history, and a small but steadily profitable avionics business, support this option."

The task force had also investigated a fourth option in which a separate wholly owned affiliate, with dedicated resources and P&L responsibility, would be set up in each country for commercial aviation activities and report to

Phoenix headquarters. But analysis soon revealed that this approach would be prohibitively expensive in many countries.

Reflecting on these various options, Mr. Verrant noted that "whatever organization we recommend must be capable of winning the commitment of the different parties involved. And nearly every option has the potential of disappointing people who will be key in implementing it." The task force recommendations were due by July 1.

Exhibit 1   Honeywell, Inc.: International Organization for Commercial Avionics (A)

Avionics Product Categories and Competitors

Products	H/S Participation	Competitors
Autopilots	Sperry	Collins Bendix/King
Displays	Sperry	Collins Bendix/King SFENA Thomson-CSF
Flight management computers	Sperry	Global Universal Aviation Navigation Smiths/Lear-Siegler
Flight reference systems	Honeywell, Sperry	Collins Litton
Surveillance and warning systems	Sperry	Collins Bendix/King 3M Safe Flight
Inertial navigation systems	Honeywell	Litton Delco
Radio	(Planned)	Collins Bendix/King

Exhibit 2   Honeywell, Inc.: International Organization for Commercial Avionics (A)

Collins Air Transport Division Marketing Organization

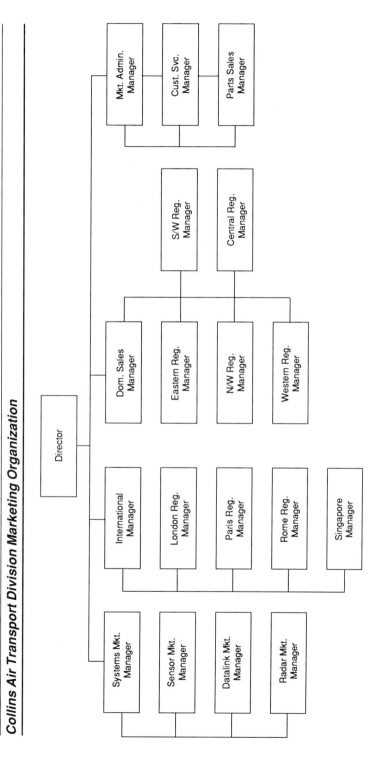

Exhibit 3 Honeywell, Inc.: International Organization for Commercial Avionics (A)

King Radio Division Marketing Organization

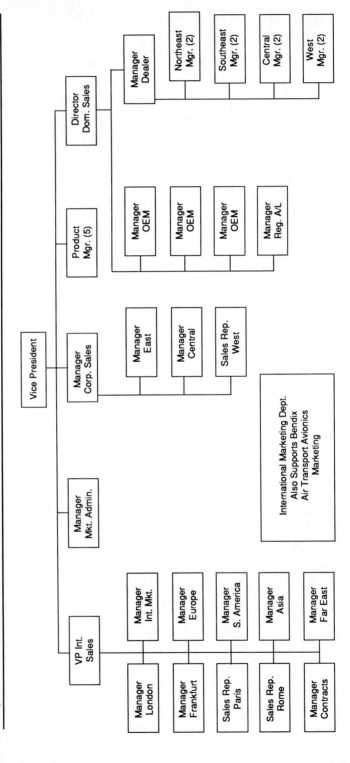

Exhibit 4 Honeywell, Inc.: International Organization for Commerical Avionics (A)

Honeywell Organization

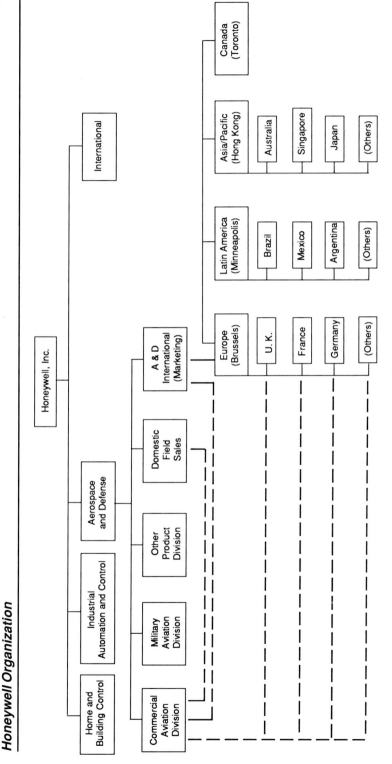

Dotted lines show some of the necessary relationships involved in selling CAvD products.

Exhibit 5 Honeywell, Inc.: International Organization for Commercial Avionics (A)

Sperry Aerospace Organization

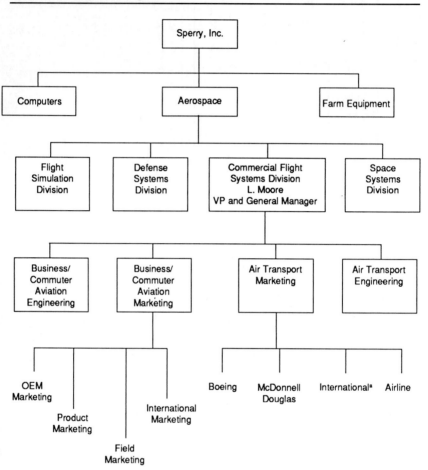

aSee detailed organization chart on p. 771.

(continued)

Exhibit 5 (continued)

Air Transport Marketing

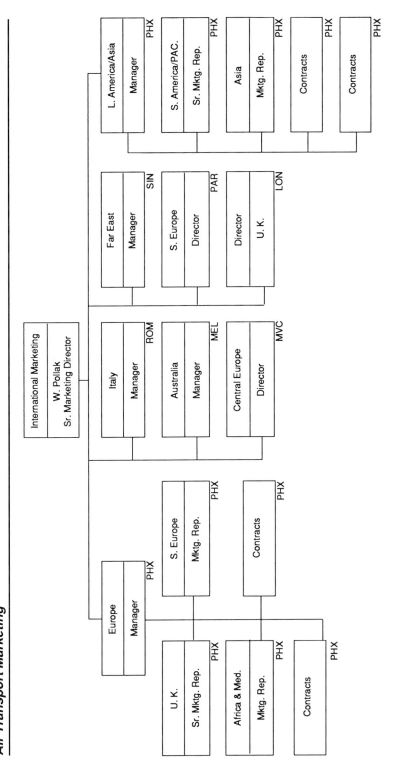

Exhibit 6   Honeywell, Inc.: International Organization for Commercial Avionics (A)

Memo on Commercial Avionics Market from Sperry FSG Management

All sales of aircraft and equipment are transacted in U.S. dollars.

Universal industry language is English.
  - Air traffic control
  - Business
  - Documentation: specifications, operating manuals, etc.

Aircraft are operated throughout the world.
  - No borders: often several countries per day

Industry associations which develop specifications for equipment, maintenance, etc. all have worldwide membership.
  - E.g., Aerospatiale uses same equipment as Boeing.

Most non-U.S. air carriers operate U.S. buying offices.
  - Airlines and aircraft manufacturers demand to deal directly with home office of equipment manufacturers.

U.S. avionics manufacturers dominate world market.
  - Honeywell/Sperry, Rockwell Collins, Allied-Bendix have 85% of world market.

Other avionics manufacturers treat market as global.
  - Collins and Bendix maintain integrated marketing and customer support organizations and facilities encompassing all non-U.S. as well as U.S. customers.

Aircraft Manufacturers

Air Transport
  - Three major manufacturers
    - Two in U.S. (Boeing and McDonnell Douglas)
    - One in Europe (Airbus)

Business Jets
  - Five major manufacturers
    - Two in U.S. (Gulfstream and Cessna)
    - One in Canada (Canadair)
    - Two in Europe (Dassault and British Aerospace)

Commuter Aircraft
  - Six major manufacturers
    - One in Canada (DeHavilland)
    - Four in Europe (Aerospatiale, Saab, British Aerospace, and CASA)
    - One in Brazil (Embraer)

Getting the Marketing Job Done

Case 28
Imperial Distributors, Inc. (B)

In December 1986, Mr. Michael Sleeper, president of Imperial Distributors, a service merchandiser in the New England area, was reviewing a possible reorganization of Imperial's sales and marketing organization. Mr. Sleeper was considering a reorganization as a means of improving sales and service while also reducing the amount of daily "firefighting" that involved the firm's top management. (See Case 18, Imperial Distributors, Inc. (A) for background about the company, the industry, and recent developments.)

Some weeks earlier, Mr. Sleeper had asked a consultant to consider possible changes in Imperial's organization. The consultant had studied the organizations of a number of other service merchandisers in different parts of the country and had recommended a revised structure for Imperial's field organization. Mr. Sleeper had to decide whether to adopt these recommendations and, if so, how to implement them.

Alternative Service Merchandiser Sales Organization

In reviewing possible changes for Imperial, the consultant had investigated how other service merchandisers organized their field sales and service operations. In particular, he focused on four firms that Mr. Sleeper had identified as profitable and respected in the industry for the ability of their top management. These firms were: A-B Drug Sales, Jay-Link, Inc., Gator Wholesale, and Mighty Merchandisers, Inc.

A-B Drug Sales

A-B Drug Sales (A-B) was located in Harrisburg, North Carolina, and had 1985 sales of approximately $40 million. A-B had initially focused on sales to drug stores and pharmacies within supermarkets, but HBA and GM items for supermarkets currently comprised most of A-B's business.

A-B divided sales and marketing as indicated in Exhibit 1. Sales consisted of 5 zone managers, 15 district managers, 11 zone merchandisers, and 105 driver route reps. Each district manager had from 4 to 8 (with an average of 7) route reps reporting to him or her. Sales responsibilities were allocated as follows. Zone managers were responsible for developing business at key accounts, calling on potential new accounts, and meeting sales forecasts and expense budgets for their assigned territories. The district managers had primarily operational responsibilities; they supervised the route reps, worked with them in the stores, and (in the words of one A-B manager) "attended to the daily needs and concerns of the reps and their stores." In addition, reporting to the zone managers were zone merchandisers who filled in on routes when necessary, did store resets, and also a limited amount of on-the-job training of new route reps.

Separate from sales was marketing where a vice president supervised three key account executives and a purchasing organization. The account executives did not supervise route personnel who serviced those assigned accounts; their responsibilities were promotional planning, customer relations, and coordination of meetings, resets, new product introductions and other matters with their assigned accounts. Commenting on the organization, A-B's president noted:

> The split between sales and marketing is partly a function of personalities and my concern about managing and monitoring closely our purchases and inventory position. Our marketing vice president comes from a supermarket purchasing background and is good at managing all aspects of purchasing and inventories; he's less adept at sales. In addition, a few years ago, our inventory situation got out of hand and caused us to lose money; since then, I've preferred keeping the purchasing function reporting to myself or someone else who's in close touch with the big accounts that tend to drive our high-volume purchases.

Jay-Link, Inc.

Jay-Link, Inc., located in Rock Island, Illinois, had 1985 sales of about $85 million. Jay-Link's president, a graduate of Harvard Business School, had purchased the company 10 years previously.

Jay-Link's sales organization (see Exhibit 2) had 1 sales manager (who reported to the president), 2 regional managers, 27 district managers, and 174 route reps. Each district manager had at least one assistant district manager (ADM), and 7 districts had 2 assistant managers, for a total of 34 ADMs. At any one time, according to the president, there were no more than three or four trainees throughout the company. In addition, Jay-Link had 7 key account executives (a relatively recent addition to the organization) and two assistant regional managers.

Regional managers reportedly spent about two-thirds of their time in the home office and one-third on the road. They were responsible for new business development, meeting sales budgets, and (in the words of one regional manager) "firefighting." Assistant regional managers were two recent graduates of local MBA programs; they performed a variety of administrative tasks for the regional managers and also analyzed field operations with an eye toward improving deployment, promotions, co-op advertising programs, and other matters. District managers spent most of their time in the field, working with route reps and often doing store resets themselves. Assistant district managers covered unfilled routes on a given day and provided support and assistance to the district managers on a variety of other store and administrative tasks.

Jay-Link also had 10 merchandisers who reported to the regional managers and performed major resets at stores. These merchandisers specialized in a given area of HBA or GM and were involved in merchandising and promotional programs for their areas. Seven key account executives were responsible for promotions, ad campaigns, public relations, and ongoing relationships with major accounts; the account executives reported to regional managers and did not supervise directly route reps for their assigned accounts. Jay-Link had 174 route reps covering that number of routes; route reps were compensated entirely through a commission based on 20% of the gross profit generated by the route.

Gator Wholesale

Gator Wholesale, based in Greenville, North Carolina, had 1985 sales of approximately $30 million in a geographical selling area about two-thirds the size of Imperial's. Gator's president had recently reorganized the firm's sales organization because "I was concerned about selling expenses and overhead swamping a company of our size." Gator's current sales organization (see Exhibit 3) separated merchandisers from the field sales and service force. Thus, Gator's vice president of Sales had both a sales manager and merchandise manager reporting to her.

The merchandise manager was reportedly on the road four days weekly. He reported to the vice president of Sales, but also had dotted-line responsibilities to the Purchasing Department; Gator's vice president of Purchasing noted that the merchandise manager "brings me ideas and concerns on a regular basis, and I try to address those ideas and concerns in our purchasing strategy." The merchandise manager supervised four merchandisers who focused on different areas of HBA and GM; the merchandisers normally accompanied supervisors for major store resets and setups of new departments.

The sales manager supervised four district managers, who in turn made headquarters calls on accounts and managed the supervisors and route reps but did not themselves set stores. Each district manager had two supervisors reporting to him or her; and each of the eight supervisors managed about seven route reps. In addition to field supervision, the supervisors also worked in the stores doing resets but did not make headquarters calls and were not responsible for new business development.

Gator had 56 route reps (and, at the time, two trainees), who were compensated according to a combination of base salary and commissions tied to a percentage of the sales volume generated by their routes.

Mighty Merchandisers, Inc.

Mighty Merchandisers (MM) was among the largest service merchandisers in the country with 1985 sales of about $300 million. MM had been acquired by a larger corporation (whose main business was distribution of various items to a variety of retailers, including supermarkets) about two years previously. MM was based in Arkansas but distributed throughout approximately 20 states in the central, northern, and eastern parts of the country. MM's sales department (see Exhibit 4) was broken into three major areas: Eastern, Midwest, and Northern regions. For purposes of comparison, the consultant focused on MM's Northern sales region, since its numbers and customer base were closest to Imperial's.

The Northern sales area had 121 routes and 3 regional managers who managed 10 division managers who in turn managed 10 division merchandisers. The regional managers reported to a sales vice president for the Northern area.

Each divisional manager had between 9–13 driver reps reporting to him or her. Companywide, MM was the most productive of the four companies from the standpoint of sales overhead versus number of active routes. At MM, driver reps owned their own vans, paid for their own gas, insurance and expenses, and were compensated entirely through commissions based on gross sales revenues generated by the assigned route. Moreover, each divisional manager was a profit center within the company and, in addition to base salary, was compensated through an incentive program based on the gross profits generated by the routes in his or her division. MM's vice president of Sales described the division manager's job as "primarily a shirtsleeve position: the division manager gets heavily involved in selling new business and maintaining customer relations with current accounts. By contrast, the division merchandisers focus on designing, setting up, and maintaining store displays and are not involved in selling."

Commenting on MM's organization, Mr. Sleeper noted:

> MM has compensated its salespeople through commissions since the company began. Imperial, on the other hand, has traditionally had a different relationship with its field salespeople: base salary is a high proportion of our route rep's compensation and commissions are tied to sales volumes in individual categories. Our direct competition in New England also compensates its field people through a combination of salary and commission. In addition, while MM distributes the same basic product categories we do, their customer base is more heavily weighted toward smaller independent stores in the Midwest, whereas our customer base is increasingly composed of large supermarket chains. Chains have tighter delivery schedules and, in general, are more demanding in their required levels of service than independent stores. An all-commission structure could therefore cause intolerable service problems. Finally, MM has quite a few promotions specialists that are part of their central organization. This is overhead, and probably their large volume justifies these specialists.

Exhibit 5 provides a numerical comparison of the four organizations studied by the consultant with comparable figures for Imperial's sales organization.

Recommended Organizational Structure

In recommending a revised organizational structure for Imperial's field operations, the consultant cited his primary objective as "putting in place an organization to provide quality service to Imperial accounts while developing specific accountability for sales, expenses and gross profit." The following paragraphs are excerpts from the consultant's report.

> *Goals.* The goals of this recommended structure are 1) to put the strongest managers available in key line positions; 2) to measure each unit by sales productivity and profit contribution; 3) to reward managers on the basis of sales productivity and profit contribution; 4) to provide "vice presidential" decision makers to key accounts and thus protect and strengthen our business with those accounts; 5) to allow for continued profit and growth.
>
> *Plan.* The heart of the recommended structure is the establishment of three geographical divisions (in place of the current four regions), each headed by a vice president and further subdivided into a number of "areas" or districts. In addition, sales goals and compensation for route reps would be changed to reflect a new emphasis on increasing sales volume. Thus, the recommended plan of action is as follows:
>
> 1. Establish three geographical divisions within Imperial:
>   a) North
>   b) Central
>   c) Southern and Semi-Service Accounts
>
> 2. Each division would be headed by a vice president accountable for sales and profits in the division and directly involved with accounts generating more than $2 million in sales annually. Geographically, the Southern Division (i.e., southern Massachusetts, Connecticut and Rhode Island) contains a large portion of Imperial's semi-service accounts; these semi-service accounts would be the responsibility of a manager who in turn reported to the Southern vice president.
>
> 3. Each divisional vice president would be responsible for developing new business within the division's geographic location; new business targets would be established annually and incentive compensation for divisional vice presidents in part tied to attainment of these targets.
>
> 4. Each division would be a separate profit center and operate with its own budget. Each "area" within the division would also operate and be measured as a profit center.
>
>   In a number of instances, an area would be synonymous with a key account, and the area manager (or account manager) would operate and be measured as a profit center. Accounts whose store locations span the geographical boundaries of a division would be handled in the following

manner: the stores of such accounts would be serviced by route person- nel located at the most geographically appropriate depot, and the division responsible for that account would be credited with the sales to those stores and charged for the proportionate expenses of servicing those stores.

5. Each area (or key account) P&L would be specified as follows:

HBA Sales
HBA Gross Profit

GM Sales
GM Gross Profit

Specialty Food Sales
Specialty Food Gross Profit
 Total Sales
 Total Gross Profit
 Less Rebates
 = Real Gross Profit
 Less Expenses:
  ■ Area Salaries
  ■ Area Commissions
  ■ Vehicle Expenses
  ■ Proportionate Share of Depot Expenses
  ■ Fuel, Transportation
  ■ Fixturings
  ■ Fringe Benefits Charges
  ■ Miscellaneous Expenses
 Area Profit Contribution

In this P&L statement, "Sales" would be defined as service, semi-service or no service; while "Gross Profit" would be defined as the difference be- tween what Imperial paid for an item and the price at which it sold that item to the customer.

6. Area P&Ls would be consolidated into a divisional P&L with appropriate charges for divisionwide salaries (vice president, secretarial, and trainees) and expenses (e.g., division management's expenses, conven- tions, etc.).

7. Division P&Ls would be consolidated with a LUVS division P&L (i.e., bill- ings and appropriate expenses for Imperial's sales to its LUVS retail out- lets) and the total of all divisional P&Ls consolidated into a corporate sales P&L.

8. Each divisional vice president, and each area manager within each division, would be compensated through a base salary (equal to their cur- rent salary) and incentive compensation based on a) Sales Contribution (40% of total incentive compensation), b) Profit Contribution (40% of total incentive compensation), and c) New Business Development (20% of total incentive compensation). The exact mix of incentive compensa- tion components would vary by division and area, depending upon the mix of business and the potential (as judged by the divisional vice presi-

dent in consultation with the vice president of Sales) for new business development.

9. Route reps' compensation would be revised to emphasize incremental sales over past performance on a route. Currently, Imperial's district managers establish annual goals on a route, based on sales forecasts. Under this plan, forecasts would be eliminated, and goals established based on last year's sales on that route (or account). Then, Imperial would pay to the route rep (in addition to salary and the current commissions on sales volumes) a bonus of 50% of the incremental sales on that route (or account). Further, this bonus would be paid quarterly and so based on the year-ago sales figure for that route in that quarter.

   This bonus system should provide a visible, ongoing incentive to increase sales at the store level for established accounts. Further, it is easy to understand, relatively quick to implement, and—at 50% of all incremental sales—fairly dramatic in its potential impact on route reps' total compensation. I also expect that turnover among route reps and the percentage of returns could be lower under this compensation system.

Exhibit 6 provides an outline of the recommended organizational structure. In this structure, the total number of routes remained the same as in the field organization. In place of the current 9 sales supervisors there were 12 area managers; the consultant believed that the current 9 sales supervisors and 3 key account managers would hold these positions. In place of the current 4 regional managers, there were 3 divisional vice presidents. In place of the current 14 merchandisers, there were 12 merchandisers, one for each area. The average number of route reps reporting to an area manager would vary, depending upon the size (in terms of sales revenue) of the area or account; on average, one merchandiser and 5.25 reps would report to each area/account manager.

The consultant also believed that the average number of trainees at Imperial should decrease under the recommended structure, because "the clearer lines of P&L responsibility, the added incentives for area managers to manage revenues and expenses closely, and the smaller number of routes and route reps reporting to each area manager should improve the quality of sales supervision in the field and reduce turnover." Thus, assuming that on average there were two trainees at Imperial at any given time, the consultant estimated the ratio of total sales management and support personnel to routes as .48 under the recommended structure (i.e., 63 active routes and a total of 30 sales management and support personnel: 1 sales vice president, 3 divisional vice presidents, 12 area/account managers, 12 merchandisers, and an average of 2 trainees).

Conclusion

Reflecting on the proposed reorganization, Mr. Sleeper commented:

> I have a number of objectives in any reorganization of our field sales and service efforts. We need to build greater selling capabilities, both within existing ac-

counts and for developing new accounts. We also need to increase our operating effectiveness at the store level. I believe we need to reduce the number of support people in our sales organization, as well as the rate of turnover in the field. Finally, I'd like the sales department to operate more self-sufficiently, without as much need for senior management involvement in daily operating matters at the store level.

We're seeing a shift in our business and competitive environment, and this proposed organization seemingly adds overhead at a time when those shifts mean increasing price and margin pressures on Imperial. In addition, this organization would mean 3 sales vice presidents in contrast to the one sales VP we now have. How would that work in terms of the people issues involved? I'm not sure I have two additional people who are currently ready for that level of P&L responsibility, and we've had problems before in adding upper-level people from the outside. They must learn the many details of the service merchandising business and also the many details of working smoothly with our field people on a daily basis.

Another concern I have is the different kinds of measures being proposed. The new VPs and area managers would have P&L responsibility and so presumably would be concerned with managing their field expenses. But the route reps, who actually do the bulk of our business, would be looking at potentially big bonuses based solely on incremental sales volumes. Is this combination simply inconsistent or a healthy check-and-balance for the organization?

The implications of this organization for our available resources also concern me. The proposed organization is still relatively flat at the top, with 7 people reporting directly to me. We have other management requirements to address, and this proposal would use most of our available people and capital resources. In addition, I'm not sure how this reorganization would help in new-business development efforts. It seems to focus on growing our sales to existing customers and I believe new account development is crucial for us.

My feeling has always been that accountability and performance are less a function of structure and more a matter of the incentives, understanding, and ability in the field. I like the proposed change in route reps' compensation: the bonus system for incremental sales could provide a big incentive, and doesn't require additional managers to implement. My initial instinct is to adopt the change in field compensation but scrap the rest of the proposed organizational changes.

Exhibit 1   Imperial Distributors, Inc. (B)

A-B Drug Sales: Field Organization

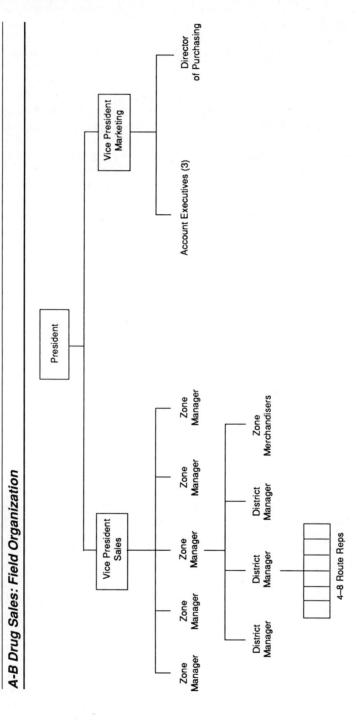

Exhibit 2 Imperial Distributors, Inc. (B)

Jay-Link, Inc.: Field Organization

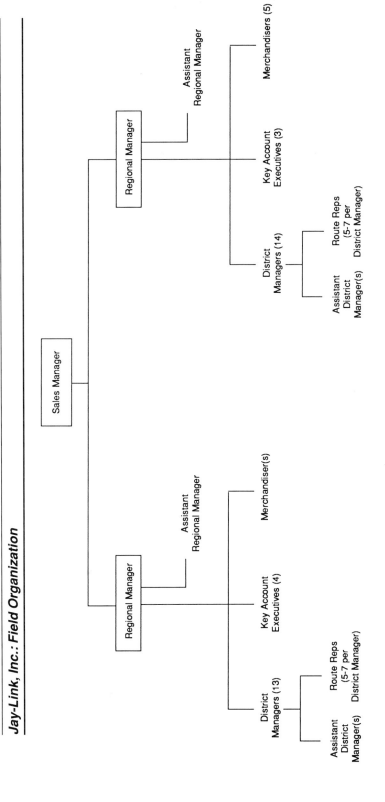

Exhibit 3 Imperial Distributors, Inc. (B)

Gator Wholesale: Field Sales Organization

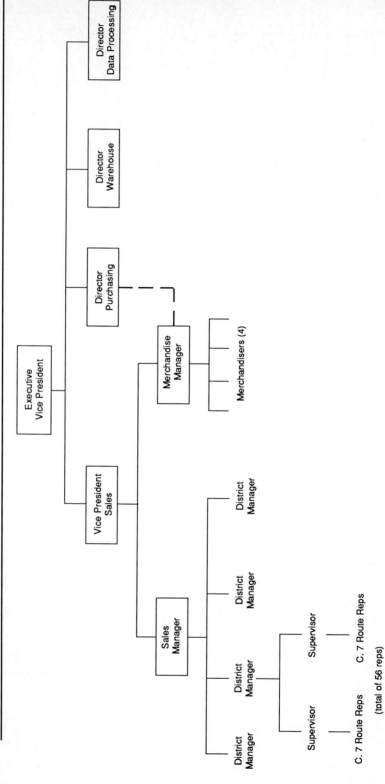

Exhibit 4 Imperial Distributors, Inc. (B)

Mighty Merchandisers, Inc.: Field Sales Organization

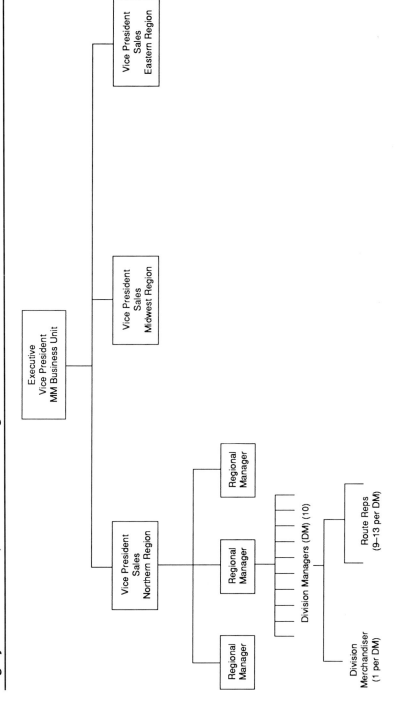

Exhibit 5 Imperial Distributors, Inc. (B)

Comparison of Different Service Merchandisers' Marketing Organizations

Company	No. of Routes	Sales/Marketing Management: Vice President, Regional, Zone	District Managers	Assistants to District Managers	Merchandisers	Account Managers	Average No. of Trainees	Average Report Ratio: Route Reps per Sales Supervisor	Total No. in Sales Organization	Ratio of Sales Management and Support Personnel to No. of Routes
A-B Drug Sales	105	7	15	—	11	3	4	7:1	145	.38
Jay-Link, Inc.	174	3 (+2 Assistant Regional Managers)	27	34	10	7	4	6:1	261	.50
Gator Wholesale	56	2	4	8	4 (+1 Merchandise Manager)	—	2	7:1	77	.375
Mighty Merchandisers										
Northern	121	4	10	—	10	—	3	12:1	148	.22
Midwest	225	6	13	—	13	—	5	17:1	262	.16
Eastern	267	8	18	—	18	—	6	15:1	317	.19
Imperial Distributors	63	5	9 Sales Supervisors	—	14, 9 Senior, 5 Junior	2	4	7:1	97	.54

Exhibit 6 Imperial Distributors, Inc. (B)

Imperial Distributors: Proposed Field Sales Organization

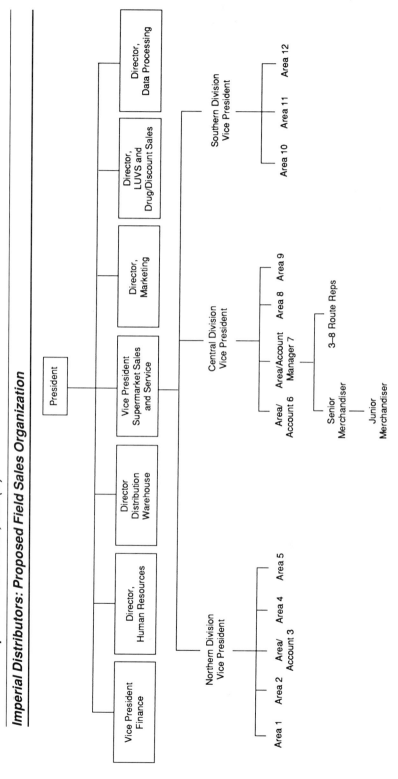

Case 29
Pepsi-Cola Fountain Beverage Division: Tea Breeze

In May 1987, Mr. John Knight, director of new product development at Pepsi-Cola Fountain Beverage Division (FBD) faced several decisions concerning Tea Breeze, FBD's new iced-tea fountain syrup. Mr. Knight had spent a year on the project, and R&D had been involved for two years. The product had been taste-tested across the nation and test-marketed in Las Vegas since July 1986. Production issues seemed to be under control, but marketing issues were becoming complicated.

A divisional planning meeting, attended by FBD's top management, was scheduled for mid-May. An important part of the agenda would be Mr. Knight's recommendations concerning national rollout of Tea Breeze and, if a national rollout were recommended, at what price, to what kinds of target accounts, and with what marketing plan designed to foster bottlers' support for the new product.

Pricing was especially complex. Any recommended price would have to consider suggested price to the consumer, the margins to the retailer, bottler, and FBD, and prices of competing products such as other tea syrups, leaf tea, and perhaps carbonated soft drink syrups also sold to bottlers and fountain accounts.

Furthermore, any marketing plan would need to recognize what Mr. Knight called "the potential 'Catch-22' in our business": bottlers were often hesitant to take on a new product without guarantees of purchase from existing accounts, while many FBD accounts were hesitant to sign contracts without guarantees of commitment from local bottlers. A related problem was that some Pepsi bottlers

Associate Professor Frank V. Cespedes and Research Associate Jon E. King prepared this case as the basis for class discussion rather than to illustrate either effective or ineffective handling of an administrative situation. Certain company data, while useful for discussion purposes, have been disguised.

were prohibited by third-party agreements from carrying Tea Breeze, because they were currently carrying competing products. Finally, FBD had never before introduced a new product; all FBD products had been initially developed and introduced by Pepsi's Bottle & Can Division (B&C), which focused on soft drink consumers rather than fountain accounts such as restaurants, hotels, and other institutions where consumers purchased beverages.

Mr. Knight believed that, if marketed properly, Tea Breeze had significant volume and strategic potential for FBD. "Many current and potential accounts," he noted, "do far more business in iced tea than in soft drinks." In addition, Mr. John Cranor, president of FBD, had recently emphasized that "new products will be critical for FBD. For example, Slice (a fruit juice drink introduced by B&C) accounted for 40% of the division's volume gain during its first year. New products can also influence the marketplace's perception of FBD as an innovator. In addition, tea in particular can be big and profitable business for us, as well as a wedge for opening up many new fountain accounts for other FBD products."

Pepsi-Cola

Pepsi-Cola Company produced and marketed a broad line of carbonated soft drinks (CSDs). Its parent corporation, PepsiCo, Inc., was a $9 billion company which also owned four large restaurant chains as well as Frito-Lay, Inc., a leading snack-food company. Pepsi had franchised about 470 local bottlers who bought CSD concentrate from Pepsi-Cola, manufactured syrup for fountain accounts, and bottled beverages for other retailers.

Pepsi-Cola USA's soft drink operations were divided among three units: the Bottle & Can Division (B&C), Pepsi Bottling Group (PBG), and the Fountain Beverage Division (FBD). These divisions represented about $3 billion in sales. B&C marketed CSDs to consumers through retailers such as grocery stores and any other vendors of canned or bottled soft drinks. PBG operated the 150 franchised bottlers owned by the company; each was run individually by a general manager, similar to any independent franchised bottlers. (See Exhibit 1 for organizational data.) Pepsi's major competitor was the Coca-Cola Company, whose domestic soft drink sales were roughly equal to Pepsi's. Coca-Cola also had an extensive set of franchised bottlers, but those bottlers had no part in Coke's fountain business, which was managed separately and delivered through independent food service industry distributors.

Fountain Beverage Division

FBD was responsible for sales of beverage syrup to fountain accounts, most of which were restaurants and other food service companies. Although FBD established contracts with such companies, deliveries were made to and from the local Pepsi bottling franchises, and bottlers decided individually whether or not to carry any new Pepsi product. For local accounts (those wholly operating within a single bottler's territory), the bottler could establish syrup prices, but for larger cross-territory accounts, the price was established by FBD. Accounts paid for their CSD deliveries through one of two ways: "charge customers" were extended credit by FBD and these customers paid FBD directly for deliveries made by bottlers; other accounts paid cash-on-delivery to the local bottler, who then forwarded the appropriate portion of these revenues to FBD. In both cases, bottlers were compensated for deliveries by FBD, not the accounts. FBD's account customers included both company-owned stores within a designated national account as well as stores owned by franchisees of such accounts. Typically, national account customers paid lower prices for CSDs than smaller, independent customers due to the purchasing power wielded by large national accounts and the intense competition among CSD suppliers for these customers.

FBD had existed for less than a decade, and few reps or managers had been with the division for more than two years. Of FBD's 300 people, 150 were in sales and 40 in marketing; the rest were in finance and systems operations. A National Accounts group served FBD's largest accounts, and a small New Business Group focused on the largest potential accounts in the market. The rest of the field sales force was organized geographically, each district sales manager (sales representative) responsible for the large accounts in a given area. These accounts fell into the range between the 14 largest National Accounts and the local accounts which were wholly within the borders of a single bottler's territory. The reps were also responsible for concentrate sales to the 1–10 bottlers in their geographic areas.

FBD had about $200 million in concentrate sales to bottlers in 1986 and was growing at over 8% per year. Sixty-nine percent of volume came from national and field contracts, the rest from accounts sold by the local bottlers; altogether, Pepsi products accounted for 29% of the $10 billion retail fountain market. Much of Pepsi's share came from sales to quick-serve restaurants (QSRs). (See Exhibit 2 for FBD performance figures.)

Tea Breeze Development

Iced tea was first examined in early 1985 by Mr. Ronald Tidmore, then head of FBD (later president of Pepsi USA), as a possible means of expanding FBD's product line. Some managers believed fountain outlets wanted full-line suppliers rather than several suppliers delivering portions of the beverage line. Ms. Nancy Vorbach, R&D manager in charge of Tea Breeze's formulation, noted: "Industry journals and reports often touch on issues that can lead to new ideas and new directions. One article might mention the size of the national tea market, another may note retailer dissatisfaction with current product options, and a third might point out present buying trends and possible applications of new technology." A gradual collection of such information, and the sheer market volume of iced tea (10% of the entire fountain market), prompted Mr. Tidmore to propose examining the market more closely.

Research and Development

Mr. Bennett Nussbaum, vice president for technical operations at PepsiCo, commented, "Pepsi is a marketing company: the annual report says so every year on the first page. But even in a marketing company, somebody has to make the product." When Mr. Nussbaum took over operations in 1984, he greatly expanded R&D activity and personnel (from 60 to 150 by 1987), and instituted regular inter-departmental meetings as project reviews for non-R&D managers. "This forced people to communicate: Pepsi is not a formal company, driven by memos and meetings; I think I wrote one memo last year." Within the next two years, Pepsi introduced the first CSD with fruit juice (Slice), and the first diet sodas with aspartame (a new artificial sweetener); both products set standards in the industry.

Research and development at Pepsi included technical troubleshooting for plants and bottlers. Ms. Vorbach commented: "A large part of product development is knowing the processes involved; our client is the bottler, and his is the consumer. We have to understand the bottler very well, what works for him, and what doesn't."

Due to freshness and inventory concerns, Pepsi delivered its concentrates to bottlers weekly. The new tea product was intended to be produced on existing bottler production equipment, and thus require little incremental investment by the bottler. However, resetting production lines was always a concern to bottlers, who typically operated a single syrup production facility. Each week, every syrup flavor would be run through the line and therefore several times weekly the line would have to be stopped, equipment flushed and sanitized, the ingredients reset, and a new syrup run started. More products meant more time, attention, and resets for the bottler. Mr. Nussbaum noted:

> No new product will ever be as quick and easy for the bottler to produce as original Pepsi. Artificial sweeteners take longer to dissolve than sugar; juices demand special sanitation facilities; and new products demand resetting production lines more often. A new product therefore needs a critical mass of sales volume for it to be attractive to bottlers, who are always concerned about the limited number of dispensers and space in fountain outlets, the shelf life of the product, and the efficiency of their own production run. These are facts of life in this business; any new product will face these demands.

First Glance

In early 1985, FBD management asked Pepsi's B&C Group to underwrite tea development and then offer it to FBD: this was the way FBD had acquired all of its current products. But B&C was not interested: Tea was an "unstable" flavor which easily picked up other tastes including those of aluminum and steel, two common B&C packaging materials. Also, the amount of preservatives necessary for iced-tea in bottles and cans could make the product taste acidic or "chemical." (For fountain service, however, these potential problems were greatly reduced.) In addition, some brand managers pointed out that since fountain outlets had a limited number of nozzles (typically 4–6), a tea product might limit the number of nozzles dedicated to soft drinks.

Before B&C's rejection of the tea project, focus groups generated some initial observations. Ms. Vorbach recalled:

> In general, people who liked iced tea loved it and felt strongly about their personal ways of making it, which diverged widely. This raised another issue with B&C managers, since Pepsi's policy is to make a consistent, standard product across regions. Also, budgets were being tightened at the time, so tea became a lower priority. A new product at Pepsi needs a champion, and iced tea didn't have one yet.

Second Start

Later in 1985, Ms. Jennifer Noonan joined B&C marketing from Frito-Lay. She became responsible for development of new products oriented toward new technologies and new categories of business. She resurrected the tea investigation and hired consultants to study various possibilities such as carbonated iced tea or adding fruit flavors or juice. Ms. Vorbach recalled that "focus groups looked at Slice Tea (with fruit flavors and carbonation) and produced a curious result: consumers loved the taste but hated the idea." The studies were inconclusive, so Ms. Noonan focused on other projects, again leaving iced tea development at a standstill.

Round Three

Mr. John Knight had been in marketing at Frito-Lay where he reported to Mr. Cranor. He then left the company to join a small restaurant start-up which eventually went bankrupt. He then joined FBD in 1985. Mr. Cranor became president of FBD in 1986. In early 1986, FBD management expressed serious interest in a fountain-only product, and in February Mr. Knight began to focus on tea as a possibility. The stated objectives of adding a tea product were to expand into a new high-volume cold beverage category, to increase gallonage and average delivery size for the bottlers, and to broaden the range of Pepsi products for the fountain service industry.

The Iced Tea Market

Mr. John Swanhaus, VP of marketing at FBD, had hired a consulting firm to examine retailers' and bottlers' perspectives on iced tea; the report was presented just as Mr. Knight took on the project. The report noted that iced tea was the third most frequently ordered beverage in restaurants (after CSDs and coffee), accounting for a volume 22% as large as all fountain CSDs combined. Most iced tea sold in restaurants was fresh brewed leaf tea, which accounted for 75% of the 140 million gallons of iced tea fountain sales in 1985.

Powdered mixes accounted for 18% of the market and syrup for 7%.[1] Consumption of all types of iced tea tended to be highest during the summer months, with high volume potential in all regions but especially in the Southeast. (See Exhibit 3 for data on product forms.)

Growth for the category in 1985 was approximately 5% overall, with leaf growing at 11%, powder dropping by 24%, and syrup decreasing 12%. Traditional leaf tea demanded time and attention to prepare, was usually dispensed by hand from a pot, and would lose freshness in hours. Since the process was rarely automated, flavor and strength could be inconsistent; tea became cloudy and bitter after about 4 hours. Storage for brewed tea was cumbersome (usually in large urns) and, because it was brewed in batches, could easily mismatch demand by running out in peak hours and being wasted at store closing. Powder offered long shelf-life, but dissolving was inconsistent and often messy. Preparation and storage of powdered iced tea was almost as time-consuming and cumbersome as for brewed leaf tea and powdered teas suffered from poor taste. Syrup iced teas offered fountain outlets some benefits of convenience and ease of operations: the product could be stored for weeks, dispensed through an automated system, and required minimal time or care. Pepsi bottlers were equipped to produce syrup, so this was the segment specifically addressed in product research.

Thirstea, Inc. produced the most successful of the iced tea syrups, while Lipton, Maryland Club (a regional subsidiary of Coca-Cola), Continental Beverages, and General Foods' Maxwell House division also sold tea syrups to bottlers. Coca-Cola had once announced a national rollout of fountain iced tea, but no product reached the market. In fact, no major supplier had had notable success selling tea syrup, and Maxwell House had recently closed its sales unit for its product. Most tea syrup was sold to institutional accounts such as school and hospital cafeterias, and 90% of that was presweetened. Most national restaurant chains established a list of approved tea vendors (supplying leaf, powder or syrup), and allowed individual outlets their choice of which approved vendor to use.

Field interviews indicated that many fountain operators had strong views about freshly brewed leaf tea: many believed it tasted better than existing powdered and syruped iced tea and had merchandising appeal based on freshness and "organic" qualities. In addition, average retail prices for sweetened, fresh-brewed iced tea were about $3.60/gallon, and the leaf tea material costs to the fountain operator were about $0.31/gallon; syrup costs to the fountain operator were generally two to three times higher than for leaf.

In analyzing the iced tea market, Mr. Knight found skews in demand among different regions and types of stores (see Exhibit 4). Iced tea was particularly

---

[1]Syrup was mixed with five parts of water to produce retail gallonage, so the total market of 140 million retail gallons of iced tea represented the equivalent of 23 million gallons of syrup; total tea syrup sales in 1985 were less than two million gallons.

popular in sit-down restaurant chains, and 16 states in the Southeast accounted for two thirds of demand. Thirty-two percent of iced tea servings across the country were made unsweetened, but only 10% of the servings in the Southeast were unsweetened.[2] Further analysis indicated that the large-run volume tea accounts were not the accounts where Pepsi was currently strong, suggesting that tea could be complementary to CSD sales. Further, from his time at Frito-Lay, Mr. Knight knew that route delivery costs were roughly the same for a small as for a large account, and believed that bottlers' route economics could be improved by adding tea. Iced tea could therefore not only increase revenues but also improve the efficiencies of FBD's existing distribution system, allowing for the penetration and development of many smaller as well as large national accounts.

Product Formulation

Soon after taking on the tea project, the development team decided to package the tea syrup in a five-gallon plastic "bag-in-a-box" (BIB) similar to the one Lipton used, thus avoiding any issues concerning "metallic" tastes. To avoid constraints tied to the limited number of beverage dispensers at fountain outlets, it was decided to provide a separate dispenser for the product. (Existing tea dispensers in outlets were typically separate from soda dispensers, so space demands on the store would not be increased.)

Meanwhile, Ms. Vorbach's R&D group worked on developing an iced tea fountain syrup product that would compare in taste with Lipton's product. (Coincidentally, Pepsi's flavoring group had already begun work on tea flavorings, since the Middle East unit at Pepsi International had independently expressed interest in a tea product.) Ms. Vorbach decided to focus on a standard, unsweetened product, allowing each consumer to add sweetener as desired. Pepsi had never before produced an unsweetened product, but Ms. Vorbach argued that unsweetened iced tea would allow for more personal variation and also lower the costs of producing the syrup.

R&D then prepared product prototypes and tested them with "sensory groups" (i.e., focus groups which tasted, smelled, and evaluated new beverages). The results were positive and, after making some changes in the formulation, tests indicated that Pepsi's product had achieved parity with Lipton's. The product was then tested against freshly brewed iced tea. It did well with heavy iced tea drinkers, but light drinkers generally preferred brewed iced tea. Ms. Vorbach accepted heavy users as the important consumers and best judges, but Mr. Knight argued that "heavy users are the worst judges: they'll drink anything that's available."

Another issue arose over whether to presweeten the tea. Ms. Vorbach was in favor of the unsweetened product formulation, but Mr. Knight argued that consumers, despite their range of sweetener preferences, would rather not take

---

[2]These figures were available through Crest, a food-service demographics database.

the trouble of adding sweetener: dissolving sugar (or artificial sweeteners) in iced tea was far slower than in hot tea. Mr. Knight believed a sweetened tea was essential since the greatest potential demand was in the Southeast,[3] which exhibited a strong preference for pre-sweetened tea. Mr. Knight therefore went to division management to resolve the issue and received agreement on a sweetened syrup.

At this point, the level of sweetness became an issue. Sweetness was chemically measured in "brix." Brand Pepsi-Cola, for example, had a brix of 11, while Lipton's tea syrup had a brix of 6.2. Ms. Vorbach had targeted a brix of 8 for iced tea, but Mr. Knight wanted a brix of 12. Company policy required a single standard, so field engineers tested sweetness levels and suggested a brix of 8–10 as a reasonable range. Ms. Vorbach noted that sweetness preferences varied by region and the usual procedure was to "look for a happy medium, or at worst, the point least offensive to most people." However, Mr. Knight was not convinced:

> There really is no standard of identity with iced tea, because heavy tea drinkers are exposed to every variety of sweetness in their areas. During the summer of 1986, I had a Harvard MBA working in my group, and she spent a portion of her time collecting samples of existing tea brews at sites across the country for chemical analysis. She found that one reason brewed tea is used in many places is because heat is needed to dissolve all the sugar customers want; existing cold tea syrups didn't accommodate this preference, but our formulation could. In the end, the product was formulated with a brix of 10.

Branding and Merchandising

Competing tea syrups were not branded (other than with company names), but Pepsi's policy was to brand all its products. Unfortunately, company attorneys rejected dozens of names proposed by Mr. Knight's group, until the product was approaching deadline. Finally Mr. Knight went back to one of the original choices (Tea Breeze) and told the lawyers to buy the rights from a confectioner using a similar name (Sea Breeze).

Another important step was to develop merchandising for the product. Earlier it had been decided to provide a separate tea dispenser, so R&D chose a standard, functional unit. Mr. Knight was not impressed with the utilitarian design, but he had been intrigued by a ceramic teapot-shaped dispenser he had seen on the market. He contacted the manufacturer and had them develop a proprietary version for Tea Breeze. The bulk of the countertop unit was decorative; the working parts besides the nozzles were hidden beneath and behind the counter (see Exhibit 5). These units cost $300 each; FBD arranged

---

[3] Highest iced tea consumption was in the following states: Virginia, Tennessee, Mississippi, Alabama, Georgia, North Carolina, South Carolina. Almost as high were Louisiana, Arkansas, Texas, Oklahoma, Kentucky, West Virginia, and Florida.

to split that cost with the bottler who installed the dispenser, and offer it free to the retailer as a promotion.

Market Testing

Mr. Knight had no demands put on him to deliver positive financial results until fiscal year 1988: he had freedom to develop the product as needed, as long as he worked on internally generated funds after 1986. Once labwork was complete, the new product needed to be run through a bottler in order to test its manufacturability and discover any pitfalls.

The first bottler to take on Tea Breeze was in Las Vegas in July 1986. Mr. Knight noted, "It was a natural place to take a gamble." The tester was a Pepsi Bottling Group (PBG) bottler which carried a tea product of such poor quality that it was costing the bottler business: the bottler had lost 100 of its 180 tea accounts in the past year. With Tea Breeze, the account base rose back to 127 accounts by the end of 1986, and several fresh brew accounts were converted to Tea Breeze syrup on the basis of the convenience of using the simple fountain system rather than the brewing process. The proprietary dispenser was also accepted: more than one operator stated, "If I have to take the tea to get the pot, I'll do it."

Flavor concentration was also tested at the Las Vegas bottler: new tubes and pumps were installed to insure a pure flavor, and dispenser flow problems were corrected with minor redesign. But further problems arose when Tea Breeze began expanding to other bottlers in the area. Ms. Vorbach received complaints which testing eventually indicated came from poor outlet and bottler operations.

B&C monitored all bottlers constantly by demanding samples at various stages in the bottling process; there were rigid standards to be met at each level. But FBD had not historically monitored bottlers' fountain operations, and Ms. Vorbach noted that even if bottlers were monitored by FBD, it was difficult to insure quality procedures in the stores themselves. For instance, an outlet might have in their tea fountain used tubing which had caught the taste of some other beverage. This was a special problem for tea because of its light taste.

Other complaints surfaced simply because of bottlers' and vendors' inexperience with the product. Some complained that the product was weak (because of its light color compared to CSD syrups). Others sanitized the system as recommended and then found the tea tasted like sanitizer because they had not rinsed the system thoroughly. But Ms. Vorbach noted that "once a bottler has his system working properly for tea, his entire operation will be noticeably improved."

Expansion

Mr. Knight then proposed rolling the product out through the South and West during the first quarter of 1987, and through the rest of the country by mid-year, in order to hit the summer peak consumption. By January 1987, he had started Tea Breeze service at independent bottlers in Tuscaloosa, Alabama, and Dyersberg, Tennessee, and had contracts from 13 other independent bottlers to pick up the product. Pepsi Bottling Group had also agreed to add more bottlers to the field test of Tea Breeze, including the large Los Angeles bottler.

The project was reviewed by FBD management in January 1987 and it was decided to continue the test market expansion. But suddenly PBG pulled back on its commitment because of other pressing problems, and the Los Angeles bottler declined until FBD could first provide large volume guarantees.

Pricing

Mr. Knight felt price incentives were needed to generate volume. Although bottlers could sell syrup to local accounts at any price they set, any chain business was contracted by FBD at a price determined at headquarters. For these contracts, the bottlers were encouraged by FBD to serve the accounts, but could not alter the price. In general, prices to chains were discounted about 25% from the prices typically charged to small accounts.

Mr. Knight noted three benchmarks in his search for a successful pricing policy. One was the typical costs of soft drink syrup to fountain accounts: about $8.23 per gallon to small (local) accounts, discounted to about $6.14 to national accounts. Concentrate and sweetener costs to the bottler for a gallon of soft drink syrup averaged $2.69 and $1.12. In Las Vegas, Tea Breeze had sold at $6.48 per gallon to large accounts and $7.76 per gallon to small accounts, while concentrate and sweetener costs to the bottler were $2.84 and $1.24 per tea syrup gallon.

The second benchmark was Lipton's iced tea product which typically sold at $5.40 per gallon to restaurants, and $2.09 per syrup gallon to bottlers.[4] However, Tea Breeze ingredients would cost FBD about $.95 per syrup gallon. Mr. Knight noted that, "Given this cost structure, I have to assume that Lipton is accepting lower margins on their iced tea fountain product than we demand for our CSDs. As a result, we may have to accept lower margins on Tea Breeze than we are accustomed. But my boss, John Cranor, was not convinced. John said that we can justify a higher price to the bottler because of our ability to deliver national account business."

The third benchmark was the total cost (to the retailer) of brewed tea, which included the leaves, labor, sweetener, and wastage. This figure was estimated at $0.84 unsweetened per brewed gallon, and $1.23 sweetened; equivalent syrup prices (noting that one syrup gallon produced six gallons of

---

[4]Some syrup manufacturers such as Continental and Maxwell House sold syrup instead of concentrate to bottlers, eliminating bottler's needs for production and packaging equipment. Although the per-gallon prices to bottlers carrying such syrups were higher than the concentrate prices (per syrup gallon), there was an average savings on labor, packaging and overhead of $0.55 per gallon.

iced tea) would be $5.02 per gallon unsweetened and $7.38 sweetened. Mr. Knight noted that there were some less tangible benefits to the outlet for having a product that was convenient to dispense. Since large accounts were sold consistently on price, he decided to try for a discount price of $5.06 (implying a small account price of $6.75).

However, restaurant customers typically did not calculate their costs in terms of total operating costs of brewed iced tea. Cost of Goods Sold was their only margin measure; labor was considered overhead and waste was virtually ignored. Mr. Weinberg, director of FBD's New Business Development Group, explained, "Most restaurants are run on gut reactions; it's hard to change their minds on anything. There is also not a lot of information available on fresh brew wastage, so it is hard to argue about it." To compete with leaves on that basis, the syrup would have to sell at $1.25 per gallon plain or $3.56 sweet, clearly an unacceptable price. (Exhibit 6 is Mr. Knight's cost calculation of brewed tea. The "6 Fresh Gallon" figures are for direct comparison to a syrup gallon, which yielded 6 retail gallons.)

In fact, headquarters FBD managers reviewing the Tea Breeze project were not enthusiastic about any of the parity-price figures Mr. Knight had derived. They argued for higher prices (a discount price to large accounts of $6.75/gallon and a small-account price of about $8.98). But Mr. Knight was worried that sales reps would not be motivated by this development: "Pepsi reps are used to selling by undercutting Coke's price, not selling at a premium." He was especially concerned with sales force reaction, because unlike other Pepsi products, Tea Breeze currently had no quota or bonus for reps to achieve. Yet these reps were the people who would (or wouldn't) sell Tea Breeze to bottlers and chains.

Motivating Bottlers and Salespeople

The planning meeting in May 1987 was closing in. Mr. William Hober, VP of sales at FBD, liked the idea of iced tea but told Mr. Knight to sell the bottlers first before trying to sell it to customers. Mr. Swanhaus (VP of marketing) disagreed, "FBD has to sell a certain amount of volume before bottlers will take on the product. They want us to provide them with profitable products, and they know that a new product needs a critical mass to be profitable. Besides, if you don't sell it to retailers, the bottlers are irrelevant."

Mr. Hober suggested, "Tea will not have the consumer pull that other Pepsi products do because this product is not advertised by B&C the way the others are. But we can sell against tea leaves to retailers on points such as sanitation and flavor consistency, and bottlers can be shown that there is a market available 22% of the size of the entire soft drink market. We can start by selling one bottler in the area and then showing the others in that area how well that bottler is doing with Tea Breeze." Mr. Knight believed this sales strategy would take a great deal of time; it also concentrated on local business rather than emphasizing FBD's strength in large accounts. He believed price incentives were likely to encourage more action, and demand less step-by-step involvement with individual bottler operations.

In February 1987, Mr. Knight learned that Lipton had recently established a national accounts sales team for its tea product and had successfully sold tea syrup to Pizza Hut, a large national sit-down restaurant chain owned by PepsiCo. Mr. Knight had been hoping to sign Pizza Hut on as an early Tea Breeze customer; the Lipton contract was sure to delay any contract with Pizza Hut, and it also indicated that Lipton was aggressively seeking large chain business. This further complicated selling strategy to bottlers by undermining FBD's ability to quickly deliver national account business.

Sales Force

Mr. Knight developed for FBD's sales force a packet of selling aids, including a comprehensive market overview, a sample bottler presentation, a sample retailer presentation, flyers for local sales, and a complete technical bulletin. The sales literature noted that fountain customers had three major criteria for choosing a tea product (taste, consumer preference, and consistency), and suggested emphasizing the following points: Tea Breeze was made with real tea; it was rated equal to brewed iced tea by heavy tea drinkers in blind taste tests; and the dispensing system measured exact syrup volumes, maintaining a strict consistency from glass to glass, day to day.

The literature also noted that convenience and consistent quality were the product's key benefits, so that accounts with high volume and limited time and space (e.g., convenience stores and restaurants in shopping malls) were likely initial targets. Of all sales proposals to retailers around Las Vegas and Tuscaloosa, 53% had resulted in orders, typically with immediate closure at $6.40–$7.75 per gallon.

By spring 1987, feedback from several QSR chains testing the product was positive, and established Tea Breeze accounts uniformly expressed high satisfaction. Mr. Knight stressed to salespeople that volume for Tea Breeze would not cannibalize current Pepsi CSD sales, and could total from 5–15% of an area's beverage market. The proprietary dispenser was also very popular with the trade and cost them nothing; it was therefore a powerful selling tool.

Mr. Knight noted that bottlers should respond to several other advantages. Iced tea was a product with a proven market, and since it was complementary to CSDs, it improved route productivity by expanding marginal accounts. Also, the new dispenser allowed addition of a new syrup into an outlet without shutting out an existing flavor, and FBD would underwrite 50% of all tea-related store equipment costs (i.e., $150 of the dispenser system's $300 price). In addition, Tea Breeze was produced and packaged along standard Pepsi lines, allowing for easy integration into the plant and distribution operations.

Mr. Weinberg offered additional reasons to push Tea Breeze:

> Tea can be used as an entrance into new accounts. It can open relations with outlets that are locked into Coke's other products. Tea can be a testing ground for

these customers. It gives them a reason to listen to a sales pitch from Pepsi, and to try Pepsi's service. It is also very big in cafeterias (a group of restaurants where Pepsi has been weak), and big in the south, Coke's heartland. Tea won't be a blockbuster for us, but it can be an important wedge.

Final Proposal

The immediate decision was whether or not to recommend the national roll-out of Tea Breeze. If he chose to do so, Mr. Knight had to convince the management review committee that Tea Breeze would be strategically and financially sound by the end of 1988, which meant achieving bottler and national account commitments, as well as providing strong revenues and margins for FBD and the bottlers. Specifically, he needed to present answers to the most current and pressing questions: Where should marketing efforts (and the limited resources available) for Tea Breeze focus? What should be the respective roles of FBD's field sales force (which focused on local bottlers and large accounts), and the National Accounts group (which focused on the largest chain accounts) in any marketing plan for Tea Breeze? What criteria should guide pricing policy, and what pricing structure would satisfy the requirements of FBD, its bottlers, and target fountain accounts? (Exhibit 7 provides an abbreviated timeline of the Tea Breeze project.)

Exhibit 1   Pepsi-Cola Fountain Beverage Division: Tea Breeze

Corporate Organization

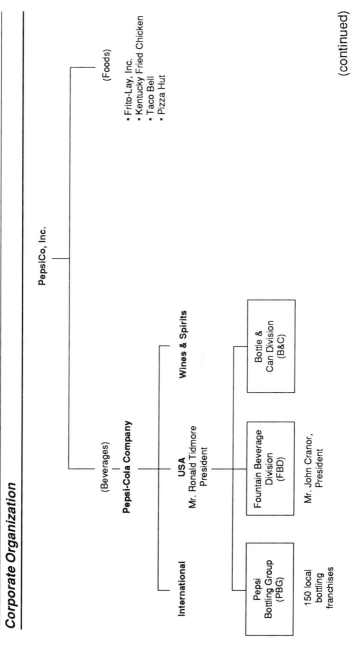

(continued)

Exhibit 1 (continued)

FBD Organization

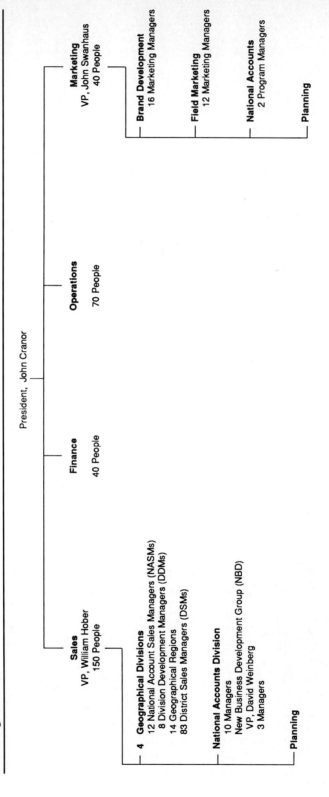

President, John Cranor

Sales
VP, William Hober
150 People

4 **Geographical Divisions**
12 National Account Sales Managers (NASMs)
8 Division Development Managers (DDMs)
14 Geographical Regions
83 District Sales Managers (DSMs)

National Accounts Division
10 Managers
New Business Development Group (NBD)
VP, David Weinberg
3 Managers

Planning

Finance

40 People

Operations

70 People

Marketing
VP, John Swanhaus
40 People

Brand Development
16 Marketing Managers

Field Marketing
12 Marketing Managers

National Accounts
2 Program Managers

Planning

Exhibit 2 Pepsi-Cola Fountain Beverage Division: Tea Breeze

FBD Performance by Channel

Channel	1986 National Volume	1986 % of National Volume	1986 Pepsi National Share	1986 Non-Pepsi National Volume	1982–86 National Volume Growth Rate	1982–86 Pepsi Volume Growth Rate	Economic Returns Pepsi/Bottler	1986 Local Volume[a]
Quick service restaurant	118 MM gals.	51.9%	37.7%	73.5 MM gals.	7.7%	16.1%	Marginal/ Good	6 MM gals.
Sit-down restaurant	29	12.7	7.4	26.9	1.2	1.2	Marginal/ Good	34
Cup vending	25	11.0	23.5	19.1	0.7	(1.0)	Good/ Negative	19
Convenience stores	22	9.9	37.8	13.7	7.4	6.8	Good/Good	1
Institutional feeders	10	4.5	12.6	8.6	1.2	(1.7)	Good/Good	5
Theaters	8	3.7	13.0	6.9	2.3	(1.1)	Good/Good	1
Sports arenas	7	3.0	11.7	6.2	4.5	(13.5)	Negative/ Negative	2
Hotels	5	2.0	12.2	4.4	(3.6)	2.7	Good/Good	4
Cafeterias	3	1.4	4.0	2.9	3.5	(7.1)	Good/Good	3
Totals	227 MM gals.	100%	28.5%	162.2 MM gals.	5.0%	10.6%		75 MM gals.

a Volume available to local, bottler-managed accounts.

Exhibit 3 Pepsi-Cola Fountain Beverage Division: Tea Breeze

Product Forms by Market

	Total	Northeast	Central	South	West
Brewed	75.0%	55.5%	62.5%	91.6%	85.3%
Syrup	7.1	14.5	7.3	3.6	4.9
Powdered	17.9	30.0	30.2	4.8	9.8
	100.0%	100.0%	100.0%	100.0%	100.0%

Operators' Reasons for Using Current Forms of Tea System

Type of Tea	Account's Reasons for Using Current Form of Tea—by Rank			
	Most Important	Second	Third	Last
All types/ overall	Quality taste	Customer preference	Consistency	Storage
Brewed	Quality taste	Customer preference	Cost	Storage
Powdered	Convenience	Cost	Quality taste	Customer preference
Concentrate	Quality taste	Convenience	Storage	Customer preference

Iced Tea Seasonality Indices

January	59	July	168
February	53	August	149
March	84	September	126
April	101	October	99
May	119	November	85
June	108	December	52

Crest Geographic Tea Development Patterns

	% of Nat'l CSD Consumption	% of National Iced Tea Consumption	Index	Iced Tea as % of Total Beverages
New England	4.1	1.2%	29	2.1
Mid-Atlantic	13.7	5.3	39	3.5
East North Central	19.1	8.8	46	4.3
West North Central	6.5	5.2	80	7.2
South Atlantic	18.1	30.5	169	16.1
East South Central	7.6	11.7	154	17.2
West South Central	12.6	25.1	199	21.2
Mountain	5.5	4.8	87	8.5
Pacific	12.8	7.4	58	5.0
	100.0%	100.0%	100	9.8

Source: NRA Cold Beverage Monitor.

Exhibit 4   Pepsi-Cola Fountain Beverage Division: Tea Breeze

Beverage Breakdown by Channel

	% of National Consumption of Iced Tea	% of National Consumption of CSDs	Index
Fast food/drive-in	26.9	55.4	48
Family type	42.5	20.3	209
Take-out	3.1	10.8	29
Cafeteria	8.3	2.8	296
Coffee shop	2.8	1.8	156
Atmosphere/specialty	15.4	7.6	203
All other	1.0	1.4	71
	100.0%	100.0%	100

Exhibit 5   Pepsi-Cola Fountain Beverage Division: Tea Breeze

Tea Breeze™ Iced Tea Dispenser

Exhibit 6 Pepsi-Cola Fountain Beverage Division: Tea Breeze

Price Comparisons
(large accounts)

| | Comparison with Other Syrups (Per Syrup Gallon) | | | | | | | | |
| | Pepsi | Diet Pepsi | Mountain Dew | Weighted Average[a] | Tea Breeze | Lipton | Lipton | Continental | Maxwell House |
							(Syrup sold to bottler premade)		
Cost to retailers	$6.21	$5.91	$6.08	$6.14		$5.40[b]	$5.40–8.10	$5.40–8.10	$8.37
Cost of concentrate to bottler	(2.31)	(4.31)[c]	(2.88)	(2.69)		(2.09)[b]	(3.54)[d]	(3.35)[d]	(4.86)[d]
Cost of sweetener to bottler	(1.32)	0.0	(1.40)	(1.12)	(1.24)	(0.84)	(1.13)	0.0[e]	(1.08)
Bottler margin	2.58	1.60	1.80	2.33		2.47	0.73–3.43	2.05–4.75	2.43
Bottler packaging costs	0.55	0.55	0.55	0.55	0.55	0.55	0.0	0.0	0.0
Mfr. cost of ingredients				0.97	0.93	0.93 est.			
Mfg. margin				1.72		1.16 est.			

Notes: FBD typically discounted prices to the largest National Accounts by $0.33 per syrup gallon.
Expected volume per outlet: 230 syrup gallons for national accounts; 133 for local.
Expected equipment costs per outlet: $150 to bottler, $150 to FBD.
[a] Average of all Pepsi brands weighted by each brand's market volume.
[b] Most competitive—figures varied widely.
[c] Presweetened concentrate.
[d] Syrup instead of concentrate.
[e] Unsweetened.

Exhibit 6 (continued)

Fresh Brewing Costs to Retailers

	Unsweetened		Sweetened	
	1 Fresh Gallon	6 Fresh Gallons[b]	1 Fresh Gallon	6 Fresh Gallons[b]
Ingredients				
Tea	$0.209	$1.254	$0.209	$1.254
Sweetener[a]	—	—	0.209	1.254
Labor [a] (6 minutes at $4.70/hour)	0.47	2.82	0.47	2.83
Cost of Ingredients and labor	0.679	4.07	0.89	5.34
Wastage[a,c] (87.5% yield)	0.101	0.61	0.12	0.73
Total	**0.78**	**4.68**	**1.01**	**6.07**

[a]Estimate: figures varied widely.

[b]This is provided as a benchmark for syrup pricing. One syrup gallon yielded six retail gallons, so syrup gallon equivalents were six times fresh gallon figures.

[c]This factor reflected that a gallon of brewed tea was rarely fully used, due to spoilage and overbrewing.

Exhibit 7 *Pepsi-Cola Fountain Beverage Division: Tea Breeze*

Tea Breeze Development Timeline

Early 1985	Ronald Tidmore (FBD) first examines iced tea; Development rejected by B&C; Initial consumer preference tested.
Mid-1985	Jennifer Noonan (B&C) investigates tea possibilities: carbonation, fruit flavors, etc.; project rejected.
Early 1986	Consultant's report extends understanding of tea market: retailer criteria, product mix, etc. Declares tea productive for bottlers. John Knight (FBD) takes on management of iced tea product. Research indicates skews in demand due to geography, season, and type of outlet.
Spring 1986	Product formulated, tested, reformulated. Sweetness contested. Tea Breeze brand name established; proprietary dispenser developed.
July 1986	Las Vegas BPG test markets Tea Breeze. Account base increased; sold successfully against leaf tea. Production issues ironed out.
Fall 1986	Tea Breeze expanded to two other bottlers; 13 others signed on for early 1987.
January 1987	FBD accepts expansion of test markets. PBG withdraws from future testing. Mr. Knight analyzes pricing benchmarks and recommends competitive price; FBD management urges premium pricing.
February 1987	Lipton National Accounts Sales Team signs a contract for tea sales to Pizza Hut.
May 1987	Mr. Knight expected to present proposal on future of Tea Breeze.

Case Index

Actmedia, Inc., 168–95
Alloy Rods Corporation, 286–313
Amerisource, 25–50
Becton Dickinson & Company: VACUTAINER Systems Division, 314–37
Capital Cities/ABC, Inc.: Spot Sales, 381–405
Carolina Power & Light Company, 569–97
Cole National Corporation: Turnover, 105–136
Cooper Pharmaceuticals, Inc., 94–104
Cox Cable (A), 196–218
Cox Cable (B), 219–32
Dorio Printing Company, 51–70
Fieldcrest Division of Fieldcrest Mills, Inc.:
    Compensation System for Field Sales Representatives, 137–59
Frito-Lay, Inc. (A), 481–504
General Electric: Customer Service, 598–630
Honeywell, Inc.: International Organization for Commercial Avionics (A), 745–72
IBM Marketing Organization (A): Changes in Structure, 632–54
IBM Marketing Organization (B): Process, 655–65
Imperial Distributors, Inc. (A), 505–32
Imperial Distributors, Inc. (B), 774–87
MCI: Vnet (A), 432–52
MCI Communications Corporation: National Accounts Program, 406–31
Pepsi-Cola Fountain Beverage Division: Marketing Organization, 699–722
Pepsi-Cola Fountain Beverage Division: Tea Breeze, 788–807
Peripheral Products Company: "The Gray Market for Disk Drives," 533–59
Procter & Gamble Co. (A), 666–98
Springs Industries: Apparel Fabrics Division, 358–80
Turner Construction Company, 724–44
Westinghouse Electric Corporation (A), 249–72
Westinghouse Electric Corporation (B): Control House, 273–85

Index

A

Account executives, in sales
    coordination, 350
Account management, 339–40
Account managers, role of, 349
Accounts. *See* Major Accounts
Account selection, 8, 340–46
Acquisitions, 234, 339
Actmedia, Inc., as case study, 165
"Administrative simplicity," in
    functionally focused organization,
    471, 472
Advertising. *See also* Marketing
  in functionally focused organization,
    467–68
  of MCI, NAP, 425, 429
Advertising managers, 621
Affiliated Purchasing Group (APG), 247
Agents, in multichannel systems, 238
Alloy Rods Corp., as case study, 247–48
Amerisource, Inc., as case study,
    22, 23
Analytical process, in market-focused
    organization, 467
Apple, 31
Arpac Corp., 445

B

"Bargain basement" customers, 343
Becton Dickinson & Co. (BD)
  as case study, 248
  VACUTAINER Systems Div. (BDVS),
    247–48
Behavior, of sales representatives, 163.
    See also Buyer Behavior; Customer
    behavior
Benefits
  vs. features, 465
  vs. product, 461
Bonuses, 89. *See also* Compensation
    systems
Boundary spanners, 20–21
Boundary spanning
  and capacity planning, 474
  inventory, 474
  new product introduction, 474–75

AT&T (American Telephone and
    Telegraph), 354
Automation, 235. *See also* Computer
    industry
Awareness, in buyer-seller relationships,
    347

physical distribution, 474
product line and, 474–75
requirements of, 473–74
sales forecast, 474
"Bounded rationality," 619
Brand assistants, 460
Brand share, 459
Brand volume, 459
Brokers, in multichannel systems, 238
Bundled purchasing agreements, 235
Bureaucracy, inherent nature of, 461
Business units, and financial resources, 243–44
Buyer behavior, and marketing strategy, 473. *See also* Customer behavior
Buyer-seller relationships, developing, 346–48
Buying center, 344
Buying decisions, 236
Buying process
  and deployment decisions, 162
  for major accounts, 343–46

C

Call capacity, index of, 164
Capital Cities/ABC, Inc., as case study, 354
Carolina Power & Light Company (CP&L), as case study, 566
Capacity planning, and boundary spanning, 474
"Carriage trade" customers, 343
Centralization
  vs. decentralization, 12
  of marketing efforts, 622–23
Chain accounts, 113–14
Chandler, Alfred, 618
Channel management, 7–8
Channels. *See also* Multichannel systems
  and control of resources, 242–45
  definition for, 233
  functions of, 236
  relations of, 239–41
Closure, in functionally focused organization, 470
Cole National Corp., as case study, 92
Combination stores, 339

Commercial Aviation Div., (CAvD), Honeywell, as case study, 623
Commission rate, 90
Commission system, salary/incentive mix, 89. *See also* Compensation systems
Commitment, in buyer-seller relationships, 347
Communications systems
  boundary spanning in, 477
  in market-focused organization, 467
Compensation systems
  decisions regarding, 88
  incentive component of, 89
  and sales coordination, 351
Computer industry, market segments of, 464
Computerization, of operations, 235
Computer technologies, and account selection, 341
Concentration, industry, 235
Conflict resolution, mechanisms of, 477
Control systems, in sales management, 82, 83, 84
Cooper Pharmaceuticals, Inc., (CPI), as case study, 91
Coordination, in marketing strategy, 472
Corey, E. Raymond, 618–19
Corporate planning systems, 17
Cost accounting systems, 564
Cox Cable Communications, as case study, 165–67
"Creeping overhead growth," 462
Cross-selling, 352
Customer behavior, and sales tasks, 78
Customer encounters, management of, 4, 79, 91
Customer goods firms, marketing organization of, 460
Customer information, and deployment, 160–61
Customer maintenance costs, in account selection, 341–42
Customer relationships, 57
Customers
  "aggressive," 343
  multinational, 339
  nature of, 461
  across product lines, 350

Customer service, 11
    definition of, 560–62, 567
    and internal marketing, 562–64
    organizational issues of, 564–66
Customer value, 563–64, 565

D

Data gathering, in market-focused
    organization, 467
Decentralization
    of Capital Cities Communications,
        398
    of marketing efforts, 622–23
Deciders, in buying process, 344–45
Decision making
    in account selection, 343
    informal influence over, 479
Decision-making unit (DMU), 343–44
Delivery salesperson, 77
Demand, creation of, 78
Deployment
    Actmedia case, 165
    Cox Cable cases, 165–67
    definition for, 160
    and focus, 160–62
    in sales management, 6
Differentiation, in marketing dept., 471
Disk-drive industry, 479
Disk drives. *See* Computer Industry
Dissolution, in buyer-seller relationships,
    347–48
Distribution. *See also* Channels
    and boundary spanning, 473
    and control of resources, 242–45
    in multichannel systems, 238–39
Distribution decisions, and marketing
    mix, 7–8
Distributors
    captive vs. independent, 238
    primary function of, 237
    traditional economic role of, 237–38
Dorio Printing Co., as case study, 22–23
Drucker, Peter, 163
Duplication, in market-focused
    organization, 465
Du Pont's Textile Fibers Division, 456

E

Effectiveness
    definition for, 162
    vs. efficiency, 163
    measuring, 162–64
80/20 rule, 8
"Empire building," in functionally
    focused organization, 471
Environment
    external vs. internal market, 10
    sales force, 82, 83, 84
Evaluation systems, for salespeople,
    90–91
Exchange, in buyer-seller relationships,
    346
Expansion, in buyer-seller relationships,
    347
Expense-to-revenue ratio (E/R ratio),
    selling, 163
Exploration, in buyer-seller
    relationships, 347

F

Fieldcrest Mills Inc., 92–93
Field marketing
    changing requirements of, 12
    management of, 21
    recruitment in, 86
    requirements for, 1–2
    selection process, 86
Field sales organization, and market
    specialization, 465
Field sales representatives, boundary
    role of, 76
Field studies, in marketing, 3–4
"Firefighting," 479
Floppy disks. *See* Disk-drive industry
Fountain Beverage Div. (FBD),
    Pepsi-Cola, as case study, 625–26
Frito-Lay, Inc. (FLI), as case study,
    478–80
Function, organizing marketing by, 457,
    467–72
Functionally focused organization,
    467–69
    example of, 468
    strengths of, 457, 469

success of, 471–72
vulnerabilities of, 457, 470–71

G

General Electric Corp., as case study,
    566–67
General Foods, Post Division, 468–69
Goal setting, in sales coordination,
    351–52
"Gray market," for PPCo products,
    479–80

H

Hawks, Chuck, 246
Honeywell, Inc., Commercial Avionics,
    626, 627
Honeywell International. *See also*
    Commercial Aviation Div.
Human resource policies
    in functionally focused organization,
        471
    in market-focused organization, 467

I

IBM (International Business
    Machines), 11
    as case study, 623, 624
    field marketing organization of, 623
Iced tea market. *See also* Fountain
    Beverage Div.
Imperial Distributors, Inc., as case study,
    479, 623, 627–28
Implementation
    definition for, 17
    in marketing, 3–4
    strategy for, 18–19
Incentive component, in compensation,
    89. *See also* Compensation systems
Industries Group, Westinghouse Electric
    Corp., 245, 246
Industry
    computerization of, 235
    concentration, 235
    distributors of, 238
Influences, in buying process, 344
Integration, in market department, 471

International sourcing strategies, 234
Inventory, and boundary spanning, 474

J

Just-in-time inventory management
    (JIT), 234–35

K

Knight, John, 628
Kupfer, Robert, 626

L

Labor pool, 88
Laissez-faire philosophy, 23
Levitt, Theodore, 563
Liaison, product manager as, 459
Light-duty liquid detergents (LDSLs),
    625
Lincoln Electric Co., 247
Little general manager, 461

M

Major accounts
    buyer-seller relationships in, 346–48
    buying process for, 343–46
    case studies, 353–56
    defined, 338–39
    management of, 338
    sales coordination for, 348–53
    selection of, 340–46
    size of, 342
    training for, 352–53
Management. *See also* Sales management
    account, 8, 339–40
    channel, 7–8
    just-in-time, 234–35
    of major accounts, 338
    in multichannel systems, 238–39
    strategy for, 17
Manufacturers, and marketing, ,474
Manufacturer's rep, in multichannel
    systems, 238
Manufacturing, and market-focused
    organizations, 465
March, James G., 619

Market. *See also* "Gray market"
consumer-goods, 350
external vs. internal environment for,
10
and organizational structures, 619
organizing marketing by, 457, 464–69
and sales tasks, 78
Market-focused organization, 462–67
vs. product-focused organization, 466
strengths of, 457, 464–65
success factors of, 467
vulnerability of, 457, 465–67
Marketing. *See also* Field marketing
boundary-spanning nature of, 20–21,
75–76, 473
customer encounters in, 20
customer service in, 560
entangling alliances involved in, 241
formal organization in, 455
implementation in, 3
interactive nature of, 167, 475, 476
internal, 562–64
managing resources for, 8–9
and manufacturing, 474
nature of, 12
organization and control systems for,
11–12
packaged-goods, 165
selling and, 73
strategy for, 3–4, 17
structure underlying, 11
varieties of organizations for, 457
vertical, 462–63
Marketing managers
conflicting goals of, 619–20
generic functions of, 621
"Marketing myopia," 620
Marketing organization
centralization and decentralization of,
622–23
components of, 620–22
formal, 455
functionally focused, 467–72
functions of, 620–22
importance of, 1
market-focused, 462–67
product-focused, 456, 458–62
purpose of, 2–3
Marketing productivity analysis, 162

Marketing strategy. *See also* Strategy
and buyer behavior, 3–4, 17, 473
coordination in, 472
definition for, 17
and deployment, 161
and managing customer encounters,
4–5
prominence of distribution in, 7
resource dependence of, 475
Market managers
focus of, 464
problems of, 466
role of, 463, 473–74
Market management organization,
example of, 463
Market segment, 462
Marks & Spencer (M & S), 353
Materials management, just-in-time, 339
Matrix organizations, 455
MBA students, 629
MCI Communications Corp., 354
McMurray, Robert, 77
Mergers, 234, 339
Missionary salesperson, 77
Motivation, and management, 80–81
Multichannel systems
control of resources in, 242–45
direct sales force in, 236
growth in, 233–36

N

National Account Managers (NAM), of
MCI, 350
National Accounts Program (NAP) of
MCI, as case study, 355
Nature vs. nurture, in sales
management, 6

O

Operations, computerization of, 235
Order cycle
functions involved in, 562
typical, 562–63
Order size, in account selection, 341
Order taker, 77
Organizational structures, 19, 619
Outcome dimension, of marketing, 478

P

Packaged-goods firms
  marketing activities of, 165
  marketing organization of, 456,
    465–66
  product management at, 461
  trade promotions of, 462
Packaged Soap & Detergent Division
    (PS&D), P&G, 625
Pepsi-Cola, as case study, 623. *See also*
    Fountain Beverage Div.
Perceptions, in buying process, 345
Performance evaluation, 90
  in functionally focused organization,
    470
  process, 91
Peripheral Products Company (PPCo),
    as case study, 479–80
Personal selling, cost of, 234
Planning, of marketing, in functionally
    focused organizations, 469
Post Division, General Foods, 468–69
Power, in buying process, 345
Prestige accounts, 342. *See also* Major
    accounts
Priorities, in buying process, 345
Process, definition for, 618
Process dimension, of marketing, 477
Procter & Gamble, 11. *See also* Light-duty
    liquid detergents
  as case study, 623, 624–26
Producers, in multichannel systems, 241
Product
  vs. benefit, 461
  and boundary-spanning role, 474–75
  definition for, 561
  organizing marketing by, 456–62
Product-focused organization, 456–62
  strengths of, 457
  vulnerabilities of, 457
Product management organization
  example of, 458
  strengths of, 460
  success of, 462
  vulnerabilities of, 460–62
Product managers, 463
  focus of, 464

  role of, 458–59
Product mix, in account selection, 341
Profits, and market orientation, 464
Program management, in marketing,
    620–21
Promotion managers, 621
Promotions. *See also* Advertising;
    Marketing
Purchase process, initiators of, 344
Purchasers, in buying process, 345

Q

Quality control, in multichannel
    systems, 245
Quantity of effort, 81

R

R&D (research and development), and
    technical service, 561
Recruitment, 86
  and personal abilities, 80
  and sales effort, 79
  training decisions and, 87
Redeployment, 162
Resellers, in multichannel systems, 239
Resource dependence, and marketing
    strategy, 475
Resource managers, 621

S

Salaries. *See* Compensation systems
Salary/incentive mix, 89
Sales, 81. *See also* Selling
Sales coordination, 348–53
Sales force. *See also* Deployment
  compensation, 222
  of CPI, 94–95
  direct, 236
  focus of, 6
  measuring effectiveness of, 7
  in product marketing organization,
    458
Sales forecasts, and boundary spanning,
    476

Sales jobs, classification of, 77–78
Sales management, 73, 233
  analysis of, 84
  basics of, 91
  compensation, 88
  importance of, 1–2
  motivation in, 80–81
  in multichannel systems, 245
  nature vs. nurture in, 6
  objectives of, 76
  process of, 4
  and salesperson, 5–6
  studying, 6
  systems for, 82–84
Salespeople. *See also* Recruitment;
    Selection process; Training
  approaches of, 56–63
  behavior of, 163
  boundary role of, 75–76, 356
  characteristics of, 74–75
  and compensation systems, 351
  delivery, 77
  demand created by, 78
  evaluation of, 90–91
  missionary, 77
  order takers, 77
  recruitment of, 63–64
  research on, 74–75
  technical, 77–78
  training of, 87
Sales performance, measuring
    effectiveness of, 81, 163–64
Sales tasks, managing, 78–82
Satellite dish, 200
Seaboard Insurance Co. (SIC), 355
Selection process, 86. *See also* Salespeople
  training decisions and, 87
Selling
  as art, 88
  costs of, 234
  cross-selling, 352
  "head-of-state," 538
  personal, 234
Service. *See also* Customer service
  company definition of, 565
  technical vs. customer, 561
"Service culture," 566

Service merchandising industry, 479
  marketing organizations in, 786
Service programs, 565
Simon, Herbert A., 619
Situational dimension, of marketing,
  475, 478
Sloan, Alfred P., 623
Specialization
  in functionally focused organization,
    469
  and market-focused organizations, 465
Sperry Aerospace, avionics business of,
  627
Spot Sales, ABC-TV, as case study, 354
Springs Industries, as case study, 353–54
Staffing, and sales coordination, 352–53.
    See also Recruitment
Star, Steve H., 618–19
Strategy. *See also* Marketing strategies
  account, 8
  definition for, 617
  evolution of, 19
  implementation and, 18–19
  in marketing, 3–4
Structural dimension, of marketing, 477
Structure, definition of, 617, 618
Super stores, 339
Supplier-reseller relationships, 239–41,
  241
Suppliers
  intermediaries and, 242
  in multichannel systems, 239
Support services, in marketing
  organization, 621

T

"Target markets," 21
Tea Breeze, as case study, 628–29
Technical salesperson, 77–78
Technical service, 561
Technology, mass-storage, 534
Trade-off analysis, in account selection,
  343
Trade promotions, in functionally
  focused organization, 468
Training, marketing

decisions in, 87
and personal abilities, 80
in product management
   organization, 460
and sales coordination, 352–53
and sales effort, 79
Transactions, in buyer-seller
   relationships, 346
"Transaction-specific assets," 89
Turner Construction Co., as case study,
   623, 626, 627

U

Users, in buyer process, 345
User-customers
   behavior of, 236
   purchasing behavior of, 241

V

Virtual networks (Vnet), of MCI, as case
   study, 355–56

W

Warehouse stores, 339
Wealth of Nations, The (Smith), 471–72
Westinghouse Electric Corp., 245. *See
   also* Industries group
Westinghouse Electric Supply Corp.,
   (WESCO), as case study, 246
Wholesalers, 237
   sales volume of, 233

Y

"yield rate," 80